CONTAINING ARAB NATIONALISM

THE NEW COLD WAR HISTORY

JOHN LEWIS GADDIS, EDITOR

CONTAINING ARAB NATIONALISM

THE EISENHOWER DOCTRINE
AND THE MIDDLE EAST

Salim Yaqub

THE UNIVERSITY OF NORTH CAROLINA PRESS | CHAPEL HILL AND LONDON

Manufactured in the United States of America
Designed by April Leidig-Higgins
Set in Monotype Garamond by Copperline Book Services

Some material in the book is drawn from Salim Yaqub,
"Imperious Doctrines: U.S.-Arab Relations from
Dwight D. Eisenhower to George W. Bush," *Diplomatic
History* 26, no. 4 (Fall 2002): 571–91; used here by
permission of Blackwell Publishing.

The paper in this book meets the guidelines for permanence
and durability of the Committee on Production Guidelines for
Book Longevity of the Council on Library Resources.

Library of Congress Cataloging-in-Publication Data
Yaqub, Salim.
Containing Arab nationalism: the Eisenhower Doctrine and
the Middle East / Salim Yaqub.
p. cm. — (The new Cold War history)
Includes bibliographical references and index.
ISBN-13: 978-0-8078-2834-2 (cloth: alk. paper)
ISBN-13: 978-0-8078-5508-9 (pbk.: alk. paper)
1. Middle East—Foreign relations—United States. 2. United
States—Foreign relations—Middle East. 3. United States—
Foreign relations—1953–1961. 4. Arab nationalism.
I. Title. II. Series.
DS63.2.U5 Y37 2004   327.73017'4927'09045—dc22   2003017879

cloth   08 07 06 05 04   5 4 3 2 1
paper   11 10 09 08 07   6 5 4 3 2

To Fawzi Yaqub, Penny Williams Yaqub,
and the memory of Dorothy Seibert Yaqub

CONTENTS

CONTENTS

ILLUSTRATIONS AND MAPS

Iraq's new leaders   258

Eisenhower and Nasser meet in New York   266

MAPS

ILLUSTRATIONS AND MAPS

ABBREVIATIONS

CIA	Central Intelligence Agency
ICA	International Cooperation Administration
ICP	Iraqi Communist Party
NATO	North Atlantic Treaty Organization
NEA	Bureau of Near Eastern, South Asian, and African Affairs
NSC	National Security Council
NSP	National Socialist Party
PL	Public Law
PPS	Parti Populaire Syrien (Syrian Social Nationalist Party)
UAR	United Arab Republic
UN	United Nations
UNEF	United Nations Emergency Force
UNF	United National Front
UNOGIL	United Nations Observer Group in Lebanon

MAP 1. The Middle East in the late 1950s

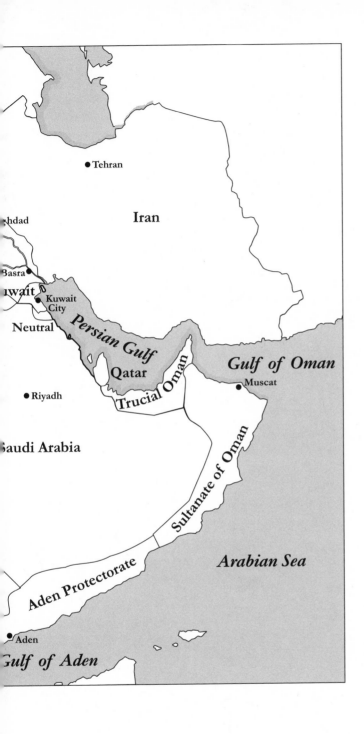

INTRODUCTION

On 5 January 1957 U.S. president Dwight D. Eisenhower addressed a joint session of Congress to warn of a grave crisis in the Middle East. The region, he said, was in danger of falling under the control of the Soviet Union, and the United States had to do all it could to help Middle Eastern nations keep their independence. Eisenhower asked Congress to pass a resolution authorizing him to pledge increased economic and military aid and even direct U.S. protection to any Middle Eastern nation willing to acknowledge the threat posed by international communism. Two months later Congress passed the requested resolution in slightly modified form. By then the policy embodied in the legislation was universally known as the Eisenhower Doctrine. The doctrine marked America's emergence as the dominant Western power in the Middle East, a role the United States continued to play long after the policy itself had been abandoned.

The immediate catalyst of the Eisenhower Doctrine was the Suez war of late 1956, in which Britain, France, and Israel had spectacularly failed to reverse Egypt's nationalization of the Suez Canal Company. As a result of this fiasco, Britain was widely regarded as having forfeited its status as the preeminent Western power in the Middle East. Eisenhower and his secretary of state, John Foster Dulles, believed that Britain's humiliation had left a "vacuum" in the region that the Soviet Union would fill unless the United States took action. One way the Soviets could conceivably fill the vacuum, though U.S. officials agreed this was improbable, was by direct military intervention in a neighboring country like Turkey or Iran. A far more likely scenario was that the Soviets would increase economic and military aid and develop closer political ties to Arab states. Already Egypt and Syria had concluded military and economic agreements with the Soviet bloc. With

Britain's Arab allies now facing overwhelming political pressure to shun their discredited patron, there was a danger that other Arab countries would soon follow Egypt's and Syria's example.

Officially, then, the Eisenhower Doctrine was aimed at protecting the Middle East from Soviet encroachment; in this sense it was merely a more specific application of the general containment doctrine with which the United States had waged the Cold War for a decade. But the Eisenhower Doctrine also sought to contain the radical Arab nationalism of Egyptian president Gamal Abdel Nasser and to discredit his policy of "positive neutrality" in the Cold War, which held that Arab nations were entitled to enjoy profitable relations with both Cold War blocs. As Eisenhower and Dulles saw it, "positive neutrality" was neither. They believed that Nasser had in fact grown so hostile to the West that he had become, albeit perhaps unwittingly, a tool of Soviet expansionism. (In July 1958 Eisenhower privately remarked that Nasser "is a puppet [of the Soviets], even though he probably doesn't think so.")[1] Rather than cooperate with Egypt, as it had done until recently, the United States would now try to strengthen conservative Arab regimes—like those of Iraq, Saudi Arabia, Lebanon, and Libya—and reinforce their pro-Western tendencies. Through economic aid, military aid, and explicit guarantees of American protection, the administration hoped to encourage such governments to side openly with the West in the Cold War, thus isolating Nasser and his regional allies, among them the Syrian government and Nasserist opposition parties in other Arab countries. The administration pursued this strategy until late 1958, when it reluctantly concluded that Nasserism was too politically powerful to be successfully opposed and that the United States should instead seek an accommodation with that movement.

WHILE HISTORIANS HAVE by no means ignored the Eisenhower Doctrine, their treatments have tended to be either piecemeal or cursory. Ray Takeyh, Erika G. Alin, Irene L. Gendzier, David W. Lesch, and Robert B. Satloff have written studies confined to the formulation of the Eisenhower Doctrine or to individual crises associated with that policy.[2] Nigel John Ashton, Fawaz A. Gerges, Zachary Karabell, and Ritchie Ovendale have treated the doctrine as a whole, but only as part of larger studies.[3] This book offers the first comprehensive account of both the formulation and the implementation phases of the Eisenhower Doctrine. Examining the doctrine at some length and in its entirety is the best way to illuminate its underlying political dynamics, which tend to remain obscured when the policy is treated too briefly or as a series of discrete case studies. Those political dynamics, in turn, offer insight into the psychological and moral dimensions of U.S.-Arab relations, not just in the 1950s but in later decades as well.

Essentially, what occurred in 1957 and 1958 was a political struggle between the United States and the Nasserist movement over the acceptable limits of Arabism, that is, over what should be seen as falling within the mainstream of Arab politics and what should be regarded as marginal or extreme. Each party—the United States on one hand and the Nasserist movement on the other—tried to put together a broad coalition of Arab states that shared its basic foreign policy orientation. Each party sought to define that orientation in such a way that those *not* sharing it would seem beyond the pale of acceptable Arabism. For the United States the cardinal issue was international communism. If a critical mass of Arab states could be induced to declare their opposition to international communism—to "stand up and be counted," as the phrase went at the time—then those Arab governments advocating positive neutrality in the Cold War could be marginalized. The Nasserist movement stressed "Western imperialism" and Zionism, insisting that those Arab governments with close ties to Britain or France (or, increasingly, the United States itself) were themselves outside the mainstream of Arab politics, discredited by their association with the great powers' "imperialist" policies and support for Israel.

One might wonder, of course, why the Eisenhower administration ever thought it could prevail in such a contest. Although none of the Arab states was a democracy, Arab governments did have to consider domestic Arab opinion, which could not be expected to oppose international communism as vehemently as it opposed Western imperialism and Zionism. Whereas the first threat was theoretical and remote from Arab concerns, the other two were actual and immediate. Eisenhower and Dulles believed, however, that the events of late 1956 had created a historic opportunity for the United States. By opposing aggression against Egypt during the Suez war, the United States had demonstrated that it was a fair and just power, more interested in upholding the rights of weak nations than in excusing the misdeeds of its allies and friends. The Soviet Union, meanwhile, had shown its true colors by brutally suppressing the Hungarian uprising. Gratitude toward the Americans and revulsion against the Soviets would now enable the United States to put together a majority coalition of pro-American, anticommunist Arab states, leaving Egypt and Syria with the choice of either joining that coalition or facing growing isolation in the region. Or so Eisenhower and Dulles hoped.

Grasping these political calculations is essential to understanding the

Eisenhower Doctrine as a whole. Some scholars have viewed the military dimensions of the doctrine too narrowly and thus have been mystified as to their purpose. Referring to the security arrangements that the Eisenhower administration made with conservative Arab regimes, Ray Takeyh finds it "hard to see how such networks, with their demarcation lines and trip-wires, could regulate the movement of ideas. Nasser did not achieve his aims by dispatching the Egyptian armed forces, but appealed directly to the inhabitants of these states by promising a new dawn in Arab history."[4] In fact, the Eisenhower Doctrine's security arrangements were not intended to "regulate the movement of ideas" or even, primarily, to deter overt Egyptian aggression. Their main purpose was to increase the confidence of pro-U.S. governments (partly by enabling them to combat Egyptian-sponsored subversion), thus emboldening them to stand openly with the United States in the Cold War. The Eisenhower administration realized that the Nasserist challenge was essentially political, and so, too, was the American counteroffensive, even in its military aspects.

Takeyh is correct, however, in stressing that the Eisenhower Doctrine did not represent a fundamental repudiation of Britain's policies and role in the Middle East. While U.S. officials saw the Suez fiasco as demonstrating Britain's inability to serve as the Western standard-bearer in the region, they still hoped to preserve the remnants of British power and influence in the Arab world; the loss of those remnants would only enlarge the perceived regional vacuum and invite further Soviet encroachment. The Eisenhower Doctrine did represent, as Takeyh puts it, "America's attempt to reintegrate Britain back into the regional political order," albeit under conditions of U.S. preeminence. Indeed, on some occasions in the post-Suez years, the United States favored a higher degree of unilateral British involvement in the region than Whitehall itself thought wise.[5]

For the most part, the British accepted their newly subservient role, consoling themselves that the Eisenhower Doctrine amounted to a belated acknowledgment of the Nasserist threat against which they had long inveighed. The Eisenhower administration rewarded such acquiescence by increasingly taking the British government back into its confidence, and by late 1957 the two nations' Middle East policies were being closely coordinated at the highest levels. The broad trend was still one of British decline in the Middle East, but that process was to be far slower than most observers could have predicted in the immediate aftermath of Suez. Not until the early 1970s would Britain withdraw the last of its military forces from the Arab world.

In evaluating the overall success of the Eisenhower Doctrine, one must distinguish between the policy's ultimate objective and the strategy employed to achieve that objective. The ultimate objective was to prevent a Soviet takeover of the Middle East, and since such a takeover never occurred, it has to be said that the objective was achieved. But the strategy behind the policy—discrediting Arab figures deemed "soft on communism" by promoting other Arab figures who were conspicuously anticommunist—failed miserably. Fortunately for the Eisenhower administration, the strategy was so ill chosen in the first place that its failure did not compromise the ultimate objective, a point to which we shall return.

The anti-Nasserist strategy failed for two main reasons. First, Eisenhower and Dulles had drastically overestimated America's political strength in the Arab world while underestimating that of Nasserism. Suez notwithstanding, the United States had no intention of repudiating its alliance with Britain and France or its support for Israel's existence and security—stubborn realities that prevented the United States from gaining the wholehearted support of Arab public opinion. Nasser's own regional popularity, by contrast, soared in the aftermath of Suez. Thus any Arab figure seeking to align himself with U.S. Cold War policies, or to oppose Nasserist policies at U.S. instigation, could be successfully branded an enemy of Arabism by Nasserist propagandists. Conservative Arab leaders sometimes played the Arabism card themselves, reminding their audiences that the Soviet Union, too, had supported the creation of the state of Israel, thus implying that radical nationalists were "soft on Zionism." The fact that Moscow had since adopted a stridently pro-Arab position on the Arab-Israeli conflict, however, limited the effectiveness of this charge.

Behind the scenes, Nasser's popularity gave Egypt another crucial advantage over its Arab rivals. Within the diplomatic corps and government ministries of the conservative Arab regimes were numerous individuals who secretly sympathized with Egypt's policies and were willing to share confidential information about their own governments with Egyptian officials.[6] While much of this information was useless gossip, some of it was sufficiently valuable to enable Egypt to anticipate and counter hostile political initiatives that its Arab rivals were contemplating.

The second reason Eisenhower's anti-Nasserist strategy failed was that the conservative Arab leaders were unable or unwilling to play their assigned roles. Usually those leaders were too fearful of domestic or regional opinion to take a strong stand in favor of the United States or against Nasserism. Even when they *were* prepared to take such a stand, they were too suspicious of one another to do so as a bloc. The most celebrated case in point was the long-standing feud between Saudi Arabia and Hashemite

"Say, What If She Doesn't Want Her Honor Protected?"

The cartoonist Herblock questions the Arabs' receptivity to the Eisenhower Doctrine, January 1957. (Herbert Block, *Herblock's Special for Today* [New York: Simon and Schuster, 1958], 124)

Iraq, but there were other rivalries—between Saudi Arabia and Lebanon, between the Iraqi and Jordanian branches of the Hashemite dynasty, and within the Saudi and Iraqi governments—that also obstructed conservative unity.

A related problem was that many conservative Arab leaders saw the Eisenhower Doctrine as an opportunity to advance local agendas that were

INTRODUCTION

not necessarily compatible with U.S. objectives in the Middle East. Both King Hussein of Jordan and King Saud of Saudi Arabia declined to endorse the Eisenhower Doctrine unconditionally, pleading that the political cost of such a gesture would be too great. Each king, however, convinced the Eisenhower administration that his general orientation was sufficiently pro-Western to warrant major U.S. political support for him. Hussein used that support to establish, for decades to come, the supremacy of the palace in Jordanian political life, while Saud tried, far less successfully, to use American support to enhance his regional prestige and to strengthen his bid to shift the line of royal Saudi succession away from his brothers and toward his own sons. Iraq and Lebanon formally endorsed the Eisenhower Doctrine, but they demanded American concessions in return. Iraqi prime minister Nuri al-Saʻid pushed relentlessly for U.S. backing of Iraqi efforts to acquire portions of northeastern Syria—pressure to which Dulles briefly succumbed in early 1958. Lebanese president Camille Chamoun sought U.S. support for an ill-considered plan to amend his country's constitution so that he could remain in office for another presidential term. Although U.S. officials privately doubted the wisdom of Chamoun's scheme, they felt politically obliged to endorse it as a reward for Chamoun's embrace of the Eisenhower Doctrine.

Because of these circumstances—the political weakness of the United States, the political strength of Nasserism, and the independent proclivities of the conservative Arab regimes—the Eisenhower administration was unable to achieve Nasser's regional isolation. Despite apparent successes for the strategy in the early months of its implementation, serious difficulties arose in the summer of 1957, and by the summer of 1958 the strategy was in shreds. Egypt had merged with Syria to form the United Arab Republic (UAR), vastly increasing Nasser's power and terrifying the conservative Arab regimes; King Saud had virtually abdicated his throne in favor of a brother committed to placating Nasser; the Iraqi regime had been overthrown by army officers who appeared to be Nasserist in orientation; the Lebanese and Jordanian regimes had come to the brink of collapse, rescued only by the intervention of American and British forces; throughout the Arab world, the forces of radical nationalism seemed to be running rampant. Eisenhower and his advisers could do little more than gape in disbelief at the magnitude of the apparent political disaster.

Actually, things were not as bad as they seemed. The political triumph of Nasserism in 1958 did not automatically redound to the Soviets' benefit. To the contrary, by early 1959, just months after having vanquished his conservative Arab foes, Nasser was publicly feuding with the Soviets, accusing them of interfering in internal Arab affairs. Quite unexpectedly, Nasserism had become a barrier to, rather than an avenue of, further Soviet penetration of the region. The result of this transformation was a modest rapprochement between the United States and the UAR that continued for the remainder of Eisenhower's term and into that of his successor.

Thus, in the end, the Eisenhower administration was the beneficiary of its own prior miscalculation. Having chosen an unsuitable strategy to begin with, it did not suffer unduly when that strategy collapsed. Such irony was typical of the administration's Middle East policy, which seemed always to hover in some twilight zone between achievement and failure, between subtlety and naïveté. Eisenhower and Dulles thought long and hard about the challenges of Arab nationalism, and they responded to them with a policy of considerable intricacy, sophistication, and internal coherence. Yet the whole edifice rested on a basic misreading of the Nasserist movement, on a drastic underestimation of its power and independence. Nasser himself was bemused by the contradiction. "The genius of you Americans," he once said to businessman and Central Intelligence Agency (CIA) agent Miles Copeland, "is that you never made clear-cut stupid moves, only *complicated* stupid moves which make us wonder at the possibility that there may be something to them we were missing." Copeland writes that Nasser, who attributed the Eisenhower Doctrine solely to Dulles, saw that policy as "one of the shrewdest mistakes ever made by a Great Power diplomat."[7]

OVER THE LAST TWO DECADES there has been growing scholarly interest in the role of cultural differences and cultural antipathies in defining America's relations with the Arab world. Such analyses can tell us much about the cultural and psychological environments in which policies have been formulated, but they should be treated with caution. Americans and Arabs have indeed been divided by vast cultural differences, giving rise, at times, to considerable mutual antagonism. These facts tell us relatively little, however, about the actual content of the Eisenhower administration's policies toward the Arab world. The United States and the Arab countries did have markedly different diplomatic styles in the 1950s, but this was due less to separate cultural heritages per se than to differences in power and geopolitical circumstance. While the United States and the Nasserist movement did take sharply divergent positions on several international questions, that divergence had less to do with clashing values than with conflicting applications of shared values.

At one end of the spectrum of culture-oriented scholars are those who warn that Arabs and Muslims harbor a fundamental hostility to the West that Westerners ignore at their peril. Such hostility, these scholars allege, derives less from disagreements over specific issues than from a deep-seated, and not entirely rational, rejection of everything the West represents: secularism, liberalism, relativism, and modernity. Since the rejection of the West is existential, the argument goes, Western nations can do little to appease Arab and Muslim wrath.[8]

In recent years this "clash of civilizations" thesis has been most often applied to Islamist movements in the Middle East, North Africa, and South Asia, but in 1964 Bernard Lewis used a version of it to explain radical Arab nationalism and its attitude toward the United States. Lewis rejected the proposition that Arab nationalists' hostility to the United States was primarily due to the latter's association with Zionism and European imperialism. After all, the Soviet Union had largely escaped such hostility despite its own complicity in Israel's creation and despite its long record of imperial rule over Muslim lands, a record not shared by the United States. A more satisfying explanation, Lewis wrote, could be found "if we view the present discontents of the Middle East not as a conflict between states or nations, but as a clash between civilizations. The 'Great Debate,' as Gibbon called it, between Christendom and Islam has been going on, in one form or another, since the Middle Ages." Arabs were especially prone to atavistic anti-Westernism, Lewis argued, because they lacked the political experience of non-Arab Middle Easterners: "Old sovereign states like Turkey and Persia have developed consistent foreign policies based on national interests and rational calculations; Arab policies are still at the mercy of a mood of ethnic and communal collectivism, which treats the West as a collective enemy."[9]

A quarter of a century later, in an article on the sources of anti-Western sentiment in the Muslim world as a whole, Lewis reiterated this basic argument. Opposition to imperialism and Zionism could not account for Muslim hostility toward the United States, Lewis claimed, because America's connection to those phenomena was too tenuous. The real explanation was far more profound: "This is no less than a clash of civilizations—the perhaps irrational but surely historic reaction of an ancient rival against our Judeo-Christian heritage, our secular present, and the worldwide expansion of both." Lewis's themes (and phrasing) were soon amplified in a provocative article and book by Samuel P. Huntington, who argued that Muslim hostility toward the West (and vice versa) has turned less on specific political or economic grievances than on "broader intercivilizational" antagonisms that have been centuries in the making.[10]

The problem with the "clash of civilizations" thesis, however, lies in its glib dismissal of precisely those concrete grievances. For Arab nationalists during the Cold War era (and for Islamists more recently), opposition to Zionism and Western imperialism was a genuine cause of anti-U.S. sentiment, not merely a cover for deeper antipathies. It is true that Eisenhower's relations with Israel were relatively chilly; but his predecessor had played a key role in Israel's creation, and his successors would tilt dramatically in favor of the Jewish state. It is true that the United States itself was not a colonial power in the Middle East or North Africa; but it was closely aligned with nations that were, and since the 1980s it has projected military power directly into those regions. Moreover, the United States has strongly supported local authoritarians, like the Shah of Iran and the Saudi ruling family, who have oppressed their own citizenry and plundered or squandered their nations' wealth.

It is also true that, during the Cold War, Arab nationalists were generally less critical of the Soviet bloc than they were of Western powers, but such a posture was consistent with reasoned opposition to Zionism and Western imperialism. Although the Soviets supported Israel in the early years of its existence, they abandoned that position in the early 1950s and stridently championed the Arab cause thereafter. Although Moscow subjugated the states of Eastern Europe and even some Muslim lands in Central Asia, it did not dominate the Arab countries themselves, instead offering them economic and military aid. Such circumstances could not fail to influence Arab attitudes. In November 1956, following the Soviet Union's brutal suppression of the Hungarian uprising, Syrian president Shukri al-Quwatli told a U.S. diplomat that the "situation in Hungary is not our affair, and I do not care if 50 Budapests are destroyed."[11] Al-Quwatli's disregard for the victims of Syria's benefactor may have been callous and unprincipled, but it was hardly irrational.

The spectacular emergence of Osama bin Laden in the late 1990s, and especially his apparent sponsorship of the terrorist attacks of 11 September 2001, has clearly enhanced the credibility of those stressing "broader intercivilizational" differences. In bin Laden, after all, we have a figure even more committed to the "clash of civilizations" thesis than Huntington. The implications of 11 September will be discussed at greater length in the Epilogue. Suffice it to say here that bin Laden and his operatives represent a tiny and extreme minority in Arab politics. Moreover, while bin Laden's message occasionally strikes a chord with wider Arab audiences, it does so primarily by stressing standard political grievances against the United States and its regional allies: Israel's continuing occupation of Palestinian lands, Washington's support for authoritarian Arab regimes, and the devastation of Iraq by economic sanctions and war. Such critiques are often exaggerated or unfair, but they do suggest that Arab opinion as a whole is more concerned with America's political behavior than with its civilizational status.

AT THE OTHER END of the culture-oriented spectrum are those who see the deep-seated hostility as emanating primarily from the Western side. Since the publication in 1978 of Edward W. Said's *Orientalism*, there have been numerous studies documenting and analyzing European and American cultural biases and stereotypes regarding the Middle Eastern "Other"; most of these studies argue, implicitly or explicitly, that such perceptions have had a profoundly distorting effect on Western policies toward the Middle East.[12] While these arguments are more typically directed at contemporary U.S. policy, scholars have occasionally projected them backward in time. Said himself finds that "the notion of Arab people with traditions, cultures, and identities of their own is simply inadmissible in the United States. . . . This morbid, obsessional fear and hatred of the Arabs has been a constant theme in US foreign policy since World War Two." In a more detailed study, Douglas Little contends that between 1945 and 1970 "orientalism and anticommunism . . . put the American eagle on a collision course with the sphinx of Arab nationalism." Seeing Arabs as "treacherous, unreliable, and vulnerable to Soviet subversion," U.S. policymakers failed to accord Arab nationalism the respect it deserved.[13]

As Little ably demonstrates, the documentary record from the 1950s is full of disparaging remarks made by U.S. officials about Arabs. What is less clear is the extent to which such anti-Arab sentiment actually explains the Eisenhower administration's policies toward the Arab world. One difficulty that immediately arises is that of distinguishing the documented anti-Arab sentiment from the blanket condescension with which top administration officials regarded Others in general, be they Arabs, Jews, Europeans, or U.S. congressmen. There is nothing surprising about Eisenhower's view that Arabs and Israelis "have built up an emotionalism that at times borders on the hysterical," but the president also felt that "the British have never had any sense in the middle east." Dulles complained that America's European allies were "selfish." In their various disputes with former and present colonies, he charged, Europeans "are so involved in emotionalism that nothing less than a comparable emotionalism on our part will satisfy them." Dulles also decried the "emotionalism . . . of a good many Zionists in this country who feel that we ought to, in effect, give a blank check to Israel."

Equally pathetic were U.S. congressmen who bowed to the "pressure of the Jews" and were "jealous among themselves."[14] Apparently Eisenhower and Dulles alone were capable of transcending the fanaticism and small-mindedness of human affairs.

Even if we were to grant that anti-Arab prejudice is of a different order from the generic condescension outlined above, we would still need to establish that the former had a significant impact on U.S. Middle East policy. That, however, is a difficult case to make, at least with respect to the Eisenhower years. Social psychologists have shown (and common sense would suggest) that prejudiced individuals are capable of disregarding negative ethnic or cultural stereotypes and behaving in a nondiscriminatory manner when other priorities—like the easing of their consciences or the avoidance of the appearance of bigotry—so dictate.[15] It stands to reason that prejudiced American policymakers, responding to a similar set of moral and political pressures, could make similar adjustments when dealing with foreign nations. Any antipathies such officials may have harbored toward a particular national or ethnic group would likely have been tempered by a sense of propriety and fair play and, more importantly, by the recognition that manifestly discriminatory behavior could damage America's international image.

Such constraints have not applied, of course, during periods when extreme bigotry was common or when the United States faced little international pressure to behave in a nondiscriminatory way. Both conditions were present in the antebellum years, when the U.S. government refused, on racial grounds, to conduct diplomatic relations with the predominantly black nation of Haiti. Similarly, as we shall see in the Epilogue, since the early 1980s it has become increasingly clear that the Arab states as a whole lack the strength, unity, and strategic leverage to pressure or threaten the United States in any fundamental way. Consequently the United States has grown more willing to disregard Arab opinion and to take actions that, arguably, reflect discriminatory attitudes toward Arab peoples.

In the 1950s, however, U.S. officials still believed that Western actions deemed harmful to Arab interests might elicit a hostile and concerted Arab reaction. In April 1956 Dulles told congressional leaders that the United States should not become a major arms supplier of Israel because doing so "would alienate the Arabs and result in cutting off Arabian oil. This in turn would greatly weaken Europe economically and bring NATO [North Atlantic Treaty Organization] to a standstill. All the gains of the Marshall Plan would be cancelled and Europe would be forced to turn to the Soviet Union for economic survival and for its oil imports. Thus we would save

Israel but lose Europe." That same month Eisenhower told British military officials "that he had been spending much time reading up [on] the history of Arab nationalism and the wars of the crusades. Europe had suffered for a thousand years from the last Islamic surge and . . . we (repeat we) could not afford another."[16] While such fears were based on a stereotype of Arabs as a vengeful horde, they often prompted U.S. officials to treat Arab concerns with greater deference than they might have otherwise.

The Eisenhower Doctrine in particular seems to owe little to anti-Arab prejudice. True, the doctrine reflected the view that Nasserism was incapable of true neutrality in the Cold War, suggesting, perhaps, a dismissive attitude toward Arab capabilities. In other ways, however, the doctrine flew in the face of prevailing anti-Arab stereotypes, which were often invoked to convey the futility of relying on the Arabs to resist international communism. A 1950 State Department report, quoted by Little, remarked that "the Near East is vulnerable to communistic exploitation" mainly because such "natural deterrents . . . as religion, a modern social system, a flourishing economic life, and a democratic political structure, are weak or lacking." Eisenhower probably would have agreed with this statement, but he used the Eisenhower Doctrine to cultivate the region's "natural deterrents" anyway. Dulles expressed doubt about "the ability of the Arabs to unite for any constructive purpose," but that did not stop him from encouraging the conservative Arabs to unite. In early 1958, when opposition to the doctrine was starting to build within the U.S. government, a National Security Council (NSC) paper noted that "the 'stand up and be counted' character of the [Eisenhower] Doctrine is incompatible with traditional Arab reluctance to be committed." The doctrine, in other words, had failed to take into consideration the moral cowardice of the Arabs. In June 1959 Eisenhower himself grumbled, "If you go and live with these Arabs, you will find that they simply cannot understand our ideas of freedom or human dignity."[17] Eisenhower's doctrine had been based on a more hopeful assessment of Arab capacities.

Since the 1990s, scholars of orientalism have extended their analyses to gender, arguing that Western imperialists and neoimperialists "feminized" Middle Easterners by ascribing to them such "unmanly" characteristics as weakness, irrationality, hysteria, emotionalism, cowardice, and self-indulgence. In the early 1950s, Mary Ann Heiss writes, U.S. and British officials recoiled from the histrionic public style of Mohammed Mosadeq, Iran's nationalist prime minister, dismissing him as "feminine" and "not manly enough for international politics." Such disparaging views of Mosadeq "made it much easier for Anglo-American officials to discount his position"—and ultimately depose him. In a study of American images of Israel from 1948 to 1960, Michelle Mart notes that "while Jews were increasingly depicted as masculine insiders in American popular and political culture, Arabs were increasingly depicted as unmasculine outsiders." Unlike their tough, smart, forthright, and dependable Israeli counterparts, Arabs appeared in such discourses as incompetent, excitable, cowardly, and devious. "A corollary stereotype," Mart adds, "is the licentious Arab male." This "sex-crazed" figure "was unmanly because he was out of control—a wild monster as opposed to a mature adult."[18]

Although gendered portrayals of Arabs do abound in the postwar U.S. diplomatic record, it is difficult to know what, if anything, their existence tells us about American policies toward the Arab world. Certainly such "tropes of gender" are not unique to American depictions of Arabs. Scholars have found similar portrayals of "natives" in the discourses of Americans in South Asia, of Britons in Bengal, of French in Vietnam, of Dutch in Indonesia, and of Spaniards in Mexico.[19] Nor have such categories been applied solely to Third World peoples. As Frank Costigliola has shown, during the Cold War U.S. officials frequently juxtaposed images of the NATO allies "as effeminate, effete, or otherwise lacking in robust masculinity" against images of the United States as virile and rational. These dichotomies, Costigliola argues, "map[ped] the supposedly natural inequality of the conventional sex-gender system onto the domain of the Western alliance, thereby further legitimating U.S. hegemony."[20] From the outset, then, one hesitates to make too much of the fact that Arabs were feminized when so many others received similar treatment.

Nor is it easy to make political sense of the disparate ways U.S. officials applied gendered categories *within* the Arab world. Arab figures in the 1950s were feminized or masculinized (or both) with little regard to their standing in Washington. In 1957 CIA director Allen Dulles, Foster Dulles's brother, complained that pro-Western Syrian army officers lacked "guts or courage," but he still apparently supported their effort to mount a coup.[21] Lebanese president Camille Chamoun and Iraqi prime minister Nuri al-Sa'id appear variously in Anglo-American documents as "courageous" and "hysterical," as "resolute" and "difficult," yet both of them enjoyed almost unwavering American and British support.[22] The two Arab leaders most nearly conforming to the manly ideal as defined by the American political elite were King Hussein and Nasser, the first a close ally of the United States, the second a sharp antagonist. In 1957, when the twenty-two-year-old Hussein decisively ousted pro-Nasser figures from his government and army, American observers celebrated the king's transformation "from boy to man."[23]

For decades thereafter, Hussein's reputation for physical courage would be deeply ingrained in the American official imagination. Meeting Nasser for the first time in September 1960, Eisenhower found the Egyptian leader a model of military bearing: "impressive, tall, straight, strong, positive." Two years earlier, noting that Nasser's attitude toward Israel was often more conciliatory than that of his conservative Arab rivals, Undersecretary of State Christian A. Herter had detected "a healthy element in the fact of an Arab strong man of such stature that he does not need to compete with other Arab countries in baiting the Israelis."[24]

Equally irrelevant to official policy were American stereotypes about Arab sexual licentiousness, an unmanly quality in Mart's scheme. Certainly such images had little bearing on Eisenhower's decision to forge a close political alliance with Saudi Arabia's King Saud, the one Arab leader whose sexual behavior gave some credence to the stereotypes. Saud had innumerable wives and concubines, and he spent much of his time on royal peregrinations seeking to marry and impregnate as many Saudi women as possible, the better to cement the political allegiance of his subjects. (The ease with which women could be married and divorced made it possible for Saud to take countless brides without exceeding, at any given time, the four-wife limit.)[25] Saud's promiscuity may have embarrassed Eisenhower,[26] but it did not keep the president from trying, in 1956 and 1957, to transform the pro-American Saud into a pan-Arab leader. Nasser, by contrast, had poor relations with Washington, even though his wholesomeness was never doubted by U.S. officials. A former U.S. ambassador to Egypt later remembered Nasser as "a great family man," "clean as a whistle," and "very fond of his children, used to plan his vacations so he could take them to the beach."[27] Saud, with his 107 acknowledged offspring, would have had a hard time organizing such an excursion.

A THIRD CLAIM, less contentious than either the "clash of civilizations" or the anti-orientalism argument, has been that the Eisenhower administration faltered in the Middle East because it failed to approach the region on its own cultural terms. Diane B. Kunz hints at such a criticism when she describes the administration's Johnston Plan (an attempt to ease Arab-Israeli tensions by encouraging Jordan and Israel jointly to develop the Jordan River Valley) as "very American in its emphasis on technical problem solving and money to overcome intractable political and religious differences." More explicitly, Matthew F. Holland argues that the Middle East has a distinct "diplomatic culture" whose very nature prevented the Eisenhower administration from achieving major successes in the region. According to Holland, who in turn draws on the work of L. Carl Brown, that "diplomatic culture" consists of a set of axioms that have governed Middle Eastern diplomacy since the early nineteenth century: alliances shift constantly "in a bewildering series of tactical moves"; Middle Eastern actors repeatedly enlist the support of great powers, ensnaring them in local controversies in which they have little at stake; Middle Eastern states exhibit "an exasperating refusal to compromise on minor points"; and everyone sees international politics as a zero-sum game.[28]

In this context, however, the use of the term "culture" can be misleading.[29] The tendencies Holland describes have indeed characterized Middle Eastern diplomacy in the modern era, but they have no particular connection to Arab, Islamic, or Middle Eastern civilization. Rather, they have been the stock-in-trade of most small countries not permanently dominated by a single big power. Holland is much nearer to the mark when he writes that Nasser "played the traditional role of a weak player by playing one big power off against the other." Eisenhower saw the matter in similarly general terms, describing Egypt's recalcitrant approach to the Suez crisis as one of the many "tyrannies of the weak" that his administration had to endure.[30]

This is not to say that cultural or religious features specific to the region played no role in the struggle over the Eisenhower Doctrine, but the process was less straightforward than one might expect. Islam, for example, was scarcely an issue in the Eisenhower administration's confrontation with the Nasserist movement, whose outlook was largely secular. Eisenhower tried to make it an issue by promoting the regional leadership of King Saud, whose formal duties included the protection of Islam's holy places, but the effort went nowhere. Saud's Islamic credentials did not translate into significant political influence in the Arab world. To the contrary, they occasioned a bitter U.S.-Saudi dispute over Israel's maritime use of the Gulf of Aqaba, to which Saud objected on Islamic grounds. Saud saw the Aqaba issue as "a question of life and death," while Eisenhower thought the king was being "almost childish" over the matter, "particularly when he talks about Allah."[31] If the United States was engaged in any clash of civilizations, it was with one of its own allies, not the Nasserist movement.

At the same time, there were undeniable differences in how the United States and the Nasserist movement saw their own roles in the Middle East and in the standards of international conduct they claimed to accept. In April 1956 Dulles told a group of U.S. foreign service officers that "the United States is, I suppose, the only country in the world which has foreign policies which are not primarily designed for its own aggrandizement. Almost every other country is thinking primarily [of] how it can develop it-self, generally at the expense of somebody else. The United States is not thinking of the thing that way. We have enough and are not eager to have more." Virtually every other nation, Dulles continued, "is emotionally in-volved in some international controversy, and it wants to be able to have the United States backing it." But the United States, being the only nation truly able to see the big picture, had both the luxury to avoid taking sides in such controversies and the duty to try to resolve them through patient diplomacy.[32] Much as "consensus" historians of the era argued that the lack of feudal and aristocratic heritages had spared the United States from European-style class conflict, so Dulles maintained that global preemi-nence allowed the United States to eschew the self-aggrandizing posture of most other nations.[33] "I believe," he remarked in congressional testimony a year later, "that the United States is freer than almost any great nation has ever been from the temptation to abuse its power for selfish purposes." In-deed, the United States was freer from that temptation "than any other na-tion in the world today except some of the very smallest nations."[34]

Dulles's rhetoric is hyperbolic and self-serving, but it does lend some in-sight into the Eisenhower administration's posture in the Middle East. Be-cause the United States had no colonies or former mandates in the Middle East and did not rely directly on the region's oil, it could afford to take a more detached approach to the area's problems than could Britain, France, or the Middle Eastern nations themselves. The United States did see Mid-dle Eastern disputes largely in global terms, favoring peaceful and, if nec-essary, gradual resolutions over sudden, violent upheavals that the Soviet Union might exploit. The United States did take a relatively dispassionate view of the bitter conflicts that pitted the Israelis against the Arabs, the French against the Algerians, and the British against the Egyptians and the Saudis (though it was almost always more partial to the British than to any of these other antagonists). U.S. officials were genuinely dismayed by the emotional rhetoric and intransigent positions adopted by all parties to these disputes.[35]

To the Nasserist movement, however, and to those familiar with its re-quirements, it was unrealistic to expect the Arabs to place a similar value on tranquillity and conciliation while engaged in a historic struggle for self-determination and dignity. In 1958 Johns Hopkins University professor Elie Salem, who would later serve as Lebanon's foreign minister, wrote a memorandum to U.S. agriculture secretary Ezra Taft Benson calling for an American accommodation with Arab nationalism. "Present Arab history," Salem wrote, "is one of action not of thought. The military is highly respected, strong action is desired. This will lead to turbulence and violent change. . . . One cannot fight these tendencies. In fact, one must be prepared for them." When the Eisenhower administration protested that the UAR's use of propaganda, threats, and subversion amounted to "indirect aggression" against its neighbors, UAR ambassador Moustafa Kamel replied that the "concept of indirect aggression . . . is not recognized by most Arabs"; with the Arab world undergoing a social and political revolution, such legalisms were beside the point. To U.S. criticism of UAR propaganda, Egyptian journalist and Nasser confidant Muhammad Hasanayn Haykal replied that the "UAR is conscious of its weakness vis-à-vis great powers and that [the] propaganda to which Arab masses [are] receptive is about its only available device." If the UAR were in a stronger position, Haykal said, its propagandists "would speak with [the] polished restraint of Selwyn Lloyd," Britain's foreign secretary.[36]

Still, it would be a mistake to conclude that, as a general proposition, Americans have been culturally disposed toward dispassionate problem-solving and Arabs culturally disposed toward uncompromising partisanship. The temperamental differences described above resulted mainly from differences in power and geopolitical position, a reality recognized on both sides. Haykal, as noted, attributed the UAR's reliance on propaganda to its position of weakness. Dulles denied that Washington's high-mindedness meant that "the United States is morally superior to other people. We are big enough, we are strong enough so that we don't have to be [self-aggrandizing]."[37]

At other times, and on other issues, Americans have been given to extremely passionate engagement in political causes, and Arabs have tried to finesse what others have seen as fundamental, even irreconcilable, political differences. As Nasser himself liked to point out, the circumstances of America's founding spawned a patriotic rhetoric no less passionate than his own country's; a nation reared on "Don't tread on me" and "Give me liberty or give me death" should not have been so disdainful of Nasserist slogans. Americans also seemed to have forgotten what it was like to be a small, struggling nation imposed upon by stronger nations and vulnerable to fluctuations in the global balance of power. The United States, too, had once resorted to the "tyrannies of the weak," playing great powers against one another. Even the denunciation of imperialist bogeymen for domestic political advantage—a technique Nasser perfected in the 1950s—had American precedents. As former secretary of state Dean Acheson observed in 1958, "Nasser runs against us the way Big Bill Thompson 'ran' against King George V in Chicago."[38]

U.S. diplomacy in the 1950s was no less prone to high emotion and extravagant commitment. The Eisenhower administration could take a relatively detached view of the Arab-Israeli dispute and the controversies rooted in European imperialism because it had less at stake in those disputes than did the primary contestants. The administration was far more concerned with preventing such disputes from spinning out of control—and thus threatening Western access to Middle Eastern oil—than with upholding the interests of any given party. But there was another conflict in which the United States *was* a passionate partisan and that it could never reduce to a matter of technical problem-solving: the Cold War. Where that struggle was concerned, the United States was so committed to victory that it repeatedly exempted itself from the legalisms and restraints it urged in other arenas, as the people of Iran, Guatemala, and Syria learned all too well.[39]

Scholars have recently questioned the extent to which American policymakers in the 1950s were bound by Cold War thinking in their dealings with the Third World. In those regions, the argument goes, U.S. policymakers were equally preoccupied with racial and cultural issues and with "North-South" concerns such as population growth, famine, drought, and modernization.[40] Elsewhere in the Third World, U.S. policymaking may well have been as multidimensional as some historians now suggest. In the Middle East, however, preoccupation with the Cold War was pervasive, crowding out or co-opting most other concerns. To be sure, Eisenhower and his top advisers occasionally fretted over the threat of resurgent Islam or responded favorably to the optimistic projections of modernization theorists. But not only were such remarks vastly outnumbered by direct references to the communist challenge; they were themselves usually couched, implicitly or explicitly, in Cold War terms.[41] Actions, too, are revealing: only after Nasser began publicly feuding with the Soviets in 1959 did U.S. relations with the UAR markedly improve.

U.S.-Arab relations in the 1950s were highly asymmetrical in most respects, but they were symmetrical in the following sense: Each party—the United States on one hand and the Nasserist movement on the other—was moved by two competing sets of values. The first set was associated with the vanquishing of evil: honor, sacrifice, solidarity, steadfastness, simplicity, and moral absolutism. The second set was best suited to conciliation and deal-making: patience, pragmatism, empathy, compromise, subtlety, and moral relativism. Each party could find in its history positive precedents for either approach. Americans could invoke the wars they had fought against tyranny and aggression, but also the cautioning spirit of George Washington's Farewell Address and the historical commitment of the United States to the freedom of the seas and to the arbitration of foreign conflicts.[42] Nasserists could look back on the impressive military performance of the Prophet Muhammad's early successors and of Salah al-Din, but also on the commercial heritage of the region and on the long experience of Arab leaders in manipulating and maneuvering among the great powers.[43]

In the 1950s the United States and the Nasserist movement applied their shared values inversely, each urging compromise where the other demanded commitment. The Americans wanted the Arabs to be conciliatory toward Zionism and European imperialism but partisan in the Cold War. The Nasserists insisted on their right to make deals with the communist bloc even as they demanded U.S. support for the Arab positions against Zionism and imperialism. Dulles explicitly rejected the proposition that America's friends could engage in rational bargaining with both Cold War blocs, warning an Egyptian diplomat in 1957 that "if a country came and indicated that it was in a good bargaining position and that if we did not give them what they wanted, they could get it from the Soviet Union, we were not interested in that sort of a relationship." Having begun his tenure at the State Department by demanding "positive loyalty" from his employees, Dulles was not about to tolerate "positive neutrality" on the part of foreigners. It was the Nasserists' failure to show sufficient deference to this sentiment that made the Eisenhower Doctrine seem necessary in the first place. The issue was moral as well as geopolitical: President al-Quwatli's professed willingness to see fifty Budapests destroyed scandalized U.S. officials, further convincing them of the need to educate Arab opinion about the evils of international communism.[44]

For their part, Nasserists defended positive neutrality with both pragmatic and high-minded arguments. Fruitful relations with both Cold War blocs would enable the Arabs to develop their economic and military strength much more fully than they could through exclusive relations with either bloc. A policy of nonalignment was also "the best way to serve the cause of peace and bring an end to the Cold War," as Nasser put it in a 1957 interview.[45] At the same time, Nasserists criticized the United States for urging Arabs to compromise in their struggles against European imperialism and Zionism. How could one split the difference between independence and foreign domination? How could one allow an interloper even part of the land he had seized? Privately, most Arab leaders acknowledged that removing the vestiges of imperialism required patient negotiation and that trying to dismantle Israel would be impractical. In public discourse, however, the moral high ground usually belonged to those taking the most defiant view.

Indeed, the distinction between public and private expression was a recurrent theme in U.S.-Arab relations. Behind closed doors, U.S. and Arab officials occasionally professed sympathy for each other's positions while insisting that they were powerless to make such sympathy public. Speaking to a U.S. diplomat in January 1957, Nasser admitted that he was concerned about the "growing strength [of the] Communist movement in Egypt. . . . [But w]hat would happen if he stood up and said [the] Soviets were [the] greatest threat when the Egyptian people saw them as helpful and sympathetic[?] People can be led but only up to a point." On a subject as grave as the threat of international communism, Dulles had little patience for such dissembling. "If Nasser attaches importance to U.S.-Egyptian friendship," he warned Egypt's ambassador, ". . . he must be willing to pay a domestic political price for such friendship." But things looked rather different when European imperialism was the issue. Urged by an Arab League official "to support the Arab position in the debate on Algeria in the [United Nations] General Assembly," Dulles demurred, remarking "that the public position we might find it necessary to take would probably not reflect exactly our private position. . . . We could do more effective work privately and quietly rather than having the issue become even more involved and complex through public debate."[46] There was a time and place for moral clarity, and a time and place for creative ambiguity.

Ironically, then, the United States and the Nasserist movement were divided by a shared moral dualism whereby the virtue of promoting international harmony vied with the imperative of shunning repugnant adversaries. This dualism was primarily expressed in attitudes toward third parties, be they Soviet, Israeli, British, or French. There was, however, an additional tension that Americans and Nasserists experienced concerning their dealings with one another. From early 1956 on, each of the two antagonists was under enormous compulsion to press its advantage against the other. Doing so was not only psychologically satisfying but potentially reassuring to pugnacious regional allies. The United States faced constant pressure from the Iraqi and Lebanese governments to toughen its line against Egypt and Syria. Nasser privately grumbled about "Egyptian and Syrian hotheads" who urged him to ratchet up his rhetoric against conservative Arab regimes —pressure to which Nasser all too often succumbed.[47]

Sometimes, however, figures on both sides saw the wisdom of conciliation. A U.S. State Department policy study in March 1958 recommended that the United States work harder to avoid public controversy with Nasser, who "continues to represent the answer to the prayers of many Arabs." After each of the major crises associated with the Eisenhower Doctrine, Eisenhower himself would briefly muse about improving relations with Nasser, though without sufficient conviction to change the course of U.S.

policy. In May 1957, after pro-American forces had scored a political victory in Jordan, al-Quwatli privately aired his misgivings over Egyptian and Syrian newspapers' furious reaction to the setback. Such vituperation, al-Quwatli maintained, was merely increasing the regional isolation of the radical Arab camp. Egypt and Syria would do well to follow the example of Britain, which was now seeking to restore its shattered relations with Egypt: "England . . . is a great nation, yet when it suffered a big defeat [in the Suez war] it did not lash out emotionally but rather worked for understanding in order to achieve whatever result was possible."[48]

As al-Quwatli's comment implied, such self-criticism occasionally transcended pragmatic considerations and touched on starker questions of honor and decency. In the spring of 1956, against a backdrop of rapidly deteriorating U.S.-Egyptian relations, U.S. ambassador to Egypt Henry A. Byroade privately wrote that he was "appalled" by the Eisenhower administration's heavy-handed use of economic pressures to compel a more favorable Cold War position in Cairo. Such an approach, Byroade protested, "really seems to me unworthy of our country's traditions." In November 1957 Ahmed Hussein, Egypt's ambassador to the United States, confessed to an American diplomat that the Egyptian government's verbal attacks on King Hussein were "undignified and disgraceful and [were] blackening Egypt's face in [the] world."[49] On both sides of the divide, however, these franker sorts of introspection were rare.

The struggle over the Eisenhower Doctrine was largely a moral conflict, but one that occurred within a shared moral framework. The United States and the Nasserist movement each proclaimed the virtues of national liberation, political independence, economic empowerment, and international harmony, but they disagreed over when and where those values were at stake. Both parties were willing to consider conciliation with each other, provided it did not compromise their own security, alliances, or basic sense of fairness. Leaders on both sides were rational, resourceful, and selectively principled men, moved less by the need for cultural vindication than by a common desire for justice and advantage. Theirs was a clash of interests and priorities, not of civilizations.

THE UNITED STATES AND THE
ARAB MIDDLE EAST, 1941–1956

Between late 1941, when the United States entered World War II, and late 1956, when it helped force an end to the Suez war, official American attitudes toward the Middle East underwent a radical transformation. In 1941 the United States had minimal political contact with Middle Eastern countries; by late 1956 American officials believed that only the United States could keep the region from falling under Soviet domination. During World War II, Americans first became convinced that the security of the United States depended on keeping the Middle East out of hostile hands. In the decade after the war, the U.S. government hoped that Britain would remain primarily responsible for this task. Two issues, however, Zionism and Western imperialism, aroused Arab resentment against the West and created opportunities for Soviet political encroachment, raising doubts in American minds about Britain's long-term ability to hold the region for the West. In late 1956 Israel, France, and Britain—nations embodying the perceived threats of Zionism and European imperialism—invaded Egypt and dramatically increased anti-Western feeling in the Arab world. With the region's political orientation now in doubt, the U.S. government decided it would have to take the lead in upholding the Western position in the Middle East.

Official U.S. concern over the political and strategic orientation of the Middle East began with America's entry into World War II. Prior to that time, American interests in the region had been almost entirely missionary, philanthropic, educational, and commercial. After it entered the war, the United States shared its allies' determination to prevent the Middle East from falling under Axis control. Should that happen, Germany and Japan would be able to link up with each other along Asia's southern rim, cutting off Russia's southern supply route through the Persian Gulf; they would also gain access to the region's enormous oil reserves. To prevent the Axis powers from making significant military or diplomatic gains in the area, the United States participated in several wartime initiatives. It joined Britain and the Soviet Union in occupying Iran to keep that country from falling under German control. It joined Britain in using economic pressure to limit neutral Turkey's dealings with Germany. It worked to keep Saudi Arabia well-disposed toward the Allies by opening a U.S. legation in Jidda and declaring the kingdom eligible for Lend-Lease aid. The overtures to Saudi Arabia caused friction with the British, who suspected the United States of seeking to monopolize Saudi oil opportunities, but Washington and London eventually worked out a modus vivendi for extracting and marketing Saudi oil.[1]

Harry S. Truman, president from 1945 to 1953, never saw Middle Eastern affairs as a priority in foreign policy, preoccupied as he was with the revival of Western Europe and the containment of Soviet communism. U.S. involvement in the Middle East had vastly increased during the war, but Britain remained the preeminent Western power in the area. Whether by treaty arrangement, by direct military occupation, or by protectorate status, most nations of the Arab Middle East were still under British domination as of 1945. British military bases dotted the region. Western European economic recovery, in which the United States had a vital stake, increasingly depended on continued Western access to Middle Eastern oil, but the United States itself was not dependent on that oil.[2]

Complications arising from Arab resentment against Zionism and imperialism, however, soon challenged American complacency. In February 1947 the British government, which had governed Palestine as a mandate since 1920, determined it could not resolve competing Zionist and Arab claims and turned the matter over to the United Nations (UN). That fall the UN General Assembly voted to partition Palestine into Jewish and Arab states, a move bitterly opposed by the Arabs, who saw the imposition of a Jewish state in Palestine as a usurpation of Arab national rights. Fighting broke out between Zionists and Palestinian Arabs. Following Israel's declaration of independence in May 1948, Egypt, Syria, Jordan, Lebanon, and Iraq went to war against the new state, but the Zionists, better armed and better organized, fended off the attackers and acquired more territory than had originally been allotted to them. By the time armistices were concluded in 1949, some 750,000 Palestinians had fled or been driven from their homes; most of them settled in squalid refugee camps in neighboring Arab countries. Israel and the Arab states generally abided by the armistices, but they were far from peace. Israel refused to relinquish the additional territories it had seized or to permit large-scale repatriation of Palestinian refugees. The Arab states refused to make peace with Israel as long as it held to these positions.

Against the advice of most of his foreign policy advisers, Truman supported the creation of Israel, first by endorsing the partition plan and then by recognizing the newly proclaimed Jewish state.[3] These actions had a corrosive effect on U.S.-Arab relations. The failure of Arab armies to prevent the uprooting of Palestinians was traumatic to Arabs everywhere. For many Arab commentators, the least painful way to explain this defeat was to portray Israel as a creation of Western imperialism designed to re-enslave the Arab world just as it was on the verge of gaining true political liberty. There was nothing new in criticizing Western imperialists; the novelty lay in including the United States in such company. Decades of philanthropy and political disinterestedness had given the United States a relatively benign reputation in the Arab world. U.S. support for Israel's creation turned much of that goodwill into bitter resentment.[4] For decades to come, such resentment would be an inescapable fact of life in Arab politics. Any Arab leader enjoying friendly relations with the United States could now be labeled "soft on Zionism" by his Arab rivals. In the 1950s President Eisenhower would sometimes blame the existence of Israel for the difficulty he was having in cultivating pro-American leadership in the Arab world. "Except for Israel," he remarked in July 1958, "we could form a viable policy in the area."[5]

Although Truman never regretted the creation of Israel, he was well aware of the complications resulting from that development. One consequence was the ever-present danger of a recurrence of Arab-Israeli hostilities, which could threaten Western access to Middle Eastern oil and give the Soviets an opportunity to make political and military inroads into the region. In the Tripartite Declaration of May 1950, the United States joined Britain and France in pledging to sell the Israelis and the Arabs only such arms as were necessary for internal security and self-defense. The three powers also resolved to intervene to prevent Israel or the Arab states from altering the territorial status quo by force. The Tripartite Declaration was intended not only to prevent another round of Arab-Israeli violence but to keep the antagonists oriented toward the West. An outright ban on Western arms sales might have prompted the Arabs or the Israelis to turn to the Soviet Union for arms. A limitation of such sales, the three powers hoped, would leave both parties sufficiently satisfied to remain loyal to Western suppliers while still denying them the means to engage in major hostilities.[6]

With the sudden increase in international tensions following the outbreak of the Korean War in June 1950, the Truman administration sought to organize Middle Eastern states to resist a possible Soviet attack. Egypt seemed the logical nucleus of such an effort: it was strategically located as the land bridge between Asia and Africa; it contained the Suez Canal, which linked the Mediterranean and Red Seas; it had a huge population and considerable cultural and political influence throughout the Arab world; and Britain already had an extensive military base in the Suez Canal zone. In 1951 the administration endorsed Britain's proposal for an allied Middle East Command that would be based in Egypt and in which the Egyptians would participate.[7]

The effort to establish the Middle East Command only intensified antiimperialist sentiment among Egyptians, who had endured British occupation since 1882. In late 1951 a wide segment of Egyptian society—workers, students, political activists, and even army and police units—rose up in rebellion against the British presence in Egypt, staging guerrilla attacks on British troops and acts of sabotage against British transportation and communications facilities in the Suez Canal zone. In early 1952 massive rioting and looting against British and European institutions in Cairo resulted in scores of deaths. Neither King Farouk nor the successive parliamentary governments with which he shared power were willing to suppress the popular uprising, so limited discipline was imposed by the British themselves, further inflaming the situation. The Egyptian crisis aroused opposition to the Middle East Command proposal throughout the Arab world. It also cleared the way for dynamic new leadership in Egypt.[8]

On 23 July 1952 a group of dissatisfied Egyptian officers known as the Free Officers seized control of the Egyptian army and government in a nearly bloodless coup.[9] The Free Officers forced the abdication of King Farouk, who went into exile. The monarchy was formally abolished the following year. The Free Officers' politics were obscure at first. Their proclaimed objectives were simply to stamp out corruption, compel Britain to withdraw from Egypt, and restore dignity to the nation. Yet even this vague program distinguished the Free Officers from Farouk and the established politicians, many of whom had been tainted by recent corruption scandals and all of whom stood accused of failing to oust the British. The Free Officers' nominal leader was Muhammad Naguib, a respected general, but real power rested with a group of younger officers operating behind the scenes, especially a thirty-four-year-old lieutenant colonel named Gamal Abdel Nasser.[10]

The Truman administration was enthusiastic about the new regime.[11] The Free Officers seemed dedicated and pragmatic, more interested in addressing Egypt's domestic needs than in whipping up anti-British sentiment in the region. The new government expressed a desire for friendly relations with the United States and cracked down on communist activists who had taken part in the anti-British disturbances, prompting Moscow to denounce the regime as reactionary. There were even indications that Egypt might now be willing to join a Middle East defense organization. In September 1952 U.S. secretary of state Dean Acheson remarked that "in Egypt things are going so well . . . there must be a catch in it."[12] It remained for the Eisenhower administration, which took office four months later, to discover just where the catch, or catches, lurked.

WHEN DWIGHT D. EISENHOWER was elected to the presidency in November 1952, much of his popular appeal lay in his status as a nonpolitician uncorrupted by the ways of Washington. He was, in fact, as savvy as they came. Garry Wills writes that Eisenhower's years in the peacetime army, "where ambition is thwarted of its natural object (excellence in war) and falls back on jealousy and intrigue," had been as rigorous a political training as any electoral career. Eisenhower did eventually attain "excellence in war," but here, too, the achievement was largely political: working productively with vain and headstrong leaders and bringing harmony to an often discordant alliance. After the war Eisenhower continued to rub shoulders with powerful and influential men, serving as chief of staff of the U.S. Army, president of Columbia University, and supreme commander of the armed forces of NATO.[13]

Eisenhower's secretary of state was John Foster Dulles. The grandson of one secretary of state and the nephew of another, Dulles had participated in international conferences since the first decade of the twentieth century. In the 1920s and 1930s he had been a partner at the New York law firm of Sullivan & Cromwell, specializing in European debt and reparations issues. In the 1940s Dulles served as a foreign policy adviser to Republican presidential candidate Thomas E. Dewey and as a U.S. delegate to the newly formed UN. In 1950 Truman appointed him chief U.S. negotiator for the peace treaty with Japan, which was concluded the following year. By 1952 Dulles was widely regarded as the Republican Party's chief foreign policy adviser.[14]

Scholars have long noted that, while it seemed at the time that Dulles dominated the new administration's foreign policy and Eisenhower followed his lead, just the opposite was true.[15] One can, however, take the point too far. Diane B. Kunz provides a useful qualification when she writes that Eisenhower made foreign policy decisions "to the extent he wished it, which varied depending on the subject."[16] There were broad areas of foreign policy of which Eisenhower chose to remain only generally aware, content to let Dulles handle day-to-day operations. In Middle East affairs, it was usually only during major crises that Eisenhower took a direct, sustained interest in diplomacy.

Ultimately, though, Eisenhower was in charge of foreign policy, and the wide discretion he granted Dulles could always be taken back. No one knew this better than Dulles himself, who never forgot the bitter experience of his uncle Robert Lansing, Woodrow Wilson's secretary of state. Lansing had sometimes behaved insubordinately, causing Wilson to ignore his advice and eventually dismiss him from the cabinet. "Lansing might as well have lived on the moon," Dulles remarked in 1957, "as far as influencing Wilson's decisions went."[17] Dulles was determined to avoid that fate.

Scholars have contrasted the optimism, pragmatism, and flexibility of Eisenhower with the pessimism, moralism, and rigidity of Dulles.[18] This view, too, needs to be qualified. Of the two men, Eisenhower was more likely to advocate compromise with America's adversaries, but he was also more easily talked out of his positions. On several occasions in the late 1950s, Eisenhower tentatively proposed seeking an accommodation with Nasser, only to yield to Dulles's forceful rebuttals.[19] Eisenhower's unfamiliarity with the details of U.S. diplomacy made it difficult for him to prevail in such exchanges. Of course, on matters of sufficient importance to him, Eisenhower could and did get his way without argument.

Dulles's rigid moralism, though real, was specific and limited. Some scholars have seen Dulles's international approach as an extension of his unwavering Protestant faith,[20] but a more convincing interpretation treats the legal profession as the overarching model for his diplomacy.[21] Depending on the situation, a legal approach could encourage either flexibility or inflexibility. Dulles publicly extolled America's alleged adherence to fixed principles of international behavior. One of the qualities that made the Soviets and their allies so contemptible, he maintained, was their refusal to adhere to any international standards. The vigorous repetition of such claims did make Dulles seem rigid and censorious, like some "international prosecuting attorney," as Eisenhower privately complained. At the same time, Dulles prided himself on his ability to maneuver within internationally accepted limits, to play the game successfully without violating its rules. When it came to international law, he told the cabinet in July 1958 as U.S. marines were swarming onto the beaches of Lebanon, "you can usually find what you want to find in terms of what you are capable of doing."[22] Whether playing to the jury of international opinion or manipulating the technicalities of international law, Dulles remained true to his original profession.

In the Middle East the Eisenhower administration's fundamental objectives were the same as the Truman administration's: maintaining Western access to the region's oil reserves and strategic positions while denying them to the Soviet Union. Yet Eisenhower and Dulles also thought that the prior administration had been excessively partial to Israel, an attitude that had heightened the Arabs' sense of grievance against the West and given the Soviets an opportunity to increase their political influence in the area. While committed to Israel's survival and security, Eisenhower and Dulles resolved to follow a more "even-handed" policy. In practice, this meant encouraging the Israelis to make modest territorial concessions in exchange for peace with the Arabs. The Eisenhower administration did not, however, favor a return to the 1947 partition plan or the wholesale repatriation of Palestinian refugees, preferring that most of them be resettled in other Arab lands.[23]

The Eisenhower administration was ambivalent about Britain's future role in the area. While committed in principle to full political independence for Middle Eastern countries, the administration feared that too rapid a withdrawal of British power and influence would leave those countries susceptible to Soviet blandishments and pressure. The United States might then have to step into the breach, an unwelcome prospect for an administration seeking to control government spending, avoid complications with Congress, and concentrate on more pressing international questions. Ideally, Britain itself would work out a modus vivendi with the Arab states that would allow it to remain the dominant Western power in the area. "We seek neither the removal [n]or the replacement of British influence," noted a November 1953 State Department position paper, "but rather its strengthening by effective adjustment to present-day realities."[24]

U.S. actions in neighboring Iran reveal the determination of the Eisenhower administration to keep the region as a whole oriented toward the West. In 1951 the Iranian parliament had voted to nationalize the facilities of the Anglo-Iranian Oil Company. Shortly thereafter Mohammed Mosadeq, the main architect of Iran's nationalization policy, was elected prime minister. The British government, a half-owner of the Anglo-Iranian Oil Company, tried to cripple Iran's economy through an embargo. The Truman administration had little regard for Mosadeq, but it did see him as a barrier to communist domination of Iran. The Eisenhower administration took a dimmer view, seeing Mosadeq's solicitation of Soviet aid, his association with the communist Tudeh Party, and his efforts to weaken the pro-Western shah as paving the way for a Soviet takeover.[25] In the summer of 1953 the U.S. CIA and British intelligence helped organize massive pro-shah demonstrations in major Iranian cities. With U.S. and British encouragement, Iranian armed forces placed Mosadeq under house arrest, causing his regime to collapse. The shah, who days earlier had fled the country, returned to Iran, and a pro-shah politician became prime minister. The nationalization of Iranian oil facilities remained formally in effect, but a consortium of foreign oil companies was allowed to control and market Iran's oil, with the Anglo-Iranian Oil Company surrendering a large share of the operation to American oil companies. Iran became a major recipient of U.S. economic aid.[26]

Elsewhere in the region, where the threats of communism and radical nationalism were less immediate, the United States could take a calmer approach. In May 1953 Dulles visited Cairo, where Egyptian leaders told him that they saw Britain and Israel as a much greater menace to Egyptian sovereignty than the Soviet Union. Concluding that an Egyptian-based Middle East defense organization was not politically feasible, Dulles encouraged the region's "Northern Tier" nations—Turkey, Iran, and Pakistan—to conclude an anti-Soviet defense pact that would receive Western support and cooperate closely with NATO, which Turkey had recently joined. Perhaps Iraq and Syria could eventually be induced to adhere to such a pact. U.S. policy toward Egypt, meanwhile, would be aimed at alleviating Arab grievances concerning British imperialism and Zionism. After facilitating a negotiated withdrawal of British forces from Egypt, the Eisenhower administration would coax Egypt to lead the other Arab states toward a comprehensive peace settlement with Israel.[27]

The administration achieved the first part of this strategy in mid-1954, when Egyptian and British officials initialed a withdrawal agreement, to be formally concluded that fall. Britain pledged to withdraw all of its troops from Egypt by 1956 and to maintain the Suez base with civilian personnel. Britain retained the right to reoccupy and use the base in the event of an armed attack on Egypt, Turkey, or any signatory to the Arab Collective Security Pact.[28]

In late 1954 Colonel Nasser supplanted General Naguib as Egypt's publicly acknowledged leader. The son of a postal clerk in Alexandria, Nasser had grown up amid the nationalist and anti-imperialist ferment of interwar Egypt. As a teenager he took part in anti-British demonstrations, occasionally running afoul of local authorities. In 1937, at age nineteen, Nasser joined the Egyptian army, where he won rapid promotion. Two events during Nasser's army career deepened his sense of shame over Egypt's helplessness in the face of hostile outside forces. In 1942 British troops and armored cars surrounded the royal palace, forcing King Farouk to appoint a government that supported the allied war effort. In 1948–49 Nasser served with the Egyptian army in Palestine, where he was shocked by his superiors' incompetence, dishonesty, lack of preparation, and failure to coordinate with other Arab armies. As early as 1942 Nasser had begun meeting clandestinely with other young officers to discuss army reform. After the Palestine fiasco, Nasser and his compatriots concluded that the Egyptian government itself had to be drastically reformed or even overthrown. In 1950 Nasser was elected president of the Free Officers' executive committee.[29]

While still an obscure officer, Nasser had impressed his colleagues with his intelligence, personal magnetism, and capacity for hard work. After he entered the limelight in late 1954, these qualities were supplemented by the more conspicuous gift of public oratory. By the mid-1950s Nasser had developed an appealing rhetorical style that blended classical with colloquial Egyptian Arabic, humor with vitriol, and candor with sloganeering. Thanks to Radio Cairo's powerful signal and to the growing availability of inexpensive radio sets, Nasser's voice could be beamed to millions of listeners in Egypt and in neighboring Arab states. U.S. officials found Nasser's rhetoric crude and bombastic, especially when compared with his calm and reasonable demeanor in private.[30] While this reaction partly reflected a different cultural standard for public discourse, it was mostly due to the anti-Western content of Nasser's speeches. In 1959, when Nasser began shrilly attacking the Soviet Union, no one in Washington accused him of demagoguery.

Nasser's pan-Arab philosophy would not achieve its fullest expression until after 1956, but by early 1955 the core principles of that philosophy were in place. The first principle was that the Arabs were a single people sharing a common destiny. Although Nasser was in no hurry to see formal mergers of Arab states, he called for a common Arab policy to meet the common threats of Zionism and Western imperialism. The unstated assumption was that Egypt itself should determine the content of that policy. The second principle, which followed from the first, was that the Arab nations had to rid themselves of all vestiges of European imperialism and colonialism. This imperative was most pressing in the case of France's colonial rule of Algeria, where an armed rebellion against the French had erupted in 1954, but it also applied to Britain's relations with its Persian Gulf protectorates and to its defense treaties with Iraq, Jordan, and Libya —treaties Nasser saw as thinly disguised instruments of imperial domination. The third principle was social and economic justice. Arab governments had to act positively to eradicate poverty, illiteracy, disease, and peonage. They should curtail feudal and imperial privileges, if necessary through the expropriation of lands and property and the nationalization of resources and industries. By enacting new land reform measures, Egypt had already begun to show the way.[31] The implication was that oil-rich Arab states should now do their part by nationalizing oil installations and sharing the wealth with poor Arabs everywhere.

The final Nasserist principle was nonalignment in the Cold War. Although Nasser ruthlessly suppressed communist activities within Egypt itself, he insisted that the Arabs should not have to take sides in the East-West contest; rather, they should be free to trade with, receive economic aid from, and purchase arms from both Cold War blocs. This principle was later dubbed "positive neutrality" to suggest that the Arabs, far from being passive onlookers, were active shapers of their own destiny. Nasser's posture was strongly influenced by that of Indian prime minister Jawaharlal Nehru, who had emerged as a powerful advocate of nonalignment in the Cold War and as a role model for leaders of other developing nations.[32] Over the next few years the advocates of nonalignment, who also included Yugoslav president Josip Broz Tito, Indonesian president Sukarno, and Ghanaian president Kwame Nkrumah, formed an influential bloc in world affairs. In practice the nonaligned camp tended to be more critical of Western than of communist powers, both because of the long history of Western subjugation of nonwhite peoples and because communist China itself was a model for emerging nations.

Initially, though, Nasser seemed to expect that the Western powers would be the ultimate beneficiaries of Egyptian neutrality. A September 1954 Egyptian policy statement argued that, if the Arab states were allowed to form an entirely indigenous collective security system, eventually "the masses would be convinced that the West is no longer intending to conquer the Arabs, and ties built on solid friendship will arise that are stronger than any written pact." Such friendship would be impossible, however, if the Arab states were pressured to join a Western-sponsored pact.[33]

The Soviets, meanwhile, had begun a Middle East policy calculated to ingratiate themselves with Egyptians and Arabs. In the early years of the

Cold War, the Soviet Union had shown little interest in cultivating friendships with the Arab states, discouraged by the extent of Western influence in those states and by the Arabs' apparent aversion to communism. The Soviets had supported the creation of Israel, seeing it as a more promising vehicle for the promotion of Soviet interests in the area. But in the early 1950s, and especially after the death of Soviet leader Joseph Stalin in 1953, the Soviet Union began courting the Arabs, exploiting their resentment over Western support for Israel and over Anglo-American efforts to establish a regional defense organization. In 1953 and 1954 Moscow voted frequently with the Arab states in the UN, stepped up its trade with Arab states, and began enticing Egypt with modest offers of economic and military aid. These changes were part of a more general evolution in Soviet foreign policy whereby the Soviets abandoned their professed belief in the inevitability of armed conflict between communism and capitalism and replaced it with a call for peaceful competition between the two systems. One way the Soviets planned to compete was by establishing political, economic, and military ties with nationalist and independence movements previously dismissed as "bourgeois nationalist." The stress on peaceful competition became especially pronounced after early 1955, when Nikita Khrushchev, a forceful advocate of that approach, emerged as the Soviet Union's unrivaled leader.[34]

The Arab world to which both Nasser and Khrushchev began appealing in the mid-1950s was undergoing a familiar social and political transformation: a revolution of rising expectations. With the exceptions of Palestine, Algeria, and Britain's Arabian protectorates, by 1955 all of the Arab countries had achieved or were about to achieve national independence.[35] The establishment of the UN, the decline of European imperialism, the emergence of Afro-Asian nations, and the growing importance of Middle Eastern oil had convinced Arabs everywhere that they could determine their own destiny and play a major role in world affairs. They were also learning to expect more from their national governments. Whatever their other ideological commitments, most Arab governments were statist, committed to managing economies and monopolizing public utilities. Due largely to government initiative, rates of literacy and school attendance were rising throughout the Arab world, and there was a general improvement in living standards, albeit more so in the cities than in the countryside. Displaced by rural overpopulation and the mechanization of agriculture, Arab peasants were flocking to the cities, forming a new and increasingly politicized urban proletariat. In 1960 more than half the population of most Arab countries was less than twenty years old.[36]

By the mid-1950s, then, politically conscious Arabs were inclined to be restless and impatient. They had gained nominal independence and now wanted the real thing. In the coming years Nasser's message of solidarity, independence, social justice, and positive neutrality would be enthusiastically received throughout the Arab world, much to the dismay of conservative Arab regimes, whose close ties to the West made them natural targets of Nasser's rhetoric. The Eisenhower administration, too, would worry about the proliferation of Nasserist ideology, especially its neutralist element. U.S. officials feared that Arab neutralism could ultimately result in a Soviet takeover of the Middle East or, failing that, in the denial to the West of the region's strategic positions and oil reserves.

It was in five Arab nations lying to Egypt's east—Iraq, Jordan, Saudi Arabia, Syria, and Lebanon—that Nasserist influence would arouse the most vigorous and sustained controversy with the United States. Each of those nations would figure prominently in one or more of the political crises associated with the Eisenhower Doctrine. Iraq, a rival of Egypt since the days of the pharaohs, was Nasser's bitterest Arab foe. Governed as a British mandate in the 1920s, Iraq gained its independence in 1932, but Britain retained considerable influence in Baghdad. An Anglo-Iraqi defense treaty of 1930 allowed Britain to operate air bases in the country. By 1955 Iraq's nominal leader was nineteen-year-old Faisal II of the Hashemite dynasty, which claimed descent from the Prophet Muhammad. But Faisal's uncle, Crown Prince 'Abd al-Ilah, was widely seen as the real power in the land. Also dominant was Prime Minister Nuri al-Sa'id, who had the support of the royal family and large landowners. The Iraqi government derived a quarter of its revenues from oil sales and invested much of this money in large-scale agricultural development. Because of its resistance to land reform measures, however, the government never won wide popular support for its development schemes. Iraq's deep ethnic divisions exacerbated the government's predicament, and the regime increasingly relied on the army to hold the country together. Nuri himself seemed to believe that the road to salvation lay in Iraqi expansion, whether by the annexation of portions of northeastern Syria or by the formation of an Iraqi-Syrian-Jordanian federation dominated from Baghdad. U.S. officials worried about Nuri's unpopularity, but they admired his forthright support for the West and opposition to the Soviet Union.[37]

Jordan, too, was ruled by the Hashemite dynasty. Jordan's origins lay in the Kingdom of Transjordan, created during the division of Ottoman territory at the end of World War I. Transjordan had been governed as a British mandate until 1946, when it gained its independence by signing a defense treaty with Britain similar to the Anglo-Iraqi treaty of 1930. After independence, Britain continued to exert influence on Jordan by maintaining the Jordanian Arab Legion, a largely Bedouin army led by British officers. During the first Arab-Israeli war, the Arab Legion occupied and held the West Bank, which Jordan later annexed, thus acquiring a Palestinian majority consisting mostly of impoverished refugees. In 1951 King Abdullah I, who had reigned since the early 1920s, was assassinated in retribution for his prior compromises with the Zionist movement. In 1953, following the brief reign of Abdullah's son Talal, who was forced to abdicate on account of mental illness, Talal's eighteen-year-old son Hussein became king. By 1955 Jordan's prospects were extremely bleak. The country had almost no natural resources, faced the daunting task of caring for the Palestinian refugees, and was ruled by an inexperienced king. Few of Jordan's inhabitants, whether Palestinian or Jordanian, appeared to feel any primary allegiance toward the Hashemite throne.[38]

Saudi Arabia was a bitter rival of Hashemite Iraq and Jordan. In the mid-1920s forces loyal to Ibn Saud, the first king of the modern Saudi state, had expelled Hussein, the Hashemite Sharif of Mecca, from the Hijaz in Western Arabia. Britain established Hussein's sons Faisal and Abdullah, the grandfathers of Kings Faisal II and Hussein, respectively, as the rulers of Iraq and Transjordan. In 1926 the modern Saudi state was established under a constitution granting total power to the king, who was to govern under Islamic law. In the 1930s American oil companies began extracting and marketing Saudi Arabia's stupendous oil reserves. Under the aegis of the parent Arabian American Oil Company, those companies played a crucial role in Saudi development, providing most of the kingdom's revenues and infrastructure. During World War II the United States came to appreciate Saudi Arabia's strategic value not just as a source of oil but as a location for military bases, and soon thereafter the U.S. Air Force began leasing the Dhahran air base. In the early 1950s the Saudi government demanded, and was granted, a 50 percent royalty on the value of oil extracted from the country. A controversial decision by the U.S. Treasury Department allowed the oil companies to deduct from their U.S. taxes the full value of the royalty paid to Saudi Arabia—permitting, in effect, the transfer of American taxpayers' dollars to the Saudi government without consent of Congress. In 1953 Ibn Saud died and was succeeded by his son Saud, who lacked his father's shrewdness and dynamism.[39]

Syria had gained formal independence from France in 1944. Thereafter it had suffered from profound political instability, wracked by a succession of military coups. The main antagonists in Syria's power struggles were the

Arab summit meeting in Beirut, November 1956. *Left to right*: King Faisal II
of Iraq, King Hussein of Jordan, President Shukri al-Quwatli of Syria, King
Saud of Saudi Arabia, and President Camille Chamoun of Lebanon.
(© Bettmann/CORBIS)

army, the large landowning families, and a cluster of new ideological parties, of which the Ba'th, or Resurrection, party was the most dynamic. The
Ba'thists advocated vigorous opposition to Western imperialism and the
creation of a single, unified Arab state to be governed according to socialist principles. The Ba'thists were more committed to formal Arab unity
than Nasser was, but they shared his views on most other inter-Arab questions. Because their influence in Syria exceeded their numbers, they were
able, in combination with other left-leaning parties, to prod successive Syrian governments to follow a pro-Egyptian foreign policy. From early 1955
until early 1958, when it merged with Egypt to form the UAR, Syria was
Egypt's closest ally. The Ba'th Party had chapters in Iraq, Jordan, and
Lebanon that played influential roles in the political oppositions of those
countries.[40]

In inter-Arab politics, Syria had special significance as a perceived "swing
state" that could vastly enhance the power and influence of whichever Arab
state—Egypt, Iraq, or Saudi Arabia—won and kept its allegiance. After
early 1955 Syria was firmly in Egypt's camp, but Hashemite Iraq never
stopped trying to wrest Syria away from Egypt. Saudi Arabia initially supported Syria's alliance with Egypt, preferring it to an Iraqi-Syrian coalition,
but later tried to supplant Egypt as Syria's primary Arab ally and sponsor.

Lebanon, which France had severed from Syrian territory during the mandate period, was a patchwork of autonomous religious communities: Maronites, Sunnis, Shiites, Druze, Greek Orthodox, and others. Since achieving formal independence in 1944, Lebanon had been governed on the basis of an unwritten "National Pact," which recognized the reality that most Lebanese owed their primary allegiance not to the nation but to their religious sects. The National Pact distributed political power among Lebanon's religious groups in proportion to their demographic strength, with certain positions going to certain groups; thus the president was always a Maronite, the prime minister always a Sunni, and the speaker of parliament a Shiite. Lebanon's religious divisions were exacerbated by a political split between those insisting that Lebanon be oriented toward the West and those calling for closer ties with other Arab countries. Camille Chamoun, Lebanon's president since 1952, was in the former camp, but initially he had followed a circumspect foreign policy, seeking cordial relations with Arab leaders of all persuasions and avoiding obvious identification with the West.[41] This cautious approach did not survive the general polarization of Arab politics that started in early 1955. By late 1956 Chamoun was one of the most conspicuously anti-Nasserist and pro-Western Arab leaders.

In the latter half of the 1950s, forces coalesced in each of these countries—sometimes openly, sometimes secretly—to promote Nasser's program of radical Arab nationalism. Often the Ba'thists provided the organizational backbone for such efforts, but Nasser was the figure with whom the rank-and-file overwhelmingly identified. Occasionally, when Egypt's interests were directly at stake, operatives employed by Egyptian diplomatic or military missions subverted the institutions of fellow Arab states. In other instances Syrian agents engaged in such activities. Arab communist parties, always small and usually illegal, were sometimes influential in pro-Nasser coalitions, but only to the extent that they subordinated (or appeared to subordinate) communist doctrine to Arab nationalism; communists violating this rule were typically ostracized. By no means was Nasser the instigator of every nationalist disturbance convulsing the Arab Middle East in those years, but it is possible to speak of a regionwide "Nasserist movement" to which Nasser gave inspiration, approval, and, occasionally, direct guidance.

IN 1955 THE TWIN GRIEVANCES of imperialism and Zionism acquired new force in Arab politics, permitting, for the first time, significant Soviet penetration of the region. Nasser, not surprisingly, was the chief exploiter of both grievances. Exacerbating anti-imperialist resentment was the formation of the so-called Baghdad Pact. In February 1955 Turkey and Iraq concluded a mutual defense treaty. The Eisenhower administration strongly supported the Turkish-Iraqi pact and hoped it would be the nucleus of a Northern Tier defense organization that the Western powers could support without actually joining. Britain, however, seeing an opportunity to revive the Anglo-Iraqi treaty of 1930 (which had become discredited as a relic of the mandate period) and to reassert its influence among other Arab states, joined the pact in April. Pakistan and Iran adhered later that year.[42]

Nasser violently opposed the Baghdad Pact. He believed he had reached an implicit understanding with Britain that the latter, upon concluding the agreement to withdraw its forces from Egypt, would allow Egypt a breathing spell in which to establish a purely indigenous Arab defense organization. British membership in the Baghdad Pact seemed to violate that understanding. Moreover, the pact could be expected to strengthen Iraq, Egypt's traditional rival for Arab leadership. Iraq, indeed, bore the brunt of Nasser's reaction. After failing to convince the Arab League to oppose the pact, Nasser launched a vigorous propaganda campaign to vilify Iraq and prevent other Arab countries from following its lead. Nasser's most immediate success was in Syria. In February Syria's pro-Iraqi government fell and was replaced by a left-leaning, neutralist regime, dashing Baghdad's hopes of winning Syria's early adherence to the pact. The following month Egypt, Syria, and Saudi Arabia formed a rival defense pact. Although the ESS Pact, as it became known, had little military effectiveness, it both exposed and increased Iraq's political isolation in the Arab world.[43]

Nasser was able to make his case against the Baghdad Pact before a wider audience in April, when he attended a conference of African and Asian political leaders in Bandung, Indonesia. Most of the attendees at Bandung were neutralist, and Nasser was feted as an emerging leader of the nonaligned camp. Nasser made the most of the occasion, convincing the conference to adopt a resolution favoring the Arab position on Palestine and to insert a clause in the final communiqué denouncing "arrangements of collective defence to serve the interests of any of the big powers," a clear reference to the Baghdad Pact.[44]

The Eisenhower administration was taken aback by Nasser's harsh reaction to the Baghdad Pact. To deprive Nasser of additional grounds for complaint, the administration refrained from joining the pact and urged a moratorium on further Arab membership. Both U.S. reactions were dismaying to the British, who regarded the adherence of the United States and other Arab countries as essential to the Baghdad Pact's long-term survival.[45] Over the next two years, pact membership would continue to be a subject of Anglo-American controversy.

Arab-Israeli tensions also intensified in 1955. Since the spring of 1954 there had been an increase in infiltrations into Israel from the Egyptian-administered Gaza Strip, both by Palestinian individuals and by Egyptian military personnel.[46] The Egyptian government insisted that such activities were unauthorized and that it was doing all it could to stop them. To induce Egypt to work harder at this task, Israel engaged in small-scale reprisals against civilian and military targets in Gaza. By early 1955, alarmed by Nasser's growing assertiveness elsewhere in the region, Israeli leaders had concluded that sharper retaliation was in order. On 28 February, following the murder of an Israeli civilian by Egyptian intelligence agents, the Israeli army attacked an Egyptian military camp in Gaza, destroying several buildings and killing thirty-eight Egyptians and Palestinians. After another Israeli raid in August, Egypt for the first time officially authorized commando raids into Israel. That same summer Egypt tightened its four-year-old blockade on Israeli shipping through the Gulf of Aqaba, Israel's maritime outlet to the Indian Ocean.[47]

Since late 1954 the Eisenhower administration had joined Britain in pursuing a major diplomatic initiative, known as Project ALPHA, to achieve an Arab-Israeli peace settlement. From the start the administration had concentrated on enlisting Egypt, the most influential Arab state, as the primary Arab participant in such a process. The escalation of Egyptian-Israeli tensions in the spring and summer of 1955 gave fresh urgency to the quest for peace. In a 26 August speech, Dulles called for a settlement whereby the Arab states, in exchange for territorial "adjustments" and compensation of Palestinian refugees (who were to be settled in other Arab lands), concluded peace treaties with Israel. Dulles pledged that the United States would mediate between the parties, help to finance the compensation and resettlement of refugees, and guarantee the peace treaties. The Egyptian and Israeli governments reacted cautiously to Dulles's speech, asking to see further details before committing themselves on the U.S. plan.[48]

Both by pursuing Project ALPHA and by seeking to limit Arab membership of the Baghdad Pact, the United States had hoped to minimize Nasser's sense of grievance against the West. Nasser, however, desired a more robust solution to the twin problems of Israel and the pact. Throughout the summer of 1955, Nasser pressed the United States to sell heavy arms to Egypt, threatening to turn to the Soviet Union if his request was denied. The Eisenhower administration feared that an arms sale to Egypt would have to be paired with a similar sale to Israel, setting off a dangerous arms race in the region. Not wishing to rebuff Nasser outright, the administration made him an offer he was bound to refuse: arms sold at nondiscount prices, payable only in hard currency. Dulles evidently doubted that Nasser really would turn to the Soviets or that, if he did, the Soviets would sell him much. This was a serious miscalculation. In September 1955, using Czechoslovakia as an intermediary, Egypt and the Soviet Union concluded a cotton-for-arms barter deal publicly valued at about $86 million. The U.S. Defense Department later calculated that, correcting for the Soviets' drastically discounted prices, the actual value was $200 million. More important than the monetary value was the marked increase in Soviet influence in the Middle East. "Earlier we had no access to the Arab countries," Soviet deputy premier Anastas Mikoyan recalled in 1957. "But then we sold arms to Egypt, we bared our teeth to our enemies, and . . . now they cannot any longer resolve the issues of the Near East without us."[49]

Dulles considered the Soviet arms deal "as irresponsible as giving a lethal weapon to children to play with." But the Eisenhower administration was not willing to give up on Nasser and thus drive him further into the Soviets' embrace. There were indications, moreover, that Nasser himself was uneasy over the arms deal and might be receptive to counterbalancing overtures from the West. Accordingly, the administration took two actions aimed at renewing Nasser's ties with the Western camp. The first was to show a more active interest in the Aswan Dam project, an ambitious Egyptian scheme to regulate the Nile's flow so as to increase agricultural yield and produce hydroelectric power. For some years the United States had considered financing the project along with Britain and the World Bank. Now, with Egypt drifting closer to the Soviet orbit, U.S. officials revisited the issue with greater seriousness. In December 1955 the U.S. and British governments submitted a formal funding offer to the Egyptian government, which withheld its acceptance pending negotiation of some of the terms. The second U.S. response was to push harder for an Arab-Israeli settlement. In January 1956 the administration sent Robert B. Anderson, a former deputy secretary of defense and close friend of Eisenhower, on a secret mission to the Middle East, code-named GAMMA. Anderson's task was to meet separately with Nasser and Israeli prime minister David Ben-Gurion to seek a workable formula for a peace settlement.[50]

Meanwhile the Western position in the Middle East suffered a further setback, this time in Jordan. In late 1955, against U.S. advice, the British government urged King Hussein to bring Jordan into the Baghdad Pact, and Hussein provisionally agreed to do so. In December Britain sent General Gerald Templer, chief of the imperial general staff, to Amman to discuss terms of adherence. Templer's visit aroused fierce opposition among Hussein's subjects, especially the Palestinians, who made up two-thirds of Jordan's population. After Prime Minister Sa'id al-Mufti was obliged to resign, Hussein made matters worse by replacing him with Hazza' al-Majali, a strong advocate of Jordanian adherence to the Baghdad Pact. Violent demonstrations, supported by Egyptian propaganda and Saudi cash, swept the country. By 20 December al-Majali, too, had been forced to step down, and Hussein had changed his mind about joining the pact.[51]

British policy toward Jordan soon suffered another humiliating blow. In early March 1956, in a further effort to appease local opinion, Hussein dismissed the Arab Legion's British commander, Lieutenant General John Bagot Glubb. Though formally answering to Hussein, Glubb had been seen as a symbol of British domination. British prime minister Anthony Eden was convinced that Nasser had engineered Glubb's ouster, and he dismissed any suggestion that domestic Jordanian politics may have influenced Hussein's decision. "I want [Nasser] destroyed," he said to Minister of State Anthony Nutting, according to the latter's 1967 memoirs. In 1984 Nutting claimed that Eden had actually used the word "murdered," not "destroyed."[52]

The Americans themselves were losing patience with Nasser, though their favored remedy fell far short of homicide. Anderson had made no headway in his mediation efforts, a failure the Eisenhower administration blamed mostly on Nasser. During Anderson's initial meetings with Nasser and Ben-Gurion, held in their respective countries in January, the two leaders had sharply disagreed on both procedural and substantive matters.[53] Still, there had been an implicit understanding that, should Nasser and Ben-Gurion find a mutually acceptable formula, Nasser would recommend it to other Arab leaders. By early March, however, Nasser was backing away from this understanding. Even if Egypt and Israel could agree on an approach, he told Anderson on 5 March, "Egypt will not put the proposal forward as its own idea" in discussions with other Arab governments. Instead, some third party, like the United States or the UN, would have to present the proposal to each of the other Arab countries, and they in turn must be free to propose modifications. This condition, Anderson reported to Washington, was "a completely new and discouraging element" and suggested that Nasser did not believe a settlement was currently feasible. "To date this has been the most disappointing conference since the beginning of the mission." Anderson left the Middle East the next day.[54]

Why did Nasser balk? The most plausible explanation was offered by Anderson, who believed that Nasser "would like to see war avoided but . . .

is not willing to assume aggressive leadership to avoid it," since doing so "would endanger his prestige in the Arab world." Nasser worried that Iraqi leaders, stung by Egyptian propaganda attacks on the Baghdad Pact, would be quick to vilify him should he advocate any compromise with Israel. As Nasser told Anderson on 4 March, "The Baghdad Pact divides the Arab world in such a way as to make it extremely dangerous for any single Arab leader to take bold action . . . in [a] settlement with Israel." Nasser even apparently feared for his personal safety, telling Anderson the next day, "I am unwilling to gamble my future or that of my country in any circumstances similar to the Abdulla incident"—a reference to the assassinated Jordanian king. Some State Department analysts, however, took a much harsher view of Nasser's motives, arguing that the new availability of Soviet arms had caused Nasser to lose interest in a peace settlement and perhaps even to contemplate "a war of annihilation against Israel as soon as he feels that victory is assured."[55]

In diary entries on 8 and 13 March, Eisenhower vented his own frustration with Nasser. During Anderson's mission, he wrote, "Nasser proved to be a complete stumbling block. . . . Because he wants to be the most popular man in all the Arab world, he . . . has to consider public opinion in each of the other countries. The result is that he finally concludes he should take no action whatsoever [to reach peace]—rather he should just make speeches, all of which must breathe defiance of Israel." Soviet military assistance, Eisenhower believed, was reinforcing such intransigence. "The Arabs, absorbing major consignments of arms from the Soviets, are daily growing more arrogant and disregarding the interest of Western Europe and of the United States in the Middle East region." Thus, rather than encouraging Nasser to lead the Arab world in opposing Soviet influence and making peace with Israel, the United States should try to forge a pro-Western Arab coalition to oppose him. "If Egypt finds herself thus isolated from the rest of the Arab world, and with no ally in sight except Soviet Russia," Eisenhower predicted, "she would very quickly get sick of that prospect and would join us in the search for a just and decent peace in that region."[56]

Later that month Eisenhower asked Dulles to draw up a new set of guidelines for Middle East policy. The resulting memorandum, dated 28 March, revealed the extent to which official Washington had soured on Nasser. Dulles's memo proposed a series of U.S. actions "to let Colonel Nasser realize that he cannot cooperate as he is doing with the Soviet Union and at the same time enjoy most-favored-nation treatment from the United States." Still, "we would want for the time being to avoid any open break which would throw Nasser irrevocably into a Soviet satellite status and we would want to leave Nasser a bridge back to good relations with the West if he so desires."[57] In keeping with the Greek theme, Dulles's proposals were dubbed the OMEGA plan.

Dulles's memorandum first outlined a series of steps, some to be coordinated with Britain, that the United States could take against Egypt itself: denying export licensees to U.S. and British companies wishing to sell arms to Egypt, dragging out negotiations on Western financing of the Aswan Dam, continuing to delay action on pending Egyptian requests to purchase U.S. grain and oil under Public Law (PL) 480,[58] and deferring any decision on further U.S. economic assistance to Egypt. According to a more detailed State Department memorandum of the same date, the United States would not draw Nasser's attention to these measures but would simply let them unfold, thus leaving "an opportunity for Nasser to reverse his previous policies" should he so choose.[59]

Dulles's memorandum next listed steps that the United States could take regarding other Middle Eastern countries: bolstering pro-Western governments in Lebanon and Libya, shoring up Britain's position in Jordan, giving increased support to the Baghdad Pact without actually joining it, strengthening U.S. relations with Saudi Arabia, and, while continuing to deny export licenses to U.S. firms wishing to sell major weapons to Israel, looking favorably on such sales by other Western countries, thereby deterring a potential Egyptian attack.[60]

Ideally, the above measures alone would force Egypt to rethink its anti-Western posture. If not, the United States could proceed to "more drastic action." In the versions of the 28 March memorandum available in official archives, the substance of this final recommendation has been censored, prompting scholars to speculate that the proposed drastic action may have included the overthrow of the Nasser regime. But a verbatim transcript of the document made by the political scientist Louis M. Gerson reveals no such recommendation. Instead, the memorandum speaks of "manipulating U.S. cotton export and import policies in a manner which would lead seriously to impede Egyptian cotton exports," "making facilities available to other countries for interference by jamming of hostile radio broadcasts" from Egypt, and consulting with Britain about a "possible change of government in Syria to one more friendly to Iraq and the West." A coup in Damascus, not Cairo, lay at the outer limits of official U.S. contemplation that spring.[61] All of these measures, Dulles implied, would leave Egypt so impoverished and isolated that it would have to abandon its radical policies or forfeit its influence in the Arab world.

Reviewing Dulles's memorandum on 28 March, Eisenhower said "he was inclined to agree with all of the suggestions," though he thought greater attention should be paid to U.S.-Saudi relations. The United States, he said, should consider "build[ing] up King Saud as a figure with sufficient prestige to offset Nasser." Eisenhower's suggestion was a more ambitious formulation of a policy the State Department was already advocating: working to prevent the "critical contradictions in Saudi national policy" from damaging U.S. interests in the region. Although the Saudi government was deeply anticommunist and had close military and economic ties to the United States, it was intensely hostile to Britain and Hashemite Iraq, a sentiment it shared with Nasserist Egypt. Since early 1955 Saud had supported Egypt's anti–Baghdad Pact campaign in the Arab world, using his wealth to bribe anti-Hashemite politicians and fund anti-Hashemite newspapers and demonstrations. Saudi money had played a major role in the recent riots in Jordan and in the defeat of Syria's pro-Iraqi government in February 1955. Saud had also echoed Nasser's anti-imperialist rhetoric and even defended Egypt's decision to purchase arms from the Soviet bloc. By March 1956 the State Department's Bureau of Near Eastern, South Asian, and African Affairs (NEA) was proposing "a sustained effort to detach Saudi Arabia from Egyptian influence," and Dulles was seeking ways "to draw [the] Saudis into [the] same orbit as Iraq."[62]

Eisenhower shared these objectives but now took them a step further. Instead of simply shifting Saud from one camp to the other, the United States should try to build him up as an anti-Nasserist pan-Arab leader in his own right. Saud's key advantage, Eisenhower believed, was Saudi Arabia's centrality to Islam. "I do not know the man," the president wrote in his diary on 28 March, but "Arabia is a country that contains the holy places of the Moslem world, and the Saudi Arabians are considered to be the most deeply religious of all the Arab groups. Consequently, the King could be built up, possibly, as a spiritual leader. Once this were accomplished we might begin to urge his right to political leadership." As Keeper of the Holy Places of Islam, Saud was well placed to "disrupt the aggressive plans that Nasser is evidently developing." A few days later a British diplomat, after meeting with Dulles, reported to London that Eisenhower favored "building up King Saud as 'monkey monk' of the Arabs"—perhaps a garbling of Dulles's use of the American expression "high muck-a-muck."[63]

Separating Saud from Nasser was a feasible objective; building him up as a pan-Arab rival of Nasser was not. Neither Saudi Arabia nor Saud was in a strong position to project political leadership in the Arab world. Saudi Arabia's dependence on the infrastructural services of the Arabian American Oil Company made it vulnerable to the charge of being an American vassal. Its heavy reliance on the labor and expertise of non-Saudi Arabs, especially Egyptians, exposed it to Egyptian political pressure, whether through the intercession of pro-Egyptian advisers in Saud's court, through the influence of Egyptian teachers in Saudi Arabia, or through the persistent threat of Egyptian-incited unrest among non-Saudi laborers.[64] Saud himself was an amiable but inexperienced leader, largely ignorant of affairs beyond his borders. His personal lifestyle, a gaudy spectacle of opulence and debauchery, scandalized many non-Saudi Arabs, making it difficult for them to regard the king as a serious contender for regional influence. Clearly Saud was no match for Nasser, and Eisenhower was naive to suppose that the king's religious credentials could make up for this fact.[65]

While few U.S. officials shared Eisenhower's enthusiasm for pitting Saud against Nasser, the more modest goal of separating the two leaders had wide support within the administration. And it was on the latter objective, and on the prospect of a "change of government in Syria," that American officials would set their sights in the spring and summer of 1956. Even after the eruption of the Suez crisis had focused the world's attention on Egypt, the disruption of the ESS Pact would remain a major U.S. goal.

There was a danger, however, that an Arab-Israeli war would break out before the effort to isolate Nasser could get under way. Thus, concurrently with the March reassessment of Nasser, NEA proposed that the executive branch "prepare a draft of a Joint Congressional Resolution which would authorize the President to use military force if necessary in case of aggression by Israel or the Arab states." Dulles rejected the proposal, arguing that "the Middle East situation was very confused, and . . . hostilities might break out under circumstances which would not make it possible clearly to identify the aggressor."[66] The idea of a congressional resolution would be revived after the Suez war, albeit with a different threat in mind.

IN EARLY APRIL Dulles met with British embassy officials to discuss the new U.S. policy for the Middle East. Although the British were less optimistic about eventually bringing Nasser around, they endorsed the idea of quietly squeezing Egypt and bolstering its regional rivals. The British also privately doubted "the extent to which Saudi Arabia can be built up as an anti-communist force," but they shared the basic objective of separating Saud from Nasser. The Eisenhower administration meanwhile approved Canadian and French sales of additional military aircraft for Israel. Such third party sales, the State Department believed, would allow for the containment of Nasser's ambitions with minimal complications elsewhere in the Arab world. As previous sales of French aircraft to Israel had shown, the "Arab reaction is less excited if [the] arms are not directed from [the] US even though it is known that US consent was required."[67]

The British already had a plan for Syria. By late March the British spy agency MI6 had devised an ambitious scheme, code-named "Straggle," for achieving the overthrow of the Syrian government. Working primarily through the Iraqis, the British proposed to funnel money to pro-Iraqi politicians in Syria, stir up unrest among Syrian tribes, and infiltrate the country with members of the Parti Populaire Syrien (PPS), the right-wing Syrian Social Nationalist Party based in Lebanon. These activities, MI6 hoped, would set the stage for pro-Iraqi officers to execute a coup or, failing that, provide a pretext for the Iraqis themselves to intervene militarily and set up a friendly government in Damascus. The PPS hoped that former Syrian dictator Adib al-Shishakli, who was then in Paris, would agree to head up the new government. In July al-Shishakli arrived in Beirut for discussions with the PPS.[68]

The Americans, however, were not yet ready for such drastic measures. While conceding that a Syrian coup might eventually be necessary, they first wanted to try a more modest plan: secretly encouraging pro-Western Syrian politicians to achieve power by constitutional, or at least not overtly violent, means. If successful, these politicians could then purge the Syrian government and army of leftists and orient the country toward the West. The principal Syrian politician through whom U.S. officials hoped to work was Mikhail Ilyan, a pro-Iraqi Christian from Aleppo. In late July, Wilbur Crane Eveland, the CIA's point-man on Syria, met with Ilyan in Damascus and urged him to produce a detailed plan for strengthening pro-Western forces in Syria. Meanwhile, Eveland convinced Lebanese president Camille Chamoun to see to it that al-Shishakli, whose plotting the Americans regarded as an obstacle to their scheme, was spirited out of Lebanon. Britain, Iraq, and the PPS nevertheless continued their planning for a Syrian coup.[69]

Meanwhile, a much larger drama was unfolding over the Aswan Dam. In early April the U.S. and British governments agreed to delay negotiations over financing the dam so as "to keep Nasser guessing" about his standing with the West.[70] Over the next few months, however, several developments convinced Dulles that the United States should pull out of the project altogether: Egypt's decision to open diplomatic relations with the People's Republic of China, growing opposition to the Aswan Dam project within the U.S. Congress,[71] and Nasser's implied threat to turn to the Soviets for funding should Western terms prove unsatisfactory, a ploy that outraged Dulles. At the same time, Dulles believed that, because of the austerity that Egypt would need to impose on itself to repay such heavy loans, the Egyptian people would grow to resent their creditors; perhaps it would be better to let the Soviets be cursed with this role. On 19 July the United States withdrew its offer to help finance the dam, and over the next few days Britain and the World Bank followed suit.[72]

Although Nasser apparently was not surprised by the Aswan Dam decision, he was outraged by the abrupt manner in which it was conveyed to his government and by Dulles's public intimation that the United States had withdrawn the offer because the Egyptian economy could not sustain such an ambitious undertaking. Dulles's statement, Nasser believed, was a gratuitous slap at Egypt's dignity and perhaps even an effort to undermine the Cairo regime. On 26 July, addressing a huge audience in Alexandria, Nasser announced that Egypt had nationalized the Suez Canal Company and would use the canal's toll revenues to finance the construction of the Aswan Dam. With this decision, Nasser said, "Arab nationalism has been set on fire from the Atlantic Ocean to the Persian Gulf." Nasser's declaration was applauded throughout the Arab world.[73]

The nationalization of the Suez Canal Company was legal in that Egypt pledged to compensate the company's shareholders at prevailing market rates. Britain, however, saw the act as politically, economically, and strategically intolerable and vowed to reverse it by any necessary means, force included.[74] France, already angered by Nasser's support of the Algerian rebels, echoed Britain's insistence that the nationalization could not stand. Despite some ambiguities at the margins, the general thrust of American thinking on this question was clear: The seizure of the canal company was a regrettable act, and vigorous efforts must be made to reimpose a measure of international control over the canal. But the use of force to achieve this goal would only make matters worse, inflaming the Arab world against the West and giving the Soviets an opportunity to increase their influence in the area. In August and September the United States took the lead in convening two international conferences, both in London, to find a formula for the international administration of the canal that would be acceptable to Egypt and the major maritime nations. Nasser, however, rejected any solution that fell short of full Egyptian sovereignty over the canal.[75]

Even as it tried to shield Egypt from military attack, the Eisenhower administration continued its efforts to isolate Nasser in the Arab world. In some ways the canal crisis facilitated this task. By August King Saud was rethinking his alliance with Nasser. Saud was disturbed that Nasser had failed to consult him before nationalizing the Suez Canal Company and thus exposing Egypt to Western attack. Not only would such an attack trigger Saudi Arabia's obligations under the ESS Pact of 1955, it could well result in a ces-

President Nasser returns to Cairo from Alexandria, where he has announced
Egypt's nationalization of the Suez Canal Company, August 1956.
(© Hulton-Deutsch Collection/CORBIS)

sation of oil shipments through the Suez Canal, damaging the Saudi economy. Saud also worried that general Arab enthusiasm over Egypt's nationalization decree would stimulate similar demands for the nationalization of
oil installations in Saudi Arabia and for the distribution of Saudi wealth
among poorer Arab states.[76]

An indication of Saud's displeasure with Egyptian policy was his willingness to mend fences with Hashemite Iraq, an attitude encouraged by both
the Americans and the British. In August and September Saud hosted a series of Iraqi delegations culminating in a brief visit to Saudi Arabia by Iraqi
King Faisal. According to the Iraqi government, Saud told the Iraqis that
"Nasser had started this fire without consulting his Arab neighbors," that
"Nasser's ambition was to become the Napoleon of the Arab world," and
that "solid cooperation between the ruling Families in Iraq and Saudi Arabia" was now necessary.[77]

Eisenhower sought to capitalize on Saud's growing estrangement from
Nasser. In late August he sent Robert Anderson on another secret mission
to the Middle East, this time to Saudi Arabia. Anderson's main task was to
convince Saud to intercede with Nasser on behalf of an eighteen-power
proposal for international administration of the Suez Canal, but the envoy
also sought to widen the rift between Saud and Nasser.[78] Meeting with the

king and his brother, Crown Prince Faisal, Anderson warned that Nasser's behavior over Suez was damaging the West's confidence in the canal as a reliable shipping route. Unless such confidence were restored, Western nations would have to seek alternative shipping routes from the Middle East. But this, Anderson continued, would drive up the price of Middle Eastern oil, creating an incentive for Western nations to purchase oil elsewhere. The West might even "be forced by necessity, [the] 'mother of invention' [to] produce new sources [of] energy"—a veiled reference to nuclear power. Saud seemed impressed by this argument, but Faisal, who apparently had been reading up on the subject (and whose suspicion of U.S. motives far exceeded Saud's), dismissed the notion that nuclear energy could soon replace petroleum, thus calling Anderson's bluff.[79]

In any event, Saud could not venture far from a position of unconditional support for an Egypt menaced by Western powers. Saud made it clear to Anderson that any Saudi mediation of the dispute had to proceed on the basis of Egyptian sovereignty over the Suez Canal. On 7 September Saud wrote to Nasser offering to intercede with the United States "in a confidential and personal way" to find a resolution to the crisis compatible with Egyptian interests. According to Egyptian journalist and Nasser confidant Muhammad Hasanayn Haykal, Saud's letter caused Nasser to fear that the king was "on the verge of changing from an ally into an intermediary." On 23 September Nasser flew to Dammam, Saudi Arabia, and warned Saud against U.S. efforts to drive a wedge between them. Obligingly, Saud joined Nasser in a public communiqué "supporting Egypt completely in its attitude" toward the canal crisis. At least for the time being, Saud had been prevented from charting an independent course.[80]

The Eisenhower administration also continued its efforts to wrest Syria from Egypt's embrace. For reasons that are not entirely clear, by late summer the administration had decided to endorse a Syrian coup after all, while still apparently hoping to avoid Iraqi intervention. Around September the CIA authorized Eveland to give Mikhail Ilyan £500,000 Syrian (about $140,000), to be distributed among disaffected Syrian officers who would seize control of Syria's major cities, frontier posts, and radio stations. Meanwhile, the PPS leaders and the Iraqis had devised an elaborate plan of their own for dislodging the Syrian regime. As a PPS paramilitary force seized Homs and key strongholds in Damascus, forces loyal to Salah al-Shishakli, Adib's brother, would take over Hama. Simultaneously, Druze and Alawite tribes in Syria, armed by Iraq, would rebel against local authorities. It is unclear whether Ilyan was coordinating his plans with the PPS and the Iraqis, but his great-power sponsor was certainly coordinating with theirs. In the second week of October, State Department and CIA officials met in Washington with their counterparts from the British Foreign Office and MI6 to discuss Operation Straggle. Both sides agreed that the coup attempt should take place at the end of October.[81]

Egyptian and Syrian officials were vaguely aware of the unfolding conspiracy against the Damascus regime. In late September Egyptian diplomats began receiving reports, first from an unnamed source in the U.S. State Department and later from a Lebanese politician, that the United States and Britain were plotting a coup operation in Syria aimed at installing Adib Shishakli as president, at "taking Syria out of the Egyptian camp," and at "totally eliminating in Syria the power of the communists."[82] Meeting with Egyptian ambassador to Syria Mahmud Riad on 15 October, Syrian prime minister Sabri al-'Asali said that his government had received similar reports and was closely monitoring the activities of Ilyan's political associates in Syria. Al-'Asali was frustrated, however, by the lack of detailed information and told Riad that he had "come to expect that anything might happen in Syria, though he cannot pinpoint the location of the blow."[83]

By now a far more ambitious conspiracy was being hatched against Egypt itself. In September French and Israeli officials met secretly in Paris to discuss joint military action to remove the Nasser regime and seize control of the Suez Canal. In London in mid-October, French officials presented Prime Minister Eden with an outline of the French-Israeli plan. Israel would attack Egypt in the Sinai Peninsula and begin advancing on the Suez Canal. Britain and France would then demand that Israel and Egypt withdraw their forces from the canal area. If either party refused the ultimatum—as Egypt was sure to do since the canal lay within its own sovereign territory—British and French forces would seize the canal, ostensibly to protect it from damage in the fighting. On 24 October, in what became known as the Protocol of Sèvres (named for the suburb of Paris in which it was drawn up), British, French, and Israeli leaders finalized and approved the plan. The Israeli attack was set to begin on 29 October.[84]

The conspirators further agreed that the United States would receive no advance notice of the scheme. The thinking seems to have been that, while the Americans would never approve such an operation in advance, they would probably accept it as a fait accompli given their own dislike of Nasser, their sense of solidarity with the allies, and their fear of opposing Israel on the eve of the upcoming presidential election, in which Eisenhower was seeking a second term.[85] This was, it turned out, a fatal miscalculation.

The British also neglected to disclose their intentions to the Iraqis, who, along with the Americans, were already collaborating with them on Operation Straggle. The British apparently assumed that Iraq, too, would retro-actively endorse an attack on Egypt. Since late July Iraqi leaders had privately urged Britain not to rule out the use of force in reversing Nasser's nationalization decree, which had stimulated pro-Nasser and antiregime sentiment inside Iraq. "It was a mistake to believe," Prime Minister Nuri al-Saʿid told a British diplomat in late August, "that a strong line or use of force would unite the Arab World against the West. There would be demonstrations, but that would be the end of it and afterwards the situation would improve."[86] Of course, had Nuri known that Britain planned to collaborate with Israel, he would not have been so sanguine. Iraq was already risking exposure by its participation in Operation Straggle. Should Britain, Iraq's ally, now attack Egypt in league with Israel, the political danger to the Iraqi regime would vastly increase. Failure to grasp this reality was another major error on Britain's part.

THE SUEZ WAR BEGAN on 29 October, when Israeli forces crossed into the Sinai, overwhelmed Egyptian border posts, and quickly advanced across the peninsula. The next day Britain and France issued their planned ultimatum, demanding that Israel and Egypt withdraw to within ten miles of either side of the Suez Canal and permit Anglo-French forces to occupy the canal zone. Israel predictably accepted the ultimatum, and Egypt, equally predictably, rejected it out of hand. On 31 October British and French airplanes began bombing Egyptian airfields near the canal zone.[87]

The Eisenhower administration reacted first with dismay over the Israeli assault and then with shock and outrage over the evident British and French collusion. Convinced that the United States would lose standing in the world if it failed to uphold Egypt's sovereignty, the administration strongly opposed the tripartite attack in the UN, even voting alongside the Soviet Union. After Britain and France used their vetoes to block action in the Security Council, the United States introduced a resolution in the General Assembly demanding that Britain, France, and Israel cease hostilities at once and that Israel withdraw behind the armistice lines. The resolution passed overwhelmingly, along with a Canadian resolution providing for a United Nations Emergency Force (UNEF) to enter the canal zone once the fighting had stopped. On nationwide television Eisenhower chided Egypt's attackers for acting outside the framework of the UN.[88] Meanwhile, at the peak of the crisis, Dulles was hospitalized with severe abdominal pains, later diagnosed as stomach cancer. Dulles would not return to the State Department until early December. Undersecretary of State Herbert Hoover

Jr., son of the former president, would serve as acting secretary in Dulles's absence.[89]

The attack on Egypt was doubly objectionable to U.S. officials because it diverted international attention from dramatic events in Eastern Europe. Earlier that October, encouraged by Nikita Khrushchev's de-Stalinization campaign and by recent reforms in Poland, Hungarian students had risen up in revolt against the Soviet military presence in Hungary. By month's end, Soviet forces had begun withdrawing from Budapest, and Imre Nagy, Hungary's new reformist prime minister, had announced that Hungary would leave the Warsaw Pact. It briefly seemed as if the Soviets had lost their nerve and that their entire alliance system might unravel. With the world's attention fastened on Western aggression against Egypt, however, the United States was ill equipped to take political advantage of the disarray in the communist world, and the Soviets were soon emboldened to reimpose control over their renegade ally. On 4 November the Soviet Union launched a massive military assault on Hungary, killing thousands of dissidents and driving tens of thousands more into exile. By 8 November the uprising had been crushed and Nagy arrested; he was later executed. Hopes for the peaceful liberation of Eastern Europe were dashed, not to be resurrected for a decade.[90]

The Suez war also interfered with Operation Straggle, whose execution had likewise been scheduled for late October. On the evening of 29 October, upon hearing of Israel's invasion of the Sinai, Mikhail Ilyan passed word to his coconspirators that the coup attempt in Syria must be immediately aborted, lest the operation be discredited by association with the Israeli attack. Ilyan then fled to Beirut, not knowing if his message had been received. It did not matter; Syrian authorities had long been monitoring the unfolding conspiracy and now moved to apprehend the suspected coup plotters. Before dawn the next morning, a furious Ilyan appeared at the doorstep of Eveland's Beirut apartment. "How," the Syrian demanded, "could you have asked us to overthrow our government at the exact moment when Israel started a war with an Arab state?" Only with difficulty was Eveland able to convince Ilyan that the CIA had not been privy to the Israeli attack.[91]

On 5 November Anglo-French paratroopers began landing at Port Said, at the canal's northern entrance, and were shortly followed by amphibious forces. Already, however, pressures were being applied that would soon force Britain and France to abandon their venture. Days earlier, Nasser had closed the Suez Canal by sinking blockships loaded with cement, and Syrian saboteurs, with the connivance of their government, had destroyed pumping stations for the Iraq Petroleum Company's oil pipelines in Syria. Western Europe was almost entirely deprived of Middle Eastern oil.[92] Prior to the crisis, in anticipation of such a cutoff in the event of war, U.S. and British officials had devised plans for emergency oil shipments from the Western Hemisphere to Western Europe. The Eisenhower administration now refused to activate those plans until Britain and France called off the attack on Egypt. At the same time, an international run on the pound had begun to erode Britain's gold reserves. The United States blocked Britain's application to borrow gold from the International Monetary Fund as long as the attack on Egypt continued.[93]

The Soviets, meanwhile, were applying pressures of their own. On 5 November the Soviet government publicly proposed that the United States and the Soviet Union conduct a joint military intervention on Egypt's behalf if Britain, France, and Israel failed to withdraw their forces within three days. The United States immediately rejected the proposal as "unthinkable." That same day, the Soviets issued public warnings to the British and French governments implying that the Soviet Union would launch missiles against Britain and France unless they ceased their attacks on Egypt. The Soviets publicly urged the Israeli government "to come to its senses before it is too late."[94]

The Eisenhower administration did not know what to make of the Soviet statements. While it was tempting to dismiss them as an attempt to divert international attention from the slaughter in Hungary, no one could rule out that something more serious was afoot. The threat to rain missiles on London and Paris was far-fetched, but the possibility of Soviet intervention in the Middle East was less so. After all, Eisenhower observed, "the Soviets are scared and furious, and there is nothing more dangerous than a dictatorship in this state of mind. He referred to Hitler's last days in this connection." Eisenhower was particularly worried that the Soviets might send military aircraft to Syria, from which raids could be launched against targets elsewhere in the region. He ordered the CIA to send U-2 reconnaissance flights over Syria to monitor the situation.[95]

Election day, 6 November, went well for Eisenhower. At noon came word that the U-2 flights had detected no Soviet planes on Syrian airfields. Eisenhower also learned that Britain had finally agreed to a cease-fire, obliging France to follow suit. (Israel had agreed to a cease-fire the previous day.) By evening, early returns were pointing to a landslide reelection victory for Eisenhower, who was to win by a margin of nearly 10 million

A child stands amid ruins of Port Said, Egypt, shortly after
the cease-fire in the Suez war, November 1956.
(© Bettmann/CORBIS)

votes. Both houses of Congress, however, would remain in Democratic
hands.[96]

As the cease-fire took hold, the dust settled to reveal a truly odd situation. Britain and France had occupied the canal zone, but their political and
economic dependence on the United States had been exposed to the world;
Britain now seemed finished as the preeminent Western power in the Middle East. The Suez Canal, whose reliable operation the Anglo-French action had been intended to safeguard, was temporarily useless. Egypt had
suffered a humiliating military defeat at Israel's hands and was under occupation by three hostile powers, but because Britain and France had joined
the attack, Nasser was being hailed throughout the Arab world as a heroic
resister of great-power aggression. The United States had gained considerable prestige in the region for defending Egypt's sovereignty, but so had the
Soviet Union, whose denunciations of Egypt's attackers had delighted Arab
audiences. Although U.S.-Soviet cooperation in the UN had raised hopes for
an easing of Cold War tensions, those tensions were actually intensifying as
U.S. officials now fretted about possible Soviet military intervention in the

Middle East, a scenario made more credible by Moscow's ruthless crushing of the Hungarian uprising. For most Western observers, this disorienting jumble of circumstances pointed to a single inescapable conclusion: the United States must now take the lead in rescuing the Western position in the Middle East.

BIRTH OF A DOCTRINE,
NOVEMBER 1956–JANUARY 1957

The two months following the cease-fire of 7 November 1956 confirmed what many already suspected: Britain and France had forfeited their positions as leading Western powers in the Middle East. During the previous week international diplomatic pressure had forced Britain, France, and Israel to halt their attacks on Egypt. Over the next several weeks a continuation of that pressure, especially economic pressure by the United States, forced Britain and France to agree, on 3 December, to an unconditional withdrawal from Egypt. By 22 December British and French troops had fully evacuated the country. Israel continued to occupy the Sinai Peninsula and the Gaza Strip. Pending a settlement of its legal status, the Suez Canal remained closed and under Egyptian control.

Of the two European powers, Britain suffered the larger demotion. Having started from a position of greater regional prominence, it had farther to fall. In the weeks following the attack on Egypt, Britain's extensive interests in the Arab world came under wholesale assault. Ordinary Arabs harassed British subjects, boycotted British products, disrupted British institutions, and destroyed or vandalized British property. The Egyptian government seized British companies and expelled or detained British subjects. Egypt, Syria, and Saudi Arabia severed diplomatic relations with Britain. Even Arab states traditionally friendly to Britain were obliged to distance themselves from the "imperialist aggressor." The Jordanian government began the process of ending its treaty relationship with Britain. The Iraqi regime, itself verging on collapse, loudly denounced the attack on Egypt and came close to leaving the British-sponsored Baghdad Pact.

Almost from the moment this angry Arab reaction began, Eisenhower administration officials agreed that the resulting reduction in British power and influence would create a diplomatic, political, and military vacuum in the Arab world. They also agreed that the United States had to fill that vacuum before the Soviets filled it themselves, and that a major U.S. initiative must be launched for this purpose. Initially Eisenhower hoped to combat Soviet influence in the Arab world through an approach that was indirect and relatively benign: securing the friendship of an Arab world already united in opposition to the Soviet Union. Events in the region soon cast doubt on this prospect, however, and in early December Eisenhower acquiesced in the formulation of a tougher regional policy. Under the new approach, which became popularly known as the Eisenhower Doctrine, the United States would not only issue a direct challenge to the Soviet Union but seek to deepen and exploit existing divisions in the Arab world.

ON 8 NOVEMBER Eisenhower recorded his thoughts on a new U.S. policy for the Middle East. The president was in a buoyant mood. On 6 November he had been overwhelmingly reelected to a second term in office; on 7 November the cease-fire in the Suez war had gone into effect. Now, as Eisenhower considered possible U.S. measures to "minimize the effects of the recent difficulties and . . . exclude from the area Soviet influence," his optimism and confidence were evident.[1]

To accomplish the first task, Eisenhower wrote, the United States should seek a "rapid restoration of pipe line and Canal operation" so that the flow of Middle Eastern oil to Western Europe could resume as soon as possible. The United States should also push for negotiations in the UN to prevent a renewed outbreak of fighting, and it should provide surplus food and other humanitarian relief "to prevent suffering" in the region.[2]

To combat Soviet influence in the Middle East, Eisenhower continued, the United States should blanket the area with negative publicity about the recent Soviet suppression of the Hungarian revolt. Each Middle Eastern country must understand "what can be in store for it once it falls under the domination of the Soviets."[3] The United States should also offer positive inducements to Middle Eastern countries. It could offer Egypt technical and financial assistance in repairing the damage caused by the war, as well as arms and training missions "in return for an agreement that it will never accept any [additional] Soviet offer" of military aid. Washington might even reconsider financial assistance for the Aswan Dam project, the issue that had sparked the Suez crisis in the first place. Meanwhile, the United States could provide a large economic loan to Israel and make it an arms offer "of exactly the same type we could make with Egypt." It could also improve its "economic and friendly ties" with Iraq, Jordan, Saudi Arabia, and Lebanon.[4]

On 13 November Eisenhower instructed the State Department to produce a major study of future Middle East policy. Because Secretary Dulles was still on sick leave (he would not return to work until early December),[5] Eisenhower communicated his wishes through Acting Secretary of State Herbert Hoover Jr. and State Department counselor Douglas MacArthur II, the department's liaison with the White House (and nephew of the famous general). The president said that "we should study, as a matter of urgency, what we could & should do for Iraq, Jordan, Saudi Arabia, Libya, & even Egypt." Though Eisenhower spoke of "holding out the carrot as well as the stick," he seemed far more interested in the former than in the latter, calling for an economic assistance program "of considerable proportions" for the Middle East. "We must take the leadership in trying to save these countries and orient them toward the West," he said, "because the British and French have forfeited their position there and have no influence." "I am very anxious to see the constructive side of what we are going to do out there."[6]

What is striking about Eisenhower's comments, both in his memo of 8 November and in his marching orders five days later, is his apparent confidence that the United States could combat Soviet influence in the Arab world without resorting to coercion. There would be no need for direct warnings to the Soviets or undue pressure on the Arabs. Once foreign forces had left Egypt and the dispute over the Suez Canal had been resolved—tall orders, to be sure—the Arab states could be persuaded to keep the Soviets at arm's length. By highlighting Soviet brutality in Hungary, the United States could convince Arab governments that Soviet aid was a dangerous trap. By extending its own offers of military and especially economic aid, it could secure the Arabs' political allegiance. Even Egypt, the Arab country most responsible for legitimating Soviet influence in the region, could be induced to shun the Soviets in exchange for U.S. support.

This last prospect had important implications for U.S. Middle East policy. Under the OMEGA plan of March 1956, the administration had sought to isolate Nasser by bolstering and uniting his conservative Arab rivals. Even during the Suez crisis, as the United States tried to dissuade Britain and France from using military force against Egypt, American political warfare against Nasser continued. Once real war erupted, however, the United

States and Egypt found themselves on the same side. If that community of interests could now continue, there would be little point in reviving the OMEGA plan. Eisenhower did not put it in these terms, but in early to mid-November he seemed eager to avoid resuming OMEGA.

It is easy to understand why Eisenhower would want to prevent an open confrontation with the Soviets and a confrontation of any sort with Nasser. The former would intensify the Cold War, while the latter would antagonize Arab public opinion. Requiring lengthier explanation is Eisenhower's belief that his administration could avoid these two pitfalls and still successfully combat Soviet influence in the Arab world.

A major reason for Eisenhower's confidence was the considerable prestige the United States seemed to have gained by opposing aggression in the Suez war—a recurrent theme among U.S. officials at the time. Shortly after the United States publicly condemned the attack on Egypt, U.S. ambassador to the UN Henry Cabot Lodge told Eisenhower of the "tremendous acclaim for the President's policy" in the UN, especially among Afro-Asian delegates. In mid-November Eisenhower remarked that as a result of Suez "everyone in the world says . . . the United States has gained a place she hasn't held since World War II." On 5 November U.S. ambassador to Egypt Raymond A. Hare reported that he was "now convinced that [as] far as Egypt and possibly other Arab states are concerned [the] US has suddenly emerged as a real champion of right." Hare saw an "opportunity to reestablish our position in [the] N[ear] E[east] area in [a] way which would not have seemed possible only [a] short week ago." About the same time, a State Department talking paper noted that "United States prestige is at its highest in the Arab states since 1948."[7]

Also encouraging to Eisenhower were the perceived constraints on his adversaries, both in Moscow and in Cairo. Eisenhower was convinced that Moscow's suppression of the Hungarian uprising had "served throughout most of the world to convict the Soviet[s] of brutal imperialism" and would thus retard the growth of Soviet influence in the Arab world. On 7 November, shortly after hearing of the Soviets' public offer to defend Egypt militarily (see Chapter 1), Eisenhower expressed "considerable confidence that the Arab leaders see the danger of the Russians coming into the situation supposedly in support of the Arab position."[8]

Nasser, too, seemed to be in a poor position to challenge U.S. policy in the Middle East. Egypt's military defeat in the Suez war had driven its regime to the brink of collapse, and Nasser had expressed gratitude for U.S. efforts to halt the attack on his country. On 2 November he even apologized to Ambassador Hare for having doubted the Americans' ability to act independently of Britain in the Middle East.[9] True, over the following week Nasser quickly regained, even increased, his political fortunes in the Arab world.[10] But there was reason to believe that Nasser would now be more inclined to take a pro-American line, either because he was genuinely grateful to the United States or because he recognized its new political power in the region. On 8 November Egyptian journalist Muhammad Hasanayn Haykal, a confidant of Nasser, told an official at the U.S. embassy in Cairo that Nasser "realizes that he must make a choice [between the Americans and the Soviets] and has chosen the course of full cooperation with the United States." That same day Nasser told Hare that, while Britain and France were finished in the region, "a United States steering an independent course should have no special difficulty in reaching an understanding with Egypt and other Arab states."[11]

In early to mid-November, then, Eisenhower's operating assumptions regarding the Arab world were that the United States was politically strong, that the Soviets were politically weak, and that Nasser, therefore, would be politically compliant. Each of these assumptions, however, would be seriously challenged by events in the days and weeks to come. Consequently, as U.S. officials began active planning for a new Middle East policy in late November, they did so in a far grimmer mood than the one in which Eisenhower had commissioned their work.

U.S. OFFICIALS WERE not wrong to believe that the United States had gained considerable goodwill in the Arab world, though they did exaggerate the phenomenon. In the first few days of the Suez war, the Eisenhower administration's resistance to the attack on Egypt drew expressions of gratitude from Arab leaders and commentators across the political spectrum. King Saud said that "what President Eisenhower had done is right and wise." Former secretary general of the Arab League 'Azzam Pasha told Ambassador Lodge that the United States had "won a place in the heart of all Arabs which they will never forget." Nasser himself reportedly remarked that the "US has won [the] area without firing a shot," while the Egyptian newspaper *al-Ahram* predicted that "President Eisenhower's finest hours are at hand," now that the United States had abandoned its imperialist allies and had resumed its former role as "a fighter for freedom."[12]

On the whole the gratitude was genuine, though its motivation varied according to circumstance. For Nasser and the Arab left, there was the simple recognition that U.S. action had helped frustrate an attempt to destroy the Egyptian regime. For conservative Arab leaders, the outlook was more complicated. Few of those leaders would have regretted Nasser's downfall, and some of them even privately relished the effectiveness of the initial Israeli onslaught in Sinai. After meeting with Lebanese president Camille Chamoun on 30 October, the U.S. ambassador to Lebanon reported that Chamoun "was obviously pleased by [the] discomfiture which they [*sic*] as yet unopposed Israeli movement was causing Nasser."[13] The subsequent entry of Britain and France into the conflict, however, threw the conservative regimes into political jeopardy. Despite those regimes' harsh condemnation of the Anglo-French intervention, their close ties to the West convicted them in the eyes of large sections of their citizenry. This was especially true of Iraq, the only Arab member of the British-sponsored Baghdad Pact; a wave of popular disturbances in early November came close to overturning the Iraqi regime. "While many high-ranking military officers have not been altogether displeased to see NASSER get a bloody nose," the U.S. embassy in Baghdad reported on 5 November, "most Iraqi officials have been outraged at what they regard as a ruthless betrayal by the British."[14] The U.S. stand on Suez was thus a godsend to conservative Arabs, since it partially rehabilitated the West, and by extension the pro-Western regimes, in Arab public opinion. "Were it not for the noble stand of America on this matter," proclaimed an Iraqi newspaper editorial on 2 November, "the Arab world would wash its hands of the west."[15] Right and left, Arab opinion leaders could unite in applauding the American stand.

It appeared, moreover, that pro-U.S. sentiment was not confined to a narrow political elite but extended to broader segments of Arab society. "Feeling in [the] street is [the] highest ever known," a Saudi official told the U.S. ambassador to Saudi Arabia; "everyone is happy about American policy." In Benghazi, Libya, U.S. diplomats reported that "Eisenhower is rapidly obtaining heroic stature" among ordinary townspeople. The embassy in Baghdad noted that "all signs would now seem to indicate that the mass of Iraqis, even the most uninformed and illiterate, have begun to make the distinction between Americans and 'the Western imperialists.'"[16]

That distinction was being made throughout the Arab world. During the Suez war, Syrian saboteurs destroyed pumping stations for pipelines belonging to the British-affiliated Iraq Petroleum Company while leaving intact pipelines belonging to the U.S.-affiliated Trans-Arabian Pipeline Company. Individual Americans fared better as well. For British subjects (and Americans thought to be British), walking the streets of an Arab city could be a minor ordeal. Adults glowered at them and cursed them under their breath; small boys taunted them and deliberately jostled them in crowded walkways.[17] Americans, however, were singled out for cordial treatment.

The U.S. ambassador to Jordan found that "Jordanians went out of their way to thank Americans in Amman for US support in [the] face of aggression." A Jordanian member of parliament refused to shake hands with an American journalist, assuming him to be English; upon learning the journalist's true nationality, "the MP stuck out his hand, smiled warmly and said, 'you people will still win the Arabs' friendship.'" During an air-raid alert in Cairo, grim Egyptian bridge sentries broke into smiles at the sight of the American flag on the hood of an embassy car.[18]

Arab gratitude was not enough, however, to ensure lasting Arab support for U.S. policy in the region. That could happen only to the extent that U.S. actions were deemed compatible with the main currents of articulate Arab opinion, as expressed by politicians and commentators throughout the region. In the short term, Arab opinion leaders demanded the immediate and unconditional withdrawal of all foreign forces from Egypt. Over the longer term, they insisted on Egyptian sovereignty over the Suez Canal, the eradication of all vestiges of European imperialism in the area, the restoration of Palestinian rights and the limitation of Israeli power and territory (if not the dismantling of Israel itself), and freedom for the Arabs to secure military and economic aid from sources of their own choosing. To protect its own overriding interest—keeping the Middle East from falling under Soviet control—the Eisenhower administration could and did meet the Arabs' short-term demand, even at the cost of major discord with its allies. But it was loath to embrace the Arabs' long-term demands, and U.S.-Arab relations were bound to suffer once this became obvious.

Even at the height of the U.S.-Arab honeymoon in early November, Arab leaders expressed dismay that the United States was not acting more vigorously on Egypt's behalf. Prior to the 7 November cease-fire, the demand was for the United States to force an end to the Anglo-French attack. On 6 November the U.S. embassy in Amman reported that the "Jordanian attitude is turning to one of 'fine words are good but when is [the] US going to take action that will stop [the] British and French[?]'" Once the cease-fire had been announced, Arab officials began urging that the United States compel Britain and France to withdraw unconditionally from Egypt. On 10 November a Saudi official told a U.S. diplomat, "You . . . should force your children (France and England) immediately to withdraw from Egypt," lest the American position in the region "unavoidably suffer." U.S. diplomats in Iraq, Lebanon, and Libya relayed similar warnings.[19]

The Soviets' public statements of 5 November—the ultimatum to Britain and France and the proposal for a joint U.S.-Soviet intervention on Egypt's behalf—provided further incentive for the United States to seek an early withdrawal from Egypt. Both statements were extremely popular in the Arab world, and the ultimatum in particular was widely credited in Arab opinion with forcing Britain, France, and Israel to accept the subsequent cease-fire. In Beirut an informal U.S. embassy poll of ordinary Lebanese revealed a "widely held belief [that the] Soviet ultimatum produced [the] 'cease fire.'" Traveling in Jerusalem in early December, *Foreign Affairs* editor Hamilton Fish Armstrong found that this version of events "is believed by our nice and friendly room servant at the American Colony, by the taxi chauffeur and guide, and by our friends who live in the Old City, refugees from near Lake Tiberius [*sic*]."[20] Syrian prime minister Sabri al-'Asali, one of the few remaining conservatives in his government, told a U.S. diplomat on 8 November that he had "attended [an] informal reception of well-wishers" at the Soviet embassy the day before and had been "shocked to see the low type of callers who came in flocks and droves." Reports from Baghdad and Jidda indicated that, even among pro-Western businessmen, intellectuals, and government officials, there was widespread support for the Soviet gestures and a feeling that the United States had been too timid in opposing the attack on Egypt.[21] Somehow, the United States would have to regain the political initiative.

The Soviet pronouncements had implications transcending public relations. While most U.S. officials discounted the threat to launch missiles against Britain and France, they could not entirely rule out Soviet intervention in the Middle East itself, either directly or through the sending to Egypt of Soviet "volunteers," a euphemism for Soviet elite military personnel sent to fight with the armed forces of a client state.[22] The 7 November cease-fire did not end this worry. For the rest of November, Britain and France resisted international demands that they withdraw immediately from Egypt, seeking to condition their withdrawal on a prior commencement of dredging operations to reopen the Suez Canal and on an opportunity to contribute their own troops to the UN peacekeeping force scheduled to occupy the canal zone. As long as Anglo-French forces refused to withdraw, the possibility remained that fighting would resume, in which case the Soviets might be compelled to back up their bold words with action.[23]

The Eisenhower administration believed that both aspects of the Soviet challenge—the growth of Soviet popularity in the Arab world and the potential for Soviet military intervention—could best be addressed by compelling Britain and France to withdraw from Egypt unconditionally. For the rest of November the administration pushed for this result through an extraordinary exertion of diplomatic and economic pressure on its allies: supporting a UN General Assembly resolution demanding an immediate and unconditional Anglo-French withdrawal; refusing to supply Western Europe with oil, now in short supply due to the closure of the Suez Canal and to the destruction of the Iraqi pipeline in Syria; and blocking Britain's attempts to withdraw gold and dollar reserves from the International Monetary Fund.[24] On 3 December Britain and France finally succumbed to the pressure and agreed to an unconditional withdrawal from Egypt, a pledge they would fulfill later that month. Israel, however, refused to vacate the Sinai Peninsula and the Gaza Strip.

U.S. prodding of the allies brought a fresh surge of pro-American feeling in the Arab world. Across the political spectrum, Arab leaders and commentators extolled Eisenhower's "principles" and "noble attitude in support of right and justice."[25] American diplomats, travelers, and residents in the area were astonished and moved by the praise ordinary Arabs heaped on the United States and Eisenhower.[26] It was all too easy to be carried away by such expressions. Describing the scene in Jordan, an American Christian relief official wrote, "It is the common man who evinces this revival of faith in the USA. The policeman on his beat salutes me as a fellow country-man of Eisenhower. . . . The students are aware of the new spirit in world politics. Everywhere there is new hope because of America's stand for justice and international law." Arabs generally, the official predicted, "will go along with Eisenhower in whatever constructive efforts he may undertake to solve the basic problems of the Near East."[27]

This last remark was wildly unrealistic. A closer examination of public statements by Arab leaders and commentators reveals a far less deferential attitude toward the United States. Arab opinion leaders continued to be gratified by U.S. behavior, but as they speculated about future U.S.-Arab relations in late November and early December, they stressed that their support for the United States was provisional and that Washington could keep the Arabs' friendship only if it made significant changes in its Middle East policy.

On the Arab-Israeli issue, Arab commentators agreed that the United States could not content itself with compelling Israel's withdrawal from Egyptian territory; it must confront the problems resulting from Israel's very creation. At the conciliatory end of this consensus were those urging the United States to force Israel's compliance with the 1947 UN resolution partitioning Palestine (which had allotted Israel a significantly smaller area than it currently occupied) and subsequent UN resolutions calling on Israel to repatriate Palestinian refugees. Much of the Nasserist press in Lebanon followed this line. At the defiant end of the consensus were those insisting that true peace was impossible as long as Israel existed at all, an argument presented most vigorously by the Iraqi government.[28]

Both positions were nonstarters as far as the Eisenhower administration was concerned. Although Eisenhower and Dulles were not, as American leaders went, warm supporters of Israel, they were committed to protecting its existence and security. Moreover, while the Eisenhower administration did favor Israeli territorial concessions to Egypt and Jordan, it had no intention of returning to the 1947 partition plan or of forcing Israel to repatriate large numbers of Palestinian refugees, preferring that they be resettled in other Arab lands.

Privately, some Arab leaders held views not too far from the U.S. government's. Secretary general of the Arab League 'Abd al-Khaliq Hassuna believed that compromise was possible between the Arabs' "old shibboleths re [the] 1947 resolution" and Israel's insistence on retaining all of the territory it had acquired by 1949. But it was the public statements that set the tone for Arab politics, and those statements proclaimed a standard for U.S. behavior that the Eisenhower administration could not be expected to meet.[29]

On the subject of future relations between the United States and its Western allies, there were similar portents of U.S.-Arab discord. Again Arab commentators fell into two main groups: those congratulating the United States for supposedly severing all ties to British and French policies in the Middle East, and those warning it of the dire consequences of failing to do so.[30] Implicit in both positions was the assumption that Britain and France had few, if any, legitimate political interests in the Arab world. This was hardly the American view. While realizing that Britain could no longer be considered the primary Western power in the Middle East, the Eisenhower administration had no desire to see the termination of Britain's treaties with Iraq, Jordan, and Libya or of its protectorate relations with Persian Gulf ministates. Such a liquidation of British assets would only enlarge the strategic vacuum in the area, increasing the opportunities for Soviet penetration. Regarding Algeria, the administration believed that France would probably have to negotiate with Algerian nationalists on the basis of short-term autonomy leading to eventual independence, but it was reluctant to press this opinion on France for fear of straining the Western alliance. In view of the damage to the alliance caused by the Suez war, the administration was now especially eager to restore relations with Britain and France. "We must face the question," Eisenhower told his advisers on 21 November, "what *must* we do in Europe and then the question, how do we square this with the Arabs?"[31] There was sure to be dismay in the Arab world once these priorities became clearer.

Americans living and working in the Arab world sensed this danger. In Amman in late November, Hamilton Fish Armstrong found "some uneasiness" among U.S. embassy officials that relations with Britain and France would be restored too rapidly, thus "cut[ting] in half the prestige we have gotten in these parts by our strong anti-colonial and anti-war position." There was even fear of mob violence against American institutions. In early December the elderly proprietor of an American-run children's hospital in Jerusalem told Armstrong "that if Eisenhower suddenly made a pro-British statement her 36 years of work at the hospital would be forgotten in a wild rush of anger."[32] Such apprehensions, while exaggerated, were not entirely baseless. The resumption of U.S. economic assistance to Britain and France in early December, after those two countries had agreed to withdraw from Egypt but before they had actually done so, was blasted by Arab commentators as a "reward for aggression."[33] The sentiment did not bode well for future cooperation between the United States and the Arab world.

If U.S.-Arab relations in general were destined for some decline, U.S.-Egyptian relations in particular were already in free fall. As we have seen, at the time of the cease-fire there had been reason to believe that Nasser would have to assume a more pro-U.S. posture. In mid- to late November, however, a series of perceived Egyptian transgressions convinced Eisenhower and his advisers that Nasser was fundamentally hostile to U.S. interests in the Arab world. Egyptian military attachés were implicated in violent subversive activities against the Libyan and Lebanese governments. The Egyptian military attaché in Syria was suspected of operating an autonomous paramilitary organization that, in league with Syrian security forces, was menacing Western-affiliated oil installations and the lives of conservative Syrian politicians.[34] Radio Cairo stepped up its propaganda war against Nasser's conservative Arab rivals, especially the Iraqis, who were accused—with some justice—of having attempted to overthrow the Syrian government (see Chapter 1). And while Nasser insisted he had no plans to invite Soviet volunteers into Egypt, he refused to rule out such an invitation should Britain and France fail to withdraw soon enough from his country.[35]

Nasser's domestic behavior was equally distasteful to U.S. officials. By early December the Egyptian government had deported about 250 stateless Jews residing in Egypt, on the pretext that they were potential Israeli collaborators. It had also sequestered all British- and French-owned property in Egypt and expelled large numbers of British and French nationals. Many of these deportees were people of Cypriot, Lebanese, or Maltese origin who had lived in Egypt all their lives and whose British or French citizenship was largely a technicality. Meanwhile, Egypt refused to authorize the dredging of the Suez Canal as long as British and French forces remained in Egypt, causing some U.S. officials to suspect Nasser of prolonging the crisis for his own political benefit.[36]

There was no excuse for the mistreatment of British, French, and Jewish residents of Egypt, but it is hard to fault Nasser for using other means at his command—such as threatening to request Soviet intervention and impeding clearance of the canal—to pressure Egypt's attackers to end their military occupation. Somewhat less clear is Nasser's culpability for subversive acts in neighboring countries. In November both Lebanon and Libya experienced a wave of bombings and other forms of sabotage, directed mostly at British institutions and properties. The Lebanese and Libyan governments charged that the Egyptian military missions assigned to their countries had provided logistical support for the attacks. Egyptian authorities denied the Lebanese government's accusation, though U.S. officials were convinced of its veracity. As for the Libyan case, on 1 December Nasser admitted to Ambassador Hare that the Egyptian military attaché in Libya "had gotten out of line, especially following the attack on Egypt, and he (Nasser) had been too preoccupied with other matters to give [the] matter [the] necessary attention until it reached [an] advanced state." While it is possible that Nasser had been unaware of the military attaché's specific transgressions, it seems unlikely that the attaché would have acted as he did without some indication of official approval.[37]

Whatever the merits of Washington's brief against Nasser, by late November U.S. officials were losing patience with the Egyptian leader. American action, they believed, had almost single-handedly rescued the Cairo regime from oblivion, and now Nasser was repaying the United States by attacking its friends, courting its enemies, and obstructing a reasonable settlement of the crisis.

The cumulative effect of such thinking was to vindicate those U.S. officials who had been least disposed to accommodate Nasser—acting secretary Hoover, CIA director Allen Dulles, and chairman of the Joint Chiefs of Staff Arthur W. Radford—and to undermine or convert those who had taken a more hopeful view.[38] Hare's cables continued to give Nasser some benefit of the doubt, but his counsels were falling out of favor in Washington.[39] Eisenhower, who earlier that month had envisioned a new and constructive relationship with Egypt, by 20 November was grumbling about "the great undependability and unreliability of Nasser" and again stressing "the importance of building up King Saud" as a regional counterweight to the Egyptian leader. At month's end there was general agreement in the NSC "that, once the British and French had announced their departure decision, all possible heat should be turned on Nasser" to force him to "behave himself and to proceed with clearing the Canal." State Department planners were calling for an effort "to isolate Egypt" and "to undermine Nasser." White House staffers were referring matter-of-factly to "our ultimate objective of peacefully eliminating Nasser."[40]

U.S. attitudes toward Soviet moves in the region likewise hardened that November. At the time of the Suez war, the perceived threat of Soviet encroachment had fallen into two categories: the short-term threat of outright Soviet intervention on Egypt's behalf, and the long-term threat of strengthened Soviet political, economic, and military ties to Arab countries. In the first half of November the Eisenhower administration had hoped to counter both threats indirectly. By compelling an immediate Anglo-French withdrawal from Egypt, it would remove the pretext for outright Soviet intervention. By exploiting Arab dismay over Soviet behavior in Hungary, it would dissuade Arab states from considering future Soviet aid offers. Events in the second half of November, however, eroded American confidence that Soviet encroachment in either the short term or the long term could be prevented by indirect means alone.

The main factor inviting immediate Soviet intervention was the continuing military occupation of Egypt. The longer British, French, and Israeli forces remained in the country, the more likely it became that hostilities would resume and that Egypt would ask the Soviets to send volunteers to its aid. On 3 December Britain and France did commit to an unconditional withdrawal from Egypt, but until that withdrawal was completed—which would not occur until 22 December—U.S. officials had to worry that a resumption of fighting might create a pretext for Soviet intervention after all. Israel's refusal to withdraw from the Sinai Peninsula and the Gaza Strip posed similar dangers.[41]

Equally disquieting was the threat of Soviet encroachment over the long term. On 29 November U.S. intelligence analysts concluded that the Suez war had "worked to increase the influence of the USSR in the area, and to enhance considerably Soviet opportunities to undermine the Western position there."[42] Due to the popularity in the Arab world of the Soviets' rhetorical support for Egypt, and to the Arab public's relative indifference to events in Hungary, Arab leaders could court the Soviet Union with little fear of public censure.[43] In late November the Jordanian parliament unanimously recommended that the government establish diplomatic relations with the Soviet Union, although the Jordanian cabinet delayed implementing the proposal for the moment. Around the same time Allen Dulles complained in the NSC that Nasser, despite earlier pledges to favor the United States over the Soviet Union, was "playing both sides against the middle" by "negotiating for new arms from the Soviet bloc."[44]

The most dramatic increase in Soviet influence was in Syria, where the collapse of Operation Straggle in late October, combined with the surge of anti-Western feeling in response to the Suez war, had permitted leftist and pro-Soviet figures to consolidate their power in the government and army. On 10 November CIA director Allen Dulles warned that "a Communist coup might be pulled off" in that country, resulting in "a Syrian invitation to Moscow to send troops into Syria" and in "Syria's becoming a Soviet base of operations in the area."[45] By mid-November U.S. intelligence had concluded that a direct Soviet takeover of Syria was unlikely—but only because Moscow now deemed it unnecessary. With the increasingly leftist orientation of the Syrian government and army, the Soviets could gain a major foothold in the region simply by meeting Syrian requests for military and economic assistance.[46]

The problem of Syria's pro-Soviet tilt was amplified by the possibility that others might overreact to it. Turkey was alarmed by Syria's leftward drift, and U.S. officials were alarmed by Turkey's alarm. In a secret memorandum of 14 November, Turkey warned the United States that the Soviets were "systematically proceeding to seize hold of Syria" in order "to surround and isolate Turkey" and to "destroy the Baghdad Pact." A Soviet-dominated Syria would subject neighboring Iraq to unrelenting "pressure" (presumably in the form of subversion and propaganda) to withdraw from the Baghdad Pact. Iraq's withdrawal from the pact would force Iran to follow suit, leaving Turkey entirely surrounded by hostile or ineffectual states. Moreover, the Turks continued, the fact that the West had permitted such erosion would convince the remaining Middle Eastern countries "that their lands are considered an 'expendable area,'" sapping their will to resist Soviet domination.[47]

To the Eisenhower administration these fears seemed overstated, but there was a distinct possibility that Turkey might act on them. In its 14 November memorandum, Turkey declared that it "considers it a sacred duty to take all the required steps" to eliminate the dangers "jeopardizing Turkey's independence and existence." U.S. officials interpreted this statement as signaling Turkey's desire to remove the Syrian government by force.

Such a venture, warned U.S. ambassador to the Soviet Union Charles E. Bohlen, "would have all the dangers . . . of renewal [of Anglo-French] hostilities with Egypt"—that is, possible military conflict with the Soviets and increased Arab bitterness toward the West.[48]

To secure the Middle East against both short-term and long-term Soviet encroachment, U.S. officials began considering the idea of publicly warning the Soviet Union to stay out of the region. Such a warning could serve several purposes: preventing the Soviets from intervening in Egypt or from pressing their political advantage in Syria; dissuading Nasser from seeking direct Soviet protection; obviating a Turkish reaction to Syria's leftward drift (or, failing that, keeping the Soviets from reacting to Turkey's reaction); and reassuring other Middle Eastern countries that the United States did not consider them an "expendable area."

On 17 November Eisenhower proposed to Dulles that the best way to prevent the Soviets from sending volunteers to the Middle East would be for the president "to make a statement to the effect that if the Russians should do this he would immediately call a special session of Congress. . . . He believed the Russians knew enough of our Constitutional procedures to be able to assess the great significance of such a move. He felt it would be a strong warning without, at the same time, committing us to any particular action. The Secretary thought this would be a useful thing to do." In a 10 November conversation with State and Defense Department officials regarding growing Soviet influence in Syria, Chairman Radford had said "that the U.S. would have to draw the line somewhere." He thought a congressional resolution similar to the Formosa Strait Resolution of January 1955 (which had authorized the executive branch to take whatever action it saw fit to protect Taiwan and neighboring islands from communist China) "would be necessary to put the Soviet Union on notice" in Syria. On 30 November Harold Stassen, Eisenhower's special adviser on disarmament, said that the United States had to "check any move by Nasser in turning toward the USSR. . . . We must say [to the Soviets], as we had said in the matter of the Chinese Communist threat to the offshore islands, 'You just can't move into this picture.'" From Moscow, Ambassador Bohlen recommended that the Eisenhower administration make "a general statement of U.S. intention to assist any victim of aggression in the Middle East."[49]

It would be some weeks before these various proposals coalesced into the general warning against Soviet encroachment contained in the Eisenhower Doctrine. Already in late November, however, some of the main features of the final version had begun to emerge: resort to congressional action, emulation of the Formosa Strait model, professed concern for victims of aggression, wide regional scope, and deliberate vagueness.

At a more basic level, the hardening attitudes toward Nasser and the Soviets reveal the extent to which the Eisenhower administration had abandoned, by late November, the more hopeful outlook the president himself had taken earlier that month. When Eisenhower wrote his 8 November memorandum, U.S. officials were still euphoric over pro-American sentiment in the Arab world. The Soviets had just shown their true colors in Hungary, and the political impact of their 5 November statements had not fully registered with U.S. officials. Nasser's attitude toward the United States, and that of Arabs generally, appeared grateful and cooperative. Given these three assumptions—American popularity, Soviet unpopularity, and Nasserist cooperation—it was easy for Eisenhower to imagine that the United States, simply by opening its coffers and publicizing "the slaughter in Budapest," could convince the Arab countries to spurn Soviet aid offers and align with the West. The United States would not need to challenge the Arabs' sovereign right to make deals with the Soviets; the Arabs would reject that option on their own.

Events in mid- to late November, however, had seriously challenged Eisenhower's three assumptions. Though gratified by U.S. defense of Egyptian sovereignty, Arab opinion leaders had treated that defense less as a major achievement in itself than as a promising first step that had to be followed by many others. Yet the remaining steps demanded of the United States amounted to a repudiation of its basic Middle East policies. Obviously the Eisenhower administration could not pass such a test.

Although Eisenhower was slow to grasp the weaknesses of his first assumption,[50] those of his other two were harder to ignore, and together they sufficed to make his earlier vision unworkable. By late November it was clear that Arab appreciation for Soviet gestures on Egypt's behalf generally outweighed Arab dismay over events in Hungary. This fact had created an atmosphere in which pro-Soviet Arab figures, especially in Syria, could increase their political power. With Soviet fortunes on the upswing, Nasser had abandoned his earlier deference to the United States and was again courting Moscow. Two of the hoped-for impediments to Soviet encroachment—Soviet unpopularity and Nasserist cooperation with the United States—had obviously failed to materialize. It appeared that the United States would have to block such encroachment itself, both by warning the Soviets to stay out of the region and by reviving its pre-Suez war policy of isolating Nasser and his Arab allies.

Yet the very circumstance that made such stiff measures necessary also made them less likely to succeed. If America's political position in the region was not strong enough to ensure the Arabs' automatic allegiance, then efforts to compel such allegiance would probably further weaken the American position, exposing Washington to the charge of seeking to impose its Cold War priorities on the region. The Eisenhower administration was aware of this problem and, as we shall see, did its best to circumvent it. Devising a new Middle East policy in late November and early December, U.S. officials sought a formula that would allow the United States to combat Nasserist influences without appearing to do so. This effort at deception was rather ingenious on paper; it remained to be seen if it would succeed on the ground.

ON 21 NOVEMBER, in response to the president's request a week earlier, Acting Secretary Hoover gave Eisenhower a memorandum outlining future U.S. policy in the Middle East. Although few of Hoover's long-term proposals would be adopted, they did suggest the anti-Nasserist strategy that the Eisenhower administration would follow (or rather resume) in dealing with the post-Suez Arab world.

In the memo, Hoover identified the main U.S. objectives in the Middle East as (1) denying the region's oil resources and strategic positions to the Soviet Union and (2) keeping those assets available to the West. He further noted that France was "no longer able to play a constructive role in the area" and that Britain's position in the region was so "seriously prejudiced by its action against Egypt . . . that the US must assume leadership in maintaining and restoring the Western position in the area." Hoover outlined several short- and long-term measures for exercising such leadership. The short-term measures were largely concerned with eliminating the most immediate sources of friction in the area in order to deny the Soviets opportunities to increase their regional influence. These measures included resolving the Suez Canal dispute, seeking the reopening of the canal and the repair of oil pipelines in Syria, resuming the search for an Arab-Israeli settlement, and seeking to "reduce Saudi Arabian financial support for extremist [i.e., anti–Baghdad Pact] elements in Syria and Jordan."[51]

The long-term measures revealed a harder side of U.S. policy: a determination to weaken Nasser's political hold on the Arab world. The United States, Hoover wrote, should "utilize all appropriate opportunities to isolate Egypt and reduce Nasser's prestige and influence." It should "further strengthen Saudi Arabia and reduce its ties with Egypt" and "possibly encourage a federation of Iraq, Syria and Jordan under Iraqi leadership," along with "a North Africa confederation from Libya to Morocco as a counterpoise to Egypt."[52] The strategy behind these proposals—weakening and isolating Egypt by bolstering and uniting rival Arab regimes—was essentially the same strategy that the Eisenhower administration had pursued in the spring and summer of 1956.

While resumption of the anti-Nasser strategy was by now widely supported within the administration, Hoover's talk of conservative Arab federations was too ambitious to merit serious consideration. Devising more feasible proposals was no easy task, however, especially as Dulles was on sick leave and would remain so until early December. Lacking Dulles's decisiveness and authority, Hoover was unable to unite the State Department behind a more workable set of proposals, and the president's time was increasingly taken up with mediating the department's internal debates. "Nobody in State could make up their mind," Eisenhower grumbled after an exhausting session on 21 November; "he would be so glad when Dulles came back."[53]

Still, by early December administration officials had developed three distinct options for Eisenhower's consideration. Under the first option, the United States would join the Baghdad Pact; under the second option, it would encourage the creation of a new, pro-Western regional grouping; under the third option, the one that ultimately prevailed as the Eisenhower Doctrine, the United States would also seek a coalition of pro-Western nations, but it would do so through a series of bilateral security agreements, not a formal organization.

Conspicuously absent from this list of alternatives was any proposal for a high-level effort to resolve the Arab-Israeli dispute, an omission strongly criticized by commentators and politicians in the months to come and by historians decades later.[54] This omission reflected the Eisenhower administration's suspicion that such a settlement was currently unattainable. The collapse of Project ALPHA in March 1956 had led Eisenhower and Dulles to discount the prospects for an Arab-Israeli peace agreement, and the violence of the Suez war only strengthened their pessimism. On 2 November Eisenhower wrote to a friend that "the Arab-Israel quarrel . . . seems to have no limit either in intensity or in scope. Everybody in the Moslem and Jewish worlds is affected by it." Two months later Dulles told an aide that he had been reading the Old Testament and had concluded "that the root of the problem could not be eradicated. . . . It did not make sense that he could solve problems which Moses and Joshua with Divine guidance could not solve." Neither Eisenhower nor Dulles was eager to stake American prestige on such slim odds. In its future dealings with the Middle East,

Eisenhower said on 23 November, the United States should avoid "being so bound as in the past by the Arab-Israeli dispute."[55]

This posture becomes more understandable when one considers Arab and Israeli attitudes in the weeks following the Suez war. Across the political spectrum, Arab leaders agreed that Israel's attack on Egypt had so inflamed Arab opinion that no Arab leader could publicly contemplate a settlement at present.[56] As a Syrian Foreign Office representative confided to a U.S. diplomat in late December, "Arab government leaders in present circumstances must appear even more extreme than [the] public which [is] thoroughly aroused against Israel in light [of the] recent aggression."[57] The lack of trust among Arab leaders tended to magnify the importance of Arab public opinion on this issue. Any Arab leader showing a willingness to treat with Israel risked being denounced as a traitor by his Arab rivals and exposed to the public's wrath. It was no accident that the Iraqi regime, the Arab government most compromised in the eyes of its own people, was now taking the hardest public line on Israel.[58] In mid-December Nasser told Hare that "Egypt could not take [the] lead [in making peace] for fear of Iraqi exploitation." To be sure, most of the Arab leaders counseling patience believed that significant progress could be made within two or three years, once anti-Israel sentiment had ebbed. Defining the outer limits of pessimism for the era, a Lebanese businessman gave *Time/Life* executive C. D. Jackson "a rude jolt" by predicting "that real peace was impossible in the foreseeable future, possibly as long as ten years."[59]

Though the Israeli government claimed greater interest in an Arab-Israeli settlement, its own behavior and posture were hardly conducive to such an outcome. Israel's recent attacks on Sinai and Gaza had been massively disproportionate to any provocation from the Arab side, and now Israel was demanding a victor's peace. Speaking before the Israeli Knesset on 7 November, Prime Minister David Ben-Gurion declared that "the Armistice Agreement with Egypt is dead and buried and will never be resurrected." He also maintained that Israel would not permit the stationing of UN peacekeeping forces "in its territory or in one of those territories which Israel now occupies" and even hinted that his country would take permanent possession of some of the Arab lands it had seized.[60] Privately, Israeli diplomats took a somewhat softer line on this last point (and in early 1957 Israel would be forced to relinquish the captured territories in any case).[61] Nevertheless, Israel's defiant public posture further diminished the prospects for an Arab-Israeli settlement, reinforcing U.S. inclinations to forgo the quest for such a settlement as a major policy option in late 1956.

Of the three options the administration did consider, the simplest was for the United States to join the Baghdad Pact.[62] The principal advocates of pact membership were Chairman Radford, the joint chiefs, Secretary of Defense Charles E. Wilson, and the American ambassadors to the pact countries, whose governments were themselves clamoring for U.S. adherence. They all argued that the United States had to join the Baghdad Pact to save it from collapse. Britain's attack on Egypt had gravely discredited the pact, which was widely seen in the region as an instrument of British power. Unless that stigma could be removed, it would be increasingly difficult for the pact's area members, especially Iraq, to remain associated with the organization. Were the Baghdad Pact to disintegrate, the West would lose a crucial means of checking Soviet and Nasserist ambitions. Only U.S. adherence, the argument went, could demonstrate that the pact was not an imperialist tool while still providing it with an adequate security guarantee.[63]

Leading State Department officials agreed that the Baghdad Pact had been discredited but saw this as an argument against U.S. adherence.[64] The pact was in such disrepute, they claimed, that U.S. membership could not possibly redeem it; to the contrary, the United States would be sullied by association with the pact. The State Department further argued that "adherence would provide Israel with a pretext for renewed demands for a U.S. security guarantee," which the Eisenhower administration did not want to give, and that the U.S. Senate was unlikely to approve U.S. pact membership without such a concession to Israel. A final objection was that Saudi Arabia, with which the United States was trying to improve relations (and whose king Eisenhower was again promoting as a counterweight to Nasser), saw the Baghdad Pact as an instrument of Hashemite aggrandizement and would thus strongly oppose U.S. adherence to it.[65]

As an alternative to pact membership, officials at the State Department's NEA and Policy Planning Staff proposed the formation of a new grouping of Middle Eastern states. The idea was "to submerge the Baghdad Pact" in a new, larger organization consisting primarily of the Baghdad Pact countries, Saudi Arabia, and Lebanon, and perhaps also Jordan, Libya, Sudan, Ethiopia, and Yemen. Israel would be excluded, because of "the strong anti-Israel sentiments of most of the area states." The new organization would be founded on a "Middle East Charter" that "would specifically recognize the danger posed by International Communism and express a determination to cooperate in self defense against this threat." The United States would offer charter members "substantially increased economic aid" and military assistance sufficient "to maintain internal security and to permit limited resistance to aggression." Upon proclamation of the charter, the United States would announce that it viewed "any threat by international Communism against the independence or territorial integrity of the participating states as seriously endangering international peace and would consult with them in the event of Communist attack on any member with a view to taking appropriate measures in accordance with our constitutional processes. . . . We might seek a joint resolution endorsing the Executive's action [in making such a pledge]." Britain and France should be persuaded "for the time being [to] avoid injecting themselves in the Middle East and to leave the US the primary responsibility of restoring the Western position in the area." That way, the United States could "make a unilateral declaration of protection" of charter states unencumbered by association with European imperialism.[66]

The charter proposal thus contained the three main elements of what later emerged as the Eisenhower Doctrine: economic aid, military aid, and the possibility of unilateral, congressionally sanctioned U.S. intervention to thwart a "Communist attack" on a Middle Eastern country. Where the new proposal differed from the Eisenhower Doctrine was in the very idea of binding the protected countries in a formal organization.

There was another, less obvious respect in which the charter proposal anticipated the Eisenhower Doctrine: its determination to combat Nasserism and Arab radicalism under the guise of official impartiality. The authors of the charter proposal had little doubt that Nasser and the Syrians were adversaries of the United States. Among the stated reasons for forming a new organization were to "circumscribe Nasser's power and influence" and to "close off access to Soviet arms for Egypt and Syria." At the same time, the authors recommended that Egypt and Syria be invited to join the new organization. "In the unlikely event that the two countries did accept the invitation, this in itself would constitute a rebuff for the USSR and a notable reversal of recent Egyptian and Syrian positions." A far more probable scenario was that both countries, unwilling to jeopardize their beneficial relations with the Soviets, would refuse to join the anticommunist organization, in which case "their rejection of the invitation would serve to isolate them from the rest of the area and to emphasize their close ties with the Soviet bloc." The United States could oppose Nasser and the Syrians without seeming to do so. The authors of the charter proposal were taking a page out of Truman's book: in 1947 the Truman administration had invited the Soviet Union to participate in the Marshall Plan, fully expecting that Moscow would decline the offer and thus bear the onus of having rejected a constructive Western initiative.[67]

The charter proposal did not, however, enjoy unanimous support within the State Department. In a 3 December memorandum, Undersecretary of

State for Political Affairs Robert D. Murphy wrote that creating a new organization would "arouse the suspicions of countries in the area and certainly those outside the area." Murphy especially doubted that King Saud, whose support was "key" to any successful U.S. policy, would be receptive to such a scheme. "He and other Moslems could well regard the proposal as a project of American power politics." Murphy also thought that forming a new grouping from which Israel was excluded "would give rise to strident opposition in some quarters" unless the United States offered Israel a similar security guarantee.[68] In other words, the formation of a new organization would entail many of the same problems as would U.S. adherence to the Baghdad Pact.

Dulles, too, had his doubts. Returning to work on 3 December, the secretary did speak favorably of U.S. "financial support to a balanced organization of Arab countries perhaps through some mechanism analogous to that of the Marshall Plan." Over the following week, however, Dulles began having second thoughts. Creating a new organization would be a vast and delicate undertaking, "full of delays and pitfalls." It was doubtful, moreover, that the United States could devote the necessary energy to the task until after the achievement of a Suez Canal agreement, which, Dulles realized, "would be slow in coming and therefore the question is whether the situation in the area will hold together until Suez is buttoned up." Timing aside, the secretary "did not have much faith in the ability of the Arabs to unite for any constructive purpose. . . . The only thing the Arabs were unified on was their hatred of Israel and, temporarily, their opposition to France and the UK."[69]

Dulles's doubts centered mainly on the feasibility of creating a formal organization in the region. The secretary did not dispute that the Arab states should be encouraged to assume public postures that were explicitly anticommunist (and thus implicitly anti-Nasserist) or that the United States should be prepared to guarantee, via a congressional resolution, the security of avowedly anticommunist Middle Eastern states. Accordingly, Dulles proved receptive to the idea of pursuing the latter two initiatives bilaterally — that is, by seeking parallel understandings with individual Middle Eastern states without requiring those states to make any formal commitment to one another. Under the bilateral scenario the U.S. executive branch would be authorized, by congressional resolution, to offer economic aid, military aid, and security guarantees to individual Middle Eastern countries proclaiming their opposition to international communism. Murphy had hinted at such an approach in his 3 December memorandum, in which he wrote that "substantial bilateralism in the area" would be preferable to the formation of a new organization. By 7 December Dulles had likewise concluded that in the coming months the United States should make security arrangements "on a bilateral basis and thus should not try the Charter idea yet."[70]

There was another advantage to a bilateral approach that, while not explicitly mentioned in the documents, can be surmised from the general situation. By steering clear of any formal organization, whether an existing one like the Baghdad Pact or a hypothetical one like the Middle East Charter, the Eisenhower administration could further insulate itself from regional criticism and suspicion. The charter proposal, as we have seen, was partly intended as a mechanism for combating Nasser and the Syrians without appearing to do so. Since the proposed regional organization would be officially open to Egyptian and Syrian membership, the United States could publicly disavow any hostility to those countries. The bilateral approach involved a similar charade: although Egypt and Syria would be invited to denounce international communism in exchange for U.S. aid, it was expected that both countries would decline the invitation and thereby reveal the extent of their fealty to Moscow. By forgoing a formal organization, however, the bilateral approach carried the deception a step further. Not only could the administration deny that it was trying to organize the region against Egypt and Syria; it could deny that it was trying to organize the region at all—even as it sought to unite potential rivals of Egypt and Syria through a series of bilateral agreements. Whereas the charter proposal envisioned an actual pact that was surreptitiously opposed to Egypt and Syria, the bilateral approach envisioned a *virtual* pact with the same covert mission. Instead of just one layer of deniability, Washington would have two.

Now that Dulles had decided in favor of the bilateral approach (or "the Resolution," in administration parlance), he needed to convince Eisenhower that this course was preferable to either Baghdad Pact adherence or the charter proposal. Dulles's task was simplified by the fact that Eisenhower showed no interest in the charter proposal and liked the Resolution. But the president also favored adherence to the Baghdad Pact and thought adherence and the Resolution could be combined. In an 8 December telephone conversation with the president, Dulles argued that U.S. adherence to the pact would bring pressure on the administration to provide a similar security arrangement for Israel. If the United States succumbed to that pressure, the pact's Middle East members would be politically undermined, defeating the whole purpose of U.S. adherence. Dulles added that the "evidence we have at the moment is that Saudi Arabia would not join [the] BP." Eisenhower, who earlier in the conversation had spoken of Saudi adherence to the pact as a precondition for U.S. adherence, "said then he agreed you would have to go ahead with the 3rd alternative (the Resolution)" on its own. He authorized Dulles to begin working on a proposed resolution to be presented at the start of the new Congress in January.[71] The administration would remain formally uncommitted to any policy option until later that month, but for all practical purposes the decision had been made.

Immediately after securing Eisenhower's endorsement of the resolution proposal, Dulles enlisted the State Department to prepare the administration's request for congressional authorization. Dulles was scheduled to leave Washington that same day to attend a NATO conference in Paris, but he had already produced a rough draft of the request, which he instructed his subordinates to revise in his absence. Over the following week, a special task force headed by Murphy deliberated over the shape and scope of the new Middle East policy.[72]

One issue Murphy's task force considered was whether the request for a congressional resolution should "be tied to Communist imperialism" alone or "also relate to possible conflict between the states of the Middle East," a reference to the Arab-Israeli conflict. The latter alternative was not a new idea. In March 1956 the administration had considered requesting "a Joint Congressional Resolution which would authorize the President to use military force if necessary in case of aggression by Israel or the Arab states." Murphy's task force concluded, however, "that the proposed resolution should be tied only to Communist imperialism." Reporting to Dulles on 15 December, following the secretary's return to Washington, Murphy acknowledged that there were hostilities in the region unrelated to communism; still, "Communist imperialism" was "the main source of difficulty at the present moment." Moreover, the centrality of the communist threat was "recognized by the American people and their representatives in the Congress. We consider it unlikely that the latter would approve a resolution not aimed specifically at Communist imperialism." Focusing solely on communism, Murphy added, would link the new Middle East policy more closely with other U.S. initiatives overseas, signaling to friend and foe alike "that the United States is prepared to move in that area as it is in Europe under NATO and in Asia under SEATO [Southeast Asia Treaty Organization] and other Far Eastern arrangements."[73] It was a fateful decision. In the months and years to come, Arab critics would portray Washington's exclusive focus on Soviet-sponsored aggression as a tacit endorsement of Israeli aggression, a politically devastating charge in the Arab world.

Murphy's task force also decided that the administration should not specifically name the countries that would be eligible for U.S. aid and protection under the new program. Potential recipients should be identified simply as "the countries of the Middle East," and "the Middle East" itself should remain undefined. Though the task force did not explain this decision, it probably feared that naming eligible nations could pose problems with geographically peripheral states. Afghanistan was a case in point. The weakness, impoverishment, and location of that country made it both militarily vulnerable to and economically dependent on the Soviet Union. Were Afghanistan to be named as a potential beneficiary of a U.S. security guarantee, it would probably have to decline the offer, damaging American prestige. But excluding Afghanistan from the list of eligible nations might convince the Soviets that they could do as they pleased in that country. Tunisia and Morocco posed another dilemma. Unilaterally placing them on the list of potential recipients might antagonize the French; leaving them off might foreclose opportunities for combating Nasserism or communism in North Africa.[74] The obvious solution was to avoid issuing any list at all, allowing potential recipients of U.S. aid and protection to establish their eligibility simply by asking for help.

Dulles accepted the task force's recommendations, and in an 18 December memorandum he listed the main features of the new program.

> We have in mind that Congress would be asked to give the President authority:
>
> 1. To cooperate with and assist any nation or group of nations in the general area of the Middle East in the development of economic strength dedicated to the maintenance of national independence.
>
> 2. To undertake programs of military assistance and cooperation with any nation or group of nations in the general area of the Middle East upon request of their governments. . . .
>
> 3. To employ the armed forces of the United States in taking measures . . . to protect the territorial integrity and political independence of such nation or group of nations against Communist armed aggression.

To enable economic and military assistance, Congress would be asked to grant the executive branch greater discretion in spending funds already appropriated for Middle East aid for fiscal year 1957. Congress would also be notified of the administration's intention to request, at a later date, the appropriation of $400 million in Middle East aid to be available over the next two fiscal years. The proposed resolution would not in itself require the appropriation of any new funds.[75]

If a single objective united all the features of the new policy, it was to reassure Middle Eastern governments and peoples that friendship with the United States would be profitable and safe, a point U.S. officials stressed repeatedly to Congress over the following weeks. Increased economic assistance, they said, would build up the economies of Middle Eastern countries and ensure "that those who are oriented toward freedom and democracy will see a way of improving themselves" through cooperation with the United States. Increased military assistance would strengthen "loyal security forces," better enabling them to defend their countries against foreign-sponsored subversion. U.S.-supplied weapons would be a visible reminder of the U.S. security commitment.[76]

Even the interventionist provision was concerned less with paving the way for any specific U.S. action than with increasing the self-confidence of pro-Western governments in the area. By convincing Turkey, Iran, and Pakistan (all close neighbors of the Soviet Union) that the United States would defend them if they came under Soviet attack, the Eisenhower administration hoped to keep those countries firmly in the Western camp. Such reassurance would also, U.S. officials hoped, prevent Turkey from responding unilaterally to Syria's radicalization.[77]

The extent to which friendly Arab states would be similarly reassured depended, of course, on what the term "Communist armed aggression" meant. If it meant Soviet aggression alone, then the Arab states would derive limited benefit from the U.S. guarantee, since none of them seemed in danger of direct Soviet attack. If, however, the term also meant aggression by a Middle Eastern state acting as a Soviet proxy, then the guarantee was more meaningful. Syria, for example, had not yet succumbed to Soviet domination, but U.S. officials believed it was moving in that direction. Syria was bitterly denouncing Iraq for having attempted to overthrow the Damascus regime, and Iraq feared these attacks might take a violent turn. Under this looser definition of "Communist armed aggression," a Syrian armed attack on Iraq could conceivably trigger U.S. intervention on Iraq's behalf. Such a prospect would reassure the Iraqi regime, reinforcing its pro-Western orientation. U.S. officials clearly favored the looser definition of "Communist armed aggression"—and soon replaced the term with one that was open to an even broader interpretation: "overt armed aggression from any nation controlled by international communism."[78]

The funding provision was also included mainly for psychological reasons. Since the resolution itself would not entail any new appropriations, there was no need for it to mention funding at all. Dulles nevertheless felt that the resolution should explicitly allude to the $400 million that the executive would later be requesting for the next two years. Such a statement would be valuable "for scenery purposes," tangibly demonstrating to Middle Eastern audiences the strength of U.S. resolve.[79]

A 20 December White House meeting, attended by Eisenhower, Dulles, Radford, and others, revealed that the administration had abandoned all pretense of considering alternatives to the proposed resolution. Radford explained that the joint chiefs "had proposed adherence to the Baghdad Pact simply to take some major action quickly. They support the present proposal." Eisenhower, too, was fully behind the resolution, permitting Dulles to lead the meeting through a detailed discussion of the mechanics of the new policy and the manner of its unveiling.[80]

In his reactions to Dulles's handiwork, Eisenhower showed greater sensitivity to Arab and world opinion than did his secretary of state. Discussing the resolution's interventionist provision at the 20 December meeting, Eisenhower "asked if it would be desirable to specify that we would intervene only at the request of the countries concerned, since the countries might otherwise take offense at the statement." Dulles objected that such a requirement would deprive the United States of flexibility, since "a sudden coup might result in displacing the government which could make the request." But Dulles agreed to study the matter, and he later followed Eisenhower's suggestion.[81] On 22 December Dulles gave Eisenhower a draft he had prepared of the request for congressional authorization. Eisenhower read the draft in Dulles's presence and pronounced it a "good paper," but he also crossed out Dulles's tactless references to the Arab states as "divided" and to the UN security system as "somewhat undependable." To Dulles's statement that the best way to avoid U.S. military intervention would be "to make clear our purpose," Eisenhower appended "and our readiness to cooperate fully with friends in the Middle East."[82] On 2 January he told Dulles that the message should emphasize "the mild language of seeking peace," and Dulles accordingly inserted a number of soothing passages not found in earlier drafts: a more emphatic statement of America's commitment to peace, a statement supporting UN efforts to resolve the Arab-Israeli dispute, and a pledge of nonaggression against the Soviet Union itself.[83]

By now Eisenhower had decided to make the request for authorization in person before a joint session of Congress. He would deliver the speech at the end of the first week in January, even before his state of the union address, thus demonstrating the seriousness with which he regarded the new policy.[84]

A final revision by Eisenhower concerned references in the speech to U.S. readiness to fill the "vacuum" created by the reduction of Anglo-French power and influence in the Middle East. Reviewing Dulles's draft on 22 December, Eisenhower had passed over the term without comment. A few days later, however, Dulles granted "background" interviews to reporters

A Lebanese cartoon spoofs Washington's notion of a vacuum in the Middle
East, May 1957. The caption reads, "Daughter: My life is all a vacuum. . . .
I don't know how to fill it. Mother: Fall in love with an American . . . "
(al-Sayyad [Beirut magazine]; reprinted in al-Musawwar
[Cairo newspaper])

in which he spoke of a "dangerous vacuum" in the area. Dulles's remarks
were picked up by newspapers in the Arab world, and Arab politicians and
commentators, especially on the left, criticized the "vacuum" statement as
a slight to the Arabs' own political institutions and security arrangements.[85]
Actually, a number of Arab leaders, including some in Egypt and Syria, had
themselves recently alluded to a "vacuum" or "gap" in the region due to
the reduction of British and French influence, but almost all of these statements had been made in private.[86] On 4 January the U.S. embassy in Amman reported "universal opposition" to the term among the Jordanian
public and urged that "some other phraseology" be found to justify the new
policy. Whether or not Eisenhower learned of this recommendation, sometime between 4 and 5 January he crossed out the word "vacuum" wherever it
appeared in the text of his speech to Congress.[87] But the damage had been
done. In the months to come, Arab critics of the new policy would seldom
tire of reminding their audiences of Dulles's gaffe.

Eisenhower's revisions reflected a well-founded concern about likely

Arab reactions to the new U.S. policy. Weeks earlier, Eisenhower had envisioned a benign scenario in which the Arab states banded together to exclude Soviet influence and align with the United States. Now he was about to launch a political initiative that directly challenged the Soviet Union and sought to deepen and exploit existing divisions in the Arab world. Many Arabs, already dismayed by U.S. moves to restore relations with Britain and France, were sure to see the new policy as an attempt to frustrate their quest for pan-Arab unity, to curtail their sovereign right to seek assistance wherever they saw fit, and to impose an alien agenda on the region.

The problem of Arab public opinion would plague the Eisenhower Doctrine throughout its brief life, but this was not the only challenge facing the new policy in January 1957. A more immediate hurdle in the doctrine's path lay on Capitol Hill, where the first session of the Eighty-fifth Congress was about to begin.

LAUNCHING THE DOCTRINE,

JANUARY–APRIL 1957

In January 1957 the Eisenhower administration began laying the basis for implementing its newly formulated Middle East policy. Most immediately this involved securing congressional passage of the Middle East Resolution, a task that proved unexpectedly difficult. Although the resolution cleared the House of Representatives in relatively short order, it languished in the Senate for two months, facing withering scrutiny by Democrats. As Senate debate extended into February, it became entangled with events in the Middle East itself, where U.S. officials were preoccupied not only with presenting the new policy to skeptical Arab audiences but with removing the political wreckage of the recent Suez war.

The administration generally met its foreign and domestic challenges. It convinced the Israelis to complete their withdrawal from Arab territories occupied in the war, clearing the way for the repair of Iraqi oil pipelines in Syria, the reopening of the Suez Canal, and thus the restoration of Western Europe's economic lifeline. It induced a handful of Arab governments to offer provisional endorsements of the Eisenhower Doctrine and avoided for the moment any outright rejections. It mended its frayed relations with Britain, which now acknowledged U.S. preeminence in Western Middle East policy. And in early March the Middle East Resolution passed the Senate and was signed into law by the president.

Through it all, Eisenhower and Dulles were dismayed by the antagonisms, foreign and domestic, aroused by their actions in the Middle East.

Instead of causing the two men to rethink their approach, however, such dissension served only to reinforce their self-righteousness. As they saw it, any difficulties their Middle East policy faced resulted not from its own faults but from the pettiness, selfishness, and blindness of its critics. This was a consoling belief, but it obstructed clear thinking about the Eisenhower Doctrine.

ON 5 JANUARY Eisenhower appeared before a joint session of the newly seated Eighty-fifth Congress to unveil his Middle East initiative. The recent Suez war, Eisenhower said, had sharply aggravated existing tensions in the Middle East. The resulting instability had enabled the Soviet Union to increase its power and influence in the area, with the ultimate aim of "dominating the Middle East." If this trend continued, the "free nations" of the area could lose their independence. Only outside help could prevent this.[1]

Who should provide such help? The president did not have to mention that Britain and France were now too discredited for the job. The UN, though effective in addressing the transgression of smaller states, "cannot be a wholly dependable protector of freedom when the ambitions of the Soviet Union are involved." The Soviets could always use their veto in the Security Council to block undesirable action by that body, as they had just done in the case of Hungary. For the Middle East to remain free of Soviet domination, "the United States must make more evident its willingness to support the independence of the freedom-loving nations of the area," and that willingness could be most convincingly demonstrated by a congressional resolution.[2]

Such a resolution, Eisenhower said, "would, first of all, authorize the United States to cooperate with and assist any nation or group of nations in the general area of the Middle East in the development of economic strength dedicated to the maintenance of national independence. It would, in the second place, authorize the Executive to undertake in the same region programs of military assistance and cooperation with any nation or group of nations which desires such aid." The third provision was to gain the most attention. It would authorize "the employment of the armed forces of the United States to secure and protect the territorial integrity and political independence of such nations, requesting such aid, against overt armed aggression from any nation controlled by International Communism."[3]

Eisenhower disavowed any eagerness for battle, saying, "It is my profound hope that this authority would never have to be exercised at all." Indeed, such prior authorization would actually decrease the likelihood of

President Eisenhower unveils the Eisenhower Doctrine before a joint session of Congress, 5 January 1957. (© United Press)

hostilities, since it would convince the Soviet Union and its Middle Eastern supporters that any aggression on their part would be vigorously resisted. Hostile governments, Eisenhower said, "will know where we stand."[4]

Even before Eisenhower's 5 January speech, the American press had dubbed the anticipated Middle East policy the Eisenhower Doctrine. Critics of the administration scoffed at the name. Democratic senator Hubert H. Humphrey of Minnesota saw nothing in the policy "which should distinguish it as a doctrine in the sense of the Monroe Doctrine and the Truman Doctrine" and began referring to Eisenhower's initiative as "the so-called doctrine." Eisenhower himself tried to get the State Department to use the term "American Doctrine" instead, but State Department officials resisted this suggestion, arguing that "Eisenhower Doctrine" was too firmly entrenched to be easily replaced. They also warned that switching to "American Doctrine" might rankle Latin American governments, which "have historically resented the use of the term 'American' as applicable only to the USA."[5] So the president's name became permanently attached to the initiative.

Personal modesty aside, Eisenhower must have been pleased to see his policy elevated to the ranks of presidential doctrines—especially the Truman Doctrine, on which his own initiative was partly modeled. In 1947 President Harry S. Truman had asked Congress to appropriate $400 million in economic and military aid to Greece and Turkey, to secure them against the perceived threats of communist subversion and aggression. In his accompanying message to Congress, Truman declared that "it must be the policy of the United States to support free peoples who are resisting attempted subjugation by armed minorities or by outside pressures." Unveiling his own doctrine to Congress a decade later, Eisenhower specifically invoked the Truman Doctrine, implying that the current proposal was a continuation of that effort. As in 1947, Eisenhower urged, the United States must again support free peoples resisting attempted subjugation. Also as in 1947, the task could best be accomplished through close cooperation between Congress and the executive. The fact that Eisenhower, too, was asking for $400 million (to be appropriated for fiscal years 1958 and 1959) was a further reminder of the Truman Doctrine.[6]

A more recent precedent was the Formosa Resolution of early 1955. In the fall of 1954 the People's Republic of China had begun shelling the Nationalist-held offshore island of Quemoy. The Eisenhower administration believed that Quemoy and another offshore island, Matsu, were potential stepping stones for a Chinese assault on Formosa (Taiwan) or the nearby Pescadores. In January 1955 Eisenhower requested, and Congress overwhelmingly passed, a resolution authorizing the president "to employ the Armed Forces of the United States as he deems necessary for the specific purpose of securing and protecting Formosa and the Pescadores against armed attack." Congress's decisive action, combined with Eisenhower's and Dulles's blunt nuclear threats, seemed to get results.[7] In the spring of 1955 Communist China called for negotiations with the United States and soon thereafter ended its shelling of Quemoy.[8] For Eisenhower the lesson was clear: when Congress and the president stood together, communists took heed.

Eisenhower also labored to make his doctrine a showcase of bipartisanship—an essential task, since both houses of Congress remained under Democratic control. At a 1 January meeting with Democratic and Republican legislative leaders, held to give Congress advance notice of the impending Middle East initiative, Eisenhower urged the lawmakers to set aside partisan considerations, pledging in return that "no quest[ion] of partisanship will move me one inch." In his 5 January speech Eisenhower noted that in past crises "the President and the Congress have united, without partisanship, to serve the vital interests of the United States and of the free world. The occasion has come for us to manifest again our national unity in support of freedom." In a further bid for Democratic support, on 7 January the president announced that former Democratic congressman James P. Richards of South Carolina, a recent chairman of the House Foreign Affairs Committee, would serve as the administration's special ambassador for the Eisenhower Doctrine, charged with explaining the policy to Middle Eastern governments.[9] Eisenhower's invocation of the Truman Doctrine was of course another attempt to disarm the opposition.

If Eisenhower thought these gestures would placate the Democrats, however, he was to be sorely disappointed. Indeed, to the extent that the congressional debate over the Eisenhower Doctrine resembled foreign policy debates of the Truman era, it was the poisonous feuds of the early 1950s, not the bipartisan legislative achievements of the late 1940s, that came most readily to mind. In early 1957 Democrats were in no mood for a bipartisan foreign policy. Many of them remained bitter over their party's defeat in the 1956 presidential election and were anxious to even the score; all aspects of administration policy, including foreign affairs, would now receive sharp scrutiny. Moreover, with the popular Eisenhower barred from seeking a third term, the Democrats had high hopes of winning the presidency in 1960, and several Democratic senators—Humphrey, John F. Kennedy of Massachusetts, and majority leader Lyndon B. Johnson of Texas—were already positioning themselves to run for their party's nomination. These men would seek national exposure by criticizing Eisenhower's foreign policy.

Reinforcing the shift toward greater partisanship among Democrats was a change in Senate leadership. In 1956 Democratic senator Walter George of Georgia, chairman of the Senate Foreign Relations Committee, had decided not to run for reelection. A forceful advocate of a bipartisan foreign policy, George had, in the previous congress, used his authority to ensure Senate cooperation with Eisenhower's overseas initiatives. But George's replacement as chairman, eighty-nine-year-old Theodore Francis Green of Rhode Island, had a more modest conception of his own legislative role, seeing himself less as an architect of foreign policy than as a mediator of conflicting views among the members of his committee. Green's passivity meant that individual Senate Democrats would be much freer than before to attack the administration's foreign policy.[10]

Democrats were especially partisan when it came to the Middle East, whose current instability they blamed on bankrupt Republican policies.

The standard Democratic critique went something like this: The Eisenhower administration had reacted to Egypt's seizure of the Suez Canal Company (itself a direct consequence of Dulles's clumsy dealings over the Aswan Dam) by appeasing Nasser, belittling the concerns of Britain, France, and Israel, and behaving in a generally duplicitous manner. To avoid losing votes in the upcoming presidential election, the administration had misled the American people as to the seriousness of the crisis, creating the impression that a peaceful resolution was imminent. When Britain, France, and Israel had finally resorted to force against Egypt (a regrettable but understand- able act), Eisenhower and Dulles had ostentatiously opposed the move, joining forces with the Soviets to humiliate America's allies. Incredibly, Eisenhower and Dulles had then treated this betrayal as the highest expres- sion of international morality, showing little concern for the fact that the Western alliance was in shambles. As New York governor Averell Harri- man, a Democratic elder statesman, privately remarked in late November, the attack on Egypt "was a tragic blunder. However, that does not relieve the Administration of its responsibility for double dealing and failure to understand the British, French and Israeli emotion—and now its smug and self righteous attitude and position."[11]

Democrats were further outraged that such a dismal performance had been rewarded with electoral success. The outbreak of the Suez war in the closing days of the campaign had caused a reflexive surge of support for Eisenhower—a "sudden rush to support the author of their anxiety," as Adlai Stevenson, the defeated Democratic presidential candidate, called it. "If ever a President was the beneficiary of events due in part to his own mistakes," Senator Humphrey consoled Stevenson in late November, "it was Eisenhower."[12]

The unveiling of the Eisenhower Doctrine in early January was, to Dem- ocrats, yet another indication of the administration's bad faith. "This whole thing is nothing short of outrageous," Humphrey complained in late Jan- uary. "First we were all hoodwinked by the Administration's reports on the Middle East. At least every attempt was made to keep us deceived about the critical situation there. Then as the peace slogans began to die out a bit following elections, we were presented with an 'urgent' proposal"—to ad- dress what the administration had suddenly decided was a grave crisis in the region. On 5 January the Democratic Advisory Committee noted that "the situation [in the Middle East] has been dangerous for many months— including the recent campaign months during which the Administration was lulling the public with assurances that the outlook for peace in the Middle East was never better." While welcoming the fact that the administration had "finally recognized publicly the great danger in the Middle East," the committee warned that Eisenhower's current proposals would receive "close and thorough scrutiny."[13]

On 7 January the House Foreign Affairs Committee, chaired by Thomas S. Gordon of Illinois, opened hearings on the proposed Middle East resolution. Appearing as the first witness, Dulles warned "that it would be a major disaster if that area were to fall into the grip of international communism." To prevent this fate, Congress and the administration must jointly proclaim their determination to defend the Middle East.[14]

A flurry of skeptical questions greeted Dulles's testimony. Wouldn't the resolution be a pre-dated declaration of war? No, Dulles replied, it would be "a declaration of peace because I do not believe that peace can be preserved unless we make it clear in advance that if aggressors attack the freedom of other countries . . . we are going to do something about it." Other members objected that the resolution did not deal with the problem of subversion, widely seen as the most likely avenue of Soviet penetration. Dulles countered that the resolution, by strengthening the economies of Middle East nations and easing governments' fear of direct military attack, would make it harder for subversion to succeed. Yet another concern was the geographical vagueness of the plan. Precisely which countries did the administration propose to protect? "There is always danger in drawing a line on the map," Dulles replied. Doing so would have the effect of telling the Soviets, "'It is all right if you take over this country; we will not mind as long as you do not take over the other.'" Dulles's remark was a veiled reference to former secretary of state Dean Acheson's infamous "defensive perimeter" speech of early 1950, which many had criticized as an unwitting invitation to communist North Korea to invade its southern neighbor.[15]

On 10 January Acheson made his own appearance before the House Foreign Affairs Committee. Acheson personally loathed Dulles and believed his actions in the Suez crisis had been a disaster for the Western alliance.[16] Now taking aim at the Eisenhower Doctrine, he charged that the president's message to Congress was both superfluous and inadequate: superfluous because it sought authorization for the exercise of war powers already inherent in the presidency, and inadequate because it failed to address more immediate problems such as Soviet-sponsored subversion, the Arab-Israeli conflict, and the ongoing dispute over the Suez Canal. "The President has himself said, 'This program will not solve all the problems of the Middle East,'" Acheson observed. "Conservatively speaking, that is the outstanding understatement of 1957." Acheson's testimony delighted the administration's opponents and foreshadowed much of the later criticism of the Eisenhower Doctrine.[17]

The following week the Senate Foreign Relations and Armed Services Committees began joint hearings on the proposed resolution. Dulles was again the lead witness, appearing successively on 14 and 15 January. Like Acheson and House Democrats, Senate Democrats criticized the resolution's failure to address local problems in the Middle East. Some conservative southern Democrats, led by Armed Services chairman Richard Russell of Georgia, objected to the resolution's economic provisions and proposed that they be severed from the resolution and resubmitted as a separate bill (which could then be rejected without jeopardizing the rest of the president's program). Estes Kefauver of Tennessee, the Democrats' vice presidential nominee in 1956, complained that the resolution made no provision for consultation with U.S. allies.[18]

Still, critics of the Eisenhower Doctrine faced powerful obstacles. Not only was Eisenhower himself immensely popular, but the American people, on balance, seemed to support his proposals.[19] There was also a widely shared assumption that, whatever the actual merits of the program, Congress simply could not refuse a presidential request made in the name of combating international communism, lest U.S. credibility be eroded. This impression was powerfully reinforced on 13 January when, much to Acheson's dismay, former president Truman released a public letter stating that Congress had "no alternative but to go along with the President in this program." Even newspapers critical of the Eisenhower Doctrine tended to support its approval by Congress.[20]

Bowing to political realities, on 25 January the House Foreign Affairs Committee reported out a resolution virtually identical to the administration's. On 30 January the full House approved the bill by a vote of 355 to 61. The impressive majority masked considerable dissatisfaction. "The sentiment was expressed repeatedly," *Congressional Quarterly* reported, "that although Members disliked the resolution they felt obliged to vote for it because of the psychological effect its defeat would have throughout the world."[21]

The Senate has always been more insulated from public pressure than the House. It has also been predisposed, both by its rules and by its traditions, to take a more critical stance on the executive branch's foreign policies. In 1957, moreover, the Senate Foreign Relations and Armed Services Committees included a handful of energetic and opinionated Democrats —Russell, Humphrey, J. William Fulbright of Arkansas, Mike Mansfield of

Montana, and Wayne Morse of Oregon—who strongly objected to the administration's proposed resolution. (Senators Kennedy and Johnson, who sat on the Foreign Relations and Armed Services Committees, respectively, were sharply critical of administration policy in general but less so of the Eisenhower Doctrine in particular.) These facts alone ensured that Senate approval of the measure would be neither quick nor easy.

On the other hand, Senate committee Democrats were not in full accord over what was wrong with the resolution. True, most Senate Democrats agreed that the resolution slighted important local issues in the Middle East. Most also agreed that all the talk of bipartisanship was a sham—that the administration merely wanted to ensure that the Democrats would share the blame if the new policy failed. Beyond these criticisms, however, little united the Senate Democrats. Russell favored the standby authority for using force but opposed the measures for economic and military aid. Mansfield and Morse disliked the unilateral commitment to defend the Middle East and wanted a multilateral commitment involving the UN. Fulbright thought the economic aid provisions too piecemeal and favored a more ambitious and integrated program. Regarding standby authority, Fulbright called the doctrine a "blank check" for "naked Executive power." Yet he also joined Mansfield in stressing the opposite danger: explicitly authorizing the president to use force in one area would cast doubt on his ability to use force in all other areas where such authorization was absent, dangerously weakening the presidency.[22] Humphrey and Morse warned that military aid to Arab states would threaten Israel's security.[23]

With their criticisms so scattered, Senate Democrats could offer no coherent alternative to the Eisenhower Doctrine. What they could do was embarrass the administration by dragging out the hearings and dwelling on the inadequacies of its Middle East policies. "While, in the main, we will have to go along with the so-called doctrine," Humphrey wrote a friend on 21 January, "we are going to make it quite clear that it doesn't get at the problems and that it is not a policy." Acheson likewise predicted that Congress "will probably pass the worst part of the resolution, but not until Dulles has been pretty thoroughly taken apart." Accordingly, in mid- to late January committee Democrats proposed numerous amendments to the resolution, each of which would have to be debated and voted on before the committees could consider the resolution as whole. By late January informed observers were predicting that another month would pass before the resolution cleared the full Senate.[24]

One of the more naked attempts to frustrate the administration was made by Senator Fulbright. On 24 January, when Dulles appeared for a third time at the joint Senate hearings, Fulbright blasted Dulles's recent performance in the Middle East and proposed that no vote be held on the resolution until Dulles had provided the committees with a "white paper" accounting for his conduct in the region over the past four years. Fulbright was clearly attempting to replay, in reverse, the domestic politics resulting from the fall of China to communism in 1949. In the wake of that debacle, Acheson's State Department had released a massive white paper to explain its actions in China. Republicans had attacked the document as "a 1,054-page whitewash" of an incompetent, defeatist, and perhaps even disloyal policy, aspersions from which the Democrats had never fully recovered.[25] Now it was payback time. Having taunted the Democrats by asking, "Who lost China?" the Republicans themselves would have to answer, "Who is losing the Middle East?"

Immediately grasping Fulbright's purpose, Republican committee members chided Fulbright for indulging in "delaying tactics" and placing the Senate "in the position of Nero"—fiddling while the Middle East burned. Dulles objected that producing a white paper would "take many months" and "open old wounds." Fortunately for Dulles, Chairman Green of the Foreign Relations Committee shared these objections and, on this occasion at least, was willing to exercise his authority. Over the next few days Dulles and Green worked out a deal that neutralized Fulbright's proposal: a white paper would be produced, but its chronology would span the entire previous decade, allowing some of the blame for the Middle East crisis to be pinned on the Truman administration; also, the review would not hold up the Senate's consideration of the Eisenhower Doctrine.[26]

Things went less well for Dulles at the 25 January session, when, in an attempt to defend the unilateralism of the doctrine, the secretary made a serious gaffe. Why, Senator Morse demanded, were "American boys" being asked to go it alone in the Middle East? Shouldn't the burden of defending the region be shared by Britain, France, "and the other countries whose oil we are going to save"? Dulles replied that Britain and France were so unpopular in the Middle East that their participation in such a venture would be a political liability: "If I were an American boy, as you put it, going to fight in the Middle East, I would rather not have a British and a Frenchman, one on my right hand and one on my left. I think I would be a lot safer under different conditions than that."[27]

It was a sensible answer, couched in the clumsiest possible terms. Dulles seemed to be disparaging the fighting ability of America's allies, which was not his intention. The British especially were infuriated by the remark, and it took several days of cajolery by U.S. officials, including Eisenhower's personal intervention with visiting British defense secretary Duncan Sandys, before Whitehall was placated. The Democrats had a field day with Dulles's blunder. The usually stoic Dulles was distressed by the criticism and told Eisenhower that his experience with the Senate committees made him "sympathize with guys that get put in police court." The committees' favorite technique, Dulles said, was to grill a witness for hours at a time until he finally made a slip—"And they say Ha! Now we've got you."[28]

Meeting with Republican congressional leaders on 29 January, Eisenhower expressed outrage that Dulles could be "subjected to such a bitter partisan attack." "Glad you mentioned the bitter partisanship," replied Indiana representative Charles Halleck. "This is more than anything we ever did." In the Truman era, Halleck said, the Republican-controlled Congress had confined its criticism to the administration's policies; it had not personally attacked Secretary Acheson the way the Democrats were now savaging Dulles. (Only in a Republican crowd could such a howler have gone unchallenged.) "If these guys want a bipartisan foreign policy," Halleck continued, "we ought to lay it on the line" and expose the Democrats' bias.[29] There were partisan advantages to be had in securing a monopoly on bipartisanship.

MEANWHILE, FOREIGN GOVERNMENTS were registering their own reactions to the Eisenhower Doctrine. On 9 January British prime minister Anthony Eden, discredited by Suez and in poor health, resigned and was replaced by Chancellor of the Exchequer Harold Macmillan. Macmillan, who had worked with Eisenhower in North Africa during World War II, was determined to repair relations with the United States, and getting along with the Americans meant getting along with the Eisenhower Doctrine. Like many British officials, Macmillan regarded the doctrine as too little, too late: too little because it did not explicitly address the threat of pro-Soviet subversion in the Middle East, and too late because it arrived after the Soviets had already made significant political and strategic gains in the area. The fact that the Eisenhower Doctrine had been substituted for U.S. adherence to the British-sponsored Baghdad Pact further disappointed the Macmillan government. As Macmillan later wrote in his memoirs, however, the doctrine "at least marked a return to the world of reality" and an end to the "unnatural flirtation, amounting to a liaison, . . . between Russian and American representatives at the United Nations." The doctrine could also be seen as a belated endorsement of Britain's long-standing hostility to Nasserism. Macmillan and his advisers suppressed their misgivings and gave strong official backing to the Eisenhower Doctrine.[30]

Western governments as a whole were likewise officially supportive. The French government endorsed the Eisenhower Doctrine, though it privately urged the United States not to make any unilateral decisions with respect to North Africa and criticized the doctrine's failure to address regional issues like the Arab-Israeli conflict and the dispute over the Suez Canal.[31] The remaining NATO members also welcomed the new policy, albeit with varying degrees of enthusiasm.[32]

The Soviet Union blasted the Eisenhower Doctrine as an effort to exploit and dominate the Middle East for the benefit of "American monopolies." Such a policy was not only unjust but dangerous, since the peoples of the area were sure to resist it. "Undoubtedly this Doctrine is a step toward war," Soviet defense minister Marshal Georgi Zhukov warned on 5 February. A week later the Soviet Foreign Ministry issued its own Middle East plan, which called on the major powers to pledge noninterference in the internal affairs of Middle Eastern states, to withdraw all their troops from the area, to dismantle their military bases there, and to offer economic aid to area countries with no strings attached. U.S. officials dismissed the plan as one-sided, noting that the Soviet Union, unlike the Western powers, had neither troops nor bases in the region to begin with. The real purpose of the Soviet plan, White House press secretary James C. Hagerty charged, was to "discredit or stop the Eisenhower plan for the Middle East."[33]

Among non-Arab Middle Eastern states, Israel was temporarily uncommitted on the Eisenhower Doctrine. While Israeli officials praised the doctrine as well intentioned, they noted that its exclusive concern with communist aggression gave Israel no protection against attacks from the Arab states, none of which could credibly be described as "controlled by international communism." The Israelis were also uneasy over the prospect of increased military aid to Arab states. Iran, Turkey, and Pakistan strongly supported the doctrine, both individually and in their capacity as Baghdad Pact members, but urged that every effort be made to resolve the Arab-Israeli conflict, lest the Soviet Union continue to exploit Arab bitterness. They also insisted that the Eisenhower Doctrine was no substitute for U.S. adherence to the Baghdad Pact.[34]

The Eisenhower administration was most concerned about the doctrine's reception in the Arab world. Early reactions in the Arab press ranged from bitterly hostile to cautiously supportive. Across the political spectrum, Arab commentators criticized the same perceived flaws of the doctrine: its underlying assumption that a political and strategic vacuum existed in the region (see Chapter 2) and its fixation on the threat of communist, rather than Western or Israeli, aggression. Where Arab commentators did fundamentally differ was in their assessment of U.S. motives. Leftists and Islamic conservatives saw the Eisenhower Doctrine as an instrument of Western exploitation and domination. Centrists and pro-Western conservatives saw it as a well-meaning but flawed effort to bring security and prosperity to the area. Hardly any commentators supported the policy without reservation.[35]

Official Arab reactions were variously critical, supportive, and uncommitted. Egypt, which led the critics, had been suspicious of the doctrine even before its formal unveiling. On 31 December, commenting on news reports of the forthcoming initiative, Egyptian ambassador to the United States Ahmed Hussein wrote that the new policy might well be "aimed at warning the Arab states against following . . . the Egyptian policy" of accepting aid from the Soviet bloc. Eisenhower's 5 January speech, with its exclusive focus on the communist threat, confirmed Hussein's fears. On 9 January Nasser told U.S. ambassador to Egypt Raymond A. Hare that, while the growth of domestic communism in Egypt was a real concern, "there was no danger from Soviet aggression. . . . If [the] President had referred to aggression in general, he would have been understood." Nor was Nasser willing to denounce the Soviets "when the Egyptian people see them as helpful and sympathetic"; doing so would only undermine his domestic position. Another Egyptian complaint, voiced by Muhammad Haykal, concerned the Eisenhower administration's freezing of Egyptian dollar assets in American banks and its refusal to accept Egyptian pounds for U.S. wheat (in retaliation for Egypt's nationalization of the Suez Canal Company). These measures, Haykal said, left Egypt "no alternative but to turn to [the] Soviet Union."[36] How, under these circumstances, could Egypt cooperate with a policy aimed at severing Arab ties to the Soviet bloc?

Nevertheless, Egypt avoided an outright rejection of the Eisenhower Doctrine. Nasser had reason to be cautious. Rejecting the doctrine could rule out future U.S. economic assistance, forcing Egypt into a position of utter dependence on the Soviet Union.[37] Nasser also may have feared more drastic retaliation should his opposition to the new policy be too strenuous or immediate. The Eisenhower administration's recent plotting against the Syrian government was, as we have seen, no secret to Egyptian officials. Thus Nasser sought to delay for as long as possible any irrevocable decision on the Eisenhower Doctrine.

Syria's position on the doctrine was even more hostile than Egypt's. With Soviet aid levels increasing and domestic leftists in the ascendancy, hardly any Syrian official was willing to praise the new initiative in public. On 10 January the Syrian cabinet denounced the "vacuum" theory and insisted there was "no trace of international communist danger in our country." Yet Syria stopped short of an outright rejection of the doctrine, as it, too, apparently feared the consequences of an open break with the United States.[38]

A small number of Arab leaders strongly supported the Eisenhower Doctrine. Lebanese president Camille Chamoun privately pledged that he was behind the doctrine "one hundred percent," a position publicly echoed by Lebanese foreign minister Charles Malik. Tunisian president Habib Bourguiba, in an 11 January speech, predicted that the Eisenhower Doctrine would be "decisive for the strengthening of peace and removal of fear from the hearts of weaker peoples." The Libyan government was circumspect in public, though the U.S. embassy in Tripoli reported private "hand-rubbing at [the] prospect [of] increased assistance." Iraqi prime minister Nuri al-Sa'id expressed "warm approval" of the initiative and told a U.S. diplomat of his "pleasure" that the United States was "embarking on [a] strong M[iddle] E[ast] policy designed to benefit free world interests."[39]

Not all of Nuri's motives were so lofty. Nuri also hoped to translate increased U.S. involvement in the region into support for Iraqi efforts to acquire portions of northeastern Syria. Those areas, Nuri claimed, had been arbitrarily awarded to Syria in the aftermath of World War I, despite their historical autonomy from the Ottoman *vilayet*, or province, of Syria. In early January Nuri requested U.S. backing for an Iraqi initiative to reopen the boundary issue in the UN General Assembly, predicting that the inhabitants of those areas, if granted a plebiscite, would opt for inclusion in Iraq. The State Department strongly objected to this proposal and warned that it would expose Iraq to intensified Egyptian and Syrian propaganda attacks and allow the Soviets to pose as the "champions of Syria." Nuri agreed to take no further action on the matter without consulting the United States. "However," he added, "if Egypt and Syria refuse [to] cooperate with [the] new U.S.–Middle East policy . . . and if [a] commie government takes control in Syria, his project might be seriously considered as [a] means of embarrassing [the] government of Syria."[40]

Nuri's urgings foreshadowed what was to be a recurring problem for the Eisenhower administration. Days earlier Dulles had told congressional leaders that, under the Eisenhower Doctrine, "the United States would focus solely on the Russian threat, making certain of keeping clear of internal squabbles" in the Middle East.[41] Over the next year and a half, however, precisely the opposite would happen. In Iraq, Jordan, Syria, and Lebanon, the doctrine would repeatedly draw the administration into thorny local disputes it much preferred to avoid.

There were two other conservative Arab leaders who remained, in January 1957, uncommitted on the doctrine: Jordan's King Hussein and Saudi Arabia's King Saud. Hussein was in an especially delicate position because, while he was personally pro-American, a pro-Nasser Jordanian cabinet had just come to power, and articulate Jordanian opinion was generally critical of the Eisenhower Doctrine. Hussein responded to this dilemma by publicly implying to his own people that he opposed the doctrine while privately implying to the U.S. embassy that he supported it. It was impossible to predict which tendency would ultimately prevail as Jordanian policy.[42]

Saud, too, was being pulled in two directions simultaneously. On one hand, the outbreak of the Suez war, with its dire economic and political consequences for Saudi Arabia, had confirmed many of Saud's worst misgivings about Nasser.[43] This fact, combined with the Saudi government's close economic and military ties to the United States, its strong opposition to communism, and its gratitude for the U.S. position in the Suez war, encouraged Saud to look kindly on the Eisenhower Doctrine. Discussing the forthcoming initiative with a U.S. diplomat on 2 January, Saud said "he had high hope [that the] 'Eisenhower Doctrine' would meet vital area needs." Meanwhile, Saud urged Syrian president Shukri al-Quwatli to prevent the Syrian press from criticizing the new policy until Eisenhower had a chance to present it to Congress, a request al-Quwatli granted.[44]

On the other hand, embracing the doctrine could be politically costly to Saud. While the king did not have to worry about domestic opinion—the Saudi government had a virtual monopoly on such expression—he had aspirations for pan-Arab leadership that made him sensitive to regional opinion. Saud could not afford to be perceived as opposing Nasser, whose regional popularity had soared in the aftermath of Suez. A Saudi diplomat warned the State Department in late January "that unless the King supports the Egyptians in the area he would get into a position which would threaten his own influence." Regarding the Eisenhower Doctrine in particular, Saud had difficulty defending the policy to other Arab leaders once its contents had been revealed and its shortcomings publicized. During a 5–7 January visit with Saud in Riyadh, al-Quwatli and Syrian foreign minister Salah al-Din al-Bitar forcefully criticized the vacuum theory and the doctrine's failure to address noncommunist aggression. Saud had to acknowledge that these were valid concerns, and for the rest of January his position was one of seeking "clarification on [the] Eisenhower Doctrine before fully accepting" it.[45]

While the Eisenhower administration tended to be fatalistic about King Hussein, it was not about to let Saud slip through its fingers. Indeed, with the easing of the Suez crisis in late 1956, Eisenhower had resumed his quixotic scheme to transform Saud into a pan-Arab leader to rival Nasser. "If we could build [Saud] up as the individual to capture the imagination of the Arab World," Eisenhower wrote Dulles in December, "Nasser would not last long." About this time Eisenhower invited Saud to pay a state visit to the United States in early 1957, and Saud accepted. The official purpose of the visit was to conclude negotiations over the renewal of the U.S. lease on the Dhahran airfield, but Eisenhower also hoped to use the occasion to enhance Saud's standing in the Arab world.[46] With the promulgation of the Eisenhower Doctrine at the turn of the new year, the president acquired the additional goal of securing Saud's active support for the doctrine.

Saud remained cautious as he prepared for his trip to Washington. On 17–18 January he met in Cairo with Nasser, King Hussein, and Prime Minister Sabri al-'Asali of Syria. The four leaders signed a joint memorandum reiterating the now familiar Arab complaints about the Eisenhower Doctrine's reliance on the vacuum theory and exclusive focus on the communist threat.[47] Saud later assured U.S. officials that, while in Cairo, he had defended the United States and warned his colleagues against excessive friendship with the Soviet Union.[48] Saud nevertheless endorsed the critical memorandum and agreed to present it to the U.S. government when he visited Washington.

Saud, whose visit to the United States lasted from 29 January until 8 February, proved an irresistible target for domestic critics of the administration. In New York City, where Saud briefly stopped before flying on to Washington, Democratic mayor Robert Wagner drew noisy local applause by refusing to bestow the city's customary honors on the king, in protest against Saudi Arabia's toleration of slavery and its restrictive laws against Jews and Catholics.[49] The task of escorting Saud on his New York rounds fell to federal officials, whose efforts were marred by pickets, catcalls, and even a mock slave auction. In Congress, Saud's visit provided a focus for critics of the Eisenhower Doctrine. With his enormous wealth, his extravagant lifestyle, and his authoritarian rule, Saud was almost a caricature of the reactionary Arab potentate that Eisenhower's new policy seemed bent on promoting. "A vast array of air-conditioned Cadillacs, luxurious palaces, slaves, concubines, and revelry beyond imagination, provide for the amusement of the royal household while the populace languishes in poverty," charged George McGovern, then a Democratic House member from South Dakota. "Do we build strength against communism by contributing American tax dollars to perpetuate this kind of feudal despotism?" "Our Middle Eastern 'policy' is in pretty sad shape," jeered Humphrey, "if it relies on the assurances and alleged friendship from the King of Saudi Arabia." The

Eisenhower Doctrine, Democrats claimed, amounted to a "bribe" or "baksheesh" for the likes of Saud.[50]

Eisenhower's own impressions upon meeting Saud were ambivalent at best. The president was fascinated by the exotic ways of his guest, lingering over such colorful details as Saud's practice of hunting "with falcons—not guns at all" and his "reference to Allah in almost every passage of a conversation." Less charming to Eisenhower was Saud's habit of lavishing gold watches, hundred dollar bills, and other extravagant gifts on his American handlers, causing embarrassment to the administration and legal headaches for the State Department. The musky odor of Saud's robes "nearly suffocate[d]" the president. As a potential statesman, Saud struck Eisenhower as "not unintelligent" and "more than anxious to be decent and honest." But he was also "strictly medieval" and showed little understanding of the modern world. When Eisenhower tried to explain to Saud the fundamentals of development economics, "most of this was lost on him."[51]

Still, Eisenhower remained convinced that Saud was the man to take on Nasser, and he told Republican congressional leaders on 5 February that he could "see nothing to show he's not the person we should tie to." Eisenhower insisted that Saud's religious authority, based on his stewardship of the Islamic holy places at Mecca and Medina, would suffice to overcome his personal shortcomings: "he's a natural as keeper of [the] Holy Places."[52]

Eisenhower's attachment to Saud was not entirely self-deceiving, though it was partly that. It also grew out of the realization that no other conservative Arab leader could make a more plausible bid for pan-Arab leadership. Nuri was discredited by Iraq's membership in the British-sponsored Baghdad Pact; Chamoun was the Christian president of a tiny, divided country; Bourguiba was too geographically removed from the Arab heartland to wield much influence over Arab affairs; Hussein seemed ill equipped to shape events in his own country, let alone those of the Arab world. Meeting with British defense minister Duncan Sandys on 1 February, Eisenhower noted the lack of alternatives to Saud: "The King is the only one the President sees now as a possible 'stone' on which to build."[53]

Substantively, Saud's visit went well. In exchange for increased economic and military assistance, Saudi officials agreed to extend the American lease on the Dhahran airfield for another five years.[54] Saud also appeared to have shed some of his reservations about the Eisenhower Doctrine, privately assuring Eisenhower and Dulles that "once the ideas and motives behind the Doctrine were explained and made clear to the Middle Eastern peoples, all opposition would melt away and everyone would be ready to cooperate

Eisenhower hosts a state visit by King Saud, February 1957.
(Dwight D. Eisenhower Library)

with the United States." Publicly, Saud hailed the Eisenhower Doctrine as "a good one which is entitled to consideration and appreciation" by Arab states.[55]

Equally encouraging were Saud's efforts to mend fences with Iraq. On 6 and 7 February the king met privately with Iraqi crown prince 'Abd al-Ilah, who was also visiting Washington. According to a report received by the State Department, the discussions between the two men were "frank and cordial" and yielded "general agreement on every issue but that of the Baghdad Pact." Each leader invited the other to visit his country, and their governments prepared to exchange ambassadors for the first time. Saud also "issued instructions to all of his diplomatic missions that they are no longer to engage in any propaganda or other activities directed against Iraq."[56] Inasmuch as uniting the conservative Arab states was one of the unstated goals of the Eisenhower Doctrine, the Saudi-Iraqi rapprochement was welcome news.

There were, however, ambiguities in Saud's stance to which Eisenhower should have paid closer attention. The four-power memorandum that Saud had brought with him from Cairo (and that he himself had signed) not only criticized the Eisenhower Doctrine but accused the West of waging "Economic War" on the Arab states and of supplying Israel with arms while deny-

King Saud meets with Crown Prince 'Abd al-Ilah in Washington, D.C., February 1957. (© Bettmann/CORBIS)

ing them to the Arabs. Such policies, the memorandum claimed, forced some Arab states to turn to the Soviets for help. During his U.S. visit, Saud did not personally repeat these charges, but he did not repudiate them, either. Similarly, while Saud echoed U.S. concerns about the dangers of establishing close ties to the Soviets, he was reluctant to criticize any specific Egyptian or Syrian moves in this direction, telling Eisenhower "that reports of the leanings of Nasser and the President of Syria toward the Soviets have been greatly exaggerated."[57] This was hardly the Eisenhower administration's view, and the disagreement was far from trivial.

Another ill-heeded warning sign was the Saudi government's ambiguous position on the Eisenhower Doctrine itself. The Saudi-American joint communiqué released at the end of Saud's visit did not explicitly recognize the threat of "international communism." At the insistence of the Saudis, the communiqué stated that "any aggression against the political independence and territorial integrity of [Middle Eastern] nations and the intervention from any source in the affairs of the states of the area would be considered endangering peace and stability."[58] This modification, designed to satisfy Arab critics who disliked the Eisenhower Doctrine's exclusive concern with communist aggression, raised some doubt over whether Saudi Arabia had formally endorsed the doctrine. Indeed, Saudi officials later assured the Egyptian government that the U.S.-Saudi agreements reached in Washington implied no such endorsement. Appreciating the delicacy of Saud's position, however, the Eisenhower administration did not press for a less equivocal statement. Saud's attitude seemed basically friendly to the new policy, and that was the important thing.[59]

ANOTHER ISSUE TO INTRUDE on Congress's consideration of the Eisenhower Doctrine was U.S.-Israeli relations. By late January Israel had withdrawn from most of the Sinai Peninsula, but it refused to vacate either the Gaza Strip or Sharm al-Shaykh, a strategic point at the tip of the peninsula overlooking the Gulf of Aqaba's Strait of Tiran. Before the Suez war, Gaza had been the source of Egyptian-supported *fedayeen* raids into Israel, and the Israelis were determined to keep the strip from reverting to Egyptian control. The Israelis also hoped to develop their southern port of Eilat, lying on the Gulf of Aqaba, as an outlet for trade with Asia and East Africa. (Because Israeli shipping could not pass through the Suez Canal, those areas were difficult to reach from Israel's Mediterranean ports.) Securing Israeli maritime access to the Indian Ocean required that the Egyptians be prevented from reoccupying Sharm al-Shaykh and resuming their blockade on shipping to and from Eilat. In late January the Israelis declared that they would withdraw from Gaza and Sharm al-Shaykh only on two conditions: that they be allowed to participate in the civil administration and policing of Gaza, and that they receive international assurances of freedom of passage through the Strait of Tiran.[60]

While the Eisenhower administration had some sympathy for Israeli concerns, it insisted that Israel's withdrawal from Gaza and Sharm al-Shaykh be entirely unconditional. Anything less would further anger the Arabs and permit the Soviets to increase their influence in the area. More concretely, Nasser was refusing to reopen the Suez Canal as long as Israel remained in Gaza and Sharm al-Shaykh, a position echoed by the Syrian government with respect to the Iraqi oil pipelines. In early February, with U.S. support, the UN General Assembly passed a resolution calling on Israel "to complete its withdrawal behind the armistice demarcation line without further delay." The administration threatened to support UN economic sanctions against Israel should it refuse to comply with the resolution.[61]

The administration's position caused an uproar in Congress. In separate statements, Senate minority leader William F. Knowland, a California Republican, and Senate majority leader Johnson charged that it would be immoral to impose sanctions on Israel unless the Soviet Union were similarly

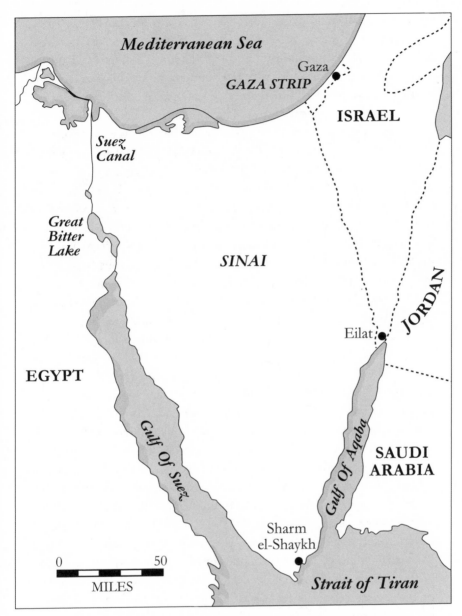

MAP 2. The Sinai Peninsula and the Gulf of Aqaba

punished for its own outrages in Hungary. Knowland's and Johnson's criticisms were loudly echoed by House and Senate members of both parties. To Dulles, the congressional rebellion demonstrated "the terrific control the Jews had over the news media and the barrage which the Jews have built on Congressmen." Actually, fear of offending American Jews was but one motive among many; others included suspicion of the UN, hostility to the Soviet Union and Egypt, and genuine sympathy for Israel's position.[62]

According to a later account by the journalists Rowland Evans and Robert Novak, Senator Johnson warned the administration that if the UN voted sanctions against Israel with U.S. support, the Eisenhower Doctrine would die in the Senate. There is no evidence, however, that Johnson or any other senator made such a threat. Throughout the crisis over Gaza and Sharm al-Shaykh, Senate consideration of the Eisenhower Doctrine continued at about the same lugubrious pace established in January, and in mid-February the Foreign Relations and Armed Services Committees reported out an amended version of the bill for consideration by the full Senate.[63]

Even without explicit threats, however, the campaign against sanctions was strong enough to extract a significant concession from the Eisenhower administration. In an 11 February aide-mémoire to the Israeli government, the State Department acknowledged that the Gulf of Aqaba "constitutes international waters and that no nation has the right forcibly to prevent free and innocent passage in the Gulf and through the Straits giving access thereto." If Israel withdrew to the armistice lines, the United States would support Israeli maritime rights in that waterway. It would also push for the stationing at Sharm al-Shaykh of the United Nations Emergency Force (UNEF), which the General Assembly had already voted to place along the Egyptian-Israeli border and armistice demarcation line. These arrangements would allow UNEF not only to intercept *fedayeen* raids from Gaza but to prevent Egypt from resuming its blockade against Israeli shipping.[64]

The concession on the Gulf of Aqaba angered the Arab states, which saw the gulf as an Arab mare clausum and believed that lifting the blockade against Eilat was tantamount to rewarding Israel for its aggression against Egypt. Saud, who had just returned to the Arab world, was especially aggrieved, since his interests in the Gulf of Aqaba were religious as well as political. Saud feared that Israel's use of the gulf could provoke armed conflict in that waterway, possibly disrupting pilgrim traffic to Mecca. As Keeper of the Holy Places of Islam, Saud believed he had a sacred duty to Muslims everywhere to keep the Israelis out of the gulf. It was "a question of life and death," he wrote Eisenhower in mid-February.[65] Having championed Saud on the basis of his religious status, Eisenhower was now getting more than he had bargained for.

Israeli prime minister David Ben-Gurion was gratified by the U.S. concession on Aqaba but remained unhappy with the UN's proposed arrangements for Gaza. UNEF's presence on the Gaza-Israel border, Ben-Gurion believed, would not provide sufficient insurance against *fedayeen* attacks; only direct Israeli administration of Gaza could do that. Meeting with the

U.S. ambassador to Israel on 18 February, Ben-Gurion urged that the United States use its influence to delay a sanctions vote in the UN, buying Israel some time to work out a better deal on Gaza. Dulles was furious at the Israelis' failure to accept the deal he had offered; "they are crazy not to do it," he privately fumed on 19 February.[66]

In a nationally televised address the next evening, Eisenhower expressed "keen disappointment" with Israeli behavior. It was unacceptable, he said, "that a nation which invades another should be permitted to exact conditions for withdrawal." As long as Israel persisted in its current stance, "the United Nations has no choice but to exert pressure upon Israel to comply with the withdrawal resolutions." Democratic congressmen immediately blasted the president for "making a whipping boy out of Israel" and for placing the issue of withdrawal on "a put-up-or-shut-up basis." In a 21 February speech in the Israeli Knesset, Ben-Gurion accused the UN of practicing "perverted justice" and reiterated that Israel would not withdraw from Gaza or Sharm al-Shaykh until it had received prior guarantees that neither area would revert to Egyptian control. Behind the scenes, however, Eisenhower's tough speech prompted a flurry of negotiations among Israeli, American, and French diplomats in search of a formula that would allow the Ben-Gurion government to comply with the UN resolution but still maintain its public commitment to Israeli security, thus appeasing hard-line critics at home. That effort would bear fruit a week later.[67]

U.S. insistence on a full Israeli withdrawal had been motivated by a desire to placate the Arab states. Dulles "did not see how we could have any influence with the Arab countries if we could not get the Israelis out of Egypt."[68] Securing Arab goodwill seemed especially imperative in the latter half of February, as the Eisenhower Doctrine approached a crucial hurdle in Arab politics. At the end of the month Egyptian, Syrian, Saudi, and Jordanian heads of state were scheduled to meet again in Cairo to coordinate foreign policy. Much seemed to hinge on the attitude of Saud. A strong defense of the Eisenhower Doctrine on Saud's part would vindicate Iraq and Lebanon, which had already revealed their support of the doctrine, and strengthen the domestic position of King Hussein, who was facing stiff leftist opposition at home; these outcomes, in turn, would isolate Egypt and Syria. Saud's failure to defend the doctrine, conversely, would strengthen the radical states and weaken the conservative ones.

Mindful of the stakes, for much of February Iraqi and Egyptian spokesmen had skirmished over the meaning of Saud's recent visit to the United States; the Iraqis tended to exaggerate, and the Egyptians to minimize, the extent of Saud's alignment with Washington. On 9 and 10 February Radio

Baghdad asserted that Saud had embraced the Eisenhower Doctrine, an act of "wisdom" and "sagacity." Three days later Radio Cairo cautioned that it was "too early yet to draw any conclusions" about Saud's position. Privately, the Egyptian Foreign Ministry's Arab Bureau advised that the upcoming conference be managed in such a way as "to combat the views expressed in the political statements that have come out of Baghdad." This could best be accomplished, the bureau suggested, by getting Saud to share in a joint communiqué favoring Egypt's positions on the Eisenhower Doctrine, the Baghdad Pact, and the proper "bases for unity" among the Arab states.[69]

The Cairo conference, which took place on 26–27 February, generally went according to the Arab Bureau's plan. Saud did try to make a case for the Eisenhower administration's good intentions, but the Egyptians skillfully deflated him by noting the economic pressures that the Western powers, including the United States, were placing on Egypt. Saudi representative Yusuf Yasin later confessed to Ambassador Hare that the Saudis "had not only been at [a] loss [to] defend [the] US position but had been convinced of [the] justice of [the] Egyptian case."[70] The conference communiqué strongly reflected Egyptian views. While commending "the desire of the government of the U.S.A. to maintain friendly relations with the countries of the Middle East," the communiqué endorsed the principle of nonalignment in the Cold War, criticized the West for failing to distinguish between nationalism and communism, claimed that Egypt's strengthening ties to the Soviet Union were the result of Western economic pressure, insisted that Israeli shipping be kept out of the Gulf of Aqaba, and condemned the Baghdad Pact as an instrument of foreign domination.[71] Only the last two issues directly concerned Saudi Arabia. Egyptian diplomats in Arab states expressed relief over the communiqué, assuring Cairo that this sentiment was shared by public opinion in the host countries. A Saudi official admitted to Hare that the "communiqué was [a] sorry product as far as [the] Saudis [were] concerned but was [the] best they could do in [the] circumstances."[72]

Meanwhile, the crisis over Gaza and Sharm al-Shaykh was finally nearing resolution. On 26 February French foreign minister Christian Pineau proposed a clever formula for securing Israel's compliance with the UN withdrawal resolution. Israel would announce its intention to withdraw unconditionally from Gaza and Sharm al-Shaykh but say it was doing so on the following "assumptions": that UNEF would be deployed in Gaza, that the UN, not Egypt, would take over the civilian administration of the strip, that these arrangements would continue until a permanent settlement on Gaza had been achieved, and that Israel would be free to respond as it saw fit should Gaza again become a base for *fedayeen* attacks. In a 1 March speech before the UN General Assembly, Israeli foreign minister Golda Meir made the announcement suggested by Pineau. Days later Israel began withdrawing its forces, and by 11 March it had completely vacated Sinai and Gaza.[73]

The "assumptions" under which Israel completed its withdrawal proved only partially valid, but it made little difference in the end. No sooner had Israel vacated Gaza than Egypt began moving civilian administrators back into the strip. The Israelis bitterly complained to the Eisenhower administration, only to be reminded that the 1949 Egyptian-Israeli armistice agreement had given Egypt administrative rights in Gaza. Egypt's decision was unfortunate, the administration said, but not illegal, and it certainly was not grounds for military retaliation by Israel.[74] Israel's basic requirements were satisfied in any case: UNEF was deployed on the armistice demarcation line separating Gaza from Israel, on the Sinai-Israel land border, and at Sharm al-Shaykh. These deployments prevented the resumption of *fedayeen* raids from Gaza and of Egypt's blockade against Israeli shipping through the Strait of Tiran. UNEF would remain in both places for the next decade.

Israel's concession in early March prompted the Syrian government to permit the Iraqi Petroleum Company to begin repairing its damaged pipelines in Syria. Once again, Iraqi oil would flow to tankers on the Mediterranean coast, providing relief to the economies of Iraq and Western Europe.[75] But the Suez Canal remained closed for the time being, pending a resolution of its legal status.

BACK IN WASHINGTON, the debate over the Eisenhower Doctrine was also nearing conclusion. On 13 February the Middle East Resolution cleared the Senate Foreign Relations and Armed Services Committees and began wending its way through the full Senate. On 5 March the Senate approved the resolution by a vote of 72-19. By now, the resolution had acquired a number of amendments that displeased the Eisenhower administration, which nonetheless accepted the Senate version to avoid further debate. On 7 March the House overwhelmingly approved the Senate version, thus obviating a conference and sending the bill directly to the White House, where Eisenhower signed it two days later.[76] Exactly nine weeks after its urgent unveiling, the Eisenhower Doctrine became the law of the land.

The most important Senate amendment, sponsored by Mike Mansfield, changed the wording of the interventionist provision.[77] The administration had requested that the president be "authorized to employ the Armed Forces of the United States" to protect Middle Eastern nations from Soviet or Soviet-sponsored aggression. Mansfield, echoing Acheson's testimony before the House Foreign Affairs Committee, objected that such a provision would be superfluous because the president already had sufficient constitutional authority to use the armed forces to protect the nation's security. Worse still, explicitly "authorizing" the president to use force in one area would cast doubt on his ability to use force in all other areas where such authorization was lacking. Mansfield proposed that the relevant passage be replaced with the phrase, "the United States is *prepared* to use armed forces." That way, the resolution could not be interpreted as altering the relationship between Congress and the president with respect to the use of force.[78]

The Mansfield amendment's most consequential feature, however, would be its opening statement: "The United States regards as vital to the national interest and world peace the preservation of the independence and integrity of the nations of the Middle East." At the time, few paid much attention to this seemingly innocuous passage, but in July 1958 it would be the sole provision of the Eisenhower Doctrine that the administration could invoke in justifying its military intervention in Lebanon.[79]

As for the interventionist provision as a whole, its most sweeping legacy lay further in the future. Just as the Middle East Resolution recalled the earlier Formosa Resolution, so it anticipated the later Gulf of Tonkin Resolution. In 1964, seeking a legislative vote of confidence in his Vietnam policy, President Lyndon Johnson convinced Congress to pass a joint resolution consciously modeled on the Middle East Resolution.[80] (The Vietnam resolution was even briefly known as the Johnson Doctrine for Southeast Asia.) Like its 1957 predecessor, the Gulf of Tonkin Resolution did not actually "authorize" the president to use the armed forces; rather, it expressed broad political support for any measures he might take, including military ones, to repel "armed attack" against U.S. forces in Southeast Asia and to assist in the defense of friendly nations in the area.[81] The Gulf of Tonkin Resolution helped set the stage for a disastrous military commitment in Vietnam and was blamed, in retrospect, for permitting a dangerous expansion of presidential powers. It was the legislative climax of the "imperial presidency," an institution partly created by the Eisenhower Doctrine.

THE PASSAGE OF THE Middle East Resolution permitted the Eisenhower administration to concentrate more fully on selling its new policy to Middle Eastern governments. On 12 March former congressman Richards, Eisenhower's special ambassador for the Eisenhower Doctrine, began his tour of Middle Eastern countries. Yet two problems from the Suez crisis remained unresolved: the breakdown in relations between the United States and Britain, and the disputed status of the Suez Canal. Over the next several weeks, as Richards sought regional converts to the new doctrine (an effort described in Chapter 4), Eisenhower and Dulles had to attend to this unfinished business.

From 20 to 23 March Eisenhower and Dulles met with their British counterparts in Bermuda to discuss the range of Anglo-American concerns, including Middle East policy. Immediately after the meeting, Eisenhower reported to congressional leaders "that in all of the many conferences that he had attended in peace and war, this one gave him about the finest feeling as to the competence of the participants and the trust that could be put in them." Eisenhower did get along famously with Prime Minister Macmillan, his wartime colleague. "Between formal meetings," Macmillan's biographer writes, "the two statesmen popped in and out of each other's rooms in the Mid-Ocean Club, sometimes in pyjamas, chatting like old school chums."[82]

Substantively, agreement at Bermuda was far from uniform, though it was clear that the British had little choice but to acquiesce in American desires. The United States agreed to join the military committee of the Baghdad Pact but declined to join the pact outright, much to the disappointment of British officials. The British were also thwarted in their efforts to continue their anti-Nasser campaign. Eisenhower wrote in his memoirs that Macmillan and Foreign Secretary Selwyn Lloyd were so "obsessed with the possibilities of getting rid of Nasser" that "Foster and I at first found it difficult to talk constructively" with them about Suez. In his diary account of the Bermuda meeting, the president was more specific: "The British mentioned the existence of a secret Egyptian plot for executing a coup to dispose of Nasser. They apparently thought we knew a great deal about it and wanted us to make some public statement against Nasser in the hope that this would encourage the dissident Egyptians." The British could not make such a statement themselves, since "manifestly anything the British said against Nasser would only make him stronger in the area."[83]

Although hostility to Nasser remained a linchpin of U.S. Middle East policy, Eisenhower and his advisers had little interest in deposing him by force. Such an attempt, they feared, would turn the entire Arab world against the West, leaving an open field to the Soviets. Moreover, with negotiations for reopening the Suez Canal still pending, this was hardly an opportune time to move against Nasser. In a review of Egyptian policy earlier that month, the Eisenhower administration had decided to continue its policy of "correct but unhelpful relations with Egypt": maintaining the current economic pressure without precipitating an open break.[84] This approach

The Americans and the British mend fences in Bermuda, March 1957.
Left to right: Selwyn Lloyd, Eisenhower, Harold Macmillan,
and John Foster Dulles. (AP/Wide World Photos)

might not yield much progress in the short run, but it could, if continued over time and augmented by diplomatic and political pressures, eventually compel Nasser to modify his anti-Western posture.[85]

Accordingly, Eisenhower told the British at Bermuda that the United States would take no action, verbal or otherwise, to support the Egyptian coup plotters.[86] As the president noted in his diary, "We brought out that if the United States had to carry the burden for the Western world of negotiations with Nasser for a Canal settlement, we had better keep our mouths shut so far as criticism of him was concerned, at least for the moment." The British, "while earnestly retaining the hope that Nasser would come to some bad end," agreed that the West had little choice but to work with Nasser toward a canal settlement.[87]

Indeed, Nasser's physical control over the Suez Canal gave him enormous leverage, which not only protected him from Western-sponsored attack but allowed him to dictate the terms of the canal's reopening. Since the Suez war, the position of Britain and France had been that all canal dues should be paid not to Egypt but to an international authority like the World Bank, whereas Egypt insisted on collecting the dues directly. In early February Dulles proposed that the international authority turn over half the canal dues to Egypt, with the other half impounded pending a final settlement, but Egypt rejected this formula as well. Britain and France then considered boycotting the canal but had to abandon the scheme when it became clear that other user countries would not cooperate. By the time of the Bermuda meeting, Britain and the United States were resigned to the likelihood of full Egyptian sovereignty over the canal.[88]

In mid-April the Suez Canal reopened under Egyptian control. The United States and Britain decided to use the canal and to allow their ships to pay dues directly to the Egyptian canal authority. Both countries, however, protested the new arrangement, and the United States continued its freeze on Egyptian assets pending resolution of the Suez Canal Company's claims against Egypt. In late April the United States took the matter before the UN Security Council, and so the dispute dragged on.[89] By early summer the canal controversy was largely forgotten, as the United States and the Arab world were embroiled in fresh crises.

A CERTAIN SMUGNESS HAD always been a feature of Eisenhower's and Dulles's foreign policy, and this was especially so in early 1957. In their recent conflicts with Arabs, Israelis, Europeans, and U.S. congressmen, Eisenhower and Dulles had become further convinced of the pettiness, irrationality, and selfishness of human affairs—and of their own administration's unique ability to transcend such failings. In mid-January Eisenhower wrote Indian prime minister Jawaharlal Nehru that Middle Eastern nations "have built up an emotionalism that at times borders on the hysterical." The United States, by contrast, was prepared "to make considerable sacrifices" to ease tensions in the region, "and in return we want nothing whatsoever except the confidence" that the area would be prosperous and secure. In early March Dulles told West German foreign minister Heinrich von Brentano "that most countries' attitudes . . . reflect their natural affinities rather than principles. The United States, however, felt that its position in the world today was such that it must base its policy on certain fundamental principles rather than let our position be governed by what countries we liked or by historic friendships. This was not an easy position to take and it was possibly the first time in history such a position had in fact been taken." At a "background" press conference at the Bermuda meeting later that month, Dulles criticized Nasser's conception of sovereignty as amounting to "the right to . . . step on other people's toes with impunity. But we all know, who have some maturity in these matters, that sovereignty—its best expression—involves the harmonizing of policies, coordinating them and working for the common good."[90] Would that all governments shared the Eisenhower administration's "maturity."

In domestic politics, Eisenhower's and Dulles's view was much the same: congressmen, like foreign governments, were too petty and self-aggrandizing to serve the common good; only the administration was sufficiently broad-minded to do that. On bipartisanship, Dulles claimed, the administration's record "is second to none"; its consultations with Congress "have been far more frequent & infinitely more informative than ever before. But the Congress itself is not well organized—they are jealous among themselves." Eisenhower complained of the Democrats' "bitter partisan attack" on administration policy. Eisenhower and Dulles were especially disgusted by Congress's noisy reaction to proposed sanctions against Israel. "Congressional pressure against them is rising rapidly," Dulles remarked in mid-February. "Votes are the only reason." "It was disheartening," Eisenhower sighed, following a discussion of the Israeli crisis with congressional leaders, "to know that political considerations entered so much into decisions of such high ranking leaders." Democrats were not the only culprits: Senator Knowland's opposition to sanctions, Dulles believed, was due to the fact that "K is running for the Presidency. . . . The pressure of the Jews largely [ac]counts for Knowland's attitude."[91]

There was, of course, a good deal of hypocrisy in such talk. A government that had conspired to overthrow the constitutional leaders of Iran and Guatemala was hardly a standard-bearer of international restraint. An administration that had appeased Senator Joseph R. McCarthy was in a poor position to disdain others for succumbing to domestic pressures.[92] Yet there can be little doubt that Eisenhower and Dulles genuinely hoped to reduce tensions and increase living standards in the Middle East. Not only would these achievements be good things in themselves; they would make it harder for communism or radical nationalism to make further gains in the area, in turn reducing the likelihood of the West's losing access to the oil reserves or strategic positions of the Middle East. Supporting UN peacekeeping efforts, pumping dollars into Middle Eastern economies, and helping friendly Middle Eastern nations defend themselves against internal and external threats—all this seemed justified on both moral and practical grounds.

Yet it was on both of those grounds—morality and practicality—that the Eisenhower Doctrine would be found wanting. Time and again, under the doctrine, the Eisenhower administration would give its support to the authoritarian, aggressive, and provocative behavior of conservative Arab leaders, eroding the moral basis of the new U.S. policy. By itself, this moral failing probably would not have sufficed to defeat the Eisenhower Doctrine, especially given Eisenhower's and Dulles's conviction that abandoning the Middle East to the depredations of international communism would have been a far greater sin. But the moral problem would soon become a practical problem, too. By giving aid and comfort to unpopular Arab leaders, by opposing popular Arab efforts to tap the resources of the communist world, and by failing to offer explicit guarantees against Israeli aggression, the Eisenhower Doctrine would alienate much of Arab public opinion, and Arab governments, whatever their real sentiments, would find it extremely difficult to embrace the doctrine in the face of such hostility. Arab audiences would take moral offense at Eisenhower's new policy, and this would contribute to its undoing.

THE CONSERVATIVE MOMENT,
MARCH–JUNE 1957

For a few weeks in the spring and early summer of 1957, the Eisenhower Doctrine seemed to be a success. Although few Arab governments endorsed it unequivocally, the doctrine did contribute to the political realignment of the Arab world and to the consolidation of an emerging anti-Nasserist camp. With Washington's encouragement, Jordan's young King Hussein decisively ousted Nasserist figures from his government and army. Also assisting Hussein were the conservative rulers of Iraq and Saudi Arabia, who set aside their bitter rivalry to cooperate with each other in aiding a fellow monarch. Lebanon's pro-Western president Camille Chamoun, with clandestine help from the CIA, crushed his pro-Nasser rivals in parliamentary elections. By June the conservative Arab regimes had banded together in a quasi-alliance, and Arab radicals were on the defensive. In celebrating these achievements, however, the Eisenhower administration was prone to underestimate the resiliency of its adversaries, the fragility of its friends, and thus the vulnerability of its own political gains in the Arab world.

CONGRESS'S PASSAGE OF the Middle East Resolution on 9 March cleared the way for former congressman James P. Richards, Eisenhower's special ambassador for the Eisenhower Doctrine, to begin his tour of Middle Eastern and North African countries.[1] Richards, whom *Newsweek* dubbed

James P. Richards (right) meets with Eisenhower and Dulles after returning from his special mission to the Middle East, May 1957. (Dwight D. Eisenhower Library)

the "traveling salesman for the Eisenhower Doctrine," had two official tasks. The first was to convince as many nations as possible to endorse the policy. Ideally, the State Department instructed Richards, a country would indicate its endorsement by unequivocally recognizing "the menace of international communism." Realistically, though, "we would not wish to jeopardize the possibility of gradually moving a country into taking a stand against international communism by too firm an immediate position." Thus Richards should be flexible in evaluating each country's attitude. Richards's second task was to establish, following discussions with governments endorsing the doctrine, amounts of U.S. economic and military assistance. Since the State Department had already made broad allocations for such aid, Richards's discretion was limited.[2] The two official objectives concealed a pair of deeper purposes: discrediting Nasserism in the Arab world by exposing its unwillingness to recognize the communist threat, and breaking Nasser's monopoly on pan-Arab leadership by building up his conservative rivals.[3]

Richards, whose mission lasted from 12 March to 7 May, met with a mixed reception in the region. Lebanon, Libya, Ethiopia, Tunisia, and the Baghdad Pact countries endorsed the doctrine unconditionally, though several of these countries, especially Libya, Iran, and Iraq, complained that their aid packages were much smaller than expected.[4] Saudi Arabia accepted $20 million in economic aid but avoided an unequivocal endorsement of the Eisenhower Doctrine. In the joint communiqué issued during Richards's visit to Riyadh, the Saudis insisted on mentioning "other forms of imperialism," as they had done during King Saud's visit to Washington.[5] Morocco and Israel expressed interest in the Eisenhower Doctrine and American aid but withheld unconditional endorsement of the doctrine.[6] Sudan, whose government was split between pro-Western and pro-Egyptian factions, both rejected the doctrine and declined American aid. A political crisis in Jordan in late April prevented Richards from visiting that country, which later secured U.S. aid on a different statutory basis.[7]

Two other countries that Richards might have visited but did not were Syria and Egypt. While Syria's open hostility to the Eisenhower Doctrine ruled out a stop in that country, Egypt's position was more ambiguous. For most of the mission's duration, Cairo, which had yet to reject the Eisenhower Doctrine outright, expressed vague interest in receiving Richards but declined to issue a formal invitation. Evidently Nasser wanted to bear neither the indignity of requesting U.S. assistance nor the onus of rebuffing it. The Eisenhower administration was equally reluctant to deal an affront and went through the motions of soliciting an invitation. The Jordanian crisis put an end to such pretenses, and in early May Eisenhower recalled his special ambassador.[8]

AT THE TIME THE Eisenhower Doctrine was being formulated in December 1956, few could have predicted that Jordan would be a testing ground for the new policy. Many U.S. officials had grave doubts about Jordan's ability to survive as a nation. A recent creation of Britain, Jordan seemed to lack historical justification and political legitimacy. Israel, Iraq, Syria, and Saudi Arabia had historical claims or present designs on portions of its territory. Jordan was utterly dependent on outside support, and its current patron, Britain, which furnished a $35 million annual subsidy under the terms of the 1946 Anglo-Jordanian treaty, had been discredited in the region. Most destabilizing of all, two-thirds of Jordan's population were Palestinians, either settled inhabitants of the West Bank, which Jordan had annexed in 1950, or refugees who had arrived after the creation of Israel. Most of these Palestinians, and many Jordanians as well, had little stake in Jordan's continued existence as a Hashemite kingdom. They instead looked to pan-

Arab nationalism, symbolized by Nasser, as a more promising avenue to the restoration of Palestinian rights and the liberation of the Arab people from imperial domination.

Since his coronation in 1953 at age eighteen, Jordan's King Hussein had been mindful of this growing nationalist mood and had made frequent rhetorical concessions to it. Throughout 1956, however, Hussein had been obliged to make substantive concessions as well. In January he was forced by domestic disturbances to rescind his provisional decision to bring Jordan into the Baghdad Pact. In March 1956 he further mollified the left by dismissing the Arab Legion's British commander, Lieutenant General John Bagot Glubb. In October Hussein permitted unusually free parliamentary elections. Held against the backdrop of the escalating Suez crisis, the elections yielded a victory for the National Socialist Party (NSP). The NSP was a mildly reformist party, but in the heat of the campaign, and lacking firm ideas of its own, it had allied itself with the left and run on a radical nationalist program. In recognition of the election's results, Hussein invited NSP leader Sulayman al-Nabulsi to form a government. Al-Nabulsi's cabinet, unveiled just as the Suez war was beginning, contained six NSP members, three independents, and one member each of the Ba'th Party and the procommunist National Front Party. The cabinet's radical members, egged on by supporters in the parliament and among the public (especially West Bank Palestinians), began pushing al-Nabulsi to move further left—and thus into conflict with the conservative king.[9]

Over the next six months three personalities, each heading a crucial Jordanian institution, helped shape the country's future. Prime Minister al-Nabulsi was an intelligent and committed Arab nationalist but not an effective leader. He had sound political instincts but lacked the strength of character to act on them. Al-Nabulsi recognized that many of his colleagues and supporters would, if not restrained, pursue dangerously polarizing policies, and he did at first show some inclination to restrain them. Later, however, when holding back the left proved unpopular, he abandoned the effort and lost control of events. The second important figure was Major General 'Ali Abu Nuwar, who became commander of the Arab Legion (now reorganized as the Jordan Arab Army) following Glubb's dismissal. Abu Nuwar was at the forefront of a group of young Jordanian officers who filled the positions vacated by Glubb's British subordinates, and he liked to portray himself as the central figure in this historic process of *ta'rib*, or Arabization. Actually, Abu Nuwar was apolitical and pragmatic to the point of being mercenary. His main interest was establishing a power base in the Jordanian army, and he would attach himself to any patron likely to further that goal. For a time Hussein seemed to be such a patron, but as the king's position grew more precarious, the general began looking elsewhere.[10]

The third important figure was Hussein himself, now twenty-one. As of late 1956 the king was still untested, but he soon demonstrated his personal dominance over al-Nabulsi and Abu Nuwar. Like al-Nabulsi, Hussein was a crowd-pleaser who avoided taking unpopular stands. Like Abu Nuwar, he could be opportunistic and devious. But Hussein had additional reserves of courage, conviction, ruthlessness, and resolve that, combined with his more self-protective traits, allowed him to prevail over his Jordanian rivals. Hussein took his role as bearer of the Hashemite legacy extremely seriously, and he was prepared to take enormous risks, to others and himself, for that legacy's preservation.[11]

In November 1956 the main task facing Jordanian politicians was securing the country's financial future. In the post-Suez mood, virtually all Jordanians agreed that the Anglo-Jordanian treaty would have to go, taking the subsidy with it. Within that consensus was a dispute between those demanding unilateral "abrogation" of the treaty and those preferring negotiated "termination." Favoring the first course were radical nationalists in parliament and the cabinet who hoped to sever ties irrevocably with the West, leaving Jordan no choice but to seek support from other Arab states—a necessary first step toward political integration with them. Favoring the second course was Prime Minister al-Nabulsi, who, though also committed to Arab unity, was loath to end the British subsidy before finding a replacement; a negotiated termination would at least buy him some time. Meanwhile, unbeknownst to al-Nabulsi, Hussein and Abu Nuwar were angling for American patronage. Both men had reason to fear an Arab aid agreement paving the way to political integration: the king stood to lose his throne; the officer, his fiefdom in the Jordanian army. In November Hussein and Abu Nuwar separately told U.S. officials that they preferred to replace the British subsidy with American aid. Failing that, they warned, Jordan would have to turn to Egypt and Russia for help.[12]

Robert Satloff describes these maneuverings as a race to determine Jordan's future political orientation, with the palace rushing to acquire an American commitment before the radicals could sever Jordan's remaining ties to the West. By the end of the year neither side had won a complete victory, as both the al-Nabulsi cabinet and the U.S. State Department refused to be stampeded into any early commitments. In late November the cabinet resisted the parliament's unanimous recommendation that Jordan unilaterally abrogate the Anglo-Jordanian treaty and establish diplomatic relations with the Soviet Union and communist China. The cabinet not only opted for negotiated termination but made termination conditional on an offer of aid from Arab countries. On the matter of diplomatic relations with the Soviet Union and China, it agreed merely to "study the recommendation."[13]

For its part, the State Department was cool to Hussein's and Abu Nuwar's appeals for American sponsorship, giving little reason to hope that the United States would increase its assistance to Jordan.[14] The department probably suspected that the two men were bluffing when they threatened to turn to Moscow should Washington disappoint them. Even if the threat was genuine, Dulles was uncharacteristically sanguine about the consequences of a Soviet takeover of Jordan. Meeting in Paris with British foreign secretary Selwyn Lloyd on 10 December, Dulles argued that satellites not contiguous to Soviet territory could be "pinched off" by the West and that the Russians, knowing this, were "not prepared to make a big investment in areas which they could not hold." Then there were the old doubts about Jordan's viability. "The brutal fact," the secretary told the British ambassador to the United States on 24 December, "was that Jordan had no justification as a state." It did not follow, Dulles hastened to add, "that this was the moment to liquidate it," but it did follow that there should be limits on any American commitment.[15]

By this time the administration was putting the finishing touches on the Eisenhower Doctrine, which both recognized the possibility of and provided the mechanism for increased U.S. military and economic aid to Jordan. U.S. officials nevertheless hoped that such aid would prove unnecessary. While acknowledging that the Anglo-Jordanian treaty could not continue unchanged, the State Department urged Jordan to reach a new understanding with Britain, perhaps on terms more respectful of Jordanian sovereignty, rather than end the treaty relationship outright. Such a renewal of ties would make a major American commitment unnecessary. At most the department envisioned "a modest increase" in nonmilitary U.S. aid to Jordan, with Britain (and possibly Saudi Arabia and Iraq) meeting the balance of Jordan's needs.[16]

Britain, however, now believed that its treaty with Jordan had outlived its usefulness. At the Paris meeting on 10 December, Selwyn Lloyd told Dulles that "our money spent there is wasted, except that it may keep out worse money," referring to possible Soviet aid. King Hussein, Lloyd predicted, would probably emulate his father and "go mad." All the British hoped to do was keep Jordan in friendly hands as they shored up their remaining positions in Iraq and the Persian Gulf. They wanted the Americans to assume responsibility for Jordan. But the Eisenhower administration resisted this

suggestion, as it did the entreaties of Hussein, Abu Nuwar, and its own ambassador to Jordan, Lester D. Mallory.[17]

Meanwhile Egypt, Syria, and Saudi Arabia, which in 1955 had formed
the ESS Pact, renewed an earlier offer to extend aid to Jordan. Given the public excitement the offer generated among Jordanians, Hussein could scarcely
afford to refuse it outright. Initially, Hussein planned to go through the motions of negotiating an ESS aid package while holding in reserve the trump
card of an American offer, to be produced in the event the negotiations
failed. In light of American stinginess, however, the king now had to take
the ESS offer more seriously. On 27 December, after hearing Mallory convey another rejection of Jordan's request, Hussein vented his frustration.
Mallory reported that the king "said looking at me almost in personal appeal that what he had really hoped for was a backstop. He had not necessarily expected a firm response of financial assistance at this moment but
an indication of favorable consideration would have been helpful." Hussein said that "he had tried to hold the line here and to keep [the] country
oriented to [the] west," but "this would be increasingly difficult and the
outcome doubtful" in view of America's attitude.[18]

CLEARLY THE EISENHOWER DOCTRINE did not signal any major American commitment to preserving the Hashemite kingdom. But it did, in the
months to come, help bring such a commitment into being. By its mere existence, the doctrine contributed to Jordan's internal polarization, which in
turn led to a showdown between Hussein and the al-Nabulsi cabinet. Hussein's success in that showdown cleared the way for American underwriting
of his regime. Ironically, when the U.S. subsidy did finally materialize, it could
not be identified with the Eisenhower Doctrine, but by that time Washington was prepared to be flexible.

The unveiling of the doctrine in January 1957 revived Hussein's hopes
for increased U.S. aid. But the king also had to consider Jordanian public
opinion, which was generally hostile to the U.S. initiative. Radicals and communists blasted the doctrine as rapacious imperialism. Islamic conservatives denounced it as an "infidel" intrusion into the Moslem world. Pro-
Western moderates and conservatives, who in principle welcomed a larger
American role in the region, objected to the notion of a vacuum in the Middle East and to the obsession with Soviet, rather than European or Israeli,
aggression.[19] Hussein's response to the dilemma was a delicate balancing
act. After hearing Eisenhower's 5 January speech, Hussein confided to Mallory that "it was cause for satisfaction that any gap in [the] Arab world

which might be filled from outside would be [filled] by those concerned with right and justice." Describing his meeting with Mallory to the Jordanian press, the king claimed to have told the ambassador "that the Arabs would not permit any foreigner to fill the vacuum" in the region. Mallory noted the discrepancy but took an indulgent attitude. The important thing, he reminded the State Department, was Hussein's "obvious approval of [the] President's declaration and willingness to receive aid."[20]

Now that the Americans themselves had officially broached the subject of aid, Hussein sought to extricate himself from the ESS agreement, which was to be concluded in Cairo later that month. On 9 January Mallory learned, via a "trusted source," that Hussein planned to sabotage the ESS talks by demanding the "guaranty of 'a certain sum' which he doubted possible." Once the talks failed, Hussein would form a new government that would crack down on communists and Ba'thists, thus securing his throne and "facilitat[ing] closer relationships with [the] US especially in working out any aid assistance."[21]

Exactly what happened at the Cairo talks is unclear. Perhaps the Jordanians never demanded the "certain sum." Perhaps that sum did not exceed what the ESS powers were prepared to offer. In any event, on 19 January Jordan, Egypt, Saudi Arabia, and Syria signed the Arab Solidarity Agreement, which pledged the ESS powers to give Jordan £12.5 million Egyptian (about $43.5 million) annually for ten years.[22] The agreement cleared the way for negotiations to terminate the Anglo-Jordanian treaty. The talks began on 4 February.

Despite Hussein's failure to make an early switch to the Americans, the Eisenhower Doctrine did play a part in his later showdown with the al-Nabulsi cabinet, ultimately permitting Jordan's reorientation toward the West. The doctrine was one of a cluster of issues over which the cabinet and the palace fought to determine government policy and, by extension, Jordan's constitutional identity. The fact that Jordan's constitution did not clearly spell out the cabinet's and the palace's respective roles in national policy created an opportunity for either party, simply by seizing the initiative, to expand its power in practice.[23] Since November, radicals in the cabinet and parliament had moved to relax Jordan's ban on local communist activity and had pushed for diplomatic relations with the Soviet Union and Red China. In January they acquired a third goal: forcing Jordan's rejection of the Eisenhower Doctrine. Victory on these three issues would establish the cabinet's political supremacy over the king, reducing him to a figurehead if not abolishing the monarchy altogether. Al-Nabulsi shared this goal, even as he tried with diminishing success to persuade his allies to pursue it more slowly. Hussein wanted to block recognition of Russia and China, resuscitate the ban on local communists, and position Jordan to take advantage of American largesse. Doing these things would keep maximum power in royal hands, securing Jordan's future as a Hashemite kingdom.

In the early weeks of 1957 the three issues of local communism, diplomatic recognition, and the Eisenhower Doctrine proved a combustible mix. On 2 January, reacting to early news reports of the doctrine, Ba'thist minister of state for foreign affairs Abdullah al-Rimawi denounced the new policy. A week later two leaders of the procommunist National Front publicly congratulated Hussein for supporting the "Arab nation in condemning American imperialist plots." In his reply Hussein deftly evaded the trap, neither confirming nor denying that this was his position, but he added that there was "no place among us for preachers of materialistic principles or doctrines differing from our religious teachings." On 31 January Hussein sent a public letter to al-Nabulsi urging him to combat communist influences in Jordan. "The Arab nation has not yet forgotten," Hussein wrote, "that the Eastern camp . . . helped our enemy to usurp a precious part of the Arab homeland, namely dear Palestine." Just as Hussein turned aside the invitation to repudiate the Americans, so al-Nabulsi wanted no part of any suppression of the communists, which would divide his coalition; he neither rejected nor heeded the king's directive. On 5–8 February Jordanian security forces, at the palace's behest, closed the Amman office of the Soviet news agency Tass, banned all "Communist propaganda," and impounded copies of al-Jamahir, the National Front's newspaper. On 18 February Hussein ordered the press to stop criticizing the Eisenhower Doctrine and instructed the cabinet to take no steps toward recognizing communist states. Al-Rimawi defied the king on both counts, declaring the cabinet's adherence to "positive neutrality" and its categorical rejection of the assumptions supposedly underlying the Eisenhower Doctrine, though not of the doctrine itself.[24]

On the surface there was considerable agreement between Hussein and al-Nabulsi, with each leader trumpeting his undying support for Arabism and his opposition to Zionism and imperialism. Since both leaders wanted a smooth termination of the Anglo-Jordanian treaty, neither dared take any action that might disrupt the termination talks. All knew, however, that the truce could not last. On 6 February Hussein told Mallory that "after treaty talks are over he planned to make [a] move" that "would be very definite and substantial," perhaps including the removal of "extremist Cabinet members" whom al-Nabulsi was unable or unwilling to control.[25] Al-Nabulsi, too, was preparing for a showdown, apparently calculating that a successful treaty termination, for which he was the primary Jordanian negotiator, would make him sufficiently popular to prevail over the king.[26]

By mid-February Mallory believed that "a new political situation is emerging in Jordan" and that Washington had an opportunity to put the kingdom "on the side of the west." "The battle is now joined," the ambassador cabled Washington on 13 February. "At least one champion is in the lists in [the] person [of] King Hussein." The administration should support Hussein against al-Nabulsi, who "shows no disposition to dispense with Communist and Bathiyiin supporters in government." But it was unclear how much or how soon the United States could strengthen the king's hand. While U.S. officials doubted that the Arab Solidarity Agreement would remain in force for long, the agreement had, for the time being, obviated direct U.S. military aid to Jordan. Alternatively, the administration could reinforce Saudi Arabia's growing estrangement from its ESS partners. This would not only undermine the Arab Solidarity Agreement (a major impediment to Jordan's reorientation toward the West) but reassure Hussein that he was not alone in his struggle against radical Arab nationalism. Perhaps, Mallory wrote, if King Saud scored a diplomatic victory at the Cairo conference in late February, Hussein's internal position would improve.[27] But the Cairo conference yielded no such victory (see Chapter 3), and Saud's break with Egypt and Syria was indefinitely postponed.

A third possibility was increased economic aid to Jordan under the Eisenhower Doctrine, a course Mallory recommended in his 13 February cable. There was some ambiguity on Mallory's part over whether this aid would be a means to or a reward for Hussein's victory over al-Nabulsi. Suggesting the latter expectation was Mallory's remark, "If aid [is] requested following [a] pro-Eisenhower doctrine stand, I recommend it be granted." Yet Mallory also saw the manipulation of Eisenhower Doctrine aid as an instrument for supporting Hussein in an ongoing struggle with al-Nabulsi: "If King Hussein can keep Jordan in [the] western camp he should in our own interest be supported. If [the] Prime Minister seeks to defy [the] King, inhibit his powers, or depose him, we need [the] possibility [of] withdrawing aid. . . . Aid should be a useable diplomatic tool and weapon."[28] The latter scenario was made plausible by the fact that the al-Nabulsi cabinet had not flatly rejected the Eisenhower Doctrine. (On 6 March al-Nabulsi would even issue a cautious invitation for Richards to visit Jordan.)[29] It was not inconceivable that the al-Nabulsi cabinet might accept some doctrine-related economic aid, which the United States could then use as leverage to support Hussein.

The State Department accepted Mallory's general recommendation and proposed "increasing our economic aid to Jordan by a small amount" within the framework of the Richards mission. In February and March, however, the department attached no special urgency to this task. Little could be done before Richards reached Jordan, which was not expected to occur until sometime in April.[30] Moreover, the conviction that Jordan was, in the words of a 31 January Joint Chiefs of Staff committee report, "of limited strategic value to the United States" died hard. As of 23 March Dulles still found it "questionable whether the integrity of Jordan was vital to the security of the United States."[31] Finally, challenges elsewhere in the Middle East—compelling Israel's withdrawal from Sinai and Gaza and securing the reopening of the Suez Canal—consumed most of the energy American policymakers devoted to the region.

Events soon forced Washington to pay closer attention to Jordan. The conclusion of the Anglo-Jordanian negotiations on 13 March opened a new, dangerous phase in Jordanian politics.[32] Now that a major issue uniting Hussein and al-Nabulsi had been removed, the prime minister's efforts to restrain the opposition, increasingly feeble of late, collapsed altogether, reinforcing Hussein's own conviction that a showdown was necessary. The treaty's end was greeted by three days of public celebrations, undeterred by heavy rains (a consequence, some charged, of Britain's seeding the clouds above Cyprus and Israel). Political groups across the spectrum participated in the demonstrations, though Western diplomats took special note of pro-communist and anti–Eisenhower Doctrine banners and slogans. In late March al-Nabulsi delivered a series of speeches calling for Jordanian federation with Egypt and Syria, and his cabinet unilaterally recognized the Soviet Union and communist China. Hussein continued to hint at a coming rupture with the cabinet, confiding to the Turkish ambassador that "extraordinary developments could be expected soon."[33]

Matters came to a head early the next month. On 7 April the cabinet sent the palace a list of royal advisers it wanted the king to remove. Hussein complied. On 10 April al-Nabulsi submitted an additional list of advisers slated for dismissal, including Chief of the Royal Diwan Bahjat al-Talhuni, one of Hussein's closest aides. The king refused, demanding the cabinet's resignation. Al-Nabulsi and his colleagues resigned, confident that Hussein would be unable to form a government without the support of the NSP. Initially, events bore them out. For the next three days Hussein tried different combinations of ministers, but each arrangement collapsed when one faction or another withdrew its support.[34]

Worse still for Hussein, the army leadership was growing restless. By early April Major General Abu Nuwar had evidently concluded that Hussein's power was ebbing and that some accommodation with al-Nabulsi's forces was in order. Whether Abu Nuwar and his officer colleagues hoped to oust Hussein in a coup or simply to prod him to give more ground to the left, they clearly sought to put heavy physical pressure on the king. On 8 April the First Armored Regiment took up positions at key intersections on the outskirts of Amman. Learning of this, Hussein personally ordered that the armored cars return to their base. The regimental commander obeyed the order. Abu Nuwar assured Hussein that the maneuver had been a routine exercise to monitor traffic to and from the capital, but Hussein was unconvinced. On 13 April, with the king still unable to form a cabinet, Abu Nuwar warned Hussein that "unless a Cabinet satisfactory to the people and all parties is formed . . . , then I and my colleagues will not be responsible for anything that happens."[35]

That evening, fighting broke out at the army base camp at Zerqa, some fifteen miles northeast of Amman. The cause of the fighting remains unclear. According to Hussein, whose account was generally accepted by Western diplomats and journalists (and later by Western historians and biographers), insubordinate officers under Abu Nuwar ordered their troops to move against the palace, but the troops, largely loyalist Bedouin, resisted the orders and turned against the officers.[36] According to Hussein's critics, the king himself sparked the loyalist mutiny by falsely informing the Bedouin troops that Abu Nuwar and his men had just launched a coup against the monarchy.[37] What is undisputed is that Hussein, upon hearing of the disturbance, immediately drove out to Zerqa, insisting that Abu Nuwar, who professed ignorance of any plot, accompany him in a separate car. On the way they met a truckload of Bedouin soldiers, who cheered the king and denounced Abu Nuwar. Terrified, Abu Nuwar got Hussein's permission to return to the capital. The general rushed back to the palace, only to find it surrounded by loyalist forces, who placed him under virtual house arrest.[38]

Hussein pressed on to Zerqa, where he found a chaotic scene. Though the gunfire had subsided, no one was in command, and rumors were flying that the king was dead. In his old Chevrolet, Hussein circulated through the camp and personally rallied the troops, jumping from the car to wade into crowds, allowing the men to mob and embrace him, climbing onto the hood to address the men—everywhere giving evidence that he was alive and in command. Staged or not, it was an impressive performance. Word of the king's presence spread quickly through Zerqa. By midnight all the allegedly insubordinate officers were either captured or on the run, and the entire camp was under Hussein's control.[39]

The Zerqa incident has been the subject of myth and countermyth. In his memoirs Hussein claimed to have thwarted "a deeply laid, cleverly contrived plot to assassinate me, overthrow the throne and proclaim Jordan a republic." Leftist critics accused the king of engineering a royalist coup against officers whose only crime was Arab nationalism.[40] The truth seems to lie somewhere between these two versions. Even if the officers had no concrete plan to overthrow the king, there did exist in the army a general atmosphere of insubordination in which a coup could have developed had Hussein not acted.[41] Whatever the intentions of Abu Nuwar and his comrades, two things are clear: that they overestimated their support within the army as a whole, and that they underestimated Hussein's ability to exploit their misreading.

In the days after the Zerqa incident, Hussein moved quickly to secure his throne. Keeping the palace under heavy guard, he brought in loyal Bedouin troops to patrol the capital. Though tempted to have Abu Nuwar executed, he allowed the discredited chief of staff safe passage out of Jordan and replaced him with Major General 'Ali al-Hiyari, whom he instructed to carry out a purge of the army. About a dozen suspect officers were arrested or suspended, while others fled the country, mainly to Syria. A week later al-Hiyari himself defected to Damascus, warning of "a great plot against Jordan" by palace officials and "non-Arab" military attachés, a veiled reference to U.S. army attaché Lieutenant Colonel James L. Sweeney, a frequent target of the radicals.[42] Al-Hiyari's betrayal delighted Hussein's rivals but did not seriously impede the military reorganization, and by 22 April the king could tell Mallory that the army was "well under control." Hussein also resumed his efforts to find a viable cabinet. On 15 April Husayn Fakhri al-Khalidi, a conservative Palestinian, formed a new government. Except for al-Nabulsi, who became foreign minister, every member of al-Khalidi's cabinet was a Hashemite loyalist by reputation. Shaken by the events at Zerqa, the National Socialists did not contest the arrangement, though parties to their left opposed it.[43]

By now the Eisenhower administration had shed its complacency about Jordan and was eager for Hussein to succeed in shoring up his regime. Still, it realized that any direct U.S. action might brand Hussein an American puppet. Even before the Zerqa incident, U.S. officials had encouraged Saudi Arabia and Iraq to give tangible support to Hussein and had discouraged Israel from disrupting that support.[44] In the days after Zerqa, each country did as the United States wished. American intercession may not have been the principal cause of all these actions—it is doubtful, for example, that either the Saudis or the Iraqis needed much encouragement—but the administration could take heart from the emergence of a regional coalition supporting Hussein.

Saud's help was the most dramatic. Since the Suez war, Jordan had allowed Syria and Saudi Arabia to station troops on its soil, the former near the northern town of Irbid and the latter at the Red Sea port of Aqaba and in the Jordan Valley.[45] On 14 April, the day after Zerqa, the Syrians began moving south, officially on a rotation maneuver but actually, Hussein believed, in a belated effort to support Abu Nuwar's coup. Hussein wanted to counter the maneuver but was fearful of diverting loyal troops from the capital, where their services were most needed. In a timely gesture, Saud placed his forces in Jordan under Hussein's command, giving Hussein the capability to strike northward. Meanwhile, one of Hussein's top aides phoned Syrian president Shukri al-Quwatli to protest the troop movements. Al-Quwatli denied any hostile intent but saw to it that the soldiers returned to their quarters in northern Jordan. Hussein was certain that the Saudi-Jordanian united front had forced Syria to back down.[46] Days later, possibly at American instigation, Saud reportedly rushed Hussein a grant of about $250,000 (unrelated to ESS money) so that the king could pay the Jordanian army and further cement its loyalty.[47] On 22 April Saud sent Hussein the first semiannual installment of ESS aid, £2.5 million sterling. (Neither Egypt nor Syria had made any payments.) Nasser, a U.S. embassy informant reported, now believed that Saud was "playing [the] American game in [the] Mid-East."[48]

The Iraqis, too, lent Hussein a hand. In mid-April they began massing forces at H3, an oil pumping station on the Iraqi-Jordanian border, signaling their intention to intervene if Hussein's position worsened. The danger of such intervention was that the Israelis might see it as a menacing move and react by seizing the West Bank of the Jordan River. Thus Iraq, using the U.S. State Department as an intermediary, assured the Israeli government that the border maneuvers were aimed solely at "stabilizing" Jordan and posed no threat to the Jewish state. Meeting with the U.S. ambassador to Israel on 19 April, Israeli foreign minister Golda Meir agreed that the status quo in Jordan ought to be preserved, adding that Hussein was "displaying real courage." She assured the ambassador that "there is no need to worry about us if our security [is] not threatened."[49]

It was not enough for Hussein to purge the armed forces and secure regional support. He still needed to meet the challenge posed by Jordan's domestic political institutions. From Hussein's perspective, the al-Khalidi cabinet was the worst of both worlds: sufficiently pro-Hashemite to provoke the opposition, but insufficiently resolute to keep it at bay. On 22 April a "national congress" composed of 23 parliamentary deputies and 200 opposition party delegates (including the National Socialists, who had withdrawn their support for the al-Khalidi cabinet) met in the West Bank town of Nablus. The national congress issued resolutions demanding Jordan's federation with Egypt and Syria, the reinstatement of purged army officers, the removal of "all conspiratorial, traitorous, and corrupt elements" from government, the expulsion from Jordan of Mallory and Sweeney, and the rejection of the Eisenhower Doctrine. The congress also called strikes and demonstrations for 24 April. On the appointed day Jordanians took to the streets, though their numbers were less impressive and their scuffles with police milder than many had expected. "I've seen worse at Ebbets Field," an American journalist quipped. According to Mallory, opposition to the Eisenhower Doctrine was the "central theme" of the disturbances. Later that evening the al-Khalidi cabinet resigned, citing its lack of parliamentary support.[50]

Egypt, too, was joining the fray. Throughout the spring Nasser's government had kept a low profile over Jordan, apparently reluctant to enter a fresh controversy while the Suez Canal dispute was still pending. On 4 April, as the showdown between Hussein and the cabinet loomed, the Egyptian embassy in Amman commented that "both the palace and the government are responsible for the current situation" and urged "that the Egyptian press not plunge into this controversy." For the next couple of weeks the Egyptian media did remain relatively quiet on Jordan.[51] But after about 20 April, with the canal functioning under Egyptian control and Hussein purging his ranks of Nasserist officials, Cairo abandoned its caution and publicly embraced the anti-Hussein movement. Egyptian news outlets not only criticized the palace but spread false rumors about the Jordanian crisis in an apparent effort to complicate Hussein's predicament.[52] When the Jordanian government's radio station refused to cover the National Congress's 22 April demands, Radio Cairo used its powerful signal to broadcast them throughout Jordan.[53]

By 24 April Hussein had concluded that cracking down on the opposition was both necessary and possible: necessary because his domestic rivals had abandoned all pretense of loyal opposition and were openly challenging the king's authority, and possible because the army was under Hussein's control and regional forces were poised to check any Syrian interference. But Hussein also wanted protection against possible Israeli intervention. Early that evening, through a CIA contact in Amman, he informed Washington of his intention to impose martial law on the West Bank, suspend constitutional rights, and denounce Egyptian and Syrian activities in Jordan. He asked if he could rely on American support if Israel or the Soviet Union intervened. Though the chances of Soviet intervention were infinitesimal, Hussein recognized that no request for American help could fail to mention such a threat. The same calculation apparently lay behind his simultaneous public statements blaming Jordan's difficulties on "international communism."[54]

Secretary Dulles received Hussein's private appeal early that afternoon, Washington time. He immediately phoned the president in Augusta, Georgia, interrupting a golf game, and secured Eisenhower's agreement to honor Hussein's request. Dulles then met with Israeli ambassador to the United States Abba Eban and urged that Israel "exercise great restraint and not use Jordan events as a pretext for action." Within hours the Israeli government had given the desired assurances.[55] At 5:30 P.M. White House press secretary James Hagerty announced that both Eisenhower and Dulles saw "the independence and integrity of Jordan as vital," using the language of the Mansfield amendment to the Middle East Resolution. Eisenhower ordered the Sixth Fleet to the Lebanese coast, and the State Department encouraged Turkey to move some of its forces to the Turkish-Syrian border.[56]

The Eisenhower administration believed it was running acceptable risks. No one expected direct Soviet intervention.[57] A more conceivable scenario was a Syrian attack from the north, to which the United States could respond by invoking the Eisenhower Doctrine, on the theory that Syria was "controlled by international communism." Early on 24 April, before Hussein issued his appeal, Foster Dulles had asked Allen Dulles what would happen if the United States intervened in Jordan. Allen said he "doubt[ed] anyone would fight us. An effective American intervention would do the trick." He did "not think the Syrians want to tangle with Jordan," let alone with the United States. While agreeing that action under the Eisenhower Doctrine would probably be unnecessary, Foster told the Israelis that the United States was prepared to invoke the doctrine, hoping to convince them to sit tight if Syria intervened after all.[58]

Emboldened by the American gestures, Hussein cracked down on the opposition. Around 10:00 P.M. on 24 April he met with trusted royalist politicians and formed a new government, with Ibrahim Hashim as prime minister and Samir al-Rifa'i (the cabinet's de facto leader) as deputy premier and foreign minister. Shortly after 2:00 the following morning, Jordan radio announced curfews in Amman, Irbid, Jerusalem, Nablus, and Ramallah. From balconies and upstairs windows, Amman residents watched as steel-helmeted troops took control of the city. In a predawn radio address to the nation, the king blasted communism, the al-Nabulsi cabinet, and, for the first time in public, Egypt's government. He warned "anybody who tries [to] create disturbances that [the] severest penalties will be meted out to him." Later that morning the palace issued decrees banning political parties and placing the police under army command. Additional decrees on 28 April suspended parliament and proclaimed martial law throughout the kingdom, not just in the West Bank as originally proposed. The martial law decree established military courts and appointed military governors authorized to search, arrest, and imprison suspected violators of the martial law regime. In the days to come, the government rounded up hundreds of its opponents, including al-Nabulsi and most of his cabinet. Other opposition figures fled the country or went underground.[59]

FEW U.S. OFFICIALS recoiled from Hussein's assault on civil and political liberties. Shortly after he received Hussein's 24 April appeal, Dulles remarked that the proposed crackdown was "a good tough program and if it works it will be wonderful for us." As Hussein proceeded to impose his will, Eisenhower applauded the king's "gallant fight to eject subversive elements from his government and country." In late April Mallory wrote that "firm implementation [of the] new decree providing for martial law will be one of [the] strongest instruments in achieving order out of potential chaos." By mid-May Mallory was less enthusiastic, reporting with dismay on the military courts' harsh treatment of "small-fry offenders," like the shoeshine boy who received a fifteen-year prison term for distributing "Communist leaflets." The ambassador, however, was concerned less with the injustice of the punishments than with the possibility that the Jordanian public would have "negative reactions to such sentences." In any event, Mallory's qualms were the exception. Most high-ranking U.S. officials saw Hussein's crackdown as a measured response to a mortal threat to his kingdom's survival, posed by local subversives who were not only agents of Syria and Egypt but also, in Eisenhower's words, "puppets of the Kremlin."[60]

This interpretation was oversimplified. Local communists were generally subservient to Moscow, but they were hardly the dominant element in the Jordanian opposition. It was the Ba'thists, with their stronger commitment to Arab unity and their more numerous contacts in neighboring Arab countries, who posed the real threat to the throne. (The National Socialists had the largest following in Jordan but lacked ideological coherence and organizational drive; for want of a clear program of their own, they generally followed the Ba'thists' lead.) Syria had provided some logistical support to the anti-Hussein movement,[61] but not much. The Syrian army's southward move on 14 April, hours after Hussein had already secured Zerqa, seemed more of an afterthought than part of a carefully prepared plot, and it ended at the first sign of royal resistance. Radio Cairo belatedly championed the anti-Hussein forces, but it did not malign the king personally or call on the Jordanian people to revolt, as it had done during the Baghdad Pact riots sixteen months earlier. "Nasser has not yet thrown his Sunday punch," Mallory observed on the afternoon of 24 April. The punch never came.[62]

In the days after 24 April, as Hussein demonstrated his resolve, Egypt and Syria further distanced themselves from the anti-Hussein movement. The Syrians assured Hussein that their brigade in northern Jordan served at Jordan's pleasure and would be withdrawn immediately upon Hussein's request. Following consultations with Nasser in Cairo, al-Quwatli and a delegation of Egyptian and Syrian leaders flew to Saudi Arabia. The visitors told King Saud that Syria and Egypt were not opposed to Hussein or to royalty but merely objected to unwise actions the king had taken on bad advice.[63] Nasser pledged noninterference in Jordan's internal affairs and promised Hussein a "free hand to do as he wished with any culprits found." Such conciliatory gestures must have frustrated conservatives in the region who hoped to benefit from further polarization. Iraqi prime minister Nuri al-Sa'id wished "that Nasser could at least be maneuvered into openly espousing [the] Communist cause. That would go a long way to break his influence in [the] Middle East." Lebanese foreign minister Charles Malik thought that Jordan should demand the withdrawal of the Syrian brigade. He "hoped that Syria would refuse to withdraw her troops, since the sooner the problem presented by Syria came to a clash, or a showdown, the better."[64] Egypt and Syria avoided handing their enemies such pretexts.

Indeed, Hussein's victory had brought about a period of self-criticism within the Nasserist camp. In May 1957 Nasserist Jordanian parliamentarians, now exiled in Damascus, admitted to Syrian and Egyptian officials that the Jordanian left had overplayed its hand, giving "Hussein sufficient excuses for implementing his plan" of declaring martial law. They also complained that Egyptian propaganda attacks in the wake of Hussein's victory were alienating Jordanian moderates "who might be won over to our side." Al-Quwatli believed that Hussein himself was not beyond salvaging. "Is it advisable," he asked the Egyptian ambassador in Damascus, "that some newspapers, especially Syrian ones, continue to attack Hussein personally and with such great severity? . . . King Hussein has won the battle for now by striking at the popular forces, and . . . it might be advisable to work in every way to prevent him from being swept entirely in a direction contrary to us, and to work to stop him at this point and to try to gain time."[65]

Still, if the Eisenhower administration misdiagnosed the domestic threat to Hussein and exaggerated the regional one, it was basically right about the seriousness of the king's predicament. An implacable opposition movement, though mainly domestic and noncommunist, did seem poised to land a crippling blow to Jordan's monarchy. On 21 April Mallory observed that Hussein's alternatives were "rapidly narrowing down to [a] choice by [the] King of military rule or abdication, unless he [is] assassinated first."[66] While the opposition might have settled for constitutional monarchy, an option Mallory omitted, it was clearly determined to strip the king of significant executive power. Jordanian public opinion strongly supported the opposition. To allow Jordanian politics to run their course was to ensure, at the very least, a drastic erosion of royal power. Only force could prevent that fate.

Of course, this meant that the United States, in supporting Hussein, was opposing representative government in Jordan. Any qualms U.S. officials may have had about this fact, however, were swept aside by a wave of euphoria over Hussein's victory, and by a growing sense of Jordan's importance to America's position in the region. U.S. officials had recently questioned Jordan's strategic value to the United States, and months later they would question it again. But Press Secretary Hagerty's 24 April statement that Eisenhower and Dulles saw "the independence and integrity of Jordan as vital" accurately reflected administration thinking at the time. "It can be a decisive thing," Dulles said early the next day. "If [Hussein] can stand up against this it will be a serious setback to pro-Communist elements in Syria and Egypt." Eisenhower agreed that if Hussein's victory held, "the position of the West will be immeasurably strengthened." Mallory was even more rapturous, at least until the harshness of the martial law regime caused him second thoughts. Hussein's triumph, he wrote on 3 May, made it "possible to foresee the countering of Communist activity in [the] Arab World, the shifting of alignments in Syria, close cooperation of Iraq, Jordan and Saudi Arabia, the negation of Nasser's influence and protection of [the] Persian Gulf militarily. With a little rosy tinted optimism one can speculate on so quieting things that eventual settlement of the Palestine problem may be possible." Although few of Mallory's colleagues went that far, there was general agreement that events in Jordan marked a turning point.[67]

The reassessment of Jordan's importance to the United States went hand in hand with a reassessment of Hussein's personal qualities. Months earlier U.S. officials had seen Hussein as a likable but shallow youth whose passion for sports cars exceeded his concern for matters of state. Richard H. Sanger, counselor at the American Embassy in Amman, had pronounced the

young king "one of the most charming sophomores." Hussein's courageous actions in April, however, deeply impressed American observers.
Overnight, it seemed, the "boy king" had become a man. On 22 April
Time/Life executive C. D. Jackson, an occasional adviser to Eisenhower,
marveled at "the startling news that King Hussein has decided to be a man
and a monarch on our side." Columnist Joseph Alsop, who was in Amman
that April, celebrated the "transformation of King Hussein from boy to
man."[68] In early May Sanger's college metaphor surfaced in *Time* magazine,
which quoted an "admiring American observer," probably Sanger, as saying
that Hussein had "completed his sophomore year in the fastest time on
record."[69] On 25 April Eisenhower commented that "the young King was
certainly showing spunk" and asked Dulles to give him "anything he needs
in the way of encouragement."[70]

Under Dulles's prodding, the administration rushed to grant Eisenhower's
request. It is possible that the secret CIA payments to Hussein, later revealed to have started sometime in 1957, began that very week.[71] Of greater
importance, because it was public and probably much bigger, was the official aid package that American and Jordanian representatives negotiated.
On the evening of 25 April the State Department instructed Mallory to receive "urgently from the King his further views as to how we might most
effectively give substance [to] our earnest desire [to] help him." The resulting aid agreement, concluded in Amman on 29 April, committed the United
States to assuring Jordan's "freedom" and maintaining its "economic and
political stability." The administration pledged to give Jordan $10 million in
Mutual Security funds, unrelated to Eisenhower Doctrine money, to be
disbursed through the International Cooperation Administration (ICA). ICA
officials complained that the agreement violated their mandate to dispense
aid only on a nonpolitical basis. According to former State Department official Richard B. Parker, however, "Dulles rode roughshod over the agency
thanks to presidential backing," and "they went along."[72]

In choosing this funding method, the administration indulged Hussein's
desire to avoid public identification with the Eisenhower Doctrine. On 23
April the king had requested that Richards's visit to Jordan, which the
country's crisis had long delayed, be put off indefinitely. The next day, just
prior to imposing martial law, Hussein told reporters that Jordan did not
need outside help, saying, "I think we can handle the situation ourselves."[73]
Over the following week, the king publicly denied he had accepted the
Eisenhower Doctrine, insisting that his own position on the doctrine was
actually less hospitable than that of al-Nabulsi, who had issued the initial
invitation to Richards. Hussein maintained that all U.S. aid was "completely

King Hussein poses in his new Mercedes-Benz sports car
at the Jordanian Royal Palace in Amman, 1957.
(AP/Wide World Photos)

unconditional" and that Jordan remained committed to a "pure Arab" policy.[74] Privately, Jordanian foreign minister Samir al-Rifa'i pleaded with Mallory for more U.S. aid, noting that Jordan had "virtually adhered" to the Eisenhower Doctrine. Virtual adherence was good enough for the administration, which agreed to defer Richards's visit and to continue aiding Jordan outside the framework of the Eisenhower Doctrine.[75]

With some reluctance, over the next two months the United States replaced Britain as Jordan's primary source of aid. Hoping to avoid "emerging as Jordan's sole supporter," the Eisenhower administration initially tried to get Iraq and Saudi Arabia to share the burden. Much to the administration's irritation, however, Iraqi prime minister Nuri al-Sa'id begged off on the grounds that Iraq was "short of cash." Saudi Arabia had already paid its first installment of ESS aid and was unwilling to pledge more.[76] Egypt and Syria did remain, for a time, formally committed to aiding Jordan under the Arab Solidarity Agreement, but they soon found a pretext to renege on their pledges.[77] In June 1957, having found no major cosponsors, the United States agreed to supplement its initial grant, which had been earmarked for economic use only, with $10 million in military aid and another $10 million in economic aid. By 1958 U.S. aid to Jordan was about $40 million per year, and it remained at that level for the rest of Eisenhower's presidency.[78]

Underlying Washington's growing commitment to Jordan was the frank recognition that Hussein's political survival and Jordanian democracy were, for the foreseeable future, mutually incompatible. As Mallory cabled the State Department in November 1957, "Popular rule in Jordan is mostly an illusory hope. . . . [The] west can not afford at this time to assist [the] free exercise of democratic processes," as "such freedom now could lead only to [the] complete loss of Jordan to [the] western cause through almost immediate alignment with Egypt and Syria." In the meantime, "it must . . . be assumed that [the] King feels he will be able to continue ruling regardless of popular support as long as he has [a] loyal army."[79]

IN THE WAKE OF THE Jordanian crisis, the realignment of the Arab world that had begun the previous year and that the Eisenhower Doctrine had aimed to encourage rapidly intensified, with a softening of old rivalries and a hardening of new ones. Convinced by Hussein's close call that Arab monarchs of every stripe faced a common threat in Nasserism, Saud hastened to ease the Saudi-Hashemite rivalry. In mid-May he made a state visit to Baghdad, where he assured the Iraqis that although he still would not join the Baghdad Pact, he now understood the reasons for its existence. Saud also expressed an interest in forming a "new alignment" in the Arab world, designed, he implied, to isolate Egypt and Syria. In late April Egypt finally rejected the Eisenhower Doctrine.[80] In May the Egyptian news media stepped up their criticism of the United States and the West. Egypt also discharged a propaganda barrage against Hussein. Egyptian cartoonists portrayed the diminutive king as a cowering dwarf, and Radio Cairo verged on open incitement of the Jordanian people. Given Hussein's newly powerful position, however, such provocations were more irritating than dangerous. By late May the king felt sufficiently confident to request the evacuation of Syria's brigade in northern Jordan, a move he had previously avoided for fear of enraging the Jordanian left.[81]

U.S. officials welcomed the regional realignment and saw it as a vindication of U.S. policy. They agreed that "the rapprochement between King Saud and Iraq was a most favorable development largely attributable to the Saud visit to the US and to the Richards Mission." At a North Atlantic Council meeting in Bonn in early May, Dulles acknowledged Soviet "progress in penetrating Egypt and Syria. . . . Now that the United States had taken the problem in hand, however, the Secretary expected a reduction in

Egyptian cartoon derides King Hussein, May 1957. The caption reads,
"The situation in Jordan!" Manacled figure on left is labeled
"The people of Jordan." (*al-Tahrir* [Cairo newspaper])

Soviet influence in the long run." Back in Washington, Eisenhower speculated that Arab governments would soon "bring pressure on Nasser to
change his ways and induce in him a more decent attitude toward the Western world."[82]

By early summer there were signs that American economic pressure on
Egypt was taking its toll and that Egypt was growing dissatisfied with its
trade relations with the Soviet bloc. The U.S. embassy in Cairo reported that
the Egyptians were "showing greater reluctance to cooperate with the Soviets as prices of bloc goods have risen sharply, shipments have been delayed, and the quality of wheat delivered has deteriorated." Allen Dulles
cited "evidence that Egyptian dissatisfaction with Nasser had been growing," especially among shopkeepers and the middle class, who chafed under
the government's economic controls. There were even "some indications
of a division of view in the armed forces, although this was not very clear as
yet." In late May an unofficial emissary of Nasser—the prominent Egyptian businessman Muhammad Ahmad 'Abbud, or "'Abbud Pasha," who
was then visiting the United States—got word to Eisenhower that Nasser
"is feeling a bit 'pinched' by his present relationship" with the Soviets and
"would like to be more friendly with [the United States] provided he could
bring this about without humiliation to himself." Eisenhower was intrigued
by the overture and suggested that Dulles meet with 'Abbud, but the secretary declined, apparently determined to hold out for a more decisive victory.[83]

By June 1957 the polarization of the Arab world had reached a climax. Hussein's visit to Baghdad and Saud's to Amman fueled speculation about the emergence of a "royalist axis," consisting of Jordan, Iraq, and Saudi Arabia, which along with Lebanon seemed increasingly willing to criticize Egypt and Syria openly. Accusations flew between the rival camps. The Syrians charged the Saudis with trying to organize a pro-American coup in Syria. Jordan charged Egypt with attempting to assassinate Jordanian officials and members of the royal family. Weeks earlier, Saudi officials had expelled an Egyptian diplomat on suspicion of involvement in a plot to kill Saud.[84] Allen Dulles found both the Jordanian and the Saudi accusations credible, and Eisenhower suggested that Hussein and Saud be told "that the best defense was a good counterattack." Iraq, the Egyptian embassy in Baghdad confidentially reported, was engaged with Syrian exiles and Bedouin tribes in "a conspiracy to overturn the regime in Syria." Lebanon accused Egyptian diplomats of meddling in its parliamentary election campaigns by bankrolling large antigovernment demonstrations. Malik urged the Eisenhower administration to denounce such behavior, but the administration declined, fearing that such a statement would "be construed as internal interference on the eve of elections."[85]

In fact, the United States was already interfering in Lebanon's June elections, which were widely seen as a referendum on the Eisenhower Doctrine. President Chamoun's warm embrace of the doctrine in January 1957 and his hosting of Richards the following March had infuriated the Lebanese opposition, which generally, but not exclusively, represented the country's Muslim population. The opposition saw Chamoun's actions as a violation of Lebanon's unwritten National Pact of 1943, which had been intended to address the close division of Lebanon's population between Christians and Muslims and between those favoring Lebanon's orientation toward the West and those calling for closer ties with other Arab countries. In addition to dividing political power among Lebanon's religious communities, the National Pact forbade the national government to make any international commitments that might upset the internal confessional and political balance. To the opposition, Chamoun's endorsement of the Eisenhower Doctrine was an illegitimate attempt to move Lebanon closer to the West against the interests of the country's Muslim and Arab-oriented citizens.[86]

In April 1957 thirty opposition leaders, most of them Muslims, formed the United National Front (UNF). The UNF demanded that Chamoun's cabinet immediately resign in favor of a "neutral" cabinet whose main task would be to supervise Lebanon's parliamentary elections, scheduled for June 1957. It also insisted that the caretaker cabinet refrain from making any agreement with a foreign power, pending the outcome of the elections. The government rejected these demands. Throughout the spring the UNF staged boisterous demonstrations, to which Lebanese security forces responded with increasing violence. Because the parliament elected in 1957 would a year later select Lebanon's next president, who would then serve a six-year term, most agreed that the elections would determine the country's geopolitical orientation. With stakes like these, outside interference was inevitable. Egypt and Syria secretly agreed to provide "material assistance" to Lebanese opposition newspapers. Meanwhile, CIA agent Wilbur Crane Eveland passed bundles of cash to President Chamoun, who distributed the funds among candidates of his choosing. The Eisenhower administration also arranged for some of the military equipment Ambassador Richards had promised Lebanon in March to be airlifted into the country "prior to the June 9 Lebanese elections." On the day the polls opened, a shipment consisting of thirty-seven jeeps and twelve 106-millimeter recoilless rifles was ostentatiously paraded down the streets of Beirut.[87]

In the elections, held on four successive Sundays in June, pro-government candidates won two-thirds of the parliamentary seats. Even before the polls closed, U.S. officials began to suspect that their efforts to secure a pro-American parliament had been overkill. At a 20 June NSC meeting Allen Dulles reported "that the second Sunday election in Lebanon had gone entirely as desired. Indeed, from the Western point of view it had almost gone too well. The opposition to the current regime had been almost entirely eliminated, and the opposition did include some good men." Dulles had a point. Good men or not, many of the defeated candidates were fixtures in Lebanese politics who had acquired large, loyal followings over years of public service. Suddenly these politicians had been stripped of power and their constituents deprived of representation—a volatile state of affairs. Moreover, the sheer scale of the government's victory was to many Lebanese prima facie evidence of Chamounist tampering. Even Phalange Party leader Pierre Gemeyal, a government supporter, admitted in an interview that "the parliament which has just been given to us, represents in my opinion, only ten percent of the population of the country—at the moment the real parliament is in the street." The UNF rejected the election results, and some of its armed supporters began engaging Lebanese gendarmes in sporadic clashes in the mountains.[88] Clearly, the Eisenhower administration's victory in Lebanon was a qualified one.

So, too, was its success in winning over Saud. Though the substance of Saud's policies on Nasserism now generally favored the American position, the king was wary of close public identification with the United States,

since such an open display might expose him to Nasserist attack. While praising the Eisenhower Doctrine during his recent visit to Washington, Saud
had, like Hussein, avoided formal adherence to the doctrine. Saud was also
in the habit of making anti-imperialist and anti-Zionist speeches that were
no less strident than Nasser's. Although some American officials were dismayed by these concessions to Nasserism, most agreed that as long as the
content of Saud's policies was pro-American, his rhetorical gestures in the
other direction could do little harm.[89]

But there was one issue over which the difference was not simply rhetorical: Israeli maritime rights in the Gulf of Aqaba. As we have seen in Chapter 3, the United States and Saudi Arabia were on opposite sides of this
question. The United States maintained that the gulf was an international
waterway from which Israeli and Israeli-bound vessels could not be barred;
Saudi Arabia insisted it was a closed Arab sea. Saud held to the general
Arab position that allowing Israel to use the gulf, which had been closed to
that country before the Suez war, was tantamount to rewarding Israel for
its aggression against Egypt. But the king also argued that Israel's use of
the gulf threatened pilgrimage routes to Mecca and that, as Keeper of the
Holy Places of Islam, he had a duty to Muslims everywhere to protect that
waterway from alien intrusion. The Eisenhower administration had been
aware of Saud's position on the gulf since February, but it was not prepared
for the vehemence with which the king pressed his case. Nasser, better appreciating the potential for U.S.-Saudi tension over Aqaba, had shrewdly
encouraged Saud to be the Arabs' spokesman on the issue.[90]

For much of the spring the Saudi-American disagreement over Aqaba
had been muted, but it became more pronounced after early May, when Israeli naval vessels began using the gulf, a move the Saudis denounced but
dared not counter with force. Saud was unmoved by Eisenhower's assurance that the United States would permit no interference with pilgrim
traffic. He likewise resisted the Eisenhower administration's suggestion that
Saudi Arabia take the issue to the World Court. Meeting with U.S. ambassador to Saudi Arabia George E. Wadsworth in late June, Saud proposed a
simpler solution: "Ask the President and the Secretary to change their policy on Aqaba."[91]

In a 27 June phone conversation with Eisenhower, Dulles grumbled that
"Saud is acting as the head of the Moslem religion and not as head of state."
Eisenhower said that Saud "is funny—almost childish particularly when he
talks about Allah." Of course, it had been largely for Saudi Arabia's religious pretensions that Eisenhower had sought to promote Saud in the first
place, a fact the president now seemed to forget. Nevertheless, Eisenhower

was now alive to the political dangers of the Aqaba dispute. As he wrote Dulles that day, "I am truly getting a bit uneasy about the increasing stiffness of King Saud's attitude with respect to the Gulf of Aqaba. . . . The seriousness of the matter in my mind arises from the fact that he seems to have been making so much progress to lead most of the Arab world toward the Western camp. I think we better do some very hard thinking on this matter."[92]

Hard thinking was indeed in order, not just on Saud but on the whole American policy. In applying the Eisenhower Doctrine, the United States was implementing a two-part strategy for weakening Nasserism. First, it sought to discredit Nasserists within the Arab world by exposing their unwillingness to recognize the threat of international communism. Second, it sought to break Nasser's monopoly on pan-Arab leadership by bolstering and uniting conservative Arab leaders. The Eisenhower administration had made little headway with the first part of the strategy. The equivocal Arab response to the Eisenhower Doctrine had blurred the distinction between acceptance and rejection, ensuring that no Arab country would lose standing with its neighbors simply because it had refused to denounce international communism. The second part of the strategy had found greater success. With American help, Chamoun, Hussein, and Saud had strengthened their internal positions, had drawn closer to one another, and were now checking Nasserism on several fronts. Yet even here the United States faced a basic problem: not only was it politically safe to oppose the Eisenhower Doctrine, but it could be politically dangerous to embrace it. Both Hussein and Saud had adjusted to this reality by withholding formal endorsement of the doctrine, and Saud had gone further by opposing the United States over the Gulf of Aqaba. In the summer and fall of 1957 Saud's lack of cooperation would seriously hamper American policy in the area. Chamoun, however, was refusing to moderate his pro-Western position and was continuing to force his will on a divided population. He, and Lebanon, would pay the price for this a year later.

THE SYRIAN CRISIS,
JULY−DECEMBER 1957

The second half of 1957 brought a dramatic reversal of fortune for the Eisenhower administration's Middle East policy. In the spring the administration had learned what the Eisenhower Doctrine could do. In the summer and fall it learned what the doctrine could not do. In Jordan and Lebanon the Eisenhower Doctrine had helped conservative regimes consolidate domestic power and move closer to the West. During the Jordanian crisis in particular, the doctrine had provided a security umbrella under which pro-Western regimes could cooperate with each other to rescue one of their own. The Syrian crisis of the summer and fall of 1957 posed more rigorous tests. Could the doctrine prevent a radical regime from consolidating domestic power and moving closer to the Soviet Union? Failing that, could it be used to induce the conservative Arab states to cooperate with one another to remove that regime?

It turned out that the Eisenhower Doctrine could do neither of these things. Worse still, in attempting to use the doctrine to dislodge the Syrian government, the Eisenhower administration helped unleash a regional crisis that quickly escaped its control to become a world crisis as well. For a moment in October, war between the superpowers was a real possibility. Disaster was averted, but not before the administration had almost completely lost the initiative in shaping inter-Arab politics. Ironically, the very loss of U.S. initiative had, by the end of the year, created new possibilities for combating Soviet influence in the Arab world. This surprising turn of events may have brought some solace to the administration, but it was the beginning of the end of the Eisenhower Doctrine.

AS WE SAW IN CHAPTER 4, the polarization of the Arab world reached a climax in June 1957. Almost immediately thereafter, however, contrary tendencies began to emerge. Though Jordan's and Lebanon's relations with Egypt and Syria remained hostile, Iraq and Saudi Arabia enjoyed a modest rapprochement with the radical camp. On 8 June the Iraqi cabinet of pro-Western stalwart Nuri al-Sa'id resigned, to be replaced on 20 June by a new cabinet under 'Ali Jawdat al-Ayyubi.[1] Jawdat was a thoroughly conventional figure, committed to the monarchy and partial to the West. But he was also convinced that the regime's internal position would be improved by more cordial relations with Egypt and Syria. Thus, without altering Iraq's basic pro-Western orientation—in particular the country's membership in the Baghdad Pact—Jawdat set out that summer to "remove the clouds in the Arab atmosphere" through a series of conciliatory gestures. His government refrained from publicly criticizing the radical camp, stopped jamming Egyptian and Syrian radio broadcasts in Iraq, and said it would participate in Egyptian and Syrian trade fairs later that summer. Egypt and Syria moderated their anti-Iraqi propaganda attacks.[2] It is unclear what Iraqi King Faisal and his uncle Crown Prince 'Abd al-Ilah thought of Jawdat's conciliatory posture at first, though they would strongly oppose it months later.[3] Both men, however, were summering in Istanbul and unable to exert day-to-day control over the cabinet.

Saudi Arabia's relations with the radical camp were also improving. In June anti-Saudi statements by Syrian officials had caused the Saudi government to close its embassy in Damascus and freeze Syrian assets in Saudi banks. In July the Syrians realized their error and issued a series of conciliatory statements to and about the Saudis, prompting the Saudis to reopen their embassy and begin unfreezing Syrian accounts. Meanwhile, Saud's disagreement with the United States over the Gulf of Aqaba permitted a rapprochement between Saudi Arabia and Egypt, since both countries were littoral states with identical positions on the dispute. On 8 July Saudi deputy foreign minister Yusuf Yasin, a top adviser of Saud, declared that Saudi Arabia would follow Egypt's policy of "active neutralism" and avoid all foreign pacts. On 21 July Saudi Arabia resumed previously suspended trade talks with Egypt. Privately, Saud assured an Egyptian diplomat that he still despised the Hashemites, especially that "drunkard" 'Abd al-Ilah, who "covets the throne of the Hijaz to this day."[4] All of these diplomatic developments stood the radical camp in good stead for facing the next major political crisis in the Arab world, over the nature and orientation of the Syrian regime.

ALTHOUGH THE EISENHOWER administration had worried about Syria's growing radicalization since early 1955, this feeling intensified in the immediate aftermath of the Suez war, as Syrian politics lurched to the left. Popular outrage over the attack on Egypt, combined with the exposure of Operation Straggle (see Chapter 1), discredited pro-Western Syrian politicians and strengthened radical ones. In early December the Syrian Ba'thists, supported by local communists, called for the formation of a "national parliamentary front" to protect the country from foreign plots and purge it of traitors. President Shukri al-Quwatli and Prime Minister Sabri al-'Asali, themselves conservatives, could ill resist the public pressure, and in late December al-'Asali conducted a cabinet reshuffle whose main effect was to consolidate leftist forces within the government.[5] About fifty conservative politicians were put on trial for participation in Operation Straggle, a development that strengthened the Syrian army, which was entrusted with conducting the trials. The army, in turn, was increasingly falling under leftist control.[6]

In foreign affairs Syria was growing more hostile to the West and friendlier to the Soviet bloc. Like Egypt and Saudi Arabia, Syria had severed diplomatic relations with Britain and France at the start of the Suez war. About the same time, Syrian army saboteurs, with official connivance, had blown up pumping stations for the pipeline carrying Iraqi oil to the Mediterranean, compounding Western Europe's difficulty in importing Arab oil. The Syrian government also refused to criticize the Soviets' suppression of the Hungarian revolt and even forbade the Syrian press to cover to the event. When U.S. ambassador to Syria James S. Moose protested to al-Quwatli about Syria's position on Hungary, the president retorted that the "situation in Hungary is not our affair, and I do not care if 50 Budapests are destroyed."[7] It was not hard to guess at the reasons for such a stance. By mid-November U.S. intelligence analysts estimated, Syria had received from the East bloc 20–25 MiG-15 fighters, 130 T-34 tanks, and more than 200 armored personnel carriers—and the arms flow seemed to be continuing. Moose told an American visitor of seeing columns of Czech transport vehicles on the roads near Damascus, their cargoes hidden under spotless tarpaulins. "A clean tarpaulin in an Arab country," Moose explained, "means a piece of armor just received from abroad." If clean tarps meant foreign arms, foreign arms meant foreign advisers. By late November CIA director Allen Dulles had acquired "hard intelligence to indicate the presence in Syria of a considerable number of technical personnel" from the East bloc.[8]

Nevertheless, the Eisenhower administration was not ready to panic. An open bid for power by Syrian communists, though possible, seemed unlikely to succeed. "This could be stopped," said Allen Dulles on 15 November, "because there is still plenty of pro-Western sentiment in Syria." Even if a communist takeover occurred, U.S. officials argued, the resulting regime would be vulnerable to a U.S.-sponsored campaign of subversion. Discussing Syria with British ambassador to the United States Harold Caccia in late December, Foster Dulles used a telling analogy. The secretary recalled saying "that, in my opinion, it was not feasible for the Soviets to maintain a satellite with which they did not have geographical continuity. I felt that resources could be developed to bring about a change of a satellite under these circumstances. I spoke of what had happened in Guatemala where the Government was sought to be supported by shipment of arms from Poland. . . . A Communist-controlled government had been eradicated without any military action whatsoever on the part of the United States."[9]

For the moment, however, such talk remained speculative. According to U.S. intelligence, it was doubtful that the Soviets even wanted a direct communist takeover of Syria, since such a move might provoke a violent response from the West or its regional allies. The Soviets seemed to be content with a gradual increase of their influence in Syria, and the United States could meet that challenge by more traditional diplomatic means.[10] Moreover, there appeared to be some dissension within the Damascus regime itself, a fact the administration might exploit to keep Syria from drifting further left.

A case in point was the Syrian government's muddled, though ultimately negative, reaction to the Eisenhower Doctrine. In early January President al-Quwatli instructed the Syrian press to refrain from attacking the new policy until Eisenhower had formally presented it to Congress. Meeting with Ambassador Moose on 4 January, however, Syrian foreign minister Salah al-Din al-Bitar sharply criticized the doctrine. Days later political director of the Syrian Foreign Office Ghalib al-Kayyali, upon receiving a U.S. embassy briefing on the new policy, "expressed considerable personal admiration for [the] ideas and principles embodied therein." But on 9 January al-Kayyali told a U.S. embassy official that the Syrian government's Ministerial Committee, charged with studying the Eisenhower Doctrine and submitting a report to the full cabinet, had reacted "in an unfavorable way" to al-Kayyali's representations on behalf of the doctrine. On 10 January Syrian newspapers carried a statement, attributed to Syrian Foreign Office sources, saying that the Syrian government needed to study the policy carefully before issuing any reaction. Moose speculated that the statement represented a Foreign Office attempt to keep the cabinet from issuing a hasty rejection.[11]

If so, the ploy failed. That same day the Syrian cabinet released a statement rejecting the notion of a vacuum in the Middle East and insisting that there was "no trace of international communist danger in our country." Al-Kayyali assured the U.S. embassy that the cabinet's statement was "'favorable' in that [it] does not . . . constitute [a] flat rejection and leaves [the] door open [to] further Syrian consideration [of the] Eisenhower program." This charitable interpretation became harder to defend on 24 January, when Acting Foreign Minister Khalil Kallas not only reaffirmed the cabinet's 10 January declaration but castigated the Eisenhower Doctrine as a threat to Middle East peace, an attack on the right of national self-determination, and a plot to subject the region to Western exploitation. Even al-Kayyali had to admit that the prospects for Syrian cooperation with the doctrine were practically nil.[12]

A related issue was whether Ambassador Richards should include Syria on his Middle Eastern itinerary. The Syrian government refused to issue a formal invitation to Richards but indicated that it would not object if he chose to visit Syria anyway. "If you want results," al-Kayyali told a U.S. embassy official on 9 January, "make as few conditions as possible, don't be rigid about formalities and don't expect Syrian leaders to take [the] initiative." Moose advised Washington that it would be a "psychological error" for Richards to go to Syria without a formal invitation, since the United States would seem to be "begging it [to] accept aid." Syria never did issue a formal invitation, and Richards did not visit Syria.[13]

Even after Syria's virtual rejection of the Eisenhower Doctrine, however, the Eisenhower administration had reason to cooperate with Damascus. It still needed Syria's authorization for the Iraq Petroleum Company to begin repairing its pipeline in Syria. The Syrians insisted that no oil could pass through the pipeline until Israel withdrew from the Sinai Peninsula and the Gaza Strip. U.S. officials grumbled over this condition but were obliged to accept it. The administration also hoped to reach an understanding over the fate of Syrian politicians convicted of involvement in Operation Straggle, many of whom had been sentenced to death.[14] In Moose's view the Syrian government was using the death sentences to "drive home to moderate Syrians that no Syrian who opposes the present regime can feel secure." The administration urged other Arab leaders, especially King Saud, to lobby the Syrians for clemency. On 6 March, following Israel's announcement that it would withdraw from Sinai and Gaza, the Syrian government authorized Iraq Petroleum Company technicians to begin repairing the pipeline. That same day it commuted the death sentences of five defendants to life imprisonment.[15] Apparently it was still possible to do business with Syria.

Nevertheless, the administration could do little to prevent the further entrenchment of Syrian leftists or the strengthening of Syria's ties to the East bloc. In mid-March the Syrian government awarded a contract to a Czech company to build an oil refinery in Syria. Around the same time President al-Quwatli, army chief of staff Nizam al-Din, and a handful of pro-Western officers caused an uproar by proposing that pro-left army intelligence chief 'Abd al-Hamid al-Sarraj and other like-minded officers be transferred to less sensitive posts. Local observers saw the transfer proposal as an attempt to orient the regime toward the United States. The Eisenhower administration clearly wanted the transfers to take place, though there is no evidence that it tangibly aided the effort. By early April, however, the pro-Sarraj forces had prevailed, and al-Sarraj and most of the targeted officers were allowed to remain at their posts. "No one there has guts or courage," Allen Dulles lamented.[16]

Over the following month U.S.-Syrian relations dramatically worsened. The two nations were on opposite sides of the Jordanian crisis in late April. U.S. officials briefly hoped that King Hussein's victory would strengthen pro-Western elements in Syria, but Syria's parliamentary by-elections in early May, to replace four members of the Chamber of Deputies arrested for their alleged involvement in Operation Straggle, dashed that prospect.[17] Though the elections mattered little to the overall composition of the 142-seat chamber, they were widely seen as a referendum on the Syrian government's increasingly radical orientation. Contesting the elections were two opposing coalitions, the pro-government National Grouping and the conservative Coalition National Front.[18] It was a measure of the prevailing mood that neither coalition supported the Eisenhower Doctrine. While the National Grouping derided the doctrine—"the vacuum is in Eisenhower's head," one of its posters proclaimed—the Coalition National Front largely ignored it.[19] In the election campaign as in the recent army crisis, U.S. officials took a strong partisan interest only to be disappointed.[20] Through a combination of superior organization and government favoritism, National Grouping candidates won three of four races.[21]

By mid-May Ambassador Moose had lost all confidence in the pro-Western officers, large landowners, religious leaders, and businessmen who

THE SYRIAN CRISIS

formed the base of the Syrian opposition. These figures showed "no sign of competent and courageous leadership nor of [a] spirit of sacrifice and hard-work in [their] ranks" and thus were powerless to prevent the leftist government from "snuggl[ing] up close to [its] Soviet protector in economic, military, [and] political affairs." Rather than pinning its hopes on the opposition, Moose suggested, the Eisenhower administration should accept the fact that Syria was, essentially, lost. The administration might even gain a propaganda advantage from this setback by focusing world attention on Syria as a "Soviet tool and base of Communist operations" and by unfavorably comparing Syria's situation with Jordan's.[22]

Washington, however, was not ready to write off Syria. Replying to Moose on 28 May, the State Department argued that a policy of quiet pressure might yet bring Syria around. Among the measures the department was considering were suspending U.S.-Syrian exchange programs, stalling on Syrian requests that required U.S. government licensing (such as for aircraft spare parts), and even "assigning low priority" to Syrian requests for assistance in administering the Salk antipolio vaccine.[23] Ignoring Moose's disparaging assessment of the Syrian opposition, the department reaffirmed its policy of "discreetly encourag[ing] elements opposed" to the Damascus regime. Allen Dulles, too, thought the situation was "not hopeless" and urged that the administration "start new planning" in Syria.[24]

In the weeks following Syria's by-elections, a siege mentality seemed to envelop the country. Domestically the leftist regime had consolidated its power; regionally it had suffered a series of setbacks. Jordan and Lebanon had purged their governments of radicals and Nasserists. Saudi Arabia had turned against the radical camp and improved relations with Hashemite Jordan and Iraq. Turkey had shown its hostility by gathering forces on the Turkish-Syrian frontier during the Jordan crisis. On each of its borders Syria now faced a potential foe. Syria's economy was in sharp decline, partly because of the inhibiting effect its regional isolation was having on trade with and investment from neighboring countries, and partly because of the government's diversion of public funds to pay for East bloc arms. That diversion, Moose reported in mid-May, "has caused [a] virtual cessation of public works projects," and the "lack [of] luxury goods, tourists, [and] business gives Syria some aspects [of an] Iron Curtain economy." The situation was so dire that U.S. intelligence analysts briefly feared that radical army officers, seeking to stifle growing criticism of leftist mismanagement, might overthrow the civilian government and rule with an iron hand.[25]

But leftist officers did not launch a coup that summer. Instead the Syrian government sought relief in foreign policy. The first sign of this effort was

Syria's decision in late June and July to improve relations with Saudi Arabia and Iraq, as outlined earlier in this chapter. To some extent the initiative reflected the particular interests of President al-Quwatli and Prime Minister al-'Asali, old-school politicians with extensive personal, political, and financial ties to conservative Arab governments.[26] But rapprochement could be justified on "progressive" grounds as well. On 4 July al-Quwatli told Egyptian ambassador to Syria Mahmud Riad that it would be better "to delay for as long as possible manifestations of hostility" toward the conservative Arab governments, as this would relieve Syria of the necessity of fighting on too many fronts at once. Riad agreed with al-Quwatli's assessment.[27]

The fact that Saudi and Iraqi leaders themselves were willing to mend fences with Syria was "disheartening" to U.S. officials, especially as it served to isolate King Hussein, whose relations with Syria and Egypt remained terrible. On 12 August U.S. ambassador to Jordan Lester D. Mallory complained that "King Saud appears more quiescent in his support of Hussein and more tolerant of Syrian extremism. Iraq also appears to be leaving Hussein to hold the bag."[28]

The second initiative to address Syria's isolation was even more disheartening to the Eisenhower administration. In late July Syrian defense minister Khalid al-'Azm led a delegation to Moscow, where he warned Soviet vice premier Alexsei Kosygin that Syria's economic troubles were threatening its ability to oppose Western schemes in the region. Al-'Azm said that "foreign propaganda" was calling attention to Syria's economic situation and unfavorably comparing it to that of pro-Western Iraq. There was a danger that such propaganda would succeed in "turning naive and innocent public opinion [in Syria] away from supporting Syria's liberationist policy, especially if the government is forced to impose heavy taxes to face the financial crisis." Without help from abroad, Syria might have to abandon its progressive stance. Al-'Azm's appeal was effective. On 6 August the Syrian and Soviet governments announced an agreement committing the Soviets to buying a large portion of Syria's agricultural and textile surpluses and to providing a long-term loan to finance development projects in Syria.[29]

Though the administration did not realize it at the time, the Moscow agreement opened a fissure within Syria's ruling leftist coalition and, indeed, within the radical Arab camp as a whole. Al-'Azm, the chief proponent of the agreement, saw the deal as a historic opportunity to develop Syria's hydraulic infrastructure, upgrade its transportation system, modernize its farming techniques, exploit its mineral resources, and thus propel the country into a new phase of economic growth.[30] Also favoring the agreement were communists and non-Ba'thist military leaders; the latter apparently assumed that Soviet loans and markets would support larger budgets for the Syrian military. The Ba'thists, however, while publicly praising the Moscow agreement, privately objected that al-'Azm had exceeded his authority in Moscow and had moved Syria too close to the Soviet camp. Nasser, too, was disturbed by the Moscow agreement. He believed that it compromised "positive neutrality" and challenged Egyptian dominance over Syrian affairs.[31] Clear only in retrospect, the emerging split within the radical camp initially eluded U.S. officials, who in the immediate aftermath of the Moscow agreement criticized the Syrian leadership as a whole for its willingness "to accept Soviet influence blindly."[32]

Had the Eisenhower administration known at the time about the split between Ba'thists and communists, it might have encouraged that development by quietly cultivating the Ba'thists. But the administration had already opted for a cruder solution—or so a handful of Syrian army officers later alleged. Sometime around early July, the officers claimed, a small group of U.S. embassy officials, under the direction of second secretary for political affairs Howard E. Stone, began recruiting individual Syrian officers for participation in a scheme to take over the army, purge it of leftist leaders, overthrow the current regime, and replace it with a rightist one under exiled former president Brigadier General Adib al-Shishakli. Unbeknownst to the American operatives, some of the officers immediately reported these contacts to their superiors, who instructed them to keep meeting with the Americans and to report back to Syrian authorities on the progress of the conspiracy. In early August the Americans allegedly arranged for each of the conspiracy's Syrian ringleaders, General al-Shishakli and Syrian military attaché in Rome Colonel Ibrahim al-Husayni, to make a brief visit to Syria in heavy disguise. While there, al-Shishakli and al-Husayni met clandestinely with the recruited officers, assuring them that the U.S. government backed the coup and that they, the recruits, would thrive under the new regime. All the while, of course, Syrian authorities were monitoring the unfolding conspiracy.[33]

Although almost all of the relevant U.S. documentation remains classified, such evidence as does exist generally supports the officers' allegations. In 1991 Robert C. Strong, who was counselor at the U.S. embassy at the time of the alleged plot, acknowledged to author Bonnie F. Saunders that in 1957 Stone was "head of the CIA section" at the embassy and that Vice Consul Frank Jeton, another embassy official implicated by the Syrian officers, was "his deputy."[34] Charles W. Yost, who became ambassador to Syria in late 1957, recalled in 1978 that "in Syria, before I arrived, the CIA had tried to pull off a coup, support its military people who were planning a coup." Former CIA agent Wilbur Crane Eveland, who was stationed in Beirut at the time, later wrote that the CIA had used Lebanon as a transit point for smuggling al-Husayni into Syria, where the colonel was to "meet secretly with . . . key Syrian agents and provide assurances that Shishakly would come back to rule once Syria's government had been overthrown."[35] While neither Yost nor Eveland directly participated in the alleged coup attempt, each, presumably, was close enough to the event to have had access to authoritative information about it.

Moreover, the scenario presented by the Syrian officers in their subsequent court testimony was generally plausible. According to a summary of the officers' allegations, Stone tried to enlist an officer in the coup effort by saying that Syria's economy "had deteriorated because of the wrong policy of the Syrian Government and the spread of communism. He said . . . things might be different if communism was eliminated, as in neighboring Arab states such as Iraq, Jordan, and Lebanon. That is, if Syria linked up with the American side and Egypt was isolated from the Arab group." When pressed on the Palestine issue, Stone acknowledged "that Israel had become a fait accompli and was created to remain. He said that if the Arab countries, including Syria, would join the American side there would be no Zionist menace because America and its allies would withhold arms from the area and work to create tranquillity in it." Stone added that the Arabs should put the Zionist issue aside until they had eliminated the more pressing threat of international communism. These remarks reflected some of the main features, official and unofficial, of U.S. Middle East policy in 1957: isolating Egypt, guaranteeing Israel's existence, discouraging an Arab-Israeli arms race, and subordinating pursuit of an Arab-Israeli peace settlement to containment of international communism. Had Syrian authorities fabricated the officers' allegations for domestic political purposes, one suspects that they would have found more incriminating words to put in the mouths of U.S. operatives. The Americans depicted in the officers' testimony only dimly resembled the fiendish backers of Zionism and imperialism to whom the consumers of Syrian propaganda had grown accustomed.[36]

In its public statements, the State Department avoided addressing the allegations individually and dismissed the entire account as "a complete fabrication." Confidentially, however, the department did offer a fairly specific and substantive defense.[37] First, the department argued that parts of the officers' account—for example, the assertion that the United States was prepared, once the coup succeeded, to support Syria's annexation of Lebanon and Jordan—were preposterous. The department also produced a 13 August news report that quoted Syrian officials in Rome (presumably supporters or employees of Colonel al-Husayni) as saying that al-Husayni had been in Italy throughout the period in which he allegedly traveled to Syria. Finally, U.S. officials proposed a powerful motive for Syria's military leadership to have fabricated the charges: to silence criticism at home. By now the U.S. embassy in Damascus was just learning of the Ba'thists' unhappiness with the Moscow agreement. Perhaps, the embassy speculated, the pro-Soviet "army clique," fearing that the Ba'thists would join the conservatives in publicly opposing the deal, had found it necessary to concoct "some startling danger to Syria . . . to overcome resistance to [the] Moscow accord."[38]

The administration's defense, however, is also vulnerable to cross-examination. It is indeed extremely unlikely that any U.S. official would have spoken in support of Syrian annexation of neighboring countries. But the recruited officers did not claim that the American operatives endorsed such a course. Rather, one of the recruits, Captain Abdullah Atiyyah, testified that al-Husayni said to him, outside the Americans' hearing, that the United States would "let us invade Lebanon and attach it to [the] motherland. . . . Jordan to follow." Al-Husayni also allegedly said, "Look here Abdullah. I did not participate cheaply. They are going to give us $400 million. . . . Americans are donkeys and we must avail ourselves of [the] opportunity and have money from them." Thus what appears at first glance to be a fantastic distortion of American intentions becomes, upon closer scrutiny, a more plausible account of a boastful Syrian colonel trying to impress a junior officer. As for the 13 August report from Rome, it does seem to provide al-Husayni with a powerful alibi. But the apparent basis for the Syrian officials' statement was the fact that al-Husayni's "passport showed no indication that he had been out of Italy" since 20 July; according to Atiyyah's testimony, al-Husayni entered Syria on a forged Saudi passport.[39] On the final point—that Syrian leaders had a powerful motive to invent "some startling danger to Syria"—the allegations did allow Syrian military leaders to silence, for a time, domestic criticism of the Moscow agreement. Still, this does not prove that they fabricated the charges. It may simply explain the eagerness with which they seized the opportunity provided by a botched foreign conspiracy.

Until the relevant documents are declassified, it will probably be impossible to determine with absolute certainty the accuracy of the officers' charges, or to explain the anomalies and implausible assertions in the existing accounts.[40] The available evidence, however, suggests that U.S. embassy officials probably did sponsor a coup attempt within the Syrian military. To put it in legal terms, there is preponderant evidence, though not proof beyond a reasonable doubt, for reaching such a judgment.

WHATEVER THEIR MERITS, the sensational allegations drastically transformed U.S.-Syrian relations. On the evening of 12 August, Syrian authorities announced over the government-controlled Syrian Broadcasting Station that they had just thwarted a "mean imperialist plot" by U.S. embassy officials, specifically naming Stone and Jeton. That night about thirty armed Syrian security guards surrounded the embassy building. The next day the Syrian Foreign Office ordered Stone, Jeton, and U.S. military attaché Colonel Robert Molloy to leave the country within twenty-four hours.[41] The U.S. State Department retaliated by naming Syria's ambassador in Washington, Farid Zayn al-Din, and the second secretary of its embassy, Yassin Zakaria, personae non gratae.[42] The department also announced that Ambassador Moose, who was in the United States on leave, would not return to his post.

The officers' accusations accelerated the radicalization of Syrian politics. Though reduced in number, Syrian security forces kept up their vigil outside the U.S. embassy, monitoring and occasionally harassing local employees and visitors. The Ba'thists put aside their misgivings about the Moscow agreement and joined the army and the communists in denouncing U.S. meddling in Syrian internal affairs. Virtually all Syrian newspapers, even those ordinarily critical of the regime, gave top billing to the conspiracy. On 15 August Colonel 'Afif Bizri, whom U.S. officials described variously as "a known Communist" and "a Communist sympathizer," replaced Nizam al-Din as army chief of staff. Dozens of lesser officers were removed from their posts, some to be replaced by suspected communists. Army intelligence chief 'Abd al-Hamid al-Sarraj began a vigorous campaign of detaining and interrogating Syrians whose loyalties were deemed suspect. Al-Quwatli left for Egypt amid rumors that he would soon resign and that Khalid al-'Azm would replace him as president. On 19 August Secretary Dulles, having returned from vacation the day before, reviewed the Syrian situation and pronounced it "wholly unacceptable."[43]

Syria's Arab neighbors seemed to agree. In the week following the officers' accusations, King Hussein, Iraqi prime minister 'Ali Jawdat, and Lebanese foreign minister Charles Malik all told U.S. diplomats that Syria's radicalization directly threatened the security of their governments. King Saud, though unavailable to meet personally with the U.S. ambassador, passed word to the United States that he was "very worried," especially about the fate of the Saudi pipeline in Syria. Even Nasser, it was reported, believed the Syrians had gone too far in courting the Soviets.[44]

Syria's non-Arab neighbors were even more disturbed. Israeli prime minister David Ben-Gurion insisted that Israel was the "ultimate target of [the] weapons which [the] USSR is pouring into Syria" and urged that the United States make a "bold move" to check Soviet ambitions. Turkish prime minister Adnan Menderes told the U.S. ambassador to Turkey that "from today it is not a mistake to consider Syria a part of [the] USSR. . . . Therefore to deal with Syria will mean to deal with the USSR." Turkey was willing "to take appropriate measures" against Syria, but it could not do so "unless [the] USA takes [a] definite position and decisions."[45] Stand behind us, Menderes hinted, and we will solve the problem.

Such sentiments, U.S. officials believed, presented a rare opportunity to set things right in Syria. "We should capitalize on the present alarm felt by our friends over the situation in Syria," Dulles said on 19 August, "an alarm which tends to subside over a period of time. We could not consider that time is on our side."[46] Adding to the sense of urgency was the feeling that any pro-Western reaction should occur before Syria could further solidify its ties with the Soviet Union.

In a series of White House meetings over the next several days, Eisenhower, Dulles, and other officials worked out a broad plan of action for Syria. The records of these meetings, most of which were not released until the late 1990s, provide a much clearer picture of the Eisenhower administration's response to the Syrian crisis than had been available to previous historians. In 1992 David W. Lesch characterized that response as "devoid of ideas."[47] Actually, the administration had plenty of ideas, though they may not have been terribly good ones.

The essence of the administration's plan was stated by Eisenhower at the 21 August meeting: the United States would "urge that friendly Arab nations band together, and using such excuses as necessary, move to eliminate the Syrian government." To generate the necessary excuses, those friendly Arab nations would join Turkey in massing troops on their borders with Syria. Having thus dispersed Syria's defenses, they would goad Syria into committing "aggression" against one or more of its neighbors. Once Syria had done so, the United States would declare Syria to be communist-controlled, and Iraq, possibly with Jordan's help, would launch a military assault on Syria resulting in the overthrow of the Damascus regime. For the sake of Arab public opinion, it was highly preferable that Iraq and Jordan be able to accomplish this task alone. As a precaution, however, Turkey should "stand ready to carry the matter through to a swift conclusion should it start to bog down." The United States would provide Syria's attackers with additional military supplies and diplomatic support in the UN. Washington would also ensure that neither the Soviet Union nor Israel intervened in the crisis. To promote this general approach, and to encourage Syria's neighbors to translate it into a more detailed operational plan, on 24 August Eisenhower sent deputy undersecretary of state for administration Loy W. Henderson, an old Middle East hand, on a special mission to the region.[48]

A great deal depended, of course, on what was meant by "Syrian aggression," the action that was to trigger a U.S.-supported assault on Syria. It was unlikely that Syria would commit aggression in the ordinary sense of overt, unprovoked, organized attack across an international border, but U.S. officials were relying on a much looser definition of the term. Meeting in Istanbul in late August with Menderes and Hussein (who, along with the Iraqi royal family, happened to be visiting that city), Henderson suggested that retaliation against Syria need not await aggression in the usual sense. Mere "Syrian provocations," which presumably could include minor border incidents and small-scale acts of sabotage, would be sufficient grounds for retaliation.[49]

A message Dulles received on 24 August from an unnamed U.S. official in Rome (possibly Allen Dulles) suggested how such "provocations" might be elicited.[50] While acknowledging the gravity of the Syrian crisis, the official insisted that "we still have substantial assets for [a] longer range fresh approach to the situation." For example, "all border states of Syria are hostile to [the] present Syrian regime. . . . This hostility over [a] period of time should produce pressures, economic and other, border incidents, sabotage, etc." The official did not spell out how "border incidents" might be an "asset," but presumably they could justify an attack on Syria. (And of course the massing of hostile troops on Syria's borders would greatly increase the likelihood of such "incidents.") Another "asset" the official mentioned was the existence of Iraqi and Saudi pipelines in Syria. If the Syrians moved to damage those pipelines, as they had done to the Iraqi line during the Suez war, they would "alienat[e] both Saudis and Iraqis" and "give us [a] better position for action." The pipelines "are therefore a kind of hostage in reverse." As Eisenhower put it more bluntly on 26 August, "If Syria were to blow up the pipelines, they would give Iraq every justification to attack."[51]

Once U.S. officials had become this eager to find a pretext for attacking Syria, the temptation to manufacture one was hard to resist. On 29 August Henderson met in Beirut with British ambassador to Lebanon George Middleton. The two diplomats agreed that "one way of putting pressure on

Syria would be to seek assurances about future Syrian intentions as regards the uninterrupted transit of oil . . . across her territory. The enquiry about Syrian intentions might be framed in such a way as to needle the Syrians into taking some foolish action which would justify intervention in the internal affairs of that country; this was a doubtful gambit as the Egyptians and Russians would no doubt both advise against it. But it was just worth exploring." In mid-September the Egyptian embassy in Baghdad informed Cairo, "We have learned that Prince 'Abd al-Ilah proposed sending some saboteurs secretly into Syria to blow up the oil pipelines" and thus provide Iraq with "an acceptable excuse for taking action against Syria, with the assistance of traitorous elements there." The embassy reported that Prime Minister Jawdat, who was loath to antagonize the radical Arab camp, had refused to carry out 'Abd al-Ilah's scheme.[52] Another idea, proposed by 'Abd al-Ilah and Nuri al-Sa'id (the latter anxiously monitoring the situation from London), was to stir up unrest among Bedouin tribes on the Syrian-Iraqi frontier, thus setting the stage for an exploitable "border incident." Nothing seems to have come of this suggestion, either.[53]

Another concept that underwent redefinition was the Eisenhower Doctrine's triggering mechanism. In earlier, public discussion of the doctrine, it had been generally assumed that any nation against which the doctrine might be invoked would have manifested its subordination to international communism before committing an act of aggression. Now, however, the administration was proposing to withhold a finding that Syria was communist-controlled until *after* it been branded an aggressor. On 25 August Dulles told congressional leaders that "we had not yet determined that Syria was under the control of international communism. . . . However, we could make that determination if politically it was desirable to do so."[54] Presumably, such a delay would enable the United States and its regional allies to prepare the attack on Syria with maximum stealth.

Eisenhower realized the plan was risky. As he wrote in his memoirs, "If Syrian aggression should provoke military action by Iraq, and a difficult campaign should bring the Turks to Iraq's aid, the Soviets might very well take this occasion to move against Turkey. Should that happen, a much larger war would be almost upon us." Eisenhower nevertheless concluded that "the alternative . . .—to do nothing and lose the whole Middle East to Communism—would be worse." Dulles thought it unlikely that the Soviets would intervene, especially if the United States made an early show of its determination to back its Middle East allies, "so that our prestige was committed before the Soviet prestige." Accordingly, Eisenhower ordered that the Strategic Air Command be placed on alert; that aircraft from Europe be sent to the U.S. base in Adana, Turkey; and that the Sixth Fleet be moved to the eastern Mediterranean.[55]

Even if the Soviets could be deterred, however, there was a danger that Arab public opinion would strongly oppose a U.S-sponsored attack on Syria. Eisenhower was anxious, therefore, to convince Arab audiences "that this action is being taken to protect Islam against militant atheism." Eisenhower hoped that King Saud, as Keeper of the Holy Places of Islam, would denounce the Syrian regime as an affront to Islam and sanctify the attack on Syria as a crusade against Soviet encroachment.[56] On 21 August Eisenhower sent an urgent appeal to Saud:

> There seems to be serious danger that Syria will become a Soviet Communist satellite. . . . Of course, under the [Eisenhower] doctrine . . . , we would sympathetically consider a request to assist any country that was attacked by a Syria which itself was dominated by International Communism. We believe, however, that it is highly preferable that Syria's neighbors should be able to deal with this problem without the necessity of outside intervention.
>
> In view of the special position of Your Majesty as Keeper of the Holy Places of Islam, I trust that you will exert your great influence to the end that the atheistic creed of Communism will not become entrenched at a key position in the Moslem world.[57]

Saud, however, had little interest in Eisenhower's jihad. In his 25 August reply, Saud acknowledged that Syrian developments were troubling but insisted that the United States and its allies were largely to blame for them. Syria, he wrote, had moved closer to the Soviets only because its "requests for arms are not being granted [by the West] while at the same time economic and military assistance to Israel is plentiful. . . . If those requests had been heeded, the situation would not have reached the present point." Saud assured Eisenhower that he would devote "my whole-hearted efforts, together with the Arab countries, to remove the danger" in Syria, but Saudi Arabia would not countenance the use of force.[58]

Evidently Saud feared that Saudi participation in an anti-Syrian campaign would be unpopular at home, a fact Saud's enemies could exploit to his detriment. On 28 August President Chamoun told Henderson, who was passing through Beirut, "that Saud was afraid of Cairo Radio, which if it attacked him could easily provoke trouble and might even stir up revolution." U.S. support for Israel, as most recently demonstrated in the Aqaba dispute, only deepened Saud's conviction that siding with the United States against Syria would be politically risky. In a 13 September letter to Eisenhower, Saud warned that the Arab people "consider that all those who assist Israel financially, militarily, and politically are antagonists and all who assist them in all these fields of action are their friends." Saudi support for a U.S.-sponsored campaign against Syria, Saud implied, would raise doubts about his own anti-Zionist credentials.[59]

Saud also believed that Syria's radicalization could be more effectively reversed without violence. In late August Saud told a Pakistani diplomat "that neighboring countries should not take up an overtly hostile attitude against Syria[,] otherwise internal Communists would be encouraged to consolidate" their position. "Action should be completely secret and directed at [the] numerous and still influential Right Wing in Syria," which, with Saudi encouragement and funds, could be induced to subvert the Damascus regime from within.[60] It is not entirely clear whom Saud meant by the "Right Wing in Syria." By some accounts Saud's hopes rested on President al-Quwatli, who had returned to resume his duties on 26 August. By other accounts the king saw Syria's conservative People's Party as the most promising agent of change. In any event, Dulles dismissed the possibility of quietly subverting the Damascus regime, remarking on 11 September "that we did not have any very valuable or potent subversive assets within Syria."[61]

The Eisenhower administration's plans for Syria were encountering difficulties on other fronts as well. The administration hoped that Iraq and Jordan would find a suitable pretext for attacking Syria. While Iraq was the preferred spearhead for such an attack, Jordan's cooperation was also considered essential. As Henderson cabled from Istanbul in early September, "It appears easier . . . for Iraqi troops to penetrate Syria through Jordan than to cover [the] vast roadless distance lying along [the] Iraqi-Syrian borders."[62] The lack of mutual trust between King Hussein and the Iraqi royal family, however, impeded Jordanian-Iraqi military coordination. Also inauspicious was Hussein's insistence on going ahead with a previously scheduled European vacation, which kept him out of the region from late August until mid-September.[63]

Even worse, Iraqi leaders were divided. 'Abd al-Ilah and King Faisal, who had been summering in Istanbul, were eager to take military action against Syria, but the government in Baghdad strongly objected to this course. Since taking office in late June, the cabinet of 'Ali Jawdat had avoided public controversy with fellow Arab states, gaining domestic popularity and a respite from Egyptian and Syrian propaganda attacks. Jawdat believed that Iraqi participation in an attack on Syria would not only reverse these political achievements but give Syria an excuse to sever the Iraqi pipeline again. Meeting with Henderson in Istanbul on 2 September, 'Abd al-Ilah admitted that he was having trouble with Jawdat, who was "weak" and "averse to making difficult decisions." The crown prince pleaded for more time to compel a better attitude in Baghdad.[64] Iraq's position remained unresolved when Henderson returned to Washington on 4 September.

Instead of abandoning hope of violently removing the Syrian regime, however, the Eisenhower administration became more convinced than ever that such an operation was necessary. Eisenhower and Dulles genuinely believed that Syria would soon become a base for Soviet-sponsored subversion of neighboring Arab countries, especially Jordan and Lebanon. The State Department had also received reports that "the Egyptians were not as concerned by Syria as it had originally been thought" and that Nasser was in no mood to help the United States rescue Syria from communism. The latter impression was correct. By early September, relying on friendly informants within the Iraqi government, Cairo was starting to piece together a generally accurate picture of Henderson's efforts to forge an anti-Syrian coalition, and Nasser had decided to throw his weight against the U.S. campaign.[65] On 8 September Nasser granted an interview with an Egyptian newspaper in which he declared his solidarity with the Syrian government. America, he said, was using the bogus threat of communism to divert Arab attention from the real threat of Israeli aggression.[66]

Also hardening the administration's attitude was the conviction, expressed repeatedly by Dulles in private meetings that September, that Syrian events were part of a broader Soviet offensive that could not go unchallenged. Dulles grimly noted the Soviets' accelerated arms deliveries to Yemen,[67] their naval maneuvers in the Mediterranean, their sudden dropping of interest in cultural exchanges with the West, their rejection of U.S. proposals at the disarmament talks in London, and the threatening tone of their recent announcement that they had successfully launched the first intercontinental ballistic missile. Khrushchev himself, Dulles said, was "an extremely dangerous man to be at the head of the state." "He is temperamental, reckless and drinks too much," often acting "under the influence of exalted moods, part natural, part induced." Whereas Stalin and his advisers had been "calculating strategists," Khrushchev "was a gambler" who was "inclined to be precipitous" and thus was "more like Hitler than any Russian leader we have previously seen." Khrushchev, in short, must not be appeased. Should the Soviets be permitted to take control of Syria, "the success would go to Khrushchev's head and we might find ourselves with a series of incidents like the experience with Hitler."[68]

There was a final reason to proceed with the anti-Syrian campaign: to head off less desirable regional initiatives. The Turks had made it clear that a Soviet-dominated state on their southern flank would be intolerable and that, if no Arab action were forthcoming, they might well act unilaterally. In early September the Turks again gathered their forces on the Syrian border.[69] The administration feared that, in a bilateral conflict between Turkey and Syria, the conservative Arab states would side with Syria. But Dulles "thought it would be dangerous to try to stop the Turks from taking action, since if we did so they would feel it was the end of their alliance with the West." Thus, rather than actively oppose a unilateral Turkish attack, the administration hoped to preempt such a move by pressing for action on the Jordanian-Iraqi side. Turkish participation might be desirable eventually, but only if it were in support of an Arab operation. In their separate accounts of the Syrian crisis, Bonnie Saunders and David Lesch erroneously suggest that the United States favored unilateral Turkish action against Syria. The available evidence clearly indicates that, while the administration's reluctance to restrain the Turks may have had the *effect* of pushing them toward unilateral action, this was not the administration's intention.[70]

The possibility of Israeli action produced a similar imperative. Although Israel had already assured the United States that it would do nothing to "create a deterioration of conditions on the frontier with Syria," Dulles doubted that the Israelis would "be indefinitely acquiescent if they thought that the Soviet Communist orbit would be extended to Syria and then to Jordan." He "hoped that there would be greater initiative on the part of some of the Arab countries so that it would not be necessary for the Israelis to act alone."[71]

For all of these reasons, in early September the Eisenhower administration launched a series of initiatives aimed at goading Iraq and Jordan to take action and at convincing Turkey and Israel to sit tight. In a 7 September public statement, Dulles reported that Henderson had found "deep concern" in the region over "the apparently growing Soviet Communist domination of Syria, and the large build-up there of Soviet Bloc arms, a build-up which could not be justified by any purely defensive means." To help secure Syria's neighbors, Eisenhower was using his authority under the Middle East Resolution to accelerate the delivery of arms previously committed to the region.[72] On 10 September the State Department sent private messages to 'Abd al-Ilah, Hussein, and Menderes pledging that, should Syria's Arab neighbors respond militarily to Syrian "provocation," the United States would provide economic assistance, additional military supplies, and diplomatic support in the UN. The message to Menderes contained a further clause urging Turkey to refrain from unilateral action, and a separate message to the Israelis urged them to take no action at all.[73]

Also about this time, the administration began working with the British government to find a diplomatic formula that would induce Syria's neighbors to pursue the anti-Syrian campaign. A secret "working group" of U.S. and British officials started meeting in Washington, and the State Department and the Foreign Office began coordinating their ambassadors' approaches to governments in the area.* Though born of the need to address the Syrian crisis specifically, these consultations soon acquired a life of their own, and U.S. and British officials would continue their close cooperation on Middle East policy long after the crisis had receded.[74]

IN PRESSING HIS CAMPAIGN against Syria, Eisenhower got exactly the opposite of what he wanted. He hoped for a speedy Arab operation that reversed Soviet gains in the region without provoking a crisis with the Soviet Union itself. Instead he got peace initiatives from the Arabs and a war of words with Moscow. By mid-October the superpowers were locked in a dangerous confrontation, albeit one ignored by most Cold War historians.[75]

On 10 September Soviet foreign minister Andrei Gromyko publicly accused the United States of trying, via the Henderson mission, to organize a regional attack on Syria. Gromyko warned that if Turkey continued to gather its troops on the Syrian border, it "might find herself at the bottom of a precipice." The official State Department rejoinder avoided the main thrust of Gromyko's remarks and focused instead on his formulaic denunciations of the Eisenhower Doctrine, comparing them to Soviet attacks on such previous U.S. initiatives as the Truman Doctrine, the Marshall Plan, and NATO. "We had hoped for better things," the statement continued, "but it seems that the Soviet Communists are in all respects confirmed reactionaries who can only replay the old wearisome tunes of which the world has grown tired." On 13 September Soviet premier Nikolai A. Bulganin sent a public note to Menderes warning him not to assume "that a military adventure against Syria could be in some manner localized." In a 19 September speech marking the opening of the twelfth session of the UN General Assembly, Dulles decried Soviet efforts "to intimidate Turkey."[76]

U.S. officials would have been even more dismayed had they known what

---

*As this book went to press, a 17 September 1957 document came to light revealing that the Anglo-U.S. working group recommended the "elimination" of 'Abd al-Hamid al-Sarraj, 'Afif Bizri, and Syrian Communist Party leader Khalid Bakdash (*Guardian*, 27 Sept. 2003). The document was discovered in the papers of Duncan Sandys, Macmillan's defense secretary, by Dr. Matthew Jones of the University of London, who kindly shared his findings with me.

the Soviets were saying in private. On 18 September a Soviet embassy official in Damascus told an Egyptian diplomat that he had confidential information that the United States was planning "to exploit the Turkish mobilization on the Syrian border and the Sixth Fleet now present near Syrian shores to engage in an aggression against Syria with Turkey's assistance." In mid-October Khrushchev told a Syrian diplomat that the United States was urging a reluctant Turkey to attack Syria.[77] Both charges were false, suggesting the Soviets either were passing along reports that they genuinely but mistakenly believed or, more likely, were conjuring up a nightmare scenario that their own public threats could later be said to have averted.

Meanwhile, a series of Saudi and Iraqi diplomatic initiatives helped ensure that there would be no Arab military action against Syria. Even after Saud's rebuff of Eisenhower's 21 August appeal, the president continued to feel that "we should do everything possible to stress the 'holy war' aspect" by enlisting Saud. But on 7 September, the day Eisenhower spoke those words, Saud arrived in Beirut, where he met with Lebanese officials and, according to a report received by the British government, "emphatically rejected the idea of a resort to force" against Syria. Saud then left for West Germany to receive medical treatment. In his absence Saudi officials publicly pledged solidarity with Syria should it become "the target of aggression."[78]

In Iraq Jawdat, too, was stepping up his opposition to the anti-Syrian campaign, which threatened his own government's political health. As he complained to a British diplomat on 15 September, "We are asked to slope arms and march off to Syria with no guarantee against Israel for the future which is the one thing which might make the venture in some degree palatable to public opinion. Communism is certainly a danger for us all but so is Zionism for the Arabs and as we see it, the former is supported by the Soviet Union and the latter by [the] United States, Britain and France. We are caught in between."[79] Days earlier, Jawdat had privately assured Cairo and Damascus that they need not fear "any harm or offense from the Iraqi government as long as he is at its head." In mid-September Jawdat sent Iraqi senate president Jamil al-Midfa'i to Syria "to learn the true situation" there. U.S. and British diplomats agreed that al-Midfa'i "will be an entirely useless emissary and quite incapable of assessing the situation." From the Anglo-U.S. perspective the mission was worse than useless: its most conspicuous result was al-Midfa'i's pledge that Iraq would support Syria against any outside aggressor, even another Baghdad Pact country like Turkey.[80]

Arab diplomacy gained further momentum following Saud's return to the region on 25 September. Saud had accepted an invitation from al-Quwatli to stop first in Damascus to assess the situation for himself. Al-

Quwatli hoped to elicit from Saud a public statement supporting the Syrian government. Dulles was alert to this possibility and remarked gloomily that the Syrians would probably "pull the wool over [Saud's] eyes" and prevent him from detecting the true extent of Soviet penetration. Lebanese foreign minister Charles Malik agreed that Saud's visit to Syria "might do harm. King Saud . . . was weak and tended to share the views of the last person he had spoken to." Jawdat, on the other hand, followed Saud's lead by hastily joining him in Damascus on 26 September.[81]

Much as Dulles and Malik had feared, the effect of Saud's and Jawdat's visit was to certify the Syrian regime as a legitimate Arab government entitled to the solidarity of fellow Arab states. Both visitors later claimed that they privately criticized Syrian political and military leaders for their growing dependence on East bloc aid and their excessive hostility to the West. Speaking publicly in Damascus, however, Saud denied that Syria could "in any way constitute danger to any of its neighbors," and Jawdat pledged that "Iraq will not stand with its hands tied in the face of aggression befalling Syria or any other Arab country." Saud's diplomacy was a sharp rebuke to U.S. policy. "When King Saud has been built up as the great Arab anti-Communist warrior," observed a British diplomat, "it is not easy to explain away statements by the Saudis that Syria is no threat to the Arabs."[82]

Arab public opinion responded extremely favorably to Saud's rhetorical support for Syria, a fact the conservative regimes dared not ignore. Jawdat had already thrown in his lot with Saud, and Nuri and the palace seemed powerless to stop him. Hussein, too, had to modify his stance. After returning to Amman on 12 September, Hussein had taken a tough line on Syria, responding vigorously to Syrian propaganda attacks and expressing dismay at the timidity of other Arab states. Following Saud's and Jawdat's visit to Syria, however, Hussein realized he had to soften his position or face isolation in the Arab world, and he grudgingly accepted a Saudi-brokered propaganda truce with Syria.[83] By mid-October both the Jordanian and the Lebanese governments had issued statements pledging support for Syria in the event it was subject to external aggression. The conservative Arabs, Dulles complained, were genuinely alarmed by the situation in Syria "but won't say so out loud. It is hard for us to say it's dangerous when they say the opposite."[84]

Another effect of Saud's diplomacy was a dramatic, if short lived, increase in the king's regional stature. To all appearances, Saud's visit to Damascus had averted an imminent attack on Syria. A wave of relief and gratitude now swept the Arab world. On 10 October Saud began a state visit to Lebanon, where the press acclaimed him as "the Desert Lion" and the "embodiment of Arab nationalism." Tens of thousands lined his motorcade route; politicians of all persuasions courted his favor. Saud even seemed poised to eclipse Nasser in inter-Arab politics—the purpose of Eisenhower's whole effort to build up the king. The difference, of course, was that Saud had achieved his new status by resisting U.S. efforts in the region. As if to underline that fact, on 6 October the Saudi government announced that it had never formally endorsed the Eisenhower Doctrine.[85] This was not news to the U.S. government, but the timing of the announcement was embarrassing.

Saud's moment of triumph was brief in any case. On 13 October Nasser landed about 1,500 Egyptian troops at the Syrian port city of Latakia, ostensibly to protect Syria against Turkish aggression. Although the move seemed to come out of nowhere, Nasser had planned it weeks earlier in secret consultations with 'Afif Bizri and 'Abd al-Hamid al-Sarraj, the Syrian army's chief of staff and intelligence chief, respectively. The Egyptian army's sudden appearance on Syrian soil dramatically transformed the atmosphere of inter-Arab politics. "By this spectacular move," Patrick Seale writes, "'Abd al-Nasir had broken out of the isolation with which Sa'ud had threatened him and had demonstrated that no settlement could be reached in the Middle East without him. . . . Saud's efforts at mediation seemed overnight timid and irresolute in contrast with 'Abd al-Nasir's wholehearted commitment to the Syrian cause." Saud could do little more than complain that Nasser and al-Quwatli, his nominal ESS allies, had neglected to consult him about the intervention in advance. Through emissaries, al-Quwatli assured Saud that Syria's civilian government itself had "not known about the presence of Egyptian forces until after they had arrived in Syria" —a striking admission, if true, of al-Quwatli's political irrelevance.[86]

With Egyptian troops now occupying Syria, hostile intervention by other Arab countries had become unthinkable, and the outright removal of the Damascus regime grew increasingly difficult to imagine. Robert Strong, counselor at the U.S. embassy in Damascus, wrote on 16 October that "United States efforts to persuade moderate Arab leaders to take an overt hard line toward Syria hav[e] failed. . . . Force is ruled out." A running joke at the embassy that fall captured, perhaps inadvertently, the growing sense of impotence and resignation: "Que Serraj, Serraj; whatever will be, will be."[87]

Nasser's intervention may indeed have ruled out Arab military action for once and for all, but it did not deter Turkish aggression. As Saud scoffed to an American diplomat, the small number of Egyptian troops was "ridiculously inadequate to contribute to any defense of Syria." There was reason to believe, however, that Turkey was being deterred already. On 14 September Egyptian ambassador to the Soviet Union Muhammad al-Quni commented that, following Bulganin's 13 September note to Menderes, "Syria has acquired a guarantee of its security. . . . Nothing remains for the other states but to abandon their policy" of seeking the removal of the Syrian government. In early October the Egyptians got word that Syrian foreign minister Salah al-Din al-Bitar, who was then in New York, "had learned from many sources in America" that the only thing deterring a Turkish attack on Syria was "America's and Turkey's belief in the seriousness of Russia's threat to Turkey." In his memoirs Ba'thist leader Akram al-Hawrani writes that "the most important thing [for Syria] was the soundness of the assessment of the Soviet position. . . . We believed that Turkey, which lay on the borders of the Soviet Union, would be very cautious" in view of Moscow's position.[88]

Providing further assurance was Khrushchev's 7 October interview with *New York Times* reporter James Reston, in which Khrushchev warned the United States that the Soviet Union would not tolerate a Turkish attack on Syria. "If war breaks out," he said, "we are near Turkey and you are not. When the guns begin to fire, the rockets can begin flying and then it will be too late to think about it." Khrushchev's threat, coming six weeks after the testing of a Soviet intercontinental ballistic missile and just three days after the launching of the Soviet satellite *Sputnik*, was enthusiastically received throughout the Arab world and reinforced the widespread belief that Turkey would not dare to lay a hand on Syria.[89]

In fact, Turkey's political leaders seemed generally unimpressed by Khrushchev's threat, though American officials took it more seriously. Telling a U.S. diplomat of a similar warning Khrushchev had issued on 8 October, Turkish foreign minister Fatin Rustu Zorlu "laughed sardonically" and said the "Soviets [were] trying [to] scare Turkey and [the] west."[90] In a 14 October memorandum to Dulles, Undersecretary of State Christian A. Herter reported that despite "doubts and hesitations on the part of the [Turkish] military," Turkish civilian leaders "wanted to go it alone in Syria." Herter wrote that Allen Dulles, James P. Richards, Henderson, and William M. Rountree, the assistant secretary for Near East affairs, all agreed with him "that action on the part of Turkey alone, particularly if overt and convincing aggression on the part of Syria cannot be shown, would lead us into an extremely serious situation." If the United States acquiesced in the attack, it would incur the wrath of the Arab world and many other nations. If it sought to compel Turkey's withdrawal through a UN resolution, à la Suez, it would be letting down yet another NATO ally. Even worse, Herter warned, should Turkey attack Syria, "Russia would feel herself for prestige reasons forced

Call To Prayer

The cartoonist Herblock ridicules Arab reverence for Soviet achievements
in rocket science, October 1957. The "muezzin" atop the missile is
Soviet leader Nikita Khrushchev. (Herbert Block, *Herblock's Special
for Today* [New York: Simon and Schuster, 1958], 101)

to attack Turkey, thereby precipitating an open, full-scale conflict between ourselves and Russia. The consensus of opinion here seems to be that Russia has definitely committed her prestige through the Khrushchev interview with Reston and through her notes and statements to Turkey in this respect." The challenge was to find a way to "keep Turkey from going it alone on some very flimsy pretext, without going back on our implied or actual commitments."[91]

It is possible that Herter and his colleagues were mistaken and that the Turks, for their own reasons, were exaggerating their eagerness to move against Syria.[92] Throughout the Syrian crisis, Turkish officials had lobbied Washington for increased economic and military aid, arguing that events in Syria were forcing Turkey to divert precious resources to its defense. Raising the specter of unilateral Turkish intervention, with all its attendant dangers, may have been Ankara's way of increasing the pressure.[93]

Even absent any hostile intent on Turkey's part, however, the situation was all too dangerous. As long as Turkey's forces remained mobilized on the frontier, there was a possibility that a border incident might spark a general shooting war with Syria, which in turn could ignite a wider conflagration. In early to mid-October the U.S. State Department received disturbing reports about the restlessness of Turkish troops stationed on the Syrian border. One report noted that the soldiers had "expressed the desire to 'get this thing over with' stating they wanted either to get on with the job of invading Syria or to return to their home stations." The Syrian forces themselves were operating on a hair trigger, inclined to place the most sinister interpretation on any Turkish movements they observed. Over the same period there were several reported incidents in which Turkish and Syrian forces exchanged gunfire across the border, though the skirmishes apparently resulted in few casualties.[94] On 18 October Dulles remarked that while he saw no signs of imminent war, "the situation is explosive. If it happens it will be an accident."[95]

Dulles, however, was still reluctant to urge restraint on the Turks, for fear of undermining their confidence in the Western alliance. Unlike his colleagues, moreover, the secretary claimed to be unmoved by the Soviet threat. On 15 October he told British foreign secretary Selwyn Lloyd, who was visiting Washington, that he "did not believe that the Russians would, in fact, intervene, if there was action in Syria." *Sputnik* notwithstanding, Dulles insisted that the Soviets were still too weak militarily to contemplate a war with the United States.[96] Two days later Dulles told Lebanese officials, "The United States is relatively immune from injury by the USSR, but the Soviet Union is not immune to complete devastation by the United States. Accordingly, we have no intention of being bluffed by the USSR, although of course we do not seek a world war." The surest way to prevent such a war was to leave the Soviets in no doubt as to the consequences of their actions. On 16 October Dulles publicly warned that a Soviet attack against Turkey "would not mean a purely defensive operation by the United States, with the Soviet Union a privileged sanctuary from which to attack Turkey."[97] Destruction would be visited on Soviet soil itself.

Dulles may have discounted the Soviet threat, but he was deeply apprehensive about the political consequences of a Turkish attack on Syria, which might well result in an "Arab world united and strongly backed by the Soviet Union against all manifestations of Westernism." This fear apparently overrode Dulles's reluctance to restrain Turkey. (Another possibility is that Eisenhower, whose own views are not clear from the available documents, insisted that Dulles take the Soviet threat more seriously.) On 20 October Dulles instructed U.S. ambassador to Turkey Fletcher Warren to meet with Prime Minister Menderes and urge, in the gentlest terms, that Turkey stand down. Warren was to "suggest that every effort be made to insure that Turkish forces now located along [the] Turkish southern border be deployed in such [a] way as to minimize [the] possibility of incidents arising from their disposition." On 22 October Warren spoke as instructed to Menderes and other Turkish officials. The Turks insisted "that the danger is greater than ever in Syria" but agreed not to "make any move without [the] closest consultation with Washington."[98]

Ankara's assurances decreased the likelihood of a deliberate, unilateral Turkish attack on Syria. Because Turkish troops remained mobilized on the border, however, the threat of accidental war persisted. In late October and early November there was a fresh spate of reported border incidents, including unsuccessful attempts by Syrian antiaircraft gunners to shoot down Turkish warplanes flying over northern Syria.[99] The border remained a dangerous flashpoint until Turkish forces were withdrawn in mid-November.

Meanwhile, the Syrian dispute had spread to the UN. On 16 October the Syrians submitted a complaint to the General Assembly about Turkey's troop concentrations. The Syrians also requested that the assembly establish an impartial commission to investigate the border region. Dulles feared that allowing the assembly to establish such a commission without prior reference to the Security Council, where the United States had the veto, would set "a dangerous precedent." Moreover, the Turkish territory to be investigated contained U.S. military installations "of the most highly sensitive character . . . and it would be disastrous to have anything exposed."[100]

On 20 October the Eisenhower administration was rescued from its predicament by Saud's public offer to mediate between Syria and Turkey. Turkey accepted the offer, and preliminary news reports indicated that Syria did as well. Seizing the opportunity, on 22 October the U.S. and Turkish delegations requested a delay in the General Assembly's consideration of the Syrian complaint, including the request for a border investigation, pending the outcome of mediation. Over Syrian and Soviet objections, the assembly granted a one-day delay.[101]

By this time uncertainty had arisen over Syria's actual position on Saudi mediation. While the Saudis claimed that al-Quwatli had personally accepted Saud's offer, Damascus radio insisted that the Syrian government had rejected it. The contradiction may have reflected divisions within the Damascus regime or simply the Syrians' recognition that Saud's offer placed them in a bind. As a British diplomat observed, "Should the Syrians refuse, they will not help their case in the United Nations, particularly with the Arab delegation. Should they accept, it will still be difficult for them to argue effectively that urgent and drastic action by the Assembly is required." In fact, both of these things happened. Syria's rebuff of Saud was just clear enough to saddle Syria with the onus of having thwarted a promising Arab initiative, and just ambiguous enough to permit the Americans to argue for further postponement. With a slim hope apparently remaining for Syria's acceptance of mediation, the General Assembly agreed to take no action until 1 November.[102]

Khrushchev, however, perhaps sensing that the political tide was starting to turn against his Syrian allies, now wanted an exit from the crisis. On 29 October, in what he called "a gesture toward peace," Khrushchev appeared unannounced at a reception at the Turkish embassy in Moscow. Holding up a chubby finger, the Soviet leader said, "If you look at this as a compass needle, you can say it has gone a little way toward peace." On 1 November, apparently concluding that they could no longer count on strong Soviet backing, the Syrians allowed the General Assembly to shelve their complaint. Thereafter the crisis steadily receded. Although Syria continued over the coming weeks to sound the alarm against Turkish aggression, and although border incidents continued to occur, the superpowers themselves were increasingly disengaged from the dispute. In mid-November Turkey withdrew its troops from the Syrian border.[103]

FOR THE UNITED STATES, of course, the problem of Soviet influence in Syria remained. The Eisenhower administration was running out of ideas, however, and was forced to yield much of the initiative to others. Britain was playing an increasingly important role. The Bermuda conference in March had created an atmosphere conducive to Anglo-American cooperation in the Middle East, but in practice such cooperation had been limited at first. In April and July there were talks between the State Department and the Foreign Office aimed at coordinating the two countries' Middle East policies, but the contacts remained at the middle level.[104] It took the Syrian crisis to produce high-level Anglo-American collaboration in the Middle East. Overwhelmed by the complexity of its self-assigned task— spurring the Arabs, harnessing the Turks, restraining the Israelis, and scaring off the Soviets—the Eisenhower administration increasingly relied on British advice and support. During the Syrian crisis itself, most of that consultation was confined to tactical questions, but by late October the administration was ready to entertain a British proposal for a fresh strategic approach to the problem.

That approach, which Selwyn Lloyd called "containment plus," involved bolstering Syria's neighbors while quietly encouraging Syrian opposition figures to subvert the leftist regime from within. Such a strategy would require greater patience than had the American plan, but it would also be less provocative. Since mid-September Lloyd had quietly lobbied the Eisenhower administration on the merits of containment plus, while taking pains to eschew strident advocacy. "We must be very careful to avoid any suggestion of pushing [the administration]," Lloyd cautioned British ambassador to the United States Harold Caccia on 4 October. But "once the Americans have come to the conclusion that immediate action in Syria is out of the question and that 'containment plus' is the only policy for the time being, we shall need to get down to further detailed planning." Three weeks later Lloyd's prediction had come to pass. On 25 October, during a visit to Washington, Lloyd and Prime Minister Harold Macmillan discussed Middle East policy with Eisenhower and Dulles. Dulles acknowledged "that the policy of 'containment plus' was the correct one."[105] It was time to hunker down and plan for the long haul.

On the "containment" side the Americans and the British agreed that the two countries most in need of bolstering were Jordan and Lebanon. It was assumed that the Syrians, no longer fearing a Western-sponsored attack, would increase their subversion of Jordan and Lebanon, perhaps to the point of sponsoring coup attempts in those countries. Thus Jordan and Lebanon would need greater material and diplomatic assistance from the West. The Americans and the British worried, however, that such assistance might not be enough. Already in the 25 October meeting there was talk of a joint Anglo-American military intervention in Jordan or Lebanon if either country requested it. Macmillan believed that such an intervention could succeed if it were done swiftly and decisively, "before world reactions became too strong." Eisenhower said "that he would be quite prepared to order that provided the appeal for help from the Jordan or the Lebanon came to the United States and the United Kingdom jointly."[106] The exchange is remarkable for two reasons: first, because it shows how early the Americans and the British began contemplating the actions they were to take in July 1958; second, because it shows how heavily the United States had come to depend on Britain's partnership.

There is no record that the four leaders discussed the "plus" side of the new policy, but other documents suggest that the idea was to rely on Syrian political dissidents and ethnic minorities to destabilize the Damascus regime from within. These figures would receive money, arms, and encouragement from neighboring governments, which were to take their own initiative in coordinating the subversion of Syria. Throughout the Syrian crisis Arab politicians had speculated about various arrangements: the Iraqis might aid the frontier tribes; the Turks might aid the Alawites; the Lebanese might aid the Christians and the Druze; the Saudis might aid the People's Party and the Druze; the Jordanians were already believed to be arming the Alawites and the Druze. Presumably containment plus would build on these or similar relationships.[107]

By mid-October conservative Arab leaders were already concerting along such lines. Saud, as we have seen, was furious with Nasser and the Syrians for failing to consult him prior to the Egyptian intervention in Syria. Meeting with Iraqi and Lebanese officials in Beirut, Saud said that "the present régime in Syria was a danger to the whole Arab world" and would have to be removed. He spoke of forming "a special 'top secret' committee" of Saudi, Iraqi, Lebanese, and Jordanian representatives aimed "at fomenting an internal movement in Syria which could at an appropriate stage be supported by the Arab neighbors of Syria," though such support could not include direct military action. By late October the Jawdat government, too, was ready for a tougher line on Syria, partly because the palace was exerting greater pressure in this direction and partly because the Syrians' rejection of Saudi mediation had tarnished their image in the Arab world, making opposition to the Damascus regime less politically risky.[108] Evidently U.S. officials did not directly participate in any of this planning, preferring to leave the initiative to the conservative Arabs. "For the immediate future of our relations with Syria," Assistant Secretary Rountree wrote on 29 October, "we hope to achieve a degree of dégagement that will permit the moderating influences of Saud and others to be most effective."[109]

It was remarkable what a little "dégagement" could accomplish. Months earlier the threat of a U.S.-sponsored attack on Syria had brought a closing of the ranks within the radical Arab camp. Now the removal of that threat allowed for a gradual reemergence of intraleft rivalries. In November and December both Nasser and the Syrian Ba'thists expressed anxiety over growing Soviet influence in Syria. As in early August, Nasser feared that such influence would undermine positive neutrality and threaten his own control over Syrian affairs, while the Ba'thists worried that the Moscow agreement, which had been followed by an implementing accord in late October, was mortgaging the country's future to the Syrian-Soviet relationship. But now the Ba'thists had an additional cause for concern: that the Soviets' public support for Syria had so enhanced the popularity of Syrian communists as to threaten the Ba'thists' own domestic position.[110]

By December British and American diplomats were receiving numerous reports of Nasser's and the Ba'thists' growing unhappiness with the communists. Ba'thist leader Akram al-Hawrani, the newly elected president of the Syrian Chamber of Deputies, reportedly told Lebanese journalists "that he was a convinced anti-Communist" who "hoped eventually to be able to lead Syria into the anti-Communist camp."[111] On 11 December Nasser sent Egyptian journalist Muhammad Hasanayn Haykal to U.S. ambassador to Egypt Raymond A. Hare with a "very serious and urgent message."[112] Nasser, Haykal reported, "is now convinced [that Syrian army chief of staff 'Afif] Bizri [is] a communist and that something must be done about it."[113] Nasser insisted, via Haykal, that the "responsibility is Egypt's and that Egypt should tackle it with courage and vigour." He asked only that the United States "keep hands off Syria for a maximum period of three months" during which Egypt would, by undisclosed means, rectify the situation.[114] Though suspecting Nasser of some sinister hidden motive, the State Department instructed Hare to give him an "affirmative response. . . . While we obviously cannot bind ourselves not to take action re Syria in [the] next three months[,] . . . we wish [to] avoid impeding any Egyptian efforts to bring about change" in that country. The administration was no longer in a position to threaten Syria in any case, so it had little to lose by letting Nasser himself try his hand at a solution.[115]

LATE 1957 WAS A GRIM TIME for the Eisenhower administration. The beginnings of an economic recession eroded Americans' confidence in Eisenhower's domestic leadership. The Little Rock, Arkansas, crisis of September, in which the president reluctantly used federal troops to enforce the court-ordered desegregation of public schools, further diminished Eisenhower's popularity, especially among southern whites. But the event also exposed American racial injustices to global scrutiny and thus damaged U.S. prestige among nonwhites abroad. "The effect of this in Asia and Africa," Dulles lamented, "will be worse for us than Hungary was for the Russians." The launching of *Sputnik* in early October, followed by a second Soviet satellite in early November, convinced many that the United States was losing the space race to the Soviets—an impression reinforced when America's answer to *Sputnik*, the Vanguard rocket, exploded on the launching pad in early December. Domestic critics accused the administration of letting down the nation's defenses. There were calls for Dulles's resignation and, for the first time, sustained public criticism of Eisenhower himself. C. D. Jackson, Eisenhower's occasional speechwriter and adviser, felt "that the Administration is floundering around without any purpose or direction" in international affairs. "The American cocksureness is shaken," reported Ambassador Caccia. The sense of infirmity at the top took on a poignant personal quality in late November when Eisenhower suffered a mild stroke that temporarily garbled his speech.[116]

Eisenhower weathered the crises. He refused to panic over *Sputnik*, stood by his secretary of state, and recovered so rapidly from his stroke that he was able, that December, to attend a summit meeting in Paris for NATO heads of state. Yet no amount of personal resilience could fully banish the feeling that, in the words of one chronicler, "Washington was governed by old, tired, unimaginative men."[117]

Such exhaustion and malaise also afflicted middle-level American officials concerned with the Arab world, abetting a growing disenchantment with received U.S. policy. The Eisenhower Doctrine, an October 1957 intelligence estimate noted, was "probably believed by almost all Arabs to indicate American preoccupation with Communism to the exclusion of what they consider to be the more pressing problems of the area." Another study lamented that "the [Eisenhower] Doctrine, with its 'stand up and be counted' character with respect to international Communism, is incompatible with the Arab brand of 'neutralism,' and traditional Arab reluctance to be committed." Out of earshot of their superiors, some U.S. officials were more blunt. Speaking to an Egyptian diplomat in Damascus, an assistant U.S. Air Force attaché "criticize[d] the policy of Mr. Dulles, . . . saying that this policy had prevented America from reaping the fruits of its position against aggression" during the Suez war. When another Egyptian diplomat made a similar observation to U.S. ambassador to Saudi Arabia Donald R. Heath, the latter agreed that "America had made many mistakes that must be corrected."[118]

Eisenhower himself was having doubts about his Middle East policy, though he was not inclined to exert strenuous efforts to change it. On 13 November, two weeks prior to his stroke, the president wrote to Dulles, "Do you think there would be any percentage in initiating a drive to attempt to bring back Nasser to our side?" Shrewdly playing on Eisenhower's continuing softness for Saud, Dulles warned that such an effort might arouse the king's jealousy. Eisenhower agreed "that we could not of course be disloyal to King Saud or attempt to push Nasser into leadership ahead of Saud"—and then dropped the matter.[119]

Eisenhower's uneasiness, however, was well founded. The Syrian crisis had mercilessly exposed the inadequacies of the Eisenhower Doctrine as an instrument for shaping Arab politics. More basically, it had discredited the doctrine's underlying political strategy and revealed America's political weakness in the Arab world. Events in 1957 had shown that, while the Eisenhower Doctrine could help a conservative regime consolidate domestic power and move closer to the West, it could not prevent a radical regime from consolidating its own power and moving closer to the Soviet bloc. The Eisenhower administration had hoped that regional isolation would compel Syria to moderate its pro-Soviet stance, but just the opposite had happened. Thus the attempt to sponsor a coup within the Syrian army (if indeed it occurred) was a tacit admission that the administration's previous efforts had failed. When the administration then sought a solution beyond Syria's borders, it was further hampered by the fact that the Eisenhower Doctrine contained no mechanism for recapturing an errant regime. The administration's subsequent plan for retrieving Syria bore little relation to the doctrine's actual provisions. Only by cynically reinterpreting those provisions—by redefining "aggression" and reducing the determination of communist control to a matter of tactical convenience—could the administration pretend otherwise.

The United States was unable to bring off the deception because the Syrian crisis also exposed the unreliability of the conservative Arab regimes. The administration had assumed that the conservative regimes, if given proper assurances and support, would be prepared to take decisive action against Syria, but the Iraqi and Saudi governments, designated to spearhead the effort, were not up to task. Both governments feared for their oil pipelines in Syria; both believed that public opinion in their own countries would not tolerate a U.S.-supported Arab attack on Syria; both had begun to enjoy better relations with the radical camp and were unwilling to return to open antagonism. Iraq's and Saudi Arabia's refusal to participate in the American scheme forced Jordan and Lebanon to follow suit. Arab inertia, combined with U.S. reluctance to discourage a NATO ally, increased the likelihood of unilateral Turkish action, in turn raising the specters of Soviet retaliation and superpower conflict. Fortunately the Syrian crisis did not escalate to global war, but it did discredit the basic political strategy of the Eisenhower Doctrine: seeking to isolate Nasserists and radicals by encouraging Arab conservatives to oppose them openly.

The unreliability of the conservative regimes was rooted in a deeper problem: the political weakness of the United States in the Arab world. Just a year earlier the Eisenhower administration was convinced that its opposition to aggression in the Suez war had won it enormous prestige among the Arabs. Yet it was now clear that Arab governments, mindful of Arab opinion, were loath to be seen as doing America's bidding. U.S. efforts to achieve the isolation or removal of the Syrian government not only brought a closing of the ranks within the radical camp but forced the conservative regimes to declare their solidarity with Syria. Only after the administration temporarily abandoned such efforts in late 1957 did things begin to move in its direction. Relieved of U.S. pressure to oppose the Syrians openly, the conservative Arabs became more willing to cooperate with one another in quietly subverting the Damascus regime. Freed from the fear of a U.S.-sponsored attack on Syria, Nasser and the Ba'thists began signaling their own readiness to oppose Soviet and communist influences. It remained to be seen if anything would come of these Arab initiatives, but the illusion of American mastery was gone.

THE NASSERIST ONSLAUGHT,
JANUARY—APRIL 1958

The first three months of 1958 were a period of triumph for Nasserism. The Egyptian-Syrian union in February and the popular jubilation it inspired throughout the Arab world dramatically enhanced Nasser's political and strategic position, terrifying conservative Arab leaders. The Iraqi-Jordanian federation, hastily arranged in reaction to the Egyptian-Syrian initiative, met with a tepid reception in the region, further underlining Nasserist hegemony. King Saud's own reckless response to the Egyptian-Syrian union forced his virtual abdication of the Saudi throne, handing Nasser a decisive victory in his two-year rivalry with the king. By mid-spring, conservative forces throughout the Arab world were in disarray.

The American reaction to the Nasserist onslaught was halting and ambivalent. To the Eisenhower administration, the Egyptian-Syrian union was cause for both dismay and encouragement. Thus the initial U.S. response included simultaneous efforts at disruption and accommodation. As the extent of Nasser's success became clearer, the administration moved more decisively toward accommodation, formally recognizing the Egyptian-Syrian union and gently discouraging Arab allies from trying to sabotage it. In March the administration conducted a policy reassessment whose main thrust was to undermine the anti-Nasserist foundations of the Eisenhower Doctrine. But acting on that reassessment was easier said than done: it proved extremely difficult to improve relations with Nasser without upsetting relations with conservative Arab allies. There could be no easy retreat from the Eisenhower Doctrine.

AS WE SAW IN CHAPTER 5, by late October 1957 conservative Arab leaders seemed willing to cooperate with one another in clandestinely opposing Syria's leftist regime. But over the next several weeks, apparently as a result of lingering mistrust between the Saudis and the Hashemites, the initiative fizzled. In late November a Jordanian diplomat told U.S. ambassador to Jordan Lester D. Mallory that "those endeavoring to change the Syrian regime had received money from King Saud, however not in any large amount. Money which had been anticipated from Iraq had not been forthcoming." Moreover, "the pull back of Turkish troops from the Syrian border was of very considerable importance in discouraging moderate elements and in relieving the extremists from preoccupation." Thus the timetable for changing the Syrian regime "had been set far back and there were no present hopeful signs." In early December the Egyptian embassy in Amman privately alleged that the Jordanian government was trying to stir up dissension among Circassian officers in the Syrian army, but otherwise there were few signs of cross-border interference.[1]

The anti-Syrian effort suffered a further setback when Iraqi King Faisal visited King Saud in mid-December. According to the Egyptian embassy in Baghdad, which had good intelligence on internal Iraqi deliberations, the delegation accompanying Faisal was sharply divided over Syrian policy and aired its differences before Saud. Former prime minister Tawfiq al-Suwaydi, representing the views of Crown Prince 'Abd al-Ilah, proposed that Iraq, Jordan, and Saudi Arabia band together in an "Arab front" to oppose Egypt and Syria. Prime Minister 'Ali Jawdat al-Ayyubi, out of favor with the palace but still in power, interjected that such a venture would be contrary to Iraqi policy. Faced with the disagreement, Saud sided with Jawdat and refused to discuss al-Suwaydi's proposal. By month's end the Iraqi palace had replaced Jawdat with the more tractable 'Abd al-Wahhab Murjan, uniting the Iraqi leadership behind a tougher Syrian policy. Saud, however, had lost all interest in joint Saudi-Iraqi action to change the Syrian government.[2]

But by now the Syrian government was being changed from within, as much of the Syrian establishment clamored for political union with Egypt. The Egyptian-Syrian merger was a complex affair born of an odd mixture of idealism and power politics, of fear and self-confidence. The original advocates of union were the Syrian Ba'thists, who had long regarded Arab unity as an integral part of their political program. Only through the establishment of a pan-Arab state, they believed, could socialism and national liberation be fully achieved. Since the mid-1950s the Ba'thists had considered an Egyptian-Syrian union to be the most viable nucleus of such a superstate, partly because Nasser's foreign policy so closely matched their own and partly because Egypt was in a position to obstruct any union from which it was excluded. In early 1957, with the Ba'thists' power and influence on the rise, federal union with Egypt became official Syrian policy. For the next several months, however, the government made no effort to enact such a union, and there was little reason to regard the policy as anything more than a symbolic gesture.[3]

All of that changed in the aftermath of the Syrian crisis. As the external threat to Syria receded, tensions resumed between the Ba'thists and the Syrian communists. The Ba'thists were alarmed by the communists' growing popularity due to the Soviet Union's ostentatious defense of Syria during the crisis. The communists seemed poised to make big gains in the municipal elections scheduled for mid-November and in the parliamentary elections the following year, clearing the way for their ally, Defense Minister Khalid al-'Azm, to make a plausible bid for the presidency. An alternative Ba'thist fear was that the communists might be emboldened to attempt a coup. Though the effort would probably fail, it could well provoke a domestic right-wing counterattack or a military intervention by Syria's neighbors. One way the Ba'thists sought to block the communist advance was to boycott the municipal elections, a move resulting in their cancellation. Another Ba'thist maneuver was to demand immediate fulfillment of Syria's formal commitment to federal union with Egypt. Only Nasser, the Ba'thists believed, had the power and stature to keep the communists in check. The call for union was soon echoed by some conservative Syrian parties, which either shared the Ba'thists' alarm over the communists' ascendancy or believed that Nasser's intervention would be the only way to limit the Syrian army's interference in politics.[4]

For all the domestic anxieties it reflected, however, the unity movement also grew out of a sense of confidence in Syria's international position. In late November Syrian unionists told Egyptian ambassador to Syria Mahmud Riad that, while fear of a negative Turkish or Western reaction had once been a powerful obstacle to an Egyptian-Syrian union, this was no longer the case. Now that the Soviet Union had publicly committed itself to Egyptian and Syrian security (during the Suez war and the Syrian crisis, respectively), Turkey and the West would be unable to act against the union "for fear of igniting a world war."[5] Syrian unionists were correct in their prediction that Moscow would publicly support an Egyptian-Syrian union

—even at the expense of local communists—but they were wrong to assume that this fact alone would deter the West and its allies from seeking to disrupt such a union.

The Egyptian government was caught off guard by the unity movement and tried to slow it down. As of the fall of 1957, Egypt had reason to be satisfied with the territorial and political status quo in the Arab world, since it afforded Egypt considerable influence over the foreign policy of other Arab states—formally through the Egyptian-dominated Arab League and informally through propaganda and subversion—while sparing it any administrative duties beyond its own borders. Egypt had already placed itself on record as favoring union with Syria, but it had cautioned that such a union could not be consummated until the two countries had achieved economic, cultural, and military integration, which would probably take several years. In late November, after receiving Ambassador Riad's reports on the rise of pro-union sentiment in Syria, the Egyptian Foreign Ministry's Arab Bureau recommended that Egypt adhere to its go-slow policy, as "this will give Egypt enough time for sufficient study of the matter." According to Muhammad Haykal, as late as January 1958 Nasser remained convinced that any Egyptian-Syrian union would require at least five years' preparation.[6]

Egypt, however, was powerless to slow the pace of events in Syria, where union with Egypt was wildly popular. In early December Riad reported that the entire Syrian political establishment was engaged in "a public auction" over union, with each party trying to outdo its rivals in extolling the project. Later that month the communists escalated the bidding by calling for a comprehensive merger between Egypt and Syria, not just a federal union as the Ba'thists and others advocated. The communists apparently calculated that Nasser would reject such a proposal, in which case they would have thwarted the union effort—whose anticommunist implications they well understood—even while posing as its most ardent supporters. Not to be outdone, the Ba'thists themselves took up the cry for comprehensive unity. For years Ba'thist intellectuals had argued that a loose federal arrangement, with due respect for local traditions and institutions, would give the Egyptian-Syrian union the best chance of thriving in the long run and of inducing other Arab states to join. But in the frenzy of the political bidding such qualifications were cast aside.[7]

In January the leadership of the Syrian army decisively intervened in favor of comprehensive unity. Paradoxically, this decision reflected both the divisions within the army leadership and the leadership's collective desire to overcome those divisions. With no single figure commanding the allegiance of the whole officer corps, the army leadership had split into pro-

Ba'thist, procommunist, and other politically motivated factions. These factions tended to support union with Egypt for much the same reasons as did their respective civilian allies. As a group, however, the army leaders were alarmed by the intensity of their own disagreements, which had occasionally verged on violence. Union with Egypt, they believed, would impose Nasser's discipline on the officer corps and prevent it from disintegrating. It is also possible, as Patrick Seale writes, that army leaders considered "a union with Egypt, where the army had triumphed over all rivals, . . . the best guarantee of their own rule at home."[8]

On 12 January, without consulting the civilian government, fourteen senior army officers flew to Cairo, leaving behind a note to be delivered to the government in their absence. The note called for the immediate implementation of "comprehensive unity with Egypt" resulting in the formation of a unitary state with a single flag, capital, president, legislature, judiciary, and military. The note also ominously predicted that "any government or group neglecting to implement this unity will bear the consequences of its action before the Arab people as a whole." Meeting with Nasser on 15 January, the officers described the desperate situation in the Syrian army and appealed for immediate union.[9]

According to Haykal, who offers the fullest firsthand account of Nasser's discussions with the officers, Nasser initially gave little encouragement to his petitioners. He said that strengthening Egypt was his priority for the foreseeable future and that, in any event, "I cannot agree to discuss such matters except with a responsible, legal, and constitutional government." The officers agreed to send an emissary to Damascus who would return with convincing proof that the Syrian government supported their demand. On 16 January Syrian foreign minister Salah al-Din al-Bitar, one of the founders of the Ba'th Party, arrived in Cairo. Meeting that night with Nasser and the Syrian officers, al-Bitar strongly endorsed comprehensive unity, calling it "a means to Syria's stability for which there is no substitute."[10]

At the end of this second meeting, which lasted until dawn, Nasser told al-Bitar and the officers that he would, after all, consent to an immediate and comprehensive merger. But Nasser had two conditions. First, all political parties in Syria had to dissolve themselves, as their counterparts in Egypt had already done. Second, all Syrian army officers had to withdraw from politics, or resign their commissions if they chose to remain politically active. These conditions were clearly designed to eliminate the two main sources of potential political rivalry to Nasser, thus facilitating his control over the proposed union.[11]

Even under those advantageous conditions, however, it is not entirely clear why Nasser should have reversed himself on such a crucial matter. The most plausible explanation is that offered by Seale: "'Abd al-Nasir's aim since 1955 had been to control Syria's foreign policy—but not to assume responsibility for her Government. Arab solidarity rather than political union was his declared objective. It was only when the first was threatened that he was persuaded to contemplate the second. Indeed, only when his alliance with Syria was endangered by anarchy in the Syrian army, and by the vulnerability of his Ba'thist friends to attack from both left and right, was he driven to intervene." If this was the case, then the Syrian petitioners' very presence in Cairo must have been powerful evidence to Nasser of the desperate situation in Syria. Haykal provides some support for Seale's view when he quotes Nasser as telling the Syrians at the second meeting, "I am prepared to accept the principle [of immediate union]. I accept in fulfillment of the Syrian people's demand and, frankly, because I fear that Syria might be lost."[12] Having concluded that immediate union was necessary, however, Nasser ensured that it took place under the most favorable circumstances possible. Hence his insistence on the dissolution of Syria's parties and the political neutralization of its army.

Once Nasser had given his consent, the Egyptian-Syrian union was accomplished with remarkable speed. Al-Bitar and the officers were taken aback by Nasser's conditions but, having committed themselves so fully to union, had little choice but to accept them. On 21 January they returned to Damascus to present Nasser's terms to the Syrian government. For the next several days in Damascus, a confusing power struggle ensued in which some of the main protagonists retreated from previously held positions. The communists, seeing that their all-or-nothing tactic had failed to prevent union—and aghast at Nasser's insistence on the dissolution of all political parties—now took up the cry for a loose federation. Many Ba'thists were equally unwilling to commit party suicide, and they, too, demanded that the federal approach be revisited. Reflecting such misgivings, on 25 January the Syrian cabinet sent al-Bitar back to Cairo to request that Nasser withdraw his conditions and consider a looser association.[13]

But there was no stopping the drive toward comprehensive unity. Nasser refused to soften his position, and he was firmly backed by the Syrian army leaders, who hinted that any failure to satisfy Nasser's conditions might prompt them to take matters into their own hands. The Syrian cabinet immediately dropped its reservations and began preparing for unity on Nasser's terms. The Ba'thists also bowed to the inevitable, consoling themselves that the ban on political parties would break the communists' power without seriously eroding their own. Even if the Ba'th party were formally dissolved,

Crowds in Cairo cheer as Shukri al-Quwatli and Nasser ride to the signing
ceremony for the formal merger of Egypt and Syria, February 1958.
(© Bettmann/corbis)

they reasoned, individual Ba'thist leaders were sure to be given prominent positions in the new government in recognition of their historic role in bringing the union about. On 30 January the entire Syrian cabinet flew to Cairo
to work out the final terms of the union. On 1 February, to noisy applause
in both Cairo and Damascus, the Egyptian and Syrian governments proclaimed the formation of the United Arab Republic, subject to ratification by
plebiscites in Egypt and Syria. Three weeks later Egyptian and Syrian voters overwhelmingly approved the ratification of the UAR. (The vote in Egypt
was so lopsided that the number of spoiled ballots exceeded the number of
ballots cast against the merger.) The two electorates also agreed—again,
overwhelmingly—that Nasser would serve as the UAR's first president.[14]

The Egyptian-Syrian union was a bitter defeat for the Syrian communists.
Forced to choose between rescuing local communists and preserving good
relations with Egypt and Syria, the Soviet Union had pragmatically opted
for the latter. Not only did the Soviet government offer strong public support to the union, but it instructed communist parties in the Arab world
that "it considers President 'Abd al-Nasir's resistance to the Eisenhower
Doctrine and the Baghdad Pact sufficient in itself to require the support of

communist parties for the United Arab Republic." Local communists were simply to "disregard" the fact that the coming merger would end the party's legal activities in Syria.[15]

It was not clear at first that Syrian communists would peaceably accept such an outcome. In late January Ambassador Riad fretted that the communists might resort to "armed insurrection" to prevent implementation of the union, a fear heightened by the fact that many communist activists, through their membership in the officially sanctioned Popular Resistance Organization, had already been issued arms by the Syrian government. In early February, following reports of street fighting between communists and Ba'thists, Syrian authorities disarmed communist members of the organization. As a result of such precautions—or perhaps because the danger had been exaggerated in the first place—the communists failed to mount any tangible resistance to the merger. Though communist activity in Syria continued clandestinely, it amounted to little more than the dissemination of propaganda against Nasser, whom the communists denounced as an "opportunist who gets what he wants from [the] USSR and then turns on friends."[16]

A far more important consequence of the Egyptian-Syrian union was an end to the decade-long struggle waged by Egypt, Iraq, and to a lesser extent Saudi Arabia over Syria's geopolitical orientation. It is true that by the mid-1950s Syria had generally aligned its foreign policy with Egypt's. Even so, Syria's political institutions had been sufficiently porous to permit Iraq and Saudi Arabia considerable influence over Syrian affairs; the possibility had remained that either of those countries, through blandishments or subversion, might eventually induce Syria to end its alliance with Egypt. But the creation of the UAR, especially under Nasser's stringent conditions, closed the traditional avenues of Iraqi and Saudi influence. This fact, combined with Egypt's newly acquired control over the oil pipelines in Syria, represented a dramatic political and strategic victory for Nasser.

ALTHOUGH NASSER'S TRIUMPH in the struggle for Syria was significant enough in its own right, few observers at the time expected matters to end there. This was as true of the union's supporters as of its opponents. In neighboring Arab countries, despite official bans on pro-UAR expression, news of the impending Egyptian-Syrian merger was widely celebrated in newspaper editorials, demonstrations, parades, and other public displays.[17] Much of this favorable outpouring treated the new union not as a finite entity but as the nucleus of a pan-Arab superstate whose formation was now inevitable. The nationalist Iraqi newspaper *al-Hurriyya* pronounced the union "a starting point for the future." Signs appearing on the streets of Kuwait proclaimed, "We Welcome the Unity and Our Entrance into It." "Abdel Nasser, President of the united Arab nation, . . . will come to our rescue," the Lebanese newspaper *Beirut-Masa'* breathlessly predicted. "Soon the frontiers of [the] Syro-Egyptian union will be only 50 kilometers from Beirut. . . . Isn't Abdel Nasser at our gates?"[18]

Nasser's enemies had to ask themselves the same question. Meeting with U.S. diplomats in late January and early February, conservative Arab leaders expressed deep alarm over the prospect of Syria's absorption by Egypt. Lebanese foreign minister Charles Malik saw the merger as a Soviet-backed "plot by Nasser to extend Egyptian hegemony beyond Africa into western Asia." Unless the United States used "every possible means" to oppose the scheme, Lebanese Nasserists "would be emboldened to seek [a] change in government with [the] ultimate aim of joining [the] new Syro-Egyptian union." Iraqi Crown Prince 'Abd al-Ilah and Prime Minister 'Abd al-Wahhab Murjan were "deeply disturbed at [the] prospects [of] having Nasser on Iraq's borders and athwart [its] oil lines" in Syria. While Jordan's King Hussein doubted that a "real" union between Egypt and Syria could be achieved, he worried that "even [a] 'paper federation' would have tremendous appeal throughout [the] Arab world especially among west bank refugees." This, in turn, "would make Jordan's position precarious."[19]

The Eisenhower administration's own reaction to the Egyptian-Syrian union was far less categorical. Two factors complicated that response. The first was the uncertain orientation of the union itself. The second was a divergence of views between Dulles and the administration as a whole, a disagreement accentuated by the fact that from 22 January until 1 February, the period in which the administration formulated its initial position on the union, Dulles was away from Washington and traveling in the Middle East, making statements and pledges occasionally at odds with policy deliberations back home.

In Dulles's absence the State Department arrived at an equivocal assessment of the nature and implications of the Egyptian-Syrian union. A 25 January report by the State Department's NEA concluded that the union was largely an anticommunist initiative (a view seconded days later by the CIA) and would consequently be beneficial to the United States in the short term. In the long term, however, NEA feared that the new union "would facilitate Nasser's domination of the Arab world," weakening conservative forces in the region. In any event, NEA acknowledged, "we are . . . not in a position effectively to prevent some kind of union from taking place if both countries desire it."[20]

Dulles took a much dimmer view of the situation, as can be seen in his remarks at the Baghdad Pact Council meeting in Ankara. Addressing a restricted session on 28 January, Dulles said that the Egyptian-Syrian union was "almost certainly backed up by Russia" and that if consummated it "would create great danger that Jordan and Lebanon would be absorbed, putting Iraq and Saudi Arabia in peril." It was clear, he said, that the United States and the Baghdad Pact "ought to oppose such a union." As in the recent Syrian crisis, however, "any initiative must be taken by an Arab State and not by a non-Arab State," though "the United States would support any Arab initiative" against the union.[21]

Dulles was prepared for drastic measures. Earlier in the 28 January session, former Iraqi prime minister Nuri al-Saʿid, who headed the Iraqi delegation, had hinted that Iraq should be permitted to annex portions of northeastern Syria. Picking up on Nuri's suggestion, Dulles proposed "that some part of Syria might wish to secede and join Iraq. If there were any such idea Iraq should follow it up and could count on United States backing." According to the State Department's later account of the session, Dulles specifically promised the Iraqis "that if out of the confusion and dissensions which might accompany the effort to force Syria to amalgamate with Egypt there came an attack on Iraq mounted with Soviet weapons, and perhaps volunteers, then the US on request would be prepared to intervene under the Eisenhower Doctrine. This discussion took place within the context of Nuri's suggestion that parts of Syria might secede and join Iraq and be received into Iraq and that this would give rise to an attack." It is unclear whether Syrian military operations within the breakaway Syrian areas would or would not be considered "an attack on Iraq." Even if they would not, Dulles's encouragement of Iraqi expansionism was extremely reckless.[22]

Perhaps Dulles regretted his indiscretion, for at the Baghdad Pact Council's 29 January session he took a more cautious line, remarking that multilateral Arab action would be preferable to unilateral Iraqi action. "If Iraq alone opposed [the union]," he said, "it would be accused of acting on [the] influence of non-Arab B[aghdad] P[act] powers."[23] The council agreed that Iraq should "work out a united position" with Jordan, Saudi Arabia, and Lebanon. Cooperation among these four countries should proceed on two fronts simultaneously. First, they should consider banding together in a rival federation offering "an alternative expression of Arab unity." Second,

THE NASSERIST ONSLAUGHT

they "should actively cooperate with . . . each other in promoting opposition to union inside Syria." Still, Dulles did not entirely repudiate his pledge of the day before. If multilateral Arab action proved impossible, he said, unilateral Iraqi action "would be better than doing nothing."[24]

Dulles was obliged to make a further retreat following his return to Washington in early February, as it became clear that his colleagues did not share his harsh assessment of the Egyptian-Syrian union. At the 6 February meeting of the NSC, CIA director Allen Dulles said that "the intelligence community does not believe that the USSR was behind the move toward union. . . . Indeed, the evidence that we have indicates opposition to the union by the Syrian Communists. Moscow has been puzzled as to what attitude to take." At that same meeting, Foster Dulles implicitly acknowledged his misreading of the situation when he said that "there had been practically no solid intelligence at Ankara as to how this union had actually come about . . . , and the U.S. Delegation accordingly felt very isolated and very much in the dark." Moreover, "there was strong pressure on the United States to speak out against the union." Dulles's explanation, writes Nigel John Ashton, "has almost the flavour of an apology."[25]

Dulles had already adopted a more cautious approach to the new union. On 5 February he instructed NEA, via his special assistant Joseph N. Greene Jr., that the United States should not rule out "extending the hand of friendship" to the UAR. "If the Soviets are hesitant about their attitude toward the Union, it might be a favorable opportunity for us." Dulles also noted, however, that "a close appraisal of the vulnerabilities of the new Union . . . might lead to the conclusion that it is more open to disruption than to blandishment," in which case the United States should "wait a while to see whether the other Arab States can agree on a common course of action, which course we might then back."[26] Though Dulles did not yet accept NEA's view that the union was unstoppable, he had abandoned any notion of encouraging unilateral Iraqi action.

The Iraqis, however, would not let Dulles forget his recent pledges in Ankara. On 6 February a cable arrived from the U.S. embassy in Baghdad conveying an urgent message from 'Abd al-Ilah. Implementation of the Egyptian-Syrian union, the crown prince claimed, "would place Iraq completely at Nasser's mercy," given the latter's control over Iraqi oil pipelines in Syria. To prevent this dire outcome, 'Abd al-Ilah proposed "giving encouragement to tribal leaders in Syria (he mentioned Shammar and Druze elements), who were already unhappy with [the] turn of events, to revolt or at least call for support from friendly neighbors against [the] union. This would give Iraq [an] opportunity to intervene with effective force in order

to help [the] Syrians free themselves from Nasser's machinations and establish their own free government." Having set up the "free government,"
Iraqi forces would then withdraw from Syria. 'Abd al-Ilah wanted to know
if the United States would support such an operation.[27]

'Abd al-Ilah's proposed initiative placed Dulles in an awkward position.
On one hand, it was just the sort of unilateral Iraqi action the secretary had
encouraged in Ankara—and had never entirely repudiated in the Iraqis'
presence even after second thoughts had set in. On the other hand, Dulles
was now more convinced than ever that any Iraqi effort to disrupt the
union must have the support of other Arab states, especially Saudi Arabia.
On 7 February, however, Saud had written Eisenhower to say that the union
should not be opposed as long as it enjoyed popular support in Egypt and
Syria and did no harm to its neighbors.[28] Nor was there reason to believe
that either Jordan or Lebanon would back the Iraqi plan.[29] Finally, the administration had "no reports of any widespread opposition in Syria to the
union," while its information on the Syrian tribes "indicates they have recently been largely isolated and subjected [to] strict surveillance and control
by [the] Syrian military." Begun under these circumstances, an Iraqi operation could quickly bog down.[30]

On 8 February the State Department cabled a reply to 'Abd al-Ilah that,
without directly dissuading the Iraqis from taking action, listed the above
obstacles to the proposed scheme and strongly implied that its implementation would be ill advised. 'Abd al-Ilah accepted the U.S. position without
protest.[31]

By now Dulles had all but given up on derailing the Egyptian-Syrian
union. That same day he wrote Eisenhower that "so far we have received
little or no evidence that our Arab friends are able or willing to formulate
common action" to disrupt the union. It also seemed likely that one or
more Arab countries would recognize the UAR as soon as its formation had
been ratified by plebiscite, in which case "we could not justifiably withhold
our recognition of the United Arab Republic without renouncing our traditional policy on Arab unity and without giving offense to the popular appeal of Arab nationalism."[32] Eisenhower authorized the State Department
to recognize the UAR upon ratification.[33]

MEANWHILE, WITH PROSPECTS dwindling for disruptive action against
the UAR, a less provocative Arab response had started to take shape. In late
January, reacting to early reports of the impending Egyptian-Syrian union,
King Hussein had sent identical letters to Saud and Iraqi King Faisal pro-

posing a Jordanian-Iraqi-Saudi federation. Such a federation would provide an outlet for rising pan-Arab enthusiasm among the populations of the three kingdoms, would preempt efforts by Egypt and Syria to draw Jordan into the UAR, and would show that conservative Arabs could play the unity game as well. Saud gave Hussein a discouraging reply, insisting that Saudi Arabia could not federate with Jordan and Iraq as long as the latter remained in the Baghdad Pact. Nor was Hussein's proposal universally popular with Iraqi officials. A group of politicians led by Nuri al-Sa'id thought that federating with Jordan—with its hopeless economy, its huge Palestinian population, and its border with Israel—would create nothing but headaches for Iraq. The Iraqi palace, however, was convinced that the political benefits of federation would outweigh its costs, and on 7 February King Faisal accepted Hussein's invitation to visit Jordan. Four days later Faisal and a delegation of Iraqi officials arrived in Amman for unity talks. The immediate goal of the talks was to work out a bilateral federation between Iraq and Jordan. Once this had been accomplished, Saudi Arabia's membership in the new grouping (or at least its approval of it) could be sought as well.[34]

For the second time in as many weeks, a pair of Arab governments hastily laid the groundwork for union. At the start of the Amman talks, in an obvious bid for Saudi approval, the Jordanians said that federation would be impossible unless Iraq withdrew from the Baghdad Pact. The Iraqis rejected the demand, however, and the Jordanians backed down, insisting only that the new federation not extend Baghdad Pact membership to Jordan.[35] The two sides then quickly agreed on the bases for unity. As the term "federation" implied, the Iraqi-Jordanian union would be looser than its Egyptian-Syrian counterpart. Iraq and Jordan would strive for complete unification of their foreign policies, substantial integration of their military and diplomatic services, and eventual coordination of their economic and fiscal policies. But each country would retain its independent national status, each king would keep his throne, and the domestic affairs of each country would remain under the jurisdiction of its cabinet and parliament. The union's affairs would be run by a federal government consisting of an executive and a legislative council, the latter to be selected by the parliaments of both countries. The Iraqi king would be the permanent chief executive of the union, an arrangement Hussein accepted with much reluctance.[36] On 14 February the main features of the Iraqi-Jordanian federation, or the Arab Union, as it was now known, were publicly unveiled.

The U.S. State Department responded cautiously to the declaration of the Arab Union. The department's initial public statement on the union—

noting that the United States welcomed any moves toward Arab unity that considered the wishes of the peoples concerned and contributed to the welfare and stability of the region—was identical to its statement on the formation of the UAR. Though privately pleased by the Iraqi-Jordanian move, the department feared that a public U.S. endorsement of the federation would expose it to the charge of being "western-inspired."[37]

The State Department was right to be concerned about the Arab Union's political vulnerability, for the union generated little public enthusiasm either at home or in the region. On 21 February the U.S. embassy in Baghdad noted the "lack of any popular demonstrations hailing the new union" in Iraq. Three days later the U.S. embassy in Amman reported that, while "expectations of economic gain for Jordan" had generated some popular interest in the federation, "public demonstrations of enthusiasm have been obviously lacking in spontaneity and conviction." Most West Bank Palestinians, a State Department intelligence report glumly observed, were "Convinced They Are In The Wrong Union."[38] Elsewhere in the Arab world, public support for the Arab Union was similarly faint. A U.S. diplomat in Kuwait concluded that the "majority [in] Kuwait is emotionally more attached to [the] UAR than to [the] Arab Union." The U.S. embassy in Beirut found that "in private discussions Christians express considerabl[y] more enthusiasm for [the] federation as [a] counter to [the] UAR than do their newspapers," which praised the Iraqi-Jordanian union only in bland terms. Saud echoed this reticence, privately assuring the Iraqis and the Jordanians that he favored the Arab Union over the UAR, while publicly taking a neutral stance between the two unions.[39]

On the other hand, criticism of the Arab Union tended to be mild as well. Egyptian, Syrian, and Lebanese press commentary, while predominantly negative, was less excoriating than dismissive. Critics belittled the new federation as a bogus imitation of the Egyptian-Syrian union, "void of feeling and sentiment."[40] Compared to the vicious rhetoric of past crises, this was gentle fare indeed.

In part, the mild tone of the commentary against the Arab Union seems to have been set by Nasser himself. In the immediate aftermath of the proclamation of the union, Nasser refrained from personally criticizing the new federation and instead sent a congratulatory public letter to King Faisal. Nasser's cordial gesture may well have been a signal to Egyptian and Syrian journalists (whose coverage was later emulated by journalists elsewhere in the Arab world) to moderate their criticism of the Iraqi-Jordanian union. Nasser had good reason to placate his enemies. In mid-February the Egyptian embassy in Baghdad, citing "sources in contact with Prince 'Abd al-

Ilah," reported that the crown prince had been deeply shaken by the proclamation of the UAR. "The sources add that he has lately increased his drinking . . . , that he is not in control of his nerves, and that he is liable to engage in any crazy political action" to disrupt the Egyptian-Syrian union.[41] Soothing words out of Cairo might keep the Iraqis at bay during the crucial weeks in which the UAR was being established and consolidated.

Such an approach was in keeping with Nasser's behavior on other fronts at the time. According to reports later received by U.S. intelligence, in mid-February Nasser counseled West Bank Palestinians temporarily to refrain from taking "direct action" against the Arab Union. A State Department intelligence analyst speculated that Nasser "did not want to offend King Saud"—whose public neutrality he valued—"by moving too fast to upset the status quo, particularly by undermining a monarchy." The analyst further speculated that Nasser, "having been catapulted into his own union with Syria before he had expected it, . . . has his hands full bringing order to the chaotic Syrian political scene."[42] This was no time for a public crisis with Arab kings.

It is possible that Nasser was simply delaying his inevitable political offensive against the Arab Union until after he had consolidated his power at home. Even if this was Nasser's intention, however, the Iraqis' behavior in the interim was sufficiently provocative to make his later attacks seem reactive. Since early February Iraqi leaders had been convinced that, once the UAR was ratified by plebiscite, Nasser would strike out at Iraq either by severing its pipeline in Syria or by allowing Iraqi oil to flow only on extortionate terms, wreaking havoc on the Iraqi economy. The belief that a UAR attack was inevitable seems to have blinded the Iraqis to the conciliatory nature of Nasser's initial attitude toward the Iraqi-Jordanian federation—or convinced them that this stance could not possibly be sincere. Consequently, in mid- to late February Iraqi leaders not only rebuffed Nasser's gestures but took actions that infuriated Nasser and his allies. Faisal replied to Nasser's congratulatory message, but in less cordial terms.[43] When Nasser promised that the UAR would recognize the Arab Union, the Iraqis and the Jordanians failed to reciprocate. Worse still, Iraqi leaders privately pressured the United States and the other Baghdad Pact countries not to recognize the UAR, a fact that soon got back to Nasser.[44] In a final affront, Iraqi leaders were quoted in the international press as saying that the Arab Union was "more natural" than the UAR and that Syria would soon be incorporated into the former.[45]

The Iraqi indiscretions gave Nasser an excuse to end his self-imposed restraint, with sharply polarizing results in the region. In late February Nasser began an extended visit to Syria to help celebrate the ratification of the Egyptian-Syrian union. Before cheering throngs in Damascus, Nasser castigated the Arab Union as an implacable enemy of Arab nationalism, referring to Iraqi and Jordanian leaders as "Arab traitors" whose own people would soon "settle accounts with them." Nasser's denunciations unleashed an all-out propaganda war between the two rival unions lasting well into the following summer and involving the most inflammatory accusations. Arab Union Radio charged that Nasser had proposed inviting Israel to join the UAR. An Iraqi magazine published a doctored photograph showing a smiling Nasser standing side by side with Moshe Dayan, chief of staff of the Israeli Defense Forces. A Cairo magazine expressed doubt about the Hashemites' claim to be descended from the Prophet.[46]

By March the mutual hostility was taking more concrete forms. Jordanian border officials harassed Syrian citizens attempting to enter Jordan, and vice versa. The UAR consul in Jerusalem was expelled on the charge of "stirring up discontent against the government" of Jordan. The printing press of a pro-government Jordanian newspaper was damaged in a bomb blast. King Hussein blamed the Syrians, saying to a British diplomat that "Jordan could play with fireworks as well, and would retaliate." 'Abd al-Ilah told British ambassador to Iraq Michael Wright of his determination not only to strengthen the Arab Union but to "bring over Syria, by the use of force if there was no other way." Otherwise, "the situation could not be held in Iraq for any long period. . . . Rather than succumb it would be better for the Hashemites to go down fighting honourably." In keeping with this tougher mood, in early March the Iraqi palace invited Nuri, a consistent advocate of a harder line against Nasserism and Arab radicalism, to resume his duties as prime minister. Nuri came out swinging, boasting to the press that he had been struggling for Arab independence "before Nasser was out of his swaddling clothes"—which was literally true.[47] Nuri's reappointment, Ambassador Wright observed on 4 March, "show[s] that Iraq has firmly taken up the challenge delivered by Colonel Nasser in his speeches in Damascus."[48]

Nasser, however, was not done delivering that challenge, for the next day he made a fresh accusation that both widened and intensified the public crisis in the Arab world. From the balcony of his Damascus guesthouse, Nasser told a crowd of supporters that King Saud had just been caught in an attempt to sabotage the Egyptian-Syrian union. Nasser claimed that Syrian intelligence chief 'Abd al-Hamid al-Sarraj had recently been approached by an emissary of Saud who had urged him to lead a coup in Damascus resulting in Syria's repudiation of the union with Egypt. Allegedly, Saud's emissary had paid al-Sarraj £1.9 million and had offered to pay him an additional £2 million if he successfully engineered Nasser's assassination. Though loyal to the UAR, al-Sarraj had pretended to go along with the scheme in order to collect damaging evidence against Saud. At a subsequent press conference, al-Sarraj displayed copies of checks drawn on the Arab Bank in Riyadh.[49]

While parts of this account may have been exaggerated, the available evidence suggests that Saud had been involved in a coup attempt in Syria—but that the United States was not, as some have alleged, complicit in the effort.[50] On 3 March, two days before Nasser made his accusation, Saudi Keeper of the Privy Purse 'Abd Allah al-Tubayshi asked U.S. ambassador to Saudi Arabia Donald R. Heath to inform Eisenhower and Dulles that "a successful military revolution would take place within a few days in Syria." That same day the U.S. consul in Damascus cabled Washington that he had "serious doubts [about the] bona fides" of the Saudi-supported plot in Syria; the effort appeared to be a UAR sting operation designed to entrap Saud.[51] On 4 March the State Department passed word to al-Tubayshi that "such information as is available to us indicates little organized opposition" in Syria. Al-Tubayshi "expressed appreciation for [the] Department's warning [against] entrapment" but said that Saud was confident the "revolutionary movement would shortly be launched and be successful." As Allen Dulles reported the day after the exposure of the plot, "While King Saud has been cautious in his official and outward dealings with Egypt and Syria, he has also engaged in intrigues against the leaders of these countries which have now been unmasked by Serraj and Nasser. . . . We had tried to warn Saud, vainly, that he was falling into a trap."[52]

The exposure of Saud's intrigues not only destroyed the king's credibility in the region but threw the Eisenhower administration into a state of near-panic. Repeated incessantly on Radio Cairo that March, Nasser's accusation was widely believed in the Arab world, including in Saudi Arabia. The resulting discredit to Saud, and by extension to all conservative Arab leaders, caused the administration to fear that the entire Western position in the area was on the verge of collapse. At the 13 March NSC meeting Allen Dulles reported "that Saud's position had become critical as the result of his implication in the plot to assassinate Nasser." While noting that "Saud was such a wily individual that . . . he would probably pull through," Dulles warned that "developments in Saudi Arabia had made the position of Jordan and Iraq even more shaky" than before. "The situation in the Near East generally was very grave indeed from the Western point of view. It was plain that Nasser had caught the imagination of the masses throughout the entire area."[53]

Eisenhower, who was present at the NSC meeting, "inquired whether, if King Saud asked for Western assistance and we responded with military forces, the situation could be stabilized." A discussion ensued about the applicability of the Eisenhower Doctrine. Undersecretary of State Christian A. Herter reminded the group that the doctrine could be invoked only "if there were a finding that International Communism constituted a threat to Saudi Arabia." Eisenhower replied that "we simply could not stand around and do nothing and see the whole area fall into the hands of Communism" —the expected outcome, presumably, of further victories for Nasserism. Treasury Secretary Robert B. Anderson agreed "that, whether or not the Eisenhower Doctrine was thought to be applicable to the present situation in the Near East, the loss of Near Eastern oil to the West, particularly to Europe, would be catastrophic." Therefore, "we should make it clear to the world that the United States or NATO would not tolerate" such a prospect.[54]

As it happened, the Saudi royal family obviated U.S. intervention in the Middle East (at least for the time being) by taking matters into its own hands. Saud's brothers were already resentful of the king's financial mismanagement, which had pushed the country toward bankruptcy, and of his secretive governing style, which had excluded them from his counsels. Worse still, Saud had appointed some of his sons to sensitive government posts, arousing suspicions that he hoped to shift the line of royal succession away from his brothers and toward his own offspring.[55] Saud's bungling over Syria was the last straw. In late March Saud's brothers met with the king and forced him to turn most of his executive functions over to Crown Prince Faisal. For the rest of the decade, Saud would be little more than a figurehead.[56]

Eisenhower and his advisers tried to think positively about Faisal's ascendancy—a difficult task given Faisal's reputation in the West as an appeaser of Nasser. After meeting the crown prince in Washington the previous September, Eisenhower had remarked that Faisal "was stupid in their conversations."[57] At the 27 March NSC meeting, however, Eisenhower recalled only "that Feisal had been extremely pleasant in his contacts in Washington." Secretary Dulles noted "that Feisal had mellowed." Allen Dulles considered the crown prince "definitely anti-Communist." "Pro-American and smart as hell" was Vice President Richard M. Nixon's verdict.[58]

These friendly assessments were not entirely unwarranted. Faisal had every intention of continuing his government's vigorous opposition to communism and of maintaining its close military and economic ties to the United States and the West. Moreover, Faisal far outclassed his brother in intelligence, self-discipline, and political experience, as evidenced by the speed with which his austerity measures subsequently helped to restore Saudi finances. But Faisal also saw the dangers of the anti-Nasser policies that Saud had fitfully pursued over the preceding year and a half. If the kingdom was to survive, it would have to lower its profile in the region. On 18 April Faisal announced that Saudi Arabia would take a neutral stance in the conflict between the UAR and the Arab Union. Egyptian diplomats were initially skeptical of Faisal's pledge, but in the coming months it would grow increasingly clear that Faisal had meant what he said.[59]

Saudi Arabia's new stance had obvious drawbacks for the Western position in the Arab world. An 8 April U.S. intelligence estimate had already predicted that Saudi neutrality would result in "the elimination of one of the major indigenous elements hostile to Nasser and the devitalization and isolation of the newly formed Arab Union."[60] But the likely alternative to a Saudi accommodation with Nasser—the collapse of the Saudi monarchy and perhaps of other pro-Western Arab regimes—was even less pleasant to contemplate.

BY MID-SPRING Nasser dominated the Arab world as never before. With Syria formally added to his domain, he now controlled the main avenues through which Arab oil passed to the West. Egypt's merger with Syria had had the further effects of frustrating a long-standing Iraqi ambition and driving Saud to a politically suicidal reaction. Nasserists in Lebanon, Iraq, Jordan, and the West Bank daily threatened the stability of conservative Arab regimes, whose own popularity was on the wane. Iraqi leaders were pathetically (and prophetically) "acting as though they expected [to] be gone in six months." To be sure, there were obstacles in the path of Nasserism's advance to which the Eisenhower administration could look with some comfort. In Jordan, for example, the UAR would have to think twice about moving too aggressively lest Israel react by seizing the West Bank.[61] But it was the impediments to American action that were most obvious to administration officials. At the 13 March NSC meeting Eisenhower complained "that there seemed to be no action that we could take to brighten the picture in the Middle East. He wanted to do something but in each direction he turned he saw stumbling blocks."[62]

In their frustration, administration officials entertained wild schemes for containing Nasser. Perhaps, Treasury Secretary Robert Anderson proposed on 20 March, the United States could advocate the withdrawal of the UN peacekeeping forces stationed in Sinai and Gaza since early 1957; Nasser "might not . . . be quite so bold if he thought [the Israelis] would come back into Egypt." Two weeks later Dulles wondered aloud about making "a big effort to get those Upper Nile waters into the control of friendly hands, and then have a position to threaten Egypt in that way to offset their threat to the West through the Suez Canal and pipelines etc."[63] Nothing, thankfully, came of either of these suggestions, presumably because U.S. officials concluded that threatening the Egyptian people with invasion or famine might not, after all, be the most politic thing to do.

By this time, however, a more realistic set of options had emerged. In mid-March Undersecretary Herter had asked NEA to draw up new recommendations for Middle East policy in light of the recent setbacks. The resulting paper, completed on 24 March, proposed a two-part strategy for blocking Nasser's drive to dominate the Arab world. On one hand, the United States should continue its previous policy of "stiffen[ing] the spines of friendly countries in the area through economic and military assistance" and "encourag[ing] them to collaborate in resisting Nasser's expansionism." On the other hand, the United States should avoid unnecessary public controversy with Nasser, who "continues to represent the answer to the prayers of many Arabs." It might even be desirable to improve relations on some fronts, such as by relaxing existing U.S. restrictions against the UAR regarding exports, cultural exchanges, and private relief efforts. Likewise, without abandoning its basic commitments, the United States should avoid overly dramatic demonstrations of support for its friends in the area, whose popularity tended only to decrease as a result. In a veiled reference to Eisenhower's unsuccessful effort to build up Saud, NEA urged that the United States "avoid becoming inextricably identified with and attached to specific individuals, whose departure from the scene would mean that the whole basis of the United States position in a particular country would disappear overnight."[64] These recommendations amounted to a significant relaxation of the anti-Nasser policy that the United States had followed for the better part of two years and on which the Eisenhower Doctrine had largely been based.

It is unclear whether Dulles formally endorsed the NEA study, but over the next several weeks the Eisenhower administration did follow the general formula of placating Nasser while quietly bolstering the conservative Arabs. In theory, there was no necessary inconsistency between these two objectives. In practice, it proved extremely difficult to pursue both of them simultaneously. U.S. moves to placate Nasser angered and demoralized pro-Western Arab leaders, raising the possibility of their ultimately losing confidence in the United States. Washington's encouragement of pro-Western leaders emboldened those leaders to take provocative positions on local and regional questions, increasing the likelihood of violent conflict between them and local Nasserists—and thus of renewed antagonism between the United States and the UAR.

In late March the State Department began consulting with Raymond Hare, the U.S. ambassador in Cairo, about an approach to Nasser to discuss a gradual improvement in relations. By mid-April the approach had been finalized: Hare was to tell Nasser that the United States would again allow U.S. companies to sell military spare parts, radio equipment, and civilian aircraft to the UAR; that it was prepared to resume cultural exchange programs with the UAR; and that it would "give sympathetic consideration" to the return of private American relief organizations to Egypt. Hare was also authorized to say that, should the UAR respond favorably to these gestures, the United States "would be prepared to take additional measures." Those measures, which Hare was not to reveal to Nasser just yet, included the sale of surplus wheat to the UAR, U.S. assistance with economic development programs, and training in the United States for UAR military personnel. On 25 April Hare conveyed the message to Nasser, who "said he welcomed our approach and wished again [to] give assurance that he desired good relations" with the United States, though he expressed some skepticism that the United States was genuinely ready for rapprochement.[65]

In a fortunate coincidence, at the end of the month the Suez Canal Company finally settled its dispute with the Egyptian government (see Chapter 1), prompting the U.S. government to release Egyptian assets frozen in American banks since July 1956. Dulles insisted that the unfreezing was a legal matter that had no direct bearing on UAR-American political relations, but the decision undeniably improved the atmosphere between the two countries.[66]

Conservative Arab leaders were disturbed by the improvement in UAR-American relations. Following a press conference on 8 April in which Dulles had said that the United States was "getting along" with Nasser, Samir al-Rifa'i, deputy prime minister and de facto leader of the Jordanian cabinet, complained to a U.S. diplomat that "any attempt [to] 'get along with Nasser' appeared ridiculous in [the] eyes of US friends [in the] Middle East" in view of Nasser's ongoing reliance on Soviet military and economic assistance. Charles Malik told U.S. ambassador to Lebanon Robert McClintock that Lebanon and other pro-Western countries "would be relieved and grateful" to learn that the "shift in US POLICY toward Egypt did not imply 'selling them down the drain'. . . . This being said, Malik could not hide [his] pessimism." At a NATO meeting in Copenhagen in early May, British foreign secretary Selwyn Lloyd warned Dulles that "our friends would abandon us if Nasser seemed to derive benefits from his behavior."[67]

Meanwhile the Eisenhower administration pursued the other half of its two-part strategy: quietly fortifying the conservative Arab regimes. In April the administration agreed to substantial increases in U.S. economic assistance to Lebanon, Jordan, and Iraq. (The Iraqi-Jordanian federation would not go into effect until the following month.) The United States also cooperated with Britain in supplying the three countries with fighter aircraft on a grant basis. U.S. officials hoped that the aircraft deliveries, in addition to offering military benefits, would allow the recipient countries "to demonstrate publicly that states cooperating with the United States and the West will be assisted by the United States in achieving legitimate defensive positions."[68]

Bolstering Jordan and Iraq was nevertheless a frustrating business. The two states failed to achieve even the limited integration promised in February. When the Arab Union officially came into being on 19 May, Hussein refused to relinquish direct control over the Jordanian army and security forces for fear of compromising their ability to defend the throne. He also declined to merge Jordan's Foreign Ministry with Iraq's, apparently reluctant to be associated with such Iraqi foreign policies as Baghdad Pact membership. The Iraqis resisted fiscal integration to avoid assuming full responsibility for Jordan's budget deficit. The State Department worried that Jordan's and Iraq's unwillingness to make the necessary concessions would allow Nasserists to portray the Arab Union as a "sham."[69]

There was also the ever-present risk that the Iraqis would treat increased U.S. support as a license to engage in reckless behavior beyond their borders. Well after the ratification of the Egyptian-Syrian union, Iraqi leaders continued to hint to U.S. and British officials that some sort of Iraqi action in Syria, aimed at wresting that country from the UAR, would be necessary to ensure political stability in Baghdad. Such talk was worrying to the U.S. and British governments, both of which now firmly opposed violent action against Syria. "The major difficulty here since January," Ambassador Wright cabled London on 23 June, "has been to maintain the resolution and spirit of the Iraqis in the face of the creation of the United Arab Republic while at the same time preventing them from taking any rash step over Syria or Kuwait."[70]

For the Iraqis had also turned a covetous eye to the southeast. Throughout the spring of 1958 Nuri insisted to American and British diplomats that the union with Jordan had saddled Iraq with a crushing financial burden that could be eased only by the incorporation of oil-rich Kuwait into the Arab Union. By June Nuri was threatening to resign if the British and Kuwaiti governments failed to satisfy this demand. Meeting with Eisenhower, Dulles, and other U.S. officials in Washington on 9 June, British prime minister Harold Macmillan remarked that Nuri's position on Kuwait "will play right into Nasser's hands," since the Kuwaiti population, which included many Egyptian, Syrian, and Palestinian immigrants, was sure to resist entry into the Arab Union. Dulles agreed, adding "that Nuri's personality has become a liability in recent times." Both sides were adamant that Nuri be discouraged from seeking the annexation of Kuwait, and they hoped he would be satisfied with recent increases in U.S. and British economic assistance to the Arab Union. After all, a British official remarked, "Nuri wants money more than he does Kuwait." But Nuri seemed to want both equally, and to the end of his days (which admittedly were numbered) he continued to demand the incorporation of Kuwait into the Arab Union.[71]

Of all the Eisenhower administration's Arab friends, however, it was Camille Chamoun whose behavior proved most trying. By the spring of 1958 Chamoun's personal ambitions and combative style had sharply polarized both Lebanese and Arab politics, provoking a violent conflict that threatened his own political survival. By summer the Eisenhower administration would have to choose between the aggravation of sustaining an increasingly discredited figure and the infamy of forsaking a loyal ally in need. The administration's choice would run counter to much of its recent thinking about the Arab world, temporarily negating its own efforts to deemphasize the Eisenhower Doctrine. But the choice would also expose further inadequacies of the doctrine and thus ultimately strengthen the case for its abandonment.

THE LEBANESE CRISIS,

APRIL–JULY 1958

On its face, U.S. policy toward Lebanon in the spring and summer of 1958 seems puzzling at best, senseless at worst. For several months U.S. officials gave unstinting support to a political leader whom they increasingly distrusted and whose personal ambitions they privately opposed, in the name of a policy they were trying to abandon. The United States then launched a massive military intervention to bring stability to a country whose immediate political crisis seemed on the verge of resolution. No sooner was the venture under way than U.S. forces nearly blundered into hostilities with the army of the nation they had allegedly come to save. Back home, the American intervention was linked in the public mind with a foreign policy doctrine that was almost wholly inapplicable to the crisis at hand.

Equally perplexing is how little American actions seemed to reflect the recent changes in the Eisenhower administration's thinking about the Arab world. In the spring of 1958 the administration had rededicated itself to bolstering pro-Western Arab regimes. At the same time, it had implicitly acknowledged that one of the main assumptions underlying the Eisenhower Doctrine—that the United States could benefit politically by dividing the Arab world along ideological lines—was mistaken. Almost invariably, the resulting polarization had occurred at the expense of the United States and its conservative Arab allies. It was time, the administration realized, to take a more conciliatory attitude toward the Nasserist movement, emphasizing areas of common ground between it and the United States. From this standpoint the aggressively anti-Nasserist posture of Lebanese president Camille Chamoun had become a liability, and there was good reason for the United States to distance itself from that position, even if it could not repudiate it altogether. Nevertheless, in the spring and summer of 1958 the administration gave Chamoun unquestioning support, culminating in the dispatch upon his request of thousands of American marines to Lebanon.

There was, however, a deeper logic to U.S. behavior toward Lebanon. Chamoun had been one of the few Arab leaders to embrace the Eisenhower Doctrine. This fact had acquired a life of its own quite apart from the doctrine's future viability. Right or wrong, Chamoun now symbolized the U.S. commitment to freedom and independence, and it was imperative for the United Sates that he avoid public failure. Quietly phasing out the Eisenhower Doctrine was one thing; permitting the conspicuous defeat or collapse of one of its chief Arab defenders, another thing altogether. In the latter event, the administration believed, U.S. prestige could suffer irreparable damage not only in the Middle East but throughout the world. Thus the United States would have to do what it could to prevent Chamoun's political demise. Even more importantly, it would have to convince international audiences that it was prepared to risk everything—the lives of its men, the friendship of the Arabs, even the peace of the world—for the sake of an embattled ally.

AS WE SAW IN CHAPTER 4, events in the first half of 1957—the Chamoun regime's early embrace of the Eisenhower Doctrine and its suspiciously lopsided victory in the June parliamentary elections—had sharply polarized Lebanese politics. To many Lebanese, especially those partial to the Nasserist-leaning UNF, it seemed that Chamoun and his foreign minister Charles Malik were determined to drag Lebanon into the Western camp against the wishes of much of the Lebanese population.

In the summer and fall of 1957 the Lebanese opposition to Chamoun expanded to include the Third Force, a group of moderately pro-Western Muslim and Christian politicians who either resented Chamoun's efforts to increase his own power at the expense of traditional local leaders or believed that Chamoun's wholehearted alignment with the West was upsetting the country's delicate internal balance. Ideologically, the Third Force and the UNF had little in common, but both groups believed that Chamoun had to go.[1]

There was nothing simple about the dispute between Chamoun and his combined opposition. The opposition was predominantly Muslim, but not exclusively so. A number of prominent Christian leaders, including Maronite patriarch Paul Ma'ushi, were active in its ranks. The Chamounists included a handful of Muslims, most notably Prime Minister Sami al-Sulh. Moreover, while the opposition liked to portray itself as "progressive" and the government as "reactionary," and while some opposition leaders were genuinely committed to political liberalization and economic justice, Chamoun himself could be seen as a progressive modernizer, devoted to improving the performance of the central government and to weakening the hold of conservative rural chieftains.[2] Views on foreign policy were a somewhat more reliable guide to the internal dispute. In general, Chamounists favored openly aligning Lebanon with the West in defiance of Nasser, while anti-Chamounists rejected this course. The latter group, however, was divided between those who opposed Chamoun's foreign policy on its merits and those who supported it in principle but feared that Lebanon could not afford to resist the Nasserist tide so publicly.

In early 1958 Lebanon's internal political situation rapidly deteriorated. The proclamation of the UAR in early February provided a focus for pro-Nasser and anti-Chamoun sentiment in Lebanon, raising fears within the Lebanese government that leftist politicians, supported by Egypt and Syria, might try to overthrow the Chamoun regime and drag Lebanon into the new union. The Egyptian government repeatedly assured U.S. officials that it had no interest in exacerbating tensions in Lebanon or in pressuring that country to join the union, and the available evidence suggests that these assurances were sincere. Reporting to Cairo in early February, Egyptian ambassador to Lebanon 'Abd al-Hamid Ghalib spoke of the necessity of "curbing the recalcitrance of extremists on the Muslim side," whose noisy demands for Lebanon's inclusion in the UAR were merely strengthening Chamoun's hand. The Egyptian Foreign Ministry's Arab Bureau agreed, adding that the Egyptian news media should be urged "not to arouse confessional strife" in Lebanon but, rather, to calm the situation there. Later that month U.S. intelligence received reports that Nasser had "counseled his Moslem supporters in the Lebanon to refrain from provocative action."[3] All these recommendations were in keeping with Egypt's general strategy of avoiding unnecessary controversy with the conservative Arab states during the crucial weeks in which the UAR was being consolidated.

Excitement in Lebanon over the Egyptian-Syrian union ebbed considerably in March, but by now a more serious controversy was engulfing the country. Since the previous year, anti-Chamounists had charged that Chamoun planned to use his newly enlarged majority in the Chamber of Deputies to force through a constitutional amendment allowing him to run for reelection as president. According to the Lebanese constitution, the president could not serve for two consecutive terms. Chamoun's refusal to either confirm or deny the charge convinced many Lebanese that he did indeed plan to amend the constitution—an accurate suspicion, as later events were to show. In January 1958 a handful of Third Force politicians publicly accused Chamoun of seeking reelection. More ominously, in late March a special congress of UNF and Third Force leaders issued a manifesto warning that any attempt by Chamoun to amend the constitution "will justify the people in imposing their will by all means at their disposal."[4]

Ironically, it was the domestic issue of presidential succession, not public excitement over the Egyptian-Syrian union, that internationalized Lebanon's internal divisions in 1958. In February Nasser warned businessman and former CIA operative Miles Copeland that Egypt's pledge to refrain from interfering in Lebanese affairs was subject to one qualification: "If Chamoun should seek re-election Egypt would oppose [him] and would spend money and exert pressure to defeat Chamoun."[5] Chamoun's failure to rule out reelection would prompt Nasser to make good on his threat, further deepening the crisis.

The United States was in a quandary over Chamoun's rumored desire to succeed himself. In cables to Washington in late February and early March, Robert McClintock, the new U.S. ambassador in Beirut, outlined the dilemma. On one hand, an effort to amend the constitution would be strongly opposed not only by most Muslims but also by many Christians, further isolating Chamoun. Such a fate could be avoided if Chamoun simply stepped down at the end of his term and made way for a pro-Western successor. On the other hand, McClintock continued, "we cannot very well dictate to Chamoun in this situation," presumably because such action would demoralize pro-Western elements throughout the region. Indeed, should the president insist on amending the constitution and running again, "we must see that he wins and wins handsomely," since Chamoun's defeat in such a contest would "be interpreted as a disavowal of his foreign policies including open support of [the] US and [the] Eisenhower Doctrine." The State Department accepted this assessment and instructed McClintock to sound out Chamoun on the possibility of finding a pro-Western successor. While agreeing that a Chamoun candidacy, if declared, had to receive U.S. support, the department hoped the situation would not reach that point.[6]

Chamoun, however, refused to take the hint. Discussing possible successors with McClintock on 5 March, Chamoun "went through [the] process of elimination, ticking off one by one potential candidates"—this man was weak, that one corrupt, the other unelectable in the Chamber of Deputies. "Ergo, by this he came to [the] conclusion [that the] only politician who could lead [the] country and evaluate its present foreign policies was himself." McClintock reluctantly concluded that the United States "can come to only one answer: We should support Chamoun." The State Department agreed "that it would be undesirable [to] attempt further to dissuade him" from running again. Administration officials were not happy with this decision, but it seemed preferable to any of the alternatives.[7]

In April hopes surfaced that the Eisenhower administration might be rescued from its predicament. As opposition to a constitutional amendment increased, Chamoun privately acknowledged that there was one figure to whom the presidency might be entrusted after all: Lebanese army chief of staff General Fu'ad Shihab. Shihab, a moderately pro-Western Maronite, was not a bad choice from Washington's standpoint. While critical of Chamoun's extravagant identification with the West, the general was committed to maintaining Lebanon's independence in the face of Nasserist pressures from within and without. He was strongly supported by the army and widely respected in the country at large. Moreover, despite frequent disavowals of political ambition, Shihab seemed willing to consider assuming the presidency if this were the only way to resolve the political crisis. When the British ambassador to Lebanon discussed the presidency with Shihab in mid-April, the general "smiled and said he had never worn a silk hat but might be willing to try." By 23 April the U.S., British, and French ambassadors were agreed that, while Shihab would probably promote Western interests less forcefully than Chamoun, he was—for that very reason—the "candidate most likely to ensure internal and external security" for Lebanon.[8]

By early May, however, the Shihab boomlet had fizzled, and it again appeared that the United States would have to support Chamoun. On 4 May McClintock collaborated with his British and French counterparts on a "joint appreciation" of the political situation in Lebanon. "General Chehab," the ambassadors reported, "is clearly unwilling to accept presidential succession from [the] hands of Chamoun and thereby incur a political debt." Shihab would run only as an independent or opposition candidate. Chamoun, however, would brook neither independence nor opposition and thus was "almost certain to seek amendment of [the] constitution and stand for re-election."[9] The president would make his final decision on or about 7 May. Assuming Chamoun did choose to succeed himself, the ambassadors advised, "we consider we shall have to support Chamoun despite the known risks." McClintock's copy of the appreciation was forwarded to Dulles at a NATO foreign ministers' meeting in Copenhagen. Dulles discussed the matter with British foreign secretary Selwyn Lloyd and French representative Jean Laloy, and all three agreed that Chamoun's reelection bid had to be supported. Dulles informed McClintock of the decision, adding "that if we do back Chamoun we should do so wholeheartedly."[10]

On 7 May Chamoun met with McClintock and, as expected, said that he had definitely decided to seek reelection. His government would shortly introduce the necessary constitutional amendment in the Chamber of Deputies. McClintock pledged that the United States would do what it could to support Chamoun, especially by helping Lebanese security forces quell the domestic disturbances Chamoun's decision was likely to provoke. McClintock told Chamoun "to have his security people get in touch with their opposite numbers in the [U.S.] Embassy" to see about acquiring additional equipment for the Lebanese police and gendarmerie. McClintock also agreed to join his British and French colleagues in urging Shihab "to do his duty in maintaining internal security."[11]

Before Chamoun had a chance to announce his electoral plans, Lebanon erupted in civil war. On 8 May Nasib al-Matni, a Maronite journalist who had been harshly critical of the Chamoun regime, was shot dead by unknown assailants. Blaming al-Matni's murder on the Chamounists, the UNF demanded Chamoun's immediate resignation and joined the Third Force in calling for a general strike throughout the country. On 9–11 May there were violent clashes between demonstrators and security forces in the northern city of Tripoli, where an angry mob also set fire to a U.S. Information Service Library. On 12 May the disturbances spread to Beirut, where antigovernment forces barricaded the streets with burning oil drums and exchanged gunfire with Lebanese soldiers. On 13 May forces loyal to Druze leader Kamal Junblatt attacked the presidential summer palace at Bayt al-Din, some fifteen miles southeast of the capital. (Chamoun was not staying there at the time.) By mid-May autonomous rebel zones had sprung up throughout the country, including in Beirut.[12]

Chamoun put off his plans to introduce a constitutional amendment in the Chamber of Deputies and reverted to his previous practice of refusing to either confirm or deny that he hoped to succeed himself. The opposition remained as suspicious as ever that Chamoun secretly hankered for a second term.[13]

Meanwhile a disagreement arose between Chamoun and General Shihab over how best to deal with the rebellion. Chamoun demanded that Shihab take vigorous measures against the rebels, but Shihab refused, fearing that ordering the Lebanese army to attack the rebels would not only result in unacceptably high civilian casualties but cause the army to split down confessional and political lines—as finally did occur in the Lebanese civil war of 1975–76. Shihab also felt that, unless Chamoun publicly renounced a second term, any campaign to suppress the opposition would be seen as an effort to promote the president's political career rather than to serve the interests of the nation. Such a perception would fatally discredit the army. Thus Shihab confined himself to the more modest goals of defending key government strongholds and enabling Chamoun to serve out his present term, while privately urging a political compromise in the crisis. Throughout the civil war Chamoun received most of his armed support not from the army but from the police, the gendarmerie, and paramilitary groups attached to supportive political parties.[14]

The Lebanese rebels were concentrated in parts of West Beirut, in a central mountainous region of the country known as the Shuf, and in the vicinity of the frontier with Syria. The Lebanese-Syrian border had always been highly porous, and over the previous two years anti-Chamounist forces had received small amounts of arms and equipment from Syria. Shortly after the civil war erupted in May, the U.S. and British governments began receiving reports that such illicit transfers had dramatically increased and were being supplemented by the infiltration of armed UAR nationals.[15] Meanwhile the Lebanese government began publicly alleging that these cross-border activities amounted to massive interference by the UAR in Lebanon's internal affairs. Implicit in the Lebanese charges were two assumptions: that the infiltrations were a major cause of the Lebanese crisis, and that they were part of a deliberate campaign, directed by Nasser himself, to dominate Lebanon. These assumptions were exaggerated but not entirely baseless. While the infiltrations from Syria did not cause the Lebanese crisis, they almost certainly exacerbated and prolonged it. Similarly, while no evidence has come to light that Nasser directly orchestrated the Lebanese rebellion,[16] he clearly tolerated the infiltrations as a deliberate act of policy—and later appeared to bring an end to such activities in response to international pressure. There are also indications that Nasser used the UAR embassy in Beirut to funnel money and arms to the rebels.[17] More conspicuously, the UAR struck out at the Chamoun regime through hostile propaganda, especially the broadcasts of Radio Cairo's "Voice of the Arabs."[18]

On 13 May, in an appeal Eisenhower later described as "hysterical," Chamoun told the U.S., British, and French governments that he was considering the option of requesting military intervention in Lebanon by the three powers, which he hoped would honor such a request within twenty-four hours of its issuing. Meeting that evening to consider Chamoun's appeal, Eisenhower, Dulles, and other U.S. officials agreed that U.S. intervention in Lebanon could well "create a wave of anti-Western feeling in the Arab world" resulting in the overthrow of pro-Western governments, the closing of the Suez Canal, the sabotage of oil pipelines in Syria, and "a new and major oil crisis" for the West. On the other hand, refusing to honor a request for intervention would be even worse, since it would show to the world that the United States was not prepared to come to the defense of its allies, with disastrous implications for the Western position in the Cold War.[19]

Accordingly, the Eisenhower administration told Chamoun that U.S. forces would intervene upon request, but it also placed a series of hurdles in his path to keep him from resorting to such an appeal too readily. First, Lebanon would have to take its case to the UN before turning to the United States. Second, it would have to secure the support at least one other Arab country. Third, Chamoun should "not push his candidacy should this appear seriously to divide the support which should be counted on to preserve the integrity and Western orientation of Lebanon."[20] This last condition contained a significant loophole: as long as Chamoun could claim that his candidacy was *not* seriously dividing pro-Western forces in Lebanon, he could continue to demand U.S. support for his reelection.

One obstacle in Washington's path was the difficulty of justifying U.S. intervention under the Eisenhower Doctrine, "since that would entail a finding that the United Arab Republic had attacked Lebanon and that the United Arab Republic was under the control of international communism"—both highly dubious assertions. Dulles, however, had a partial solution to this problem. He noted that the Middle East Resolution's Mansfield amendment "stated that the preservation of the independence and integrity of the nations of the Middle East was vital to the national interests and world peace." Were the United States to intervene in Lebanon, it could invoke at least that amendment of the resolution (a provision, ironically, that the Eisenhower administration had opposed when first introduced). The remaining justification would be Lebanon's inherent right, recognized by Article 51 of the United Nations Charter, to arrange for collective self-defense against external armed attack, until such time as the UN Security Council took action to deal with the situation.[21]

As the Lebanese crisis deepened, the Eisenhower administration stepped up its consultations with the British government. Since the formation of the Anglo-U.S. "working group" in the fall of 1957, the administration had worked closely with the British to coordinate Middle East policy; the deteriorating situation in Lebanon had been a major topic of discussion. Immediately following Chamoun's 13 May appeal, U.S. and British military officials drew up a preliminary plan, code-named "Blue Bat," for an Anglo-American military intervention in Lebanon with the primary objective of supporting or reestablishing the authority of the Lebanese government. In the first stage of the plan U.S. forces—either marines aboard the Sixth Fleet or an airborne battle group flown in from Europe, or both—would secure Beirut. In the second stage British land forces would occupy other parts of the country.[22]

At the same time, the U.S. and British governments were determined to keep the French, to whom Chamoun had also issued his 13 May appeal, from taking part in any military operation. In truth France had every reason to avoid a military venture in Lebanon. Not only were French military forces tied down in North Africa, but French officials had rather more pressing concerns at the time, as the Fourth Republic was just then undergoing its final collapse.[23] Nevertheless, the consistent French position—held by both the outgoing Pierre Pflimlin government and the Charles de Gaulle regime that replaced it on 1 June—was that France simply had to respond favorably to a Lebanese request for assistance. To do otherwise would be to suffer an unacceptable loss of international prestige.[24]

U.S. and British officials were alarmed by the French attitude. France's continuing presence in Algeria, its close relations with Israel, and its role in the Suez war had made it deeply unpopular in the Arab world, even more so than Britain. French participation in any intervention would make the political costs of the operation, sure to be high in any event, prohibitive. But despite tactful warnings that their intervention in Lebanon would cause serious political difficulties, the French remained adamant about contributing a force, even if only a token one, to any Western operation. The Americans and the British were powerless to prevent the French from taking this position, but they could and did follow Selwyn Lloyd's recommendation to "keep the French completely in the dark about any military preparations we may be making."[25]

On 22 May the Chamoun regime submitted a complaint against UAR interference to the UN Security Council. While such an approach was meant to satisfy the Eisenhower administration's requirement that Lebanon take its case to the UN before requesting U.S. intervention, the two countries were in fact following different strategies. The United States believed that Lebanon should request the establishment of a UN military force to defend Lebanon against UAR attack, and that the request should be made only after Lebanon had already decided to seek Anglo-American intervention. That way the intervention could be justified as an interim measure for Lebanon's protection pending action by the Security Council. Lebanon, however, went to the Security Council well in advance of any decision to appeal for Anglo-American intervention. Apparently the Lebanese hoped that the Security Council would vote on a resolution condemning UAR interference in Lebanon; the Soviets would probably veto such a resolution, but that in itself would justify Lebanon's subsequent appeal for Anglo-American intervention.[26]

The Security Council's response to Lebanon's approach was not quite as useful as the Chamoun regime had hoped. On 11 June the Security Council voted on a Swedish resolution calling for the dispatch to Lebanon of an observation group "to ensure that there is no illegal infiltration of personnel or supply of arms or other material across the Lebanese borders." The measure passed with ten votes in favor and only the Soviet Union abstaining. On 16 June UN secretary-general Dag Hammarskjold announced the establishment of the UN Observer Group in Lebanon (UNOGIL), to be headed by an Ecuadorian former president, an Indian diplomat, and a Norwegian major general whose name, Odd Bull, delighted English-speaking journalists and earned him the nickname "Queer Steer." UNOGIL would have no authority to block any infiltration it detected. Its mission would be simply to observe and report. By late June UNOGIL was operating in Lebanon with the support of nearly a hundred military personnel from eleven countries.[27]

UNOGIL, which remained in Lebanon until December 1958, never found conclusive evidence of significant infiltration of men or arms from the UAR into Lebanon. One should not make too much of this fact, however, since both the situation on the ground and the narrowness of UNOGIL's mandate precluded an adequate investigation of cross-border activity. Most of the Lebanese areas bordering Syria were under the control of the rebels, with whom UNOGIL was obliged to negotiate for permission to inspect suspected infiltration routes; such permission was often denied. Even when UNOGIL was allowed into a rebel area, the timing of the inspection was usually announced in advance, removing the element of surprise. UNOGIL also conducted few inspections at night, when the level of UAR infiltration was believed to be at its highest. (Chamoun complained that the observers "spend their time in social clubs at night.") Similarly, the fact that UNOGIL's mandate covered only current infiltration prevented the group from discussing any infiltration that may have occurred prior to late June 1958. UNOGIL was candid about these limitations in its public reports, but its failure to document significant UAR infiltration seriously damaged the credibility of the Lebanese claims, much to the frustration of U.S. and British officials.[28]

WHILE HISTORIANS HAVE extensively chronicled American, Lebanese, and British actions in the crisis in Lebanon, they have paid less attention to the role of other international actors—in Cairo, in Baghdad, and at UN headquarters in New York. Only by considering this larger cast of characters can one fully appreciate the paralysis of U.S. policy in the face of Lebanon's deepening crisis. Lacking trust in Nasser, U.S. officials gave short shrift to a peace plan he proposed, despite its apparent reasonableness. Fearing the consequences of escalation, however, they also declined to back Iraqi efforts to rescue Chamoun. Not surprisingly, it was a non-American figure, Dag Hammarskjold of the UN, who offered the most promising formula for resolving the Lebanese crisis, though his efforts, too, would be thwarted by events occurring outside Lebanon.

In the second half of May Nasser and moderate elements of the Lebanese opposition proposed a compromise to the political impasse in Lebanon: if Chamoun publicly forswore reelection, appointed General Shihab his prime minister,[29] and granted amnesty to the Lebanese rebels, he would be permitted to serve out his current term. On 20 May Nasser assured Ambassador Hare that should the United States agree to urge this formula on Chamoun, Nasser "would be glad to use his influence with opposition leaders [to] obtain their assent." Hare was encouraged by the proposal and cabled Washington that evening, "I feel that we may have struck [a] lead which can be profitably pursued." From Lebanon, McClintock agreed that Nasser's offer merited serious consideration. Eisenhower himself later wrote in his memoirs that Nasser's terms "were not wholly unreasonable."[30]

Still, Eisenhower and his top advisers refused to endorse the proposed compromise. They were determined to deny Nasser a political success in the region, even one in which they themselves might share. "This would add to Nasser's prestige," Dulles said on 9 June, "and seriously discourage Iraq and the other pro-Western elements in the area." Eisenhower, too, "expressed unwillingness for the United States Government to act as Nasser's lackey in this matter." The Eisenhower administration was also under pressure from the British, who despite Selwyn Lloyd's private acknowledgment that the proposed compromise "would in itself not be unsatisfactory," insisted that Nasser receive no reward for his meddling in Lebanon.[31]

Accordingly, when the State Department conveyed Nasser's formula to Chamoun on 11 June, it assured him that it was doing so out of "loyalty to Lebanon and not because we endorse [the] proposal which is for Lebanon to decide. Neither can we assume any responsibility for Nasser's good faith." Chamoun promptly rejected the formula, not on substantive grounds but because "it would be a most dangerous principle for Lebanon to admit that Nasser should set out terms of settlement for its internal difficulties," and the State Department accepted Chamoun's decision as final. UAR officials were furious. Meeting with Hare on 16 June, Muhammad Haykal charged that the United States had "merely been playing Nasser for [a] sucker in order [to] neutralize him" as it prepared for military intervention in Lebanon.[32]

The Eisenhower administration may have disdained Nasser's diplomatic overtures, but it was equally resistant to Arab calls for escalation. Iraqi and Jordanian leaders were desperate for Chamoun to prevail, convinced that the political security of their own regimes depended on Lebanon's anti-Nasserist orientation and that this, in turn, depended on Chamoun's remaining in power. Iraq's leaders wanted the United States to intervene militarily on Chamoun's behalf or, failing that, to provide air cover and airlift assistance to such an intervention by the Arab Union. Characteristically, the Iraqis also saw the crisis as an opportunity for Hashemite expansion. Perhaps, Iraqi prime minister Nuri al-Sa'id told a British diplomat in mid-May, an intervention in Lebanon might result in the redrawing of that country's borders to ensure a large Christian majority. Should that happen, "Iraq would wish simultaneously to raise the question of the Upper Euphrates valley [in Syria] which . . . is inhabited by people who would prefer to adhere to Iraq and who were denied opportunity of doing so after [the] first world war."[33]

U.S. and British officials saw little merit in an Arab Union intervention, even one cleansed of expansionist motives. They doubted that the Arab Union's military forces were up to the task and feared that merely attempting to intervene would cause the Iraqi government to fall. Moreover, the provision of Anglo-American air cover and airlift assistance entailed many of the same political risks as did direct Anglo-American intervention. Baghdad's appeals were politely ignored.[34]

In mid-June the Iraqis came forth with another proposal. During a visit to Istanbul, Iraqi crown prince 'Abd al-Ilah met with the U.S. consul general to report on his contacts with Syrian exiles in that city. The exiles, 'Abd al-Ilah said, believed that a "diversionary revolutionary movement should be started in northern Syria to take UAR pressure off Lebanon." The crown prince favored the exiles' plan but "could not unilaterally approve such [a] move which would require supplies and other support Iraq could not provide." Only if 'Abd al-Ilah got assurance of U.S. logistical backing would he give the go-ahead to the Syrian exiles.[35]

U.S. officials quickly rejected this idea as well. Allen Dulles doubted that "the individuals mentioned have the potential to do this." Assistant Secretary of State for Near Eastern, South Asian, and African Affairs William M.

Rountree agreed, adding that while even an unsuccessful revolt "might contribute temporarily to easing UAR pressure on the Lebanon," it would "seriously prejudice the possibility of taking action on an appropriate occasion in the future to redress the Syrian situation itself." The State Department sent a discouraging reply to 'Abd al-Ilah, who calmly accepted the verdict.[36]

Washington's inability to resolve the crisis, by either diplomacy or force, was replicated in microcosm within Lebanon itself. In the second half of June, under pressure from Chamoun, Shihab moved somewhat more aggressively against the rebellion, but he either could not or would not deliver a crushing blow. Nor was there much movement on the political front. Back in late May, Prime Minister al-Sulh had publicly stated that the Lebanese government would seek no constitutional amendment permitting the president to succeed himself. Because Chamoun himself had failed to make such a public disavowal, however, the opposition remained convinced that he harbored ambitions for a second term. On 1 July McClintock, too, speculated "that Chamoun could easily persuade himself, given a slight upturn in his military fortunes, that he is the indispensable man who must remain in office to carry out his policies and vindicate his position." To McClintock this was a depressing prospect, but other U.S. officials seemed less dismayed. "Apparently," Allen Dulles reported to the NSC on 3 July, "Chamoun still thought it might be possible for him to pull off another six-year term. Indeed, maybe he could. He was a very courageous individual."[37]

By now, however, the most vigorous diplomatic initiative to date was under way. On 22 June Hammarskjold went to Cairo to discuss the crisis with Nasser. UNOGIL had only just begun its mission, but Hammarskjold had little doubt that arms and men were passing over the Syrian-Lebanese border. Ending that infiltration, Hammarskjold suspected, would place decisive pressure on the Lebanese antagonists to settle their dispute. Deprived of aid from the UAR, the rebels would have to modify their demand that Chamoun resign immediately. Denied the excuse that his country was under external attack, Chamoun would be obliged to renounce, publicly and unmistakably, any notion of succeeding himself in office; failing that, a demonstrable end to UAR interference would at least decrease the likelihood of Western intervention, which itself might compel Chamoun to rethink his intransigent position.[38]

Historians of the Lebanese crisis have largely ignored Hammarskjold's mission, yet its results were impressive.[39] In Cairo Hammarskjold made "a very sharp appeal" to Nasser, warning him that the UAR's actions in Lebanon could contribute to an escalation of the crisis such that "the whole area would become an area of Western-Soviet conflict." Hammarskjold also may have hinted that should the UAR's interference in Lebanon continue, he would declare the UAR an aggressor and recommend economic sanctions against it.[40] According to Hammarskjold, Nasser protested "that all he had done [since late May] was to lift the ban previously placed against Syrian activities"—a striking confession in itself. Still, Nasser promised to mend his ways. On 23 June UAR foreign minister Mahmud Fawzi told Hammarskjold that Nasser had given the Syrians "categorical instructions that as of Tuesday morning, June 24, no further supply of men or material should be made or permitted to be given to the Lebanese rebels." In return Fawzi asked only that Nasser's pledge be kept secret.[41]

Fawzi's assurance was a further admission that Nasser had authorized or tolerated Syrian-based infiltration into Lebanon, but the statement also represented a commitment Nasser was now determined to keep. In the coming days there were indications that Nasser had indeed called for an end to Syrian-based infiltration and that his orders were being obeyed. On 28 June McClintock noted intelligence reports that the "UAR has given [the] instruction to curtail infiltration of men and matériel into Lebanon."[42] On 30 June Dulles told Foreign Minister Malik, "Our intelligence sources indicated that there has been a considerable reduction or termination of infiltrations across the border. . . . The activities of the UN and Hammarskjold have brought about a large cessation of infiltration." At the 3 July NSC meeting Allen Dulles reported that "there were some signs . . . that the rebels were running out of ammunition. Maybe Nasser really has agreed not to send further ammunition to the Lebanese rebels from Syria."[43]

Irene L. Gendzier suggests that the United States intervened in Lebanon in mid-July 1958 partly to prevent a feared rebel victory. This argument fails to take into account that on the eve of the American decision to intervene, Lebanon's presidential crisis seemed on the verge of resolution—apparently a result of Hammarskjold's diplomacy. In his 30 June meeting with Malik, Secretary Dulles said that one consequence of the reported cessation of UAR infiltration had been to reinforce "the proposition that the Lebanese matter should be resolved without the use of troops from the outside." Dulles further urged, both in his talk with Malik and in instructions to McClintock, that Chamoun now work to ensure the election of a pro-Western successor by the Lebanese Chamber of Deputies, which was due to name a new president on 24 July.[44] Chamoun grumbled "that he could not be charged with thinking up a presidential slate while at the same time fighting for his life," but neither could he ignore the writing on the wall. In early July Chamoun for the first time publicly renounced a second consecutive term and reluctantly endorsed Shihab for the presidency. Shihab was now widely regarded as the only Maronite figure who could simultaneously win election in the Chamber of Deputies, command the army's allegiance, and be acceptable to large portions of the opposition. For the moment Shihab was disclaiming any interest in the presidency, but not strenuously. By 12 July both McClintock and the British chargé d'affaires were convinced that Shihab would, in the end, submit to a presidential draft.[45]

HAD THE LEBANESE been left to themselves from this point onward, they probably would have resolved the presidential crisis (if not the deeper political crisis of which it was symptomatic) without the goad of Western military intervention. But of course the Lebanese were not left to themselves. A chain of events elsewhere in the Middle East, starting with an abortive coup in Jordan and leading to a successful one in Iraq, dramatically transformed the political landscape of the region, prompting Chamoun to demand the Western intervention that Eisenhower and Dulles had long sought to avoid.

In late June Jordanian officials uncovered a conspiracy among army officers to assassinate King Hussein and overthrow the government. The dissident officers were motivated by a combination of ideological and professional grievances. Ideologically they opposed Jordan's monarchical system of government and its orientation toward Iraq and the West. They planned to set up a republic that would be severed from the Arab Union and aligned with, if not joined to, the UAR. Professionally the dissident officers, who were non-Bedouin, resented the preference in promotions given to Bedouin officers in recognition of the latter's allegiance to the throne. This custom, too, would be swept away in the planned coup.[46]

Upon learning of the conspiracy, the Jordanian government arrested the known ringleaders and launched an investigation. As a further precaution, Hussein appealed for protection from his Iraqi partners in the Arab Union. In early July the Iraqis arranged for the army's Twentieth Infantry Brigade, stationed at Jalawla' east of Baghdad, to move into Jordan to help secure the Jordanian throne. After a series of delays the brigade was ordered to begin the journey on the evening of 13 July. To reach its destination, the brigade would have to pass through Baghdad.[47]

It is one of the ironies of the failed Jordanian coup, Uriel Dann writes, "that a measure taken for Hussein's preservation became the means of destroying his would-be preservers." For unbeknownst to either the Jordanian or the Iraqi government, a far more extensive conspiracy had long been taking shape within the Iraqi officer corps, and the marching orders to the Twentieth Brigade now gave the Iraqi conspirators a priceless opportunity to strike.[48] Since the early 1950s pockets of organized discontent had been forming within the Iraqi officer corps. By early 1957 they had coalesced into a single clandestine Free Officer movement, loosely based on the Egyptian model, under the leadership of Staff General 'Abd al-Karim Qasim. The Iraqi Free Officer movement developed independently of Nasser, but it strongly supported his general outlook. The Iraqi officers were dismayed by the Hashemite regime's pro-British, pro-American, and anti-Nasserist orientation, which had isolated Iraq from the mainstream of Arab politics. While often differing with one another on timing and tactics, the officers shared the general objectives of overthrowing the existing regime, abolishing the monarchy, establishing a republic, and launching a new foreign policy based on Arab unity and positive neutrality.[49]

By July 1958 the Free Officers believed they had sufficient control over the army to mount a successful coup; all they needed was the opportunity. A military seizure of the government would require the presence in Baghdad of a large number of troops, which under ordinary circumstances would arouse the government's suspicions. The government's order to the Twentieth Brigade to proceed to Jordan by way of Baghdad was thus a godsend to the Free Officers, especially since Staff Colonel 'Abd al-Salam 'Arif, a prominent coup plotter, happened to command one of the brigade's three battalions. The coup was set to begin in the early hours of 14 July.[50]

While the Iraqi government and palace were generally apprehensive about the attitude of the military, they had no inkling of the specific plot. Faisal, 'Abd al-Ilah, and Nuri spent their final days and hours obsessively monitoring the crisis in Lebanon, pugnacious to the end. Meeting with British ambassador to Iraq Michael Wright on 12 July, Faisal and 'Abd al-Ilah lamented Britain's and America's failure to back Chamoun to the hilt. Having given up on Anglo-American action, they now hoped that Turkey would come to Chamoun's rescue. A meeting of the Baghdad Pact's Muslim members was scheduled to take place in Istanbul on 14 July, and Nuri, Faisal, and 'Abd al-Ilah were planning to attend. The Turks "were in a mood both of impatience and resolution," the king and crown prince told the ambassador. "Rather than see the Lebanon fall to the United Arab Republic . . . the Turkish Government would seriously contemplate taking action in Syria."[51]

Meeting with Nuri on 13 July, Wright found the prime minister "deeply disturbed" over Lebanon. "If Chamoun went," Nuri predicted, "no other man would be strong enough for long to keep Lebanon from the influence of the U.A.R." The United States, Nuri said, "had enunciated the Eisenhower Doctrine and now looked like running away from it." The Eisenhower administration's failure to back Chamoun "represented [a] change of policy which was likely to involve serious consequences for all concerned."[52]

Nuri's pessimism was vindicated much sooner and more dramatically than he could have foreseen. Late that night the Twentieth Brigade began moving westward from Jalawla'. Through a combination of force and subterfuge, Colonel 'Arif took control of the brigade within ten kilometers of Baghdad. Reaching the capital at dawn on 14 July, 'Arif split up the brigade and ordered its component battalions to seize the Ministry of Defense, the police station, the royal palace, and Nuri's home. 'Arif led his own forces to occupy the radio station, from which he personally broadcast the news that the monarchy had been overthrown and that Iraq was now a republic. Nuri was awakened by the sound of gunfire and managed to slip away before the officers reached his home; 'Abd al-Ilah ordered the palace guards to surrender without resistance. In the palace courtyard, officers opened fire on the king, the crown prince, and several members of the royal household, killing them instantly. The bodies were hastily buried. The murders of Faisal and 'Abd al-Ilah effectively extinguished the Hashemite dynasty in Iraq. Nuri's escape, on the other hand, frustrated and alarmed the coup plotters, who launched an intensive manhunt for the fugitive premier. Meanwhile, as word of the revolt spread, military units throughout the country threw in their lot with the Free Officers. At noon General Qasim arrived in Baghdad and set up his headquarters in the Ministry of Defense.[53]

In a response that shocked even the Free Officers, within hours of the coup tens of thousands of Baghdadi civilians, mostly young men, took to the streets, venting their fury on the old regime and its perceived supporters. Mobs ransacked the palace and Nuri's house, set fire to the British embassy, and attacked foreign diplomats and businessmen. By afternoon Qasim had imposed a curfew, which limited the popular violence but could not end it entirely. The following day 'Abd al-Ilah's body was exhumed, mutilated, dragged naked through the streets, and strung up outside the Ministry of Defense. Nuri was apprehended in a Baghdad neighborhood while attempting to flee the city disguised as a woman. He was immediately set upon by the mob and then either shot himself or was killed by his assailants. Nuri's body, too, was mutilated and dragged naked through the streets.[54]

Elsewhere in the Arab world the Iraqi coup seemed to have wide popular support, though dismay over the event's brutality may have dampened some of the rejoicing. Lebanese rebels celebrated the news by firing their guns into the air, as rebel-held radio stations recounted the details of the coup and predicted that the Chamoun regime would meet the same fate. Storekeepers on the streets of Benghazi, their radios blaring news reports from Cairo radio in defiance of police bans, served drinks and sweets to passersby. A British diplomat in Kuwait reported that the coup "was greeted with considerable popular enthusiasm, though not with celebration in the streets as had been the formation of the United Arab Republic." U.S. diplomats reported "enthusiasm in Saudi Arabia," celebrations in Arab villages within Israel, and "light expressions [of] sympathy" for the coup in Jordan and the West Bank.[55]

Conservative Arab leaders were deeply shaken by the Iraqi coup and wasted little time in seeking Western assistance. Early on the morning of 14 July King Saud, who had kept a low profile since the Syrian fiasco in March, passed word to the U.S. embassy that he was "terribly upset" over the coup. He demanded that the remaining Baghdad Pact powers intervene militarily to reinstate the Iraqi regime. Otherwise, "what is [the] use [of] all these pacts?" Later that morning Saud lodged a fresh demand with the embassy: "British and American troops should be sent to Jordan at once to save it from going [the] same way [as] Iraq." If the United States and Britain failed to act, the king warned, Saudi Arabia would conclude that "they are finished as powers in the Middle East" and be obliged to "go along with UAR foreign policy." Although Saud was far less powerful now than he had been some months earlier, his remarks attracted considerable attention in Washington.[56]

King Hussein's initial reaction to the coup was less panicked than Saud's, but it pointed toward the same basic remedy: rollback in Iraq and reinforcement in Jordan. Immediately after learning of the coup, Hussein assumed leadership of the Arab Union (as he was authorized to do in the event of Faisal's absence or incapacity) and tried to rally Iraqi military units outside Baghdad to the support of the Arab Union, on the mistaken assumption that the coup was confined to the Iraqi capital. He even arranged for Jordanian troops to begin marching on Baghdad. At the same time, Hussein attended to the preservation of his throne in Jordan. On 14 July he asked both the Americans and the British whether they would be prepared to take military action to "preserve the integrity and independence of Jordan," though he did not call for intervention just yet.[57]

Chamoun, by contrast, was already prepared to cash his blank check. On the morning of the coup Chamoun summoned McClintock and, "in a highly wrought-up mood," charged that the United States had consistently disregarded Chamoun's warnings of the radical nationalist threat. "Now however developments in Baghdad had proved him right and [the] US wrong." Chamoun, McClintock reported, "said he did not wish any more inquiries or specifications or conditions re our intervention. He would interpret our intentions by our deeds. He wanted [the] 6th Fleet here within 48 hours or else he would at last know where he stood re assurances of support from [the] West." Chamoun made a similar appeal to the French ambassador and the British chargé d'affaires, warning the latter that he would "appeal to [the] Soviet Union and to [the] UAR" if the West failed to intervene, a threat McClintock interpreted as "a derisive statement" rather than as a literal declaration of intent.[58] There was no doubting, however, the sincerity of Chamoun's desperation.

WHEN THE EISENHOWER administration received Chamoun's appeal early that same morning, Washington time, it confronted two distinct but related questions: whether to honor Chamoun's request for intervention and whether to seek to reverse the Iraqi coup. The answer to the first question was easy, if distasteful. The administration had already decided that it would have to respond favorably to a Lebanese appeal for intervention or risk losing international credibility. An answer to the second question was harder to provide, and it would be some days before one was forthcoming.

Just before 11 A.M. on 14 July, following a previously scheduled NSC meeting on civil defense, Eisenhower and his top foreign policy advisers convened in the oval office to decide how to respond to Chamoun's appeal. Robert Cutler, the president's special assistant for national security affairs, described the scene in his memoirs: "The faces and attitudes of many of those in the room reflected the crisis unrolling before them. But the President sat sprawled back in the chair behind his desk in a comfortable position, the most relaxed man in the room, listening and asking questions. I had a feeling that the President knew exactly what he meant to do." It was customary at such meetings for Eisenhower to withhold comment until each of the Dulles brothers had given an appraisal of the international scene, Allen providing an intelligence briefing and Foster a political appreciation. On this occasion, however, Eisenhower spoke up immediately after Allen Dulles completed his briefing, saying, "This is our last chance to make a move. We cannot ignore this one." According to Cutler, Secretary Dulles interjected to ask whether the president still wished to hear his political appreciation. "A little embarrassed at appearing to have passed over his closest adviser, he replied: 'Go ahead, Foster . . . please.'"[59]

Dulles reviewed the familiar arguments for and against intervention. Honoring Chamoun's request would inflame the Arab world against the West. Failing to do so would cause America's friends to question the value of U.S. commitments. "On balance," the secretary said, ". . . the losses from doing nothing would be worse than the losses from action." Dulles suspected that most of the Arab world would be lost to the West whether or not the United States acted. In the case of action, however, the United States would at least maintain the confidence of non-Arab Middle Eastern countries like Turkey, Iran, and Pakistan. Dulles also believed that failure to act in Lebanon would damage U.S. credibility with the Soviets. At present, he said, the United States had significant military superiority over the Soviet Union, but over the next few years the gap was likely to close. "If we do not accept the risk [of war with the Soviets] now, they will probably decide that we will never accept risk and will push harder than ever, and border countries will submit to them." The bottom line was that "we should send our troops into Lebanon."[60]

Dulles stressed, however, that his colleagues should have no illusions about the hazards of intervention. "If . . . we do respond to the request, we must expect a very bad reaction through most of the Arab countries—a cutting off of the pipeline, stoppage of transit through the Suez, and hostile activity throughout the area." Vice President Nixon, who two months earlier had nearly been dragged from his car by angry demonstrators in Caracas, Venezuela, added that "the[r]e may be mob violence against American embassies and Americans throughout the whole Middle East. In a way this is our greatest risk."[61]

Eisenhower brushed such concerns aside, saying "that his mind had been made up long ago. We had to act or get out of the Middle East." Of course the latter option was unthinkable: "To lose this area by inaction would be far worse than the loss in China, because of the strategic position and resources of the Middle East." There was no acceptable alternative to intervention.[62]

The documentary record thus strongly supports Douglas Little's conclusion that Eisenhower decided to intervene in Lebanon "for the same reason that Lyndon Johnson would plunge into the Vietnamese quagmire after 1964: credibility. Like LBJ, Ike believed that failure to support such pro-Western leaders as Camille Chamoun . . . would erode the United States's credibility as a guarantor and invite Soviet adventurism in the Third World."[63] As for Gendzier's claim that Eisenhower's intervention was intended, in part, to thwart an imminent rebel victory in Lebanon, none of the internal documents concerning the decision to intervene mentions such a motive.

Early that afternoon Eisenhower and the Dulles brothers met with a bipartisan group of legislative leaders. Secretary Dulles repeated the arguments he had presented in the White House meeting, further noting that the Lebanese had embraced the Eisenhower Doctrine and "feel that for that reason they have undergone extra pressure. They feel we are morally bound to help them." The administration's characterization of the threat was rather less ambiguous in the meeting with the congressmen than it had been in the oval office session. In the White House, Allen Dulles had acknowledged that there was as yet "no information that Nasser spearheaded" the Iraqi coup. To the congressmen he claimed that "the hand of Nasser in these developments is very evident." The fact that Nasser was then away on a trip to Yugoslavia, the CIA director added, was itself no exoneration, since the trip "might possibly have been a ruse to cover the Iraqi plans." Even more alarmist was Secretary Dulles's statement that the Soviet Union "is undoubtedly behind" Nasser's meddling in Lebanon and Iraq. Eisenhower did not go that far, though he insisted "that one crucial question is what the victims believe. Chamoun believes it is Soviet communism that is causing him his trouble."[64]

Eisenhower told the legislative leaders that his administration had yet to make a final decision on Chamoun's request. In reality the drive to intervene had gained so much momentum that the congressmen could have said little to derail it. Their objections were few and mild in any case. Democratic senator J. William Fulbright of Arkansas, apparently accepting the proposition that Nasser was behind the Iraqi coup, questioned only whether "this crisis is Soviet- or Communist-inspired. He said that perhaps Nasser is playing his own game." Eisenhower replied "that whatever Nasser may think he is doing, the Soviets have a tremendous interest in this." Secretary Dulles said that a prior finding of Soviet involvement was unnecessary in any event, since both Article 51 and the Mansfield amendment provided a basis for protecting nations against more general threats to their independence and integrity.[65]

Offering a broader critique were Senator Mike Mansfield of Montana (who rejected the administration's interpretation of his amendment) and House Speaker Sam Rayburn of Texas, both Democrats. They suggested that the Lebanese, Jordanian, and Iraqi crises were essentially internal disturbances, not cases of external aggression. Eisenhower "answered that they have that appearance but we know they are being fomented by Nasser under Kremlin guidance." "If we were to adopt the doctrine that Nasser can whip up a civil war without our intervention," Secretary Dulles added, "our friends will go down to defeat."[66]

The remaining nineteen congressmen in the meeting either supported the administration's position or were noncommittal, strengthening the impression that intervention was unstoppable. As a Republican participant, Senator H. Alexander Smith of New Jersey, wrote in his diary the next day, "At the meeting there seemed to be a footdragging by the Democrats— Sam Rayburn—Mike Mansfield—but a dominance by Dulles and a feeling of not letting down Lebanon."[67]

Immediately after the session with the legislative leaders, Eisenhower, Dulles, and other top officials held another meeting to finalize the manner and timing of the U.S. response to Chamoun's appeal. The group agreed that on the following day, 15 July, at 3:00 P.M. local time (9:00 A.M. Washington time), an advance battalion of some 1,700 marines would land at or near Beirut, to be reinforced over the coming days by two additional marine battalions and two battle groups stationed in West Germany. The decision to intervene in Lebanon would remain secret until "the moment we know our forces are ashore," at which time the White House would release a public statement explaining the action. Meanwhile the United States would call for an emergency meeting of the UN Security Council, where it would justify the intervention as a temporary measure to stabilize the situation until the Security Council could make its own arrangements for protecting Lebanon's independence and territorial integrity.[68]

Contrary to the original Blue Bat plan, British forces would take no part in the Lebanon operation but would be held in reserve for possible action elsewhere in the area. One advantage of this arrangement, Dulles told a British diplomat that evening, was that "it should be easier to persuade the French to hold off" from intervening in Lebanon. Were the Americans and the British to intervene jointly, the French might feel irresistible pressure to take part in the operation, if only to counteract the impression that the United States and Britain had a special understanding from which France was excluded. A unilateral U.S. intervention would make France's failure to act far less conspicuous. Sure enough, upon learning the next day that the British were not moving into Lebanon, the French also decided to refrain from intervening.[69]

Another advantage of unilateral U.S. intervention was that it allowed for a potential "division of labor" that was favorable to Washington. Although the Eisenhower administration believed that intervention in Jordan or Iraq might be desirable, it had little interest in sending U.S. forces into either country, partly because of the logistical difficulties and political risks inherent in a wider intervention, and partly because of the lack of congressional approval for any U.S. action beyond Lebanon.[70] By taking sole responsibility for Lebanon, the administration would be in a better position to ask the British to do likewise in Jordan or Iraq, should intervention in either country become necessary.

British prime minister Harold Macmillan, however, was determined to enlist the United States in any Jordanian or Iraqi operation. Speaking on the telephone with Eisenhower on the evening of 14 July, Macmillan accepted unilateral U.S. intervention in Lebanon but said that such action should be "part of a much larger operation" by both the United States and Britain. Even if the intervention were initially confined to Lebanon, he said, such a move would inflame the entire Arab world against the West, probably resulting in the destruction of oil fields and pipelines. "There is no point in running these risks unless we are going to do the whole thing together." Macmillan did not say exactly what he meant by "the whole thing," but Eisenhower assumed that he was proposing a joint Anglo-American military intervention throughout much of the Fertile Crescent. "I would not want to go further [than Lebanon]," Eisenhower protested. "If we are now planning the initiation of a big operation that could run all the way through Syria and Iraq, we are far beyond anything I have [the] power to do constitutionally."[71]

In two messages cabled to Eisenhower later that evening, Macmillan further clarified his views, though he failed to move the Americans beyond their narrow conception of the U.S. military commitment. Macmillan's first message called for "a determination between us both to protect Jordan with the hope of restoring the situation in Iraq." As the Foreign Office separately informed the British embassy in Washington, Macmillan's objective was to establish a Western force in Jordan that could then "serve the double purpose of stiffening the King's resolve and forming a bridgehead for such possible future action as may be necessary in Iraq." Macmillan's second message, referring to Hussein's hypothetical request earlier that day for Anglo-American intervention in Jordan, proposed that Hussein be urged "to make his request at once." Later that night Samuel Hood, minister of the British Embassy in Washington, showed Dulles the two messages from Macmillan. Dulles rejected Macmillan's suggestion that Hussein be urged to request Anglo-American intervention immediately, telling Hood "that this was a totally new question, not covered by our present military planning." Dulles added that, from a political standpoint, "Hussein has a better chance of pulling through without western military assistance than with it." The secretary promised, however, "to give this matter urgent study."[72]

For the moment U.S. officials were preoccupied with the impending marine landing in Lebanon, whose results they awaited with a mixture of trepidation and fatalism. In his phone conversation with Macmillan on the eve of the landing, Eisenhower admitted that "we are opening Pandora's box. We don't know what's at the bottom of it."[73] The next morning, just as the marines began wading ashore, Eisenhower told Nixon that "we had come to the crossroads. Since 1945 we have been trying to maintain the opportunity to reach vitally needed petroleum supplies peaceably, without hindrance on the part of any one." Now Nasser was trying "to get control of these supplies—to get the income and the power to destroy the Western world. Somewhere along the line we have got to face up to the issue." Success, however, was far from assured, for "we have a campaign of hatred against us, not by the [Arab] governments but by the people. The people are on Nasser's side." Earlier that morning Nixon had discussed the impending intervention with Dulles, saying, "If it works we are heroes and if not we are bums."[74]

If ever Eisenhower and his advisers were in danger of being "bums," it was in the first twenty-four hours of the operation, when U.S. forces only narrowly avoided blundering into hostilities with the Lebanese army. At 1:45 P.M. local time, McClintock informed Shihab of the upcoming landing. The general warned that U.S. intervention might cause the army to "disintegrate on confessional lines." Lebanon was "on the brink of catastrophe," Shihab said. "There is a very thin chance we can avoid going over that brink provided your soldiers stay on board their ships." Impressed by Shihab's appeal, McClintock sent an urgent communication to the operational commander of the U.S. expeditionary force, imploring him to keep the marines from coming ashore for the time being. But McClintock's message failed to reach the commander in time to prevent the scheduled landing. At 3:00 P.M. the Second Marine battalion began to disembark on the beach at Khaldi, a few miles south of Beirut, and quickly secured the nearby airport. Supporting the marines were the seventy-odd ships of the U.S. Sixth Fleet, now converging on the Lebanese coast. Aircraft from nearby carriers ferried supplies into the Beirut airport and patrolled the skies over Lebanon.[75]

As the marines went ashore, Eisenhower released a public statement announcing the operation and describing it as a measure "to protect American lives and . . . to encourage the Lebanese Government in the defense of Lebanese sovereignty and integrity." Without mentioning either provision by name, the president indicated that Article 51 and the Mansfield amendment were the legal grounds for his action.[76]

Though the amphibious landing itself was entirely unopposed—gawkers and vendors, not hostile gunmen, greeted the marines—it did not take long for the Lebanese army to show its displeasure. Many Lebanese officers were deeply affronted by the U.S. intervention, about which they had received

The first U.S. marines to arrive in Lebanon wade ashore at Khaldi, near Beirut, 15 July 1958. (© Bettmann/CORBIS)

virtually no advance notice, and some of them were determined to prevent the marines from moving beyond their initial beachhead at Khaldi. On the morning of 16 July a marine detachment attempted to move north into Beirut proper to secure the port area, the U.S. embassy, the ambassador's residence, and other American institutions. A Lebanese army force blocked the highway to the capital with tanks and artillery and refused to let the marines pass. The marine commander, citing firm orders, was equally insistent on entering Beirut. A tense standoff ensued, with the Lebanese forces training their guns on the halted marine column. McClintock and Shihab (who disclaimed responsibility for the Lebanese soldiers' actions) rushed to the scene to resolve the crisis. Eventually a compromise was reached whereby a smaller U.S. force, broken into platoons, was permitted to enter the capital escorted by Lebanese soldiers. The deal came none too soon. As McClintock confided to a British diplomat that evening, the Americans "had just reached the point of deciding to shoot their way to the port when agreement had been finally reached."[77]

The Eisenhower administration's good fortune was not confined to Lebanon. Elsewhere in the region the U.S. response to Chamoun's appeal provoked harsh denunciations and menacing gestures but little in the way of tangible opposition. Nasser, who was in Yugoslavia when the marines landed, released a statement charging that the U.S. intervention "endangers world peace and is a direct threat to the Arab countries" and warning that the UAR would forcibly resist any outside attack on the new Iraqi regime. The Syrian sector of the UAR went on high alert, canceling army leaves and busing armed civilians to the border with Lebanon.[78] But the Suez Canal remained open, oil continued to flow through the pipelines in Syria, and oil installations elsewhere in the area were undisturbed. The remaining pro-Western Arab regimes were not, as Dulles had dreaded, swept away in an irresistible tide of popular anger.

The Soviet reaction was also mainly symbolic. On 15 July, when the United States informed the UN Security Council of its intention to withdraw from Lebanon once a UN force had been established in that country, the Soviet UN delegate blasted the intervention in Lebanon as "an act of aggression against the people of the Arab world" and called for an immediate and unconditional U.S. withdrawal. In a statement released the next day, the Soviet government warned the United States against moving beyond Lebanon, noting that "the Soviet Government cannot remain indifferent to events creating a grave menace in an area adjacent to its frontiers, and reserves the right to take the necessary measures dictated by the interests of peace and security." The Soviets did not, however, threaten any specific retaliation as they had done during the Suez war and the Syrian crisis. On 17 July Moscow ostentatiously announced that Soviet military maneuvers would be held near the Turkish and Iranian borders, but these maneuvers were an annual event planned long in advance, and knowledgeable observers were not alarmed. The closest thing to actual Soviet hostilities came at the hands of Moscow demonstrators who, for an hour on 18 July, pelted the U.S. embassy with rocks, bricks, and bottles as local policemen stood by.[79]

The UAR pressed the Soviet Union to adopt a stronger stance in the crisis, but with no success. On 17 July Nasser, Foreign Minister Fawzi, and Haykal flew from Yugoslavia to the Soviet Union to meet with the Soviet leadership. According to Haykal, Nasser urged Soviet leader Nikita Khrushchev to issue a statement warning that the Soviet Union would defend Iraq or Syria if either were subject to Western intervention. Khrushchev warned that such a threat might lead to superpower conflict. "There is no politician in the world," he said, "who can have it on his conscience that he exposed his people to the horrors of a nuclear war. . . . The confrontation is political, not military, and it need not become military."[80]

Fortunately the Eisenhower administration was also interested in keeping the crisis contained within narrow bounds. In taking this cautious approach, however, it got little help from the British. On 15 July, as U.S. forces were establishing themselves in Lebanon, Hood again pressed Dulles to consider an Anglo-American intervention in Jordan, with the understanding that such an operation might continue into Iraq. Dulles again rebuffed Hood, protesting that the British plans were too vague. In a phone conversation with Eisenhower early that evening, Dulles said that the British were "asking for a blank check, which of course the President cannot give and will not give." Eisenhower grumbled that the British "can't get it through their heads" that under the American political system the president must seek congressional authority to modify or expand an existing military commitment. Nevertheless, Eisenhower accepted Dulles's suggestion that Foreign Secretary Lloyd, who had expressed a desire to come immediately to Washington to discuss Jordan and Iraq, be invited to do so.[81]

On 16 July Hussein's hypothetical request for outside intervention became actual. Sometime that day, perhaps in an effort to force the king's hand, the British embassy in Amman passed intelligence information to Hussein indicating that a UAR-supported uprising was scheduled to take place in Jordan no later than 17 July.[82] Hussein summoned the British and U.S. ambassadors and requested Anglo-American intervention to "guarantee Jordan's independence [and] integrity." Hussein's appeal for foreign intervention, Uriel Dann writes, "may have been the most humiliating decision of his public career."[83]

The British immediately agreed to honor the request, and in a long-distance call to Dulles on the evening of 16 July, Macmillan strongly urged that the United States do the same. Dulles begged off on the grounds that the Eisenhower administration had "told Congress [that] nothing beyond what was explained to them . . . would be done and we can't alter it without consultation." Macmillan then proposed that the United States contribute "an airplane or two to show we were together." Dulles agreed that "we could supply at least some air logistics" to the Jordanian operation.[84]

At noon on 17 July, Britain's Sixteenth Parachute Brigade began arriving in Amman from bases in Cyprus; troop strength eventually reached 3,700. The United States, as planned, took no active part in the operation, confining itself to logistical and rhetorical support. Jordanian prime minister Samir al-Rifa'i was distressed by the U.S. failure to intervene directly; on 18

July he told the American chargé d'affaires that U.S. troops were needed to offset "the psychological effect of having only British troops in Jordan." The Eisenhower administration remained adamant about keeping its forces out of Jordan, however, and the Jordanian regime was obliged to accept, as a cost of survival, the public disgrace of being protected by British guns alone.[85]

Yet even furnishing those guns proved a difficult and, at times, hazardous undertaking. To get the men and supplies into Jordan, British transport planes departing from Cyprus had to fly through Israeli airspace. Although Israeli prime minister David Ben-Gurion initially granted permission for British overflights, he rescinded that privilege a few days into the operation, as part of a larger effort to pressure Britain and the United States to provide Israel with a formal security guarantee. Ben-Gurion's action temporarily severed Britain's supply chain, stranding its troops in Jordan with only twelve days' worth of provisions. The British began cobbling together an alternative supply system involving maritime transport to the Jordanian port of Aqaba, initially from Cyprus via the Suez Canal and later from British-held Aden. Meanwhile, in late July, Dulles got Israeli authorization for U.S. transport planes to fly over Israel with supplies for the British forces in Jordan. These measures, along with some unauthorized British flights over Israeli territory, sufficed to keep the troops in Jordan supplied, but the incident underscored the political and logistical precariousness of Britain's Jordanian venture.[86]

Indeed, no sooner had Britain gotten its forces into Jordan than one of the main goals of the operation—rollback in Iraq—began receding from consideration. On 17 July, meeting in Washington with Dulles and other U.S. officials, Lloyd acknowledged "that if the new Government of Iraq obtains effective control of the country it would be out of the question to consider reconquering the country from the military standpoint." Since at the same meeting "it was formally agreed that there were few possibilities or figures around whom resistance in Iraq might be rallied," the logical inference was that retrieving the Iraqi situation should not be attempted.[87]

In a further irony, it took the prospect of intervention in Iraq by another Western ally—in this case Turkey—to force the Americans and the British to abandon for good any lingering hope for rollback in Iraq. This episode, traceable mainly through British documents, has escaped the notice of previous historians of the Lebanese crisis.[88] On 18 July Lloyd cabled Macmillan from Washington that "the Turks have informed the United States that they want to invade Iraq. They have asked for United States air cover." Lloyd reported that he and Dulles had discussed the matter that morning, and both had concluded "that this Turkish action would be folly. It would unite Iraq in support of the new regime. It would give the Soviet the opportunity to send in troops into Iraq in response to an invitation from the Iraqi republic. The [U.S.] military expressed doubts about Turkish capacity to the do the job speedily. On the biggest issue of all, this Turkish action might lead to a Russian invasion of Turkey and so to world war."[89]

Macmillan reacted even more strongly against the proposed Turkish action. "An attack by Turkey on Iraq," he cabled Lloyd that same day, "would be worse than folly; it would be criminal folly. . . . Apart from the dangers of real war which might be involved in a Turkish movement, there is the almost certainty of the loss of our oil supplies and all that that involves." Also contributing to Macmillan's reaction were the first glimmerings of a pragmatic assessment of the new Iraqi regime and its future relations with the West. "We must not allow our horror and resentment at the murder of our friends to stand in the way of the long-term interests of the world." While he deplored the violence of the revolution, Macmillan thought it possible "that the new Iraqi Government may be detached from Nasser and drawn gradually into our own circle, even perhaps after a period of neutralism and indecision. It would be madness to force them now into the other camp. . . . We must not allow the Turks to go berserk."[90]

Dulles and Lloyd agreed that the Turks should be immediately discouraged from moving into Iraq, a decision Eisenhower endorsed, apparently with some vigor. The president "was utterly magnificent," Eisenhower's personal secretary told a White House speechwriter that day. "He'll fuss all day about what dinner jacket to wear—really fuss—but on Iraq is as certain as can be."[91]

On 19 July the U.S. ambassador in Ankara was instructed to tell the Turkish government that the United States had grave doubts about the feasibility of the Turkish plan, both from the military standpoint (given the difficult terrain on the Turkish-Iraqi frontier) and from the political standpoint (given the likelihood that the Iraqi population would support the Iraqi regime in the event of outside attack).[92] Under no circumstances, however, was the ambassador to let on to the Turks that fear of Soviet retaliation played any part in the U.S. attitude. As Lloyd, who was privy to these instructions, explained to Macmillan that day, "Anything of this kind said to the Turks would, owing to Turkish insecurity [i.e., inability to keep secrets], certainly leak back to the Russians." On 22 July the U.S. ambassador spoke as instructed to Turkish prime minister Adnan Menderes, who assured him that all the talk of Turkish intervention "was more in [the] nature of consultation re [the] idea rather than [an] actual proposal." The ambassador reported that "so far as [Menderes] is concerned we do not have to worry over possible military action in Iraq at this time."[93]

The ominous rumblings out of Ankara had a farcical echo in Amman. Despite the fact that foreign intervention had been necessary to sustain his government at home, Hussein was still talking of marching on Baghdad to avenge his cousins' murders. On 19 July Jordanian officials, in the name of the Arab Union, delivered notes to the U.S. chargé d'affaires and the British ambassador requesting "military, economic, and political assistance to enable the Government of the Arab Union to crush this insurrection and restore affairs to their normal lawful form in the Iraqi sector."[94] In Washington later that day, Dulles and Lloyd discussed the Jordanian request and "agreed that the same objections to any action by Jordan applied as in the case of the Turks and that King Hussein must be firmly discouraged" from moving into Iraq. U.S. and British diplomats were instructed accordingly. Al-Rifa'i took the news in stride, confiding to the British ambassador "that the Note had been sent for the record," as a consolation to Iraqi members of the Arab Union parliament who were now stranded in Amman.[95] It is unclear whether Hussein himself shared al-Rifa'i's cynicism or genuinely intended to wreak vengeance in Baghdad. Given the king's curious mixture of pragmatism and impetuousness, either alternative is conceivable.

There was one other place where foreigners might have intervened but did not: Kuwait. Since the spring the popularity within Kuwait of the Egyptian-Syrian union had caused Britain to worry about the political stability of the protectorate and the continuing availability to the West of its considerable oil reserves. In June a British Foreign Office analyst speculated that Kuwaiti ruler Shaykh 'Abd Allah ibn Salim Al Sabah "might feel, in some future crisis, that the threat of Nasserism or the pull of Arab solidarity was so strong that he must place restrictions on our free access to Kuwait oil." Thus Britain might have "to intervene without the Ruler's consent."[96]

With the Baghdad coup in mid-July, the day of reckoning seemed at hand. Meeting with Dulles in Washington on 17 July, Lloyd said that the rapid success of the coup had shocked the British government, which "had never imagined that all three of the principal figures in Iraqi political life would be killed at the same time. It was even more necessary now to consider what was to be done to prevent a similar occurrence in Kuwait." Even if the ruler escaped outright removal, he might well be obliged to abdicate in favor of pro-UAR family members. Dulles agreed that it would be naive to expect that "Nasser would be content with taking over Iraq without also taking over Kuwait." Rather than passively awaiting such a takeover, it might "be more tolerable to move now before the sympathizers with the UAR have consolidated their position." Dulles and Lloyd agreed to set up another Anglo-American "working group" to study the feasibility of a British intervention in Kuwait (with or without the ruler's consent), to be supported by the landing in eastern Saudi Arabia of a U.S. marine battalion from the Far Eastern Seventh Fleet.[97]

On this matter, too, caution prevailed. On 23 July Rountree advised Dulles that British and U.S. landings in Kuwait and Saudi Arabia, respectively, "might insure temporary short-term control of the oil fields. Unless such action were requested by the Governments concerned, however, it would be likely to provoke the most adverse political reactions not only on the part of the local populations but also from the ruling families concerned. Strikes and sabotage might well threaten petroleum production which currently is proceeding normally." At Rountree's suggestion, Dulles "strongly counsel[ed] the U.K. against military occupation of Kuwait unless either (i) the ruling family were to give its prior agreement; or (ii) an emergency situation had already been created by an Iraq-type coup in Kuwait town or by a serious deterioration of public security." By now the British themselves had concluded that any disturbance in Kuwait could be handled by British forces currently stationed in Bahrain; a preemptive landing in Kuwait itself was unnecessary. By early August the ruler's domestic position seemed sufficiently stable to warrant an indefinite suspension of British plans for intervention.[98]

THUS THE EISENHOWER administration succeeded, with the help of Nasser, the Soviets, and eventually the British, in preventing the Lebanese and Iraqi crises from igniting a regional conflagration. Even so, the administration now faced a daunting and delicate task. By late July there were some 8,500 American troops in Lebanon, stationed in the vicinity of the airport and at key points in the capital. Through a combination of skill, patience, luck, and overwhelming strength, U.S. forces had established themselves in the country without firing a shot in anger, but there was no guarantee that things would continue to go so smoothly. The longer U.S. forces remained in Lebanon, the greater was the likelihood of their being drawn into hostilities with Lebanese rebels or army units, a disastrous outcome from every standpoint. Thus for the remainder of the summer of 1958, the administration's principal objective in Lebanon would be to find a political basis for withdrawing the troops consistent with its commitment to the Lebanese government and with the imperative of denying Nasser a further victory in the region.

The Eisenhower administration would also seek extrication of a different sort—from the web of assumptions and commitments formalized in the Eisenhower Doctrine. Once again the doctrine had been singularly unhelpful in a major Middle Eastern crisis. With the exception of the Mansfield amendment, for which the administration itself deserved no credit, nothing in the Middle East Resolution provided a legal basis for intervention, since the Lebanese crisis clearly was not a case of "armed aggression" by a country "controlled by international communism." To justify its actions, the United States had relied mainly on Article 51 of the UN Charter.

In a larger sense, of course, the intervention in Lebanon had everything to do with the Eisenhower Doctrine, though this fact, too, suggested the policy's failings. Chamoun's embrace of the doctrine in early 1957 had alienated much of the Lebanese population, contributing to the escalation of Lebanon's political crisis over the next year and a half. At the same time, Chamoun's willingness "to stand up and be counted" on the side of the United States in the Cold War—a rarity among Arab leaders—earned the gratitude of U.S. officials and convinced them that Chamoun's example had to be publicly vindicated. Consequently the Eisenhower administration was extremely reluctant to discourage Chamoun from taking whatever action he saw fit to improve his domestic position. Chamoun exploited the American backing to the fullest, exacerbating the local crisis and increasing the likelihood that he would eventually have to call on U.S. protection. Though the administration grew less enamored of Chamoun as the crisis wore on, it could not, in the end, fail to honor a pledge given to one of the few Arab leaders who had endorsed the Eisenhower Doctrine. Thus the doctrine bore considerable responsibility for aggravating the Lebanese crisis to the point where U.S. intervention seemed necessary, even as it failed to provide sufficient legal justification for that intervention—let alone to offer a formula for actually resolving the crisis. It was, to borrow an expression from a later generation, part of the problem, not part of the solution.

As early as March 1958 the administration had begun to question the Eisenhower Doctrine's anti-Nasserist assumptions. The ensuing Lebanese crisis interrupted that process, even as it supplied further grounds for questioning the policy. With the fading of the Lebanese crisis in the summer and fall of 1958, internal criticism of the Eisenhower Doctrine would resume with a vengeance, clearing the way for the policy's final demise.

DEATH OF A DOCTRINE,
JULY 1958–DECEMBER 1960

There is a curious symmetry between the events of 1956 and those of 1958. In the spring of 1956 the Eisenhower administration had become fed up with Nasser and had resolved to weaken and isolate him in the Arab world. The administration's subsequent opposition to the British, French, and Israeli attack on Egypt obscured and interrupted that policy but did not end it. To the contrary, the regional prestige the United States seemed to have won by defending Egypt's sovereignty emboldened the administration to take an even harder line against Nasser than it might otherwise have thought prudent. The Eisenhower Doctrine was largely an expression of this newfound confidence.

U.S. behavior in 1958 followed a similar pattern, but in reverse. In the spring of that year the administration concluded that its get-tough policy on Nasser had failed. As in 1956, however, the implications of this decision were subsequently obscured, this time by the U.S. intervention in Lebanon in July. Yet U.S. intervention—like U.S. *opposition* to intervention two years earlier—could not long divert the administration from its previously chosen course. Indeed, the anomaly again strengthened the rule: having made the supreme gesture on behalf of an anti-Nasserist ally, the administration now felt much freer to call off its confrontation with Nasser. In late 1958 the administration formally abandoned its policy of seeking to isolate Nasser by building up conservative Arab rivals.

It was not a satisfying decision. The Lebanon crisis, while demonstrating the futility and danger of confronting Nasser openly, had also deepened American resentment against the Egyptian leader. Thus by the fall of 1958 the administration was left with an essentially negative—not to say paralyzed—Middle East policy: opposed to Nasser, and opposed to opposing him. The events of late 1958 and early 1959, however, partly resolved the administration's dilemma, as a sudden deterioration in relations between the UAR and the Soviet Union caused U.S. officials to revise their view of Nasser and to suppose that Nasserism might be a barrier to, rather than an avenue of, further Soviet penetration of the Middle East. The result of this surprising turn of events was a modest UAR-American rapprochement that lasted for the remainder of Eisenhower's presidency and into the term of his successor.

ON 16 JULY 1958 Deputy Undersecretary of State Robert D. Murphy flew to Beirut on a special mission for the president. Ambassador Robert A. McClintock's attempt the previous day to delay the marine landing at Khaldi had perturbed some Eisenhower administration officials, and Murphy's mission was apparently designed to prevent any further acts of ambassadorial independence. As Dulles delicately put it in a long-distance phone call to McClintock, Murphy would "be helpful to get things straightened out and give M[cClintock] the fill-in of our thinking." The joke in the Beirut business community was that "Mr Murphy has been sent out to prevent a coup d'état in the American Embassy." Murphy's mode of transportation to Beirut—a brand-new Air Force Boeing 707 making the first nonstop flight in history between the United States and Lebanon—suggests the eagerness with which the administration sought to gain direct control at the scene.[1]

The dispatching at critical moments of special U.S. envoys to the Middle East—or "Great White Fathers," as former CIA agent Miles Copeland later called them—was by now standard administration practice. Over the previous two years James P. Richards, Eric Johnston, Robert Anderson, and Loy Henderson had all made high-profile visits to the area; in the spring of 1958 Murphy himself had undertaken a "Good Offices" mission to North Africa to help resolve a Franco-Tunisian dispute related to the Algerian war for independence. The function of these special envoys, who were typically billed as Eisenhower's personal emissaries, was to signal Washington's concern over the crisis at hand and thus expedite diplomacy. Not surprisingly, U.S. ambassadors to the countries in question often resented such intrusions, which tended to diminish their own prestige and discretion.[2]

When he landed in Beirut on 17 July, Murphy found a volatile situation.

By now nearly 7,000 marines had arrived at the Khaldi beachhead and were patrolling its vicinity in tanks and armored vehicles. (The number of marines would soon reach 14,000.) About seventy U.S. warships were at or near Beirut harbor, and a steady traffic of jets and transport planes was landing at Beirut airport. Following the close call of the day before, in which U.S. marines and Lebanese soldiers had almost exchanged gunfire, the forces of both nations were doing their best to get along. Escorted by Lebanese soldiers, the marines had moved north from Khaldi into Beirut proper. Yet the Lebanese rebels remained unmolested in their strongholds, most conspicuously in a Muslim section of central Beirut known as the Basta, and were now calling on their countrymen to "kill the invaders." Only about a third of Lebanon's territory was under government control. Militarily, though, the situation remained calm, as all anxiously awaited the Americans' next move.[3]

Immediately Murphy began meeting with Lebanese leaders to gauge their reactions to the U.S. intervention. Even among conservatives, he found, the range of opinion was wide. 'Adil 'Usayran, the pro-Western speaker of the Lebanese parliament, blasted the marine landing as a violation of Lebanese sovereignty. Prime Minister Sami al-Sulh ridiculed 'Usayran's claim and defended his government's constitutional right to request U.S. intervention. President Chamoun expressed gratitude for the U.S. action but insisted it was not enough; rollback in Iraq would also be necessary. Chamoun added that "so long as Syria was in Nasser's hands, there could be no lasting peace in [the] ME. . . . If anything were to be done against Syria militarily, it should be done with secrecy and speed."[4]

Such talk was far too ambitious for the Eisenhower administration, which was just then reaching the conclusion that any action beyond shoring up Lebanon and Jordan would be futile and dangerous. Not only should the U.S. intervention be confined to Lebanon; the intervention force should assume purely defensive positions, freeing up the Lebanese army to suppress the rebellion on its own.[5]

But even this more modest plan was proving unrealistic. In his 17 July meeting with Chamoun, Murphy was dismayed to learn that General Shihab, chief of staff of the Lebanese army, was defying Chamoun's instructions that he send the army into the Basta to suppress the rebels. "My immediate reaction," Murphy later wrote in his memoirs, "was that Chehab ought to be fired, a competent new commander appointed, and action taken to restore order and the authority of the Government." On 18 July, however, Shihab told Murphy that ordering the army to attack the rebels could well cause it to split down religious and political lines. "After some straight-from-the shoulder conversation with the General and his staff," Murphy wrote, "I became convinced that he honestly believed that if he attempted to clean up the Basta, his wobbly Army would fall apart." "Mr. Murphy, after 24 hours here," a British diplomat cabled London that evening, "is beginning to hold his head in his hands at the intricacies of the Lebanese situation."[6]

On 19 July Murphy cabled Washington with a preliminary assessment of the Lebanese situation. While the marine landing had been a military success, he observed, its "local political result is dubious. . . . The mere presence of our forces in a small coastal portion of the country seems to have brought no fundamental change in the local political climate." Though now bolstered by U.S. forces, Shihab was still balking at "energetic action to clean up the city of Beirut much less the country at large." With prospects dwindling for a military victory against the rebels, Murphy recommended that the United States work for a political solution to the crisis. Earlier that month Lebanese parliamentarians had tentatively agreed to convene on 24 July to select a new president. "We should," Murphy advised, "use whatever influence we can bring to bear . . . to ensure parliament's meeting next Thursday [the 24th] for that purpose." If the rebels could not be defeated on the battlefield, perhaps they could be appeased by the prospect of Chamoun's final departure from the presidency. With the crisis thus resolved, the United States could declare victory and withdraw its forces from the country.[7]

FROM WASHINGTON'S PERSPECTIVE, the situation in Lebanon was but one concern among many. And if the marine landing seemed to have had little effect on Lebanese politics, its positive impact on the regional scene was even harder to detect. To the contrary, the military interventions in Lebanon and Jordan appeared to have deepened the political predicament of the conservative Arab regimes. A 22 July Special National Intelligence Estimate reported that "popular feeling in the Arab world, even in such states as Saudi Arabia and Kuwait, is generally favorable to the Iraqi coup and hostile to US and UK intervention." This sentiment had given enormous impetus to radical forces throughout the area, making the domestic position of conservative governments more precarious than ever:

> The Jordanian regime is in a perilous position with widespread popular opposition. . . . Elements of a UAR-supported revolutionary organization are almost certainly still in existence. The threat of assassination still hangs over King Hussein. . . . We expect widespread

DEATH OF A DOCTRINE

disturbances on the West Bank . . . as well as harassment of British troops and public demonstrations in Amman. . . . The Saudi public . . . generally welcomed the Iraqi coup and can be expected to disapprove [of] US and UK intervention in Lebanon and Jordan. . . . The situation in Kuwait is very shaky as a result of the coup in Iraq, and there is a strong possibility that the revolutionary infection will spread there. . . . Events have increased instability in Libya and the Sudan and their governments fear the possibility of Egyptian-inspired revolts against them.

It seemed likely that the conservative regimes, simply to ensure their survival, would have to take a more accommodating attitude toward Nasserism and radical Arab nationalism.[8]

Saudi Arabia was already showing the way. While King Saud was privately "jubilant over US intervention in Lebanon," he dared not say so in public. Crown Prince Faisal—by now the real power in the land—strongly opposed the intervention, and he was determined to distance his country from the United States. In a decision that shocked King Hussein, Faisal forbade U.S. transport planes from the Persian Gulf to fly over Saudi territory with desperately needed oil supplies for Jordan. According to a report received by the UAR embassy in Jidda, on 19 July Hussein telephoned Saud to plead for a reversal of this decision. "We are kings," Hussein said, "and we must cooperate to preserve our existence." Saud demurred, confessing that "everything now is in Faisal's hands." Seeking to account for Faisal's attitude, U.S. ambassador to Saudi Arabia Donald R. Heath speculated that the crown prince "is determined on reconciliation with Nasser in order to buy temporary relief from radio attacks and, he hopes, defer an Egyptian plot to overthrow the present Saudi regime." As a UAR diplomat concluded on 20 July, shortly after meeting with Faisal, "Saudi Arabia has begun to realize that it must move with the current of liberation prevailing among the people of the Arab nation, or else the current will sweep everything away."[9]

In a 23 July conversation with Eisenhower, Allen Dulles, and other officials, John Foster Dulles used the same metaphor: "We must regard Arab nationalism as a flood which is running strongly. We cannot successfully oppose it, but we can put up sand bags around positions we must protect —the first group being Israel and Lebanon and the second being the oil positions around the Persian Gulf." Meeting with a Norwegian diplomat that same day, Dulles likened Arab nationalism to a "turbulent stream," adding that "the United States did not have the slightest intention of trying to stem it." At most the United States could "erect dikes to contain it. Later on, when the turbulence of the stream has moderated, we would hope to work with it."[10]

To the extent that Arab nationalism was associated with Nasser, however, it was difficult to see how the Eisenhower administration could "work with it." By the summer of 1958 the administration's attitude toward Nasser was more hostile than it had ever been. Dulles had always regarded Nasser with distaste, but since the escalation of the Lebanese crisis in early May, a new theme had crept into the secretary's conversations. Nasser, Dulles claimed, was "an expansionist dictator somewhat of the Hitler type who want[s] to go on from achievement to achievement," be it the nationalization of the Suez Canal, the annexation of Syria, or the latest attempt to subjugate Lebanon. Nasser was "whipp[ing] up Pan-Arabism, much as Hitler had whipped up Pan-Germanism, as a means of promoting an extension of his power." Nasser's aggressive designs "could be seen from his book 'The Philosophy of the Revolution,' just as had been the case with Hitler in 'Mein Kampf.' But these books were not taken seriously at the time they were written." Indeed, the only significant difference between Nasser and Hitler was "that Nasser, fortunately, does not himself control great military power." Even so, "he relies on the same hero myth, and we must try to deflate that myth."[11]

Eisenhower, characteristically, was more open to the possibility of treating with Nasser, but he found it difficult to maintain this stance in the face of Dulles's opposition. Following the Jordanian and Syrian crises, as we have seen, Eisenhower had gently (and unsuccessfully) prodded Dulles to consider rapprochement with Nasser. With U.S. marines now safely ashore in Lebanon, the president tried again. On 23 July he forwarded to Dulles two memoranda, one from a newspaper editor and the other from a university professor, that had found their way to the oval office.[12] Both memoranda argued that Arab nationalism was too powerful to be successfully opposed and that the United States should seek an accommodation with that movement; the editor's memo called for an effort to woo Nasser back to the American fold, saying, "We must shake Nasser loose from his convictions that his only friends are the Soviets." Eisenhower was impressed by the two papers and sought Dulles's comments on them.[13]

Two days later Dulles replied that the memoranda "contain interesting ideas, although nothing to which we have not already given much thought." On the matter of befriending Nasser, Dulles noted that "Nasser counts as his 'friends' those who help him to achieve his ambitions. These ambitions include at least a truncation of Israel and the overthrow of present governments in Lebanon, Jordan, Morocco, Tunis, Libya, the Sudan, Saudi

Arabia, etc., and replacement by his stooges. . . . We cannot honorably help him in these respects." The United States, Dulles continued, was "wholly sympathetic with Arab nationalism if it means a constructive and productive unity of the Arab peoples. Unfortunately, Nasser's brand of Arab nationalism does not seem to be leading to that." Instead of working for the welfare of his people, Nasser "tends to require an unending series of political successes."[14]

Soon Eisenhower himself was echoing these sentiments. In a 28 July reply to pastor of the National Presbyterian Church Edward L. R. Elson, who had also called for a U.S. accommodation with Arab nationalism, the president wrote, "You did not mention . . . one very complicating factor. I refer to the obviously unbridled ambition of Nasser, an ambition that seems to compel him to seek one political success after another. One of those announced ambitions is to destroy or dismember Israel. He is not a builder nor is his dedication to the best interest of the Arabs. As I see him, he wants only public acclaim at any cost, even though the cost must be paid by the people he pretends to serve."[15]

One possible response to the situation was proposed by Treasury Secretary Robert Anderson at the 31 July NSC meeting: "to dissociate Nasser from Arab nationalism." The problem, however, was that Nasser's popularity among the Arab masses seemed to have increased dramatically. Days earlier William Rountree, the assistant secretary of state for Near Eastern affairs, warned of "a strong wave of emotional 'Nasser' imperialism sweeping through the area," and Eisenhower himself expressed dismay at "Nasser's capture of Arab loyalty and enthusiasm throughout the region."[16] It was a perplexing conundrum for Eisenhower and Dulles. A nationalist movement they could not safely oppose seemed inseparable from a leader they could not "honorably help."

If one took a longer view, however, the picture was not entirely bleak. Dulles suspected that Nasser's hold on the Arab people would loosen over time. True, Nasser "had caught the imagination of the masses and was riding the momentum of success. . . . However, Nasser was not building anything permanent or lasting," and after the current excitement had subsided, "we would not find that Nasser had left a serious threat to us." Such confidence was evident in the very metaphors Dulles used to describe the current predicament. Arab nationalism might be a raging flood, but "once the torrent has run its course things will settle down much as before." Nasser might be an Arab Hitler, but what this really meant was that Nasser "went from conquest to conquest without consolidating his gains" and thus "could not be a lasting phenomenon." Allen Dulles, too, thought that "the Nasser type of Arab nationalism might not be a permanent part of the life of the Near East. Throughout history local forces in the Arab states had been very strong," and they might well reassert themselves once it was politically safe to do so.[17]

Arab oil was a case in point. At the 31 July NSC meeting Secretary Dulles reported that "all is not well between Iraq and Egypt. Egypt wants some of the oil revenues of Iraq. The Iraqis do not want to abandon their development plan financed by oil revenues in order to split these revenues with Nasser." The emerging dispute had given the British "some slight hope of leading the Iraqi government toward a moderate position." "Many Arab countries give lipservice to close relations with Nasser," Allen Dulles said, "but when it comes to dividing oil revenues . . . it is a different story."[18]

From such observations it followed that a policy of watchful waiting was the most sensible U.S. approach. Rather than launching any bold initiatives, the Eisenhower administration should lower its profile in the Arab world, try to secure its remaining assets in the area, and allow the Nasserist tide to run its course. Perhaps after the tide had begun to ebb and localist tendencies to reemerge, it might be possible to cultivate a more "constructive" nationalist leadership prepared to cooperate with the West. But for the moment, Allen Dulles advised, "we should try to buy time, in which we could see if we could find a way out of our present situation."[19] No one, as of late July, seemed to have any better ideas.

In the meantime the administration still had to deal with the practical consequences of the Iraqi coup and of the military interventions in Lebanon and Jordan, and these matters could hardly be addressed through inertia. Nevertheless, for all the vigor with which the administration approached these diplomatic tasks, its underlying objectives were essentially negative: reducing the level of chaos in Lebanon, Jordan, and Iraq; keeping the U.S. military commitment in the region to a minimum; avoiding unnecessary conflict with radical nationalists; and preventing the Soviet Union from politically exploiting the crisis.

ON 19 JULY, as noted, Robert Murphy had recommended that the United States abandon hope of a military victory against the Lebanese rebels and work instead for a political settlement. After securing the administration's consent to this approach, Murphy began consulting with Lebanese politicians to ensure that the special meeting of parliament, now rescheduled for 31 July, resulted in the selection of a pro-Western successor to Chamoun. Although Shihab was the obvious choice, his candidacy almost collapsed on 29 July, when Prime Minister al-Sulh narrowly escaped being blown to bits by a car bomb. Al-Sulh and many Chamounist deputies were furious at Shihab, whose passivity, they charged, had invited the assassination attempt. They vowed to block the general's election in parliament. Chamoun, however, wanted an end to the impasse, and he threatened to resign if the loyalist deputies failed to vote for Shihab. On 31 July the parliament convened and elected Shihab president, with the understanding that Chamoun would serve the remaining two months of his term.[20]

Shihab's election brought a significant relaxation of tensions in Lebanon. Within days rebel leaders were ordering their followers to stand down and pledging their loyalty to the president-elect. On 7 August Lebanese security forces began confiscating weapons carried by civilians in Beirut, and Shihab could tell McClintock that "there was a general trend toward a return to peaceful conditions."[21] Whether that trend would continue, permitting an orderly transfer of presidential power and a dignified withdrawal of U.S. forces, remained to be seen. But things were looking up in Lebanon.

Jordan was a different story. Britain's military occupation of the country, while securing the Jordanian throne against any immediate threat of overthrow, was deeply embarrassing to King Hussein. In the days following the British troop landing, Hussein and his prime minister, Samir al-Rifa'i, repeatedly begged the United States to take part in the operation, believing this would help remove the imperialist stigma created by Britain's unilateral intervention. The British themselves were uncomfortable with the situation and made similar appeals for U.S. participation. The Eisenhower administration declined, arguing that U.S. intervention in Jordan had not been cleared with Congress. Another reason to remain on the sidelines (not disclosed to the Jordanian government) was the administration's deep pessimism over Hussein's ability to retain his throne and even over Jordan's ability to survive as a nation. Jordan, Dulles said in late July, "was not a viable state, it lived on subsidies, and it had some 500,000 Palestinian refugees" who felt little allegiance to Hussein. Since the demise of the Hashemite monarchy seemed inevitable in any case, Dulles saw little point in staking American prestige on its survival. The administration continued, therefore, to confine its involvement in Jordan to the provision of logistical support to the British occupation forces.[22]

But doing too little for Hussein carried risks of its own. If, following the withdrawal of British troops, Hussein were overthrown by pro-Nasser Jordanians and Palestinians, the Israelis, citing Nasserist encirclement, might seize the West Bank.[23] At best such a scenario would further inflame Arab opinion against the West. At worst it could spark an Arab-Israeli war into which the superpowers might be drawn. It was essential, then, that Jordan be stabilized; the only question was how. One approach, proposed by Hussein and al-Rifaʿi on 25 July, was laughably ambitious. It involved U.S. funding for the creation of two additional Jordanian army brigades, the signing of a U.S.-Jordanian mutual defense treaty, and the establishment of a new regional defense organization consisting of Jordan, Lebanon, Saudi Arabia, Turkey, Iran, Pakistan, Sudan, Tunisia, Morocco, Libya, Italy, Greece, France, Britain, West Germany, and the United States. It would be hard to imagine a set of proposals less in tune with American priorities at the time. As Undersecretary of State Christian A. Herter privately noted on 26 July, "We would be happy if some way could be found for us to disengage ourselves from our responsibilities in Jordan with minimum political disadvantage." U.S. officials were at a loss, however, as to how this might be done.[24]

In Iraq the Eisenhower administration was showing similar reluctance to confront radical nationalists. The very act of dissuading Turkey from launching an attack on Iraq (see Chapter 7) had prompted U.S. and British officials to think pragmatically about the prospects for cooperation with the new Iraqi regime. Criticizing the proposed Turkish operation on 18 July, British prime minister Harold Macmillan acknowledged that the violence of the Iraqi revolution had been deplorable, yet he still thought it possible "that the new Iraqi government may be detached from Nasser and drawn gradually into our own circle, even perhaps after a period of neutralism and indecision." News out of Baghdad soon gave some credence to Macmillan's optimism. In the week following the coup, officials of the new regime announced that Iraq would not nationalize oil production, that it would honor existing contracts with Western oil companies, that it would recognize but not join the UAR, that it hoped to stay on friendly terms with the West, and that it would even, for the moment, remain in the Baghdad Pact. There were also indications that "moderate" figures were holding their own within the new regime and that communist influences were limited.[25] And in late July, as we have seen, the U.S. government learned that the Iraqi regime was resisting Nasser's proposal that Iraqi oil revenues be shared with the UAR.

All of these reports suggested the wisdom of seeking an understanding with Baghdad. Extending U.S. recognition to the new regime was the obvious first step. The only significant barrier to recognition was the fear of offending pro-Western governments in the region, and this concern turned out to have been exaggerated. On 30 July Murphy, who was briefly visiting Amman, raised the recognition issue with Hussein and al-Rifaʿi. Mere mention of the subject, Murphy reported, drew "emotional objections by both. . . . How could civilized nations deal with murderers et cetera?" But later that evening, outside Hussein's hearing, al-Rifaʻi "blandly said, 'well, we meant you should not recognize right away, perhaps in a month or six weeks.'" Confidential discussions with Turkish, Iranian, Pakistani, and Lebanese officials revealed a similar realism about the inevitability of official relations between the United States and Iraq. On 1 August the United States formally recognized the new regime. So much for al-Rifaʻi's decent interval.[26]

THE RAMIFICATIONS OF U.S. intervention in Lebanon were global as well as regional. As Murphy and the ambassadors worked quietly with local governments to stabilize the situation on the ground, Eisenhower and Dulles skirmished publicly with the Soviets over the proper means of resolving the Lebanese crisis. Both the U.S. and the Soviet governments agreed that the crisis should be resolved at the international level. Each government, however, sought to place that international resolution on a basis favoring its own interests.

On 15 July the Soviet Union submitted a resolution to the UN Security Council accusing the United States of "gross intervention in the domestic affairs of the people of Arab countries" and demanding an immediate withdrawal of U.S. forces from Lebanon. Two days later the United States proposed a resolution calling for the dispatch of UN peacekeeping forces to Lebanon, gradually to replace withdrawing U.S. forces. By referring to such UN action as "*additional* measures . . . to protect the territorial integrity and independence of Lebanon," Washington implied a continuity between its own intervention and the proposed UN action, attempting thereby to legitimate the former. On 18 July both resolutions failed, the Soviets' by a simple vote and the Americans' by a Soviet veto. That same day the Security Council took up a Japanese resolution that, without passing judgment on the U.S. intervention, called on the UN secretary-general to take whatever steps he deemed necessary to fulfill the purposes outlined in the Security Council's 11 June resolution (see Chapter 7). On 22 July, the Soviets vetoed the Japanese resolution as well, and the Security Council adjourned without taking any action.[27]

The Soviets, meanwhile, were pushing for great power summitry. In a 19 July public letter to Eisenhower, Soviet leader Nikita Khrushchev proposed that the heads of government of the Soviet Union, the United States, Britain, France, and India meet to discuss the Middle East crisis. Dulles thought the summit idea was "a propaganda stunt" in which the Americans would be cast as "the disturbers of peace." The British, however, favored a variation on the Soviet plan: a special meeting at the UN Security Council attended by the heads of government Khrushchev had mentioned. On 22 July Harold Macmillan proposed this alternative to the Soviet leader, who tentatively accepted it the following day. Eisenhower and Dulles disliked the British proposal, but Macmillan's unilateral overture to the Soviets had narrowed their options, and a week later Eisenhower accepted the idea of a heads-of-government meeting in the Security Council. In early August Khrushchev wrote again to Eisenhower, proposing that the meeting instead take the form of a special session of the UN General Assembly devoted to the Middle East crisis. Eisenhower accepted this proposal as well, seeing it as an opportunity to present the American case before a world audience. The General Assembly meeting was set to begin on 13 August.[28]

In anticipation of the event, Dulles asked *Time/Life* executive C. D. Jackson, an occasional outside adviser to the administration, to work with the State Department in preparing some opening remarks for Eisenhower to deliver at the meeting. Dulles intended those remarks to be primarily an indictment of Nasser's use of propaganda, subversion, and other forms of "indirect aggression" against neighboring Arab states. Jackson, however, devoted the bulk of the speech to a hopeful vision of the future, proposing a partnership between the Arab world and the West aimed at developing the resources of the Middle East to conquer drought, poverty, disease, illiteracy, and instability. This message, Jackson wrote in a memorandum to Dulles, should be "projected with a force that reaches down to the last bedouin, the last impassioned Arab egghead."[29]

Jackson's proposal drew on a number of Middle East development schemes then circulating within the U.S. government. Treasury Secretary Anderson had recently called for the establishment of an Arab Development Fund, to be financed initially by the World Bank and subsequently by an export tax on Arab oil, that could provide loans for indigenous development projects. The ICA had launched a water desalinization project in Tunisia that it hoped would serve as a model for other countries in the area. Admiral Lewis L. Strauss, a former chairman of the Atomic Energy Commission and a current adviser to the president, was advocating an ambitious scheme to improve Middle Eastern irrigation systems and locate underground water supplies through the use of radioisotopes.[30] More generally, Jackson's proposal drew on the emerging field of modernization theory, which held that by fostering economic growth in "developing countries" the West could encourage them to become more stable, democratic, and resistant to communism. One of the academics Jackson consulted in writing Eisenhower's speech was the economist Walt Rostow, an influential proponent of modernization theory.[31]

While an emphasis on economic development could be defended on the merits, it also had considerable political appeal. A network of international development arrangements could block further extensions of Nasser's power and influence. The trick, Rostow advised Jackson, was to make the offer "so attractive that it cannot be refused by Nasser with political safety," even though it "by-passes Nasser's plan to gain total direct political control over the oil regions" of the Arab world. Secretary Anderson was thinking along similar lines. "An Arab Development Fund," he predicted, "would be the kind of organization Egypt would have to go along with, but an organization which Egypt could not control. It would result in a sharing of Near Eastern wealth, but under other than Nasser's auspices." This was "the kind of thing we must do in order to demolish the Nasser myth." Admiral Strauss saw the challenge in even broader political terms. About a quarter of the earth's land surface, he informed Eisenhower in late July, was arid. "It may be mentioned that many of the 'neutralist' countries are located in the arid zone." By conspicuously helping the Arabs address their water problems, Strauss implied, the West could improve its standing with nonaligned nations generally.[32]

Despite its clear anti-Nasserist implications, Dulles was unhappy with Jackson's handiwork. Meeting on 7 August with Jackson, Herter, and other State Department officials who had assisted with the speech, Dulles objected to the downplaying of indirect aggression. "With his voice occasionally quivering with a combination of anger and anti-Communist sincerity," Jackson wrote in his diary, "[Dulles] gave us the full treatment on the implications of indirect aggression, that it existed as a technique, that we knew it had been used, that it could not be appeased without leading to direct aggression, and eventually to full scale war." Later, when Dulles and Jackson were alone, Dulles complained that Jackson's speech was abetting the natural timidity of State Department personnel: "I know your spine hasn't weakened, but that is not true of the rest of them. I have to keep stiffening them almost every day." But Eisenhower himself favored the softer approach, seeing the emphasis on economic development as the necessary "bait" to attract favorable attention in the General Assembly, and Dulles acquiesced.[33]

On 13 August Eisenhower delivered his speech at the special meeting of the General Assembly. Khrushchev had decided not to come to New York after all, but Soviet foreign minister Andrei Gromyko was in attendance, as were the foreign ministers of several other nations concerned with the crisis. Describing the scene in his diary, columnist Drew Pearson wrote, "C. D. Jackson sat in the wings as nervous as a playwright on opening night. But his star didn't fluff the lines." Following a brief and mildly worded defense of U.S. actions in Lebanon, Eisenhower unveiled his proposal for the creation of a new institution to oversee economic and infrastructural development in the Arab world. Established in consultation with the UN secretary-general and the World Bank, and receiving financial support from both Western nations and private organizations, such an institution would provide loans to Arab enterprises in industry, agriculture, education, health, and water supply. Using water as an example (and allowing optimism to get the better of him), Eisenhower noted that "much scientific and engineering work is already under way in the field of water development. . . . Atomic isotopes now permit us to chart the course of the great underground rivers. And new horizons are opening in the desalting of water. The ancient problem of water is on the threshold of solution." By these means and others, living standards in the Arab world could be dramatically improved, setting the stage for cultural and spiritual renewal as well. It would be, Eisenhower said, "a true Arab renaissance."[34]

While pledging U.S. financial support for an Arab development institution, the president was careful to disavow any "position of leadership for my own country" in such an endeavor. "If this institution is to be a success, the function of leadership must belong to the Arab States themselves."[35]

Reactions to Eisenhower's UN speech were about as favorable as could have been expected. Across the political spectrum, American politicians and commentators praised the president's initiative as constructive and humane. Latin American and NATO governments were also generally supportive, while Afro-Asian states were divided. The Soviets refrained from criticizing the substance of the development plan, though they called it a diversion from the real issue at hand: America's and Britain's lawless interventions in the Middle East. Turkey and Lebanon immediately endorsed the Eisenhower plan. Most of the remaining Arab states made encouraging noises but declined to commit themselves one way or the other. UAR officials publicly blasted the United States for failing to consult with them before unveiling the scheme. Privately, however, UAR foreign minister Mahmoud Fawzi, who had come to New York to attend the General Assembly session, told Dulles that "the U.S. should not be over-alarmed by expressions of hasty disapproval." If handled circumspectly, the development plan "could soon become a nucleus of economic sanity" in the Arab world, but it "should not have too big a U.S. flag on it."[36] Though little was made of it at the time, Fawzi's encouraging attitude suggested that UAR-American relations need not be permanently embittered.

The fate of the Arab development plan was a matter for the future; more immediately, the General Assembly had to address the crises in Lebanon and Jordan. All agreed that American and British forces should be withdrawn as soon as this was feasible. The question was on what basis the withdrawals should occur. The Soviets wanted the General Assembly to pass a resolution calling for unconditional withdrawal. The Americans and the British preferred a resolution acknowledging the problem of "indirect aggression" and containing measures to ensure the independence and integrity of Lebanon and Jordan. U.S. and British officials suspected, however, that such a resolution could not pass the General Assembly and that a compromise draft would have to be accepted.[37]

On 21 August ten Arab states introduced a resolution in the name of the Arab League. It called on members of the league to "respect the systems of government established in the other member States and regard them as exclusive concerns of these States." It also called on the UN secretary-general to consult with the nations involved in the crises and to make "such practical arrangements as would adequately help in upholding the purposes and principles of the [UN] Charter in relation to Lebanon and Jordan . . . , and thereby facilitate the early withdrawal of the foreign troops from the two countries." This cautious formula proved popular with UN delegations, and Dulles, believing that "the Arab draft was about as much as we could expect to obtain from the General Assembly," publicly embraced it. The Soviets apparently made a similar calculation, and the Arab resolution was unanimously adopted.[38]

The Arab resolution reflected, in part, an unexpected convergence of interests between the United States and the UAR. Over the previous week Foreign Minister Fawzi, apparently one of the main architects of the Arab resolution, held a series of confidential meetings with Dulles in New York. Dulles told Fawzi that if the UAR agreed to keep its hands off Lebanon and Jordan, the United States and Britain would promptly withdraw their forces from those two countries, and Fawzi, in effect, accepted Dulles's offer. Fawzi did not deny Dulles's charge that the UAR had recently interfered in Lebanese affairs, but he insisted that his government had no current interest in dominating the country and that "the UAR is ready to accept the presence of [UN] observers and to throw as much light as possible to show it is not interfering." Such disavowals were nothing new, of course, but by August 1958 a hands-off policy on Lebanon genuinely made sense from the UAR standpoint. On one hand, the Americans' willingness to intervene in Lebanon seems to have surprised UAR officials, impressing on them that the risks of meddling in Lebanon were greater than previously thought.[39] On the other hand, the UAR had already achieved a major political victory with the election of Shihab and the official foreclosing of Chamoun's ambitions. This was no time to rock the boat in Lebanon.

The New York talks also revealed that Fawzi shared some of Dulles's concerns about the likely consequences of a sudden Nasserist takeover in Jordan. Both men agreed that such a development might well prompt Israel to seize the West Bank, sparking an Arab-Israeli war. Even short of that dire outcome, there was the problem of Jordan's utter dependence on outside financial assistance. If Hussein "should be overthrown by violence and a pro-Nasser regime installed," Dulles warned, "American public opinion would preclude any [U.S.] financial aid" to Jordan. Fawzi admitted "that these considerations were very much in his mind. If Hussein should be overthrown and a new regime should ask the UAR to take over financial responsibility, the UAR could not afford to do so." A long-term solution, Fawzi proposed, might be a revival of the Jordanian-Iraqi union, which the Baghdad coup had extinguished. Dulles agreed "that this could be a logical step" provided the Israelis would tolerate it. At any rate, he "did not see a permanent future for Jordan as an independent nation." For the short term, Fawzi pledged that his government would work to calm the situation in Jordan. UAR officials "would certainly advise their friends in Jordan, particularly of Palestinian origin, to keep quiet for the time being." The UAR would also be agreeable to the stationing in Jordan of UN peacekeepers or monitors "to ensure there is no interference by the UAR or anybody else." As for King Hussein, "the UAR would not resist his staying in Jordan."[40]

Over the next several weeks, political conditions in the Arab world did become more conducive to the withdrawal of British and American forces from Jordan and Lebanon. Pursuant to the 21 August General Assembly resolution, in late August and September UN secretary-general Dag Hammarskjold visited the Middle East to consult with Arab leaders. In Amman, Hammarskjold and the Jordanians agreed that a "UN Representative Office" would be established in Jordan to investigate any alleged violations of the 21 August resolution. In Cairo, Hammarskjold extracted a commitment from Nasser to tone down the UAR's anti-Jordanian radio broadcasts; Nasser also promised to guarantee air and land access across Syrian territory to the new UN mission in Jordan. Although manifestations of UAR hostility continued—anti-Jordanian broadcasts never entirely abated, and the UAR was slow to lift its blockade on Jordanian commerce with Syria—by late September the British government was satisfied that adequate procedures were in place for monitoring UAR compliance with the UN resolution. By early November the British had withdrawn their troops from Jordan.[41]

While U.S. officials continued to believe that Nasser's short-term interests dictated a hands-off policy on Jordan, they took little comfort in this assumption. Even if Nasser himself took no action, a 28 October U.S. intelligence estimate warned, "Arab extremists both in and out of Jordan might take independent action to overthrow the regime. . . . If Hussein continues his present government and policies after the withdrawal of UK troops, we believe the chances are better than even that he will be overthrown within a few months."[42] Few observers could have imagined that Hussein's reign would continue for another four decades.

In Lebanon the gradual return to political normality continued as clandestine radio stations were shut down, government curfews were relaxed, and militiamen were disarmed. In mid-September, to assist Shihab in his negotiations with rebel leaders, the United States withdrew one of its marine battalions from the country. To facilitate the withdrawal of the remaining U.S. forces, Hammarskjold agreed to expand UNOGIL, which had been stationed in Lebanon the previous June. On 23 September Shihab formally assumed the presidency, pledging to work for the reestablishment of domestic security, the rebuilding of Lebanon's economy and infrastructure, the easing of tensions with other Arab states, "and, above all, the realization of the prompt withdrawal of foreign troops from the soil of the fatherland." On 8 October the U.S. State Department announced that all U.S. forces would be out of Lebanon by the end of the month; the withdrawal was completed on 25 October. By early December UNOGIL, too, had departed the country.[43]

Once in office, Shihab took a conciliatory attitude toward the Lebanese opposition. Of the eight members of his first cabinet, seven were anti-Chamounists and one was neutral. The Chamounists' reaction to this development was so bitter that a resumption of the civil war briefly seemed possible. In mid-October Shihab replaced his first cabinet with a more balanced one, forestalling a Chamounist revolt. Yet even the second cabinet made it clear that its policy toward the UAR would be far more accommodating than that of Chamoun's government.[44]

A case in point was Lebanon's new position on the Eisenhower Doctrine. In December 1958 Rashid Karami, Shihab's prime minister, announced that Lebanon no longer considered itself bound by the doctrine. The Eisenhower administration was not inclined to object. Dulles himself had already told the NSC that the Lebanese crisis had occurred in large part because "Chamoun had adopted an extreme pro-Western policy" and had gone "too far in embracing the Eisenhower Doctrine."[45] That the United States itself may have borne some responsibility in the matter seems not to have crossed Dulles's mind.

As for C. D. Jackson's cherished Arab development plan, nothing came of it. Even after the United States and Britain had withdrawn their forces from Lebanon and Jordan—thus removing a major political obstacle to the plan—the Arab states failed to take the initiative in devising a regional approach. In the overheated political atmosphere of late 1958, Arab governments simply could not muster the concentration, self-confidence, and mutual trust such an endeavor would have required. And the Eisenhower administration, having explicitly renounced a leadership role in the matter, felt that any American effort to push the Arabs would be poorly received. Jackson had anticipated this problem shortly after Eisenhower's UN speech. "I know that the President said that the Arabs themselves would have to take this initiative," he wrote Dulles in late August, after having returned to his regular duties at *Time/Life*, ". . . but I think we will have to take the initiative to get the Arabs to take the initiative." The administration remained passive, however, and Jackson could do little more than plead from the sidelines. "As far as I know," he wrote Dulles in February 1959, "after six months, practically nothing has been done, and the all-important element of timing has been largely lost."[46]

THE ARAB DEVELOPMENT PLAN was part of a general transition in U.S. policy on Nasserism—away from the confrontational approach formalized in the Eisenhower Doctrine and toward the more accommodationist stance of the late 1950s and early 1960s. Under the confrontational policy, the Eisenhower administration had tried to weaken Nasser and his supporters by exposing their unwillingness to denounce international communism and by strengthening their Arab rivals. By the summer of 1958 that strategy had been discredited, yet U.S. hostility to Nasser remained sufficiently great to rule out, for the moment, any move toward accommodation. While Nasser himself was too popular to be opposed, his methods and goals were too distasteful to be supported. The Arab development plan was one response to this dilemma; if Nasser could not be defeated in the political arena, then perhaps he could be bypassed economically. The utility of this approach was limited, however, by the slowness with which such a plan would take shape (if it did so at all) and by the assumption that the United States could not take the initiative. By itself, the Arab development plan was no substitute for a new Middle East policy.

A fresh policy statement, however, was already in the works. From late July to late October the NSC Planning Board formulated new guidelines for U.S. dealings with Nasser and Arab nationalism. Those guidelines would be issued in early November as NSC 5820/1. The Planning Board's principal

DEATH OF A DOCTRINE

innovation was to distinguish between vital and secondary U.S. interests in the Middle East. The vital interests were denial of the area to international communism and continued Western access to Middle Eastern oil. The secondary interests were continued availability to the West of military bases and transit rights in the area, resolution of the Arab-Israeli conflict on a basis ensuring Israel's survival, and economic and social development in the area in a manner conducive to political stability and friendly relations with the West. The Planning Board further noted that while some or all of the secondary interests might be in conflict with Arab nationalism, this was not necessarily true of the vital interests. After all, even radical Arab nationalists were committed to maintaining independence from both Cold War blocs and to using oil revenues (derived primarily from oil sales to the West) to serve the needs of the Arab people. Thus there was some basis for improved relations between the United States and Nasserism.[47]

The Planning Board was divided, however, over the proper scope of such a rapprochement. The majority position, reflecting the views of mid-level officials at the State Department and the CIA, was that the United States should recognize "Nasser's present role as leader and symbol of pan-Arab nationalism" and "seek a limited understanding with him in areas of mutual interest." The minority position, representing the views of the Defense and Treasury Departments, was that the United States should deal with Nasser "as head of the UAR on specific problems and issues affecting the UAR's immediate interests, but not as leader of the Arab world."[48]

At the 16 October NSC meeting Dulles and Eisenhower endorsed the Defense-Treasury position. Dulles thought it shortsighted and defeatist to regard Nasserism as synonymous with Arab nationalism. "There were several areas," he said, "where Nasser's goals obviously conflicted very sharply with the nationalist aspirations of various Arab states, such as Tunisia, the Sudan, and Iraq, the government of which was giving evidence that it did not wish to see Iraq absorbed by Egypt. . . . In the long run, indeed, more moderate views may prevail than the views now rampant in radical pan-Arab nationalism." Eisenhower agreed, noting

that the revenue-producing countries of the Near East . . . had a natural antipathy toward Egypt, which was not, strictly speaking, an Arab state. . . . The oil-rich Arab states of the Near East do not want to give away their revenues to Egypt, and we certainly don't want to be the agent through whom Nasser secures control of all these oil revenues. . . . Certainly there was no reason for the United States to go on and treat Nasser as the head of the whole Arab nationalist movement. If we did this, the President predicted, Nasser would become the biggest blackmailer this country ever faced.[49]

Accordingly, the final version of NSC 5820/1 favored the Defense-Treasury position on relations with Nasser, directing that the United States "deal with Nasser as head of the UAR on specific problems and issues, area-wide as well as local, affecting the UAR's legitimate interests, but not as leader of the Arab world." The statement likewise distinguished between mere "Arab nationalism" and "radical pan-Arab nationalism as symbolized by Nasser." Whereas the United States should "establish an effective working relationship" with the former, it should not be resigned to the perpetual hegemony of the latter.[50]

Still, the thrust of NSC 5820/1 was to repudiate previous U.S. efforts to thwart Nasserism, especially the policy of seeking to organize the conservative Arabs. There had been, the statement acknowledged, a "virtual collapse during 1958 of conservative resistance, leaving radical nationalist regimes almost without opposition in the area." As gracefully as possible, the United States should now distance itself from its hapless allies. It should "maintain friendly relations with the Saudi Arabian Government" while "recognizing the position of reduced influence of King Saud." It should "support the continued independence and integrity of Lebanon, but avoid becoming too closely identified with individual factions in Lebanese politics and seek discreetly to disengage from relationships that may be disadvantageous to U.S. interests." It should recognize "that the indefinite continuance of Jordan's present political status has been rendered unrealistic" and, while seeking to avoid any abrupt changes, work "to bring about peaceful evolution of Jordan's political status"—not ruling out partition or absorption—"and to reduce the U.S. commitment in Jordan." Rather than organizing an anti-Nasserist Arab front, the United States should "accept neutralist policies of states in the area when necessary, even though such states maintain diplomatic, trade, and cultural relations with the Soviet bloc (or receive military equipment)."[51] NSC 5820/1 did not repudiate the Eisenhower Doctrine itself, but it discarded the doctrine's underlying political strategy.

NSC 5820/1 UNDERSCORED the futility of confronting Nasser, not the benefits of befriending him. Those benefits were suggested by fresh developments in Iraq. Soon after the 14 July coup, a rift had developed between General 'Abd al-Karim Qasim, who had become Iraq's prime min-

DEATH OF A DOCTRINE

ister, and Colonel 'Abd al-Salam 'Arif, the new deputy premier. 'Arif, with
the support of Iraqi Ba'thists and other pan-Arab nationalists, had pressed
for Iraq's entry into the UAR. Opposing this course were many Shiites and
Kurds, who feared being absorbed into a larger Sunni Arab state, and the
Iraqi Communist Party (ICP), which was anxious to avoid the fate of its
Egyptian and Syrian counterparts. The ICP was the best organized of the
anti-unionist groups. After some hesitation Qasim—an erratic figure whose
purposes were often mysterious to Arabs and Westerners alike—threw in
his lot with the anti-unionists. He ousted 'Arif from the cabinet and later
had him arrested for "plotting against the security of the State." Ba'thist
cabinet members were likewise removed or demoted, and unionist army
officers were relieved of their commands.[52]

While Qasim himself was almost certainly not a communist,[53] his crackdown on Ba'thists and other unionists removed the principal barrier to the
ICP's expansion, and by late fall the party had achieved unprecedented
strength and visibility in Iraq. Qasim apparently believed he could accept
support from the ICP without granting it excessive domestic power, but
U.S. officials had their doubts. "While Communist infiltration probably has
not yet got out of control," a State Department intelligence analyst reported on 25 November, "the point of no return may be reached in a few
months should the Qasim regime continue on its present course."[54]

Nasser, too, was upset by Iraqi developments. Although Nasser probably had no interest in bringing Iraq into the UAR at this moment, the suppression of Iraqi unionists was a serious affront to his regional leadership.
Qasim's behavior also increased Nasser's difficulties in Syria, where Ba'thist
politicians, seeing the prospect of Iraq's incorporation into the UAR suddenly evaporate, began questioning their own commitment to the Egyptian-Syrian union. After all, writes Malcolm Kerr, "If revolutionary Iraq
would not join the union, who else would? . . . If the Syro-Egyptian union
were to stop short of expansion, then Syrians must have second thoughts
about its merits." Such nagging doubts, combined with the Syrian Ba'thists'
growing disenchantment over their newly subservient status vis-à-vis the
Egyptians, posed a serious threat to the internal cohesion of the UAR.[55] Nasser could not let Qasim's challenge go unanswered.

To signal his displeasure with Qasim's apostasy—and to suggest its alien
origins—Nasser decided to crack down on communists within his own
domain. He was determined, however, to extract an American concession
in return. On 1 December Muhammad Haykal, playing his usual role as
Nasser's emissary, approached Ambassador Hare and asked if the United
States would be willing to sell wheat to the UAR under PL 480.[56] Such a ges-

Iraq's new leaders, July 1958. *Left to right*: Deputy Prime Minister 'Abd al-Salam 'Arif and Prime Minister 'Abd al-Karim Qasim. (© Bettmann/CORBIS)

ture, Haykal said, would "help [the] UAR take [a] stronger line on [the] Commie issue." Sensing an opportunity for a new beginning in UAR-American relations (and mixing metaphors in his excitement), Hare urged that Washington "take [a] leaf out of Khrushchev's book and strike while [the] iron is hot." The State Department accepted Hare's recommendation and replied the next day that the United States would be willing to sell PL 480 wheat to the UAR. Nasser was amazed by the promptness of the American response. "He practically fell off the davenport," Hare later recalled. In late December Nasser began arresting suspected communists in Egypt and Syria and denouncing Arab communists as enemies of Arab unity.[57]

The growing UAR-Iraqi rift was dramatized for U.S. officials in mid-December when Assistant Secretary Rountree—another "Great White Father"—visited several Arab countries.[58] Rountree reported that he was cordially received by most Arab leaders, particularly "when it became apparent that I had not come to sell a new doctrine. . . . They seemed to feel that the US had . . . indicated a new willingness to allow the Arabs to solve their problems in their own way."[59]

Things went especially well in Cairo, where Rountree found "perfect order in the streets" and was "struck by the very great material progress since he had last been there." Meeting with Nasser, Rountree was "treated to all the usual arguments" about the Arabs' quest for independence and dignity. But toward the end of the session Nasser dispensed with his confident manner and, adopting the "attitude of [a] very troubled man," spoke of growing communist influence in Iraq. He said the situation was "very serious because, if [the] Communists gain control in Iraq, they will then be able [to] move into Syria and Jordan and eventually into Egypt." Nasser acknowledged that he had little experience in combating communism in foreign countries, whereas "American experience had been more extensive. Did [the Americans] have any ideas?" Rountree promised that Nasser's concerns would receive serious attention in Washington.[60]

Rountree's visit to Baghdad was far less pleasant. A huge, hostile crowd waving anti-American signs and chanting "Go home, Rountree!" greeted him at the airport. Demonstrators pelted Rountree's limousine with mud, rocks, eggs, and garbage and tried to stop the car by herding cattle into its path. The scene was all too reminiscent of Vice President Nixon's visit to Caracas the previous May, when Nixon and his party had nearly been dragged from their cars by angry mobs. Iraqi security guards trained their machine guns on Rountree as he arrived at the Defense Ministry for a tense meeting with Qasim. Rountree chided Qasim for failing to provide adequate protection for the visit. Qasim expressed regret over the demonstrations but said the Iraqi people were reacting to reports that the United States had been involved in a recent coup attempt by Nasserist Iraqi officers, a charge Rountree denied.[61] "I did not gain [the] impression," Rountree reported, "that Qassim [was] substantially reassured by my statements." Qasim, however, promised there would be "no trouble" for the remainder of Rountree's stay, and there was none.[62]

Reports of Rountree's contrasting experiences in Cairo and Baghdad made a deep impression in Washington. At the 18 December NSC meeting, Allen Dulles remarked that Qasim "is in the hands of the Communist mob," though he noted that a successful Nasserist coup was still possible. Eisenhower "said it might be good policy to help the UAR take over in Iraq. Nasser does not want to be dominated by the Kremlin." On 23 December Rountree briefed the president on his recent trip, stressing that "Nasser desires to work with us on Iraq." Eisenhower said "that Nasser could oppose Communists better than can the U.S. in the three-cornered struggle of the Middle East." At the 15 January NSC meeting the possibility of a Nasserist coup in Iraq was revisited. Gordon Gray, Eisenhower's special assistant for national security affairs, sought Dulles's assurance "that if events moved very quickly in that country, we would not prevent Nasser from moving promptly to counter Communist gains." Dulles admitted that, between Nasser and the communists, "certainly Nasser was the lesser of two evils"—this from a man who six months earlier had been likening Nasser to Hitler.[63]

By late January the UAR was feuding directly with the Soviet Union, which, seeing that Nasser had lost his monopoly on radical expression in the Arab world, was shedding its customary deference toward him. On 27 January, at the Twenty-First Congress of the Communist Party of the Soviet Union, Khrushchev criticized the UAR's recent campaign against local communists, calling it a "reactionary" undertaking. Nasser himself made no response to Khrushchev's remarks, but Haykal, writing in the Cairo newspaper *al-Ahram*, accused the Soviet Union of meddling in the UAR's domestic affairs, prompting the Soviet media to accuse the UAR of meddling in Iraqi affairs.[64]

The UAR-Soviet dispute intensified in March when Iraqi Nasserist officers, with logistical support from the UAR and tacit encouragement from the United States, tried to seize the army garrison at Mosul, the largest city in northern Iraq.[65] Pro-government paramilitary units, led by the ICP, brutally crushed the officers' revolt.[66] Incensed by the defeat, Nasser publicly charged that Iraq had fallen under a "red dictatorship," to which Khrushchev retorted that Nasser was a "passionate and hotheaded young man" who was now indulging in "the language of imperialists." Nasser responded by reminding Arab audiences that during the Suez war the Soviet ultimatum to Egypt's attackers had come too late to affect the outcome of the conflict. For nine days, Nasser said, "we had no indication of support from any foreign state, including the Soviet Union. . . . I say to Mr. Khrushchev that the passion and hotheadedness [of which he accuses me] were the only thing enabling our country to remain independent."[67]

Nasser's growing hostility toward the Soviets was welcome news to U.S. officials. Ambassador Hare almost gushed as he reminded the State Department in a 1 April cable that Nasser

has always maintained that, if [the] Soviets deviated from [their] policy of non-interference [in internal Arab affairs], he would attack them as vigorously as he had [the] West for alleged imperialism. To many this was regarded as [a] mere rhetorical exercise since it was maintained [that] Nasser had become so enmeshed with [the] Soviets that he would not have [the] courage to stand up to them, but, now that [the] Soviets have done what he had predicted they would not do, Nasser has been as good as his word. . . . In fact, to give [the] devil his due, [it] must be recognized that Nasser has dealt body blows to both [the] Communists and [the] Soviets recently which [the] West, with all its psychological warfare potential, could not equal.

Hare forbore to mention that among the "many" who had underestimated Nasser were the American president and secretary of state. The State Department shared Hare's enthusiasm for Nasser's actions, which it rewarded with an additional sale of PL 480 wheat to the UAR. Later that month the department approved a proposal by the International Bank for Reconstruction and Development to provide a $100 million loan to the UAR for improving the Suez Canal.[68]

By late April Nasser and Khrushchev had apparently concluded that their verbal duel was counterproductive and were softening their public attacks on each other. But Nasser's hostility to Qasim and Arab communism remained, as did the new community of interest between the United States and the UAR. If anything, Nasser now seemed to worry that the Americans were not taking the communist menace seriously enough. In late April Egyptian newspaper editor Mustafa Amin, whom Nasser had sent as an unofficial emissary to Washington, told Rountree that "the US may consider that Qasim is not a Communist and that [the] UAR is responsible [for driving him into the Communists' arms]. This is false. Qasim is increasingly under Communist control and in any case was a Communist Party member before the July 1958 revolt." In September 1959, at the very time that Eisenhower was hosting a high-profile visit from Khrushchev, Nasser told Hare that it was "virtually impossible for [a] non-Communist country to come to basic agreement with [the] Soviets as long they [are] so dedicated to Communist principles and convinced [that] Communism [is] destined [to] pervade [the] world. [It w]ould seem, he said, [that] there [is] some inner impulse which drives them on whether they will it or not."[69] John Foster Dulles could not have said it better himself.

DULLES, HOWEVER, HAD SINCE vanished from the scene, taking with him his polarizing approach to Arab politics. In early 1959 Dulles suffered a recurrence of the stomach cancer that had stricken him in late 1956. On 9 February, beginning what he hoped would be but a few weeks' leave of absence from his post, he entered Walter Reed Hospital. By mid-April it was clear that Dulles's condition would not improve, and Eisenhower reluctantly accepted his resignation. Undersecretary Herter became secretary of state. On 24 May Dulles died at age seventy-one, eliciting an outpouring of respect, domestic and international, that belied the controversies of his tenure.[70]

Bland, passive, and in poor health himself, Herter was no match for his predecessor. But by mid-1959 Dulles's brand of diplomacy was no longer needed, at least not in the Middle East. Forswearing bold ventures, the Eisenhower administration was now mainly concerned with avoiding any further unpleasantness in the area as it finished out its term. For this, a modest caretaker would do.

To be sure, there were some features of the emerging situation that might well have become major crises requiring the services of an experienced and forceful secretary of state, but these problems mostly corrected themselves. A case in point was the Anglo-American disagreement over how best to respond to the Nasser-Qasim feud. While Britain shared the Eisenhower administration's dismay over Qasim's courting of the ICP, into the spring of 1959 it continued to see Nasser as the primary threat to its regional interests. Still hopeful that the Iraqi regime could maintain its independence from communists and Nasserists alike—and thus serve as a bulwark against radical threats to Britain's protectorates on the Arabian peninsula—Britain initially opposed America's rapprochement with the UAR. But Qasim's continuing reliance on the ICP soon caused British officials to wonder whether Iraq really would be as cooperative as they hoped, and whether Qasim could be trusted to keep his hands off Kuwait, the most important of Britain's remaining assets on the gulf.[71] "In these circumstances," writes Nigel John Ashton, "blank opposition to any initiative taken by Nasser might not be the best method of defending British interests." By the summer of 1959 the British themselves were seeking better relations with the UAR.[72]

The Eisenhower administration was fortunate in another respect: although Qasim's tilt toward the ICP was sufficiently worrisome to bring the British around to Washington's way of thinking, it never became intolerable in its own right. From mid-1959 until Eisenhower left office in early 1961, Qasim tempered his support for the ICP with occasional crackdowns on its activities. Qasim well knew that Western Europe was the primary market for Iraqi oil, and he saw to it that existing contracts with Western firms were honored. While Qasim never made a clean break with the ICP, and while he continued to receive considerable military and economic aid from the Soviet bloc, the cumulative effect of his maneuverings was to deny the ICP a decisive victory within Iraq and to keep the Soviets at arm's length.[73] These facts, combined with the general calm now prevailing in inter-Arab relations, reinforced American passivity.

The only inter-Arab problem that did require vigorous U.S. diplomacy was the lingering hostility between Jordan and the UAR. Of all the conservative Arab states, Jordan was the most resistant to Washington's rapprochement with Cairo. "Jordan will never accept Nasser," King Hussein told a U.S. diplomat in May 1959, "whether he poses as anti-Communist or reveals himself in his true light as a dictator bent on creating an Arab empire." U.S. officials believed that Hussein continued to harbor fantasies of marching on Baghdad, overthrowing the Qasim regime, wresting Syria from Nasser's grip, and establishing a new Hashemite federation. "Devoid of reason as this proposal may be," a U.S. diplomat cabled from Amman in April 1959, "unfortunately I am convinced . . . it is [the] kind of destructive policy that [the] Hussein/Rifai regime will pursue unless definitely dissuaded."[74]

The enmity between Jordan and the UAR boiled over in the late summer of 1960. On 31 August Jordanian prime minister Hazza' al-Majali, who had replaced Samir al-Rifa'i the previous year, was killed when a time bomb exploded in his office. Blaming the UAR, Jordan mobilized troops on its border with Syria, and in early September hostilities seemed possible.[75] "If Jordan should undertake any aggressive action," the State Department cautioned Hussein, "[the] US cannot be expected to be of any assistance." Whether as a result of this warning or because he had never actually contemplated military action in the first place, Hussein soon withdrew the troops from the border, confining his retaliation to the rhetorical arena. In October he attended the annual meeting of the UN General Assembly and publicly accused the UAR of "seeking to dominate our part of the world," prompting Nasser to declare that Hussein was "traitorous." Yet even a verbal battle with Nasser was inadvisable for a leader of Hussein's vulnerabilities, and in early 1961 Hussein concluded a propaganda truce with Nasser.[76]

While the Eisenhower administration generally refrained, in the last two years of its term, from challenging Nasser on inter-Arab affairs, it was still prepared to incur his displeasure on other matters. U.S.-Israeli relations markedly improved during this period. The realization by 1958 that the conservative Arab states could not form a reliable bulwark against radical nationalism prompted a gradual reassessment of Israel's strategic potential. The issue was most sharply drawn in Jordan. For years U.S. officials had worried that Israel might react to a radical takeover in Jordan by seizing the West Bank, in turn sparking an Arab-Israeli war. But by 1958 there were indications that Nasser, fearing the same chain of events, was urging restraint on his West Bank supporters. Israel's pugnacity began to appear in a new light: "It might be a good thing," Secretary Dulles remarked in August 1958, "that the UAR was afraid of Israel." The perception that Nasser was constrained by Israeli power persisted well after UAR-American relations had begun to improve. "Even should the Egyptians revert to the ambition they had in 1957–58 of absorbing Jordan," the U.S. embassy in Amman speculated in September 1959, such a move "could quite easily be taken by Israel as a signal to achieve the long-held Zionist ambition of grabbing the part of Palestine now in Jordan," an action that "would undoubtedly lead to war."[77] While the actual outbreak of an Arab-Israeli war was to be avoided at all costs, the threat of such a war could be beneficial to Washington. "Brinkmanship" had many guises.

With this shift in perception came a more favorable U.S. attitude toward military assistance to Israel. Nasser's difficulties with Moscow did nothing to curtail Soviet military aid to the UAR. Indeed, they may have caused the Soviets to increase such assistance in an effort to placate Nasser.[78] To counter the UAR's growing arsenal, the Israelis relentlessly pressured the United States to shed its long-standing reluctance to supply Israel with arms, and the United States modestly complied. In the fall of 1958 the Eisenhower administration agreed to sell Israel military helicopters and recoilless anti-tank guns.[79] In the spring of 1960 the administration agreed to provide Israel with a $10.2 million credit to purchase electronic air-raid warning equipment in the United States. Though the administration declined Israel's request to purchase American Hawk antiaircraft missiles—for fear of angering the Arabs and exacerbating the Arab-Israeli arms race—clearly the trend was one of increasing sympathy for Israel's position. Nasser, not surprisingly, was greatly irritated by this development, and in 1960 there was a general upswing in rhetorical attacks on U.S. policy both in Nasser's speeches and in the UAR press.[80]

The Eisenhower administration was also willing to antagonize Nasser in Central Africa. In the summer of 1960 the UN sent peacekeeping forces into the Congo, following a breakdown of public order in that newly independent state. Although Nasser initially supported the peacekeeping mission and even contributed some troops to the effort, he soon came to see it as diplomatic cover for a U.S.-sponsored campaign to unseat Patrice Lumumba, the Congo's leftist prime minister. The Eisenhower administration was indeed out to get Lumumba, whom it suspected of being an agent of Moscow and whose "removal" it deemed "a high priority of our covert action." CIA plans were afoot for Lumumba's assassination. In December, with tacit U.S. support, forces loyal to Congolese army chief of staff (and later president) General Joseph Mobutu arrested Lumumba, who was later murdered in their custody. By then Nasser was publicly accusing the United States and the UN of pursuing a neocolonialist policy in the Congo.[81]

Thus, in the last two years of his administration, Eisenhower's treatment of Nasser foreshadowed the policies of President John F. Kennedy. Kennedy, too, would generally refrain from challenging Nasser on inter-Arab questions while risking his ire on other matters, such as Israel and the Congo. Despite frequent setbacks, this policy endured throughout the Kennedy years. It expired during the presidency of Lyndon B. Johnson, a casualty of Washington's growing support for Israel and the conservative Arab regimes, of increasing challenges to Nasser's leadership from within the radical Arab camp itself, and of Nasser's own reckless behavior. Squeezed from both the left and the right, in 1967 Nasser sought to escape his predicament through a dramatic—and, he apparently hoped, purely diplomatic—showdown with Israel. The effort backfired, leading to a disastrous war with Israel and to a severing of relations with the United States, an estrangement that continued until well after Nasser's death in 1970.[82]

EISENHOWER AND NASSER met for the first and only time in September 1960, when Nasser, who had come to New York to attend the annual session of the UN General Assembly, visited Eisenhower's suite in the Waldorf Towers Hotel. Eisenhower found Nasser "impressive, tall, straight, strong, positive"—an exemplary soldier. Speaking in clear, confident tones, Nasser "said he must begin by thanking the U.S. for its great help during the 1956 aggression against his country." With U.S. backing, "the UN had not only ended aggression, but had forced the aggressors to withdraw." Later in the meeting Nasser reiterated his appreciation, commending "the courage of the U.S. in standing up against the wishes of its closest allies." Reaching further into the past, Nasser said that "the Arab people . . . had been deeply moved by [Woodrow] Wilson's principles of self-determination and by the ideals of the Atlantic Charter."[83] There was no inherent conflict, Nasser implied, between Arab nationalism and American internationalism.

The remainder of the meeting, however, was devoted to a recitation of UAR-American disagreements. Nasser criticized UN operations in the Congo, which "seemed to the UAR to be actions taken against Lumumba." Such partiality could "compromise the UN's utility in the eyes of the African people" and damage U.S. standing in the Middle East, where "simple people see the U.S. and the UN as virtually the same thing." Eisenhower insisted that "the UN's first job was to insure law and order" in the Congo and "that the U.S. would support the UN when action is called for." Nasser next chided the United States for its growing willingness to sell arms to Israel. Eisenhower countered that such arms had been defensive rather than offensive, a distinction Nasser rejected. Eisenhower "agreed that Israel constitutes a terrible problem. However, Israel is. The question is how can this problem be solved without starting a war." Nasser objected "that to accept Israel as a fact would be to permit a thief to keep what he has stolen." Nasser denied, however, that he harbored any fantasies of destroying Israel. Border

Eisenhower and Nasser meet in New York, September 1960 (© Nat Fein)

rectifications and repatriation of Palestinian refugees were the remedies he favored. Agreeing to disagree, the two leaders parted on cordial terms.[84]

Appreciation for past U.S. actions, dismay over present ones—these were Nasser's themes as he bade farewell to the Eisenhower administration. In mid-November Nasser told G. Frederick Reinhardt, the new U.S. ambassador in Cairo, how pleased he was finally to have met Eisenhower, whom he had admired "since his staff college days." Eisenhower's appeal, Nasser explained, had transcended military accomplishment: "Teachers and students of military history developed strong likes and dislikes for the military personalities they studied. Then, after searching for an example, [Nasser] suddenly added that just as he had on one hand disliked Ghengis Khan, he had on the other developed a great admiration for General Eisenhower."[85]

Soon, however, Nasser was speaking in a more familiar idiom. In a 23 December Victory Day speech at Port Said, marking the fourth anniversary of the Anglo-French withdrawal from Egypt, Nasser delivered a blistering attack on U.S. policy. Recent news reports that the Israelis had secretly built a nuclear reactor lent special vehemence to Nasser's criticism of U.S. support for Israel. "The cost of every bullet aimed to kill an Arab," he charged, "is paid by America and Western imperialism." Should Israel now acquire

DEATH OF A DOCTRINE

nuclear weapons, "we would get an atomic bomb, at any price." Nasser also had harsh words for NATO, which "represents nothing but the love of tyranny and domination," as could be seen in its support for French colonialism in Algeria. Nor could the United States evade responsibility in this matter, since "the arms that France fights with come from America." In the Congo, Nasser said, the Americans "have destroyed the United Nations" by turning it into "a tool of the imperialist states." Cabling a report of Nasser's speech to Washington, Ambassador Reinhardt noted that the "US has not come in for such sharp and specific criticism for [a] long time."[86]

It is doubtful that Eisenhower saw Reinhardt's report. If he did, he may well have felt a breeze of relief, knowing that the challenges of Nasserism and Arab nationalism would bedevil him no longer.

EPILOGUE

In January 1957 the Eisenhower administration set out to redeem the Western position in the Middle East. The recent fiasco over Suez had suggested that Britain was no longer able to hold the Middle East for the West, and the region seemed in danger of succumbing to eventual Soviet domination. America's answer to this challenge was the Eisenhower Doctrine, embodied in a congressional resolution declaring the intention of the United States to give aid and protection to any Middle Eastern nation willing to acknowledge, out loud, the menace of international communism. With the Eisenhower Doctrine the United States assumed Britain's position as the dominant Western power in the Middle East, a role Washington continued to play long after the doctrine was shelved and forgotten.

Ostensibly the Eisenhower Doctrine was a mechanism for protecting the Middle East from Soviet encroachment, but its purpose was also to contain Nasser's radical Arab nationalism. Although Nasser professed neutrality in the Cold War, the Eisenhower administration believed he had grown so hostile to the West as to become, perhaps unwittingly, a tool of Soviet expansionism. Ideally, the administration hoped, U.S. pressure would force Nasser to see the error of his ways and abandon his courtship of Moscow. Failing that, conspicuous offers of U.S. aid and protection would encourage conservative Arab governments to side openly with the United States in the Cold War, leaving Nasser and his regional supporters isolated and discredited.

What made this scenario plausible was the propaganda victory the Eisenhower administration believed it had won in late 1956. By opposing British, French, and Israeli aggression against Egypt during the Suez war, the United States had proved itself to be a fair and just power, more interested in defending the rights of weak nations than in excusing the sins of its allies and friends. The Soviet Union, meanwhile, had shown its true colors by brutally suppressing the Hungarian uprising. The prevailing mood in the Arab world, U.S. officials assumed, was now one of gratitude toward the Americans and revulsion against the Soviets. Such an atmosphere would make it easier for conservative Arabs to stand with the United States and harder for radical Arabs to oppose it.

Events did not, however, bear out these hopeful projections. Because the Soviets had condemned the attack on Egypt even more forcefully than the Americans had, their suppression of the Hungarian revolt received little criticism in the Arab world. Nor could the United States secure lasting credit for its own stand during the Suez war. Nasser saw the Eisenhower Doctrine for what it was—a veiled attempt to diminish his own influence in the Arab world—and his gratitude toward Washington quickly evaporated. With Nasser's hostility on the rise, the Eisenhower administration placed its hopes in the conservative Arab regimes, seeking to unite them in a pro-American, anti-Nasserist coalition. But the populations of these countries generally supported Nasser, and the conservative regimes could not respond favorably to U.S. overtures without jeopardizing their own political standing, as the regional crises of 1957 and 1958 made clear. In late 1958 the Eisenhower administration bowed to reality and quietly abandoned the Eisenhower Doctrine, deciding instead to seek a political accommodation with the Nasserist movement. Conveniently, no sooner had Eisenhower shelved his doctrine than Nasser's own relations with the Soviet Union deteriorated, clearing the way for a modest rapprochement between Washington and Cairo that lasted for the rest of Eisenhower's term and into that of his successor.

In its broadest sense the Eisenhower Doctrine was an instrument with which the United States waged a political struggle with the Nasserist movement over the acceptable limits of Arab nationalism. The United States hoped to convince Arab audiences that international communism was inimical to the Arabs' national aspirations and that any Arab leader who failed to acknowledge this truth was unworthy of public support. Nasserists shifted the focus to Western imperialism and Zionism, insisting that those Arab figures with close ties to Britain or France (or, increasingly, the United States itself) were themselves outside the mainstream of Arab politics, discredited by their association with the great powers' imperialist policies and support for Israel. In the court of Arab public opinion, the Nasserists decisively won the argument, and Washington had to moderate its anti-Nasserist stance, which Nasser's falling out with Moscow made less necessary in any case.

These political dynamics offer insight into the psychological and moral dimensions of U.S.-Arab relations in the 1950s and challenge interpretations that stress cultural conflict. Cultural differences were important, but tensions between the Eisenhower administration and the Nasserist movement had less to do with clashing values than with differing applications of shared values. Each party was moved by two competing sets of values. The first set was associated with the vanquishing of evil: honor, sacrifice, solidarity, steadfastness, simplicity, and moral absolutism. The second set was best suited to conciliation and deal-making: patience, pragmatism, empathy, compromise, subtlety, and moral relativism. In Middle Eastern diplomacy, the two parties applied their shared values inversely, each urging compromise in precisely those areas in which the other demanded commitment. The Americans wanted the Arabs to be conciliatory toward Zionism and European imperialism but partisan in the Cold War. The Nasserists insisted on their right to make deals with the communist bloc even as they demanded U.S. support for the Arab positions against Zionism and imperialism. Freedom, justice, empathy, and understanding—these were the terms of reference for Americans and Nasserists alike. Eisenhower's feud with Nasser was not a conflict over values; it was a contest of interests, mediated by shared values.

TO CONTEMPLATE THE Eisenhower Doctrine from the vantage point of the early twentieth-first century is to be struck, first and foremost, by the vast psychological and moral changes that U.S.-Arab political relations have undergone over the last several decades. In Eisenhower's day even the angriest U.S.-Arab disputes occurred in an atmosphere of restraint and mutual deference that seems almost quaint by the standards of our own era, in which Americans and Arabs exchange bitter recriminations, vicious epithets, and on occasion, homicidal attacks. America's frequent military interventions in the Arab world in recent years, combined with tacit U.S. support for Israel's continuing occupation of Arab lands, reveal a striking disregard for the views and aspirations of the overwhelming majority of Arabs. Meanwhile, the terrorist attacks of 11 September 2001, the continuing threat posed by Osama bin Laden's al-Qa'ida network, and, more diffusely, the popularity in the Arab world of outlandish anti-American conspiracy theories suggest a level of antipathy toward the United States starkly disproportionate to any provocation from the American side. On a deeper level, however, there is a fundamental continuity between the struggles over the Eisenhower Doctrine and those of later decades. For all the bitterness of their mutual antagonism, Arabs and Americans continue to combat one another within a common moral framework, much as they did in the 1950s.

There can be no denying that over the last four-and-a-half decades, the sheer amount of hostility between Americans and Arabs has dramatically increased. In the 1950s Americans and Nasserists (the most formidable Arab opponents of U.S. policy at the time) viewed one another with antagonism, to be sure, but theirs was an oblique antagonism, resulting mainly from disagreements over third parties. The Americans considered the Nasserists naive and reckless in their dealings with the Soviets, while the Nasserists saw the Americans as excessively partial to Britain, France, and Israel. Only later did Americans and Arabs become directly hostile to one another, each party accusing the other of doing it deliberate and active harm.

For all their opposition to U.S. policy, Arabs in the 1950s continued to hope that American power would be, on balance, a force for the advancement of Arab political causes. In these years the United States was still growing into its role as a superpower, its heavy hand only beginning to be felt in the Arab world. Every Arab adult could remember a time when American interests in the Middle East were almost entirely missionary, philanthropic, educational, or commercial, and, a decade into the postwar era, America's reservoir of Arab goodwill was far from depleted. In the Eisenhower era U.S. identification with Israel was much more limited than it would be in later decades, and Arab leaders behaved as if they actually expected Washington to be evenhanded on the Arab-Israeli issue—and they were not always disappointed. Eisenhower himself was widely respected in the Arab world, and while Nasser had harsh words for U.S. policies in the 1950s, he never attacked Eisenhower the man. Not until Lyndon B. Johnson would an American president endure Nasser's personal vilification.[1]

For its part the Eisenhower administration approached its challenges in the Arab world with a caution and a restraint seldom shown by its successors. Though later developments would suggest that such fears were exaggerated, in the 1950s U.S. officials still believed that Western actions deemed harmful to Arab interests might elicit a hostile and concerted Arab reaction, like a cutoff of oil shipments to the West or a decision to forge closer ties with Moscow. This anxiety, as we have seen, underlay Eisenhower's vehement opposition to the British, French, and Israeli attack on Egypt in the fall of 1956. Even when the Eisenhower administration conducted its own intervention in Lebanon in July 1958, it acted in a mood of deep fatalism, convinced that the operation would so inflame the Arab world as to jeopardize Western oil facilities, pro-U.S. regimes, and even the lives of American residents in the area. The marines went in anyway, but they successfully avoided hostilities with any Lebanese or Arab combatants. Future U.S. interventions in the Arab world would be undertaken with far fewer qualms and far less restraint.

It was Eisenhower's misfortune to have launched his doctrine just as radical Arab nationalism was reaching its peak, and to have compounded his disadvantage by occasionally elevating the movement's power in his own mind. With the exception of John F. Kennedy, who felt obliged to treat Nasser with considerable deference, future U.S. presidents would not be bound by the same constraints.[2] In the 1960s Nasser's regional influence markedly diminished, some of it chipped away in internecine Arab disputes, some of it pulverized by the Israeli wrecking ball in 1967. At the time of his death in 1970, Nasser was still an imposing and beloved figure in the Arab world. Little, however, remained of the conviction, so confidently proclaimed a dozen years earlier, that the Arab nations would soon band together to defend their common interests and vanquish their common foes. (The excitement generated by the Arab oil embargo of 1973–74 was to be a brief and misleading exception to this rule.) In the ensuing decades Nasserism gave way to other Arab actors—whether "rogue" states like Libya and Iraq or militant organizations like Hizbullah, Islamic Jihad, and eventually al-Qa'ida—that were much more willing to take violent action against American targets. But these movements and regimes had far less regional appeal; none could hope to capture the imagination of Arabs everywhere and thus force the hands of Arab governments, as Nasser had done in his heyday.

Structural changes in the international system further diminished the potency of Arab challenges to the United States and its allies. The U.S.-sponsored Egyptian-Israeli peace process of the mid- to late 1970s subtracted Egyptian power from the Arab-Israeli equation, permitting Israel greater freedom of action elsewhere. One wonders if Israel would have invaded Lebanon in 1982 had Egyptian intervention been a realistic prospect. A decrease in the global demand for Middle Eastern oil in the 1980s, due both to conservation measures in the West and to the exploitation of non–Middle Eastern reserves, diminished the likely effectiveness of another Arab embargo, as did the Gulf Arab regimes' increasing economic and strategic dependence on the United States.[3] The disintegration of the Soviet bloc in the late 1980s and early 1990s was another decisive blow to would-be challengers of American hegemony. Moderate Arab governments, lacking the strategic leverage to extract modest concessions from the United States (such as a return to a more evenhanded policy on the Arab-Israeli conflict),

were increasingly upstaged by Arab extremists whose agendas were too outrageous for Washington to appease under any circumstances.

Thus as the twentieth century drew to a close, the United States faced increasingly audacious challenges to its position in the Arab world but far
fewer inhibitions about striking back with naked power; harsher measures
against Arab offenders were, from Washington's standpoint, both necessary
and possible. Over the last two decades the United States has asserted itself
in the Arab world in ways that would have been inconceivable in Eisenhower's day: launching military attacks against targets in Libya, Lebanon,
Iraq, and Sudan; using the veto in the UN Security Council to shield Israel
from criticism for its continuing occupation of the West Bank and the
Gaza Strip; ensuring the perpetuation of crippling economic sanctions against
Iraq; and intervening militarily to effect a "regime change" in that country.
Whatever one thinks of these actions, they hardly demonstrate a solicitous
regard for the broad currents of Arab public opinion. Granted similar freedom from the political consequences of his actions, Eisenhower, too, might
have ridden roughshod over Arab sensibilities, but this was a luxury he
never enjoyed.

In the introduction to this book, I challenged interpretations of U.S.-
Arab political relations that place cultural antipathies at their center. Such
interpretations are indeed of limited value with respect to the 1950s, but
they become harder to refute when applied to later decades. The recent
emergence in the Arab world of Islamist movements militantly critical of
the United States raises the possibility that most Arabs and Muslims do,
after all, harbor a deep-seated hostility to Western civilization itself. (Not
surprisingly, the attacks of 11 September and their aftermath have given
the work of Bernard Lewis and Samuel Huntington a new purchase on
public discourse.)[4] At the same time, Washington's diminishing regard for
Arab sensibilities has given rise to the charge that U.S. policies toward the
Middle East are strongly influenced by anti-Arab prejudice—a proposition
that cannot be dismissed out of hand.[5] Ultimately, however, neither resurgent Islam nor anti-Arab prejudice should be seen as a cause of the basic
conflict between U.S. policy and Arab opinion, though both phenomena
magnify its effects.

Certainly the rise to prominence of Islamist movements has strengthened the impression that Arab critiques of the United States and the West
are more "civilizational" than political. Arab causes that were once advanced in overwhelmingly secular terms, like Palestinian nationalism, have
in recent years taken on an increasingly religious cast.[6] It would be a mistake, however, to conclude that current anti-U.S. sentiment in the Arab world

is primarily rooted in a rejection of Western civilization and its values. Polls recently taken in Arab countries do reveal high levels of antagonism toward the United States, but two qualifications should be borne in mind. First, on several questions Arab critiques of the United States are not much different from critiques prevalent in other countries, including the countries of Western Europe. Second, the harshest Arab assessments are reserved for America's foreign policies, not its perceived values and cultural characteristics, for which many Arabs continue to express admiration. According to a 2003 survey conducted by the Pew Research Center for the People and the Press, "American ideas about democracy" enjoy a higher favorable rating in Lebanon (46 percent) than they do in Britain (45 percent), France (33 percent), Germany (39 percent), or Spain (30 percent), while "American ways of doing business" are more than twice as popular among the Jordanians (56 percent) as they are among the French (23 percent).[7]

Moreover, as Yvonne Yazbeck Haddad and others have shown, even avowedly Islamist critiques of U.S. policy tend to employ moral categories perfectly intelligible to the Western mind: opposition to foreign domination, revulsion against attacks on defenseless civilians, indignation over the defamation of Islam, and rejection of the "double-standard" (izdiwajiyya) that the United States has applied in responding to Israeli and Arab transgressions. This is not to say that such accusations are always accurate or that Islamists are not guilty of similar abuses; it is to say that the most resonant Islamist charges focus more on Washington's *behavior* than on the values supposedly underlying that behavior.[8] Osama bin Laden's own hatred of the United States seems mainly civilizational, but his propaganda materials rely heavily on standard political critiques of U.S. Middle East policy. When bin Laden charged, in a videotape released in October 2001, that "millions of innocent children are being killed in Iraq and in Palestine," he could be confident of striking a chord with Arabs of all persuasions.[9] It is true that certain values associated with the West, like secularism and gender equality, have in recent years come under attack in the Arab world. But such issues are usually peripheral to the political critiques and seldom generate the sort of outrage that invariably materializes when Washington is perceived as violating more universal standards of conduct.[10]

The second claim I have questioned—regarding the role of anti-Arab prejudice in recent U.S. policy toward the Middle East—is less easily disposed of. Although the existence of such prejudice was largely inconsequential in the 1950s, it is harder to say the same of more recent decades. The sheer scope of Washington's disregard for Arab views, aspirations, and even physical safety gives pause. Still, it would be too much to argue that the United States has acted out of simple malice toward the Arab people. A more plausible claim would be that American administrations have acted to further their strategic interests in the Middle East (and their political interests at home) and that the promotion of Arab welfare, while embraced in the abstract, has been largely incidental to these ends. In the early postwar decades, fear of offending Arab or world opinion was a major constraint on the United States, and U.S. officials took pains to craft Middle East policies that were legally and morally defensible in the international arena. Over the last quarter-century that fear has receded, and the United States can now give short shrift to foreign critiques. Current U.S. policy is not driven by any particular animus against the Arabs, but neither is it much affected by any concern for their sensibilities or well-being. In the early aftermath of 11 September, some observers speculated that the need to enlist Arab allies in the coming war on terrorism would force the United States to pay greater heed to Arab public opinion.[11] But subsequent developments—Washington's acquiescence in repeated Israeli incursions into Palestinian areas, its war in Iraq, and its ominous nuclear threats against a growing list of Middle Eastern foes—have put an end to such talk.[12]

There is, to be sure, a deeply moral element to official U.S. attitudes toward the Arab world. Arab terrorists' bloody attacks on innocent civilians provoke genuine and justifiable outrage among American leaders, as did the former Iraqi government's brutal treatment of its own people (at least after that regime had outlived its usefulness to Washington). Typically, however, such indignation is mustered only on behalf of the victims of America's enemies. Suffering resulting from U.S. policies or from the policies of allied governments merits little more than formulaic and inconsequential expressions of "regret."[13] There is nothing unique or surprising about this pattern—Arab indignation is no less selective—but it is deplorable all the same.

If there is any hope for the future of U.S.-Arab relations, it lies, paradoxically, in the very nature of the two peoples' mutual antagonism. Americans and Arabs are indeed divided by substantial cultural differences, and some of their conflicts arise from this fact. Yet the bitterest U.S.-Arab disputes —over life and death, peace and war, freedom and coercion—occur within a common moral framework, as each party condemns the other for sins recognized on both sides. It is tragic that Americans and Arabs apply their shared values so selectively and use them as weapons against one another. But the shared values endure, along with the faint hope that Americans and Arabs might someday achieve a mutually respectful and beneficial political friendship.

NOTES

ABBREVIATIONS

In addition to the abbreviations used in the text, the following appear in the notes.

AWF	Ann Whitman File, Dwight D. Eisenhower Papers
BFO	British Foreign Office
DDEL	Dwight D. Eisenhower Library, Abilene, Kans.
desp	despatch
DOS	Department of State
DWQ	Dar al-Watha'iq al-Qawmiyya (National Archives), Cairo
EFM	Egyptian Foreign Ministry
FBIS	*Foreign Broadcast Information Service*
FO	Foreign Office Files
FRUS	U.S. Department of State, *Foreign Relations of the United States*
NA	National Archives and Records Administration, College Park, Md.
PREM	Prime Ministerial Files
PRO	Public Record Office, Kew
RG 59	General Records of the U.S. Department of State, Record Group 59
tel	telegram
USARMA	U.S. Army attaché
WK	Al-Wizara al-Kharijiyya, al-arshif al-sirri al-jadid (Foreign Ministry, New Secret Archive)

INTRODUCTION

1. Memorandum of conversation, Dwight D. Eisenhower and Nathan F. Twining, 15 July 1958, *FRUS, 1958–1960,* 11:245.

2. Takeyh, *Origins of the Eisenhower Doctrine;* Alin, *Lebanon Crisis;* Gendzier, *Notes from the Minefield;* Lesch, *Syria and the United States;* Satloff, *From Abdullah to Hussein.* See also Little, "His Finest Hour?"

3. Ashton, *Problem of Nasser*, 103–89; Gerges, *Superpowers*, 79–128; Karabell, *Architects of Intervention*, 136–72; Ovendale, *Transfer of Power*, 178–215. See also Manchester, "Tangled Web."

4. Takeyh, *Origins of the Eisenhower Doctrine*, 151.

5. Ibid., xvi–xvii. In late 1956 and early 1957, for example, the United States hoped that Britain would continue its treaty relationship with (and accompanying subsidy of) the Jordanian government, but Britain terminated the treaty, forcing the United States to assume responsibility for Jordan's security and finances. In July 1958, after the United States and Britain decided to intervene militarily in Lebanon and Jordan, respectively, the British urged the Americans to take part in the Jordanian venture, but the Americans refused. For more on these events, see Chapters 4 and 7.

6. Such individuals were especially conspicuous within the Iraqi, Jordanian, and Lebanese diplomatic corps. See Egyptian Embassy, Damascus, to EFM, desp #364, 9 September 1957, WK, box 1223, folder: "3/6/4 al-ahwal al-siyasiyya fi-al-'Iraq," DWQ; Egyptian Embassy, Jidda, to EFM, desps #57, #65, #70, 1, 25 February, 9 March 1957, WK, Jidda Series, box 2, folder: "756/81/3 J1 al-taqarir al-siyasiyya lil-safara al-Misriyya fi-Jidda," DWQ.

7. Copeland, *Game of Nations*, 183 (emphasis in original).

8. Bernard Lewis, "Roots of Muslim Rage," 48, 52–60; Huntington, "Clash of Civilizations?," 31–38, 45–48; Huntington, *Clash of Civilizations*, 209–18. For additional citations and an intelligent analysis of this line of argument, see Gerges, *America and Political Islam*, 21–28.

9. Bernard Lewis, *Middle East and the West*, 134–36.

10. Bernard Lewis, "Roots of Muslim Rage," 52–60; Huntington, "Clash of Civilizations?," 22; Huntington, *Clash of Civilizations*, 209–18.

11. U.S. Embassy, Damascus, to DOS, 8 November 1956, *FRUS, 1955–1957*, 13:596.

12. Said, *Orientalism*; Said, *Covering Islam*; Stockton, "Ethnic Archetypes and the Arab Image"; Suleiman, *Arabs in the Mind of America*; Kamalipour, *U.S. Media and the Middle East*; Terry, *Mistaken Identity*.

13. Said, quoted in Anthony Arnove, introduction to *Iraq under Siege*, 13; Little, "Eagle and the Sphinx," 153, 155. Using less direct language, Little makes a similar claim in *American Orientalism*, 11, 25–33. In both works, Little is heeding his own earlier recommendation that scholars more fully "explore the cultural assumptions that shaped America's interactions with the Middle East" and the ways in which Americans after 1945 adopted an "American orientalism" and "came to shoulder 'the White Man's Burden' in the Middle East" (Little, "Gideon's Band," 498–99).

14. Eisenhower to Jawaharlal Nehru, 12 January 1957, AWF, DDE Diary Series, box 21, folder: "Jan '57 Miscellaneous (3)," DDEL; telephone call, Eisenhower and John Foster Dulles, 4 March 1957, AWF, DDE Diary Series, box 22, folder: "Mar '57 Phone Calls," DDEL; entry for 16 December 1955, reel 7, *Diaries of Dwight D. Eisenhower*; memorandum of conversation, J. F. Dulles and Lauris Norstad, 28 October 1957, RG 59, lot 64 D199, "Secretary of State's Memoranda of Conversation," box 7, folder: "Secy's M. of Con., Oct. 18–31, 1957," NA; J. F. Dulles, address to U.S. foreign service officers, 21 April 1956, Dulles Papers, box 106, folder: "Re Middle East 1956," Princeton University Library; telephone conversation, J. F. Dulles and James C. Hagerty, 18 February 1957, *FRUS, 1955–1957*, 17:196.

15. Devine, "Stereotypes and Prejudice"; Monteith and Walters, "Egalitarianism, Moral Obligation, and Prejudice-Related Personal Standards," 196–97.

16. Memorandum of conversation, J. F. Dulles and congressional leaders, 10 April 1956, *FRUS, 1955–1957*, 15:506; British Embassy, Washington, to BFO, tel #851, 3 April 1956, PREM 11/1937, PRO.

17. Little, "Eagle and the Sphinx," 155, 157; memorandum of conversation, J. F. Dulles, Selwyn Lloyd, et al., 10 December 1956, *FRUS, 1955–1957*, 12:400; enclosure to NSC 5801/1, 24 January 1958, *FRUS, 1958–1960*, 12:22.

18. Heiss, *Empire and Nationhood*, 46, 231–33; Mart, "Tough Guys and American Cold War Policy," 360, 368–69, 378–79. For Said's own early foreshadowings of such gendered analyses, see Said, *Orientalism*, 207, 286–87.

19. See, for example, Rotter, "Gender Relations, Foreign Relations"; Gouda, "Gendered Rhetoric of Colonialism and Anti-Colonialism in Twentieth-Century Indonesia," 19; Laura A. Lewis, "'Weakness' of Women and the Feminization of the Indian in Colonial Mexico"; Mark Philip Bradley, *Imagining Vietnam and America*, 49, 55; Sinha, *Colonial Masculinity*.

20. Costigliola, "Nuclear Family," 165, 167.

21. Telephone conversation, J. F. Dulles and Allen Dulles, 17 April 1957, Dulles Papers, Telephone Calls Series, box 6, folder: "Memoranda Tel. Conv.—General March 1957 to April 30, 1957 (2)," DDEL. For more on Washington's probable involvement in an attempted Syrian coup in the summer of 1957, see Chapter 5.

22. 371st meeting of NSC, 3 July 1958, AWF, NSC Series, box 10, DDEL; Eisenhower interview, Columbia Oral History Project, 61; Michael Wright to Selwyn Lloyd, 13 March 1958, FO 371/134198, PRO; memorandum of conversation, Eisenhower, Harold Macmillan, et al., 9 June 1958, *FRUS, 1958–1960*, 12:301–2; Gallman, *Iraq under General Nuri*, 9, 27.

23. For more on gendered portrayals of King Hussein, see Chapter 4. As Hussein's case suggests, tropes of maturity and immaturity were also present in American discourse, as American leaders and commentators sometimes portrayed Arab resistance to U.S. policy as evidence of immaturity. When King Saud opposed Washington's position on Israeli shipping in the Gulf of Aqaba in 1957, Eisenhower dismissed him as "childish" (see main text, below). In late 1958, when Nasser showed signs of taking a harder line on the Soviets and a softer one on the Israelis, Eisenhower "admitted that Nasser has grown up a little" (memorandum of conversation, Eisenhower, Richard M. Nixon, et al., 23 December 1958, *FRUS, 1958–1960*, 13:510). As with gendered portrayals, such imputations of immaturity may have had less to do with any particular animus against Arab culture than with the more general human tendency to see one's own behavior as normative and that of one's adversaries as irrational, immoral, immature, or otherwise objectionable, but the subject requires further study.

24. Eisenhower, *White House Years*, 584; memorandum of conversation, Eisenhower, Richard M. Nixon, et al., 23 December 1958, *FRUS, 1958–1960*, 13:510.

25. Holden and Johns, *House of Saud*, 179–80, 183; Lacey, *Kingdom*, 302; Arnold, *Golden Swords and Pots and Pans*, 72–74.

26. In June 1956 State Department officials interceded with *Time* publisher Henry R. Luce to kill a planned cover story on Saud in which the king's "sexual obsession" was to be hinted at. See attachment to Luce to Jackson, 21 April 1956, Jackson Papers, box

71, folder: "Luce, Henry R. & Clare, 1956 (4)," DDEL; Fraser Wilkins to Rountree, 1 June 1956, reel 2, *Confidential U.S. State Department Central Files, Saudi Arabia*; memorandum of conversation, Herbert Hoover Jr., John Noble, et al., 11 June 1956, RG 59, lot 64 D199, box 5, folder: "Sec Memo of Con, June 1957," NA.

27. Hare interview, Columbia Oral History Project, 43, 45.

28. Kunz, *Economic Diplomacy*, 39; Holland, *America and Egypt*, x–xiii; L. Carl Brown, *International Politics and the Middle East*, 3–18.

29. For a trenchant critique of the recent overuse of the word "culture," see Clausen, *Faded Mosaic*, 11–13, 18–34.

30. Holland, *America and Egypt*, x–xii, 67; Ambrose, *Eisenhower*, 2:333.

31. Saud to Eisenhower, 15 February 1957, AWF, International Series, box 46, folder: "Saudi Arabia, King Saud 1957 (1)," DDEL; telephone conversation, Eisenhower to J. F. Dulles, 27 June 1957, Dulles Papers, Telephone Calls Series, box 12, folder: "Memoranda Tel Conv.—W. H. March 1957 to Aug 30, 1957 (2)," DDEL. See Chapters 3 and 4 for a fuller discussion of the Gulf of Aqaba dispute.

32. J. F. Dulles, address to U.S. foreign service officers, 21 April 1956, Dulles Papers, box 106, folder: "Re Middle East 1956," Princeton University Library. See Chapter 3 for additional evidence of Dulles's belief in American exceptionalism.

33. For more on the consensus school of U.S. history, see Novick, *That Noble Dream*, 332–34, 443–44. To be sure, some of the more sophisticated consensus historians tempered their interpretations with an ironic skepticism that seldom found its way into Dulles's rhetoric. Louis Hartz, for example, argued in 1955 that the very circumstances that had allowed the United States to escape the ideological conflicts of the Old World now made it difficult for Americans to achieve the self-understanding and understanding of others necessary for meeting the global challenges of the modern era; see Hartz, *Liberal Tradition in America*, 284–88, 302–9.

34. Petersen, *Middle East between the Great Powers*, 110–11.

35. For more on American opinion leaders' efforts to distance the United States from the legacy of European imperialism in the Middle East, and on the reverberations of those efforts in American popular culture in the 1950s, see McAlister, *Epic Encounters*, 43–83.

36. Elie Salem to Ezra Taft Benson, n.d. [ca. July 1958], Dulles Papers, White House Memoranda Series, box 7, folder: "White House—Meetings with the President, July 1, 1958–December 31, 1958 (10)," DDEL; memorandum of conversation, William M. Rountree, Moustafa Kamel, et al., 5 August 1958, and U.S. Embassy, Cairo, to DOS, 24 July 1958, *FRUS, 1958–1960*, 13:467, 462.

37. J. F. Dulles, address to U.S. foreign service officers, 21 April 1956, Dulles Papers, box 106, folder: "Re Middle East 1956," Princeton University Library.

38. *President Gamal Abdel-Nasser's Speeches and Press-Interviews, 1958*, 236; Sulzberger, *Last of the Giants*, 500. William Hale "Big Bill" Thompson was mayor of Chicago in the 1910s and 1920s. Running for a third term in early 1927, at the same time that King George V of England was visiting the United States, Thompson delighted Irish- and German-American voters by threatening to punch the king "on the snoot" if he ventured to the shores of Lake Michigan; see Bukowski, *Big Bill Thompson*, 5–6.

39. For a forceful, if at times overstated, argument about the prevalence of emo-

tionalism in Eisenhower's and Dulles's Cold War policies, see Dallek, *American Style of Foreign Policy*, 187–220.

40. For a sophisticated and persuasive presentation of this argument, see Connelly, "Taking Off the Cold War Lens." For other works on foreign relations stressing race, ethnicity, culture, or the problems of modernization, see Hunt, *Ideology and U.S. Foreign Policy*; Lauren, *Power and Prejudice*; Latham, *Modernization as Ideology*; Holland, *America and Egypt*.

41. Eisenhower's remark to British military officials about Arab nationalism and the Crusades (see main text, above) does seem to draw on deep cultural fears. But the memorandum of that conversation immediately goes on to note that Eisenhower "seemed convinced that the build up of Nasser and Arab power under him was against all our interests and to the advantage of the Soviet" (British Embassy, Washington, to BFO, tel #851, 3 April 1956, PREM 11/1937, PRO). There were two main scenarios, in U.S. thinking, under which the triumph of anti-Western Arab nationalism could damage America's Cold War position. In the first case, Arab nationalist regimes might directly align themselves with the Soviet Union (or give way to regimes that did). In the second case, nationalist regimes, while remaining neutral in the Cold War, might limit or block Western access to the region's oil reserves and strategic positions, thus strengthening the Soviet Union by default.

Modernization theory, too, was pressed into service in the Cold War, in keeping with the widely shared assumption that material deprivation was a breeding ground for communist agitation. Walt Rostow's 1960 book *The Stages of Economic Growth*, a classic statement of modernization theory, was subtitled *A Non-Communist Manifesto*.

42. Just as Nasser invoked America's revolutionary heritage to justify current radical ferment in the Arab world, so he invoked America's neutralist heritage to defend Egypt's attitude toward the Cold War. "Our policy," he told members of the American Society of Editors and Commentators in 1957, "is based on positive neutralism, or, in other words, 'non-alignment' to any party or other in the present international strife. . . . You might recall that George Washington himself announced this policy . . . in what you call his 'farewell speech.' . . . Therefore it is indeed very strange to find that those who adopt this stand are accused of being Communists, because this would definitely mean that George Washington himself was a Communist" (U.S. Embassy, Cairo, to DOS, desp #785, 18 April 1957, RG 59, 774.11/4-1857, NA).

43. Hourani, *Arab Peoples*, 22–23, 84. For the salience of Islamic martial history even to predominantly secular Arab nationalist movements, see Bernard Lewis, *Islam and the West*, 140–41, 150–52; Maalouf, *Crusades through Arab Eyes*, 265.

My observations on Arab values are adapted from an analysis by the sociologist Halim Barakat, who groups contemporary Arab "value orientations" in a series of competing pairs: fatalism versus free will, shame versus guilt, collectivity versus individuality, obedience versus rebellion, charity versus justice, and so on. Barakat tends to associate the first half of each pair with "the dominant culture" in the Arab world and the second half with "the counterculture," whereas in my division of Arab values— conciliation versus righteousness—there is no necessary correlation between either half of that dichotomy and any particular segment of Arab society. See Barakat, *Arab World*, 190–205.

44. Memorandum of conversation, J. F. Dulles, Ahmed Hussein, et al., 8 October 1957, *FRUS, 1955–1957*, 17:754; Mosley, *Dulles*, 310; U.S. Embassy, Damascus, to DOS, 8 November 1956, and memorandum of conversation, Arthur W. Radford, Gordon Gray, and Robert D. Murphy, 10 November 1956, *FRUS, 1955–1957*, 13:596–97, 598.

45. Speech by Nasser, 1 June 1956, and Nasser interview, 17 September 1957, in *al-Majmu'a al-kamila*, 2:312, 584.

46. U.S. Embassy, Cairo, to DOS, 10 January 1957, and memorandum of conversation, J. F. Dulles, Ahmed Hussein, et al., 17 May 1956, *FRUS, 1955–1957*, 17:16, 17–18, 15:647; memorandum of conversation, J. F. Dulles, 'Abd al-Khaliq Hassuna, et al., 13 November 1957, RG 59, lot 64 D199, box 7, folder: "Secy's M. of Con., November 1957," NA.

47. U.S. Consulate, Damascus, to DOS, tel #2474, 4 March 1958, RG 59, 786.00/3-458, NA.

48. "Assessment of Current Situation in Near East," Tab A of Rountree to J. F. Dulles, 24 March 1958, *FRUS, 1958–1960*, 12:49; Egyptian Embassy, Damascus, to EFM, desp #163, 13 May 1957, WK, box 1223, folder: "3/6/4 al-ahwal al-siyasiyya fi-al-mamlaka al-Urduniyya al-Hashimiyya," DWQ.

49. U.S. Embassy, Cairo, to DOS, 19 April, 26 May 1956, 16 November 1957, *FRUS 1955–1957*, 15:560, 681–82, 17:800.

CHAPTER I

1. Bryson, *Seeds of Mideast Crisis*; Gaddis Smith, *American Diplomacy during the Second World War*, 99–118.

2. In 1946 it was projected that by 1951 Western Europe would be importing 80 percent of its oil from the Middle East. By the time the Eisenhower administration came into office in 1953, NATO countries were getting about 75 percent of their oil from the Persian Gulf. See Yergin, *The Prize*, 425; Saunders, *United States and Arab Nationalism*, vii.

3. For Truman's motivations in supporting the creation of Israel, see Benson, *Truman and the Founding of Israel*, 77–184, 195–96; Cohen, *Truman and Israel*, 275–81; Spiegel, *Other Arab-Israeli Conflict*, 16–47.

4. This stark change of mood in the late 1940s was especially painful for American diplomats in the Arab world, many of whom had opposed the creation of a Jewish state but now bore the burden of defending Truman's policy. Like the Arabs themselves, these diplomats saw the creation of Israel as having prevented them from reaping a long-awaited and well-deserved political success. "We had made a tremendous effort to lay the ground for good relations with the Arabs," recalled Parker T. Hart, who was an Arabist foreign service officer at the time, "and all of a sudden, when we were in a good position, all of our hopes were dashed" (Kaplan, *Arabists*, 86; for similar statements by other Arabist diplomats, see ibid., 107, 113).

5. Memorandum of conversation, Dwight D. Eisenhower, John Foster Dulles, et al., 23 July 1958, *FRUS, 1958–1960*, 12:98. For similar remarks by Eisenhower and Dulles, see memorandum of conversation, Eisenhower, Richard M. Nixon, et al., 23 December 1958, ibid. 13:510; memorandum of conversation, J. F. Dulles, Mike Mansfield, and William B. Macomber, 6 October 1957, Dulles Papers, General Correspondence and

Memoranda Series, box 1, folder: "Memos of Conversation—General—L Through M (3)," DDEL.

6. Hahn, *United States, Great Britain, and Egypt*, 101; Louis, *British Empire in the Middle East*, 583–84.

7. Ovendale, *Transfer of Power*, 32, 51–52; Hahn, *United States, Great Britain, and Egypt*, 102–3, 109–16, 122–28, 133.

8. Hahn, *United States, Great Britain, and Egypt*, 133–35; Stephens, *Nasser*, 96–102.

9. Two people were killed and eight wounded in the coup. See Nutting, *Nasser*, 43.

10. Stephens, *Nasser*, 104–8, 111.

11. Former CIA operative Miles Copeland maintains that, prior to the coup, the CIA was in contact with the Free Officers and gave them encouragement, but hardly any documentary evidence has emerged to substantiate this claim. See Copeland, *Game of Nations*, 53–60; Holland, *America and Egypt*, 22–28.

12. Hahn, *United States, Great Britain, and Egypt*, 148–51; Copeland, *Game of Nations*, 61–62.

13. Wills, *Nixon Agonistes*, 119; Kunz, *Economic Diplomacy*, 26–27. For Eisenhower's pre-presidential career, see Ambrose, *Eisenhower*, vol. 1.

14. For Dulles's pre-secretarial career, see Pruessen, *John Foster Dulles*.

15. See, for example, Immerman, "Eisenhower and Dulles," 21–27, 34–37; Divine, *Eisenhower*, 19–23; Greene, "Bibliographic Essay," 215–16.

16. Kunz, *Economic Diplomacy*, 27.

17. Knock, *To End All Wars*, 110–11, 313 n. 106, 205, 258, 336 n. 63; diary entry for 8 June 1957, Armstrong Papers, box 102.

18. See, for example, Divine, *Eisenhower*, 10–11, 21–23; Hoopes, *Devil and John Foster Dulles*, 170, 294–95.

19. For examples of Dulles's resistance to such proposals, see Chapters 4, 5, and 8.

20. Holsti, "'Operational Code' Approach to the Study of Political Leaders," 129–32. The very title of Townsend Hoopes's biography of Dulles—*The Devil and John Foster Dulles*—suggests the importance of religion in Hoopes's interpretation of Dulles's approach.

21. Hughes, *Ordeal of Power*, 204–7.

22. Immerman, introduction to *John Foster Dulles and the Diplomacy of the Cold War*, 11; cabinet meeting notes, 18 July 1958, White House Office, Office of the Staff Secretary, Cabinet Series, box 4, folder: "C-46 (1) July 18 and 25, 1958," DDEL.

23. Kunz, *Economic Diplomacy*, 31; Freiberger, *Dawn over Suez*, 52; Takeyh, *Origins of the Eisenhower Doctrine*, 11.

24. State Department position paper, 27 November 1953, *Declassified Documents*, 1986-1411.

25. Bill, *Eagle and the Lion*, 67–86; Kunz, *Economic Diplomacy*, 20–22; Ovendale, *Transfer of Power*, 70–72. In fact, recently released Soviet documents from the time suggest that Moscow saw little advantage in Mosadeq's premiership. See Gaddis, *We Now Know*, 166–67.

26. Bill, *Eagle and the Lion*, 86–97; Kunz, *Economic Diplomacy*, 32–33; Ovendale, *Transfer of Power*, 72–74.

27. Freiberger, *Dawn over Suez*, 50–54.

28. Ibid., 59–76; Ovendale, *Transfer of Power*, 75–78; Stephens, *Nasser*, 131–35. The original signatories to the 1950 Arab Collective Security Pact were Egypt, Lebanon, Saudi Arabia, Syria, and Yemen. Iraq and Jordan added their signatures in 1951 and 1952, respectively. See Ansari, *Arab League*, 98.

29. Stephens, *Nasser*, 21–90; Nutting, *Nasser*, 12–32.

30. Stephens, *Nasser*, 122; Hourani, *Arab Peoples*, 393; Nixon, *RN*, 1:308; Hare interview, Columbia Oral History Project, 43–44; Allan Evans to W. Park Armstrong, 14 August 1956, with attachment, RG 59, lot 58 D776, "Subject Files of the Bureau of Research and Intelligence (INR), 1945–1960," box 11, folder: "Egypt," NA.

31. In 1952 the new Egyptian regime promulgated a land reform law limiting individual holdings to 200 *feddans* (about 210 acres), with an additional 100 *feddans* permitted for dependents. Lands exceeding the limit were to be purchased by the government at a fixed rate in government bonds and redistributed among small farmers. See Stephens, *Nasser*, 114–17; Hourani, *Arab Peoples*, 383.

32. Seale, *Struggle for Syria*, 195–99; Ginat, *Soviet Union and Egypt*, 176–85.

33. Ginat, *Soviet Union and Egypt*, 185. See also Seale, *Struggle for Syria*, 210–11.

34. Ginat, *Soviet Union and Egypt*, 160–64; Smolansky, *Arab East*, 15–17, 24–25.

35. Morocco, Tunisia, and Sudan became independent in 1956.

36. Hourani, *Arab Peoples*, 373–75, 381–82, 384–90.

37. Marr, *History of Iraq*, 24–116; Ashton, *Problem of Nasser*, 28–30.

38. Wilson, *King Abdullah, Britain, and the Making of Jordan*; Satloff, *From Abdullah to Hussein*, 3–107.

39. Long, *Kingdom of Saudi Arabia*, 28–34; Kunz, *Economic Diplomacy*, 19–20.

40. Ashton, *Problem of Nasser*, 32–33; Seale, *Struggle For Syria*, 24–185.

41. Ashton, *Problem of Nasser*, 33–34; Qubain, *Crisis in Lebanon*, 17–21, 25–27.

42. Freiberger, *Dawn over Suez*, 94–100, 104–6; Ashton, *Problem of Nasser*, 43–51.

43. Ashton, *Problem of Nasser*, 52–53; Nutting, *Nasser*, 77–78; Stephens, *Nasser*, 143–45.

44. Nutting, *Nasser*, 100–101; Aronson, *Sideshow*, 119–21.

45. Ashton, *Problem of Nasser*, 47–48, 49–50; Freiberger, *Dawn over Suez*, 105–6.

46. Motivation for such infiltration varied widely. Many infiltrators from Gaza were Palestinian refugees who sought merely to retrieve property from their former homes, to see relatives who had remained in Israel, or to visit family graves. Other infiltrators, both Palestinian and Egyptian, entered Israel to commit acts of sabotage or murder so as to maintain a state of tension along the armistice lines, thus preventing the consolidation of an unacceptable status quo. See Tal, "Israel's Road," 61.

47. Ibid., 63–64, 69; Stephens, *Nasser*, 151–52, 165.

48. Freiberger, *Dawn over Suez*, 109–24.

49. Aronson, *Sideshow*, 125–41; Holland, *America and Egypt*, 70–72; transcript of Soviet Communist Party Central Committee Plenum, 24 June 1957, *Cold War International History Project Bulletin* 10 (March 1998): 54.

50. Memorandum of conversation, J. F. Dulles and Josip Broz Tito, 6 November 1955, Dulles Papers, General Correspondence and Memoranda Series, box 1, folder: "Memos of Conversation—General—T Through Z," DDEL; Holland, *America and Egypt*, 72–73, 75–76; Kunz, *Economic Diplomacy*, 40–46, 48–59; Freiberger, *Dawn over Suez*, 124–26, 134–37; Neff, *Warriors at Suez*, 124–25.

51. Dann, *King Hussein*, 26–29; Satloff, *From Abdullah to Hussein*, 114–23.

52. Dann, *King Hussein*, 31–34; Nutting, *No End of a Lesson*, 34; Hahn, *United States, Great Britain, and Egypt*, 201.

53. Nasser had ruled out direct negotiations with Israel, insisting on communicating through a mediator; Ben-Gurion had called for face-to-face talks. Nasser had demanded that Israel relinquish portions of the Negev Desert to Egypt and Jordan (making the two Arab states territorially contiguous) and give Palestinian refugees the choice of either returning to their former homes in Israel or receiving compensation if they settled elsewhere; Ben-Gurion had refused to consider any large territorial concession or wholesale repatriation of Palestinian refugees. See Freiberger, *Dawn over Suez*, 138–40.

54. Ibid., 145–46; U.S. Embassy, Cairo, to DOS, 6 March 1956, *FRUS, 1955–1957*, 15:305.

55. Robert B. Anderson to J. F. Dulles, 6 March 1956; U.S. Embassy, Cairo, to DOS, 5, 6 March 1956; and "United States Policy in the Near East," 28 March 1956, *FRUS, 1955–1957*, 15:311–12, 297, 306, 410.

56. Diary entries by the president, 8, 13 March 1956, ibid., 327, 342–43.

57. Memorandum, J. F. Dulles to Eisenhower, 28 March 1956, ibid., 419.

58. PL 480 was a program under which developing nations could purchase American grain, oil, and other commodities with local (usually nonconvertible) currency, a beneficial arrangement for nations suffering from shortages of hard currency.

59. Memorandum, J. F. Dulles to Eisenhower, 28 March 1956, *FRUS, 1955–1957*, 15:419; "United States Policy in the Near East," 28 March 1956, *Declassified Documents*, 1994-256.

60. Memorandum, J. F. Dulles to Eisenhower, 28 March 1956, *FRUS, 1955–1957*, 15:420–21.

61. In the early 1960s Gerson, a biographer of Dulles, was granted access to Eisenhower's papers, then located at the former president's Gettysburg farm. Gerson made a verbatim transcription of the 28 March memorandum, which was subsequently released only in sanitized form. That transcription is now located in the Louis M. Gerson Collection, University of Connecticut, Storrs, under the supervision of Professor J. Gary Clifford. For speculation that the document considered the overthrow of Nasser, see Kunz, *Economic Diplomacy*, 64–65. Freiberger even finds it "logical to conclude that Nasser was to be killed" (*Dawn over Suez*, 149). More modestly, Takeyh speculates that the OMEGA plan included covert encouragement of "opposition forces" inside Egypt; see Takeyh, *Origins of the Eisenhower Doctrine*, 114–15.

62. Memorandum of conversation, Eisenhower, J. F. Dulles, et al., 28 March 1956; memorandum of conversation, George V. Allen, Ivone Kirkpatrick, et al., 15 March 1956; and "United States Policy in the Near East," 28 March 1956, *FRUS, 1955–1957*, 15:423, 366, 417; Office of Intelligence and Research, U.S. Department of State, "The Outlook for Saudi Arabia," 13 January 1956, RG 59, lot 58 D776, box 10, folder: "Near & Middle East—1955–1956," NA, 13–17; J. F. Dulles to Eisenhower, 8 March 1956, Gerson Papers.

63. Diary entry by the president, 28 March 1956, *FRUS, 1955–1957*, 15:425; British Embassy, Washington, to BFO, tel #821, 1 April 1956, PREM 11/1937, PRO.

64. Bligh, *From Prince to King*, 62. In June 1956 the State Department estimated that there were 60,000 Egyptians in Saudi Arabia, of whom 5,000 were officers, advisers,

and instructors and the remainder laborers. See DOS to U.S. Embassy, Jidda, 21 June 1956, *FRUS, 1955–1957*, 13:379 n 1.

65. Holden and Johns, *House of Saud*, 179–80, 183; Arnold, *Golden Swords and Pots and Pans*, 72–74; Lacey, *Kingdom*, 302; attachment to Henry R. Luce to C. D. Jackson, 21 April 1956, Jackson Papers, box 71, folder: "Luce, Henry R. & Clare, 1956 (4)," DDEL.

66. "United States Policy in the Near East," 28 March 1956, and memorandum of conversation, J. F. Dulles, Roger Makins, et al., 4 April 1956, *FRUS, 1955–1957*, 15:417, 459.

67. Memorandum of conversation, J. F. Dulles, Makins, et al., 1 April 1956, and DOS to U.S. Embassy, Ottawa, 12 April 1956, ibid., 439–41, 527–28; BFO to British Embassy, Washington, tel #1898, 4 April 1956, and Selwyn Lloyd to Anthony Eden, 6 April 1956, PREM 11/1937, PRO. France sold Israel twenty-four Mystere II and Mystere IV jet fighters; Canada sold it twenty-four F-86s. See Freiberger, *Dawn over Suez*, 153.

68. Gorst and Lucas, "Operation Straggle," 585–86; Eveland, *Ropes of Sand*, 169–70; Seale, *Struggle for Syria*, 270–71.

69. Eveland, *Ropes of Sand*, 192–95, 197–98, 202–3; Gorst and Lucas, "Operation Straggle," 589.

70. Memorandum of conversation, J. F. Dulles, Makins, et al., 1 April 1956, *FRUS, 1955–1957*, 15:437; British Embassy, Washington, to BFO, tel #821, 1 April 1956, PREM 11/1937, PRO.

71. Most of the congressional opposition to Aswan Dam funding came from sympathizers with Israel, from opponents of Nasser's dealings with communist nations, or from southern politicians who feared that increasing Egypt's cotton production would harm cotton growers in their own states. See Hahn, *United States, Great Britain, and Egypt*, 203.

72. Kunz, *Economic Diplomacy*, 65–72; Hahn, *United States, Great Britain, and Egypt*, 203–5. Although the British later complained that Dulles had failed to consult them before withdrawing the Aswan Dam offer, the record shows that they were consulted about, and did acquiesce in, the U.S. decision in advance. See Hahn, *United States, Great Britain, and Egypt*, 205–6.

73. Hahn, *United States, Great Britain, and Egypt*, 206; Nutting, *Nasser*, 145–46; Freiberger, *Dawn over Suez*, 156; U.S. Embassy, Cairo, to DOS, 26 July 1956, *FRUS, 1955–1957*, 15:906–8.

74. Two-thirds of Western Europe's oil imports and a quarter of Britain's total imports passed through the Suez Canal. Moreover, because Britain held a 45 percent share in the Suez Canal Company, it stood to lose considerable revenues derived from the company's profits. Nasser's move also complicated the Eden cabinet's domestic political position, since Conservative Party backbenchers could now claim that Britain's withdrawal from the Suez base had emboldened Nasser to behave more provocatively than he otherwise would have dared. See Hugh Thomas, *Suez*, 31; Hahn, *United States, Great Britain, and Egypt*, 212–13.

75. Freiberger, *Dawn over Suez*, 161–80; Kunz, *Economic Diplomacy*, 76–115; Hahn, *United States, Great Britain, and Egypt*, 211–23.

76. Haykal, *Milaffat al-Suways*, 510–11; U.S. State Department, Office of Intelligence Research, "The Cairo-Riyadh Axis: Second Thoughts in Saudi Arabia," 10 August 1956, and British Embassy, Baghdad, to BFO, tels #954, #1049, 30 August, 15 September 1956, in Tuson and Burdett, *Records of Saudi Arabia*, 255–59, 263–64, 274–75;

U.S. Embassy, Jidda, to DOS, tel #118, 4 September 1956, *Declassified Documents*, 1994-838.

77. U.S. Embassy, Baghdad, to DOS, tel #331, 29 August 1956, RG 59, 686A.87/8-2956, NA; British Embassy, Baghdad, to BFO, tels #954, #1049, #1085, 30 August, 15, 23 September 1956, in Tuson and Burdett, *Records of Saudi Arabia*, 263–64, 274–75, 277–78.

78. For discussion of the eighteen-power proposal, see Kunz, *Economic Diplomacy*, 92; Kyle, *Suez*, 194.

79. U.S. Consulate, Dhahran, to DOS, 23 August 1956, *FRUS, 1955–1957*, 16:274; Eveland, *Ropes of Sand*, 210–12; DOS to U.S. Embassy, London, TEDUL #8, 17 August 1956, reel 6, *Confidential U.S. State Department Central Files, Egypt*.

80. U.S. Consulate, Dhahran, to DOS, 23 August 1956, *FRUS, 1955–1957*, 16:274–75; Saud to Nasser, 7 September 1956, reproduced in Haykal, *Milaffat al-Suways*, 820–21; Haykal, *Milaffat al-Suways*, 508, 510; joint Saudi-Egyptian-Syrian communiqué, 24 September 1956, in Tuson and Burdett, *Records of Saudi Arabia*, 290–91. Syrian president Shukri al-Quwatli also attended the meeting in Dammam.

81. Eveland, *Ropes of Sand*, 217–23; Gorst and Lucas, "Operation Straggle," 589–90.

82. Egyptian Embassy, Washington, to EFM, 26 September 1956, reproduced in Haykal, *Milaffat al-Suways*, 823; Egyptian Embassy, Damascus, to EFM, desp #556, 8 October 1958, WK, box 1190, folder: "2/3/6 Mu'amarat al-gharb ma' al-'Iraq didda Suriya," DWQ. The Lebanese source was former foreign minister Hamid Frangieh.

83. Egyptian Embassy, Damascus, to EFM, desp #564, 15 October 1956, WK, box 1190, folder: "2/3/6 Mu'amarat al-gharb ma' al-'Iraq didda Suriya," DWQ. An Iraqi diplomat in Damascus later told the U.S. embassy that Syrian authorities had gotten wind of the conspiracy because of lack of discretion on the part of Salih Mahdi al-Samarra'i, Iraq's military attaché in Damascus. See U.S. Embassy, Damascus, to DOS, desp #348, 25 February 1958, RG 59, 783.00/2-2558, NA.

84. Freiberger, *Dawn over Suez*, 180–83, 259–60 n. 110.

85. Ibid., 183; Hahn, *United States, Great Britain, and Egypt*, 222, 225.

86. "Egypt (and Iraq) Minute by Sir M[ichael] Wright," 30 July 1956, and British Embassy, Baghdad, to BFO, tels #881, #914, #951, 12, 20, 29 August 1956, PREM 11/1896, PRO.

87. Freiberger, *Dawn over Suez*, 187–88; Hahn, *United States, Great Britain, and Egypt*, 229–31.

88. Hahn, *United States, Great Britain, and Egypt*, 228–32; Kyle, *Suez*, 386.

89. Ambrose, *Eisenhower*, 2:366.

90. Powaski, *Cold War*, 116–17; Ambrose, *Eisenhower*, 2:362–63.

91. Seale, *Struggle for Syria*, 277–79; Eveland, *Ropes of Sand*, 226–27.

92. The only pipelines now operating in Syria were those of the Trans-Arabian Pipeline Company (TAPLINE), which carried Saudi oil.

93. Editorial note, *FRUS, 1955–1957*, 16:1011; Hahn, *United States, Great Britain, and Egypt*, 232–33; Stephens, *Nasser*, 230–31.

94. Nicolai Bulganin, messages to Eisenhower, Eden, Guy Mollet, and Ben-Gurion, 5 November 1956, and White House statement, 5 November 1956, U.S. Department of State, *United States Policy in the Middle East*, 180–81, 183–88, 182.

95. U.S. Embassy, Moscow, to DOS, 5 November 1956, and memorandum of con-

versation, Eisenhower, Herbert Hoover Jr., et al., 5 November 1956, ibid., 995, 1001; Ambrose, *Eisenhower*, 2:368.

96. Editorial note, *FRUS, 1955–1957*, 16:1011; Ambrose, *Eisenhower*, 2:369–70.

CHAPTER 2

1. Memorandum by the president, 8 November 1956, *FRUS, 1955–1957*, 16:1088.
2. Ibid.
3. Ibid. With Eisenhower's encouragement, the U.S. Information Agency circulated within Middle Eastern countries motion pictures about events in Hungary. See 303rd meeting of NSC, 8 November 1956, ibid., 1083.
4. Memorandum by the president, 8 November 1956, ibid., 1088–89.
5. At the time Dulles was still recovering from surgery at Walter Reed Hospital, where he remained until 18 November. He then went to Florida for further convalescence and returned to Washington in early December. While at Walter Reed Hospital, Dulles frequently consulted with Eisenhower and other U.S. officials.
6. Telephone conversation, Dwight D. Eisenhower and Herbert Hoover Jr., 13 November 1956; Douglas MacArthur II to Hoover, 13 November 1956; and Fisher Howe to Hoover, 14 November 1956, *FRUS, 1955–1957*, 16:1122, 1121, 12:324.
7. Telephone conversation, Eisenhower and Henry Cabot Lodge, 31 October 1956, AWF, DDE Diary Series, box 18, folder: "Oct. '56 Phone Calls," DDEL; Kyle, *Suez*, 527; U.S. Embassy, Cairo, to DOS, tel #1339, 5 November 1956, reel 10, and "Status of Near Eastern Crisis," attachment to William M. Rountree to Hoover, 7 November 1956, reel 11, *Confidential U.S. State Department Central Files, Palestine-Israel: Foreign Affairs*.
8. Bipartisan legislative meeting, 9 November 1956, AWF, DDE Diary Series, box 20, folder: "Nov '56 Miscellaneous (3)," DDEL; memorandum of conversation, Eisenhower, John Foster Dulles, and Hoover, 7 November 1956, *FRUS, 1955–1957*, 16:1052.
9. U.S. Embassy, Cairo, to DOS, 2 November 1956, *FRUS, 1955–1957*, 16:939–40.
10. For indications of Nasser's increased popularity in the Arab world, see U.S. Embassy, Baghdad, to DOS, desp #285, 5 November 1956, reel 10; U.S. Embassy, Beirut, to DOS, tel #1133, 7 November 1956; U.S. Consulate, Basra, to DOS, desp #24, 8 November 1956; and U.S. Embassy, Jidda, to DOS, tel #257, 10 November 1956, reel 11, all in *Confidential U.S. State Department Central Files, Palestine-Israel: Foreign Affairs*.
11. Memorandum for W. Park Armstrong, 8 November 1956, and U.S. Embassy, Cairo, to DOS, 8 November 1956, *FRUS, 1955–1957*, 16:1087, 1097.
12. U.S. Embassy, Jidda, to DOS, tel #218, 31 October 1956, and U.S. United Nations Delegation, New York, to DOS, tel #456, 31 October 1956, reel 10, *Confidential U.S. State Department Central Files, Palestine-Israel: Foreign Affairs*; U.S. Embassy, Cairo, to DOS, 4 November 1956, *FRUS, 1955–1957*, 16:975; *al-Ahram* editorial, 9 November 1956. See also U.S. Embassy, Cairo, to DOS, 2 November 1956, *FRUS, 1955–1957*, 16:939–40; U.S. Embassy, Damascus, to DOS, tels #1003, #1004, 1 November 1956, and U.S. Embassy, Beirut, to DOS, tel #1070, 3 November 1956, reel 10, and U.S. Embassy, Tripoli, to DOS, tel #316, 8 November 1956, reel 11, *Confidential U.S. State Department Central Files, Palestine-Israel: Foreign Affairs*.
13. U.S. Embassy, Beirut, to DOS, tel #1014, 30 October 1956, RG 59, 783.00(A)/10-3056, NA. The ambassador also noted that "various Christian personalities have ex-

pressed glee over [the] Israeli move towards Egypt" (ibid.). In Abu Dhabi about this time, sheiks of the bu Fahal family told the British political officer "that they hoped Nasser would be taught a lesson by the Israelis" ("Trucial States Diary No. 11 for the period November 1–30, 1956," *Political Diaries of the Persian Gulf*, 274).

14. U.S. Embassy, Baghdad, to DOS, desp #285, 5 November 1956, reel 10, *Confidential U.S. State Department Central Files, Palestine-Israel: Foreign Affairs*; Memorandum of conversation, Hoover and Arab ambassadors, 3 November 1956, *FRUS, 1955–1957*, 16:951; Kyle, *Suez*, 397–98; "Muscat Intelligence Summary No. 10 for the Period October 1 to 31, 1956," *Political Diaries of the Persian Gulf*, 230. In late November Chamoun complained to *Foreign Affairs* editor Hamilton Fish Armstrong, "If Israel had been allowed to deal with Nasser alone, he would be gone by now. Within 24 hours of the attack Nasser's picture had come down in every Lebanese shop window. The Egyptian army was beaten. Then Britain and France came in and Nasser's pictures all went up again. Now he is at [the] apex of prestige" (diary entry for 24 November 1956, Armstrong Papers, box 102).

15. *Al-Nas* editorial, 2 November 1956, quoted in U.S. Consulate, Basra, to DOS, desp #24, 8 November 1956, reel 11, *Confidential U.S. State Department Central Files, Palestine-Israel: Foreign Affairs*.

16. U.S. Embassy, Jidda, to DOS, tel #223, 1 November 1956, and U.S. Embassy, Baghdad, to DOS, desp #285, 5 November 1956, reel 10, ibid.; U.S. Embassy, Tripoli, to DOS, desp #191, 13 November 1956, RG 59, 773.00(W)/11-1356, NA.

17. Diary entry for 7 December 1956, Armstrong Papers, box 102; Keith Wheeler to Manuel Gottfried, 1 November 1956, Jackson Papers, box 71, folder: "Luce, Henry R. & Clare, 1956 (1)," DDEL; *Political Diaries of the Persian Gulf*, 239, 243; Holden, *Farewell to Arabia*, 24–25. Violence against British civilians, however, was rare.

18. U.S. Embassy, Amman, to DOS, tel #457, 6 November 1956, and U.S. Embassy, Cairo, to DOS, tel #1282, 2 November 1956, reel 10, *Confidential U.S. State Department Central Files, Palestine-Israel: Foreign Affairs*; Wheeler to Gottfried, 1 November 1956, Jackson Papers, box 71, folder: "Luce, Henry R. & Clare, 1956 (1)," DDEL.

19. U.S. Embassy, Amman, to DOS, tel #457, 6 November 1956, reel 10; U.S. Embassy, Jidda, to DOS, tel #257, 10 November 1956; U.S. Embassy, Beirut to DOS, tel #1133, 7 November 1956; U.S. Embassy, Tripoli, to DOS, tel #316, 8 November 1956; and U.S. Consulate, Basra, to DOS, desp #24, 8 November 1956, reel 11, all in *Confidential U.S. State Department Central Files, Palestine-Israel: Foreign Affairs*.

20. U.S. Embassy, Beirut, to DOS, tel #1133, 7 November 1956, ibid.; diary entry for 3 December 1956, Armstrong Papers, box 102.

21. U.S. Embassy, Damascus, to DOS, tel #1106, 8 November 1956; U.S. Consulate, Basra, to DOS, desp #24, 8 November 1956; and U.S. Embassy, Jidda, to DOS, tel #257, 10 November 1956, reel 11, *Confidential U.S. State Department Central Files, Palestine-Israel: Foreign Affairs*. For additional reports on Arab popular support for the Soviet gestures, see U.S. Embassy, Amman, to DOS, tel #457, 6 November 1956, reel 10, and U.S. Embassy, Cairo, to DOS, tel #1389, 7 November 1956, reel 11, ibid.; U.S. Embassy, Amman, to DOS, tel #464, 7 November 1956, reel 1, *Confidential U.S. State Department Central Files, Jordan*.

22. Special National Intelligence Estimate, 6 November 1956; U.S. Embassy, Moscow, to DOS, 5 November 1956; U.S. Embassy, Cairo, to DOS, 6 November 1956;

memorandum of conversation, Eisenhower, J. F. Dulles, and Hoover, 7 November 1956; 303rd meeting of NSC, 8 November 1956; and Special National Intelligence Estimate, 16 November 1956, *FRUS, 1955–1957*, 16:1019, 995–96, 1027–28, 1052, 1079–81, 13:603.

23. U.S. Embassy, Cairo, to DOS, 19 November 1956, ibid., 16:1164; cabinet meeting notes, 16 November 1956, White House Office, Office of the Staff Secretary, Cabinet Series, box 4, DDEL; memorandum of conversation, J. F. Dulles and Lyndon B. Johnson, 13 November 1956, Dulles Papers, General Correspondence and Memoranda Series, box 1, folder: "Memos of Conversation—General—J Through K (1)," DDEL; U.S. Embassy, Moscow, to DOS, tels #1285, #1309, 22, 24 November 1956, reel 12, *Confidential U.S. State Department Central Files, Palestine-Israel: Foreign Affairs*.

24. Kunz, *Economic Diplomacy*, 133–52. France was less vulnerable to this last form of pressure, since it had made a large withdrawal from the International Monetary Fund just prior to the Suez war. See ibid., 113–14, 192–93.

25. *Al-Ahram* editorial, 26 November 1956; interview with Akram al-Hawrani, *Ruz al-Yusuf*, 19 November 1956, 8; translation of 6 December speech by Shukri al-Quwatli, U.S. Embassy, Damascus, to DOS, desp #265, 11 December 1956, RG 59, 783.00/12-1156, NA. See also U.S. Embassy, Amman, to DOS, tel #503, 17 November 1956; U.S. Embassy, Damascus, to DOS, tel #1246, 22 November 1596; U.S. Embassy, Cairo, to DOS, tel #1786, 4 December 1956; and U.S. Embassy, Beirut, to DOS, tel #1487, 10 December 1956, RG 59, 684A.86/11-1756, 684A.86/11-2256, 684A.86/12-456, 684A.86/12-1056, NA; Foreign Ministry commentary, Damascus radio, *FBIS*, #236, 5 December 1956, A6.

26. See, for example, U.S. Embassy, Beirut, to DOS, tel #1490, 10 December 1956, RG 59, 684A.86/12-1056, NA; U.S. Consulate, Jerusalem, to DOS, desp #83, 30 November 1956, reel 1, *Confidential U.S. State Department Central Files, Jordan*; diary entry for 3 December 1956, Armstrong Papers, box 102; A. Willard Jones to "Friends," 6 December 1956, AWF, International Series, box 35, folder: "Jordan, The (4)," DDEL.

27. A. Willard Jones to "Friends," 6 December 1956, AWF, International Series, box 35, folder: "Jordan, The (4)," DDEL.

28. Press summary in U.S. Embassy, Beirut, to DOS, tel #1487, 10 December 1956, and U.S. Embassy, Baghdad, to DOS, tel #1007, 6 December 1956, RG 59, 684A.86/12-1056, 684A.86/12-656, NA. Also calling for the dismantling of Israel were Syrian Ba'th Party leader Akram al-Hawrani and elements of the Iraqi and Egyptian press. See translation of *al-Nas* editorial, 17 December 1956, U.S. Consulate, Basra, to DOS, desp #32, 19 December 1956, RG 59, 611.80/12-1956, NA; interview with Akram al-Hawrani, *Ruz al-Yusuf*, 19 November 1956, 8; *al-Ahram* editorial, 8 December 1956.

29. U.S. United Nations Mission, Geneva, to DOS, tel #587, 7 December 1956, and U.S. United Nations Delegation, New York, to DOS, DELGA 390, 21 December 1956, RG 59, 684A.86/12-756, 684A.86/12-2156, NA.

30. For commentaries in the first category, see press summaries in U.S. Embassy, Cairo, to DOS, tels #1725, #1843, 29 November, 10 December 1956, RG 59, 684A.86/11-2956, 684A.86/12-1056, NA; Foreign Ministry commentary, Damascus radio, *FBIS*, #236, 5 December 1956, A6; *al-Ahram* editorial, 26 November 1956. For the second category, see *al-Ahram* editorial, 29 November 1956; commentary by Anwar Sadat,

Cairo radio, *FBIS*, #229, 26 November 1956, A4–5. In some cases, like that of the editorialist for *al-Ahram*, a single commentator employed both rhetorical modes.

31. Wall, *France, the United States, and the Algerian War*, 14–32; memorandum of conversation, Eisenhower, George M. Humphrey, et al., 21 November 1957, *FRUS, 1955–1957*, 12:340–42 (emphasis in original).

32. Diary entries for 30 November, 3 December 1956, Armstrong Papers, box 102. The proprietor was Bertha Spafford Vester, leader and lifelong resident of the American Colony, a Christian community that since the late nineteenth century had operated philanthropic and commercial enterprises in Jerusalem.

33. Press summaries in U.S. Embassy, Beirut, to DOS, tels #1490, #1516, 10, 13 December 1956, RG 59, 684A.86/12-1356, and in U.S. Embassy, Damascus, to DOS, tel #1392, 7 December 1956, RG 59, 783.00/12-756, NA; commentary by Anwar Sadat, Cairo radio, *FBIS*, #239, 10 December 1956, A15. Shortly after Britain and France agreed to an unconditional withdrawal, the United States stopped blocking British attempts to make withdrawals from the International Monetary Fund; it also approved a $500 million Export-Import Bank loan to Britain. On 30 November, even before Britain and France committed to an unconditional withdrawal, the Eisenhower administration authorized oil shipments to Western Europe to make up for the shortfall due to the Suez war. See Kunz, *Economic Diplomacy*, 149, 162.

34. USARMA, Beirut, to DOS, CX 158, 21 November 1956, and U.S. Embassy, Beirut, to DOS, tels #1315, #1331, 23 November 1956, desp #237, 4 December 1956, reel 1, *Confidential U.S. State Department Central Files, Lebanon*; U.S. Embassy, Tripoli, to DOS, desps #191, #210, 13, 26 November 1956, RG 59, 773.00(W)/11-1356, 773.00(W)/11-2656, NA; DOS to U.S. Embassy, Damascus, 24 November 1956, *FRUS, 1955–1957*, 16:1191–92.

35. Cabinet meeting notes, 16 November 1956, White House Office, Office of the Staff Secretary, Cabinet Series, box 4, folder: "C-34 (2) November 16, 1956," DDEL; U.S. Embassy, Cairo, to DOS, 19 November 1956, *FRUS, 1955–1957*, 16:1164.

36. U.S. Embassy, Moscow, to DOS, tel #1309, 24 November 1956, and U.S. Embassy, London, to DOS, tel #2932, 26 November 1956, RG 59, 684A.86/11-2656, NA; U.S. Consulate, Alexandria, to DOS, tel #224, 20 November 1956, and U.S. Embassy, Beirut, to DOS, tel #1376, 27 November 1957, reel 12, *Confidential U.S. State Department Central Files, Palestine-Israel: Foreign Affairs*; U.S. Embassy, Cairo, to DOS, 2, 3 December 1956, *FRUS, 1955–1957*, 16:1234, 1235 n. 4; Kyle, *Suez*, 483–84. Nasser also refused to allow Canadian troops to participate in the UN peacekeeping force, arguing that their uniforms, language, and regimental names (e.g., The Queen's Own Rifles) might cause the local population to mistake them for British troops. See Kyle, *Suez*, 482; Love, *Suez*, 649.

37. U.S. Embassy, Tripoli, to DOS, desps #191, #210, 13 November, 26 November 1956, RG 59, 773.00(W)/11-1356, 773.00(W)/11-2256, NA; U.S. Embassy, Beirut, to DOS, desp #237, 4 December 1956, reel 1, *Confidential U.S. State Department Central Files, Lebanon*; U.S. Embassy, Cairo, to DOS, 2 December 1956, *FRUS, 1955–1957*, 16:1235–36.

38. For examples of Hoover's, Allen Dulles's, and Radford's views of Nasser, see memorandum of conversation, Eisenhower, Sherman Adams, et al., 5 November 1956; 303rd meeting of NSC, 8 November 1956; Allen W. Dulles to Hoover, 10 November 1956; 304th meeting of NSC, 15 November 1956; and memorandum of conversation,

A. W. Dulles, Christian Pineau, and Jean Henri Daridan, 16 November 1956, *FRUS, 1955–1957*, 16:1000–1001, 1084, 1101, 1128, 1137.

39. U.S. Embassy, Cairo, to DOS, 2 December 1956, *FRUS, 1955–1957*, 16:1234–35; U.S. Embassy, Cairo, to DOS, tel #1662, 26 November 1956, RG 59, 684A.86/11-2656, NA; memorandum of conversation, Radford and MacArthur, 29 November 1956, RG 59, lot 58 D776, "Subject Files of the Bureau of Intelligence and Research (INR), 1945–1960," box 11, folder: "Middle East Crisis—1956," NA.

40. MacArthur to Hoover, 20 November 1956; memorandum of conversation, Eisenhower, Humphrey, et al., 20 November 1956; 305th meeting of NSC, 30 November 1956; memorandum of conversation, Eisenhower, Humphrey, et al., 21 November 1956; and Rountree to J. F. Dulles, 5 December 1956, *FRUS, 1955–1957*, 16:1165, 1169, 1228–29, 12:340, 379; Hoover to Eisenhower, n.d. [21 November 1956], AWF, Dulles-Herter Series, box 8, folder: "Dulles, Foster, Nov. '56 (1)," DDEL; "Program to Counter Soviet Penetration in the Middle East," 5 December 1956, RG 59, lot 66 D487, "Policy Planning Staff Office Files," box 113, folder: "S/P Working Papers Dec 1956," NA; White House Staff Notes #46, 28 November 1956, AWF, DDE Diary Series, box 19, folder: "Nov. '56 Diary—Staff Memos," DDEL.

41. Special National Intelligence Estimate, 29 November 1956, *FRUS, 1955–1957*, 12:359–60.

42. Ibid., 353.

43. For a retrospective discussion of Arab reactions to events in Hungary, see Operating Coordinating Board report, 22 December 1956, ibid., 423.

44. Satloff, *From Abdullah to Hussein*, 157–58; 305th meeting of NSC, 30 November 1956, *FRUS, 1955–1957*, 16:1219. In early December State Department intelligence concluded that as of late October Egypt had already received about $250 million worth of arms from the Soviet bloc, including 80 MiG-15 jet fighters, 180 T-34 tanks, 100 armored personnel carriers, and assorted antiaircraft and antitank guns. See Bureau of Intelligence and Research, "Bloc Arms Shipments to Egypt and Syria," 6 December 1956, RG 59, lot 58 D776, box 11, folder: "Middle East Crisis—1956," NA.

45. A. W. Dulles to Hoover, 10 November 1956, RG 59, lot 58 D776, box 11, folder: "Middle East Crisis—1956," NA. Allen Dulles went on to write that the CIA was "intensively restudying the STRAGGLE operation with a view to reactivating it."

46. Special National Intelligence Estimate, 16, 29 November 1956, and DOS to U.S. Embassy, Ankara, 10 December 1956, *FRUS, 1955–1957*, 13:603, 12:358, 24:705. For more on Soviet aid to Syria at this time, see Chapter 5.

47. U.S. Embassy, Ankara, to DOS, tel #1123, 14 November 1956, AWF, Dulles-Herter Series, box 8, folder: "Dulles, Foster, Nov. '56 (1)," DDEL.

48. Ibid.; U.S. Embassy, Ankara, to DOS, 14 November 1956, and Rountree to MacArthur, 19 November 1956, *FRUS, 1955–1957*, 24:695–97, 703; U.S. NATO Delegation, Paris, to DOS, POLTO 1211, 26 November 1956, RG 59, 684A.86/11-2656, NA; U.S. Embassy, Moscow, to DOS, tel #1285, 22 November 1956, reel 12, *Confidential U.S. State Department Central Files, Palestine-Israel: Foreign Affairs*.

49. Memorandum of conversation, Eisenhower and J. F. Dulles, 17 November 1956; 305th meeting of NSC, 30 November 1956; and memorandum of conversation, Radford, Gordon Gray, and Murphy, 10 November 1956, *FRUS, 1955–1957*, 16:1141, 1220,

13:598; U.S. Embassy, Moscow, to DOS, tel #1292, 23 November 1956, reel 12, *Confidential U.S. State Department Central Files, Palestine-Israel: Foreign Affairs.*

50. See, for example, memorandum of conversation, Eisenhower, Charles E. Wilson, et al., 19 December 1956, *FRUS, 1955–1957*, 12:414.

51. Hoover to Eisenhower, 21 November 1956, ibid., 12:343–51. *FRUS*'s version of this document is partially censored. The censored portions can be restored by combining the versions of this document available in RG 59, 611.80/11-2156, NA, and in AWF, Dulles-Herter Series, box 8, folder: "Dulles, Foster, Nov. '56 (1)," DDEL.

52. Hoover to Eisenhower, 21 November 1956, versions in RG 59, 611.80/11-2156, NA, and in AWF, Dulles-Herter Series, box 8, folder: "Dulles, Foster, Nov. '56 (1)," DDEL.

53. Entry for 21 November 1956, AWF, Ann Whitman Diary Series, box 8, folder: "Nov. '56 Diary—ACW (1)," DDEL.

54. For criticism by contemporaries, see Chapter 3. For criticism by historians, see Stivers, "Eisenhower and the Middle East," 215–16; Gerner, "Missed Opportunities and Roads Not Taken," 103–5; Neff, *Warriors at Suez*, 442–43; Freiberger, *Dawn over Suez*, 209, 212–13.

55. Eisenhower to Everett ("Swede") Hazlett, 2 November 1956, and memorandum of conversation, Eisenhower, Hoover, et al., 23 November 1956, *FRUS, 1955–1957*, 16:944, 1180; J. F. Dulles quoted in Kunz, *Economic Diplomacy*, 158.

56. Iraqi foreign minister Burhan al-Din Bashayan, Egyptian foreign minister Mahmud Fawzi, Syrian foreign minister Salah al-Din al-Bitar, King Hussein, and Nasser all offered versions of this argument. See diary entry for 6 December 1956, Armstrong Papers, box 102; U.S. United Nations Delegation, New York, to DOS, DELGA 179, 23 November 1956; U.S. Embassy, Damascus, to DOS, tel #1307, 28 November 1956; and U.S. Embassy, Amman, to DOS, tel #569, 30 November 1956, reel 12, *Confidential U.S. State Department Central Files, Palestine-Israel: Foreign Affairs*; U.S. Embassy, Cairo, to DOS, 16 December 1956, *FRUS, 1955–1957*, 16:1318. Offering a rare dissent from the prevailing view was secretary general of the Arab League 'Abd al-Khaliq Hassuna, who thought the "moment auspicious for [an] overall settlement in [the] Middle East because of two radically new factors in [the] area: [the] high prestige of [the] UN and [that of] President Eisenhower." Unless movement toward an Arab-Israeli settlement were taken soon, Hassuna warned, the "opportunity may be lost irretrievably" (U.S. United Nations Mission, Geneva, to DOS, tel #587, 7 December 1956, RG 59, 684A.86/12-756, NA).

57. U.S. Embassy, Damascus, to DOS, tel #1566, 27 December 1956, RG 59, 684A.86/12-2756, NA.

58. On 13 November the Iraqi Foreign Ministry circulated among diplomatic missions in Baghdad a note calling for the dismantling of Israel on the grounds that regional peace was impossible as long as "the Israeli threat is not uprooted and the usurpers returned whence they came." The note was also released to the Iraqi press, which gave it extremely favorable coverage. The U.S. embassy in Baghdad believed that the ministry had issued the note mainly "to mollify outraged public opinion in Iraq and to reduce pressure on the [Iraqi] government" in the wake of Britain's attack on Egypt. See U.S. Embassy, Baghdad, to DOS, desp #319, 21 November 1956, reel 12, *Confiden-*

tial U.S. State Department Central Files, Palestine-Israel: Foreign Affairs. In mid-December, however, Iraqi prime minister Nuri al-Saʻid privately told U.S. officials that the Palestine issue "could be settled only within [the] framework of past UN resolutions," thus implicitly recognizing Israel. See U.S. Embassy, Baghdad, to DOS, tel #1075, 18 December 1956, RG 59, 684A.86/12-1856, NA.

59. U.S. Embassy, Cairo, to DOS, 16 December 1957, *FRUS, 1955–1957,* 16:1318; "Notes on Lunch," 2 January 1957, Jackson Papers, box 69, folder: "Log—1957 (1)," DDEL.

60. Kyle, *Suez,* 478. For example, Ben-Gurion referred to Sharm al-Shaykh, the strategic location in Sinai overlooking the Strait of Tiran (see Map 2), as a place that "until two days ago was called Sharm al-Sheikh and whose name is now Mifratz Shlomo" (ibid., 477).

61. On 26 November Israeli ambassador to the United States Abba Eban told State Department officials that Israel would withdraw from Sinai provided that "key points" in the peninsula were first occupied by UN forces "pending agreements between Egypt and the UN and Israel and the UN looking to the demilitarization of the Peninsula." Eban also said that, while Israel was reserving the option of annexing the Gaza Strip, it was not yet committed to that course. Israel was determined, however, to prevent Egypt from regaining control of Gaza. See memorandum of conversation, Eban, Rountree, et al., 26 November 1956, *FRUS, 1955–1957,* 16:1198–99. For more on Israel's occupation of and eventual withdrawal from Sinai and Gaza, see Chapter 3.

62. This was not a new idea. In the spring of 1956 Chairman Radford and Secretary of Defense Charles E. Wilson had lobbied for U.S. adherence to the Baghdad Pact, arguing that such a move could enhance the pact's political standing in the region. See memorandum of conversation, Eisenhower, Radford, et al., 15 March 1956, and Wilson to J. F. Dulles, 5 April 1956, *FRUS, 1955–1957,* 12:259, 267. Dulles, using many of the arguments that he and the State Department were to use in December 1956 (see main text, below), successfully defeated Radford's and Wilson's proposal; see J. F. Dulles to Wilson, 23 April 1956, ibid., 294–95. In April 1956, however, the United States did agree to join the Baghdad Pact's economic and countersubversion committees; see DOS to U.S. Embassy, Tehran, 16 April 1956, ibid., 284.

63. Rountree to Hoover, 18 November 1956; Radford to Wilson, 30 November 1956; memorandum of conversation, J. F. Dulles and ambassadors from Baghdad Pact countries, 4 December 1956; and Wilson to Eisenhower, 4 December 1956, ibid., 12:333–35, 361–63, 369–71, 372–74.

64. A prominent exception was Deputy Undersecretary for Administration Loy W. Henderson, a former head of the State Department's Near East bureau, who favored U.S. adherence to the pact. See Henderson to J. F. Dulles, 6 December 1956, ibid., 12:387–89.

65. "Statement by State of the Reasons against U.S. Adherence to the Baghdad Pact at This Time," attachment 2 of Wilson to Eisenhower, 4 December 1956, ibid., 374–6.

66. "Proposal for a New Grouping of Middle Eastern States," Tab A of Rountree to J. F. Dulles, 5 December 1956, and "Program to Counter Soviet Penetration in the Middle East," 5 December 1956, ibid., 377–82, 383–87.

67. *FRUS, 1955–1957,* 12:383–84; "Proposal for a New Grouping of Middle Eastern

States," Tab A of Rountree to J. F. Dulles, 5 December 1956, ibid., 378–79; LaFeber, *America, Russia, and the Cold War*, 59.

68. Robert D. Murphy to Rountree, 3 December 1956, *FRUS, 1955–1957*, 12:368. Murphy was responding to an earlier draft (also of 3 December) of the paper "Proposal for a New Grouping of Middle Eastern States" (see preceding two endnotes). The 5 December version of that paper satisfied none of Murphy's objections. Murphy wrote "Do not concur" on the text of the later draft and appended to it a copy of his 3 December memo to Rountree; see editorial note, ibid., 377 n. 6.

69. Memorandum of conversation, J. F. Dulles, Hoover, et al., 3 December 1956; memorandum of conversation, J. F. Dulles and Knowland, 8 December 1956; memorandum of conversation, J. F. Dulles, Hoover, et al., 7 December 1956; and memorandum of conversation, J. F. Dulles, Selwyn Lloyd, et al., 10 December 1956, ibid., 367, 397, 394, 400.

70. Murphy to Rountree, 3 December 1956, and memorandum of conversation, J. F. Dulles, Hoover, et al., 7 December 1956, ibid., 369, 394.

71. Telephone conversation, Eisenhower and J. F. Dulles, 8 December 1956, ibid., 395–96.

72. Hoover to Murphy, 10 December 1956, ibid., 398.

73. Murphy to J. F. Dulles, 15 December 1956, ibid., 410.

74. Ibid., 411. The special problems posed by Afghanistan and North Africa had surfaced in deliberations over the charter proposal. The authors of that proposal had concluded that Afghanistan, partly because of "its heavy economic involvement with the USSR," would probably decline an invitation to join a new, anti-Soviet Middle East organization. They also concluded that inviting Tunisia and Morocco to join such a grouping "would unnecessarily arouse the French" ("Proposal for a New Grouping of Middle Eastern States," Tab A of Rountree to J. F. Dulles, 5 December 1956, ibid., 378).

75. J. F. Dulles to Wilson, 18 December 1956, and memorandum of conversation, Eisenhower, J. F. Dulles, et al., 20 December 1956, ibid., 413, 416; draft #3 of the president's message to Congress, 22 December 1956, attachment to memorandum of conversation, Eisenhower and J. F. Dulles, 22 December 1956, Dulles Papers, White House Memoranda Series, box 4, folder: "Meetings with the President, Aug. thru Dec. 1956," DDEL. In his 18 December memorandum to Wilson, Dulles proposed that the $400 million be appropriated for fiscal years 1957 and 1958. (According to the system then prevailing, fiscal year 1957 had begun on 1 July 1956 and was to end on 30 June 1957.) By the time it was submitted to Congress in January 1957, however, the request had been altered to cover fiscal years 1958 and 1959 instead.

76. Statement by J. F. Dulles, 2 January 1957, *Executive Sessions*, 11, 17–18; president's message to Congress, 5 January 1957, in U.S. Department of State, *United States Policy in the Middle East*, 21.

77. Statement by J. F. Dulles, 2 January 1957, *Executive Sessions*, 11.

78. Secretary's staff meeting, 13 December 1956, RG 59, lot 63 D75, box 3, folder: "Secretary's Staff Meeting Notes 541-500, July 12, 1956–Jan. 15, 1957," NA; *New York Times*, 1 January 1957; statement by J. F. Dulles, 2 January 1957, *Executive Sessions*, 5, 10, 11.

79. Statement by J. F. Dulles, 2 January 1957, *Executive Sessions*, 23.

80. Memorandum of conversation, Eisenhower, J. F. Dulles, et al., 20 December 1956, *FRUS, 1955–1957*, 12:415–16.

81. Ibid.; draft #13 of the president's message to Congress, 4 January 1957, AWF, Speech Series, box 19, folder: "Msg. to Congress on Mid-East, 1/5/57 (2)," DDEL.

82. Memorandum of conversation, Eisenhower and J. F. Dulles, 22 December 1956, Dulles Papers, White House Memoranda Series, box 4, folder: "Meetings with the President, Aug. thru Dec. 1956," DDEL; draft #3 of the president's message to Congress, 22 December 1956, attachment to ibid. By the final version the sentence had acquired an additional conciliatory phrase: "in ways consonant with the purposes and principles of the United Nations" (president's message to Congress, 5 January 1957, in U.S. Department of State, *U.S. Policy in the Middle East*, 22).

83. Telephone conversation, Eisenhower and J. F. Dulles, 2 January 1957, AWF, DDE Diary Series, box 21, folder: "Jan '57 Phone Calls," DDEL; president's message to Congress, 5 January 1957, in U.S. Department of State, *U.S. Policy in the Middle East*, 15, 16, 21.

84. Statement by J. F. Dulles, 2 January 1957, *Executive Sessions*, 2; telephone conversation, Eisenhower and J. F. Dulles, 2 January 1957, AWF, DDE Diary Series, box 21, folder: "Jan '57 Phone Calls," DDEL.

85. Draft #3 of the president's message to Congress, 22 December 1956, attachment to memorandum of conversation, Eisenhower and J. F. Dulles, 22 December 1956, Dulles Papers, White House Memoranda Series, box 4, folder: "Meetings with the President, Aug. thru Dec. 1956," DDEL; telephone conversation, Eisenhower and J. F. Dulles, 31 December 1956, AWF, DDE Diary Series, box 20, folder: "Dec. '56 Phone Calls," DDEL; *New York Times*, 1 January 1957; *al-Hayat*, 3 January 1957; *Ruz al-Yusuf*, 7 January 1957, 4, 9; U.S. Embassy, Amman, to DOS, tel #712, 3 January 1957, and U.S. Embassy, Damascus, to DOS, tel #1622, 4 January 1957, RG 59, 611.80/1-357, 611.80/1-457, NA.

86. See, for example, U.S. Embassy, Tripoli. to DOS, tel #327, 12 November 1956, reel 11, and U.S. Embassy, Damascus, to DOS, tel #1309, 28 November 1956, reel 12, *Confidential U.S. State Department Central Files, Palestine-Israel: Foreign Affairs*; U.S. Embassy, Baghdad, to DOS, tel #1001, 5 December 1956, and U.S. Embassy, Cairo, to DOS, desp #404, 13 December 1956, RG 59, 684A.86/12-1356, NA; diary entries for 31 November, 6, 10 December 1956, Armstrong Papers, box 102; *New York Times*, 28 November 1956.

87. U.S. Embassy, Amman, to DOS, tel #721, 4 January 1957, RG 59, 611.80/1-457, NA; draft #13 of the president's message to Congress, 4 January 1957, and unnumbered draft of the president's message to Congress, 4 January 1957, AWF, Speech Series, box 19, folder: "Msg. to Congress on Mid-East 1/5/57 (2)," DDEL.

CHAPTER 3

1. President's message to Congress, 5 January 1957, in *Public Papers, 1957*, 7–10.

2. Ibid., 10–12.

3. Ibid., 12–13.

4. Ibid., 14, 15.

5. Hubert H. Humphrey to J. Arthur Pino, 5 April 1957, Humphrey Papers, Senato-

rial Files, 150.A.20.3(B), folder: "LEG: Foreign Relations *Eisenhower Doctrine*—March 1957"; Humphrey to William Styx Wasserman, Humphrey Papers, 21 January 1957, 150.A.20.4(F), folder: "LEG: Foreign Relations *Middle East*—Jan. 1957"; Fisher Howe to Robert D. Murphy, 27 March 1957, with attachments, and Roy Rubottom to Murphy, 26 February 1957, RG 59, 611.80/3-2757, 611.80/2-2657, NA.

6. President's message to Congress, 5 January 1957, in U.S. Department of State, *United States Policy in the Middle East*, 20.

7. On 15 March 1955 Dulles remarked at a press conference that the United States was prepared to use tactical atomic weapons against China in the event war broke out in the Formosa strait. Asked the next day to comment on Dulles's statement, Eisenhower told reporters, "I see no reason why they [tactical atomic weapons] shouldn't be used just exactly as you would use a bullet or anything else" (Divine, *Eisenhower*, 62).

8. Ibid., 64. Although the negotiations were inconclusive, Communist China refrained from shelling Quemoy until August 1958. The resumption of shelling at that time may have been, in part, a reaction to the U.S. intervention in Lebanon the previous month. According to a declassified Soviet document, in September 1958 China's foreign minister Zhou Enlai told Soviet foreign minister Andrei Gromyko that the purpose of the resumed shelling had been to "prove to the Americans that the People's Republic of China is strong and bold enough and is not afraid of America" following its actions in Lebanon (Gaddis, *We Now Know*, 250). For more on the 1958 U.S. intervention in Lebanon, see Chapter 7.

9. Meeting with Republican leadership, 1 January 1957, White House Office, Office of the Staff Secretary, Legislative Meetings Series, box 4, folder: "L-33 [January 1, 1957]" (brackets in source title), DDEL; president's message to Congress, 5 January 1957, and White House news statement, 7 January 1957, in U.S. Department of State, *United States Policy in the Middle East*, 23, 29.

10. Gaskin, "Lyndon B. Johnson," 341–42; Evans and Novak, *Exercise of Power*, 175. See also the British embassy's contemporaneous analysis of the congressional scene in John E. Coulson to Selwyn Lloyd, 18 March 1957, FO 371/127742, PRO.

11. Thomson and Shattuck, *1956 Campaign*, 288, 303–10; Averell Harriman to Dean Acheson, 23 November 1956, Acheson Papers, series I, box 15, folder 193.

12. Adlai Stevenson to Reinhold Niebuhr, 14 November 1956, box 60, and Hubert Humphrey to Stevenson, 26 November 1956, box 41, Stevenson Papers. See also Niebuhr to Stevenson, 27 December 1956, ibid., box 60; Thomson and Shattuck, *1956 Campaign*, 319.

13. Humphrey to Jack L. Paro, 29 January 1957, Humphrey Papers, 150.A.20.4(F), folder: "LEG: Foreign Relations *Middle East*—Jan. 1957"; *New York Times*, 6 January 1957.

14. *Congressional Quarterly Weekly Report*, 11 January 1957, 45; *Time*, 21 January 1957, 11.

15. *Time*, 21 January 1957, 11–12. In a January 1950 speech before the National Press Club, Acheson had defined the U.S. "defensive perimeter" in the Pacific as running along the Aleutian Islands to Japan and then down to the Philippines. Since South Korea lay outside that perimeter, critics later charged that Acheson's speech had left the erroneous impression that the United States would not defend that country if it were attacked.

16. Chace, *Acheson*, 260–61, 373–74.

17. *New York Times,* 11 January 1957; Robert S. Allen to Acheson, 14 February 1957, Acheson Papers, series I, box 1, folder 7; Lucius Battle to Acheson, 14 January 1957, Acheson Papers, series I, box 2, folder 26; Herbert Feis to Acheson, 14 January 1957, Acheson Papers, series I, box 10, folder 132.

18. Testimony by J. F. Dulles, 14, 15 January 1957, in *President's Proposal,* 13–18, 42–47, 80–84, 99.

19. Shortly after Eisenhower's 5 January speech to Congress, results of nationwide polls conducted by *Newsweek* and the *Wall Street Journal* suggested that the American people supported the president's proposals "overwhelmingly" (*Newsweek*) and "about three-to-one" (*Wall Street Journal*). The *Newsweek* poll revealed that support for the president's proposals was especially strong among women. Neither poll was scientific, however, and both relied on extremely small samples. See *Newsweek,* 14 January 1957, 26, 29; *Wall Street Journal,* 16 January 1957. Somewhat more reliable was a Gallup poll in early February that revealed considerable, though not overwhelming, public support for Eisenhower's proposals: on economic aid to friendly Middle Eastern countries, 70 percent of respondents approved, 19 percent disapproved, and 11 percent had no opinion; on military aid to such countries, 53 percent approved, 34 percent disapproved, and 13 percent had no opinion; on the prospect of using U.S. armed forces to repel a Soviet attack on the Middle East, 50 percent approved, 34 percent disapproved, and 16 percent had no opinion. See Gallup, *Gallup Poll,* 1467. All these data must be placed alongside a 1 February news report that mail to senators on the Foreign Relations Committee was running "8 or 9 to 1 against the 'Eisenhower Doctrine' for the Middle East." But as the author of the report cautioned, "People who are 'agin' normally write more letters to Senators and Representatives than those who are for"—a claim later substantiated by social scientists. See *New York Times,* 1 February 1957; Crabb, *Doctrines,* 174.

20. Acheson to Harry S. Truman, 15 January 1957, in McLellan and Acheson, *Among Friends,* 120–21; Acheson to Feis, 17 January 1957, Acheson Papers, series I, box 10, folder 132; *New York Times,* 13 January 1957; press analyses, in British Embassy, Washington, to BFO, desps #11 Saving and #17 Saving, 7, 11 January 1957, FO 371/127739, and in British Embassy, Washington, to BFO, desp #25 Saving, 16 January 1957, FO 371/127740, PRO.

21. *Congressional Quarterly Weekly Report,* 1 February 1957, 126.

22. Crabb, *Doctrines,* 170; *New York Times,* 23 January 1957; *President's Proposal,* 27–28, 118–19; *Congressional Record,* vol. 103, pt. 2 (1957), 1856. Fulbright's position on standby authority was not as contradictory as it may have seemed. Fulbright believed that either of the dangers he described—presidential recklessness or presidential timidity—could result from the attempt "to define in exact terms what [the president's] emergency power is." As long as that emergency power remained ambiguous, Fulbright argued, the president would have both the flexibility to react appropriately to unexpected crises and the need to justify his action to Congress or the public. While such flexibility could, in extraordinary circumstances, lead the president to exercise "a power which he does not legally possess," the president would also "be very careful to see that the necessity which he pleads to excuse his act is clear and beyond question," the better to convince Congress or the public to endorse his action after the fact. If, however, the president were granted special powers through a prior congressional authorization, he

could be far less cautious in exercising those powers and would, therefore, be more prone to abuse them. In an 11 February speech, Fulbright quoted Virginia representative Alexander White, a member of the first Congress, as saying in 1789, "It would be better for the President to extend his powers on some extraordinary occasion, even where he is not strictly justified by the Constitution, than [that] the Legislature should grant an improper power to be exercised at all times" (*Congressional Record*, vol. 103, pt. 2 (1957), 1856–57). For a fuller treatment of both the history and the merits of this argument, see Schlesinger, *Imperial Presidency*, 7–10, 23–25.

23. *Congressional Record*, vol. 103, pt. 2 (1957), 1873.

24. Humphrey to Wasserman, 21 January 1957, Humphrey Papers, 150.A.20.4(F), folder: "LEG: Foreign Relations *Middle East*—Jan. 1957"; Acheson to Feis, 17 January 1957, Acheson Papers, series I, box 1, folder 132; *New York Times*, 30 January 1957; *Newsweek*, 4 February 1957, 22.

25. *President's Proposal*, 218–19; Chace, *Acheson*, 219–20.

26. *President's Proposal*, 220–21; *Congressional Quarterly Almanac* (1957), 577. In April 1957 the State Department's Historical Division began producing installments of a chronological review of U.S. policy in the Middle East since January 1946, along with supporting documents. The installments were provided to a special subcommittee chaired by Senator Fulbright. In July, however, the project was dropped on the recommendation of Fulbright's subcommittee, which concluded that passage of the Middle East Resolution had rendered many of the questions moot. See editorial note, *FRUS, 1955–1957*, 12:445–46.

27. *President's Proposal*, 286–87.

28. British Embassy, Washington, to BFO, tels #144, #155, 26, 28 January 1957, and Harold Caccia to Harold Macmillan, 1 February 1957, PREM 11/1178, PRO; *New York Times*, 28 January 1957; meeting with Republican leadership, 29 January 1957, White House Office, Office of the Staff Secretary, Legislative Meetings Series, box 4, folder: "L-34(2) [January 23 and 29, 1957]," DDEL. About this time Dulles complained to his sister that the congressional committees "act as if I were a criminal at the bar" (Dulles, *John Foster Dulles*, 40).

29. Meeting with Republican leadership, 29 January 1957, White House Office, Office of the Staff Secretary, Legislative Meetings Series, box 4, folder: "L-34(2) [January 23, 29, 1957]," DDEL. For Republicans' personal attacks on Acheson during the Truman years, see Chace, *Acheson*, 228–29, 310–12.

30. Macmillan, *Riding the Storm*, 213–14; Ashton, *Problem of Nasser*, 110–11. For the views of other British officials, see Gladwyn Jebb to Ivone Kirkpatrick, 4 January 1956 [*sic*; 1957], FO 371/127747; British Embassy, Paris, to BFO, desp #7 Saving, 7 January 1957, FO 371/127739; E. M[ichael] Rose, "Eisenhower Plan," 28 January 1957, FO 371/127740, PRO.

31. C. Burke Elbrick to J. F. Dulles, 31 December 1956, RG 59, 611.80/12-3156, and U.S. Embassy, Paris, to DOS, tel #3300, 8 January 1957, RG 59, 611.80/1-857, NA.

32. Among these nations the Netherlands, Greece, and Turkey expressed the strongest support for the Eisenhower Doctrine, Belgium expressed the strongest reservations (but also cautious support), and Italy occupied an intermediate position. See U.S. NATO Delegation, Paris, to DOS, POLTO 1570, 10 January 1957, RG 59, 611.80/

1-1057, NA; U.S. Embassy, The Hague, to DOS, tel #1027, 11 January 1957, RG 59, 611.80/1-1157, NA; U.S. Embassy, Brussels, to DOS, tel #777, 12 January 1957, RG 59, 611.80/1-1257, NA.

33. "The Soviet Propaganda Line on the President's Middle East Plan," n.d. [ca. February 1957], Harlow Records (Pre-Acquisition), box 13, folder: "Middle East Resolution," DDEL; U.S. Consulate, Madras, to DOS, tel #171, 6 February 1957, White House Office, Office of the Staff Secretary, Subject Series, State Department Subseries, box 1, folder: "State Department—1957 (February–March) (2)," DDEL; *New York Times*, 13 February 1957. The Soviet plan also called on the great powers to commit themselves to the resolution of Middle Eastern disputes by peaceful means alone, to renounce all attempts to organize area countries into military blocs, and to agree among themselves to stop delivering arms to area countries; see *New York Times*, 13 February 1957.

34. U.S. Embassy, Tel Aviv, to DOS, tel #842, 14 January 1957, RG 59, 611.80/1-1457; U.S. Embassy, Tehran, to DOS, tel #1039, 8 January 1957, RG 59, 611.80/1-857; U.S. NATO Delegation, Paris, to DOS, POLTO 1570, 10 January 1957, RG 59, 611.80/1-1057; memorandum of conversation, J. F. Dulles, Feroz Khan Noon, et al., 21 January 1957, RG 59, lot 64 D199, "Secretary of State's Memoranda of Conversation," box 6, folder: "Secy's M. of Con., January 1957," NA; British Embassy, Ankara, to BFO, tel #62, 21 January 1957, PREM 11/1938, and James Bowker to Lloyd, 25 January 1957, FO 371/127824, PRO.

35. *Al-Hayat*, 3 January 1957; *al-Ahram* editorial, 7 January 1957; press summaries in U.S. Embassy, Amman, to DOS, tels #721, #747, #759, 4, 7, 9 January 1957, RG 59, 611.80/1-457, 611.80/1-757, 611.80/1-957, NA; U.S. Embassy, Damascus, to DOS, tels #1622, #1646, 4, 7 January 1957, RG 59, 611.80/1-457, 611.80/1-757, NA; U.S. Embassy, Cairo, to DOS, tels #2159, #2189, 7, 9 January 1957, RG 59, 611.80/1-757, 611.80/1-957, NA; U.S. Embassy, Baghdad, to DOS, tels #1198, #1206, 8, 10 January 1957, RG 59, 611.80/1-857, 611.80/1-1057, 611.80/1-1157, NA; U.S. Embassy, Beirut, to DOS, tels #1680, #1691, 10, 13 January 1957, RG 59, 611.80/1-1057, 611.80/1-1357, NA.

36. Egyptian Embassy, Washington, to EFM, desp #198, 31 December 1956, WK, box 386, folder: "203/7/1/H9 al-taqarir al-siyasa lil-safara al-Misriyya fi-Washintun," DWQ; U.S. Embassy, Cairo, to DOS, 10 January 1957, *FRUS, 1955–1957*, 17:16–18; Haykal quoted in U.S. Embassy, Cairo, to DOS, tel #2192, 9 January 1956, RG 59, 611.80/1-957, NA; Kunz, *Economic Diplomacy*, 80–81.

37. This speculation is partly based on U.S. ambassador Hare's analysis of the Egyptian scene in mid-January; see U.S. Embassy, Cairo, to DOS, tel #2252, 13 January 1957, RG 59, 611.80/1-1357, NA.

38. U.S. Embassy, Damascus, to DOS, 11 January 1957, *FRUS, 1955–1957*, 13:609–10. See Chapter 5 for a fuller treatment of domestic Syrian politics in early 1957.

39. *New York Times*, 29 January 1957; Habib Bourguiba, weekly speech, 11 January 1957, enclosure to Mongi Slim to H. Alexander Smith, 11 June 1957, Smith Papers, box 125, folder: "Jordan 1957"; U.S. Embassy, Beirut, to DOS, tel #1691, 13 January 1957, RG 59, 611.80/1-1357, NA; U.S. Embassy, Tripoli, to DOS, tel #477, 14 January 1957, RG 59, 611.80/1-1457, NA; U.S. Embassy, Baghdad, to DOS, tels #1186, #1198, 5, 8 January 1957, RG 59, 611.80/1-557, 611.80/1-857, NA.

40. U.S. Embassy, Baghdad, to DOS, tels #1186, #1225, 5, 14 January 1957, RG 59, 611.80/1-557, 611.80/1-1457, and DOS to U.S. Embassy, Baghdad, tel #1177, 10 January 1957, RG 59, 611.80/1-557 (misfiled), NA.

41. Memorandum of conversation, Eisenhower, J. F. Dulles, and congressional leaders, 1 January 1957, *FRUS, 1955–1957*, 12:434.

42. For more on Hussein's and Jordan's reaction to the Eisenhower Doctrine, see Chapter 4.

43. Egypt's decision during the war to block the Suez Canal, which remained closed until April 1957, had drastically curtailed Saudi oil shipments to the West, since cargo vessels now had to sail around the Cape of Good Hope. This inconvenience, combined with Saud's decision in early November to impose an oil embargo against Britain and France (an obligatory gesture of solidarity with Egypt), caused a 40 percent drop in Saudi oil revenues. Also threatening to Saud was the regional acclaim Nasser was now receiving for having withstood an attack by great powers; thus reinforced, Nasser seemed poised for further acts of recklessness. See Holden and Johns, *House of Saud*, 189–90; Lacey, *Kingdom*, 314–15.

44. U.S. Consulate, Dhahran, to DOS, tel #315, 3 January 1957, reel 2, *Confidential U.S. State Department Central Files, Saudi Arabia*; Egyptian Embassy, Damascus to EFM, desp #16, 6 January 1957, WK, box 249, folder: "2/3/6 B al-'alaqat al-Suriyya al-Amrikiyya fi daw' siyasat Amrika fi-al-Sharq al-Awsat," DWQ.

45. Memorandum of conversation, Herbert Hoover Jr., Abdel Rahman Azzam Pasha, et al., 23 January 1957, RG 59, lot 64 D199, box 6, folder: "Secy's M. of Con., January 1957," NA; U.S. Embassy, Jidda, to DOS, tel #382, 15 January 1957, RG 59, 611.80/1-1557, NA; U.S. Consulate, Dhahran, to DOS, tel #334, 10 January 1957, reel 2, *Confidential U.S. State Department Central Files, Saudi Arabia*; U.S. Embassy, Beirut, to DOS, tel #1776, 23 January 1957, reel 13, *Confidential U.S. State Department Central Files, Palestine-Israel: Foreign Affairs*.

46. Eisenhower to J. F. Dulles, 12 December 1956; U.S. Consulate, Dhahran, to DOS, 26 November 1956; and editorial note, *FRUS, 1955–1957*, 16:1297, 13:405, 413–14; DOS to U.S. Consulate, Dhahran, tel #179, 16 November 1956, AWF, International Series, box 46, folder: "Saudi Arabia, King Saud, 1952 through 1956 (3)," DDEL; U.S. Consulate, Dhahran, to DOS, tel #315, 3 January 1957, reel 2, *Confidential U.S. State Department Central Files, Saudi Arabia*.

47. A copy of the 18 January 1957 four-power memorandum is appended to William Morris to R. Michael Hadow, 7 March 1957, FO 371/127155, PRO.

48. U.S. Embassy, Beirut, to DOS, tel #1776, 23 January 1957, reel 13, *Confidential U.S. State Department Central Files, Palestine-Israel: Foreign Affairs*; memorandum of conversation, Eisenhower and Saud, 30 January 1957, *FRUS, 1955–1957*, 13:427.

49. *New York Times*, 29 January 1957. At the time, the Saudi government did not allow Jewish American airmen to serve at the Dhahran air base and was accused, erroneously, of prohibiting Roman Catholic chaplains from saying Mass at the base. See Arnold, *Golden Swords and Pots and Pans*, 93–94. Saudi Arabia did not formally abolish slavery until 1962, though the practice was rare by the 1950s.

50. *New York Times*, 30, 31 January 1957; meeting with GOP leadership, 5 February 1957, White House Office, Office of the Staff Secretary, Legislative Meetings Series, box 4, folder: "L-34 (3) (February 5 and 26, 1957)," DDEL; *Congressional Record*, vol.

103, pt. 1 (1957), 1368, and pt. 2, 1915; Humphrey to Dorothea R. Muller, 7 February 1957, 150.A.20.5(B), folder: "LEG: Foreign Relations *Saudi Arabia*," and Humphrey to Ruth Scop, 15 February 1957, 150.A.20.4(F), folder: "LEG: Foreign Relations *Middle East*—Jan. 1957," Humphrey Papers.

51. Meeting with GOP leadership, 5 February 1957, White House Office, Office of the Staff Secretary, Legislative Meetings Series, box 4, folder: "L-34 (3) (February 5 and 26, 1957)," DDEL; memorandum of conversation, Eisenhower and Saud, 30 January 1957, AWF, DDE Diary Series, box 21, folder: "Jan '57 Diary," DDEL; telephone conversation, J. F. Dulles and Eisenhower, 30 January 1957, Dulles Papers, Telephone Calls Series, box 11, folder: "Memoranda of Tel. Conv. W.H. Jan 1957 to February 28, 1957 (2)," DDEL; Eisenhower, *White House Years*, 117; secretary's staff meetings, 5, 7 February 1957, RG 59, lot 63 D75, and "Minutes and Notes of the Secretary's Staff Meetings, 1952–1961," box 3, folder: "Secretary's Staff Meeting Notes 501-550, Jan. 17, 1957–July 16, 1957," NA; memorandum of conversation, Eisenhower and Duncan Sandys, 1 February 1957, *FRUS, 1955–1957*, 13:444.

52. Meeting with GOP leadership, 5 February 1957, White House Office, Office of the Staff Secretary, Legislative Meetings Series, box 4, folder: "L-34 (3) (February 5 and 26, 1957)," DDEL.

53. Memorandum of conversation, Eisenhower and Sandys, 1 February 1957, *FRUS, 1955–1957*, 13:445.

54. J. F. Dulles to Eisenhower, 7 February 1957, ibid., 477–80. According to the agreement, over the next five years the United States would give Saudi Arabia $50 million in military aid, for the training and maintenance of Saudi armed forces and the construction of an air terminal at Dhahran, and $20 million in economic aid, for the development and expansion of the Saudi port of Dammam. The United States would also sell Saudi Arabia about $110 million worth of military equipment.

55. Memorandum of conversation, Eisenhower, Saud, et al., 30 January 1957, ibid., 422; *New York Times*, 7 February 1957.

56. William M. Rountree to J. F. Dulles, 12 February 1957, RG 59, 685.86A/2-1257, NA.

57. Four-power memorandum, 18 January 1957, enclosure to Morris to Hadow, 7 March 1957, FO 371/127155, PRO; memorandum of conversation, Eisenhower and Saud, 30 January 1957, *FRUS, 1955–1957*, 13:427.

58. For the text of the 8 February communiqué, see *New York Times*, 9 February 1957.

59. Egyptian Embassy, Jidda, to EFM, desp #95, 13 April 1957, WK, Jidda Series, box 2, folder: "756/81/3 J1 al-taqarir al-siyasiyya lil-safara al-Misriyya fi Jidda," DWQ. In June of that year the State Department advised the U.S. embassy in Saudi Arabia that it considered the 8 February Saudi-U.S. communiqué an "endorsement [of the] principles underlying [the] Doctrine. Dept has not regarded [a] formal announcement of acceptance as essential to [the] success [of] this program" (DOS to U.S. Embassy, Jidda, tel #1265, 28 June 1957, RG 59, 611.80/6-2857, NA).

60. Memorandum of conversation, Reuven Shiloah and Robert D. Murphy, 22 January 1957, *FRUS, 1955–1957*, 17:43.

61. Editorial note, ibid., 78; *New York Times*, 6 February 1957; Eisenhower to David Ben-Gurion, 3 February 1957, *FRUS, 1955–1957*, 17:83; Fry and Hochstein, "Forgotten Middle Eastern Crisis," 60.

62. Fry and Hochstein, "Forgotten Middle Eastern Crisis," 60; *New York Times*, 6, 10, 12 February 1957; Lyndon B. Johnson to J. F. Dulles, 11 February 1957, *FRUS, 1955–1957*, 17:139–40; Evans and Novak, *Exercise of Power*, 178–79; Kunz, *Economic Diplomacy*, 266 n. 63.

63. Evans and Novak, *Exercise of Power*, 179; *Congressional Quarterly Almanac* (1957), 577.

64. Aide-mémoire, State Department to Israeli embassy, 11 February 1957, *FRUS, 1955–1957*, 17:133.

65. Memorandum of conversation, J. F. Dulles, Yusuf Yasin, et al., 7 February 1957, ibid., 101–5; Saud to Eisenhower, 15 February 1957, AWF, International Series, box 46, folder: "Saudi Arabia, King Saud 1957 (1)," DDEL.

66. U.S. Embassy, Tel Aviv, to DOS, 18 February 1957, and telephone conversation, J. F. Dulles and Arthur Dean, 19 February 1957, *FRUS, 1955–1957*, 17:203–4, 207; Fry and Hochstein, "Forgotten Middle Eastern Crisis," 61–65.

67. Radio and television address by Eisenhower, 20 February 1957, and Knesset statement by Ben-Gurion, 21 February 1957, in U.S. Department of State, *United States Policy in the Middle East*, 304–7, 308, 311–15; *New York Times*, 21 February 1957; Fry and Hochstein, "Forgotten Middle Eastern Crisis," 66–74.

68. Telephone conversation, J. F. Dulles and William F. Knowland, 16 February 1957, *FRUS, 1955–1957*, 17:188.

69. *FBIS*, #29, #31, 12, 14 February 1957, A9, A6; memorandum, Arab Bureau, 21 February 1957, WK, Baghdad Series, box 4, folder: "752/81/3 al-taqarir al-siyasiyya lil-safara fi-Baghdad—'mukhtalif,'" DWQ.

70. BFO, "Policy of King Saud," 5 March 1957, in Tuson and Burdett, *Records of Saudi Arabia*, 364; al-'Azm, *Mudhakkirat*, 2:491–94; U.S. Embassy, Cairo, to DOS, 28 February 1957, *FRUS, 1955–1957*, 17:322.

71. The text of the Cairo conference communiqué is in U.S. Embassy, Cairo, to DOS, tel #2746, 28 February 1957, AWF, International Series, box 46, folder: "Saudi Arabia, King Saud 1957 (1)," DDEL.

72. Egyptian Embassy, Jidda, to EFM, desp #67, 3 March 1957, WK, Jidda Series, box 2, folder: "756/81/3 J1 al-taqarir al-siyasiyya lil-safara al-Misriyya fi Jidda," DWQ; Egyptian Embassy, Amman, to EFM, desp #40, 7 March 1957, WK, Jordan Series, box 1, folder: "S—'Amman," DWQ; U.S. Embassy, Cairo, to DOS, 28 February 1957, *FRUS, 1955–1957*, 17:323.

73. Fry and Hochstein, "Forgotten Middle Eastern Crisis," 69, 76, 78; UN General Assembly statement by Golda Meir, 1 March 1957, in U.S. Department of State, *United States Policy in the Middle East*, 328–32.

74. Fry and Hochstein, "Forgotten Middle Eastern Crisis," 77; memorandum of conversation, J. F. Dulles, Meir, et al., 18 March 1957, *FRUS*, 1955–1957, 17:434–39.

75. For more on the repair of the Iraqi pipelines in Syria, see Chapter 5.

76. *Congressional Quarterly Almanac* (1957), 578; telephone conversation, J. F. Dulles and Sam Rayburn, 5 March 1957, reel 6, *Minutes of Telephone Conversations*. The text of the final version of the Middle East Resolution is in U.S. Department of State, *U.S. Policy in the Middle East*, 44–46.

77. In addition to the Mansfield amendment, which was introduced in the Foreign Relations Committee, the Senate attached three amendments by roll call. The first roll-

call amendment, sponsored by Wyoming Democrat Joseph C. O'Mahoney, removed the administration's proviso that any use of force under the resolution be in keeping with the United Nations Charter, directing instead that such use of force be in keeping with the U.S. Constitution. The second amendment, sponsored by Mansfield and modified by South Dakota Republican Francis Case, required the president to give logistical and military assistance to UNEF in maintaining the Middle East truce. The third amendment, sponsored by Illinois Democrat Paul H. Douglas and modified by Alabama Democrat John J. Sparkman, reiterated the principle that U.S. military aid could be used only for self-defense by the recipient nations. See *Congressional Quarterly Almanac* (1957), 578.

78. Committee report, "To Promote Peace and Stability in the Middle East," 14 February 1957, *Executive Sessions*, 778–80 (emphasis added); *Time*, 25 February 1957, 18.

79. For more on the 1958 U.S. intervention in Lebanon, see Chapter 7.

80. See, for example, 538th meeting of NSC, 4 August 1964, *FRUS, 1964–1968*, 612. See also Senate Report No. 1329, "Promoting the Maintenance of International Peace and Security in Southeast Asia," 6 August 1964, *Senate Reports*, 88th Cong., 2d sess., vols. 1–4 (Washington, D.C.: U.S. Government Printing Office, 1964).

81. Crabb, *Doctrines*, 193–234. The text of the Gulf of Tonkin Resolution is in *Congressional Quarterly Almanac* (1964), 332.

82. Bipartisan congressional meeting, 25 March 1957, AWF, DDE Diary Series, box 22, folder: "Mar '57 Diary Staff Memos," DDEL; Horne, *Macmillan*, 25.

83. Ashton, *Problem of Nasser*, 116–20; Eisenhower, *White House Years*, 122; entry for 21 March 1957, AWF, DDE Diary Series, box 22, folder: "Mar '57 Diary," DDEL.

84. Such pressures consisted mainly of freezing Egyptian assets in U.S. banks, restricting American tourist travel to Egypt, and suspending economic and technical assistance programs.

85. "United States Objectives and Policy for Egypt," 8 March 1957, *FRUS, 1955–1957*, 17:390–91. Departing somewhat from this view was Ambassador Hare, who favored a "slightly more flexible policy" toward Egypt, for fear that the current policy might arouse international sympathy toward Nasser and undermine pro-American figures in his government. See U.S. Embassy, Cairo, to DOS, tel #2827, 8 March 1957, reel 7, *Confidential U.S. State Department Central Files, Egypt*.

86. After hearing the British request for an American verbal signal to launch the coup, Eisenhower and Dulles, having no "worthwhile information" on the scheme, "secured an evaluation from Washington. Our appraisal was that the dissidents didn't stand much chance" (entry for 21 March 1957, AWF, DDE Diary Series, box 22, folder: "Mar '57 Diary," DDEL).

87. Ibid.

88. Kunz, *Economic Diplomacy*, 177–81; Lamb, *Macmillan Years*, 26–29.

89. Kunz, *Economic Diplomacy*, 186; memorandum of conversation, Eisenhower, Herter, et al., 16 April 1957, AWF, DDE Diary Series, box 23, folder: "Apr '57 Diary—Staff Memos (1)," DDEL; Henry Cabot Lodge, statement in UN Security Council, 26 April 1957, in U.S. Department of State, *United States Policy in the Middle East*, 390–92.

90. Eisenhower to Jawaharlal Nehru, 12 January 1957, AWF, DDE Diary Series, box 21, folder: "Jan '57 Miscellaneous (3)," DDEL; memorandum of conversation, J. F. Dulles, Heinrich von Brentano, et al., 4 March 1957, RG 59, lot 64 D199, box 6, folder:

"Secy's M. of Con., Mar. 1–20, 1957," NA; transcript of "background" press conference in Bermuda, 24 March 1957, Dulles Papers, box 113, folder: "Bermuda Conference, March 29–24, 1957," Princeton University Library.

91. Telephone call, Eisenhower and J. F. Dulles, 4 March 1957, AWF, DDE Diary Series, box 22, folder: "Mar '57 Phone Calls," DDEL; meeting with Republican leadership, 29 January 1957, White House Office, Office of the Staff Secretary, Legislative Meetings Series, box 4, folder: "L-34(2) [January 23 and 29, 1957]," DDEL; entry for 20 February 1957, AWF, Ann Whitman Diary Series, box 8, folder: "Feb. '57 Diary—acw," DDEL; telephone conversations, Eisenhower and J. F. Dulles, 12 February 1957, and J. F. Dulles and James C. Hagerty, 18 February 1957, *FRUS, 1955–1957*, 17:147, 196.

92. For the Eisenhower administration's covert actions in Iran, see Chapter 1 and relevant citations. For Guatemala, see Gleijeses, *Shattered Hope*. For the administration's appeasement of Senator McCarthy, see Brendon, *Ike*, 252–53, 266, 275.

CHAPTER 4

1. Richards visited Afghanistan, Ethiopia, Greece, Iran, Iraq, Israel, Lebanon, Libya, Morocco, Pakistan, Saudi Arabia, Sudan, Tunisia, Turkey, and Yemen.

2. *Newsweek*, 29 April 1957, 54; "General Paper #4," 14 February 1957, and "General Paper #10," 9 March 1957, RG 59, lot 57 D616, "Briefing Materials Prepared for the Richards Mission to the Middle East," box 14, folder: "Mission to the Middle East, Basic Book, Ambassador Richards, General Papers," NA.

3. For indications of the anti-Nasserist and anti-Syrian purposes of Richards's mission, see "General Paper #5," 14 February 1957, RG 59, lot 57 D616, box 14, folder: "Mission to the Middle East, Basic Book, Ambassador Richards, General Papers," NA; testimony by James P. Richards, 27 May 1957, *Executive Sessions*, 555.

4. Lebanon received up to $10 million in economic development assistance and about $2.7 million in military equipment; see RG 59, lot 57 D616, box 14, Lebanon entry, folder: "General 4. Summary of Telegrams," and Rountree to J. F. Dulles, 4 April 1957, folder: "Briefing Book—Richards Mission," NA. Libya received $4.5 million in economic aid, later supplemented by an additional $2.5 million; see Rountree to J. F. Dulles, 4 April 1957, and to Christian A. Herter, 8 May 1957, U.S. Department of State, *FRUS, 1955–1957*, 12:486–87, 530–33. Iran received about $13 million in military aid and $6 million for telecommunications and railway projects; see Rountree to J. F. Dulles, 4 April 1957, U.S. Department of State, *FRUS, 1955–1957*, 488–89. Iraq received about $14 million in military aid and $2.5 million for police, telecommunications, and railway projects; see Rountree to J. F. Dulles, 16 April 1957, U.S. Department of State, *FRUS, 1955–1957*, 493–94. Tunisian prime minister Habib Bourguiba insisted that half of his $3 million aid package, which was earmarked for police and communications equipment, be in guns and tanks. Because the State Department had already promised the French it would not give Tunisia military aid, Richards refused Bourguiba's request, and Bourguiba declined the aid package altogether. Still, Bourguiba endorsed the Eisenhower Doctrine. See memorandum of conversation, Herter, Richards, et al., 13 May 1957, U.S. Department of State, *FRUS, 1955–1957*, 535; Sangmuah, "Eisenhower and Containment in North Africa," 83–84.

5. U.S. Embassy, Baghdad, to DOS, 28 March 1957, and Rountree to J. F. Dulles, 17 April 1957, *FRUS, 1955–1957*, 12:474, 495–96.

6. Morocco was then negotiating a base renewal agreement with the United States and was unwilling to commit itself on the doctrine pending the outcome of the discussions; see Rountree to J. F. Dulles, 10 May 1957, ibid., 534–35. Israel's 21 May endorsement of the doctrine made no mention of international communism, referring instead to "aggression from any quarter." Left-leaning members of Israel's governing coalition believed that nonalignment in the Cold War would better serve Israel's security interests and improve the prospects for Soviet Jewish emigration to Israel. See Yizhar, "Israel and the Eisenhower Doctrine," 60–61.

7. Rountree to J. F. Dulles, 27 April 1957, and Richards to DOS, 19 April 1957, *FRUS, 1955–1957*, 12:523, 518; Lefebvre, "United States and Egypt," 330–31.

8. Egypt entry, RG 59, lot 57 D616, box 14, folder: "General 4. Summary of Telegrams," NA.

9. Dann, *King Hussein*, 26–34, 38–41; Satloff, *From Abdullah to Hussein*, 151–54; Abidi, *Jordan*, 208, 211.

10. Satloff, *From Abdullah to Hussein*, 148–49, 154–55; Satloff, "Jekyll-and-Hyde Origins," 120.

11. The Hashemite legacy included not only claimed lineal descent from the Prophet but also the mystique of the Arab Revolt, which the king's great-grandfather, Sharif Hussein of Mecca, had led against the Ottoman Empire during World War I.

12. Satloff, *From Abdullah to Hussein*, 156–57; U.S. Embassy, Amman, to DOS, 9, 17 November 1957, *FRUS, 1955–1957*, 13:59, 61 n. 2.

13. Satloff, *From Abdullah to Hussein*, 157–58.

14. At the time, the United States was giving Jordan about $8 million annually in technical assistance and economic aid. It was also providing about $17.5 million annually to aid Palestinian refugees throughout the Arab world, over half of whom were in Jordan, mainly on the West Bank. See DOS to U.S. Embassy, Amman, 24 December 1956, *FRUS, 1955–1957*, 13:78.

15. Memorandum of conversation, John Foster Dulles, Selwyn Lloyd, et al., 10 December 1956, ibid., 13:73–75; Satloff, *From Abdullah to Hussein*, 156–58; Dann, *King Hussein*, 47.

16. DOS to U.S. Embassy, Amman, 12 December 1956, and Fraser Wilkins to Rountree, 3 January 1957, *FRUS, 1955–1957*, 13:75, 80–81.

17. Satloff, *From Abdullah to Hussein*, 158; memorandum of conversation, J. F. Dulles, Lloyd, et al., 10 December 1956, versions in RG 59, lot 64 D199, "Secretary of State's Memoranda of Conversation," box 6, folder: "Secy's M. of Con., December 1956," NA, and in PREM 11/1912, PRO; U.S. Embassy, Amman, to DOS, 22 November 1956, and DOS to U.S. Embassy, Amman, 24 December 1956, *FRUS, 1955–1957*, 13:66, 77–79.

18. U.S. Embassy, Amman, to DOS, tel #679, 27 December 1956, RG 59, 685.00/12-2756, NA.

19. Press summaries in U.S. Embassy, Amman, to DOS, tels #694, #721, #747, 31 December 1956, 4, 7 January 1957, RG 59, 611.80/12-3156, 611.80/1-457, 611.80/1-757, NA; translations of pamphlets in U.S. Consulate, Jerusalem, to DOS, desp #146,

27 March 1957, RG 59, 785.00/3-2757, NA; U.S. Embassy, Amman, to DOS, tel #712, 3 January 1957, RG 59, 611.80/1-357, NA; Satloff, *From Abdullah to Hussein*, 161–62.

20. U.S. Embassy, Amman, to DOS, tels #745, #754, 7, 8 January 1957, RG 59, 611.80/1-757, 611.80/1-857, NA; *al-Difaʿ*, 8 January 1957.

21. U.S. Embassy, Amman, to DOS, tel #767, 10 January 1957, RG 59, 611.80/1-1057, NA.

22. Satloff, *From Abdullah to Hussein*, 159.

23. Dann, *King Hussein*, 51. One could argue that the traditional practice established by King Abdullah (and long predating the 1952 constitution) had strongly favored royal absolutism, but one could also argue that Hussein himself, by allowing an unusually free election and then inviting the victors to form a government, had already begun to change the traditional practice and to move Jordan toward constitutional monarchy.

24. U.S. Embassy, Amman, to DOS, tels #712, #775, 3, 11 January 1957, and enclosure to desp #196, 5 February 1957, RG 59, 611.80/1-357, 611.80/1-1157, 785.00/2-557, NA; U.S. Embassy, Amman, to DOS, 13 February 1957, *FRUS, 1955–1957*, 13:84; Dann, *King Hussein*, 48–49. The cabinet rejected the idea that a vacuum existed in the Middle East or that "any state located outside the area . . . has any right to interfere in the Arab Homeland" outside the framework of the UN. The cabinet insisted that "defense of the Arab Homeland . . . should emanate from the area itself, and should be directed against any aggression on its sovereignty, independence, and interests" (*FBIS*, #39, 27 February 1957, A3–4).

25. U.S. Embassy, Amman, to DOS, tel #894, 6 February 1957, RG 59, 685.00/2-657, NA. *New York Times* reporter Kennett Love later maintained that the targeted "extremists" were Minister of State for Foreign Affairs al-Rimawi, Minister of Education and Culture Shafiq Irshaydat, and Minister of Agriculture ʿAbd al-Qadir al-Salih, members of the Baʿth, National Socialist, and National Front Parties, respectively. See U.S. Embassy, Amman, to DOS, desp #221, 12 March 1957, RG 59, 785.00/3-1257, NA.

26. Satloff, *From Abdullah to Hussein*, 162–63.

27. U.S. Embassy, Amman, to DOS, 13 February 1957; DOS to U.S. Embassy, Amman, 24 December 1957; and Wilkins to Rountree, 3 January 1957, *FRUS, 1955–1957*, 13:84–86, 78–79, 80.

28. U.S. Embassy, Amman, to DOS, 13 February 1957, ibid., 84–86.

29. The text of al-Nabulsi's letter of invitation has not surfaced, but according to an available summary the prime minister qualified his invitation by noting there would be a "more suitable" atmosphere for considering the Eisenhower Doctrine after Israel withdrew from Gaza and Sinai. (By 6 March Israel had announced its intention to withdraw from both areas but had not yet done so.) See Jordan entry, RG 59, lot 57 D616, box 14, folder: "General 4. Summary of Telegrams," NA.

30. Reinforcing this wait-and-see attitude was Britain's 18 February request that the United States "not make any public or private promises" to aid Jordan while negotiations to terminate the Anglo-Jordanian treaty were pending. Britain was using the possibility of continued British aid as leverage in the negotiations, and it did not want the United States to spoil this effort by introducing aid offers of its own. See memorandum of conversation, R. W. Bailey, Lampton Berry, and Richard Parker, 18 February 1957, *FRUS, 1955–1957*, 13:87–88.

31. Joint Chiefs of Staff report, 31 January 1957, *Declassified Documents*, 1980-153B; memorandum of conversation, U.S. Delegation to the Bermuda Meeting, 23 March 1957, RG 59, lot 64 D199, box 6, "Secy's M. of Con., Mar. 21–30, 1957," NA.

32. According to the termination agreement, Britain ended its subsidy, pledged to withdraw its forces from Jordan within six months, and released Jordan from a previous debt of £1.5 million; Jordan agreed to pay Britain £4.25 million over six years for facilities and stores the latter left behind. Jordan never made all of its payments. See Satloff, *From Abdullah to Hussein*, 228 n. 11.

33. Johnston, *Brink of Jordan*, 46–47; U.S. Embassy, Amman, to DOS, 29 March 1957, *FRUS, 1955–1957*, 13:88–89; U.S. Embassy, Amman, to DOS, desp #144, 22 March 1957, and tel #1129, 26 March 1957, RG 59, 785.003-2257, 685.86/3-2657, NA.

34. Dann, *King Hussein*, 52, 55–57; Satloff, *From Abdullah to Hussein*, 164–66.

35. Dann, *King Hussein*, 139; Satloff, *From Abdullah to Hussein*, 164–66; Hussein, *Uneasy Lies the Head*, 134–35, 140.

36. For Hussein's version, see *Newsweek*, 29 April 1957, 50–54; *Sunday Times*, 5 May 1957; Hussein, *Uneasy Lies the Head*, 140–46; Snow, *Hussein*, 108–11; Lunt, *Hussein of Jordan*, 38–42; Satloff, *From Abdullah to Hussein*, 166–67; Johnston, *Brink of Jordan*, 57–59.

37. *Time* magazine reported a version of this allegation as fact. Unlike Hussein's critics, however, *Time* sympathized with Hussein's overall predicament, portraying the danger posed by Nasserist and communist subversion as sufficient justification for the king's duplicity in this instance. The tone of the magazine article was one of admiration for Hussein's cunning. See *Time*, 29 April 1957, 26. Nasser himself later offered a more elaborate conspiracy theory: that the CIA passed "disinformation" to Abu Nuwar and al-Nabulsi, tricking both into thinking they could mount a successful coup against Hussein; the men attempted the coup and fell into Hussein's trap. See Copeland, *Game of Nations*, 209.

38. Satloff, *From Abdullah to Hussein*, 166–67; Hussein, *Uneasy Lies the Head*, 140–44; Snow, *Hussein*, 109–10.

39. Hussein, *Uneasy Lies the Head*, 144–46; Johnston, *Brink of Jordan*, 57–59; Snow, *Hussein*, 110.

40. Hussein, *Uneasy Lies the Head*, 126–27; U.S. Embassy, Amman, to DOS, 21 April 1957, *FRUS, 1955–1957*, 13:101.

41. Support for this position is found in the testimony of people on both sides of the Zerqa controversy. In 1989 Nadhir Rashid, commander of the First Armored Regiment and an ally of Abu Nuwar, acknowledged, "If things had had more time [to develop], a coup could have happened. But at the time, there was no plan for it. I can't say that His Majesty was wrong [in thinking that a coup was being planned]. What I can say is that if he didn't take the matter into his own hands, it could have developed. . . . Things were moving in that direction" (qtd. in Satloff, *From Abdullah to Hussein*, 167 [ellipses and brackets in source text]). In a May 1957 interview with the British Broadcasting Company, Hussein admitted that the antiroyal plot was "in the preparatory stage" (ibid., 168).

42. Hussein's rivals accused both Mallory and Sweeney of participating in Hussein's alleged plot to frame Abu Nuwar and his officers. In fact, the cables that Mallory and Sweeney sent to Washington on 13 April suggest that neither man had any inkling of

what was to happen that night. Mallory could offer nothing more definitive than "rumors . . . that General Nuwwar [is] completely on [the] side [of the] Nabulsi crowd though endeavoring [to] maintain strong relations with [the] king." He concluded that "there is little ground for optimism." Sweeney similarly noted that "Newar believes [the] King is losing and therefore is stringing along with Nabulsi, but still is trying to keep [the] King's good will. How long this situation will remain is indeterminate but should be more clear in [the] next week." Sweeney closed his cable with this ambivalent assessment of Abu Nuwar: "He is an opportunist, treacherous, highsider, and extreme nationalist; however he is one of [the] few who will take action if given proper backing but how long he would support [the] US after receiving backing is anyone's guess." See U.S. Embassy, Amman, to DOS, 13 April 1957, *FRUS, 1955–1957*, 13:90–91; US-ARMA, Amman, to DOS, tel #C-23, 13 April 1957, RG 59, 785.00/4-1357, NA.

43. U.S. Embassy, Amman, to DOS, tel #1363, 22 April 1957, RG 59, 685.00/4-2257, NA; Satloff, *From Abdullah to Hussein*, 169–70; Richard Collins to Erskine B. Graves, 15 April 1957, *FRUS, 1955–1957*, 13:94–95; Shwadran, *Jordan*, 350–51; Snow, *Hussein*, 111; Vatikiotis, *Politics and the Military in Jordan*, xvi; Dann, *King Hussein*, 59–60.

44. U.S. Embassy, Amman, to DOS, tel #1258, 12 April 1957, RG 59, 685.00/4-1257, NA.

45. The Syrians had approximately 5,000 troops in Jordan, and the Saudis had approximately 5,500.

46. U.S. Embassy, Amman, to DOS, tel #1363, 22 April 1957, RG 59, 685.00/4-2257, NA; Johnston, *Brink of Jordan*, 59–60. Al-Quwatli may at first have been ignorant of the maneuvers, which according to Johnston, "seem to have been arranged by ['Abd al-Hamid] Serraj," head of Syria's internal security forces; see *Brink of Jordan*, 59–60.

47. On the morning of 21 April Secretary Dulles told Allen Dulles, "If there was any way we could get any offer of assistance to strengthen the hand of the King [Hussein] we should try to do so." He wondered "if there was anything we could do through the Saudis. . . . If we could find a dependable way of getting the Saudis to help out that would be better than if we did it" (telephone conversation, J. F. Dulles and Allen Dulles, 21 April 1957, *FRUS, 1955–1957*, 13:102 n. 4).

48. Dann, *King Hussein*, 62; U.S. Embassy, Cairo, to DOS, tel #3307, 20 April 1957, RG 59, 785.00/4-2057, NA.

49. U.S. Embassy, Baghdad, to DOS, 15 April 1957, and DOS to U.S. Embassy, Amman, 15 April 1957, *FRUS, 1955–1957*, 13:96 n. 2, 97; U.S. Embassy, Tel Aviv, to DOS, tel #1230, 19 April 1957, RG 59, 685.00/4-1957, NA.

50. Dann, *King Hussein*, 60–61; Satloff, *From Abdullah to Hussein*, 170; Shwadran, *Jordan*, 352–55; *New York Herald Tribune*, 25 April 1957; *Time*, 6 May 1957, 31; U.S. Embassy, Amman, to DOS, tel #1390, 24 April 1957, RG 59, 785.00/4-2457, NA.

51. Egyptian Embassy, Amman, to EFM, desp #49, 4 April 1957, WK, Jordan Series, box 1, folder: "S—'Amman," DWQ; *New York Herald Tribune*, 22, 25 April 1957.

52. On 21 April the Middle East News Agency, a semiofficial Egyptian news outlet based in Amman, falsely reported that Iraqi troops had moved into Jordan. On 24 April Israeli ambassador to the United States Abba Eban told Dulles that Cairo Radio was broadcasting the same story into Israel in Hebrew, hoping "to embroil Israel" in the Jordanian crisis. Also on 24 April, Egyptian radio stations reported that Prime Minister al-Khalidi had resigned. Although al-Khalidi did resign later that night, he had not done

so at the time of the broadcasts. See *New York Herald Tribune*, 22 April 1957; memorandum of conversation, J. F. Dulles, Eban, et al., 24 April 1957, *FRUS, 1955–1957*, 13:105; U.S. Embassy, Amman, to DOS, tel #1390, 24 April 1957, RG 59, 785.00/4-2457, NA.

53. Snow, *Hussein*, 113.

54. Satloff, *From Abdullah to Hussein*, 170–71; memorandum of conversation, J. F. Dulles, Caccia, et al., 24 April 1957, *FRUS, 1955–1957*, 13:106; Parker, "United States and King Hussein," 112; *New York Herald Tribune*, 25 April 1957.

55. Parker, "United States and King Hussein," 116 n. 24; editorial note, *FRUS, 1955–1957*, 13:103; diary entry for 8 June 1957, Armstrong Papers, box 102; memorandum of conversation, J. F. Dulles, Abba Eban, et al., 24 April 1957, lot 64 D199, box 6, folder: "Secy's M of C Apr 1957," NA. According to *FRUS*, which contains a sanitized version of this document, the conversation took place from 3:32 to 3:53 P.M.; see *FRUS, 1955–1957*, 13:104–6.

56. *New York Herald Tribune*, 25 April 1957; *Newsweek*, 6 May 1957, 42; Parker, "United States and King Hussein," 112.

57. Six weeks later, referring to the possibility of Soviet intervention in Jordan, Dulles told *Foreign Affairs* editor Hamilton Fish Armstrong, "I didn't really believe in any such danger, but I saw that whether it ensued or not this was the moment for *us* to take a clear stand" (diary entry for 8 June 1957, Armstrong Papers, box 102 [emphasis in original]).

58. Telephone conversation, J. F. Dulles and Allen Dulles, 24 April 1957, Dulles Papers, Telephone Calls Series, box 6, folder: "Memoranda Tel. Conv—General March 1957 to April 30, 1957 (1)," DDEL; memorandum of conversation, J. F. Dulles, Eban, et al., 24 April 1957, *FRUS, 1955–1957*, 13:105.

59. Translation of Hussein's address, in U.S. Embassy, Amman, to DOS, tel #1403, 25 April 1957; U.S. Embassy, Amman, to DOS, tel #1410, 25 April 1957; and translation of martial law decree, enclosed with U.S. Embassy, Amman, to DOS, desp #278, 3 May 1957, RG 59, 785.00/4-2557 (2), 785.00/5-357, NA; *New York Times*, 26 April 1957; Johnston, *Brink of Jordan*, 62; Satloff, *From Abdullah to Hussein*, 172; Dann, *King Hussein*, 64.

60. Editorial note, *FRUS, 1955–1957*, 13:103; Eisenhower to Macmillan, 28 April 1957, AWF, DDE Diary Series, box 23, folder: "Apr '57 Miscellaneous (1)," DDEL; U.S. Embassy, Amman, to DOS, tels #1449, #1576, 28 April, 14 May 1957, RG 59, 785.004-2857, 785.00/5-1457, NA; telephone conversation, J. F. Dulles and Robert Murphy, 26 April 1957, reel 5, *Minutes of Telephone Conversations*.

61. In an October 1957 message to Cairo, the Egyptian ambassador in Damascus alluded to Syria's assistance to the Jordanian opposition the previous spring. The Syrian army, he wrote, "played an effective role in protecting, supporting, and extending every assistance to the nationalists, this behind the screen of the military facilities provided" to Jordan since the Suez war. See Egyptian Embassy, Damascus, to EFM, desp #300, 21 October 1957, WK, box 1195, folder: "2/3/5h ʿalaqat Suriya al-siyasiyya maʿ al-Mamlaka al-Saʿudiyya al-ʿArabiyya," DWQ.

62. Dann, *King Hussein*, 63; U.S. Embassy, Amman, to DOS, tel #1390, 24 April 1957, RG 59, 785.00/4-2457, NA.

63. U.S. Embassy, Damascus, to DOS, tels #2544, #2611, 25, 30 April 1957, RG 59,

785.00/4-2557, 785.00/4-3057, NA. Another purpose of the visit by Egyptian and Syrian officials was to assure Saud that Nasser was not plotting to assassinate him. On 19 April Saudi authorities had discovered a cache of arms in the king's Nasriyah Palace in Riyadh. The cache was linked to a Palestinian subcontractor who under interrogation allegedly confessed that he had received the arms from an Egyptian diplomat in Jidda. Both the Palestinian and the Egyptian were expelled from the country. According to the Palestinian's alleged confession, the arms were to be shipped to Iraq for use against that country's government, but Saud believed they were also intended for eliminating him. In his meeting with the Egyptian-Syrian delegation, Saud accused Nasser of direct involvement in the plot, demanding, "How could my brother treat me this way after all I have done for him!" The Egyptian members of the delegation swore to Nasser's innocence, but Saud was unmoved. See U.S. Embassy, Jidda, to DOS, desps #273, #291, 23 May, 12 June 1957, reel 6, *Confidential U.S. State Department Central Files, Egypt*; al-'Azm, *Mudhakkirat*, 2:505–6.

64. U.S. Embassy, Damascus, to DOS, tel #2611, 30 April 1957; U.S. Embassy, Baghdad, to DOS, tel #1788, 26 April 1957; and U.S. Embassy, Beirut, to DOS, tel #2710, 11 May 1957, RG 59, 785.00/4-3057, 785.00/4-2657, 685.00/5-1157, NA.

65. Egyptian Embassy, Damascus, to EFM, desps #162, #163, 13 May 1957, WK, box 1223, folder: "3/6/4 al-ahwal al-siyasiyya fi-al-Mamlaka al-Urduniyya al-Hashimiyya," DWQ.

66. U.S. Embassy, Amman, to DOS, 21 April 1957, *FRUS, 1955–1957*, 13:101–2.

67. Eisenhower to Macmillan, 28 April 1956, AWF, DDE Diary Series, box 23, folder: "Apr '57 Miscellaneous (1)," box 23, DDEL; telephone conversation, J. F. Dulles and William F. Knowland, 25 April 1957, reel 5, *Minutes of Telephone Conversations*; U.S. Embassy, Amman, to DOS, 3 May 1957, *FRUS, 1955–1957*, 13:124–25.

68. Sanger quoted in diary entry for 29 November 1956, Armstrong Papers, box 102; *New York Herald Tribune*, 26 April 1957; C. D. Jackson to Pierre Lazareff, 22 April 1957, Jackson Papers, box 69, folder: "Log—1957 (4)," DDEL. In his address to the nation on 25 April, Hussein invited precisely this sort of commentary, declaring, "I have served you as a child, and now I serve you as a man" (*Newsweek*, 6 May 1957, 42).

69. *Time*, 6 May 1957, 31.

70. Editorial note, *FRUS, 1955–1957*, 13:109. Richard B. Parker, who at the time was the Israel-Jordan desk officer at the State Department, writes, "Hussein's courage became something of a byword during this period. In one telephone conversation between Eisenhower and Dulles, . . . Dulles referred to him as 'the brave young king.' [Officer-in-Charge of Israel-Jordan Affairs Donald] Bergus, who was in Dulles's office during the conversation, reported this back to the Near East division of the State Department, and after that Hussein was referred to as the 'BYK'" (Parker, "United States and King Hussein," 116 n. 20). In later years this epithet gave way to the more condescending "PLK"—for Plucky Little King.

71. The available evidence is fragmentary but tantalizing. On 21 April the secretary told Allen Dulles, "If there was any way we could get any offer of assistance to strengthen the hand of the King we should try to do so." The secretary hoped to do this through the Saudis, and this conversation may well have led to Saud's reported payment to Hussein of $250,000 (see main text, above). During the same conversation, however, Foster Dulles predicted that Saudi involvement "would leak to Egypt and others," and thus

he may have decided on some other form of payment. On the afternoon of 24 April, shortly after Eisenhower and Dulles discussed Hussein's appeal for American support, the secretary told Allen Dulles that Eisenhower had "asked re money and the Sec told him A[llen Dulles] was taking care of it at least on a provisional basis." See telephone conversation, J. F. Dulles and Allen Dulles, 21 April 1957, Dulles Papers, Telephone Calls Series, box 6, folder: "Memoranda Tel. Conv.—General March 1957 to April 30, 1957 (1)," DDEL; telephone conversation, J. F. Dulles and Allen Dulles, 24 April 1957, reel 5, *Minutes of Telephone Conversations*; telephone conversation, J. F. Dulles and Allen Dulles, 21 April 1957, *FRUS, 1955–1957*, 13:102 n. 4. The first public disclosure of the secret CIA payments to Hussein was in the *Washington Post*, 18 February 1977.

72. DOS to U.S. Embassy, Amman, 25 April 1957, and editorial note, *FRUS, 1955– 1957*, 13:113, 118; Parker, "United States and King Hussein," 112, 116 n. 27.

73. *New York Times*, 25 April 1957; Jordan entry, RG 59, lot 57 D616, box 14, folder: "General 4. Summary of Telegrams," NA.

74. U.S. Embassy, Amman, to DOS, tels #1403, #1480, 25 April, 1 May 1957, RG 59, 785.00/4-2557, 785.00/5-157, NA.

75. U.S. Embassy, Amman, to DOS, 3 May 1957, *FRUS, 1955–1957*, 13:123–24. Richards never did visit Jordan. In July 1957 Hussein told Edward L. R. Elson, pastor of the National Presbyterian Church, that he and his advisers "did not invite Richards because they wanted to demonstrate to other Arab nations they could stand alone" (Jordan entry, Elson Papers, box 11, folder: "Journal—Europe c. 1945–1967").

76. White House Staff Notes, #128, 11 June 1957, AWF, DDE Diary Series, box 25, folder: "June '57 Diary—Staff Memos," DDEL; DOS to U.S. Embassy, London, and to U.S. Embassy, Baghdad, 6 May 1957, *FRUS, 1955–1957*, 13:126, 128; Parker, "United States and King Hussein," 113. The Saudis paid only the first installment of their pledge to Jordan.

77. That pretext was a further deterioration in Jordanian-Egyptian relations (and hence in Jordanian-Syrian relations) following Jordan's 9 June accusation that the Egyptian military attaché in Jordan had tried to instigate the assassination of Jordanian officials and members of the royal family. See Dann, *King Hussein*, 74–75; U.S. Embassy, Amman, to DOS, tel #1783, 13 June 1957, RG 59, 785.00/6-1357, NA.

78. Parker, "United States and King Hussein," 113.

79. U.S. Embassy, Amman, to DOS, tel #934, 6 November 1957, RG 59, 785.00/11-657, NA.

80. Podeh, "Struggle over Arab Hegemony," 102–3; Lesch, "Saudi Role in the American-Syrian Crisis," 36; U.S. Embassy, Cairo, to DOS, tel #3362, 26 April 1957, reel 7, *Confidential U.S. State Department Central Files, Egypt*.

81. Dann, *King Hussein*, 70, 74; U.S. Embassy, Amman, to DOS, tel #1522, 7 May 1957, reel 6, and Egyptian political cartoons (from May 1957), enclosed with U.S. Embassy, Cairo, to DOS, desp #948, 5 June 1957, reel 7, *Confidential U.S. State Department Central Files, Egypt*.

82. Memorandum of conversation, J. F. Dulles, Richards, et al., 14 May 1957, *FRUS, 1955–1957*, 12:538; memorandum of conversation, United States Delegation to the Ministerial Meeting of the North Atlantic Council, 2–4 May 1957, AWF, Dulles-Herter Series, box 8, folder: "Dulles, John Foster May 1957," DDEL; 321st meeting of NSC, 2 May 1957, AWF, NSC Series, box 8, DDEL.

83. White House Staff Notes, #133, 19 June 1957, AWF, DDE Diary Series, box 25, folder: "June '57 Diary—Staff Memos," DDEL; 321st meeting of NSC, 2 May 1957, AWF, NSC Series, box 8, DDEL; telephone conversation, Eisenhower and J. F. Dulles, 21 May 1957, AWF, Dulles-Herter Series, box 8, folder: "Dulles, John Foster May '57," DDEL; R. D. Drain to William Macomber, 22 May 1957, Dulles Papers, Telephone Calls Series, box 12, folder: "Memoranda Tel. Conv.—W. H. March 1957 to Aug. 30, 1957 (3)," DDEL.

84. Podeh, "Struggle over Arab Hegemony," 103; Lesch, "Saudi Role in the American-Syrian Crisis," 37. For the Saudi and Jordanian allegations, see nn. 63 and 77 above, respectively.

85. 326th meeting of NSC, 13 June 1957, AWF, NSC Series, box 9, DDEL; White House Staff Notes, #125, 5 June 1957, AWF, DDE Diary Series, box 25, "June '57 Diary—Staff Memos," DDEL; EFM to Egyptian Embassy, Damascus, desp #79, 1 June 1957, WK, box 1195, folder: "2/3/6 mu'amarat al-gharb wa-al-'Iraq didda Suriya," DWQ; U.S. Embassy, Beirut, to DOS, tel #2888, 31 May 1957, reel 1, *Confidential U.S. State Department Central Files, Egypt*.

86. Qubain, *Crisis in Lebanon*, 46–47.

87. Ibid., 48–51, 53–56; Egyptian Embassy, Damascus, to EFM, desp #108, 30 March 1957, WK, box 1223, folder: "3/6/3 al-ahwal al-siyasiyya fi Lubnan," DWQ; Eveland, *Ropes of Sand*, 248–53; Copeland, *Game of Nations*, 191–92; White House Staff Notes, #126, 7 June 1957, AWF, DDE Diary Series, box 25, folder: "June '57 Diary—Staff Memos," DDEL.

88. 327th meeting of NSC, 20 June 1957, AWF, NSC Series, AWF, box 9, DDEL; Qubain, *Crisis in Lebanon*, 56–59.

89. U.S. Embassy, Amman, to DOS, tel #1789, 14 June 1957; U.S. Embassy, Jidda, to DOS, tel #823, 20 June 1957; and DOS to U.S. Embassy, Jidda, tel #1265, 28 June 1957, RG 59, 786A.11/6-1457, 685.00/6-2057, 611.80/6-2857, NA.

90. R. Gordon Arneson to J. F. Dulles, *FRUS, 1955–1957*, 13:498.

91. Eisenhower to Saud, 10 July 1957, and Rountree to J. F. Dulles, 24 June 1957, *FRUS, 1955–1957*, 17:690, 657; summary of King Saud's correspondence with President Eisenhower, 19 July 1957, *Declassified Documents*, 1996-2953.

92. Telephone conversation, Eisenhower to J. F. Dulles, 27 June 1957, Dulles Papers, Telephone Calls Series, box 12, folder: "Memoranda Tel Conv.—W.H. March 1957 to Aug 30, 1957 (2)," DDEL; editorial note, *FRUS, 1955–1957*, 17:659–60.

CHAPTER 5

1. The purpose of Nuri al-Sa'id's resignation, which the palace approved, was not to signal any change in Iraqi policy but, rather, to allow the aging Nuri some rest and to give other establishment politicians a chance to govern for a while. It was widely expected that Nuri would return to the premiership in the fall. See U.S. Embassy, Baghdad, to DOS, tel #2125, 19 June 1957, RG 59, NA; "Iraq: Annual Review for 1957," 2 May 1958, FO 371/134195, PRO.

2. British Embassy, Baghdad, to BFO, tels #884, #1185, 20 July, 1 October 1957, FO 371/128041, FO 371/128230, and E. Michael Rose, "The New Iraqi Government," 24

June 1957, FO 371/128040, PRO; al-Ayyubi, *Dhikriyat*, 287–88; Lesch, *Syria and the United States*, 132–34.

3. In late June 'Abd al-Jalil al-Rawi, Iraq's chargé d'affaires in Damascus, told the Egyptian ambassador that 'Abd al-Ilah "desires to open a new page with Egypt" (Egyptian Embassy, Damascus, to EFM, desp #240, 27 June 1957, WK, box 1223, folder: "3/6/1 al-ahwal al-siyasiyya fil-'Iraq," DWQ). Al-Rawi himself, however, was a strong advocate of Iraqi-Egyptian rapprochement (as well as something of a loose cannon) and may have been exaggerating 'Abd al-Ilah's desire for better relations with Egypt.

4. Lesch, *Syria and the United States*, 129–30; Ian D. Scott to Rose, 11, 18, 25 July 1957, FO 371/128223, PRO; Egyptian Embassy, Jidda, to EFM, desp #151, 16 July 1957, WK, Jidda Series, box 2, folder: "756/81/3J al-taqarir lil-safara al-Misriyya fi-Jidda," DWQ.

5. Lesch, *Syria and the United States*, 104; Seale, *Struggle for Syria*, 282. The cabinet reshuffle excluded the People's Party and the Constitutional Front (both of which had been implicated in Operation Straggle), allowed the Ba'thists to keep the Foreign Ministry and Economy Ministry portfolios, and awarded the Defense Ministry portfolio to Khalid al-'Azm, a noncommunist but pro-Soviet politician. President al-Quwatli and Prime Minister al-'Asali remained in their positions.

6. Special National Intelligence Estimate, 16 November 1956, *FRUS, 1955–1957*, 13:602, 613 n. 4.

7. British Embassy, Beirut, to BFO, tel #1129, 12 November 1956, FO 371/121859, PRO; Egyptian Embassy, Damascus, to EFM, desp #611, 10 December 1956, WK, box 1196, folder: "2/1/5 al-barliman al-Suri," DWQ; U.S. Embassy, Damascus, to DOS, 8 November 1956, *FRUS, 1955–1957*, 13:596.

8. Special National Intelligence Estimate, 16 November 1956, and 305th meeting of NSC, 30 November 1956, *FRUS, 1955–1957*, 13:604 n. 2, 606; Moose quoted in diary entry for 29 November 1956, Armstrong Papers, box 102. Allen Dulles did not specify the number of East bloc advisers, but in April 1957 Ambassador Moose estimated that there were 150 to 200 East bloc technicians in Syria on both military and civilian assignments. See Scott to J. H. Adam Watson, 18 April 1957, FO 371/128222, PRO. In September 1957 President al-Quwatli privately assured Iraqi prime minister 'Ali Jawdat al-Ayyubi "that there were not more than eighteen Soviet technicians in Syria." Al-Quwatli did not give a figure for non-Soviet East bloc technicians. See British Embassy, Baghdad, to BFO, tel #1169, 30 September 1957, PREM 11/2119, PRO.

9. 304th meeting of NSC, 15 November 1956, AWF, NSC Series, box 8, DDEL; memorandum of conversation, John Foster Dulles and Harold Caccia, 24 December 1956, RG 59, lot 64 D199, "Secretary of State's Memoranda of Conversation," box 6, folder: "Secy's M. of Con., December 1956," NA. In 1954 a CIA-trained army of Guatemalan exiles invaded Guatemala from bases in Honduras and Nicaragua, causing the leftist government of President Jacobo Arbenz Guzmán to collapse. The event precipitating the invasion was a shipment of arms from Czechoslovakia to Guatemala via the Polish port of Stettin. See Immerman, *CIA in Guatemala*, 155–77.

As we have seen in Chapter 4, about this time Dulles was similarly arguing that the prospect of a Soviet takeover of Jordan was not a matter for serious alarm, since "noncontiguous Satellites can be 'pinched off' by the US and UK working together" (memorandum of conversation, J. F. Dulles and Selwyn Lloyd, 10 December 1956, *FRUS, 1955–1957*, 13:74).

10. Special National Intelligence Estimate, 16 November 1956, *FRUS, 1955–1957*, 13:603–5.

11. Egyptian Embassy, Damascus, to EFM, desp #16, 6 January 1957, WK, box 249, folder: "2/3/6B al-'alaqat al-Suriyya al-Amrikiyya," DWQ; U.S. Embassy, Damascus, to DOS, tels #1627, #1631, #1663, #1664, 4, 5, 10 January 1957 (2), RG 59, 611.80/1-457, 611.80/1-557, 611.80/1-1057, NA.

12. U.S. Embassy, Damascus, to DOS, tels #1676, #1749, #1781, 12, 24, 30 January 1957, RG 59, 611.80/1-1257, 611.80/1-2457, 611.80/1-3057, NA; U.S. Embassy, Damascus, to DOS, 11 January 1957, *FRUS, 1955–1957*, 13:609–10.

13. U.S. Embassy, Damascus, to DOS, tels #1663, #1668, 10, 11 January 1957, RG 59, 611.80/1-1057, 611.80/1-1157, NA.

14. DOS to U.S. Embassy, Damascus, 13 December 1956, *FRUS, 1955–1957*, 13:607–8; secretary's staff meeting, 13, 20 December 1956, RG 59, lot 63 D75, "Minutes and Notes of the Secretary's Staff Meetings, 1952–1961," box 3, folder: "Secretary's Staff Meeting Notes 451-500, July 12, 1956–Jan. 15, 1957," NA.

15. Lesch, *Syria and the United States*, 106–7; U.S. Embassy, Damascus, to DOS, desp #364, 1 March 1957, RG 59, 783.00/3-157, NA; DOS to U.S. Embassy, Cairo, 27 February 1957, and editorial note, *FRUS, 1955–1957*, 13:612–13, 613, 614; William Morris to R. Michael Hadow, 8 March 1957, FO 371/128221, PRO.

16. Lesch, *Syria and the United States*, 108–11; Seale, *Struggle for Syria*, 290; U.S. Embassy, Damascus, to DOS, tel #2202, 23 March 1957, RG 59, 783.00/3-2357, NA; Egyptian Embassy, Damascus, to EFM, desp #103, 26 March 1957, WK, box 249, folder: "2/3/6B al-'alaqat al-Suriyya al-Amrikiyya," DWQ; telephone conversation, J. F. Dulles and Allen Dulles, 17 April 1957, Dulles Papers, Telephone Calls Series, box 6, folder: "Memoranda Tel. Conv.—General March 1957 to April 30, 1957 (2)," DDEL.

17. Eisenhower to Harold Macmillan, 28 April 1957, AWF, DDE Diary Series, box 23, folder: "Apr '57 Miscellaneous (1)," DDEL; memorandum of conversation, ministerial meeting of the North Atlantic Council, 2–4 May 1957, AWF, Dulles-Herter Series, box 8, folder: "Dulles, John Foster, May '57," DDEL; U.S. Embassy, Damascus, to DOS, tel #2479, 20 April 1957, and DOS to U.S. Embassy, Tel Aviv, tel #1006, 27 April 1957, reel 1, *Confidential U.S. State Department Central Files, Jordan*; U.S. Embassy, Amman, to DOS, 3 May 1957, *FRUS, 1955–1957*, 13:124–25.

18. The National Grouping consisted of Ba'thists, communists, and left-wing members of the Independent and Nationalist Parties. The Coalition National Front consisted of the People's Party, the Muslim Brotherhood, the Arab Liberation Movement, and right-wing Independents and Nationalists.

19. U.S. Embassy, Damascus, to DOS, desp #461, 25 May 1957, RG 59, 783.00/5-2557, NA; Lesch, *Syria and the United States*, 112.

20. An August 1957 memorandum of conversation between Secretary Dulles and Ambassador Caccia suggests that the United States may have attempted to interfere in the elections. After Caccia wondered "what might be done under the general heading of covert operations" in Syria, Dulles "mentioned that we had been hopeful at least as an off-chance that some favorable development might occur at the time of the recent Syrian elections. This had not quite come off" (memorandum of conversation, J. F. Dulles, Harold Caccia, and Murphy, 19 August 1957, *FRUS, 1955–1957*, 13:243–44).

21. "Upon arrival at their customary polling places," the U.S. embassy in Damascus

reported, "Coalition National Front supporters found that their names did not appear on the voting lists and were consequently directed to other voting centers some distance away. In some cases, the process was repeated. Hence many conservatives were discouraged from voting because of lack of time or transportation. . . . There were also instances of intimidation of known Coalition National Front supporters by police" and state security agents. In Damascus, National Grouping supporters "were carried to the polls in government-owned vehicles" (U.S. Embassy, Damascus, to DOS, desp #461, 25 May 1957, RG 59, 783.00/5-2557, NA).

22. U.S. Embassy, Damascus, to DOS, tel #2779, 17 May 1957, RG 59, 783.00/5-1757, NA.

23. DOS to U.S. Embassy, Damascus, tel #2270, 28 May 1957, RG 59, 783.00/5-1757 (misfiled), NA. In *FRUS*'s version of this document, the reference to the Salk vaccine is censored; see *FRUS, 1955–1957*, 13:619.

24. DOS to U.S. Embassy, Damascus, tel #2270, 28 May 1957, RG 59, 783.00/5-1757 (misfiled), NA; telephone conversation, J. F. Dulles and Allen Dulles, 7 May 1957, Dulles Papers, Telephone Calls Series, box 6, file: "Memoranda of Tel. Conv.—General May 7, 1957 to June 27, 1957 (4)," DDEL.

25. U.S. Embassy, Damascus, to DOS, tel #2779, 17 May 1957, RG 59, 783.00/5-1757, NA; intelligence report, "Possible Leftist Coup in Syria," 17 June 1957, *Declassified Documents*, 1981-471B.

26. U.S. Embassy, Damascus, to DOS, tel #3036, 19 June 1957, RG 59, 683.00/6-1957, NA; Lesch, *Syria and the United States*, 129; al-'Azm, *Mudhakkirat*, 2:506–7. Al-Quwatli's family had long served as commercial agent in Damascus for the Saudi royal house, and al-Quwatli himself had been close to the Saudi ruling family since the 1920s. In the early 1950s al-'Asali had received a secret subsidy from the Iraqi government. He remained a senior partner in a prosperous law firm whose clients included the Trans Arabian Pipeline Company. See Seale, *Struggle for Syria*, 26, 165.

27. Egyptian Embassy, Damascus, to EFM, desp #251, 5 July 1957, WK, box 249, folder: "2/3/6B al-'alaqat al-Suriyya al-Amrikiyya," DWQ.

28. U.S. Embassy, Amman, to DOS, 12 August 1957, *FRUS, 1955–1957*, 13:158; secretary's staff meeting, 1 August 1957, RG 59, lot 63 D75, box 3, folder: "Secretary's Staff Meeting Notes 551-597, July 18, 1957–Dec. 31, 1957," NA.

29. Al-'Azm, *Mudhakkirat*, 3:18, 23; Lesch, *Syria and the United States*, 118. The promised loan amounted to £400 million Syrian (about $112 million) payable over ten years. See Scott to Rose, 8 August 1957, FO 371/128223, PRO.

30. Al-'Azm, *Mudhakkirat*, 3:6–9, 43; Seale, *Struggle for Syria*, 292–93.

31. For retrospective analysis of the split within the Syrian ruling coalition, see U.S. Embassy, Damascus, to DOS, tels #424, #564, 13, 23 August 1957, RG 59, 783.00/8-1357, 783.00/8-2357, NA; U.S. Embassy, Damascus, to DOS, desp #81, 17 August 1957, *Declassified Documents*, 1977-71G; Special National Intelligence Estimate, 3 September 1957, *FRUS, 1955–1957*, 13:675–77. For examples of Ba'thists' public praise for the Moscow agreement, see U.S. Embassy, Damascus, to DOS, tel #390, 11 August 1957, and U.S. Consulate, Aleppo, to DOS, desp #13, 27 August 1957, RG 59, 611.80/8-1157, 611.83/8-2757, NA; Salah al-Din al-Bitar, "Ahdaf al-siyasa al-Amrikiyya fi Suriya" (The goals of American policy in Syria) (1957), in Bitar, *al-Siyasa al-'Arabiyya*, 100, 107–9. In his memoirs, al-'Azm insists that he received full authorization from the

Syrian cabinet for his negotiations in Moscow, but he adds that the cabinet "took no written decision out of a desire to keep news of the trip secret" (al-'Azm, *Mudhakki-rat*, 3:9).

32. Little, "Cold War and Covert Action," 70.

33. For a comprehensive summary of the officers' allegations, see *FBIS*, #190, #191, 1, 2 October 1957, C1–17, C1–11.

34. Saunders, *United States and Arab Nationalism*, 63. Prior to serving in Syria, Howard "Rocky" Stone had worked as a CIA agent in Iran and Sudan, where his official "cover" had been employment as a foreign service officer. While in Iran, Stone had participated in the CIA-supported coup against Prime Minister Mohammed Mosadeq. He was later awarded the Distinguished Intelligence Medal, the CIA's highest career award. See Evan Thomas, *Very Best Men*, 183; *New York Times*, 15 August 1957.

35. Eveland, *Ropes of Sand*, 253–54; Yost interview, DDEL, 25–26. See also Yost, *Conduct and Misconduct of Foreign Affairs*, 161, and *History and Memory*, 236. Andrew Rathmell provides additional supporting details, but many of them come from anonymous sources and thus cannot be verified; see Rathmell, *Secret War in the Middle East*, 138–40.

36. *FBIS*, #190, 1 October 1957, C8. One might argue, of course, that Syrian authorities manufactured a nuanced and complex case precisely to achieve greater credibility with the Syrian public. But this argument presupposes a level of sophistication to which Syrian propagandists did not ordinarily aspire. From the tone of official statements and government-sponsored commentaries of the time, it is clear that Syrian authorities assumed their audiences to be most receptive to crude appeals. This is evident in the introductory portions of the conspiracy case's bill of indictment, which was read over the government-controlled Syrian Broadcasting Station. The introductory remarks were an occasion for the regime to comment on the allegations before presenting their substance. The overwrought tone of those remarks, which describe Howard Stone as an "evil force" given to "criminal lust," is in marked contrast to the detailed and factual approach of the bill of indictment's substantive portions. See *FBIS*, #190, 1 October 1957, C2–6.

37. The State Department's defense appeared in "background" interviews with journalists and in instructions to diplomats overseas, who in turn were to make the case to foreign governments.

38. DOS circular, tel #138, 14 August 1957; U.S. Embassy, Damascus, to DOS, tel #424, 13 August 1957; U.S. Embassy, Beirut, to DOS, tel #402, 13 August 1957, RG 59, 783.00/8-1357, 783.00/8-1457, NA; *Time*, 26 August 1957, 19–20; *New York Times*, 14 August 1957; briefing items, 14 August 1957, AWF, DDE Diary Series, box 26, folder: "August—1957—Memos on Appts. (2)," DDEL.

39. U.S. Embassy, Damascus, to DOS, tel #474, 16 August 1957, RG 59, 783.00/8-1657, NA; *FBIS*, #190, 1 October 1957, C11; *New York Times*, 14 August 1957.

40. A minor anomaly is Captain Atiyyah's description of the dark-haired Stone as blond; see U.S. Embassy, Damascus, to DOS, tel #474, 16 August 1957, RG 59, 783.00/8-1657. More troublesome is the assertion, in the statement by Lieutenant Colonel Khattar Hamzi, that former Syrian president Adib al-Shishakli briefly materialized in Damascus to encourage the conspirators. The current Syrian government had recently sentenced al-Shishakli, in absentia, to life imprisonment for his involvement in Operation Straggle, so such a visit would have been extremely risky. It would have been far

more sensible for al-Shishakli to have postponed his return until after the coup's success. See U.S. Embassy, Damascus, to DOS, desp #106, 5 September 1957, RG 59, 783.00/9-557, NA. Also problematic is Eveland's recollection that al-Husayni, to make his secret rendezvous with the Syrian officers, had crossed the Syrian-Lebanese border in the trunk of a U.S. embassy car; see Eveland, *Ropes of Sand*, 254. In addition to being highly implausible, Eveland's assertion is contradicted by Atiyyah's claim that al-Husayni entered Syria on a forged Saudi passport.

41. U.S. Embassy, Damascus, to DOS, tels #411, #423, 13 August 1957, RG 59, 783.00/8-1357, NA; *FBIS*, #156, 13 August 1957.

42. *New York Times*, 15 August 1957. Zayn al-Din was out of the country at the time. Zakaria was given forty-eight hours to leave.

43. U.S. Embassy, Damascus, to DOS, tels #462, #465, #510, 16 (2), 19 August 1957; U.S. Embassy, Baghdad, to DOS, tel #241, 19 August 1957; U.S. Consulate, Alexandria, to DOS, tel #90, 20 August 1957; and memorandum of conversation, Agostino Soldati, Lampton Berry, and Wells Stabler, 22 August 1957, RG 59, 783.00/8-1657, 783.00/8-1957, 783.00/8-2057, 611.83/8-2257, NA; U.S. Embassy, Damascus, to DOS, desp #81, 17 August 1957, *Declassified Documents*, 1977-71G; Seale, *Struggle for Syria*, 291, 295; Special National Intelligence Estimate, 5 September 1957, and memorandum of conversation, J. F. Dulles, Herter, et al., 19 August 1957, *FRUS, 1955–1957*, 13:676, 641.

44. U.S. Embassy, Beirut, to DOS, tels #441, #468, 16, 20 August 1957; U.S. Embassy, Amman, to DOS, tel #304, 18 August 1957; U.S. Embassy, Baghdad, to DOS, tel #228, 17 August 1957; and U.S. Embassy, Jidda, to DOS, tel #180, 17 August 1957, RG 59, 783.00/8-1657, 783.00/8-2057, 783.00/8-1857, 783.00/8-1757, 611.83/8-1757, NA; Daily Top Secret Summary, 19 August 1957, *FRUS, 1955–1957*, 13:638–39; 335th meeting of NSC, 22 August 1957, AWF, NSC Series, box 9, DDEL; British Embassy, Washington, to BFO, tel #1603, 21 August 1957, FO 371/128224, PRO.

45. U.S. Embassy, Ankara, to DOS, 21 August 1957, and U.S. Embassy, Tel Aviv, to DOS, 22 August 1957, *FRUS, 1955–1957*, 13:642–44, 648–49.

46. Memorandum of conversation, J. F. Dulles, Herter, et al., 19 August 1957, ibid., 641. See also British Embassy, Washington, to BFO, tel #1603, 21 August 1957, FO 371/128224, PRO.

47. Lesch, *Syria and the United States*, 150.

48. Memorandum of conversation, Eisenhower, J. F. Dulles, et al., 21 August 1957, and memorandum for the record, 23 August 1957, AWF, International Series, box 48, folder: "Syria (3)," DDEL; Eisenhower, *White House Years*, 198; U.S. Consulate, Istanbul, to DOS, 25, 26 August 1957, *FRUS, 1955–1957*, 13:654, 657. Henderson's mission lasted from 24 August to 4 September. Henderson stayed mainly in Istanbul, where he met with President Celal Bayar and Prime Minister Adnan Menderes of Turkey, Faisal and 'Abd al-Ilah of Iraq, and Hussein of Jordan. He also made a short visit to Beirut, where he met with President Camille Chamoun of Lebanon. For a study of Henderson's career, see Brands, *Inside the Cold War*.

49. U.S. Consulate, Istanbul, to DOS, 25, 26 August 1957, *FRUS, 1955–1957*, 13:654, 657.

50. Letter to the secretary of state, 24 August 1957, ibid., 652. The official, whose identity is censored in *FRUS*, mentioned that he had "met with Loy [Henderson] last night during [Henderson's] brief Rome stopover" on the way to the Middle East. At

the time of his departure from the United States, Henderson planned "to meet Allen Dulles secretly during the stop-over of his plane in Rome" (secretary's staff meeting, 23 August 1957, RG 59, lot 63 D75, box 7, folder: "Secretary's Staff Meeting Minutes, June 3, 1957–Dec. 30, 1957," NA). Without offering any evidence, Matthew F. Holland writes that the anonymous correspondent was "probably" CIA agent Kermit Roosevelt; see Holland, *America and Egypt*, 141.

51. Letter to the secretary of state, 24 August 1957, *FRUS, 1955–1957*, 13:652; memorandum for record, 28 August 1957, AWF, International Series, box 48, folder: "Syria (3)," DDEL.

52. British Embassy, Beirut, to BFO, tel #924, 31 August 1957, FO 371/127743, PRO; Egyptian Embassy, Baghdad, to EFM, desp #147, 13 September 1957, WK, Baghdad Series, box 4, folder: "756/81/2 al-taqarir al-siyasiyya lil-safara al-Misriyya fi-Baghdad," DWQ. The Egyptian embassy in Baghdad did not reveal how it had acquired this information.

53. BFO to British Embassy, Baghdad, tel #2219, 6 September 1957, FO 371/128225, PRO; al-Ayyubi, *Dhikriyat*, 308.

54. Memorandum of conversation, J. F. Dulles and congressional leaders, 25 August 1957, RG 59, 783.00/8-2557, NA.

55. Eisenhower, *White House Years*, 199; memorandum of conversation, Eisenhower, J. F. Dulles, et al., 21 August 1957, AWF, International Series, box 48, folder: "Syria (3)," DDEL; memorandum of conversation, J. F. Dulles and congressional leaders, 25 August 1957, RG 59, 783.00/8-2557, NA; telephone conversation, J. F. Dulles and Nathan Twining, 7 September 1957, reel 6, *Minutes of Telephone Conversations*.

56. Memorandum for the record, 23 August 1957, AWF, International Series, box 48, folder: "Syria (3)," DDEL. There was wide agreement among conservative Middle Eastern leaders that Saud's approval was key to any regional action against Syria, either because his support would benefit the operation or because his opposition would hinder it. The British also thought Saud's support was essential, for the latter reason. See U.S. Embassy, Beirut, to DOS, tel #441, 16 August 1957; U.S. Embassy, Amman, to DOS, tel #304, 18 August 1957; and U.S. Consulate, Karachi, to DOS, tel #341, 21 August 1957, RG 59, 783.00/8-1657, 783.00/8-1857, 783.00/8-2157, NA; U.S. Embassy, Ankara, to DOS, 21 August 1957, *FRUS, 1955–1957*, 13:643; BFO to British Embassy, Washington, tel #3284, 20 August 1957, FO 371/128224, PRO.

57. DOS to U.S. Embassy, Jidda, 21 August 1957, *FRUS, 1955–1957*, 13:645–46.

58. Saud to Eisenhower, 25 August 1957, AWF, International Series, box 46, folder: "Saudi Arabia, King Saud 1957 (2)," DDEL. Over the last several years the United States had, in fact, offered to sell Syria small amounts of military equipment, such as light arms and transport vehicles. Syria had consistently refused these offers, either because the prices were too high or because the offers came with conditions (e.g., that the equipment be used only for internal security and self-defense) that the Syrians considered infringements of their sovereignty. See Saunders, *United States and Arab Nationalism*, 13–14; Allen to Hoover, 8 December 1955, and U.S. Embassy, Damascus, to DOS, 5 January 1956, *FRUS, 1955–1957*, 13:559–60, 560 n 6.

59. U.S. Embassy, Beirut, to DOS, tel #563, 28 August 1957, Dulles-Herter Series, box 9, folder: "Dulles—August, 1957 (1)," DDEL; Saud to Eisenhower, 13 September

1957, AWF, International Series, box 46, folder: "Saudi Arabia, King Saud 1957 (2)," DDEL. See also British Embassy, Ankara, to BFO, tel #1011, 26 October 1957, FO 371/128238, PRO.

60. British Embassy, Ankara, to BFO, tel #785, 31 August 1957, FO 371/128225, PRO. See also British Embassy, Washington, to BFO, tel #1759, 9 September 1957, FO 371/128226, PRO; memorandum of conversation, J. F. Dulles, Lloyd, et al., 16 September 1957, PREM 11/2119, PRO.

61. British Embassy, Amman, to BFO, tel #1382, 26 August 1957, FO 371/128224, PRO; al-Ayyubi, *Dhikriyat*, 314; memorandum of conversation, J. F. Dulles, Mike Mansfield, and William B. Macomber, 11 September 1957, Dulles Papers, General Correspondence and Memoranda Series, box 1, folder: "Memos of Conversation—General—L Through M (3)," DDEL.

62. U.S. Consulate, Istanbul, to DOS, 2/3 September 1957, *FRUS, 1955–1957*, 13:672. A copy of this document in the Eisenhower Library identifies Henderson as the author. See U.S. Consulate, Istanbul, to DOS, tel #228, 2 September 1957, AWF, International Series, box 48, folder: "Syria (2)," DDEL.

63. Memorandum of conversation, Eisenhower, J. F Dulles, et al., 7 September 1957, and U.S. Consulate, Istanbul, to DOS, 2/3 September 1957, *FRUS, 1955–1957*, 13:685, 672; memorandum of conversation, J. F. Dulles, Christian Pineau, et al., 7 September 1957, RG 59, 783.00/9-757, NA; Eisenhower, *White House Years*, 200–201.

64. British Embassy, Baghdad, to BFO, tels #1018, #1028, 21, 25 August 1957, and British Embassy, Washington, to BFO, tel #1636, 26 August 1957, FO 371/128224, FO 371/128225, PRO; U.S. Consulate, Istanbul, to DOS, 2/3 September 1957, *FRUS, 1955–1957*, 13:670–71; al-Ayyubi, *Dhikriyat*, 307, 308.

65. Memorandum of conversation, Eisenhower and J. F. Dulles, 2 September 1957, and memorandum of conversation, Eisenhower, J. F. Dulles, et al., 7 September 1957, *FRUS, 1955–1957*, 13:669, 685; memorandum of conversation, Robert Hager and Stabler, 3 September 1957, RG 59, 783.00/9-357, NA; Egyptian Embassy, Damascus, to EFM, desp #324, 9 September 1957, WK, box 1223, folder: "3/2/1 al-ahwal al-siyasiyya fi-al-'Iraq," DWQ; Egyptian Embassy, Baghdad, to EFM, desp #147, 13 September 1957, WK, Baghdad Series, box 4, folder: "756/81/2 al-taqarir al-siyasiyya lil-safara al-Misriyya fi-Baghdad," DWQ. Subsequent intelligence reports on the anti-Syrian campaign appeared in Egyptian Embassy, Baghdad, to EFM, desp #172, 12 October 1957, WK, Baghdad Series, box 4, folder: "756/81/3 al-taqarir al-siyasiyya lil-safara Baghdad —'mukhtalif,'" DWQ, and Egyptian Embassy, Baghdad, to EFM, desp #276, 19 December 1957, WK, Baghdad Series, box 3, folder: "756/81/2 H2 al-taqarir al-siyasiyya lil-safara al-Misriyya fi-Baghdad 'inda al-'Iraq," DWQ.

66. *Al-Ahram*, 9 September 1957.

67. Earlier that summer a cable from the U.S. embassy in Saudi Arabia referred to a Czech arms sale to Yemen valued at approximately $3 million; see U.S. Embassy, Jidda, to DOS, 9 June 1957, *FRUS, 1955–1957*, 13:763.

68. Memorandum of conversation, Eisenhower, J. F. Dulles, et al., 7 September 1957, ibid., 687–88; memorandum of conversation, J. F. Dulles, Pineau, et al., 7 September 1957, RG 59, 783.00/9-757, NA; memorandum of conversation, J. F. Dulles, Mike Mansfield, and Macomber, 11 September 1957, Dulles Papers, General Correspondence and Memoranda Series, box 1, folder: "Memos of Conversation, L Through

M (3)," DDEL; memorandum of conversation, Dag Hammarskjold, J. F. Dulles, et al., 20 September 1957, reel 227, *John Foster Dulles State Department Microfilm Collection.*

69. Turkey increased its troop strength on the border from 32,000 to 50,000; see Eisenhower, *White House Years*, 203.

70. Memorandum of conversation, J. F. Dulles, Lloyd, et al., 16 September 1957, PREM 11/2119, PRO; memorandum of conversation, Eisenhower and J. F. Dulles, 2 September 1957, *FRUS, 1955–1957*, 13:670; memorandum of conversation, J. F. Dulles, Pineau, et al., 7 September 1957, RG 59, 783.00/9-757, NA; Saunders, *United States and Arab Nationalism*, 73; Lesch, *Syria and the United States*, 156.

71. Memorandum of conversation, Yohanan Meroz, Stuart W. Rockwell, et al., 23 August 1957, and memorandum of conversation, J. F. Dulles, Pineau, et al., 7 September 1957, RG 59, 783.00/8-2357, 783.00/9-757, NA; memorandum of conversation, J. F. Dulles and William F. Knowland, 30 August 1957, Dulles Papers, General Correspondence and Memoranda Series, box 1, folder: "Memos of Conversation—General—J Through K (2)," DDEL.

72. White House press release, 7 September 1957, RG 59, 611.80/9-757, NA. The recipients of these accelerated arms shipments were Iraq, Jordan, Saudi Arabia, Iran, and Turkey, with the first three countries receiving "overriding priority." See Special White House Staff Note, 20 September 1957, *FRUS, 1955–1957*, 13:714–15.

73. DOS to U.S. Consulate, Istanbul, 10 September 1957; DOS to U.S. Embassy, Amman, 10 September 1957; and DOS to U.S. Embassy, Tel Aviv, 10 September 1957, *FRUS, 1955–1957*, 13:691–96, 698–99, 690.

74. Ashton, *Problem of Nasser*, 128–29.

75. For general Cold War accounts making no mention of the Syrian crisis, see Gaddis, *We Now Know*; Crockatt, *Fifty Years War*; McCormick, *America's Half-Century*; John F. N. Bradley, *War and Peace since 1945*; LaFeber, *America, Russia, and the Cold War*; Larson, *Anatomy of Mistrust*; Joseph Smith, *Cold War*.

76. *Department of State Bulletin*, 30 September 1957, 525; *New York Times*, 11, 14, 20 September 1957.

77. Egyptian Embassy, Damascus, to EFM, desp #338, 18 September 1957, WK, box 249, folder: "2/3/6B al-'alaqat al-Suriyya al-Amrikiyya," DWQ; Egyptian Embassy, Damascus, to EFM, desp #398, 19 October 1957, WK, box 1190, folder: "2/3/6D al-'alaqat al-siyasiyya bayna Suriya wa-Turkiya," DWQ.

78. Memorandum of conversation, Eisenhower, J. F. Dulles, et al., 7 September 1957, *FRUS, 1955–1957*, 13:688; British Embassy, Beirut, to BFO, tel #965, 10 September 1957, FO 371/128226, PRO; Lesch, *Syria and the United States*, 174.

79. British Embassy, Baghdad, to BFO, tel #1118, 15 September 1957, PREM 11/2119, PRO. See also al-Ayyubi, *Dhikriyat*, 317–18.

80. Egyptian Embassy, Damascus, to EFM, desp #324, 9 September 1957, WK, box 1223, folder: "3/6/1 al-ahwal al-siyasiyya fil-'Iraq," DWQ; Jawdat to Jamil al-Midfa'i, 10 September 1957, in al-Ayyubi, *Dhikriyat*, 309–10; British Embassy, Baghdad, to BFO, tels #1121, #83 Saving, #85 Saving, 16, 19, 25 September 1957, FO 371/128227, FO 371/128228, PRO; Lesch, *Syria and the United States*, 174.

81. Egyptian Embassy, Damascus, to EFM, desp #337, 17 September 1957, WK, box 1195, folder: "2/3/5H 'alaqat Suriya al-siyasiyya ma' al-Mamlaka al-'Arabiyya al-Sa'udiyya," DWQ; telephone conversation, Eisenhower and J. F. Dulles, 25 September

1957, Dulles Papers, Telephone Calls Series, box 12, folder: "Memoranda Tel. Conv.—
W. H. Sept. 2, 1957 to Dec. 26, 1957 (3)," DDEL; memorandum of conversation, Lloyd
and Malik, 24 September 1957, FO 371/128230, PRO; al-Ayyubi, *Dhikriyat*, 322. Saud
was in Syria from 25 to 28 September; Jawdat was there on 26 September. They apparently met with Syrian officials separately.

82. British Embassy, Baghdad, to BFO, tels #1169, #1170, #1171, 30 September
1957, PREM 11/2119, PRO; British Embassy, Beirut, to BFO, tel #1047, 2 October
1957, FO 371/128238, PRO; Morris to Hadow, 3 October 1957, FO 371/127743,
PRO; U.S. Embassy, Damascus, to DOS, tel #921, 27 September 1957, RG 59, 786A.11/
9-2757, NA; Lesch, *Syria and the United States*, 178; al-Ayyubi, *Dhikriyat*, 324.

83. British Embassy, Amman, to BFO, tels #1446, #1460, #1461, 16, 21 September
1957 (2), PREM 11/2119, PRO; Scott to Rose, 24 September 1957, FO 371/128229,
PRO; British Embassy, Amman, to BFO, tels #1479, #1484, 30 September, 2 October
1957, FO 371/128230, PRO; *New York Times*, 20 September 1957; U.S. Embassy,
Amman, to DOS, desp #102, 1 October 1957, RG 59, 786A.11/10-157, NA; Lesch,
Syria and the United States, 179.

84. Lesch, *Syria and the United States*, 179; *New York Times*, 12, 17 October 1957; telephone conversation, J. F. Dulles and Henry Cabot Lodge, 2 October 1957, reel 6, *Minutes of Telephone Conversations*.

85. U.S. Embassy, Beirut, to DOS, tel #1120, 13 October 1957, RG 59, 786A.11/10-
1357, NA; Seale, *Struggle for Syria*, 304–5; Lesch, *Syria and the United States*, 178, 180.

86. Haykal, *Sanawat al-ghalayan*, 266–68; memorandum of conversation, Meroz and
John Dorman, 15 October 1957, RG 59, 783.0010/1557, NA; Seale, *Struggle for Syria*,
305; Egyptian Embassy, Damascus, to EFM, desp #395, 19 October 1957, WK, box
1190, folder: "2/3/6 al-'alaqat al-siyasiyya bayna Suriya wa-Turkiya," DWQ; British
Embassy, Baghdad, to BFO, tel #1244, 17 October 1957, PREM 11/2119, PRO;
British Embassy, Amman, to BFO, tel #1558, 19 October 1957, FO 371/128232, PRO.

87. Robert C. Strong to William M. Rountree, 16 October 1957, and enclosure to
U.S. Embassy, Damascus, to DOS, desp #167, 8 October 1957, RG 59, 783.00/10-
1657, 783.00/10-857, NA.

88. U.S. Embassy, Beirut, to DOS, 16 October 1957, *FRUS, 1955–1957*, 13:508; Egyptian Embassy, Moscow, to EFM, desp #125, 14 September 1957, WK, box 1190, folder:
"2/3/7A al-'alaqat al-Suriyya al-Sufiyatiyya," DWQ; Egyptian Embassy, Damascus, to
EFM, desp #376, 9 October 1957, WK, box 249, folder: "2/3/6B al-'alaqat al-Suriyya
al-Amrikiyya," DWQ; al-Hawrani, *Mudhakkirat*, 3:2399–2400. There was, to be sure,
reason to be skeptical of Soviet professions of solidarity with Syria. Early in the Suez
war, Nasser had learned from al-Quwatli, who was visiting Moscow, that the Soviet
Union was not willing to risk war to protect Egypt. It appears, however, that many
Egyptian and Syrian officials were unaware of this fact. In early 1958 Nasser related the
Suez incident to high-ranking Syrian officials, calling it a "hitherto unrevealed secret"
that he had kept from most members of his own inner circle; see U.S. Embassy, Cairo,
to DOS, tel #1953, 4 February 1958, RG 59, 786.00/2-58, NA. Even if many Egyptian
and Syrian officials had learned of this episode by the fall of 1957, they may still have
believed that Soviet threats against Turkey, which shared a border with the Soviet
Union, were inherently more credible than the prospect of Soviet hostilities against
Britain and France.

89. *New York Times,* 10 October 1957; Lesch, *Syria and the United States,* 181; Seale, *Struggle for Syria,* 304.

90. U.S. Embassy, Ankara, to DOS, tel #1050, 11 October 1957, RG 59, 661.82/10-1157, NA.

91. Herter to J. F. Dulles, 14 October 1957, Dulles Papers, White House Memoranda Series, box 5, folder: "Meetings with the President—1957 (2)," DDEL.

92. Since the early 1950s the Menderes government had been waging an extensive campaign to convince the United States to increase its aid levels to Turkey. See Harris, *Troubled Alliance,* 71–76.

93. Memorandum of conversation, J. F. Dulles, Hasan Polatkin, et al., 24 September 1957, RG 59, lot 64 D199, box 7, "Sec Memo of Con Sept. 1957," NA; DOS/U.S. Information Agency to U.S. Embassy, Ankara, 11 October 1957, RG 59, 782.5-MSP/10-1757, NA. The Turks were threatening to move in the opposite direction as well. On 19 September the Turkish ambassador to the United States told Loy Henderson "that although anti-Russian feelings are very strong among the [Turkish] people, the situation cannot be taken for granted. The high cost of living, the shortages of imported commodities, and the heavy defense expenditures are affecting people's thinking. Although most recent USSR economic offers have been turned down by the Turkish Government it is a question as to how long these offers can be resisted" (memorandum of conversation, Henderson and Ali Suat Havri Urguplu, 19 September 1957, *FRUS, 1955–1957,* 24:736).

94. *New York Times,* 9, 11 October 1957; John H. Morris to H. Daniel Brewster, 11 October 1957, RG 59, lot 58 D610, "Subject Files Relating to Turkey, 1947–1958," box 1, folder: "Turk-Syrian Relations, October 1957," NA; U.S. Embassy, Ankara, to DOS, tel #1153, 18 October 1957, RG 59, 783.00/10-1857, NA. Newspaper accounts of the border incidents refer to a small number of injuries and no deaths. In late October an Indian diplomat in Beirut told a member of the British embassy staff "that an important frontier incident about two weeks ago[,] in which about 50 people were killed, was hushed up by both sides by mutual agreement" (Scott to Rose, 31 October 1957, FO 371/128232, PRO). This claim is not confirmed by any other available source.

95. Telephone conversation, J. F. Dulles and William F. Knowland, 18 October 1957, reel 6, *Minutes of Telephone Conversations.*

96. British Embassy, Washington, to BFO, tel #2089, 15 October 1957, PREM 11/2119, PRO. Dulles also told Lloyd that he detected "an element of bluff in the Soviet attitude. . . . Although they had a certain number of heavy bombers, it was very doubtful whether they had given orders for a large scale production programme." Nor did Dulles think that "the I.C.B.M. [intercontinental ballistic missile] would be produced in quantity for some time." He believed the Soviets would remain in a position of relative weakness for at least five years.

97. Memorandum of conversation, J. F. Dulles, Malik, et al., 17 October 1957, RG 59, 783.00/10-1757, NA; *New York Times,* 17 October 1957.

98. Memorandum of conversation, Eisenhower, Macmillan, et al., 25 October 1957; DOS to U.S. Embassy, Ankara, 20 October 1957; and U.S. Embassy, Ankara, to DOS, 23 October 1957, *FRUS, 1955–1957,* 13:732, 24:738–39, 740.

99. *New York Times,* 25, 28 October, 5, 7, 9, 10 November 1957.

100. Lesch, *Syria and the United States,* 197–98; telephone conversations, J. F. Dulles

and James Wadsworth, 18 October 1957, and J. F. Dulles and Lodge, 20 October 1957, reel 6, *Minutes of Telephone Conversations*; memorandum of conversation, J. F. Dulles, Lloyd, et al., 18 October 1957, RG 59, 683.00/10-1057 (misfiled), NA.

101. Seale, *Struggle for Syria*, 306.

102. Ibid.; British Embassy, Washington, to BFO, tels #2159, #2181, 21, 23 October 1957; British Embassy, Baghdad, to BFO, tels #1275, #1296, 22, 24 October 1957, PREM 11/2119, PRO.

103. Lesch, *Syria and the United States*, 201–2; Scott to Rose, 14 November 1957; British Embassy, Ankara, to BFO, tel #1060, 14 November 1957; and Philip G. D. Adams to Rose, 5 December 1957, FO 371/128233, PRO; *New York Times*, 2, 3, 20 November 1957.

104. Ashton, *Problem of Nasser*, 122–23.

105. Memorandum of conversation, Lloyd and Richard G. Casey, 11 September 1957, FO 371/128227, PRO; memorandum of conversation, J. F. Dulles, Lloyd, et al., 16 September 1957; BFO to British Embassy, Washington, tel #3956, 4 October 1957; and memorandum of conversation, Eisenhower, Macmillan, et al., 25 October 1957, PREM 11/2119, PRO.

106. Memorandum of conversation, Eisenhower, Macmillan, et al., 25 October 1957, PREM 11/2119, PRO.

107. British Embassy, Beirut, to BFO, tel #924, 31 August 1957, FO 371/127743, PRO; memorandum of conversation, Lloyd and Malik, 24 September 1957, FO 371/128230, PRO; British Embassy, Beirut, to BFO, tel #1142, 25 October 1957, PREM 11/2119, PRO; EFM to Egyptian Embassy, Damascus, desp #135, 3 September 1957, WK, box 1195, folder: "2/3/5C al-'alaqat al-siyasiyya bayna Suriya wa-al-Mamlaka al-'Urduniyya," DWQ; al-Ayyubi, *Dhikriyat*, 314.

108. British Embassy, Beirut, to BFO, tels #1142, #1146, 25 October 1957, and British Embassy, Baghdad, to BFO, tels #1244, #1276, 17, 22 October 1957, PREM 11/2119, PRO.

109. Rountree to Strong, 29 October 1957, *FRUS, 1955–1957*, 13:737.

110. For a fuller treatment of the split between Ba'thists and communists during this period, see Chapter 6.

111. Adams to Rose, 12 December 1957, FO 371/128233, PRO.

112. U.S. Embassy, Cairo, to DOS, 11 December 1957, *FRUS, 1955–1957*, 13:744–45. In *FRUS*'s version of this document the name of Nasser's emissary is censored, but a contemporaneous British document and a slightly later American one both identify him as Haykal. See British Embassy, Washington, to BFO, tel #631 Saving, 13 December 1957, FO 371/128233, PRO; U.S. Embassy, Cairo, to DOS, 18 February 1958, *FRUS, 1958–1960*, 13:427.

113. U.S. Embassy, Cairo, to DOS, 11 December 1957, *FRUS, 1955–1957*, 13:745. In late December the Egyptian Foreign Ministry's Arab Bureau confidentially reported that Bizri "has two sisters who are considered to be members of the Communist Party, and thus he has been accused of communist leanings," implying there was no evidence that Bizri himself was a communist. Of course, Nasser may have had information about Bizri to which the bureau was not privy. See Arab Bureau, memorandum #3, 29 December 1957, WK, box 508, folder: "140/139/8H1 mashru' al-ittihad bayna Misr wa-Suriya," DWQ.

114. U.S. Embassy, Cairo, to DOS, 11 December 1957, *FRUS, 1955–1957*, 13:745. One remedy Nasser evidently was not contemplating at the time was an immediate union with Syria, though such a union did occur in February 1958 (see Chapter 6). Shortly after the union was proclaimed, Nasser told Ambassador Hare that in December 1957 "he had no thought of Egyptian-Syrian union except as something which might be worked out in five years or so" (U.S. Embassy, Cairo, to DOS, 18 February 1958, *FRUS 1958– 1960*, 13:427). Haykal and former Egyptian cabinet minister 'Abd al-Latif al-Baghdadi both confirm that such was Nasser's position about this time. See Haykal, *Sanawat al-ghalayan*, 272; al-Baghdadi, *Mudhakkirat*, 2:35.

115. Secretary's staff meeting, 12 December 1957, RG 59, lot 63 D75, box 3, folder: "Secretary's Staff Meeting Notes 551-597, July 18, 1957–Dec. 31, 1957," NA; DOS to U.S. Embassy, Cairo, 12 December 1957, *FRUS, 1955–1957*, 13:746.

116. Pach and Richardson, *Presidency of Dwight D. Eisenhower*, 175–76; *Time*, 11 November 1957, 24; Brendon, *Ike*, 344–50, 352; telephone conversation, J. F. Dulles and Herbert Brownell, 24 September 1957, reel 6, *Minutes of Telephone Conversations*; log entry, 14 October–11 November 1957, Jackson Papers, box 69, folder: "Log—1957 (4)," DDEL; Macmillan, *Riding the Storm*, 320; Hughes, *Ordeal of Power*, 247–52.

117. Hoopes, *Devil and John Foster Dulles*, 430.

118. National Intelligence Estimate, 8 October 1957, and "United States Objectives and Policies with Respect to the Near East," 30 October 1957, *FRUS, 1955–1957*, 12:609, 623; Egyptian Embassy, Damascus, to EFM, desp #407, 23 October 1957, WK, box 1190, folder: "2/3/6 'alaqat siyasiyya bayna Suriya wa-Turkiya," DWQ; Egyptian Embassy, Jidda, to EFM, desp #12, 27 January 1958, WK, folder: "756/81/3 H2 al-taqarir al-siyasiyya lil-safara al-Misriyya fi-Jidda," DWQ.

119. Eisenhower to J. F. Dulles, 13 November 1957, and memorandum for the record, 15 November 1957, *FRUS, 1955–1957*, 17:795, 796.

CHAPTER 6

1. U.S. Embassy, Amman, to DOS, desp #157, 29 November 1957, reel 2, *Confidential U.S. State Department Central Files, Jordan*; Egyptian Embassy, Amman, to EFM, desp #288, 2 December 1957, WK, box 1195, folder: "2/3/5J al-'alaqat al-siyasiyya bayna Suriya wa-al-Mamlaka al-'Urduniyya," DWQ.

2. Egyptian Embassy, Baghdad, to EFM, desps #276, #288, 19, 20 December 1957, WK, Baghdad Series, box 3, folder: "752/81/2 H2 al-taqarir al-siyasiyya lil-safara al-Misriyya fi-Baghdad 'inda al-'Iraq," DWQ. In his own account of the meeting with the Saudis, 'Ali Jawdat al-Ayyubi refers cryptically to "proposals . . . , by irresponsible people, for the formation of political blocs that the two governments were not prepared to accept" (al-Ayyubi, *Dhikriyat*, 342).

3. Seale, *Struggle for Syria*, 310–11.

4. Ibid., 316–17; British Embassy, Washington, to BFO, desp #631 Saving, 13 December 1957, FO 371/128233, PRO; Arab Bureau, memorandum #3, 29 December 1957, WK, box 508, folder: "140/139/8 H1 mashru' al-ittihad bayna Misr wa-Suriya," DWQ; Egyptian Embassy, Damascus, to EFM, desp #469, 4 December 1957, WK, box 1190, folder: "2/3/10 al-ittihad bayna Misr wa-Suriya," DWQ. The conservative

parties expressing early support for union were the People's Party, the Nationalist Party, and the Muslim Brotherhood.

5. Egyptian Embassy, Damascus, to EFM, desp #447, 20 November 1957, WK, box 1190, folder: "2/3/10 al-ittihad bayna Misr wa-Suriya," DWQ.

6. Seale, *Struggle for Syria*, 311–15; Arab Bureau, memorandum #2, 24 November 1957, WK, box 508, folder: "140/139/8 H2 mashru' al-ittihad bayna Misr wa-Suriya," DWQ; Haykal, *Sanawat al-ghalayan*, 272. 'Abd al-Latif al-Baghdadi, a former Egyptian Free Officer who was soon to be a vice president of the UAR, writes that this was Nasser's view as of December 1957. See al-Baghdadi, *Mudhakkirat*, 2:35.

7. Egyptian Embassy, Damascus, to EFM, desp #469, 4 December 1957, WK, box 1190, folder: "2/3/10 al-ittihad bayna Misr wa-Suriya," DWQ; Seale, *Struggle for Syria*, 318.

8. Arab Bureau, memorandum #3, 29 December 1957, WK, box 508, folder: "140/139/8 H1 mashru' al-ittihad bayna Misr wa-Suriya," DWQ; Seale, *Struggle for Syria*, 318–19.

9. Seale, *Struggle for Syria*, 320. The officers' note is printed in al-'Azm, *Mudhakkirat*, 3:123–25; Haykal, *Sanawat al-ghalayan*, 274–75.

10. Haykal, *Sanawat al-ghalayan*, 276–77, 278. See also al-Baghdadi, *Mudhakkirat*, 2:37.

11. Haykal, *Sanawat al-ghalayan*, 279; Seale, *Struggle for Syria*, 321–22; al-Baghdadi, *Mudhakkirat*, 2:36.

12. Seale, *Struggle for Syria*, 321–22; Haykal, *Sanawat al-Ghalayan*, 279. A couple of less convincing explanations for Nasser's turnabout have been proposed. One such explanation is that Nasser had favored an immediate union all along but played hard-to-get so as to enhance his bargaining position with the Syrians. See Roberts, *Ba'th and the Creation of Modern Syria*, 43; Gerges, *Superpowers*, 91. There is no evidence, however, that Nasser supported immediate union prior to his second meeting with the Syrian petitioners. Another explanation, offered by al-Baghdadi, is that Nasser changed his position to thwart Syrian army chief of staff 'Afif al-Bizri, who headed the officers' delegation to Cairo. According to al-Baghdadi, Nasser suspected that al-Bizri, at the behest of the Syrian communists, was calling for immediate, comprehensive unity with Egypt in the expectation that Nasser would reject the demand. Such a rejection would allow al-Bizri to take credit for having advocated Egyptian-Syrian unity, with Nasser taking the blame for having opposed it. To prevent this, al-Baghdadi writes, Nasser reversed his position at the second meeting with the Syrians; see al-Baghdadi, *Mudhakkirat*, 2:35–36. While it would have been characteristic of Nasser to be preoccupied with such tactical considerations, it is hard to believe that tactics alone sufficed to change his position on a matter of this importance. More likely, the fear of anarchy in Syria was the primary motivation for Nasser's decision to reverse course, and the desire to outflank al-Bizri and the communists reinforced that decision.

13. Nutting, *Nasser*, 216–17; Stephens, *Nasser*, 274; Seale, *Struggle for Syria*, 323.

14. Petran, *Nations of the Modern World*; Seale, *Struggle for Syria*, 322–24; al-'Azm, *Mudhakkirat*, 3:143; al-Baghdadi, *Mudhakkirat*, 2:37; *Newsweek*, 17 February 1958, 48–49; *Time*, 17 February 1958, 29; U.S. Embassy, Cairo, to DOS, tel #2178, 22 February 1958, RG 59, 786.00/2-2258, NA. According to the official tally, both ballot measures—the ratification of the UAR and Nasser's election as president—received more than 99.9 percent of the vote in both Egypt and Syria.

15. Egyptian Embassy, Beirut, to EFM, desp #22, 11 February 1958, WK, box 508, folder: "140/139/8 H2 mashru' ittihad bayna Misr wa-Suriya," DWQ.

16. Egyptian Embassy, Damascus, to EFM, desp #50, 22 January 1958, WK, box 1190, folder: "2/3/10 al-ittihad bayna Misr wa-Suriya," DWQ; U.S. Embassy, Damascus, to DOS, tels #2130, #2162, #2344, 1, 4, 18 February 1958, RG 59, 786.00/2-158, 786.00/2-458, 786.00/2-1858, NA.

17. U.S. Consulate, Jerusalem, to DOS, desp #136, 5 February 1958; U.S. Embassy, Baghdad, to DOS, tels #1262, #1296, 3, 7 February 1958; U.S. Embassy, Beirut, to DOS, tels #2628, #2629, #2674, 3, 4, 6 February 1958; and U.S. Consulate, Benghazi, to DOS, tel #131, 11 February 1958, RG 59, 786.00/2-358, 786.00/2-458, 786.00/2-558, 786.00/2-658, 786.00/2-758, 786.00/2-1158, NA.

18. U.S. Embassy, Baghdad, to DOS, tel #1280, 5 February 1958, and U.S. Consulate, Kuwait, to DOS, desp #233, 3 February, 1958, RG 59, 786.00/2-558, 786.00/2-358, NA; U.S. Embassy, Beirut, to DOS, tel #2545, 27 January 1958, reel 1, *Confidential U.S. State Department Central Files, Egypt*.

19. U.S. Embassy, Beirut, to DOS, tels #2535, #2546, 26, 27 January 1958, reel 1, *Confidential U.S. State Department Central Files, Egypt*; U.S. Embassy, Baghdad, to DOS, tel #1296, 7 February 1958, RG 59, 786.00/2-758, NA; U.S. Embassy, Amman, to DOS, 27 January 1958, *FRUS, 1958–1960*, 11:268.

20. J. Lampton Berry to Christian A. Herter, 25 January 1958, *FRUS, 1958–1960*, 13:411; 353rd meeting of NSC, 30 January 1958, AWF, NSC Series, box 9, DDEL.

21. U.S. Embassy, Ankara, to DOS, SECTO 30, 29 January 1958, reel 1, *Confidential U.S. State Department Central Files, Egypt*; British Embassy, Ankara, to BFO, tel #195, 28 January 1958, FO 371/134386, PRO.

22. British Embassy, Ankara, to BFO, tel #195, 28 January 1958, FO 371/134386, PRO; DOS to U.S. Embassy, Beirut, tel #3058, 1 February 1958, RG 59, 674.83/2-158, NA.

23. U.S. Embassy, Ankara, to DOS, 29 January 1958, *FRUS, 1958–1960*, 13:412–13. It is possible that Dulles revised his position because he had received intelligence reports in the interim suggesting the anticommunist origins of the Egyptian-Syrian union. Dulles later claimed that his initial remarks in Ankara were based on inadequate intelligence on the union (see main text, below). At some point during his stay in Ankara, Dulles discussed the Egyptian-Syrian union with Wilbur Crane Eveland, CIA director Allen Dulles's special representative in the Middle East. Eveland writes that Foster Dulles asked him, "What do the Russians think about it? They must be behind it." Eveland replied that, according to the CIA's information, the Soviets were not responsible for the union and probably secretly opposed it; Eveland also passed on Allen Dulles's advice "that open opposition by us or by the Baghdad Pact would probably give fresh impetus to the union" (Eveland, *Ropes of Sand*, 271–72). Eveland does not say precisely when this exchange took place, but it may have occurred between the 28 January and 29 January sessions of the Baghdad Pact Council meeting, thus explaining Dulles's more cautious stance at the later session.

24. U.S. Embassy, Ankara, to DOS, 29 January 1958, *FRUS, 1958–1960*, 13:412–13; British Embassy, Ankara, to BFO, tel #223, 29 January 1958, FO 371/134386, PRO.

25. 354th meeting of NSC, 6 February 1958, *FRUS, 1958–1960*, 13:409–10, 12:38; Ashton, *Problem of Nasser*, 145.

26. Joseph N. Greene Jr. to Berry, 5 February 1958, *FRUS, 1958–1960*, 13:416.

27. U.S. Embassy, Baghdad, to DOS, tel #1283, 6 February 1958, reel 1, *Confidential U.S. State Department Central Files, Egypt*.

28. Saud's 7 February letter to Eisenhower remains classified in American archives. For summaries of its contents, see DOS to U.S. Embassy, Baghdad, 8 February 1958, *FRUS, 1958–1960*, 13:420; U.S. Embassy, Jidda, to DOS, tel #754, 12 February 1958, RG 59, 786.00/2-1258, NA.

29. On 6 February the U.S. embassy in Baghdad conveyed a report by former Iraqi prime minister Muhammad Fadhil Jamali on his recent trip to Lebanon. Though "Jamali found general agreement in Lebanon that Iraq will be in mortal danger if [the] union [is] Consummated," he saw little indication that Lebanon was prepared to act against the union: "Chamoun is with Iraq in mind and spirit but [is] unable to do much and is afraid of being accused of Sectarianism if he opposes [the] union. Malik is concerned and feels his Prime Minister [Sami al-Sulh] is weak. Solh says he is with Iraq but doubts Iraq will act" (U.S. Embassy, Baghdad, to DOS, tel #1284, 6 February 1958, reel 1, *Confidential U.S. State Department Central Files, Egypt*). As for King Hussein, he was primarily concerned with forming a Jordanian-Iraqi union, which he considered a safer and more feasible alternative to covert action in Syria (see main text, below).

30. DOS to U.S. Embassy, Baghdad, 8 February 1958, *FRUS, 1958–1960*, 13:419–20.

31. Ibid.; U.S. Embassy, Baghdad, to DOS, tel #1312, 10 February 1958, reel 1, *Confidential U.S. State Department Central Files, Egypt*.

32. John Foster Dulles to Eisenhower, 8 February 1958, *FRUS, 1958–1960*, 13:421. The "traditional policy on Arab unity" was to welcome any moves toward Arab unity that considered the wishes of the peoples concerned and contributed to the welfare and stability of the region. See DOS circular #637, 21 January 1958, reel 1, *Confidential U.S. State Department Central Files, Egypt*.

33. *FRUS, 1958–1960*, 13:421, 421 n. 1.

34. U.S. Embassy, Amman, to DOS, 27 January 1958, ibid., 11:268–69; U.S. Embassy, London, to DOS, tel #4563, 3 February 1958; U.S. Embassy, Amman, to DOS, tel #592, 7 February 1958, and desp #241, 19 February 1958; and U.S. Embassy, Baghdad, to DOS, tel #1296, 7 February 1958, RG 59, 674.83/2-358, 685.87/2-758, 786.00/2-1958, 786.00/2-758, NA.

35. Jordan's capitulation was masked by a provision requiring Iraq to "re-examine" its adherence to the Baghdad Pact when Iraqi membership in the pact came up for renewal the following year. It was generally understood that, while Iraq might go through the motions of such a reexamination, it had no intention of actually changing its position on the pact. See U.S. Embassy, Amman, to DOS, desp #241, 19 February 1958, RG 59, 786.00/2-1958, NA; Dann, *King Hussein*, 79.

36. U.S. Embassy, Amman, to DOS, tels #1497, #1507, 14, 15 February 1958, and desp #241, 19 February 1958, RG 59, 786.00/2-1458, 786.00/2-1558, 786.00/2-1958, NA; Johnston, *Brink of Jordan*, 89–91. Hussein had wanted the position of chief executive to rotate between himself and Faisal, but the Iraqis insisted on keeping the position permanently in their hands. Under the confederation agreement, the Jordanian king would serve as chief executive when the Iraqi king was absent. See Johnston, *Brink of Jordan*, 90–91; Dann, *King Hussein*, 79.

37. DOS to U.S. Embassy, Amman, 13 February 1958, *FRUS, 1958–1960*, 11:274; DOS to U.S. Embassy, Amman, tels #1919, #1927, 13, 14 February 1958, RG 59, 685.87/2-1358, 786.00/2-1458, NA.

38. U.S. Embassy, Baghdad, to DOS, 21 February 1958, and U.S. Embassy, Amman, to DOS, 24 February 1958, *FRUS, 1958–1960*, 12:294, 11:276; R. Gordon Arneson to Herter, 7 March 1958, reel 2, *Confidential U.S. State Department Central Files, Jordan*. See also U.S. Consulate, Jerusalem, to DOS, desp #147, 19 February 1958, RG 59, 786.00/2-1958, NA.

39. U.S. Consulate, Kuwait, to DOS, tel #70, 24 February 1958; U.S. Embassy, Beirut, to DOS, tel #2750, 13 February 1958; U.S. Embassy, Amman, to DOS, tel #1507, 15 February 1958; U.S. Consulate, Dhahran, to DOS, tel #453, 18 February 1958; and U.S. Embassy, Baghdad, to DOS, tel #1456, 3 March 1958, RG 59, 786.00/2-2458, 786.00/2-1358, 786.00/2-1558, 786.00/2-1858, 786.00/3-358, NA.

40. Press summaries in U.S. Embassy, Beirut, to DOS, tel #2750, 13 February 1958; U.S. Embassy, Damascus, to DOS, tel #2314, 15 February 1958; and U.S. Embassy, Cairo, to DOS, tel #2079, 15 February 1958, RG 59, 786.00/2-1358, 786.00/2-1558, NA; Haykal column, *al-Ahram*, 15 February 1958.

41. U.S. Embassy, Cairo, to DOS, tel #2079, 15 February 1958, RG 59, 786.00/2-1558, NA; Egyptian Embassy, Baghdad, to EFM, desp #61, 13 February 1958, WK, Baghdad Series, box 3, folder: "756/81/2 H2 al-taqarir al-siyasiyya lil-safara al-Misriyya fi-Baghdad 'inda al-'Iraq," DWQ.

42. Arneson to Herter, 7 March 1958, reel 2, *Confidential U.S. State Department Central Files, Jordan*. See Chapter 7 for contemporaneous Egyptian efforts to avoid similar controversy in Lebanon.

43. Egyptian Embassy, Damascus, to EFM, desp #71, 14 February 1958, WK, box 1190, folder: "2/3/10 al-ittihad bayna Misr wa-Suriya," DWQ; U.S. Embassy, Baghdad, to DOS, tels #1283, #1312, 6, 10 February 1958, reel 1, *Confidential U.S. State Department Central Files, Egypt*; British Embassy, Baghdad, to BFO, tel #204, 11 February 1958, FO 371/134197, PRO. Although the text of Faisal's reply to Nasser has not surfaced, an Iraqi diplomat privately acknowledged at the time that Faisal had failed "to reply to Nasser's message . . . in comparably cordial terms" (U.S. Embassy, Damascus, to DOS, tel #2466, 3 March 1958, RG 59, 786.00/3-358, NA). See also U.S. Embassy, Cairo, to DOS, tel #2444, 20 March 1958, RG 59, 786.00/3-2058, NA.

44. DOS to U.S. Embassy, Baghdad, 21 February 1958, *FRUS, 1958–1960*, 13:431; U.S. Consulate, Damascus, to DOS, tel #2474, 4 March 1958, RG 59, 786.00/3-458, NA; secretary's staff meeting, 25 February 1958, RG 59, lot 63 D75, box 3, folder: "Secretary's Staff Meeting Notes 598-648, Jan. 2, 1958–June 27, 1958," NA. On 20 March Nasser complained to Ambassador Hare "that Iraq had adopted [a] hostile public attitude and also endeavored to persuade [the] US and B[aghdad] P[act] members not [to] recognize [the] UAR." Recording this remark in his memorandum of the conversation, Hare noted, "Nasser's information on this was surprisingly complete and accurate" (U.S. Embassy, Cairo, to DOS, tel #2444, 20 March 1958, RG 59, 786.00/3-2058, NA).

45. U.S. Embassy, Cairo, to DOS, tel #2266, 3 March 1958, RG 59, 786.00/3-358, NA; *Newsweek*, 24 February 1958, 22.

46. Speech by Nasser, 27 February 1958, in *al-Majmuʿa al-kamila*, vol. 3, pt. 1, 86–87; U.S. Consulate, Damascus, to DOS, desp #423, 18 April 1958, and U.S. Embassy, Baghdad, to DOS, desp #958, 3 April 1958, reel 6, *Confidential U.S. State Department Central Files, Egypt*; Dann, *King Hussein*, 82.

47. Dann, *King Hussein*, 82; U.S. Embassy, Amman, to DOS, tel #1612, 5 March 1958, reel 2, *Confidential U.S. State Department Central Files, Jordan*; British Embassy, Amman, to BFO, tel #251, 3 March 1958, and British Embassy, Baghdad, to BFO, tel #321, 26 February 1958, FO 371/134198, PRO; *Newsweek*, 17 March 1958, 40. In 1916, two years before Nasser's birth, Nuri joined the "Arab revolt" led by Sharif Hussein of Mecca, the great-grandfather of King Faisal II. In 1918–19 Nuri served as chief of staff to Hussein's son Prince Faisal (later King Faisal I), assisting with diplomatic discussions over the political future of the Arabs. See Gallman, *Iraq under General Nuri*, 12.

48. British Embassy, Baghdad, to BFO, tel #365, 4 March 1958, FO 371/134198, PRO.

49. Rathmell, *Secret War in the Middle East*, 148; William M. Rountree to J. F. Dulles, 14 March 1958, *FRUS, 1958–1960*, 12:719.

50. For imputations of U.S. involvement, see Eveland, *Ropes of Sand*, 273; Anthony Cave Brown, *Oil, God, and Gold*, 218.

51. U.S. Embassy, Jidda, to DOS, 3 March 1958, and U.S. Consulate, Damascus, to DOS, 3 March 1958, *FRUS, 1958–1960*, 12:714 nn. 1, 3. See also Rountree to J. F. Dulles, 14 March 1958, ibid., 719. Following the ratification of the UAR by plebiscites, the U.S. embassy in Damascus had been downgraded to consular status.

52. DOS to U.S. Embassy, Jidda, 4 March 1958, ibid., 714; U.S. Embassy, Jidda, to DOS, tel #838, 4 March 1958, reel 1, *Confidential U.S. State Department Central Files, Saudi Arabia*; 357th meeting of NSC, 6 March 1958, AWF, NSC Series, box 9, DDEL.

53. Rountree to J. F. Dulles, 14 March 1958, and 358th meeting of NSC, 13 March 1958, *FRUS, 1958–1960*, 12:719, 46; U.S. Embassy, Jidda, to DOS, tel #887, 13 March 1958, RG 59, 686.86A/3-1358, NA; U.S. Consulate, Dhahran, to DOS, tel #514, 18 March 1958, reel 1, *Confidential U.S. State Department Central Files, Saudi Arabia*.

54. 358th meeting of NSC, 13 March 1958, *FRUS, 1958–1960*, 12:46.

55. Lacey, *Kingdom*, 318–20; Bligh, *From Prince to King*, 60–61; Yizraeli, *Remaking of Saudi Arabia*, 56–58. In Saudi Arabia the title of king is transferred not through primogeniture but through a loose, and not entirely predictable, system of seniority among eligible princes, usually of the deceased king's own generation. In the 1930s King Ibn Saud had breached this tradition by naming Saud, his eldest surviving son, as his successor. But it was generally recognized that this had been an exceptional act designed to convince foreign governments that the line of succession to the Saudi throne was sufficiently orderly, and hence the monarchy sufficiently stable, to warrant diplomatic recognition of the kingdom. See Bligh, *From Prince to King*, 102–4; Holden and Johns, *House of Saud*, 178.

56. Holden and Johns, *House of Saud*, 320–22. Saud did regain some of his powers in the early 1960s, but deteriorating health prevented him from making a full comeback. He was forced to abdicate in favor of Faisal in 1964.

57. Telephone conversation, Eisenhower and J. F. Dulles, 25 September 1957, Dulles Papers, box 12, folder: "Memo Tel. Conv.—W.H. Sept. 2, 1957 to Dec. 26, 1957 (3),"

DDEL. Faisal had been in the United States from July 1957 until February 1958, receiving medical treatment. See Bligh, *From Prince to King*, 62.

58. Editorial note, *FRUS, 1958–1960*, 12:724.

59. BFO report, "Saudi Arabia: Annual Review for 1958," 9 August 1959, and broadcast statement by Faisal, 19 April 1958, in Tuson and Burdett, *Records of Saudi Arabia*, 449–50, 750; Holden and Johns, *House of Saud*, 197–202; Lacey, *Kingdom*, 321–25; Egyptian Embassy, Jidda, to EFM, desp #39, 24 April 1958, WK, Jidda Series, box, 2, folder: "757/81/3 H2 al-taqarir al-siyasiyya lil-safara al-Misriyya fi-Jidda," DWQ.

60. Special National Intelligence Estimate, 8 April 1958, *FRUS, 1958–1960*, 12:728.

61. U.S. Embassy, Manila, to DOS, 11 March 1958, ibid., 294. On 17 March Haykal had told Ambassador Hare that Egypt hoped to avoid a crisis in Jordan partly for "fear that [the] Israelis would move against Jordan" (U.S. Embassy, Cairo, to DOS, tel #2444, 20 March 1958, RG 59, 786.00/3-2058, NA).

62. Memorandum for the secretary, 15 March 1958, *FRUS, 1958–1960*, 11: item #6 (microfiche supplement).

63. Telephone conversation, J. F. Dulles and Robert Anderson, 20 March 1958, and telephone conversation, J. F. Dulles and Rountree, 3 April 1958, reel 7, *Minutes of Telephone Conversations.*

64. "Assessment of Current Situation in Near East," Tab A of Rountree to J. F. Dulles, 24 March 1958, *FRUS, 1958–1960*, 12:48–54.

65. DOS to U.S. Embassy, Cairo, 25 March 1958; U.S. Embassy, Cairo, to DOS, 1 April 1958; DOS to U.S. Embassy, Cairo, 16 April 1958; and U.S. Embassy, Cairo, to DOS, 26 April 1958, ibid., 13:437–38, 438 n. 3, 439–40, 446–49.

66. J. F. Dulles press conference, 1 May 1958, *Department of State Bulletin*, 19 May 1958, 807.

67. J. F. Dulles press conference, 8 April 1958, ibid., 28 April 1958, 684; U.S. Embassy, Amman, to DOS, tel #1846, 28 April 1958, and U.S. Embassy, Beirut, to DOS, tel #3588, 28 April 1958, RG 59, 611.84/4-2858, 611.86/4-2858, NA; memorandum of conversation, J. F. Dulles, Selwyn Lloyd, et al., 4 May 1958, RG 59, lot 64 D99, box 8, folder: "Secy's M. of Con., May—1958," NA.

68. Rountree to J. F. Dulles, 16 April 1958, *FRUS, 1958–1960*, 12:55–59.

69. U.S. Embassy, Amman, to DOS, 28 June, 19 May 1958; DOS to U.S. Embassy, Amman, 20 May 1958; Rountree to J. F. Dulles, 16 April 1958; and staff notes for Eisenhower, 16 April 1958, ibid., 11:292, 288 n. 2, 288–89, 12:58, 298.

70. U.S. Embassy, Baghdad, to DOS, 12 March 1958, ibid., 12:297; British Embassy, Baghdad, to BFO, tels #321, #1109, 26 February, 23 June 1958, FO 371/134198, PRO.

71. British Embassy, Baghdad, to BFO, tels #422, #706, #1109, 12 March, 3 May, 23 June 1958, FO 371/134198, PRO; memorandum of conversation, Eisenhower, Harold Macmillan, et al., 9 June 1958, and Rountree to J. F. Dulles, 10 June 1958, *FRUS, 1958–1960*, 12:301–2, 302 n. 2.

CHAPTER 7

1. Alin, *Lebanon Crisis*, 55–56.

2. Hudson, *Precarious Republic*, 111–13.

3. Egyptian Embassy, Beirut, to EFM, desps #16, #17, 3 February 1958, WK, box 508, folder: "140/139/8 H2 mashruʿ al-ittihad bayna Misr wa-Suriya," DWQ; Arab Bureau, "Sada iʿlan al-Jumhuriyya al-ʿArabiyya al-Muttahida fi-Lubnan," 8 February 1958, DWQ; William L. Eagleton to Stuart W. Rockwell, 21 February 1958, and U.S. Embassy, Cairo, to DOS, tel #2444, 20 March 1958, RG 59, 786.00/2-2158, 786.00/3-2058, NA.

4. Alin, *Lebanon Crisis*, 68; Qubain, *Crisis in Lebanon*, 65–66.

5. U.S. Embassy, Cairo, to DOS, tel #2031, 10 February 1958, and U.S. Embassy, Beirut, to DOS, tel #2741, 13 February 1958, RG 59, 786.00/2-1058, 786.00/2-1358, NA.

6. U.S. Embassy, Beirut, to DOS, 21 February 1958; DOS to U.S. Embassy, Beirut, 27 February 1958; and U.S. Embassy, Beirut, to DOS, 5 March 1958, *FRUS, 1958–1960*, 11:10–13, 13, 16.

7. U.S. Embassy, Beirut, to DOS, 5 March 1958, and DOS to U.S. Embassy, Beirut, 18 March 1958, ibid., 16, 17.

8. U.S. Embassy, Beirut, to DOS, 17, 22, 23 April 1958, ibid., items #15, #17 (microfiche supplement), 24–25.

9. U.S. Embassy, Beirut, to DOS, 4 May 1958, ibid., 28–30. The ambassadors' own view was that independence "would have suited our interests" while opposition "would necessarily represent a clear defeat for Chamoun's pro-western policy and is therefore undesirable" (ibid., 29).

10. U.S. Embassy, Beirut, to DOS, 4 May 1958, and U.S. Embassy, Copenhagen, to DOS, 6 May 1958, ibid., 28–30, 30–31; British Embassy, Beirut, to BFO, tel #433, 5 May 1958, PREM 11/2386, PRO.

11. U.S. Embassy, Beirut, to DOS, 7 May 1958, *FRUS, 1958–1960*, 11:31–32.

12. Qubain, *Crisis in Lebanon*, 68–69, 71–73; Gendzier, *Notes from the Minefield*, 242–45.

13. Qubain, *Crisis in Lebanon*, 86–87.

14. British Embassy, Beirut, to BFO, tels #475, #487, 12, 14 May 1958, PREM 11/2386, PRO; U.S. Embassy, Beirut, to DOS, 14 May 1958, *FRUS, 1958–1960*, 11: item #41 (microfiche supplement); Qubain, *Crisis in Lebanon*, 83–85. The two main parties providing paramilitary support to Chamoun were the Phalangist Party and the PPS.

15. Editorial note, and U.S. Embassy, Beirut, to DOS, 2 June 1958, *FRUS, 1958–1960*, 11:71, 87; British Embassy, Beirut, to BFO, tel #635, 29 May 1958, PREM 11/2386, PRO. Estimates of the number of UAR infiltrators varied widely. In late June Chamoun charged that as many as 4,000 armed Syrians and Egyptians were in Lebanon, whereas UN observers, who had entered the country in mid-June (see main text, below), put the figure at somewhere between 300 and 1,000. In interviews and memoirs years later, Lebanese rebel leaders acknowledged that their movement received some £1.3 million Egyptian (about $4.5 million) in military and other aid from Syria and that at least 500 Syrian Druze, commanded by Syrian army officers, were sent to fight alongside the forces of Lebanese Druze leader Kamal Junblatt. See Gendzier, *Notes from the Minefield*, 268–70; Qubain, *Crisis in Lebanon*, 142–43.

16. On 19 June Allen Dulles reported to the NSC "that there was strong evidence of a highly confidential nature that the United Arab Republic was providing tactical direction to the rebel forces in Lebanon," but he did not further describe the evidence;

nor did Dulles indicate whether by "United Arab Republic" he meant the central government in Cairo or officials in Syria. See editorial note, *FRUS, 1958–1960*, 11:155. Three weeks earlier, the British ambassador in Beirut had cabled London, "It is . . . reported that operations of the [Lebanese] dissidents are now being centrally controlled from Damascus, though I have no positive confirmation of this" (British Embassy, Beirut, to BFO, tel #635, 29 May 1958, PREM 11/2386, PRO).

17. In interviews years later, former Lebanese rebel leaders disclosed that 'Abd al-Hamid Ghalib, the UAR's ambassador in Beirut, had overseen the distribution of an estimated £80 million Egyptian (about $278 million) in material aid to the rebels, including 12,000 to 14,000 light arms. The monetary figure seems improbably high. See Gendzier, *Notes from the Minefield*, 268–69. 'Abd al-Latif al-Baghdadi, who at the time was one of the UAR's four vice presidents, writes in his memoirs that the UAR used former Lebanese prime minister Sa'ib Salam, a prominent figure within the UNF, as a conduit for money and arms to the Lebanese rebels. See al-Baghdadi, *Mudhakkirat*, 2:51.

18. For a sampling of Egyptian radio and press attacks on the Lebanese government during this period, see Qubain, *Crisis in Lebanon*, 220–24.

19. Eisenhower interview, Columbia Oral History Project, 61; U.S. Embassy, Beirut, to DOS, 13 May 1958, and memorandum of conversation, Eisenhower, John Foster Dulles, et al., 13 May 1958, *FRUS, 1958–1960*, 11:41–42, 46–47.

20. DOS to U.S. Embassy, Beirut, 13 May 1958, *FRUS, 1958–1960*, 11:49–50; memorandum for record, 15 May 1958 (record of 13 May conversation), AWF, DDE Diary Series, box 32, folder: "May 1958 Staff Memos (2)," DDEL.

21. Memorandum of conversation, Eisenhower, J. F. Dulles, et al., 13 May 1958, *FRUS, 1958–1960*, 11:46, 48.

22. Editorial note, ibid., 60; Ashton, *Problem of Nasser*, 151–54.

23. On 13 May, the day Chamoun issued his appeal, right-wing French officers seized power in Algeria, arousing fears that the coup would extend to France itself. Over the next two weeks much of the French establishment became convinced that General Charles de Gaulle was the only figure who could head off a right-wing takeover and still be acceptable to the country as a whole. On 1 June the French Assembly voted to make de Gaulle premier and granted him decree powers for the next six months, at the end of which he was to submit a new French constitution for ratification by popular referendum. See Cobban, *History of Modern France*, 236–39.

24. British Embassy, Paris, to BFO, tels #208, #212, #318, 14, 15 May, 17 June 1958, PREM 11/2386, PRO. The Pflimlin government had the additional worry that failing to act in Lebanon would allow domestic critics to question its patriotism. See BFO to British Embassy, Washington, tel #2738, 16 May 1958, ibid. The de Gaulle government, of course, was far less vulnerable on this score.

25. Telephone conversation, Eisenhower and J. F. Dulles, 15 June 1958, and memorandum of conversation, William M. Rountree, Charles Lucet, et al., 23 June 1958, *FRUS, 1958–1960*, 11:127 n. 3, 170–71; BFO to British Embassy, Paris, tels #913, #925, 14 May, 15 May 1958; British Embassy, Paris, to BFO, tels #212, #318, 15 May, 17 June 1958; and BFO to British Embassy, Washington, tel #2738, 16 May 1958, PREM 11/2386, PRO; BFO to British Embassy, Washington, tel #3885, 19 June 1958, and British Embassy, Washington, to BFO, tel #1699, 24 June 1958, PREM 11/2387, PRO.

26. British Embassy, Washington, to BFO, tels #1190, #1216, 17, 19 May 1958; British United Nations Delegation, New York, to BFO, tel #449, 3 June 1958; and British United Nations Delegation, New York, to British Embassy, Washington, tel #191, 9 June 1958, PREM 11/2386, PRO.

27. Editorial note, *FRUS, 1958–1960*, 11:107–8; Qubain, *Crisis in Lebanon*, 92; Eveland, *Ropes of Sand*, 179n.

28. Qubain, *Crisis in Lebanon*, 143–51; memorandum of conversation, J. F. Dulles, Malik, et al., 30 June 1958, and DOS to U.S. United Nations Delegation, New York, 11 July 1958, *FRUS, 1958–1960*, 11:185, item #155 (microfiche supplement); BFO to British Embassy, Washington, tel #4177, 1 July 1958, PREM 11/2387, PRO.

29. The elevation of Shihab, a Maronite Christian, to the premiership would have violated Lebanon's unwritten National Pact (see Chapter 1), which required that Lebanon's prime minister always be a Sunni Muslim. There were indications, however, that such a departure would have been broadly acceptable to Lebanese Muslims. See Qubain, *Crisis in Lebanon*, 86.

30. U.S. Embassy, Beirut, to DOS, 20 May 1958; U.S. Embassy, Cairo, to DOS, 20 May, 8 June 1958; and U.S. Embassy, Beirut, to DOS, 9 June 1958, *FRUS, 1958–1960*, 11:67 n. 5, 69–70, 103 n. 6 (2); Haykal, *Sanawat al-ghalayan*, 327–28; Eisenhower, *White House Years*, 268.

31. British Embassy, Washington, to BFO, tel #1483, 10 June 1958, and BFO to British Embassy, Washington, tel #3595, 11 June 1958, PREM 11/2386, PRO.

32. DOS to U.S. Embassy, Beirut, 11 June 1958; U.S. Embassy, Beirut, to DOS, 11, 13 June 1958; and U.S. Embassy, Cairo, to DOS, 16 June 1958, *FRUS, 1958–1960*, 11:108–9, 110–11, 111 n. 3, 13:452.

33. British Embassy, Baghdad, to BFO, tels #794, #829, 14, 17 May 1958, and British Embassy, Amman, to BFO, tel #538, 18 May 1958, PREM 11/2386, PRO; U.S. Embassy, Baghdad, to DOS, 4 June 1958, and U.S. Embassy, Amman, to DOS, 24 May 1958, *FRUS, 1958–1960*, 11:90, item #66 (microfiche supplement).

34. BFO to British Embassy, Washington, tel #3336, 4 June 1958, PREM 11/2386, PRO; British Embassy, Washington, to BFO, tels #1594, #1699, 17, 24 June 1958, PREM 11/2387, PRO.

35. U.S. Embassy, Ankara, to DOS, tel #3130, 18 June 1958, RG 59, 783.00/6-1858, NA.

36. Telephone conversation, J. F. Dulles and Allen Dulles, 20 June 1958, and Rountree to J. F. Dulles, 20 June 1958, *FRUS, 1958–1960*, 11:163, 12:303; U.S. Embassy, Ankara, to DOS, tel #3172, 23 June 1958, RG 59, 783.00/6-2358, NA.

37. Qubain, *Crisis in Lebanon*, 78–79, 86–87; U.S. Embassy, Beirut, to DOS, 1 July 1958, *FRUS, 1958–1960*, 11:193; 371st meeting of NSC, 3 July 1958, AWF, NSC Series, box 10, DDEL.

38. Memorandum of conversation, Hammarskjold and Lodge, 26 June 1958, *FRUS, 1958–1960*, 11:176, 179–80; British Embassy, Washington, to BFO, tel #1673, 23 June 1958, and British United Nations Delegation, New York, to BFO, tel #575, 26 June 1958, PREM 11/2387, PRO.

39. Two exceptions are Little, "His Finest Hour?," 43, and Fry, "Uses of Intelligence," 78–79, 84. Neither Little nor Fry, however, brings out the full significance of Hammarskjold's June 1958 mission to Cairo.

40. Hammarskjold to Lloyd, 9 July 1958, in British United Nations Delegation, New York, to BFO, tel #617, 9 July 1958, PREM 11/2387, PRO; memorandum of conversation, Lodge and Hammarskjold, 26 June 1958, *FRUS, 1958–1960*, 11:176. On 21 June Hammarskjold met in Amman with Samir al-Rifaʿi, now prime minister of the local Jordanian government. According to a report of the conversation received by the BFO, when al-Rifaʿi asked what would happen if Nasser refused to relieve the pressure on Lebanon, "Hammarskjold had replied that he had it in mind to seek the imposition of economic sanctions upon [the] U.A.R. and to declare them the aggressors" (British Embassy, Amman, to BFO, tel #700, 23 June 1958, PREM 11/2387, PRO).

41. Memorandum of conversation, Lodge and Hammarskjold, 26 June 1958, *FRUS, 1958–1960*, 11:176, 177; see also British United Nations Delegation, New York, to BFO, tels #575, #600, 26 June, 3 July 1958, PREM 11/2387, PRO.

42. U.S. Embassy, Beirut, to DOS, 28 June 1958, *FRUS, 1958–1960*, 11: item #139 (microfiche supplement). The intelligence reports also indicated, however, that Nasser had ordered his Lebanese allies "to continue skirmishing until July 24, [the] date when parliament has been called to elect a new president" (ibid.).

43. Memorandum of conversation, J. F. Dulles, Malik, et al., 30 June 1958, *FRUS, 1958–1960*, 11:187; 371st meeting of NSC, 3 July 1958, AWF, box 10, DDEL.

44. Gendzier, *Notes From the Minefield*, 14, 304; memorandum of conversation, J. F. Dulles, Malik, et al., 30 June 1958, and DOS to U.S. Embassy, Beirut, 29 June 1958, *FRUS, 1958–1960*, 11:187–89, 184. The British and French governments issued similar urgings to Chamoun; see U.S. Embassy, Beirut, to DOS, 1 July 1958, *FRUS, 1958–1960*, 11:192; British Embassy, Beirut, to BFO, tel #890, 1 July 1958, PREM 11/2387, PRO.

45. U.S. Embassy, Beirut, to DOS, 1, 10, 12 July 1958, *FRUS, 1958–1960*, 11:192, 204–7; British Embassy, Beirut, to BFO, tels #929, #961, #976, 5, 10, 11 July 1958, PREM 11/2387, PRO; Qubain, *Crisis in Lebanon*, 154.

46. U.S. Embassy, Amman, to DOS, 30 June, 10 July 1958, *FRUS, 1958–1960*, 11:294, 298; Dann, *King Hussein*, 86–87.

47. Dann, *King Hussein*, 87; Batatu, *Old Social Classes*, 797.

48. Dann, *King Hussein*, 87. There seems to have been no coordination between the Jordanian and the Iraqi army conspiracies.

49. Marr, *History of Iraq*, 153–55.

50. Batatu, *Old Social Classes*, 796–97, 800.

51. British Embassy, Baghdad, to BFO, tel #1263, 12 July 1958, PREM 11/2387, PRO. There had also been speculation about Turkish-Iraqi intervention in Lebanon itself. On 10 July the commandant of the Lebanese gendarmerie told McClintock that Chamoun regarded such intervention "as his last cartridge" in the battle to prolong his presidency. McClintock commented to Washington that he "would not be surprised if Chamoun may ask for aid from [the] Baghdad Pact Moslem powers" (U.S. Embassy, Beirut, to DOS, 10 July 1958, *FRUS, 1958–1960*, 11: item #154 [microfiche supplement]).

52. British Embassy, Baghdad, to BFO, tel #1265, 13 July 1958, PREM 11/2387, PRO.

53. Batatu, *Old Social Classes*, 800–802; Marr, *History of Iraq*, 156–57.

54. Batatu, *Old Social Classes*, 801, 804–5; Marr, *History of Iraq*, 157; al-Suwaydi, *Mudhakkirati*, 591; James Bowker to E. Michael Rose, 17 July 1958, FO 371/134199, PRO;

British Embassy, Baghdad (Emergency Headquarters) to BFO, tel #15, 20 July 1958, PREM 11/2368, PRO.

55. *New York Times*, 16 July 1958; Qubain, *Crisis in Lebanon*, 115; Egyptian Consulate, Benghazi, to EFM, desp #149, 15 July 1958, WK, Baghdad Series, box 5, folder: "347/1037/1 i'lan al-Jumhuriyya al-'Iraqiyya," DWQ; confidential annex, Kuwait diary #7, 20 June–28 July 1958, *Political Diaries of the Persian Gulf*, 675; synopsis of reports, 19 July 1958, AWF, International Series, box 40, folder: "Mid East, July 1958 (1)," DDEL; U.S. Embassy, Tel Aviv, to DOS, desp #55, 17 July 1958, reel 4, *Confidential U.S. State Department Central Files, Palestine-Israel: Internal Affairs*; U.S. Embassy, Amman, to DOS, tel #103, 15 July 1958, reel 2, *Confidential U.S. State Department Central Files, Jordan*.

56. U.S. Embassy, Jidda, to DOS, 14 July 1958, *FRUS, 1958–1960*, 11: items #157, #158 (microfiche supplement). See, for example, memorandum of conversation, Eisenhower, J. F. Dulles, et al., 14 July 1958, and memorandum of conversation, Eisenhower, J. F. Dulles, and congressional leaders, 14 July 1958, ibid., 212, 223; synopsis of reports, 19 July 1958, AWF, International Series, box 40, folder: "Mid East, July 1958 (1)," DDEL.

57. British Embassy, Amman, to BFO, tels #816, #827, 14, 15 July 1958, and Political Office with the Middle East Forces (POMEF), Episkopi, to BFO, tel #826, 14 July 1958, FO 371/134199, PRO; Dann, *King Hussein*, 88; U.S. Embassy, Amman, to DOS, 14 July 1958, and Harold Macmillan to Eisenhower, 14 July 1958, *FRUS 1958–1960*, 11:300, 301.

58. U.S. Embassy, Beirut, to DOS, 14 July 1958, *FRUS 1958–1960*, 11:207–8, 216.

59. Cutler, *No Time for Rest*, 363; Cutler's notes of White House meeting, 14 July 1958, *FRUS, 1958–1960*, 11: item #160 (microfiche supplement). See also memorandum of conversation, Eisenhower, J. F. Dulles, et al., 14 July 1958, *FRUS, 1958–1960*, 11:212.

60. Memorandum of conversation, Eisenhower, J. F. Dulles, et al., 14 July 1958, versions in *FRUS, 1958–1960*, 11:212–13 and item #159 (microfiche supplement). See also telephone conversation, Eisenhower and J. F. Dulles, 14 July 1958, ibid., 209.

61. Memorandum of conversation, Eisenhower, J. F. Dulles, et al., 14 July 1958, ibid., 11:212, 214.

62. Ibid., 214 and item #159 (microfiche supplement).

63. Little, "His Finest Hour?," 53.

64. Cutler's notes of White House meeting, 14 July 1958, *FRUS, 1958–1960*, 11: item #160 (microfiche supplement); memorandum of conversation, Eisenhower, J. F. Dulles, and congressional leaders, 14 July 1958, versions in ibid., 11:218–25 and item #161 (microfiche supplement).

65. Memorandum of conversation, Eisenhower, J. F. Dulles, and congressional leaders, 14 July 1958, ibid., 218–25.

66. Ibid., 218–25 and item #161 (microfiche supplement).

67. Ibid., 218–25; entry for 15 July 1958, Smith Papers, box 282, folder: "The Diary of H. Alexander Smith 1958."

68. Memorandum of conversation, Eisenhower, J. F. Dulles, et al., 14 July 1958, *FRUS, 1958–1960*, 11:226–28.

69. Ibid.; British Embassy, Washington, to BFO, tel #1903, 14 July 1958, PREM 11/2387, PRO; British Embassy, Paris, to BFO, tel #345, 15 July 1958, PREM 11/2388, PRO. The French did decide, however, to send a cruiser to Lebanese waters bearing a

small "commando" unit that was prepared, if necessary, to come ashore to protect the French embassy.

70. Memorandum of conversation, J. F. Dulles, Twining, et al., 14 July 1958; memorandum of conversation, Eisenhower, J. F. Dulles, et al., 14 July 1958; telephone conversation, Eisenhower and J. F. Dulles, 15 July 1958; and telephone conversation, J. F. Dulles and Richard M. Nixon, 15 July 1958, *FRUS 1958–1960*, 11:210, 226–27, 242, 12:321.

71. Telephone conversation, Eisenhower and Macmillan, 14 July 1958, versions in PREM 11/2387, PRO, and in *FRUS, 1958–1960*, 11:231–32.

72. Macmillan, messages to Eisenhower, 14 July 1958, and memorandum of conversation, J. F. Dulles and Samuel Hood, 14 July 1958, *FRUS, 1958–1960*, 11:235, 301, 238; Ashton, *Problem of Nasser*, 173.

73. Telephone conversation, Eisenhower and Macmillan, 14 July 1958, PREM 11/2387, PRO.

74. Memorandum of conversation, Eisenhower and Nixon, 15 July 1958, and telephone conversation, J. F. Dulles and Nixon, 15 July 1958, *FRUS, 1958–1960*, 11:244, item #180 (microfiche supplement).

75. U.S. Embassy, Beirut, to DOS, 15 July 1958, ibid., 247–49; Qubain, *Crisis in Lebanon*, 115.

76. *New York Times*, 16 July 1958. "As the United Nations Charter recognizes," Eisenhower said, "there is an inherent right of collective self-defense," which Lebanon was now invoking. The president also said that the U.S. forces "will demonstrate the concern of the United States for the integrity and independence of Lebanon, which we deem vital to the national interest and world peace" (ibid.).

77. British Embassy, Beirut, to BFO, tels #1011, #1014, #1042, 15 (2), 17 July 1958, PREM 11/2388, PRO; *New York Times*, 16 July 1958; *Newsweek*, 28 July 1958, 18; *Time*, 28 July 1958, 17; Qubain, *Crisis in Lebanon*, 116–18; U.S. Embassy, Beirut, to DOS, 16 July 1958, *FRUS, 1958–1960*, 11:253–55.

78. *New York Times*, 17, 18 July 1958.

79. Ibid., 16, 17, 18, 19 July 1958. The U.S. and British military missions in Potsdam, East Germany, were also attacked by unruly demonstrators.

80. Haykal, *'Abd al-Nasir wa-al-'alam*, 182, 187–90; Haykal, *Sphinx and Commissar*, 97–100; Haykal, *Sanawat al-ghalayan*, 370–71.

81. Ashton, *Problem of Nasser*, 173; memorandum of conversation, J. F. Dulles and Hood, 15 July 1958, *FRUS, 1958–1960*, 11:305; telephone conversation, Eisenhower and J. F. Dulles, 15 July 1958, versions in *FRUS, 1958–1960*, 11:251, 12:317 n. 1.

82. Memorandum of conversation, Eisenhower, J. F. Dulles, et al., 16 July 1958, and U.S. Embassy, Amman, to DOS, 16 July 1958, *FRUS, 1958–1960*, 11:308–10, 312–13. According to the British report, "UAR agents" both on the West Bank and in East Jordan had planned mass antigovernment demonstrations to occur on 16–17 July. These agents also "had responsive groups within [the] security forces including [the] Army who in all probability would not 'fire on their brothers' once mob action began" (U.S. Embassy, Amman, to DOS, 16 July 1958, ibid., 313).

83. U.S. Embassy, Amman, to DOS, 16 July 1958, ibid., 312–13; Dann, *King Hussein*, 91.

84. Telephone conversation, Macmillan and J. F. Dulles, 16 July 1958, *FRUS, 1958–1960*, 11:314–15.

85. Editorial note; memorandum of conversation, J. F. Dulles, Lloyd, et al., 17 July 1958; and U.S. Embassy, Amman, to DOS, 18 July 1958, ibid., 316–17, 317–18, 323–24.

86. Ovendale, *Transfer of Power*, 207–10; Tal, "Seizing Opportunities," 144–49.

87. Memorandum of conversation, J. F. Dulles, Lloyd, et al., 17 July 1958, *FRUS, 1958–1960*, 12:326.

88. For fleeting references to this event in available American documents, see DOS to U.S. Embassy, London, 18 July 1958, ibid., 11:325; "Synopsis of Reports relating to the Mid-East Crisis," 19 July 1958, AWF, International Series, box 40, folder: "Mid East, July 1958 (1)," DDEL.

89. British Embassy, Washington, to BFO, tel #1948, 18 July 1958, PREM 11/2368, PRO.

90. BFO to British Embassy, Washington, tel #4792, 18 July 1958, ibid.

91. British Embassy, Washington, to BFO, tel #1948, 18 July 1958, ibid.; DOS to U.S. Embassy, London, 18 July 1958, *FRUS, 1958–1960*, 11:325; memorandum of conversation, Eisenhower, J. F. Dulles, et al., 20 July 1958, AWF, DDE Diary Series, box 35, folder: "Staff Memos—July 1958" (1), DDEL; entry for 18 July 1958, Larson Papers, box 23, folder: "Memorandum Book July 1958," DDEL.

92. The contents of the State Department's instructions to Ankara are summarized in British Embassy, Washington, to BFO, tel #1963, 19 July 1958, PREM 11/2368, PRO.

93. British Embassy, Washington, to BFO, tel #1962, 19 July 1958, ibid.; U.S. Embassy, Ankara, to DOS, tel #322, 22 July 1958, reel 15, *Confidential U.S. State Department Central Files, Palestine-Israel: Foreign Affairs*.

94. U.S. Embassy, Amman, to DOS, 19 July 1958, *FRUS, 1958–1960*, 11:344 n. 2; British Embassy, Amman, to BFO, tel #912, 19 July 1958, FO 371/134200, PRO.

95. Memorandum of conversation, J. F. Dulles, Lloyd, et al., 19 July 1958, and DOS to U.S. Embassy, Amman, 19 July 1958, *FRUS, 1958–1960*, 11:342, 344; British Embassy, Amman, to BFO, tel #957, 22 July 1958, FO 371/134200, PRO.

96. Little, "His Finest Hour?," 49.

97. Memorandum of conversation, J. F. Dulles, Lloyd, et al., 17 July 1958; memorandum of conversation, Eisenhower, J. F. Dulles, et al., 20 July 1958; and DOS to U.S. Embassy, London, 18 July 1958, *FRUS, 1958–1960*, 12:776–78, 83, 11:326.

98. Rountree to J. F. Dulles, 23 July 1958; DOS to U.S. Embassy, London, 31 July 1958; and U.S. Consulate, Kuwait, to DOS, 3 August 1958, *FRUS, 1958–1960*, 12:93–95, 93 n. 1, 778–79; Little, "His Finest Hour?," 50.

CHAPTER 8

1. Telephone conversation, John Foster Dulles and Richard M. Nixon, 15 July 1958, and telephone conversation, J. F. Dulles and Robert A. McClintock, 16 July 1958, *FRUS, 1958–1960*, 11: item #187 (microfiche supplement), 242; Copeland, *Game of Nations*, 204; *New York Times*, 18 July 1958.

2. Copeland, *Game of Nations*, 204. For an anonymous foreign service officer's bitter denunciation of Eisenhower's reliance on special emissaries, see attachment to Robert S. Allen to Dean Acheson, 14 February 1957, Acheson Papers, series I, box 1, folder 7.

3. Murphy, *Diplomat*, 399–400; Qubain, *Crisis in Lebanon*, 118–19.

4. U.S. Embassy, Beirut, to DOS, 17, 18 July 1958, *FRUS, 1958–1960*, 11:326–27, 262.

5. U.S. Embassy, Beirut, to DOS, 19 July 1958, ibid., 333.

6. Murphy, *Diplomat*, 400–401; U.S. Embassy, Beirut, to DOS, 18 July 1958, *FRUS, 1958–1960*, 11:328; British Embassy, Beirut, to BFO, tel #1074, 18 July 1958, PREM 11/2388, PRO.

7. U.S. Embassy, Beirut, to DOS, 19 July 1958, *FRUS, 1958–1960*, 11:333–34.

8. Special National Intelligence Estimate, 22 July 1958, ibid., 12:87–93.

9. Special National Intelligence Estimate, 22 July 1958, and U.S. Embassy, Jidda, to DOS, 25 July 1958, ibid., 90, 730–32; synopsis of intelligence and State Department items, 23 July 1958, AWF, DDE Diary Series, box 34, folder: "Goodpaster Briefings—July 1958," DDEL; Egyptian Embassy, Jidda, to EFM, desp #62, 20 July 1958, WK, Jidda Series, box 2, folder: "756/81/3 H2, al-taqarir al-siyasiyya lil-safara al-Misriyya fi-Jidda," DWQ; Egyptian Embassy, Jidda, to EFM, desp #59, 20 July 1958, Jidda Series, box 2, folder: "756/81/3 S3, al-taqarir al-siyasiyya li-safarat al-Jumhuriyya fi-Jidda," DWQ.

10. Memorandum of conversation, Eisenhower, J. F. Dulles, et al., 23 July 1958, *FRUS, 1958–1960*, 12:98; memorandum of conversation, J. F. Dulles, Paul Gruda Koht, et al., 23 July 1958, RG 59, lot 64 D199, "Secretary of State's Memoranda of Conversation," box 9, folder: "Secy's M. of Con., July 20–31, 1958," NA.

11. Remarks, Western European chiefs of mission meeting, 9 May 1958, RG 59, lot 64 D199, box 8, folder: "Secy's M. of Con, May 1958," NA; memorandum of conversation, J. F. Dulles, Konrad Adenauer, et al., 26 July 1958, RG 59, lot 64 D199, box 9, folder: "Secy's M. of Con., July 20–31, 1958," NA; memorandum of conversation, J. F. Dulles and Daud, 26 June 1958, Dulles Papers, General Correspondence and Memoranda Series, box 1, folder: "Memos of Conversation—General—A Through D," DDEL; memorandum of conversation, Eisenhower, Amintore Fanfani, et al., 30 July 1958, AWF, DDE Diary Series, box 35, folder: "Staff Memos—July 1958 (1)," DDEL; 374th meeting of NSC, 31 July 1958, *FRUS, 1958–1960*, 12:129. In August 1956, shortly after Nasser nationalized the Suez Canal Company, the State Department's Office of Intelligence Research did a comparison study between Hitler and Nasser, apparently for the purpose of uncovering parallels that could be used to discredit Nasser. The intelligence office did find some similarities in the two leaders' suppression of opposition parties, their use of bombastic rhetoric, and their reliance on subversion as an instrument of foreign policy. "In general, however, analogies are scarce, in that the basic personalities and the basic political organizations of Hitler and Nasser radically differ." As a State Department official concluded in a covering memo, "I am afraid this analysis does little to assist the intended project" (Allan Evans to W. Park Armstrong, 14 August 1956, with attachment, RG 59, lot 58 D776, "Subject Files of the Bureau of Research and Intelligence [INR], 1945–1960," box 11, folder: "Egypt," NA). It is not known if Dulles ever saw the study.

12. The newspaper editor was O. Preston Robinson of Salt Lake City's *Deseret News*. The university professor was Dr. Elie Salem of Johns Hopkins University; in the 1980s Salem served as Lebanon's foreign minister.

13. Robinson to Eisenhower, 23 July 1958; Salem to Ezra Taft Benson, n.d. [ca. July

1958]; and Eisenhower to J. F. Dulles, 23 July 1958, Dulles Papers, White House Memoranda Series, box 7, folder: "White House—Meetings with the President, July 1, 1958–December 31, 1958 (10)," DDEL.

14. J. F. Dulles to Eisenhower, 25 July 1958, ibid.

15. Edward L. R. Elson to Eisenhower, 24 July 1958, and Eisenhower to Elson, 28 July 1958, box 1, Elson Papers.

16. 374th meeting of NSC, 31 July 1958; memorandum of conversation, Eisenhower, J. F. Dulles, et al., 23 July 1958; and Eisenhower to George M. Humphrey, 22 July 1958, *FRUS, 1958–1960*, 11:365, 12:130, 99. See also Special National Intelligence Estimate, 12 August 1958, ibid., 12:141.

17. Memorandum of conversation, J. F. Dulles, Adnan Menderes, et al., 28 July 1958, RG 59, lot 64 D199, box 9, folder: "Secy's M. of Con., July 20–31, 1958," NA; memorandum of conversation, J. F. Dulles, Aiichiro Fujiyama, et al., 14 August 1958, RG 59, lot 64 D199, box 9, folder: "Secy's M. of Con., August 1–14, 1958," NA; 373rd meeting of NSC, 24 July 1958, *FRUS, 1958–1960*, 12:107.

18. 374th meeting of NSC, 31 July 1958, *FRUS, 1958–1960*, 12:127.

19. Memorandum of conversation, Eisenhower, J. F. Dulles, et al., 23 July 1958, ibid., 99.

20. Murphy, *Diplomat*, 402; U.S. Embassy, Beirut, to DOS, 30 July 1958, *FRUS, 1958–1960*, 11:408–10, 411–13, 415 n. 2.

21. U.S. Embassy, Beirut, to DOS, 7 August 1958, *FRUS, 1958–1960*, 11:438; synopses of intelligence and State Department items, 1, 8 August 1958, AWF, DDE Diary Series, box 35, folder: "August 1958—Goodpaster Briefings," DDEL; Qubain, *Crisis in Lebanon*, 156.

22. U.S. Embassy, Amman, to DOS, 18, 21, 22 July 1958; Harold Macmillan to Eisenhower, 22 July 1958; memorandum of conversation, J. F. Dulles, Christian A. Herter, et al., 23 July 1958; Eisenhower to Macmillan, 23 July 1958; and 373rd meeting of NSC, 24 July 1958, *FRUS, 1958–1960*, 11:323–24, 361–62, 364, 366, 374–76, 378–79, 384; memorandum of conversation, U.S. observer delegation, Fifth Baghdad Pact Ministerial Council Session, 28 July 1958, RG 59, lot 64 D199, box 9, folder: "Secy's M. of Con., July 20–31, 1958," NA.

23. On 24 July Secretary Dulles told the NSC that he had asked the Israelis how they would react to a coup in Jordan. The "Israeli interim reply had stated that chaos in Jordan would invalidate the armistice agreement between Israel and Jordan, and leave Israel free to take the action necessary to its own security" (373rd meeting of NSC, 24 July 1958, *FRUS, 1958–1960*, 11:384).

24. Memorandum of conversation, J. F. Dulles, Herter, et al., 23 July 1958; U.S. Embassy, Amman, to DOS, 25 July 1958; and DOS to Baghdad Pact Council Delegation, London, 26 July 1958, ibid., 374–75, 398, 403–4.

25. BFO to British Embassy, Washington, tels #4792, #4833, #4854, 18, 19 July 1958 (2), and British Embassy, Baghdad (Emergency Headquarters), to BFO, tel #24, 23 July 1958, PREM 11/2368, PRO; U.S. Embassy, Baghdad, to DOS, 19 July 1958, and Hugh S. Cumming Jr. to G. Frederick Reinhardt, 20 July 1958, *FRUS, 1958–1960*, 12:328, 330.

26. U.S. Embassy, Tel Aviv, to DOS, 31 July 1958; William M. Rountree to J. F. Dulles, 23 July 1958; and editorial note, *FRUS, 1958–1960*, 11:414, 12:332–33, 334.

27. Qubain, *Crisis in Lebanon*, 93–94; editorial note, *FRUS, 1958–1960*, 11:331–2 (emphasis added).

28. Editorial notes; telephone conversation, Eisenhower and J. F. Dulles, 19 July 1958; and memorandum of conversation, J. F. Dulles, Samuel Hood, et al., 21 July 1958, *FRUS, 1958–1960*, 11:339, 422, 429–31, 340, 355.

29. "Log, July 24 to August 13, 1958," Jackson Papers, box 69, folder: "Log—1958 (2)," DDEL; Jackson to J. F. Dulles, 7 August 1958, ibid., box 77, folder: "Middle East Crisis—Presidential Speech to U.N., 8/13/58—Drafts (6)," DDEL.

30. 374th meeting of NSC, 31 July 1958, *FRUS, 1958–1960*, 12:130; James H. Smith to Jackson, 11 August 1958, Jackson Papers, box 77, folder: "Middle East Crisis—Working Papers, Results, etc. (1)," DDEL; Lewis L. Strauss to Eisenhower, 25 July 1958, AWF, DDE Diary Series, box 35, folder: "Staff Memos—July 1958 (1)," DDEL.

31. For more on Walt Rostow's influence on the Eisenhower administration, see Kaufman, *Trade and Aid*, 10, 96–99.

32. Attachment to Rostow to Jackson, 28 July 1958, Jackson Papers, box 91, folder: "Rostow, Walt W., 1958 (2)," DDEL; Lewis L. Strauss to Eisenhower, 25 July 1958, AWF, DDE Diary Series, box 35, folder: "Staff Memos—July 1958 (1)," DDEL; Anderson quoted in 374th meeting of NSC, 31 July 1958, *FRUS, 1958–1960*, 12:130–31.

33. "Log, July 24 to August 13, 1958," Jackson Papers, box 69, folder: "Log—1958 (2)," DDEL; telephone conversation, Eisenhower and J. F. Dulles, 10 August 1958, Dulles Papers, Telephone Calls Series, box 13, folder: "Memoranda of Tel. Conv.—W.H. August 1, 1958 to Dec. 5, 1958 (3)," DDEL.

34. *New York Times*, 13 August 1958; Pearson, *Diaries*, 472; address to emergency session of UN General Assembly, 13 August 1958, in *Public Papers, 1958*, 606–14.

35. Address to UN General Assembly, 13 August 1958, in *Public Papers, 1958*, 612.

36. *New York Times*, 14, 15 August 1958; *Los Angeles Times*, 14 August 1958; *New York Herald Tribune*, 14 August 1958; memorandum of conversation, J. F. Dulles, Fatin Rustu Zorlu, et al., 14 August 1958, RG 59, lot 64 D199, box 9, folder: "Secy's M. of Con., August 1–14, 1958," NA; memorandum of conversation, J. F. Dulles, Mahmoud Fawzi, et al., 14 August 1958, *FRUS, 1958–1960*, 11:472–73.

37. Memorandum of conversation, J. F. Dulles, Selwyn Lloyd, et al., 12 August 1958, *FRUS, 1958–1960*, 11:461.

38. Qubain, *Crisis in Lebanon*, 106–8, 226; editorial note, *FRUS, 1958–1960*, 11:510–11; memorandum of conversation, J. F. Dulles and Charles Malik, 21 August 1958, RG 59, lot 64 D199, box 9, folder: "Secy's M. of Con., August 15–31, 1958," NA.

39. Memorandum of conversation, J. F. Dulles, Fawzi, et al., 18 August 1958, and U.S. Embassy, Cairo, to DOS, 24 July 1958, *FRUS, 1958–1960*, 11:492, 493, 494–95, 13:463.

40. Memoranda of conversation, J. F. Dulles, Fawzi, et al., 14, 18, 21 August 1958, ibid. 11:471–72, 493–94, 508–9.

41. U.S. Embassy, Amman, to DOS, 29 August, 9 September 1958; editorial note; memorandum of conversation, J. F. Dulles, 'Abd al-Mun'im al-Rifa'i, et al., 15 October 1958; and U.S. Embassy, London, to DOS, 24 September 1958, ibid., 542 n. 2, 557–58, 587, 611, 578; Ovendale, "Great Britain and the Anglo-American Invasion," 301.

42. Special National Intelligence Estimate, 28 October 1958, *FRUS, 1958–1960*, 11:618.

43. Qubain, *Crisis in Lebanon*, 109, 156, 158; U.S. Embassy, Beirut, to DOS, 9 September 1958, and editorial notes, *FRUS, 1958–1960*, 11:556–57, 587, 599–600, 615.

44. Qubain, *Crisis in Lebanon*, 158–61.

45. U.S. Embassy, Cairo, to DOS, tel #1842, 19 December 1958, RG 59, 611.83A/12-1958, NA; editorial note, and 374th meeting of NSC, 31 July 1958, *FRUS, 1958–1960*, 11:591, 12:132.

46. Jackson to J. F. Dulles, 29 August 1958, Jackson Papers, box 69, folder: "Log—1958 (2)," DDEL; Jackson to J. F. Dulles, 9 February 1959, ibid., folder: "Log—1959 (1)," DDEL.

47. "Factors Affecting U.S. Policy toward the Near East," 19 August 1958, *FRUS, 1958–1960*, 12:145–47.

48. Ibid., 151.

49. 383rd meeting of NSC, 16 October 1958, ibid., 176–78.

50. NSC 5820/1, "U.S. Policy toward the Near East," 4 November 1958, ibid., 190, 195. Failing to note this distinction between "Arab nationalism" and "radical pan-Arab nationalism," Fawaz A. Gerges mistakenly concludes that NSC 5820/1's statement on relations with Nasser "represented a victory for the majority view" on the NSC Planning Board; see Gerges, *Superpowers*, 130.

51. NSC 5820/1, "U.S. Policy toward the Near East," 4 November 1958, *FRUS, 1958–1960*, 12:188, 190, 195–97.

52. Batatu, *Old Social Classes*, 816–18, 827–28, 835; U.S. Embassy, Baghdad, to DOS, 14 October 1958, and USARMA, Baghdad, to DOS, 4 November 1958, *FRUS, 1958–1960*, 12:345, 351 n. 1.

53. A November 1958 CIA working paper warned that "Qasim may be a member of a Communist cell." In the spring of 1959 several Arab leaders, including Nasser, King Saud, and former Iraqi prime minister 'Ali Jawdat al-Ayyubi, alleged that Qasim was a communist. See Richard H. Sanger to R. Gordon Arneson, 25 November 1958, RG 59, lot 58 D776, box 24, folder: "INR—Iraq 1957," NA; U.S. Embassy, Jidda, to DOS, 4 April 1959, and memorandum of conversation, Rountree, Mustafa Amin, et al., 30 April 1959, *FRUS, 1958–1960*, 12:413, 13:539; U.S. Embassy, Amman, to DOS, tel #2191, 13 April 1959, reel 3, *Confidential U.S. State Department Central Files, Jordan*. The dominant view within U.S. intelligence circles, however, was that Qasim was a noncommunist who had aligned himself with the ICP for tactical reasons. Still, there was considerable fear that Qasim would become the captive of the ICP. Batatu, who has done an extensive study of the political and social backgrounds of Iraqi leaders, maintains that Qasim, far from being a communist, was a left-leaning moderate who favored redistributing the country's wealth while preserving its propertied classes. See Hugh S. Cummings Jr. to J. F. Dulles, 25 November 1958, and Special National Intelligence Estimate, 17 February 1959, *FRUS, 1958–1960*, 12:354, 381–83; Batatu, *Old Social Classes*, 836–47.

54. Batatu, *Old Social Classes*, 832; Cummings to J. F. Dulles, 25 November 1958, *FRUS, 1958–1960*, 12:354.

55. Kerr, *Arab Cold War*, 18.

56. U.S. Embassy, Cairo, to DOS, 29 November, 1 December 1958, *FRUS, 1958–1960*, 13:501, 504–5. The United States had previously sold PL 480 wheat to Egypt, but both parties had allowed the arrangement to lapse in 1956.

57. U.S. Embassy, Cairo, to DOS, 1 December 1958, *FRUS, 1958–1960*, 13:505, 505 n. 5; memorandum of conversation, Eisenhower, Rountree, et al., 23 December 1958, ibid., 509; Hare interview, Columbia Oral History Project, 26; Gerges, *Superpowers*, 126, 141 n. 103; Batatu, *Old Social Classes*, 861–62; speech by Nasser, 23 December 1958, in *al-Majmu'a al-kamila*, vol. 3, pt. 1, 353.

58. Rountree visited Lebanon, Jordan, Egypt, and Iraq.

59. Rountree to J. F. Dulles, 27 December 1958, *FRUS, 1958–1960*, 12:202–3.

60. Memorandum of conversation, Roger Stevens, Rountree, et al., 20 December 1958, PREM 11/2396, PRO; U.S. Embassy, Cairo, to DOS, 15 December 1958, *FRUS, 1958–1960*, 13:505–9.

61. *Time*, 29 December 1958, 19; U.S. Embassy, Baghdad, to DOS, 16 December 1958, and 392nd meeting of NSC, 23 December 1958, *FRUS, 1958–1960*, 12:361–62, 372–73; memorandum of conversation, Roger Stevens, Rountree, et al., 20 December 1958, PREM 11/2396, PRO. On 10 December Iraqi authorities broke up a conspiracy by Nasserist Iraqi officers to overthrow the regime. U.S. officials had not taken part in the coup attempt, but they had known about it in advance. In early December an Iraqi officer attempted to enlist the U.S. embassy in the operation. Fearing the approach might be an effort to entrap the United States, the State Department instructed the embassy to remain aloof from the operation. See DOS to U.S. Embassy, Baghdad, tel #1754, 3 December 1958, RG 59, 787.00/12-358, NA; DOS to U.S. Embassy, Baghdad, 4 December 1958, *FRUS, 1958–1960*, 12:355, 355 n. 1.

62. U.S. Embassy, Baghdad, to DOS, 16 December 1958, and 392nd meeting of NSC, 23 December 1958, *FRUS, 1958–1960*, 12:362–63, 373.

63. 391st meeting of NSC, 18 December 1958; 393rd meeting of NSC, 15 January 1959; and memorandum of conversation, Eisenhower, Rountree, et al., 23 December 1958, *FRUS, 1958–1960*, 12:363, 376, 13:509–10.

64. Batatu, *Old Social Classes*, 862; Smolansky, *Arab East*, 128–29; *al-Ahram*, 29 January 1959.

65. According to both Haykal and Batatu, the UAR gave the dissident officers a radio transmitter with which to broadcast the news of the revolt. Batatu adds that the UAR promised to support the rebellion with a battalion of commandos and a squadron of MiG aircraft, should such action be necessary, but neither the commandos nor the aircraft were forthcoming. See Batatu, *Old Social Classes*, 873, 882; Haykal, *Sphinx and Commissar*, 107. Both the U.S. and the British embassies in Baghdad received advance notice of the coup attempt the day before it occurred, but they chose not to alert the Qasim regime. See U.S. Embassy, Baghdad, to DOS, tel #2537, 7 March 1959, RG 59, 787.00/3-759, NA.

66. For a detailed account of the Mosul revolt, see Batatu, *Old Social Classes*, 866–89.

67. Ibid., 863; Smolansky, *Arab East*, 132; speech by Nasser, 22 March 1958, in *al-Majmu'a al-kamila*, vol. 3, pt. 2, 501.

68. U.S. Embassy, Cairo, to DOS, 1 April 1959; DOS to U.S. Embassy, Cairo, 2 April 1959; and Rountree to C. Douglas Dillon, 29 April 1959, *FRUS 1958–1960*, 13:522, 526–27, 530–34.

69. Smolansky, *Arab East*, 132; memorandum of conversation, Rountree, Amin, et al., 30 April 1959, and U.S. Embassy, Cairo, to DOS, 19 September 1959, *FRUS 1958–1960*, 13:539, 551. See also U.S. Embassy, Cairo, to DOS, tel #3229, 29 April 1959, RG

59, 686B.oo/4-2959, NA; U.S. Embassy, Cairo, to DOS, tel G-74, 23 October 1959, RG 59, 686B.oo/10-2359, NA.

70. Dulles, *John Foster Dulles*, 227–31; Mosley, *Dulles*, 448–49.

71. Ashton, *Problem of Nasser*, 200–204. As we have seen in Chapter 6, the former Iraqi regime had also coveted Kuwait. But this attitude, while annoying to Britain, was not seen as profoundly threatening, since Iraq itself was then a close ally.

72. Ashton, *Problem of Nasser*, 203–4, 206.

73. U.S. Embassy, Baghdad, to DOS, 9 August, 10 December 1959; editorial note; and National Intelligence Estimate, "The Outlook for Iraq," 1 November 1960, *FRUS 1958–1960*, 12:474–77, 494–95, 510, 516–23.

74. U.S. Embassy, Amman, to DOS, 7 May 1959, ibid. 11:714; U.S. Embassy, Amman, to DOS, tel #2198, 14 April 1959, reel 3, *Confidential U.S. State Department Central Files, Jordan*.

75. Dann, *King Hussein*, 110–11. Dann writes that the assassination of Hazza' al-Majali "involved mainly Palestinians at the operational level" and that former Jordanian army chief 'Ali Abu Nuwwar helped plan the attack from his exile in Damascus, where he was "abetted in turn by [former Syrian intelligence chief 'Abd al-Hamid al-]Sarraj, then chairman of the executive council of the UAR Northern Region. What the connection was from Damascus to Cairo is . . . not clear" (ibid., 111; Dann cites no source for these assertions).

76. DOS to U.S. Embassy, Amman, 9 September 1960, *FRUS, 1958–1960*, 11:736; Dann, *King Hussein*, 111–12, 114–15.

77. Memorandum of conversation, J. F. Dulles, Zorlu, et al., 14 August 1958, RG 59, lot 64 D199, box 9, folder: "Secy's M. of Con., August 1–14, 1958," NA; U.S. Embassy, Amman, to DOS, 5 September 1959, *FRUS, 1958–1960*, 11:719. See also Ben-Zvi, *Decade of Transition*, 80–83.

78. Smolansky, *Arab East*, 137; Pennar, *U.S.S.R. and the Arabs*, 67–68.

79. Rountree to J. F. Dulles, 22 August, 9 October 1958, *FRUS, 1958–1960*, 13:90–91, 99.

80. Memorandum of conversation, Herter, Harman, et al., 11 April 1960; G. Lewis Jones to C. Douglas Dillon, 26 May 1960; Jones to Livingston T. Merchant, 7 July 1960; memorandum of conversation, Herter, Dillon, et al., 27 July 1960; and Armin H. Meyer to Parker T. Hart, 20 July 1960, ibid., 306, 327–28, 344–49, 356–57, 589.

81. Haykal, *Cairo Documents*, 175–78; Evan Thomas, *Very Best Men*, 222–24; Kalb, *Congo Cables*, 157–96; speech by Nasser, 23 December 1960, in *Majmu'at khutab*, 3:341.

82. For accounts of Kennedy's and Johnson's relations with Nasser, and of Nasser's relations with other Arab leaders in the mid-1960s, see Little, "From Even-Handed to Empty-Handed," 156–77; Haykal, *Cairo Documents*, 187–249; Oren, *Six Days of War*, 22–84; Lenczowski, *American Presidents and the Middle East*, 71–89, 105–15; Mufti, "United States and Nasserist Pan-Arabism," 178–83; Gerges, *Superpowers*, 145–237; Kerr, *Arab Cold War*, 106–28.

83. Eisenhower, *White House Years*, 584; memorandum of conversation, Eisenhower, Nasser, et al., 26 September 1960, *FRUS, 1958–1960*, 13:601, 602.

84. Memorandum of conversation, Eisenhower, Nasser, et al., 26 September 1960, *FRUS, 1958–1960*, 13:601–5.

85. Extract from U.S. Embassy, Cairo, to DOS, desp #342, 15 November 1960, AWF, International Series, box 53, folder: "United Arab Republic," DDEL.

86. Speech by Nasser, 23 December 1960, in *Majmuʿat khutab*, 3:337–41; U.S. Embassy, Cairo, to DOS, 24 December 1960, *FRUS, 1958–1960*, 13:609–11.

EPILOGUE

1. For more on Nasser's antagonistic relations with Lyndon Johnson, see Haykal, *Cairo Documents*, 225–49; Parker, *Politics of Miscalculation*, 103–7.

2. Little, "From Even-Handed to Empty-Handed," 156–77.

3. Yergin, *The Prize*, 717–20.

4. See profiles of Lewis and Huntington in, respectively, *U.S. News and World Report*, 3 December 2001, 40, and Kaplan, "Looking the World in the Eye."

5. See, for example, Chomsky, "Current Crisis in the Middle East" (lecture transcript): *Observer*, 14 July 2002; *Guardian*, 13 September 2002.

6. For more on the Islamicization of the Palestinian struggle, see Abu-Amr, *Islamic Fundamentalism*; Schoch, *Islamic Movement*.

7. Telhami, *The Stakes*, 39–49; Pew Research Center, "Views of a Changing World 2003" (topline results).

8. Haddad, "Islamist Perceptions," 419–33; Esposito, *Islamic Threat*, 271, 273–74.

9. *Independent*, 8 October 2001. See also *Guardian*, 8 October 2001. For bin Laden's earlier attempts to exploit Arab and Muslim anger over U.S. policies toward Iraq and Palestine, see Bergen, *Holy War*, 27, 98.

10. For a forceful defense of the salience of universal values in contemporary international relations, see Fred Halliday, *Two Hours That Shook the World*, 27, 48, 131, 216.

11. See, for example, *Los Angeles Times*, 18 September 2001, California Section, pt. 2, p. 9; *Independent*, 19 September 2001; *San Francisco Chronicle*, 4 November 2001.

12. *Washington Post*, 11 December 2002; *Los Angeles Times*, 25 January, 3 February 2003.

13. See, for example, *Guardian*, 26 January 1998; *Washington Post*, 24 October 2001; U.S. Department of State, Daily Press Briefing, 23 July 2002, ⟨http://www.state.gov/r/pa/prs/dpb/2002/12098.htm⟩; *New York Times*, 2 April 2003.

BIBLIOGRAPHY

OFFICIAL ARCHIVES

Egypt
Dar al-Watha'iq al-Qawmiyya (National Archives), Cairo
    Al-Wizara al-Kharijiyya, al-arshif al-sirri al-jadid (Foreign Ministry, New Secret
      Archive)

Great Britain
Public Record Office, Kew
    Foreign Office Files (FO 371)
    Prime Ministerial Files (PREM 11)

United States
Dwight D. Eisenhower Library, Abilene, Kans.
    John Foster Dulles Papers
    Dwight D. Eisenhower Papers, Ann Whitman File
    Bryce N. Harlow Records (Pre-Acquisition)
    C. D. Jackson Papers
    Arthur Larson Papers
    White House Office, Office of the Staff Secretary
National Archives and Records Administration, College Park, Md.
    General Records of the U.S. Department of State, Record Group 59

PERSONAL PAPERS COLLECTIONS

Dean Acheson Papers, Yale University Library, New Haven, Conn.
Hamilton Fish Armstrong Papers, Princeton University Library, Princeton, N.J.
John Foster Dulles Papers, Princeton University Library, Princeton, N.J.
Edward L. R. Elson Papers, Presbyterian Historical Society, Philadelphia, Pa.
Louis Gerson Papers, University of Connecticut, Storrs

Robert Charles Hill Papers, Hoover Institution Archives, Stanford, Calif.
Hubert H. Humphrey Papers, Senatorial Files, Minnesota Historical Society, St. Paul
H. Alexander Smith Papers, Princeton University Library, Princeton, N.J.
Adlai Stevenson Papers, Princeton University Library, Princeton, N.J.

ORAL HISTORIES

Eisenhower, Dwight D. Columbia Oral History Project, Columbia University Library, New York, N.Y.

Hare, Raymond A. Columbia Oral History Project, Columbia University Library, New York, N.Y.

Henderson, Loy W. Columbia Oral History Project, Columbia University Library, New York, N.Y.

Yost, Charles W. Dwight D. Eisenhower Library, Abilene, Kans.

PUBLISHED DOCUMENTS

Bitar, Salah al-Din. *Al-Siyasah al-'Arabiyah: Bayna al-mabda' wa-al-tatbiq* (Arab policy: Between principle and application). Beirut: Dar al-Tali'ah, 1960.

Executive Sessions of the Senate Foreign Relations Committee Together with Joint Sessions of the Senate Armed Services Committee (Historical Series). Vol. 9. 85th Cong., 1st Sess., 1957. Washington, D.C.: U.S. Government Printing Office, 1979.

Al-Majmu'a al-kamila li-khutab wa-ahadith wa-tasrihat Jamal 'Abd al-Nasir (The complete compilation of the speeches, interviews, and statements of Gamal Abdel Nasser). Beirut: Markaz Dirasat al-Wahda al-'Arabiyya, 1999.

Majmu'at khutab wa-tasrihat wa-bayanat lil-ra'is Jamal 'Abd al-Nasir (Collected speeches, declarations, and statements by President Gamal Abdel Nasser). Cairo: Maslahat al-Isti'lamat, n.d.

McLellan, David S., and David C. Acheson, eds. *Among Friends: Personal Letters of Dean Acheson.* New York: Dodd, Mead, 1980.

Political Diaries of the Persian Gulf. Vol. 20. Farnham Common, Buckinghamshire: Archive Editions, 1990.

President Gamal Abdel-Nasser's Speeches and Press-Interviews, 1958. Cairo: UAR Information Department, n.d.

President Gamal Abdel-Nasser's Speeches and Press-Interviews, 1959. [Cairo: UAR Information Department,] n.d.

The President's Proposal on the Middle East: Hearings before the Committee on Foreign Relations and the Committee on Armed Services, United States Senate, Eighty-Fifth Congress, First Session, on S.J. Res. 19 and H.J. Res. 117. Washington, D.C.: U.S. Government Printing Office, 1957.

Public Papers of the President, Dwight D. Eisenhower, 1957. Washington, D.C.: U.S. Government Printing Office, 1958.

Public Papers of the President, Dwight D. Eisenhower, 1958. Washington, D.C.: U.S. Government Printing Office, 1959.

Tuson, Penelope, and Anita Burdett, eds. *Records of Saudi Arabia: Primary Documents, 1902–1960.* Vol. 9. Farnham Common, Buckinghamshire: Archive Editions, 1992.

U.S. Department of State. *Foreign Relations of the United States, 1955–1957.* Vols. 12, 13, 15, 16, 17. Washington, D.C.: U.S. Government Printing Office, 1989–91.

———. *Foreign Relations of the United States, 1958–1960.* Vols. 11, 12, 13. Washington, D.C.: U.S. Government Printing Office, 1992–93.

———. *Foreign Relations of the United States, 1964–1968.* Vol. 1. Washington, D.C.: U.S. Government Printing Office, 1992.

———. *United States Policy in the Middle East, September 1956–June 1957.* Washington, D.C.: U.S. Government Printing Office, 1957. Reprint, New York: Greenwood, 1968.

MICROFILM AND MICROFICHE COLLECTIONS

Confidential U.S. State Department Central Files, Egypt: Foreign Affairs, 1955–1959. Frederick, Md.: University Publications of America, 1989.

Confidential U.S. State Department Central Files, Iraq: Internal and Foreign Affairs, 1955–1959. Frederick, Md.: University Publications of America, 1991.

Confidential U.S. State Department Central Files, Jordan: Internal and Foreign Affairs, 1955–1959. Frederick, Md.: University Publications of America, 1990.

Confidential U.S. State Department Central Files, Lebanon: Internal and Foreign Affairs, 1955–1959. Frederick, Md.: University Publications of America, 1990.

Confidential U.S. State Department Central Files, Palestine-Israel: Foreign Affairs, 1955–1959. Frederick, Md.: University Publications of America, 1990.

Confidential U.S. State Department Central Files, Palestine-Israel: Internal Affairs, 1955–1959. Frederick, Md.: University Publications of America, 1990.

Confidential U.S. State Department Central Files, Saudi Arabia: Internal and Foreign Affairs, 1955–1959. Frederick, Md.: University Publications of America, 1990.

Confidential U.S. State Department Central Files, the Persian Gulf States and Yemen: Internal and Foreign Affairs, 1950–1959. Frederick, Md.: University Publications of America, 1991.

Confidential U.S. State Department Central Files, the Soviet Union: Foreign Affairs, 1955–1959. Frederick, Md.: University Publications of America, 1989.

Declassified Documents Reference System. Washington, D.C.: Carrollton Press, 1980–97.

The Diaries of Dwight D. Eisenhower, 1953–1961. Frederick, Md.: University Publications of America, 1986.

John Foster Dulles State Department Microfilm Collection, 1953–1959. Princeton University Library, Princeton, N.J.

Minutes and Documents of the Cabinet Meetings of President Eisenhower, 1953–1961. Frederick, Md.: University Publications of America, 1980.

Minutes of Telephone Conversations of John Foster Dulles and of Christian A. Herter, 1953–1961. Frederick, Md.: University Publications of America, 1980.

The Papers of John Foster Dulles and of Christian A. Herter, 1953–1961: The White House Correspondence and Memoranda Series. Frederick, Md.: University Publications of America, 1986.

President Dwight D. Eisenhower's Office Files, 1953–1961. Pt. 2, *International Series.* Frederick, Md.: University Publications of America, 1990.

Al-Ahram (Cairo)
Cold War International History Project Bulletin
Congressional Quarterly Almanac
Congressional Quarterly Weekly Report
Congressional Record
Department of State Bulletin
Al-Difaʿ (Amman)
Foreign Broadcast Information Service
Guardian (London)
Al-Hayat (Beirut)
Independent (London)
Los Angeles Times
Newsweek
New York Herald Tribune
New York Times
Observer (London)
Progressive
Ruz al-Yusuf (Cairo)
San Francisco Chronicle
Sunday Times (London)
Time
The Times (London)
U.S. Department of State, Daily Press Briefings, ⟨http://www.state.gov/r/pa/prs/dpb⟩
U.S. News and World Report
Washington Post

BOOKS, ARTICLES, AND DISSERTATIONS

Abidi, Aqil Hyder Hasan. *Jordan: A Political Study, 1948–1957*. Bombay: Asia Publishing House, 1965.

Abu-Amr, Ziad. *Islamic Fundamentalism in the West Bank and Gaza: Muslim Brotherhood and Islamic Jihad*. Bloomington: Indiana University Press, 1994.

Alin, Erika G. "The 1958 United States Intervention in Lebanon." Ph.D. diss., American University, 1990.

———. *The United States and the 1958 Lebanon Crisis: American Intervention in the Middle East*. Lanham, Md.: University Press of America, 1994.

Ambrose, Stephen E. *Eisenhower*. Vol. 1, *Soldier, General of the Army, President-Elect, 1890–1952*. New York: Simon and Schuster, 1984.

———. *Eisenhower*. Vol. 2, *The President*. New York: Simon and Schuster, 1984.

Ansari, Mohammad Iqbal. *The Arab League, 1945–1955*. Aligarh, India: Institute of Islamic Studies, 1968.

Arnold, Jose. *Golden Swords and Pots and Pans*. New York: Harcourt, Brace and World, 1963.

Arnove, Anthony, ed. *Iraq under Siege: The Deadly Impact of Sanctions and War*. London: Pluto Press, 2000.

Aronson, Geoffrey. *From Sideshow to Center Stage: U.S. Policy toward Egypt, 1946–1956*. Boulder, Colo.: Lynne Rienner, 1986.

Ashton, Nigel John. *Eisenhower, Macmillan, and the Problem of Nasser: Anglo-American Relations and Arab Nationalism, 1955–59*. London: Macmillan, 1996.

Al-Ayyubi, 'Ali Jawdat. *Dhikriyat, 1900–1958* (Memories, 1900–1958). Beirut: Matabi' al-Wafa', 1967.

Al-'Azm, Khalid. *Mudhakkirat Khalid al-'Azm* (The memoirs of Khalid al-'Azm). 3 vols. Beirut: Dar al-Muttahida lil-Nashr, 1973.

Al-Baghdadi, 'Abd al-Latif. *Mudhakkirat 'Abd al-Latif al-Baghdadi* (The memoirs of 'Abd al-Latif al-Baghdadi). 2 vols. Cairo: al-Maktab al-Misri al-Hadith, 1977.

Barakat, Halim. *The Arab World: Society, Culture, and State*. Berkeley: University of California Press, 1993.

Batatu, Hanna. *The Old Social Classes and the Revolutionary Movements of Iraq: A Study of Iraq's Old Landed and Commercial Classes and of Its Communists, Ba'thists, and Free Officers*. Princeton: Princeton University Press, 1978.

Benson, Michael T. *Harry S. Truman and the Founding of Israel*. Westport, Conn.: Praeger, 1997.

Ben-Zvi, Abraham. *Decade of Transition: Eisenhower, Kennedy, and the Origins of the American-Israeli Alliance*. New York: Columbia University Press, 1998.

Bergen, Peter L. *Holy War, Inc.: Inside the Secret World of Osama bin Laden*. New York: Simon and Schuster, 2002.

Bill, James A. *The Eagle and the Lion: The Tragedy of American-Iranian Relations*. New Haven: Yale University Press, 1988.

Bird, Kai. *The Chairman: John J. McCloy: The Making of the American Establishment*. New York: Simon and Schuster, 1992.

Bligh, Alexander. *From Prince to King: Royal Succession in the House of Saud in the Twentieth Century*. New York: New York University Press, 1984.

Bradley, John F. N. *War and Peace since 1945: A History of Soviet-Western Relations*. Boulder: Columbia University Press, 1989.

Bradley, Mark Philip. *Imagining Vietnam and America: The Making of Postcolonial Vietnam, 1919–1950*. Chapel Hill: University of North Carolina Press, 2000.

Brands, H. W. *Inside the Cold War: Loy Henderson and the Rise of the American Empire, 1918–1961*. New York: Oxford University Press, 1991.

Brendon, Piers. *Ike: His Life and Times*. New York: Harper and Row, 1986.

Brown, Anthony Cave. *Oil, God, and Gold: The Story of Aramco and the Saudi Kings*. Boston: Houghton Mifflin, 1999.

Brown, L. Carl. *International Politics and the Middle East: Old Rules, Dangerous Game*. Princeton: Princeton University Press, 1984.

Bryson, Thomas A. *Seeds of Mideast Crisis: The United States Diplomatic Role in the Middle East during World War II*. Jefferson, N.C.: McFarland, 1981.

Bukowski, Douglas. *Big Bill Thompson, Chicago, and the Politics of Image*. Chicago: University of Chicago Press, 1998.

Bustani, Emile. *March Arabesque*. London: Robert Hale, 1961.

Chace, James. *Acheson: The Secretary of State Who Created the American World.* New York: Simon and Schuster, 1998.

Chomsky, Noam. "The Current Crisis in the Middle East: What Can We Do?" 14 December 2000, ‹http://web.media.mit.edu/~nitin/mideast/chomsky_lecture.html›. 15 July 2003.

Clausen, Christopher. *Faded Mosaic: The Emergence of Post-Cultural America.* Chicago: Ivan R. Dee, 2000.

Cobban, Alfred. *A History of Modern France.* Vol. 3, *France of the Republics, 1871–1962.* Harmondsworth, Middlesex, U.K.: Penguin, 1965.

Cohen, Michael J. *Truman and Israel.* Berkeley: University of California Press, 1990.

Connelly, Matthew. "Taking Off the Cold War Lens: Visions of North-South Conflict during the Algerian War for Independence." *American Historical Review* 103, no. 3 (June 2000): 739–69.

Copeland, Miles. *The Game of Nations: The Amorality of Power Politics.* New York: Simon and Schuster, 1969.

Costigliola, Frank. "The Nuclear Family: Tropes of Gender and Pathology in the Western Alliance." *Diplomatic History* 21, no. 2 (Spring 1997): 163–83.

Crabb, Cecil V., Jr. *The Doctrines of American Foreign Policy.* Baton Rouge: Louisiana State University Press, 1982.

Crockatt, Richard. *The Fifty Years War: The United States and the Soviet Union in World Politics, 1941–1991.* London: Routledge, 1995.

Cutler, Robert. *No Time for Rest.* Boston: Little, Brown, 1965.

Dallek, Robert. *The American Style of Foreign Policy: Cultural Politics and Foreign Affairs.* New York: Alfred A. Knopf, 1983.

Dann, Uriel. *King Hussein and the Challenge of Arab Radicalism: Jordan, 1955–1967.* New York: Oxford University Press, 1989.

Devine, Patricia G. "Stereotypes and Prejudice: Their Automatic and Controlled Components." *Journal of Personality and Social Psychology* 56, no. 1 (January 1989): 5–18.

Divine, Robert A. *Eisenhower and the Cold War.* New York: Oxford University Press, 1981.

Dulles, Eleanor Lansing. *John Foster Dulles: The Last Year.* New York: Harcourt, Brace, 1963.

Eisenhower, Dwight D. *The White House Years.* Vol. 2, *Waging Peace, 1956–1961.* Garden City, N.Y.: Doubleday, 1965.

Esposito, John L. *The Islamic Threat: Myth or Reality?* New York: Oxford University Press, 1999.

Evans, Rowland, and Robert Novak. *Lyndon B. Johnson: The Exercise of Power.* New York: New American Library, 1966.

Eveland, Wilbur Crane. *Ropes of Sand: America's Failure in the Middle East.* New York: W. W. Norton, 1980.

Freedman, Robert O. *Soviet Policy toward the Middle East since 1970.* 3d ed. New York: Praeger, 1982.

Freiberger, Steven Z. *Dawn over Suez: The Rise of American Power in the Middle East, 1953–1957.* Chicago: Ivan R. Dee, 1992.

Fry, Michael Graham. "The Uses of Intelligence: The United Nations Confronts the

United States in the Lebanon Crisis, 1958." *Intelligence and National Security* 10, no. 1 (January 1995): 59–91.

Fry, Michael Graham, and Miles Hochstein. "The Forgotten Middle Eastern Crisis of 1957: Gaza and Sharm-el-Sheikh." *International History Review* 15, no. 1 (February 1993): 46–83.

Gaddis, John Lewis. *We Now Know: Rethinking Cold War History.* Oxford: Clarendon, 1997.

Gallman, Waldemar J. *Iraq under General Nuri: My Recollections of Nuri al-Said.* Baltimore: Johns Hopkins University Press, 1963.

Gallup, George D. *The Gallup Poll: Public Opinion, 1935–1971.* Vol. 2. New York: Random House, 1972.

Gaskin, Thomas M. "Lyndon B. Johnson, the Eisenhower Administration, and U.S. Foreign Policy, 1957–60." *Presidential Studies Quarterly* 24 (Spring 1994): 341–61.

Gendzier, Irene L. *Notes from the Minefield: United States Intervention in Lebanon and the Middle East, 1945–1958.* New York: Columbia University Press, 1997.

Gerges, Fawaz A. *America and Political Islam: Clash of Cultures or Clash of Interests?* Cambridge: Cambridge University Press, 1999.

———. *The Superpowers and the Middle East: Regional and International Politics, 1955–1967.* Boulder, Colo.: Westview, 1994.

Gerner, Deborah J. "Missed Opportunities and Roads Not Taken: The Eisenhower Administration and the Palestinians." In *U.S. Policy on Palestine from Wilson to Clinton,* edited by Michael W. Suleiman, 81–112. Normal, Ill.: Association of Arab-American University Graduates, 1995.

Ginat, Rami. *The Soviet Union and Egypt, 1945–1955.* London: Frank Cass, 1993.

Gleijeses, Piero. *Shattered Hope: The Guatemalan Revolution and the United States, 1944–1954.* Princeton: Princeton University Press, 1991.

Golan, Galia. *Soviet Policies in the Middle East: From World War II to Gorbachev.* Cambridge: Cambridge University Press, 1990.

Gorst, Anthony, and W. Scott Lucas. "The Other Collusion: Operation Straggle and Anglo-American Intervention in Syria, 1955–56." *Intelligence and National Security* 4, no. 3 (July 1989): 576–95.

Gouda, Frances. "The Gendered Rhetoric of Colonialism and Anti-Colonialism in Twentieth-Century Indonesia." *Indonesia* 55 (April 1993): 1–22.

Greene, John Robert. "Bibliographic Essay: Eisenhower Revisionism, 1952–1992, a Reappraisal." In *Reexamining the Eisenhower Presidency,* edited by Shirley Anne Warshaw, 209–20. Westport, Conn.: Greenwood, 1993.

Haddad, Yvonne Yazbeck. "Islamist Perceptions of U.S. Policy in the Middle East." In *The Middle East and the United States: A Historical and Political Reassessment,* edited by David W. Lesch, 419–37. Boulder, Colo.: Westview, 1996.

Hahn, Peter L. *The United States, Great Britain, and Egypt, 1945–1956: Strategy and Diplomacy in the Early Cold War.* Chapel Hill: University of North Carolina Press, 1991.

Halliday, Fred. *Two Hours That Shook the World, September 11, 2001: Causes and Consequences.* London: Saqi Books, 2001.

Harris, George S. *Troubled Alliance: Turkish-American Problems in Historical Perspective, 1945–1971.* Stanford: Hoover Institution, 1972.

Hartz, Louis. *The Liberal Tradition in America: An Interpretation of American Political Thought since the Revolution.* New York: Harcourt, Brace, 1955.

Al-Hawrani, Akram. *Mudhakkirat Akram al-Hawrani* (The memoirs of Akram al-Hawrani). 4 vols. Cairo: Maktabat Madbuli, 2000.

Haykal, Muhammad Hasanayn. *'Abd al-Nasir wa-al-'alam* ('Abd al-Nasir and the world). Beirut: Dar al-Nahar lil-Nashr, 1972.

———. *The Cairo Documents: The Inside Story of Nasser and His Relationship with World Leaders, Rebels, and Statesmen.* Garden City, N.Y.: Doubleday, 1973.

———. *Milaffat al-Suways: Harb al-thalathin sana* (The Suez files: The Thirty Years' War). Cairo: Markaz al-Ahram lil-Tarjama wa-al-Nashr, 1986.

———. *Sanawat al-ghalayan: Harb al-thalathin sana* (Years of upheaval: The Thirty Years' War). Vol. 1. Cairo: Markaz al-Ahram lil-Tarjama wa-al-Nashr, 1988.

———. *Sphinx and Commissar: The Rise and Fall of Soviet Influence in the Arab World.* London: Collins, 1978.

Heiss, Mary Ann. *Empire and Nationhood: The United States, Great Britain, and Iranian Oil, 1950–1954.* New York: Columbia University Press, 1997.

Holden, David. *Farewell to Arabia.* London: Faber and Faber, 1966.

Holden, David, and Richard Johns. *The House of Saud: The Rise and Rule of the Most Powerful Dynasty in the Arab World.* New York: Holt, Rinehart and Winston, 1981.

Holland, Matthew F. *America and Egypt: From Roosevelt to Eisenhower.* Westport, Conn.: Praeger, 1996.

Holsti, Ole. "The 'Operational Code' Approach to the Study of Political Leaders: John Foster Dulles' Philosophical and Instrumental Beliefs." *Canadian Journal of Political Science* 3 (March 1970): 123–57.

Hoopes, Townsend. *The Devil and John Foster Dulles.* Boston: Little, Brown, 1973.

Horne, Alistair. *Macmillan.* Vol. 2, *1957–1986.* New York: Viking, 1989.

Hourani, Albert. *A History of the Arab Peoples.* London: Faber and Faber, 1991.

Hudson, Michael C. *The Precarious Republic: Political Modernization in Lebanon.* New York: Random House, 1968.

Hughes, Emmet John. *The Ordeal of Power: A Political Memoir of the Eisenhower Years.* New York: Atheneum, 1963.

Hunt, Michael H. *Ideology and U.S. Foreign Policy.* New Haven: Yale University Press, 1987.

Huntington, Samuel P. "The Clash of Civilizations?" *Foreign Affairs*, September 1993, 22–49.

———. *The Clash of Civilizations and the Remaking of World Order.* New York: Simon and Schuster, 1996.

Hussein, King of Jordan. *Uneasy Lies the Head.* London: William Heinemann, 1962.

Immerman, Richard H. *The CIA in Guatemala: The Foreign Policy of Intervention.* Austin: University of Texas Press, 1982.

———. "Eisenhower and Dulles: Who Made the Decisions?" *Political Psychology* 1, no. 2 (Autumn 1979): 21–38.

———, ed. *John Foster Dulles and the Diplomacy of the Cold War.* Princeton: Princeton University Press, 1990.

Johnston, Charles. *The Brink of Jordan.* London: Hamish Hamilton, 1972.

Kalb, Madeleine B. *The Congo Cables: The Cold War in Africa, from Eisenhower to Kennedy.* New York: Macmillan, 1982.

BIBLIOGRAPHY

Kamalipour, Yahya R., ed. *The U.S. Media and the Middle East: Image and Perception.* Westport, Conn.: Greenwood, 1995.

Kaplan, Robert D. *The Arabists: The Romance of an American Elite.* New York: Free Press, 1993.

———. "Looking the World in the Eye." *Atlantic Monthly*, December 2001, 68–82.

Karabell, Zachary. *Architects of Intervention: The United States, the Third World, and the Cold War, 1946–1962.* Baton Rouge: Louisiana State University Press, 1998.

Kaufman, Burton I. *The Arab Middle East and the United States: Inter-Arab Rivalry and Superpower Diplomacy.* New York: Twayne, 1996.

———. *Trade and Aid: Eisenhower's Foreign Economic Policy, 1953–1961.* Baltimore: Johns Hopkins University Press, 1982.

Kerr, Malcolm. *The Arab Cold War: Gamal 'Abd al-Nasir and His Rivals, 1958–1970.* 3d ed. London: Oxford University Press, 1971.

Khadduri, Majid, and Edmund Ghareeb. *War in the Gulf, 1990–1991: The Iraq-Kuwait Conflict and Its Implications.* New York: Oxford University Press, 1997.

Khalidi, Rashid. "Consequences of the Suez Crisis in the Arab World." In *The Modern Middle East*, edited by Albert Hourani, Philip S. Khoury, and Mary C. Wilson, 535–49. Berkeley: University of California Press, 1993.

Knock, Thomas J. *To End All Wars: Woodrow Wilson and the Quest for a New World Order.* New York: Oxford University Press, 1992.

Kunz, Diane B. *The Economic Diplomacy of the Suez Crisis.* Chapel Hill: University of North Carolina Press, 1991.

Kyle, Keith. *Suez.* New York: St. Martin's Press, 1991.

Lacey, Robert. *The Kingdom.* New York: Harcourt Brace Jovanovich, 1981.

LaFeber, Walter. *America, Russia, and the Cold War.* 5th ed. New York: Alfred A. Knopf, 1985.

Lamb, Richard. *The Macmillan Years, 1957–1963: The Emerging Truth.* London: John Murray, 1995.

Larson, Deborah Welch. *Anatomy of Mistrust: U.S.-Soviet Relations during the Cold War.* Ithaca: Cornell University Press, 1997.

Latham, Michael E. *Modernization as Ideology: American Social Science and "Nation Building" in the Kennedy Era.* Chapel Hill: University of North Carolina Press, 2000.

Lauren, Paul Gordon. *Power and Prejudice: The Politics and Diplomacy of Racial Discrimination.* Boulder, Colo.: Westview, 1988.

Lefebvre, Jeffrey A. "The United States and Egypt: Confrontation and Accommodation in Northeast Africa, 1956–60." *Middle Eastern Studies* 29, no. 2 (April 1993): 321–38.

Lenczowski, George. *American Presidents and the Middle East.* Durham, N.C.: Duke University Press, 1990.

Lesch, David. "The Saudi Role in the American-Syrian Crisis of 1957." *Middle East Policy* 1, no. 3 (Summer 1992): 33–48.

———. *Syria and the United States: Eisenhower's Cold War in the Middle East.* Boulder, Colo.: Westview, 1992.

Lewis, Bernard. *Islam and the West.* New York: Oxford University Press, 1993.

———. *The Middle East and the West.* Bloomington: Indiana University Press, 1964.

———. "The Roots of Muslim Rage." *Atlantic Monthly*, September 1990, 47–60.

Lewis, Laura A. "The 'Weakness' of Women and the Feminization of the Indian in Colonial Mexico." *Colonial Latin American Review* 5, no. 1 (June 1996): 73–94.

Little, Douglas. *American Orientalism: The United States and the Middle East since 1945.* Chapel Hill: University of North Carolina Press, 2002.

———. "Cold War and Covert Action: The United States and Syria, 1945–1958." *Middle East Journal* 44, no. 1 (Winter 1990): 51–75.

———. "The Eagle and the Sphinx: America and Arab Nationalism, 1945–1970." In *The United States and the Middle East: Diplomatic and Economic Relations in Historical Perspective*, edited by Abbas Amanat, 152–67. New Haven: Yale Center for International and Area Studies, 2000.

———. "From Even-Handed to Empty-Handed: Seeking Order in the Middle East." In *Kennedy's Quest for Victory*, edited by Thomas G. Paterson, 156–77. New York: Oxford University Press, 1989.

———. "Gideon's Band: America and the Middle East since 1945." In *America in the World: The Historiography of American Foreign Relations since 1941*, edited by Michael J. Hogan, 462–500. New York: Cambridge University Press, 1995.

———. "His Finest Hour? Eisenhower, Lebanon, and the 1958 Middle East Crisis." *Diplomatic History* 20, no. 1 (Winter 1996): 27–54.

Long, David E. *The Kingdom of Saudi Arabia.* Gainesville: University of Florida Press, 1997.

Louis, William Roger. *The British Empire in the Middle East, 1945–1951: Arab Nationalism, the United States, and Postwar Imperialism.* Oxford: Clarendon Press, 1984.

Love, Kennett. *Suez: The Twice-Fought War.* New York: McGraw-Hill, 1969.

Lunt, James. *Hussein of Jordan: Searching for a Just and Lasting Peace.* New York: William Morrow, 1989.

Maalouf, Amin. *The Crusades through Arab Eyes.* Translated by Jon Rothschild. London: Saqi Books, 1984.

Macmillan, Harold. *Riding the Storm, 1955–1959.* New York: Harper and Row, 1971.

Al-Majali, Hazza'. *Mudhakkirati* (My memoirs). Beirut: Dar al-ʿIlm lil-Malayin, 1960.

Manchester, Margaret M. "The Tangled Web: The Baghdad Pact, Eisenhower, and Arab Nationalism." Ph.D. diss., Clark University, 1994.

Mansfield, Peter. *A History of the Middle East.* London: Penguin, 1992.

Marr, Phebe. *The Modern History of Iraq.* Boulder, Colo.: Westview, 1985.

Mart, Michelle. "Tough Guys and American Cold War Policy: Images of Israel, 1948–1960." *Diplomatic History* 20, no. 3 (Summer 1996): 357–80.

McAlister, Melani. *Epic Encounters: Culture, Media, and U.S. Interests in the Middle East, 1945–2000.* Berkeley: University of California Press, 2001.

McCormick, Thomas J. *America's Half-Century: United States Foreign Policy in the Cold War.* Baltimore: Johns Hopkins University Press, 1989.

Monteith, Margo J., and Gina L. Walters. "Egalitarianism, Moral Obligation, and Prejudice-Related Personal Standards." *Personality and Social Psychology Bulletin* 24, no. 2 (February 1998): 186–99.

Morris, Benny. *Israel's Border Wars, 1949–1956: Arab Infiltration, Israeli Retaliation, and the Countdown to the Suez War.* Oxford: Clarendon, 1993.

Mosley, Leonard. *Dulles: A Biography of Eleanor, Allen, and John Foster Dulles and Their Family Network.* New York: Dial, 1978.

Mufti, Malik. "The United States and Nasserist Pan-Arabism." In *The Middle East and the United States: A Historical and Political Reassessment*, edited by David W. Lesch, 167–86. Boulder, Colo.: Westview, 1996.

Murphy, Robert. *Diplomat among Warriors*. Garden City, N.Y.: Doubleday, 1964.

Mustafa, Munawar Sbaiti. "The United States and Lebanon before and during the Lebanese Crisis of 1958." Ph.D. diss., Duke University, 1978.

Neff, Donald. *Warriors at Suez: Eisenhower Takes America into the Middle East*. New York: Simon and Schuster, 1981.

Nixon, Richard M. *RN: The Memoirs of Richard Nixon*. 2 vols. New York: Warner, 1978.

Novick, Peter. *That Noble Dream: The "Objectivity Question" and the American Historical Profession*. New York: Cambridge University Press, 1988.

Nutting, Anthony. *Nasser*. London: Constable, 1972.

———. *No End of a Lesson: The Story of Suez*. New York: Clarkson N. Potter, 1967.

Oren, Michael B. *Six Days of War: June 1967 and the Making of the Modern Middle East*. New York: Oxford University Press, 2002.

Ovendale, Ritchie. *Britain, the United States, and the Transfer of Power in the Middle East, 1945–1962*. London: Leicester University Press, 1996.

———. "Great Britain and the Anglo-American Invasion of Jordan and Lebanon in 1958." *International History Review* 16, no. 2 (May 1994): 284–303.

Pach, Chester J., Jr., and Elmo Richardson. *The Presidency of Dwight D. Eisenhower*. Lawrence: University Press of Kansas, 1991.

Parker, Richard B. *The Politics of Miscalculation in the Middle East*. Bloomington: Indiana University Press, 1993.

———. "The United States and King Hussein." In *The Middle East and the United States: A Historical and Political Reassessment*, edited by David W. Lesch, 103–16. Boulder, Colo.: Westview, 1996.

Pearson, Drew. *Diaries, 1949–1959*. Edited by Tyler Abell. New York: Holt, Rinehart and Winston, 1974.

Pennar, Jaan. *The U.S.S.R. and the Arabs: The Ideological Dimension*. New York: Crane, Russak, 1973.

Petersen, Tore T. *The Middle East between the Great Powers: Anglo-American Conflict and Cooperation, 1952–7*. New York: St. Martin's Press, 2000.

Petran, Tabitha. *Nations of the Modern World: Syria*. New York: Praeger, 1972.

Pew Research Center for the People and the Press. "Views of a Changing World 2003: War with Iraq Further Divides Global Publics." ⟨http://people-press.org/reports/pdf/185topline.pdf⟩. 15 July 2003.

Podeh, Elie. "The Struggle over Arab Hegemony after the Suez Crisis." *Middle East Studies* 29, no. 1 (January 1993): 91–110.

Powaski, Ronald E. *The Cold War: The United States and the Soviet Union, 1917–1991*. New York: Oxford University Press, 1998.

Pruessen, Ronald W. *John Foster Dulles: The Road to Power*. New York: Free Press, 1982.

Qubain, Fahim I. *Crisis in Lebanon*. Washington, D.C.: Middle East Institute, 1961.

Rathmell, Andrew. *Secret War in the Middle East: The Covert Struggle for Syria, 1949–1961*. London: I. B. Tauris, 1996.

Roberts, David. *The Ba'th and the Creation of Modern Syria*. London: Croom Helm, 1987.

Rotter, Andrew. "Gender Relations, Foreign Relations: The United States and South

Asia, 1947–1964." *Journal of American History* 81, no. 2 (September 1994): 518–42.

Said, Edward W. *Covering Islam: How the Media and the Experts Determine How We See the Rest of the World.* New York: Pantheon, 1981. Reprint, New York: Vintage, 1997.

———. *Orientalism.* New York: Vintage, 1979.

Salami, George Raymond. "The Eisenhower Doctrine: A Study in Alliance Politics." Ph.D. diss., Catholic University of America, 1974.

Sangmuah, Egya N. "Eisenhower and Containment in North Africa, 1956–1960." *Middle East Journal* 44, no. 1 (Winter 1990): 76–91.

Satloff, Robert B. *From Abdullah to Hussein: Jordan in Transition.* New York: Oxford University Press, 1994.

———. "The Jekyll-and-Hyde Origins of the U.S.-Jordanian Strategic Relationship." In *The Middle East and the United States: A Historical and Political Reassessment*, edited by David W. Lesch, 117–30. Boulder, Colo.: Westview, 1996.

Saunders, Bonnie F. *The United States and Arab Nationalism: The Syrian Case, 1953–1960.* Westport, Conn.: Praeger, 1996.

Schlesinger, Arthur M., Jr. *The Imperial Presidency.* Rev. ed. Boston: Houghton Mifflin, 1989.

Schoch, Bernd. *The Islamic Movement: A Challenge for Palestinian State-Building.* Jerusalem: Palestinian Academic Society for the Study of International Affairs, 1999.

Seale, Patrick. *The Struggle for Syria: A Study of Post-War Arab Politics.* Oxford: Oxford University Press, 1965. Reprint, New Haven, Conn.: Yale University Press, 1987.

Shwadran, Benjamin. *Jordan: A State of Tension.* New York: Council for Middle East Affairs Press, 1959.

Sinha, Mrinalini. *Colonial Masculinity: The "Manly Englishman" and the "Effeminate Bengali" in the Late Nineteenth Century.* Manchester: Manchester University Press, 1995.

Smith, Gaddis. *American Diplomacy during the Second World War, 1941–1945.* New York: John Wiley and Sons, 1965.

Smith, Joseph. *The Cold War.* 2d ed., *1945–1991.* Oxford: Blackwell, 1998.

Smolansky, Oles M. *The Soviet Union and the Arab East under Khrushchev.* Lewisburg, N.J.: Bucknell University Press, 1974.

Snow, Peter. *Hussein: A Biography.* London: Barrie and Jenkins, 1972.

Spiegel, Steven L. *The Other Arab-Israeli Conflict: Making America's Middle East Policy, from Truman to Reagan.* Chicago: University of Chicago Press, 1985.

Stephens, Robert. *Nasser: A Political Biography.* London: Penguin, 1971.

Stivers, William. "Eisenhower and the Middle East." In *Reevaluating Eisenhower: American Foreign Policy in the 1950s*, edited by Richard A. Melanson and David Mayers, 192–219. Urbana: University of Illinois Press, 1987.

Stockton, Ronald. "Ethnic Archetypes and the Arab Image." In *The Development of Arab-American Identity*, edited by Ernest McCarus, 119–53. Ann Arbor: University of Michigan Press, 1994.

Suleiman, Michael. *The Arabs in the Mind of America.* Brattleboro, Vt.: Amana Books, 1988.

Sulzberger, C. L. *The Last of the Giants.* New York: Macmillan, 1970.

Al-Suwaydi, Tawfiq. *Mudhakkirati: Nisf qarn min tarikh al-ʿIraq wa-al-qadiyya al-ʿArabiyya*

(My memoirs: Half a century of the history of Iraq and the Arab cause). Beirut: Dar al-Kitab al-ʿArabi, 1969.

Takeyh, Ray. *The Origins of the Eisenhower Doctrine: The US, Britain, and Nasser's Egypt, 1953–57.* New York: St. Martin's Press, 2000.

Tal, David. "Israel's Road to the 1956 War." *International Journal of Middle East Studies* 28, no. 1 (February 1996): 59–81.

———. "Seizing Opportunities: Israel and the 1958 Crisis in the Middle East." *Middle Eastern Studies* 37, no. 1 (January 2001): 143–58.

Telhami, Shibley. *The Stakes: America and the Middle East: The Consequences of Power and the Choice of Peace.* Boulder, Colo.: Westview, 2002.

Terry, Janice J. *Mistaken Identity: Arab Stereotypes in Popular Writing.* Washington, D.C.: American-Arab Affairs Council, 1985.

Thomas, Evan. *The Very Best Men: Four Who Dared: The Early Years of the CIA.* New York: Simon and Schuster, 1995.

Thomas, Hugh. *Suez.* New York: Harper and Row, 1966.

Thomson, Charles A. H., and Frances M. Shattuck. *The 1956 Presidential Campaign.* Washington, D.C.: Brookings Institution, 1960.

Tyson, Carolyn Ann. "Making Foreign Policy: The Eisenhower Doctrine." Ph.D. diss., George Washington University, 1984.

Vatikiotis, P[anayiotis] J. *Politics and the Military in Jordan.* London: Frank Cass, 1967.

Wall, Irwin M. *France, the United States, and the Algerian War.* Berkeley: University of California Press, 2001.

Wills, Garry. *Nixon Agonistes: The Crisis of a Self-Made Man.* Boston: Houghton Mifflin, 1969.

Wilson, Mary C. *King Abdullah, Britain, and the Making of Jordan.* Cambridge: Cambridge University Press, 1987.

Yaqub, Salim. "Containing Arab Nationalism: The United States, the Arab Middle East, and the Eisenhower Doctrine, 1956–1959." Ph.D. diss., Yale University, 1999.

———. "Contesting Arabism: The Eisenhower Doctrine and the Arab Middle East, 1956–1959." In *The United States and the Middle East: Diplomatic and Economic Relations in Historical Perspective,* edited by Abbas Amanat, 168–86. New Haven: Yale Center for International and Area Studies, 2000.

———. "Imperious Doctrines: U.S.-Arab Relations from Dwight D. Eisenhower to George W. Bush." *Diplomatic History* 26, no. 4 (Fall 2002): 571–91.

Yergin, Daniel. *The Prize: The Epic Quest for Oil, Money, and Power.* New York: Simon and Schuster, 1991.

Yizhar, Michael. "The Eisenhower Doctrine: A Case Study of American Foreign Policy and Implementation." Ph.D. diss., New School for Social Research, 1968.

———. "Israel and the Eisenhower Doctrine." *Wiener Library Bulletin* 28, no. 33/34 (1975): 58–64.

Yizraeli, Sarah. *The Remaking of Saudi Arabia: The Struggle between King Saʿud and Crown Prince Faysal, 1953–1962.* Tel Aviv: Moshe Dayan Center for Middle Eastern and African Studies, 1997.

Yost, Charles W. *The Conduct and Misconduct of Foreign Affairs.* New York: Random House, 1972.

———. *History and Memory.* New York: W. W. Norton, 1980.

ACKNOWLEDGMENTS

It has taken me much longer to research and write about the Eisenhower Doctrine than it took the Eisenhower administration to design and implement it. In all these years, I have received more than my fair share of guidance, help, encouragement, and inspiration.

This book began as a history dissertation at Yale University under the supervision of Gaddis Smith. Professor Smith was a superb advisor, unfailing in his support, encouragement, and incisive commentary and inspiring in his example as a prolific, engaged, versatile, and masterful scholar. Also serving on my dissertation committee were Diane Kunz and Abbas Amanat. Professor Kunz gave generously of her time and expertise and kindly agreed to remain on my committee after leaving the Yale faculty. She read several drafts of the dissertation and spent countless hours with me in long-distance telephone conversations, prodding me (with what success only others can judge) to think and write more clearly. Professor Amanat encouraged me to broaden the conceptual scope of the project and to include a discussion of the role of culture. A Yale conference he sponsored in the summer of 1999 gave me an excellent opportunity to try out my ideas before a wider audience of Middle East scholars. I am grateful also to Paul Kennedy for his advice and support; a timely letter from Professor Kennedy may have been decisive in cracking open the doors of the Egyptian Foreign Ministry archive. Toward the end of my time at Yale, John Lewis Gaddis came on board as an informal advisor, offering invaluable suggestions for transforming the dissertation into a book. I am honored that Professor Gaddis later proposed the monograph for inclusion in this splendid series at the University of North Carolina Press.

My research in American, British, and Egyptian archives would not have been possible without generous grants from the Yale University History Department, the Yale Graduate School, the Yale Center for International and Area Studies, the Andrew W. Mellon Foundation, and the Smith Richardson Foundation. The archivists and staff at the Yale University Library, the Columbia University Library, the Princeton University Library, the Presbyterian Historical Society, the National Archives, the Library of Congress, the Dwight D. Eisenhower Library, the Public Record Office, and Egypt's Dar al-Witha'iq al-Qawmiyya were consistently courteous, patient, and helpful. I am especially grateful to Jim Leyerzapf, Bonnie Mulinax, Dwight Strandberg, and Kathy Struss at the

Eisenhower Library and to Amal Rashid at Dar al-Witha'iq al-Qawmiyya. During my research trip to Cairo in the summer of 1998, Amir Ahmed and Amira Ahmed of the American Research Center in Egypt offered me lodgings, the services of ARCE's office, and excellent advice about navigating Egyptian archives. My parents-in-law, Richard and Jeanie Teare, and my sister-in-law, Megan Teare, put me up in their homes during frequent research visits to Washington, D.C.

I have incurred additional debts at the University of Chicago. First and foremost, it is an immense privilege to be part of such an outstanding department of history; I could not ask for a more brilliant, productive, challenging, and supportive group of colleagues. I am grateful also for the department's humane teaching load, which made it possible for me to complete the book without going on leave. Thanks to John Woods, I have another home-on-campus at the Center for Middle Eastern Studies, an ideal place for testing and refining ideas about the United States and the Arab world. Bruce Cumings and Rashid Khalidi read the entire manuscript and suggested many improvements. The participants in the Middle East History and Theory Workshop offered valuable feedback on portions of the monograph. More generally, the probing insights and questions of the students in my courses—graduates and undergraduates alike—have sharpened my own thinking about U.S.–Middle Eastern relations.

Getting the manuscript into publishable form has been a daunting task, made manageable—and at times even pleasurable—by the generous assistance of colleagues and friends. At the University of North Carolina Press, Chuck Grench guided the project with a light but sure touch, gently prodding me to broaden the book's appeal beyond a specialist audience. Amanda McMillan, Pam Upton, Stephanie Wenzel, and the late Kathy Malin handled the mechanics of publication with cheerful professionalism and patiently walked me through each bewildering stage. Peter Hahn and Fawaz Gerges carefully reviewed the manuscript and offered numerous suggestions for expanding and clarifying its arguments; Professor Hahn looked over the manuscript a second time and saved me from several embarrassing errors. Colin Wilder did a fabulous job of checking my references. My wife, Elizabeth Teare, took long hours from her own work to proofread the manuscript twice, a task she performed with frightening thoroughness. Any factual errors, typos, or infelicities now present in the text must have been added by me after these vigilant inspectors completed their work.

Over the years, I have been fortunate to know scores of dedicated, resourceful, and generous scholars who have shared their insights, findings, and research tips with me and have challenged and refined my arguments and interpretations. I could not possibly name all the people who have helped me in these ways, but I would like to make special mention of Jon Alterman, Ralph Austen, Nate Citino, Matt Connelly, Stacey Davis, Will Gray, Peter Hahn, Mary Ann Heiss, Geoff Kabaservice, David Koistinen, Robert Johnston, Doug Little, Fred Logevall, Michelle Mart, Duke Merriam, Farouk Mustafa, Jeffrey Nadaner, Timothy Naftali, Richard Parker, Terry Regier, Michael Rubin, Jeremi Suri, Trysh Travis, Bob Vitalis, and Brad Westerfield. I thank these friends and colleagues for their valuable assistance and apologize to those I have failed to mention.

I am dedicating this book to my parents, Fawzi Yaqub, Penny Williams Yaqub, and the late Dorothy Seibert Yaqub. They have encouraged and sustained me through countless enthusiasms, ambitions, pretensions, and personality changes, including my latest incarnation as a historian. They offered me priceless opportunities, which I too often squandered, to absorb the history, cultures, and languages of the Middle East. My siblings, too, have been an inexhaustible source of inspiration, friendship, support, and, at times, amused tolerance.

One of the guilty pleasures I have shared with Elizabeth is snickering at the mawkish tones in which academic writers acknowledge their spouses. So I dare not try (at least not here) to put into words all she has meant to me.

INDEX

mation of, 193, 328 (n. 36); proposed
intervention in Lebanon, 216; relations
with UAR, 195–96; U.S. attitudes to-
ward, 193–94
Arab values, 19–20, 274–76, 281 (n. 43)
Arbenz, Jacobo. *See* Guzmán, Jacobo
Arbenz
'Arif, 'Abd al-Salam, 220, 221, 257, *258*
Armed Services Committee, U.S. Senate,
94–95, 111
Armstrong, Hamilton Fish, 64, 67
Article 51, United Nations Charter, 212,
225, 228, 236, 337 (n. 76)
al-'Asali, Sabri, 50, 64, 102, 149, 154, 314
(n. 5), 316 (n. 26)
Ashton, Nigel John, 2, 191, 262
Aswan Dam project, 40, 46–47, 59, 286
(nn. 71, 72)
Attiyah, Abdullah, 157, 317–18 (n. 40)
al-Ayyubi, 'Ali Jawdat, 148, 158, 161,
163–64, 167, 168, 182, 325 (n. 2), 342
(n. 53)
al-'Azm, Khalid, 154, 158, 183, 314 (n. 5),
316–17 (n. 31)
'Azzam Pasha, 61

al-Baghdadi, 'Abd al-Latif, 325 (n. 114),
326 (n. 12), 333 (n. 17)
Baghdad Pact: and Arab Union, 193, 328
(n. 35); British interest in, 38–39, 97,
113; formation of, 38; and Iraq, 42,
58, 246; and Jordan, 40–41, 122; and
Lebanese crisis, 220, 335 (n. 51); Nas-
ser's view of, 38, 42; relationship to
Eisenhower Doctrine, 97, 98; and
Saudi Arabia, 44; and Turkey, 70; and
United States, 38–39, 76, 97, 113, 294
(n. 62)
Baghdad Pact Council, 190–91
Baghdad Pact riots, 136, 41
Bandung Conference (1955), 38
Barakat, Halim, 281 (n. 43)
Batatu, Hanna, 342 (n. 53)
Ba'th Party: in Iraq, 36, 257; in Jordan,
36, 122, 135; in Lebanon, 36; in Syria,
36, 149, 155, 177, 182–88, 257

Beirut-Masa', 189
Ben-Gurion, David, 40, 75, 108–9, 159,
232, 285 (n. 53), 294 (n. 60)
Benson, Ezra Taft, 17
Bermuda conference (March 1957),
113–14, *114*, 175
bin Laden, Osama, 10, 271, 275
al-Bitar, Salah al-Din, 101, 150, 170, 185,
186
Bizri, 'Afif, 158, 169, 177, 324 (n. 113),
326 (n. 12)
"Blue Bat" plan, 213
Bohlen, Charles E., 71
Bourguiba, Habib, 100, 103, 305 (n. 4)
Britain: Arab views of, 3, 57–58, 62, 67;
attack on Egypt, 50–53; decline of
influence in Middle East, 4, 57–58,
157; military intervention in Jordan, 7,
245; position in Arab world, 4; proposed intervention in Kuwait, 234–
35; relations with Egypt, 22; relations
with Iran, 30; relations with Iraq, 262;
relations with Israel, 232; relations
with Jordan, 124, 231, 278 (n. 5), 307
(n. 30), 308 (n. 32); and Suez Canal,
47, 114–15, 286 (n. 74); support for
Eisenhower Doctrine, 97; U.S. alliance
with, 5, 66; views of Nasser, 4, 113,
262; views of Saudi Arabia, 45; withdrawal of forces from Egypt, 57,
64–65, 67; withdrawal of forces from
Jordan, 252
Brown, L. Carl, 16
Bulganin, Nokolai A., 166
Bull, Odd, 214
Bureau of Near Eastern, South Asian,
and African Affairs (NEA), U.S. Department of State, 44, 45, 76, 189–90,
200
Byroade, Henry A., 22

Caccia, Harold, 150, 175, 178, 315 (n. 20)
Cairo conference (February 1957),
109–10, 128
Central Intelligence Agency (CIA), 30, 49,
52, 53, 138, 189, 255, 264, 283 (n. 11)

Chamoun, Camille, *36*; and Baghdad
Pact, 335 (n. 51); British views of, 14;
dispute with Shihab, 210–11; and
Egyptian-Syrian union, 328 (n. 29);
expulsion of Shishakli, 46; on Iraq,
239; on King Saud, 162; on Nasser,
215–16; political outlook of, 37; and
presidential succession, 7, 207–10,
217, 218–19, 245; requests for U.S. intervention, 211, 222–23; on Suez war,
62, 289 (n. 14); support for Eisenhower Doctrine, 100, 142, 206, 236;
on Syria, 239; on UAR infiltrations,
332 (n. 15); on UNOGIL, 214; U.S.
views of, 14, 208–9, 234
"Clash of civilizations" thesis, 9, 274–75
Coalition National Front, 152
Cold War: Arab views of, 20; U.S. preoccupation with, 19, 20
Communism: Arab views of, 3; in Egypt,
27, 32, 99; in Iran, 30; in Iraq, 257,
259, 260, 261, 262 (*See also* Iraq Communist Party [ICP]); in Jordan, 126–
27, 135; in Syria, 177, 183, 184, 186,
187–88; in UAR, 257–58; U.S. views
of, 3
Congo crisis, 264, 265, 267
Congressional Quarterly, 94
Conservative Arab governments: in Arab
countries, 37; on Arab-Israeli conflict,
5; disunity of, 5–6; on Soviet Union, 5;
on Suez war, 61–62; on U.S. relations
with Nasser, 201–2; weakness of, 5,
180, 256, 263, 270
Constitutional Front (Syria), 314 (n. 5)
Containment doctrine, 2
"Containment plus," 175–76
Copeland, Miles, 8, 208
Costigliola, Frank, 14
Cutler, Robert, 223
Cyprus, 231, 232
Czechoslovakia, 40

Dann, Uriel, 219, 231, 344 (n. 75)
Dayan, Moshe, 196
De Gaulle, Charles, 213, 333 (n. 23)

Democrats, 91–97, 102–3, 109
Dewey, Thomas E., 27
Dhahran airfield, 102, 103
Druze, 176, 332 (n. 15)
Dulles, Allen W.: on Chamoun, 217; on
Crown Prince Faisal, 198; on Egypt,
141; on Egyptian-Syrian union, 191,
327 (n. 23); on Iraq, 225, 259; on Jordan, 134; on King Saud, 197; on Lebanon, 143, 217, 218, 332–33 (n. 16); on
Nasser, 68, 70, 243–44; on oil, 244; on
Qasim, 259; on Syria, 14, 70, 150, 152,
160, 170, 216
Dulles, John Foster, *114, 120*; on American exceptionalism, 16–17, 18, 115;
on American Jews, 11–12, 107, 116;
on Arab-Israeli conflict, 39, 66, 74;
on Arab nationalism, 8, 241–43; on
Arab unity, 13, 78; assistance to British intervention in Jordan, 232; and
Baghdad Pact, 294 (n. 62); on bipartisanship, 116; on Chamoun, 253; on
colonialism, 21; congressional testimony of, 93, 94, 95–97; on conservative Arab governments, 168; on "containment plus," 175; on Crown Prince
Faisal, 198; death of, 261; on economic
aid, 82; on Egypt, 200; on Egyptian-
Syrian union, 190–92, 327 (n. 23); on
Eisenhower's UN speech, 249; on European allies, 11; on France, 226; on
Guatemala, 150; illness of, 51, 59, 74,
261, 288 (n. 5); and "indirect aggression," 248, 249; on international law,
29; on Iraq, 44, 190, 259; on Israel, 12,
165, 263; on Jordan, 124, 129, 234,
245, 251–52; and Jordanian crisis, 134,
135, 137, 309 (n. 47), 310 (n. 57); on
King Saud, 144, 168; on Khrushchev,
164; on Kuwait, 234–35; on Lebanese
crisis, 218, 223–24, 225, 247, 251–52;
on Little Rock crisis, 178; on Middle
East Charter proposal, 78–79; on
Middle East summit, 247; on military
intervention in Middle East, 83, 227,
231; on Nasser, 40, 42–43, 115, 242–

43, 255, 259–60; and "Northern Tier" strategy, 30; on nuclear weapons, 297 (n. 7); on oil, 244; personal characteristics of, 28–29; on "positive neutrality," 2, 20, 21; pre-secretarial career of, 27–28; relationship with Eisenhower, 28; on Saudi Arabia, 44; on Soviet arms sales to Egypt, 40; on Soviet threat, 100, 124, 140–41, 164, 166, 172–73, 314 (n. 9), 323 (n. 96); on Suez Canal dispute, 114–15; on Syria, 150, 315 (n. 20); on Syrian crisis, 158, 159, 161, 163, 165, 168, 172, 173; threats against Soviet Union, 173; on Turkey, 165, 173; on U.S. Congress, 12, 116; visit to Egypt, 30

Eban, Abba, 134, 294 (n. 61), 309 (n. 52)
Eden, Anthony, 41, 50, 97
Egypt: foreign residents of, 68; inter-Arab relations of, 5; Jewish community in, 67; and Jordanian crisis, 133, 309–10 (n. 52); July 1956 revolution, 26–27; land reform in, 32, 284 (n. 31); and Middle East Command proposal, 26; position on Eisenhower Doctrine, 99, 121; and "positive neutrality," 32; relations with Iraq, 148; relations with Lebanon, 68, 142, 207; relations with Libya, 68; relations with Saudi Arabia, 148; relations with Soviet Union, 1, 39–40, 141, 292 (n. 44); and Suez crisis, 1; troops in Syria, 169; union with Syria, 182–88; U.S. economic pressures on, 99, 113, 304 (n. 84). *See also* United Arab Republic (UAR)
Egypt–Syria–Saudi Arabia (ESS) Pact, 38, 45, 125, 126
Eilat, 106, 108
Eisenhower, Dwight D., *89, 104, 114, 120, 266;* on Arab culture, 13; on Arab-Israeli conflict, 11, 42, 66, 74–75, 115, 265; on Arab nationalism, 8, 13, 281 (n. 41); Arab views of, 65, 272; on Baghdad Pact, 79; on bipartisanship, 90–91; on Britain, 11, 59, 231; on

Congo crisis, 265; on Crown Prince Faisal, 198; on economic aid, 58–59; on Egypt, 16, 42, 59; on European allies, 66–67, 96; on France, 59; frustrations over Middle East policy, 199; on Israeli occupation of Sinai and Gaza, 209; and Jordanian crisis, 135, 137; on King Hussein, 138; and King Saud, 16, 44–45, 69, 101–3, 108, 144–45, 162, 167, 179, 200, 279 (n. 23); on Lebanese crisis, 224, 225; meeting with Nasser, 265–66; mild stroke of, 178; on military aid, 58–59; on military intervention in Middle East, 83, 176, 198, 224, 227; on Nasser, 15, 21, 42, 141, 179, 215, 225, 228, 242, 243, 255–56, 259, 279 (n. 23), 281 (n. 41); on nuclear weapons, 297 (n. 7); personal characteristics of, 28; on "positive neutrality," 2; pre-presidential career of, 27; and proposed Turkish intervention in Iraq, 233; reelection to presidency, 53–54; relationship with Dulles, 28; reliance on special emissaries, 238, 338 (n. 2); on Soviet Union, 53, 58, 60, 71, 225; on Syria, 159, 160, 161–62; United Nations speech of, 248–50; on U.S. Congress, 116; on U.S. State Department, 74; unveiling of Middle East Resolution, 1, 88–89
Eisenhower administration: on Algerian uprising, 66; on Arab-Israeli conflict, 29, 74; on Britain's role in Middle East, 4, 29, 66–67; on Egyptian-Syrian union, 189–90; on France's role in Middle East, 66–67; fundamental objectives in Middle East, 29, 73, 255; on Gulf of Aqaba, 106; on intervention in Lebanon, 211–12, 223–24, 272–73; on Iraqi communism, 257; on Jordan, 245; on Nasser, 67–69; on Palestinian refugees, 29, 66; relations with Egypt, 30, 39–40, 67–69, 113–14; relations with Iran, 30; relations with Israel, 29, 263–64; relative restraint of, 272–73,

276; on Suez Canal dispute, 47, 113–15; on Syria, 159–60; on Turkey, 70. *See also* United States; U.S. State Department

Eisenhower Doctrine: abandonment of, 2; and Arab-Israeli conflict, 80; Arab views of, 98–99, 116–17, 178; and entanglement in local disputes, 100; geographical scope of, 80–81; impact on Jordan, 125, 126–27; inadequacies of, 179–80, 236; naming of, 89; and NATO countries, 97–98, 299 (n. 32); and NSC 5820/1, 256; objectives of, 5, 81–83; planning of, 61, 73–84; political strategy of, 5, 7, 8, 79, 120, 179–80, 200; precursors to, 45, 71–72, 80; and president's message to Congress, 1, 83–84, 88–89, 296 (n. 82); scholarly treatments of, 2–3, 4; and U.S. public opinion, 94, 298 (n. 19). *See also* Middle East Resolution

Elson, Edward L. R., 243, 312 (n. 75)

Ethiopia, 120–21

Evans, Rowland, 108

Eveland, Wilbur Crane, 46, 52, 143, 156, 318 (n. 40), 327 (n. 23)

Faisal (Crown Prince of Saudi Arabia), 49, 198–99, 241

Faisal II (King of Iraq), 34, *36*, 48, 148, 182, 220, 221, 329 (n. 43)

Farouk (King of Egypt), 26

Fawzi, Mahmud, 218, 230, 250, 251–52

Fedayeen raids, 106, 108, 111

Foreign Affairs Committee, U.S. House of Representatives, 93, 94

Foreign Relations Committee, U.S. Senate, 94–95, 111

Formosa Strait Resolution, 71, 90, 297 (n. 7)

France: Arab views of, 3, 67, 213; attack on Egypt by, 50–53; demise of Fourth Republic, 333 (n. 23); and Lebanese crisis, 213, 226, 333 (n. 24), 336–37 (n. 69); position on Eisenhower Doctrine, 98; and Suez Canal, 47, 114–15;

U.S. alliance with, 5, 66; withdrawal of forces from Egypt, 57, 64–65, 67

Free Officers (Egypt), 26–27, 31

Free Officers (Iraq), 220

Fulbright, J. William, 94, 95–96, 225, 298–99 (n. 22)

GAMMA operation, 40, 41–42, 285 (n. 53)

Gaza Strip, 39, 69, 75, 106, *107*, 108–9, 110–11, 151–52, 274, 294 (n. 61)

Gemeyal, Pierre, 143

Gender analyses, 13–15

Gendzier, Irene L., 2, 218, 224

George, Walter F., 91

Gerges, Fawaz A., 2, 342 (n. 50)

Gerson, Lewis M., 43, 285 (n. 61)

Ghalib, 'Abd al-Hamid, 207, 333 (n. 17)

Glubb, John Bagot, 41, 122

Gordon, Thomas S., 93

Gray, Gordon, 259

Green, Theodore Francis, 91, 96

Greene, Joseph N., Jr., 191

Gromyko, Andrei, 166, 249

Guatemala, 150, 314 (n. 9)

Gulf of Aqaba dispute, 16, 39, 106, 108, 144–45, 148

Gulf of Tonkin Resolution, 112

Guzmán, Jacobo Arbenz, 314 (n. 9)

Haddad, Yvonne Yazbeck, 275

Hagerty, James C., 98, 134, 137

Haiti, 12

Halleck, Charles, 97

Hammarskjold, Dag, 214, 215, 217–18, 252, 253, 335 (n. 40)

Hamzi, Khattar, 317 (n. 40)

Hare, Raymond A., 60, 61, 68, 75, 99, 110, 177, 201, 215, 257–58, 260–61, 304 (n. 85)

Harriman, Averell, 92

Hartz, Louis, 280 (n. 33)

Hashemite dynasty, 6, 34–35, 148, 221

Hashim, Ibrahim, 134

Hassouna, 'Abd al-Khaliq, 66

al-Hawrani, Akram, 170, 177

Haykal, Muhammad Hasanayn, 18, 49,
   61, 99, 177, 184, 186, 216, 230, 257–
   58, 260, 324 (n. 112), 325 (n. 114), 331
   (n. 61)
Heath, Donald R., 178, 197, 241
Heiss, Mary Ann, 13
Henderson, Loy W., 160–61, 163–64,
   170, 238, 294 (n. 64), 318 (n. 48)
Herter, Christian A., 15, 170–72, 198,
   200, 246, 261–62
Hitler analogies, 53, 164, 242, 243, 260,
   339 (n. 11)
al-Hiyari, ʿAli, 131
Hizbullah, 273
Holland, Matthew F., 15–16, 319 (n. 50)
Hood, Samuel, 227, 231
Hoover, Herbert, Jr., 51–52, 59, 68, 73–
   74
Humphrey, Hubert H., 89, 91, 92, 95,
   102
Hungarian uprising, 3, 10, 52, 59, 69, 72,
   149, 270, 288 (n. 3)
Huntington, Samuel, 9, 274
al-Hurriyya, 189
al-Husayni, Ibrahim, 155, 157, 318
   (n. 40)
Hussein (King of Jordan), *36, 139, 141*;
   on Arab nationalism, 122; and Arab
   Union, 192–93, 202, 328 (n. 36); ascension of, 35; and Baghdad Pact, 40–
   41, 202; bleak outlook for, 35, 240–
   41, 252, 253; clandestine U.S. aid to,
   138, 309 (n. 47), 311–12 (n. 71); on
   communism, 127; on Egypt, 135; on
   Egyptian-Syrian union, 189; imposition of martial law, 134–35; inter-
   Arab diplomacy of, 102; on Iraqi-
   Jordanian union, 192–93; on Nasser,
   262–63; personal characteristics of,
   123, 234; position on Eisenhower
   Doctrine, 7, 101, 125–27, 138–39, 312
   (n. 75); reaction to Iraqi revolution,
   222, 234; relations with Syria, 154,
   158, 168; relations with UAR, 196; request for Anglo-U.S. intervention,
   231; requests for U.S. aid, 123, 125,
   133–34; requests for U.S. intervention, 245; struggle with cabinet, 127–
   29, 307 (nn. 23, 25); U.S. views of,
   14–15, 137–38, 311 (n. 70); and Zerqa
   incident, 130–31
Hussein (Sharif of Mecca), 35, 306
   (n. 11)
Hussein, Ahmed, 22, 99

Ibn Saud (King of Saudi Arabia), 35, 330
   (n. 55)
Ilyan, Mikhail, 46, 49, 50, 52
"Imperialism" issue, 3, 9, 10, 19, 20, 21,
   23, 25, 26, 30, 37, 66–67, 77, 270–71,
   280 (n. 35)
International Bank for Reconstruction
   and Development, 261
International Cooperation Administration, 138, 248
International Monetary Fund, 53, 65
Iran, 70, 82, 98, 121, 283 (n. 25), 321
   (n. 72)
Iraq: designs on Kuwait, 202–3, 262, 344
   (n. 71); economic sanctions against,
   11, 274; independence of, 34; and Jordan crisis, 132; July 1958 revolution, 7,
   220, 221–22; Mosul revolt, 260, 343
   (n. 65); Nasserist coup attempt, 259,
   343 (n. 61); new regime in, 246; position on Arab-Israeli conflict, 75, 293–
   94 (n. 58); position on Eisenhower
   Doctrine, 121; position on Lebanese
   crisis, 216; proposed Turkish intervention in, 233–34; public opinion in, 62,
   64, 194; reaction to Egyptian-Syrian
   union, 190, 191–92, 202; relations
   with Egypt, 148, 314 (n. 3); relations
   with Jordan, 154; relations with Saudi
   Arabia, 5–6, 76, 104, 140; relations
   with Soviet Union, 262; relations with
   Syria, 36, 82, 142, 148, 154, 167, 176,
   182, 188, 190, 216–17; relations with
   UAR, 258; "rogue" state status, 273;
   Saddam Hussein regime, 276; territorial ambitions of, 7, 100, 190, 202–3,
   216; union with Jordan, 192–94; U.S.

aid to, 121, 202; U.S. arms shipment
to, 321 (n. 72); U.S. hopes for, 2; U.S.-
led wars in, 11, 274

Iraqi Communist Party (ICP), 257, 260,
262, 342 (n. 53). *See also* Communism

Iraq Petroleum Company, 53, 62, 111,
151–52

Irshaydat, Shafiq, 307 (n. 25)

Islam, 16, 19, 44

Islamic Jihad, 273

Islamism, 274, 275

Israel: Arab views of, 5, 65–66; attack on
Egypt, 50–53; British overflights of,
232; independence of, 24; and Jordan
crisis, 132; nuclear program of, 266–
67; occupation of Sinai and Gaza, 57,
69, 75, 106–9, 110–11, 151–52, 294
(n. 61); occupation of West Bank and
Gaza, 271, 274, 276; position on Eisenhower Doctrine, 98, 121, 306
(n. 6); relations with Britain, 232; and
Syrian crisis, 165; threat to West Bank,
132, 199, 245, 263–64, 331 (n. 61), 340
(n. 23); U.S. aid to, 264; and U.S. diplomats, 282 (n. 4); withdrawal from Sinai
and Gaza, 110–11, 307 (n. 29)

Jackson, C. D., 75, 138, 178, 248–50, 254

al-Jamahir, 127

Jamali, Muhammad Fadhil, 328 (n. 29)

Jawdat, 'Ali. *See* al-Ayyubi, 'Ali Jawdat

Jeton, Frank, 155, 158

Johnson, Lyndon B., 91, 95, 106–7, 265,
272

Johnston, Eric, 238

Johnston Plan, 15

Joint Chiefs of Staff, 129

Jordan: alleged UAR plot in, 231, 337
(n. 82); army conspiracy in, 219; British military intervention in, 231–32,
278 (n. 5); establishment of royal supremacy within, 7; independence of,
34–35; lack of democracy in, 140; position on Eisenhower Doctrine, 121,
139, 307 (nn. 24, 29); public opinion
in, 63, 64, 65, 84, 125, 137, 194; rela-

tions with Britain, 34–35, 123, 124,
126, 129, 231–32; relations with communist China, 126, 129; relations with
Egypt, 142, 312 (n. 77); relations with
Soviet Union, 69–70, 124, 126, 129;
relations with Syria, 140, 154, 168, 312
(n. 77); relations with UAR, 262–63;
U.S. aid to, 138–40, 202, 278 (n. 5),
306 (n. 14); U.S. arms shipment to,
321 (n. 72); weakness of, 121

Jordanian Arab Legion, 35, 122

Junblatt, Kamal, 210, 332 (n. 15)

Kallas, Khalil, 151

Kamel, Moustafa, 18

Karabell, Zachary, 2

Karami, Rashid, 253

al-Kayyali, Ghalib, 150–51

Kefauver, Estes, 94

Kennedy, John F., 91, 95, 264–65, 273

Kerr, Malcolm, 257

al-Khalidi, Husayn Fakhri, 131, 309–10
(n. 52)

Khrushchev, Nikita, 33, 52, 164, 170, *171*,
174, 230–31, 247–48, 249, 260, 261

Knowland, William F., 106–7, 116

Korean War, 26, 93, 297 (n. 15)

Kosygin, Alexei, 154

Kunz, Diane B., 15, 28

Kurds, 257

Kuwait, 189, 194, 202–3, 234–35, 262

Lamumba, Patrice, 264, 265

Lansing, Robert, 28

Lebanon: civil war in, 210–11, 217; easing of tensions in, 245, 253; independence of, 37; Israeli invasion of (1982),
273; parliamentary elections in, 142–
43; position on Eisenhower Doctrine,
7, 120–21, 225, 253; public opinion in,
64, 66, 194, 206; relations with Egypt,
67, 68, 142; relations with Syria, 168;
relations with UAR, 211, 253, 328
(n. 29); sectarian divisions within, 37,
142; UAR infiltrations into, 211, 214,
216, 332 (n. 15); U.S. aid to, 143, 202;

U.S. military intervention in, 112, 226–29, *229*, 272–73, 274; withdrawal of U.S. forces from, 253

Lend-Lease aid, 24

Lesch, David W., 2, 159, 165

Lewis, Bernard, 9, 274

Libya, 43, 62, 67, 68, 100, 120–21, 222, 273, 274

Little, Douglas, 11, 13, 224, 278 (n. 13)

Little Rock crisis, 177–78

Lloyd, Selwyn, *114*; on conservative Arab governments, 202; on "containment plus," 17; on France, 213; on Iraq, 232–33, 234; on Jordan, 124; on Kuwait, 234–35; on Lebanese crisis, 215; view of Nasser, 113

Lodge, Henry Cabot, 60

Love, Kennett, 307 (n. 25)

Luce, Henry R., 279 (n. 26)

MacArthur, Douglas, II, 59

Macmillan, Harold, *114*; dealings with Khrushchev, 248; on Iraqi revolution, 233, 246; meetings with Eisenhower, 113–14, 175–76; on military intervention in Middle East, 175–76, 227, 231; on Nuri al-Said, 203; on proposed Turkish intervention in Iraq, 233; support for Eisenhower Doctrine, 97

al-Majali, Hazza', 41, 263, 344 (n. 75)

Malik, Charles, 100, 136, 158, 168, 189, 201–2, 206

Mallory, Lester D., 125, 126, 128, 131, 135, 136, 137, 140, 154, 182, 308–9 (n. 42)

Mansfield, Mike, 94, 95, 225

Mansfield amendment, 111–12, 134, 212, 225, 228, 337 (n. 76)

Marshall Plan, 77, 78

Mart, Michelle, 14, 15

al-Matni, Nasib, 210

Ma'ushi, Paul, 207

McCarthy, Joseph R., 116

McClintock, Robert, 201, 208–10, 215, 217, 218, 219, 222–23, 228, 229, 238, 245

McGovern, George, 102

Meir, Golda, 111, 132

Menderes, Adnan, 159, 233–34

MI6 (British spy agency), 46, 50

Middle East Charter proposal, 76–78

Middle East Command proposal, 26

Middle East Resolution: amendments to, 111–12, 303–4 (n. 77); congressional consideration of, 93–97; drafting of, 80–81; economic assistance provisions of, 81, 83, 88, 295 (n. 75); House approval of, 94; interventionist provision of, 81, 88, 95, 161, 212, 298–99 (n. 22); military assistance provisions of, 81, 88, 165; Senate approval of, 111. *See also* Eisenhower Doctrine

Middleton, George, 160–61

al-Midfa'i, Jamil, 167

Mikoyan, Anastas, 40

Mobutu, Joseph, 264

Modernization theory, 19, 248, 281 (n. 41)

Molloy, Robert, 158

Moose, James S., 149, 151, 152–53, 158

Morocco, 81, 121, 295 (n. 74), 306 (n. 6)

Morse, Wayne, 95, 96

Mosadeq, Mohammed, 13–14, 29–30

Moscow agreement (Syria and Soviet Union), 154–55, 177, 316–17 (n. 31)

al-Mufti, Sa'id, 41

Murjan, 'Abd al-Wahhab, 182, 189

Murphy, Robert D., 78, 80–81, 238–40, 244–45, 246–47

al-Nabulsi, Sulayman, 122, 123, 126–28, 129

Naguib, Muhammed, 27

Nagy, Imre, 52

Nasser, Gamal Abdel, *48, 187, 266*; accusation against King Saud, 196–97; on Arab-Israeli conflict, 20, 41–42, 75, 164, 265–66, 285 (n. 53); and Arab nationalism, 2; and Aswan Dam, 47; background of, 31; British coup plotting against, 113–14, 304 (n. 86); on Cold War, 20; on communism, 21, 99, 257–59, 261; on Congo crisis, 265, 267; death of, 265, 273; declining influence of, 273; on Eisenhower, 266; on Eisenhower Doctrine, 8, 99, 121; and Free Officers, 27, 31; and Gulf of Aqaba dispute, 144; inter-Arab diplomacy of, 102; on Iraq, 329 (n. 44); and Iraqi-Jordanian union, 194–96; and Jordanian crisis, 136, 308 (n. 37); on King Hussein, 263; meeting with Eisenhower, 265–66; and nationalization of Suez Canal Company, 47; on nuclear weapons, 266–67; pan-Arab philosophy of, 31–32; personal characteristics of, 31; popularity of, 4, 270; and "positive neutrality," 2, 32, 281 (n. 42); and Qasim, 257, 261, 342 (n. 53); relations with Soviet Union, 2, 7, 19, 21, 67, 72, 99, 260–61, 270, 322 (n. 88); relations with United States, 67–68, 201, 261, 264–65; rhetoric of, 31; role in Lebanese crisis, 207, 208, 211, 215, 218, 335 (n. 42); on Saud, 132; on subversion, 68; on Syria, 21, 155, 164, 177; and UNEF, 291 (n. 36); and union with Syria, 185–86, 325 (n. 114), 326 (n. 12); on U.S. history, 18, 281 (n. 42); on U.S. intervention in Lebanon, 230; on U.S. Middle East policy, 60–61, 266; U.S. views of, 14–15, 67–69

Nasserism: and Arab-Israeli conflict, 20; critique of "Western imperialism," 3, 20; influence in Arab countries, 34, 37; popularity of, 7; and Soviet Union, 8, 20; tenets of, 31–32; views on Cold War, 20

National Front Party (Jordan), 122, 127

National Grouping (Syria), 152

National Pact (Lebanon), 37, 142, 334 (n. 29)

National Security Council (NSC): meetings, 13, 69, 143, 191, 197–98, 199, 217, 218, 243, 244, 253, 259–60; NSC 5820/1, 254–56, 332–33 (n. 16), 340 (n. 23); Planning Board, 254–55

National Socialist Party (Jordan), 122, 129, 131, 133, 135

Nehru, Jawaharlal, 32, 115

Newsweek, 119–20

Nile River, 200

Nixon, Richard M., 198, 224, 228, 259

Nizam al-Din, 'Abd al-Baqi, 152, 158

Nkrumah, Kwame, 32

Nonaligned movement, 32, 38. *See also* "Positive neutrality"

North Atlantic Council, 140

North Atlantic Treaty Organization (NATO), 12, 27, 30, 80

Novak, Robert, 108

Nutting, Anthony, 41

Oil, Middle Eastern: Arab embargo of 1973–1974, 273; Arab nationalism and, 255; declining global demand for, 273; Iraqi policy on, 246, 262; lack of direct U.S. dependence on, 17; threat to Kuwaiti supply of, 234–35; U.S. interest in, 12, 19, 116, 198, 228, 255, 281 (n. 41); Western Europe's dependence on, 24, 53, 65, 198, 282 (n. 2). *See also* Pipelines, oil (in Syria)

OMEGA plan, 42–43, 45–46, 59–60

"Operation Straggle," 46, 49–50, 52, 67, 99, 149, 152, 287 (n. 83)

Orientalism (Said), 11

Ovendale, Ritchie, 2

Pahlavi, Muhammad Reza (Shah of Iran), 10

Pakistan, 82, 98

Palestinians, 24, 35, 41, 65–66, 121–22, 194, 306 (n. 14)

Parker, Richard B., 138, 311 (n. 70)

Parti Populaire Syrien (PPS), 46, 49, 332 (n. 14)

Pearson, Drew, 249–50

People's Party (Syria), 163, 176, 314 (n. 5)

People's Republic of China, 32, 46, 71, 90, 96, 124, 297 (n. 8)

Pew Research Center for the People and the Press, 275

Pflimlin, Pierre, 213

Phalange Party (Lebanon), 332 (n. 14)

Pineau, Christian, 110

Pipelines, oil (in Syria), 58, 106, 111, 149, 151–52, 160–61, 188, 191, 195, 212, 224, 230

Policy Planning Staff, U.S. Department of State, 76

Popular Resistance Organization (Syria), 188

"Positive neutrality," 2, 20, 32

Public Law (PL) 480, 43, 258, 261, 285 (n. 58), 342 (n. 56)

al-Qaʻida, 271, 273

Qasim, ʻAbd al-Karim, 220, 221, 256–57, *258*, 259, 262, 342 (n. 53)

al-Quni, Muhammad, 170

al-Quwatli, Shukri, *36, 187*; on Britain, 22; on Hungarian uprising, 10, 20; position on Eisenhower Doctrine, 101, 150; and radicalization of Syria, 149, 152, 158, 314 (n. 5); relations with Egypt, 169; relations with Iraq, 154; relations with Jordan, 132, 136; relations with Saudi Arabia, 154, 167–68, 316 (n. 26); return to Syria, 163; on Soviet advisors, 314 (n. 8)

Radford, Arthur W., 68, 71, 76, 83, 294 (n. 62)

Radio Cairo, 31, 67, 133, 136, 140, 197, 211

Rashid, Nadhir, 308 (n. 41)

al-Rawi, ʻAbd al-Jalil, 314 (n. 3)

Rayburn, Sam, 225

Reinhardt, G. Frederick, 266, 267

Reston, James, 170

Riad, Mahmud, 50, 154, 183, 184, 188

Richards, James P., *120*; as special ambassador for Eisenhower Doctrine, 91, 112, 119–21, 129, 138–39, 140, 151, 238, 305 (n. 4); on Syrian crisis, 170

al-Rifaʻi, Samir, 134, 139, 201, 231–32, 234, 245, 246, 247, 335 (n. 40)

al-Rimawi, ʻAbdullah, 127, 307 (n. 25)

Robinson, O. Preston, 339 (n. 12)

Rostow, Walt, 248–49

Rountree, William M., 170, 176, 216–17, 235, 243, 258–59, 261

"Royalist axis," 142

Russell, Richard, 94, 95

Said, Edward W., 11

al-Saʻid, Nuri: on Arab-Israeli conflict, 294 (n. 58); background of, 330 (n. 47); British views of, 14; on Eisenhower Doctrine, 100; escape of, 221; on Jordan, 139; on Iraqi-Jordanian union, 193; killing of, 221; on Kuwait, 202–3; on Lebanese crisis, 216, 220–21; on Nasser, 136, 196; political outlook of, 34; resignation of premiership, 148, 313 (n. 1); resumption of premiership, 196; on Suez crisis, 51; on Syria, 161; territorial ambitions of, 7, 34, 100, 190, 216; U.S. views of, 14

Salah al-Din, 20

Salem, Elie, 17, 339 (n. 12)

Salam, Saʻib, 333 (n. 17)

al-Salih, ʻAbd al-Qadir, 307 (n. 25)

Salk vaccine, 153

Samarraʻi, Salih Mahdi, 287 (n. 83)

Sandys, Duncan, 97, 103

Sanger, Richard H., 137–38

al-Sarraj, ʻAbd al-Hamid, 152, 158, 169, 196–97, 344 (n. 75)

Satloff, Robert B., 2, 123

Saud (King of Saudi Arabia), *36, 104, 105*; on ʻAbd al-Ilah, 148; alleged Egyptian assassination attempt on, 311 (n. 63); ascension of, 35; and Baghdad Pact, 44, 140, 193, 222; on Egypt, 105, 169; on Egyptian-Syrian union, 192; on Eisenhower Doctrine, 7, 101, 103–4, 144; Eisenhower's views of, 44–45, 103; on Gulf of Aqaba dispute, 108, 144; inter-Arab diplomacy of, 102, 169, 176; on Iraqi revolution, 222; and Jordanian crisis, 132; and King Faisal, 48; and King Hussein, 132, 154, 311–12 (n. 71); lifestyle of, 15, 45, 102; on Nasser, 48, 105, 311 (n. 63); offer to mediate Syrian-Turkish dispute, 174;

plot against UAR, 196–97; on Qasim, 342 (n. 53); relations with Egypt, 44, 48–49, 101; relations with Iraq, 132, 140, 182; relations with Jordan, 241; religious role of, 16, 103, 108, 144, 162; on royal succession, 7; on Suez crisis, 48–49; and Syria, 105, 158–59, 162–63, 167–68, 319 (n. 56); on U.S. position in Suez war, 61; visit to United States, 102–6; virtual abdication of, 7, 198, 330 (n. 55)

Saudi Arabia: Egyptian residents of, 45; foreign labor in, 45; independence of, 35; position on Eisenhower Doctrine, 101, 105–6, 121, 169, 302 (n. 59); public opinion in, 62, 64, 162; relations with Arab Union, 194, 199; relations with Egypt, 44, 142, 148; relations with Iraq, 5–6, 44, 48, 76, 104, 140; relations with Syria, 36, 142, 148, 154, 158–59, 162–63, 167–69, 174, 182, 188; relations with UAR, 194, 199; religious discrimination in, 102, 301 (n. 49); royal succession in, 330 (n. 55); slavery in, 102, 301 (n. 49); strategic value to United States of, 35; and Suez war, 101, 301 (n. 43); U.S. aid to, 103, 121, 302 (n. 54); U.S. arms shipment to, 321 (n. 72)

Saunders, Bonnie F., 155

Seale, Patrick, 169, 185, 186

September 11, 2001, attacks, 10, 271, 274

Sèvres, Protocol of, 50

Sharm al-Shaykh, 106, 109, 110–11

Shihab, Fu'ad, 209, 210–11, 217, 219, 228, 229, 239–40, 244–45, 253

al-Shishakli, Adib, 46, 50, 155, 317–18 (n. 40)

Sinai Peninsula, 69, 75, 106, 151–52, 294 (n. 61)

Smith, H. Alexander, 226

Southeast Asia Treaty Organization (SEATO), 80

Soviet Union: Arab views of, 3, 64, 69; disintegration of, 273; Middle East plan of, 98, 300 (n. 33); Nasser's dis-

agreements with, 7–8, 19; opposition to Eisenhower Doctrine, 98; as perceived threat to Middle East, 1–2, 4, 13, 63–64, 69, 71, 72; positions on Arab-Israeli conflict, 5, 10, 33; reaction to Egyptian-Syrian union, 187–88; reaction to U.S. intervention in Lebanon, 230–31, 247–48; relations with Egypt, 1, 27, 33, 39–40; relations with Syria, 1, 70, 149–50, 154–55, 177; relations with UAR, 260–61, 264; and Third World nationalism, 33; threats against Turkey, 166, 170–71, 322 (n. 88); ultimatum to Britain and France, 63–64, 322 (n. 88); U.S. views of, 69; "volunteers," 64, 67, 69, 71

Sputnik, 170, 178

Stalin, Joseph, 33, 164

Stassen, Harold, 71

Stevenson, Adlai, 92

Stone, Howard E., 155, 156, 158, 317 (n. 34)

Strategic Air Command, 161

Strauss, Lewis L., 248, 249

Strong, Robert C., 155, 169

Sudan, 121, 274

Suez Canal, 26, 47, 49, 57, 58, 111, 114–15, 212, 224, 230, 261

Suez Canal Company, 47, 115, 201

Suez war, 1, 3, 23, 51–53, 58, 269–70

Sukarno, 32

al-Sulh, Sami, 207, 217, 239, 245, 328 (n. 29)

Sullivan & Cromwell, 27

al-Suwaydi, Tawfiq, 182

Sweeney, James L., 131, 133, 308–9 (n. 42)

Syria: alleged U.S. coup attempt in, 155–58, 317–18 (nn. 36, 40); independence of, 35; and Jordanian crisis, 132, 134, 135–36, 310 (n. 61); parliamentary by-elections in, 152, 315–16 (nn. 20, 21); position on Eisenhower Doctrine, 99–100, 121, 150–51; public opinion in, 64, 70, 149, 152, 177; radicalization of, 70, 149, 153, 177, 314 (n. 5); relations with East bloc, 150, 314 (n. 8);

relations with Egypt, 36, 67, 188; relations with Iraq, 36, 82, 148, 154, 188; relations with Lebanon, 143; relations with Saudi Arabia, 36, 142, 148, 154, 174, 188; relations with Soviet Union, 1, 70, 99, 149–50, 154–55, 169, 177; relations with Turkey, 172, 173–74; "swing state" status of, 36; Turkish threats against, 70–71, 165; U-2 flights over, 53; union with Egypt, 182–88; and U.S. arms sales, 319 (n. 58). *See also* United Arab Republic (UAR)

U.S. coup attempt in Syria, 156–57; on Arab public opinion, 60; on Arab Union, 194, 202; on Arab unity, 328 (n. 32); on Baghdad Pact, 76; on Britain's role in Middle East, 29; on Egypt, 164; on Gulf of Aqaba dispute, 108; on Iraqi expansionism, 100; on Jordan, 124, 128–29; on Jordan-UAR dispute, 263; on Lebanese crisis, 208–9, 215–16; on Nasser, 21, 255, 261; on Nasserist coup attempt in Iraq, 343 (n. 61); on Richards mission, 120; on Soviet threat, 13; on Syria, 153, 165–66

U.S. Department of the Treasury, 35, 255

'Usayran, 'Adil, 239

"Vacuum" theory, 1, 4, 58, 66, 83–84, *84*, 98, 99, 102, 125, 152

Vanguard rocket, 178

Vester, Bertha Spafford, 291 (n. 32)

"Voice of the Arabs," 211

von Brentano, Heinrich, 115

Wadsworth, George E., 144

Wagner, Robert, 102

Warren, Fletcher, 173

Washington, George, 19

West Bank, 35, 121, 132, 133, 194, 195, 199, 240–41, 245, 263–64, 274

Wills, Garry, 27

Wilson, Charles E., 76, 294 (n. 62)

Wilson, Woodrow, 28, 265

World Bank, 114, 248

Wright, Michael, 196, 202, 220

Yasin, Yusuf, 110, 148

Yemen, 164, 320 (n. 67)

Yost, Charles W., 155–56

Zakaria, Yasin, 158

Zayn al-Din, Farid, 158

Zerqa incident, 130–31, 308 (nn. 37, 41)

Zhukov, Georgi, 98

Zionism. *See* Israel

Zorlu, Fatin Rustu, 170

THE NEW COLD WAR HISTORY

Salim Yaqub, *Containing Arab Nationalism: The Eisenhower Doctrine and the Middle East* (2003).

Francis J. Gavin, *Gold, Dollars, and Power: The Politics of International Monetary Relations, 1958–1971* (2003).

William Glenn Gray, *Germany's Cold War: The Global Campaign to Isolate East Germany, 1949–1969* (2003).

Matthew J. Ouimet, *The Rise and Fall of the Brezhnev Doctrine in Soviet Foreign Policy* (2003).

Pierre Asselin, *A Bitter Peace: Washington, Hanoi, and the Making of the Paris Agreement* (2002).

Jeffrey Glen Giauque, *Grand Designs and Visions of Unity: The Atlantic Powers and the Reorganization of Western Europe, 1955–1963* (2002).

Chen Jian, *Mao's China and the Cold War* (2001).

M. E. Sarotte, *Dealing with the Devil: East Germany, Détente, and Ostpolitik, 1969–1973* (2001).

Mark Philip Bradley, *Imagining Vietnam and America: The Making of Postcolonial Vietnam, 1919–1950* (2000).

Michael E. Latham, *Modernization as Ideology: American Social Science and "Nation Building" in the Kennedy Era* (2000).

Qiang Zhai, *China and the Vietnam Wars, 1950–1975* (2000).

William I. Hitchcock, *France Restored: Cold War Diplomacy and the Quest for Leadership in Europe, 1944–1954* (1998).